¶	paragraph
no ¶	no paragraph
p	error in punctuation (pp. 545–61)
paral	faulty parallelism (pp. 278–79, 532–33)
pas	unnecessary or ineffective passive construction (pp. 298–300)
prom	paragraph is faulty — try the promise pattern (pp. 211–23)
pron	error with pronoun (pp. 508–09)
pv	check point of view (pp. 87–89)
ref	vague pronoun reference (pp. 508–09)
rep	unnecessary repetition
ro	run-on sentence (p. 543)
sb	check the sentence base rule (pp. 272–73)
sp	spelling error
split	split construction (pp. 527–28)
ss	check sentence structure (pp. 306–12)
sub	faulty subordination (pp. 280–81, 533–34)
t	error in verb tense (p. 511)
th	clarify the thesis (pp. 48–50)
tr	effective transition needed (pp. 227–28)
un	unity — check for unnecessary shifts in wording, tone, or attitude
vb	error with verb (p. 511)
wdy	wordy
wr	write out — do not abbreviate or use numbers (p. 562, pp. 564–65)
ws	check your writer's stance (pp. 21–40)
X	obvious error
∧	insertion (pp. 525–26)
?	I don't understand
	Additional symbols

STRATEGIES OF RHETORIC WITH HANDBOOK

Fifth Edition

A.M. Tibbetts
Charlene Tibbetts
University of Illinois at Urbana-Champaign

Scott, Foresman and Company
Glenview, Illinois
London

An Instructor's Manual is available. It may be obtained through a local Scott, Foresman representative or by writing to the English Editor, College Division, Scott, Foresman and Company, 1900 East Lake Avenue, Glenview, IL 60025.

Library of Congress Cataloging in Publication Data

Tibbetts, A. M.
  Strategies of rhetoric.

  Includes index.
  1. English language—Rhetoric. 2. English
language—Grammar—1950-   I. Tibbetts, Charlene.
II. Title.
PE1408.T49   1987   808'.042   86–17705
ISBN 0-673-18534-6

Acknowledgments

Photography Credits—Pages 2, 74, 194, 314 © Carol Palmer. Page 490, "Windowsill Daydreaming," 1958, Reproduction Courtesy The Minor White Archive, Princeton University. Copyright © Trustees of Princeton University. In the collection of The Museum of Modern Art, New York.

Literary acknowledgments appear on pages 601–604, which constitute a legal extension of the copyright page.

PREFACE

This fifth edition of *Strategies of Rhetoric* is true to the goal we set when the first edition was published in 1969: To provide students with as much practical information about writing as can be included in a text of reasonable size. We are pleased with how well it has stood the test of time, and attribute much of its success to the changes and revisions we have made in response to suggestions from students and teachers.

Strategies of Rhetoric takes students from the *prewriting* stage through the processes of *development* and *revision*. It then helps them to apply the techniques that they have learned to a variety of writing projects. Finally, the text provides a handbook of grammar, sentence structure, punctuation, mechanics, dictionary usage, and a glossary to help with those thorny problems that arise while a piece of writing is underway.

The Theme of This Revision

When we picked the term "strategies" many years ago, we did so to stress the idea that there are many ways to achieve a well-written piece of work. At every stage of writing, options present themselves and decisions are required. The theme of this revision, stated simply, is: *Writers have choices.* At different times, and for different purposes, they will make different choices. We also believe that instructors want a textbook that gives them flexibility in organizing courses to meet student needs; this edition provides just such flexibility.

The Student's Choices

For the student, the opportunity to choose arises first in the process of finding and limiting ideas. It continues as the method for developing the idea is selected. Choice is ever-present as the student decides which words are most clear and appropriate, as sentences are written and revised, and as the paper is revised and edited.

Choice is important even in the issue of outlining. Clearly, some writers need outlines for some papers, but they may choose different techniques for different papers—from a formal outline to doodles on a piece of scratch paper to no formal shaping at all. On occasion, a successful writer may find a topic and just start to write. As we point out in the text, choices entail consequences: some good, some not as good.

The Instructor's Choices

We have organized this book around the elements of the composition — stance, organization, word choice, sentence structure. Each element of composition has its own chapter, and the chapters can be taught in order of individual preference. Whenever possible, we have tried to strike a balance among the demands made upon you, your time, and your efforts to teach composition.

We have also kept in mind the need that your students have to succeed early if they are to enjoy becoming writers. The problem is not how to teach beginning writers everything they need to know right away (that can't be done anyway), but to help them get started. Surely the process is more attractive if students think of themselves as participants in an adventure rather than as spectators at some event. The role of the instructor is to guide students in learning to make rhetorically sound choices.

Changes in the Fifth Edition

We have written a new Chapter 1, "Finding Subjects," in which we cover the major elements of prewriting: brainstorming, free writing, keeping a journal, and *hooking* an idea. The next two chapters on *stance* and *thesis* continue the themes begun in the first chapter. Here, further examples and exercises are given in which students can practice making choices in the art of prewriting.

For Chapter 4, "Shaping and Outlining Ideas," we have written a new section on "shaping" ideas. This material emphasizes the value of organizing ideas by visualizing them in a *shape* pattern — every paper taking its own special visual form on a sheet of scratch paper. We have added to this an explanation of *support diagrams*. And, finally, we discuss in detail the standard outline, which remains an excellent practical device for planning a piece of writing.

Chapter 5, "Introduction — Strategies of Development," is new to this edition. It covers, very briefly, the strategies that are presented more fully in the following four chapters. For each of the eight major strategies we have added new *revising* and *rewriting* sections with "before" and "after" examples. Students can make their revisions more meaningful by analyzing a paper's strengths and weaknesses before they begin to revise.

Chapter 10, "The Practice of Revision," is new also. It builds on the material covered in Parts One and Two, taking the student through the major devices and techniques of revising papers at all levels of writing. Note, though, that we have retained Chapter 15 on revising and editing sentences; there is so much useful material on this topic that a separate chapter is required to do it justice.

To the previous two chapters on the sentence, we have added a third, "How Meaning Matches Structure"; it includes a discussion, with exercises, of how writers fit an idea into an appropriate clausal structure.

In previous editions, we had one research chapter. We have now broken this into two, "Library Research" and "Writing the Research Paper." In Chapter 17, we follow students as they ask a question they hope to answer, write a narrative describing their research, and then follow a research strategy. On-line computer catalogs and on-line data bases are also covered in this chapter. All examples are tied to the model research paper in Chapter 18, which is on the subject of women in politics. "Writing the Research Paper" shows the student how to plan and how to write the paper. Note that we have used the latest Modern Language Association form of parenthetical documentation and have supplied examples of content notes and endnotes.

Along with the major changes listed above, we have also refreshed the text with many new examples of both student and professional writing and with new practices.

This fifth edition, like its predecessors, owes much to many people. We thank our reviewers: Ronald Corthell, Kent State University; Christine Briggs, Henry Ford Community College; Ron Nelson, Valencia Community College; George Miller, University of Delaware; Bonnie Braendlin, Florida State University; William Dyer, Mankato State University; David Barber, University of Idaho; Robert Perrin, Indiana State University.

A. M. Tibbetts
Charlene Tibbetts

OVERVIEW

PART FOUR

HANDLING SPECIAL ASSIGNMENTS   315

PART FIVE

HANDBOOK   491

CONTENTS

PART FOUR

*H*ANDLING SPECIAL ASSIGNMENTS

P *PUNCTUATION* *545*

M *MECHANICS* *562*

STRATEGIES OF
RHETORIC WITH HANDBOOK

Fifth Edition

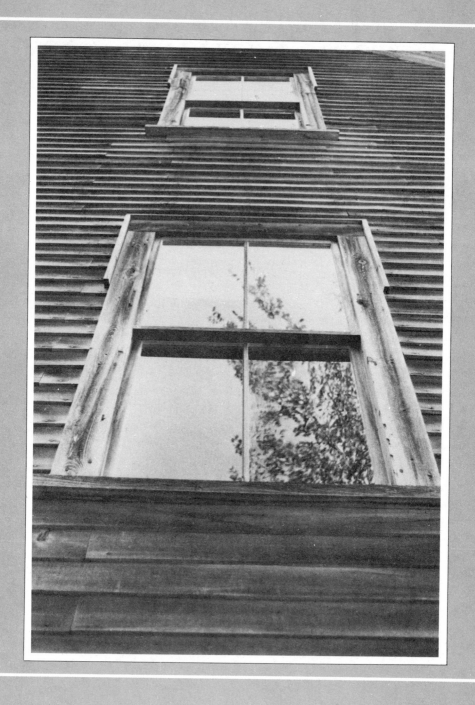

PART ONE

PREPARING TO WRITE

4

CHAPTER 1
FINDING SUBJECTS— AN INTRODUCTION

"Growl!" the student said. At least that is what she wrote (and under-lined) at the top of the page. Here is the rest of what she wrote:

I'm working on a new paper, one which is causing me a good deal of trouble. I hope it's worth the trouble. Topics and subjects for papers don't come easily to me, and when they do come, they aren't docile. I beat on them until they submit. Stop! they cry. I'll cooperate if you will just let me alone. For this new paper I have developed new techniques of harassment to get the subject tamed.

Today I feel like a hunter. I go tiptoeing around, hoping the subject won't suspect I'm coming, making sure to stay downwind; then I slowly sneak up on it, watching out for all the pitfalls of the past, when I have scared it off—I'm very superstitious. When I finally get close I pounce. The subject remains very cool through this. It pretends to ignore me. I grapple and bite. The subject must enjoy being pursued a little; it has to like my grip, I suppose.

Finally, I get it pinned down on paper, get it all written out in several pages (by now I am really sick of the thing). I hand it to someone, and they read it and say: "That's very good!" Then the subject hisses in my ear, "I told you so." I yell back, "What do you mean, Told you so? I did all the work!"

This is a chapter about finding subjects—finding, trapping, caging them; and then keeping them under control once you've got them in mind. We subtitle this chapter "an introduction" because it is just that—the beginning of a program in writing which continues through the rest of the book. At almost any stage in writing, you can "find" an idea. Ten years after you write something, you can read it over and have an idea pop into your head about the subject. Indeed, as long as you are alive, your brain never stops its process of discovering ideas. What it needs is encouragement. In that last sentence is a major theme of this chapter—and also of the following three chapters in Part One: *Preparing to Write.*

Psychologically speaking, our "needs" as writers are somewhat different. A device for finding ideas for papers may be useful to you but not to your friend, sister, or roommate. A method of organizing may satisfy your roommate but drive you to distraction. Every human being has a creative engine, but not all engines run at the same rate or on the same fuel. Accordingly, the strategies for finding ideas for subjects given here are meant to be suggestions rather than hard-and-fast rules.

Textbooks used to say that the parts of a typical writing process could be sharply outlined, one stage neatly following another:

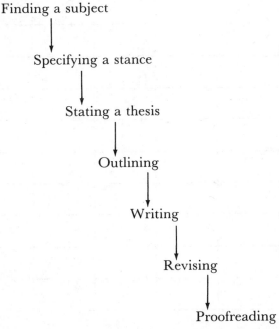

Finding a subject

Specifying a stance

Stating a thesis

Outlining

Writing

Revising

Proofreading

Recent research has shown that the writing process is rather different. If it could be diagrammed at all, it would look something like the drawing on the next page. In other words, writing is less a linear process than a complex set of processes, verbal tactics, and rhetorical strategies.

Writing Is . . .

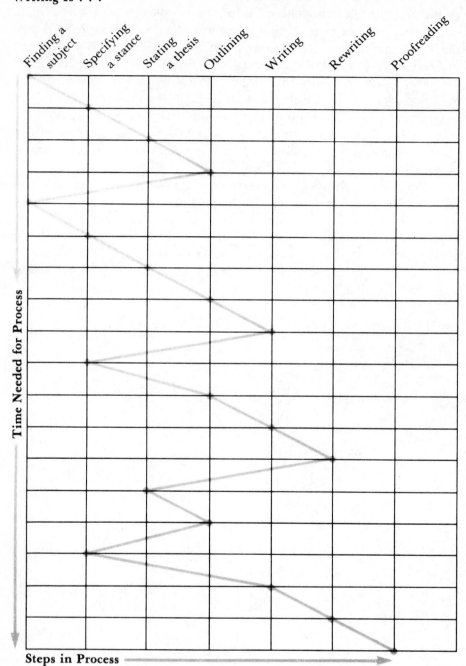

All of these tend to occur both singly and together. The subject-finding stage, for example, often seems a part of everything else. It's as if writers move forward and backward, even sideways, at the same time they inch toward the goal — a finished paper.

PATHS TO FINDING SUBJECTS

Brainstorming

Originally, *brainstorming* was a term used to describe a "conference method" for solving problems. The method has been used for many years in business. You get a group of people around a table, and they try to solve a problem — for example, to find new uses for a *resealable plastic bag.* The people around the table simply start talking and reacting to each other:

> *Joan:* "Use it for wet bathing suits."
> *Chairman:* "How about album covers for phonograph records."
> *Joan:* "Toothbrushes . . . Soap."
> *Sally:* "How about the fisherman."
> *Chairman:* "How about for bait. Live bait, you could put that in this."
> *Jim:* "How about taking something down when you go skin diving."
> *Joan:* "How about for vegetables or cheeses."
> *Chairman:* "How about using it to contain paint or coloring material."
> *Bill:* "Put the fish in it after you catch it."
> *Sam:* "Use it as a rain shoe."
> *Albert:* "How about the invalids who have to take a certain type of prescribed pill so many times a day . . . a very small package in place of a box which is cumbersome."
> *Chairman:* "Maybe it could even have little packages inside the major package."
> *Joan:* "Artists could use that for carrying pastels and oils."
> *Chairman:* "Or for their wet brushes."
> *Mary:* "Women could carry their makeup."
> *Joan:* "Yes."
> *Paul:* "Packaging food for restaurants."
> *Bill:* "Use it to take the bones home to feed the dog."
>   —Charles Whiting, *Creative Thinking*

Brainstorming is particularly valuable to the writer because it offers a technique for getting *suggestions* and *leads* for a subject. You can do it with roommates or friends. But most of us brainstorm alone, using sheets of scratch paper. Done alone, brainstorming becomes an association game on paper. You start with something—anything—and with a pencil and paper you talk to yourself (see p. 6).

```
        Here comes Mickey up the stairs wearing his Walkman

        Walkman -- radio

        radio what?  Lost.  No, stolen

        Cherie's car, they stole radio & stereo, broke into car

        (in college lot)

        parking lot

        why steal?

        why not keep from stealing?

        cars broken into often in college lots

        stop it!!!

        how to stop them from stealing (breaking into?)

        add lights

        regular patrols -- use 'em

        _____

        Prevent thefts in college lots by adding lights and

        regular police patrols.
```

Here you see an example of *controlled brainstorming,* in which at first you let your thoughts freely associate, writing down whatever comes to mind. But after a few phrases appear, you gently apply pressure and *shape* some of the material as it emerges. But not too much pressure at first. Only when the ideas tend to get specific should you come to a conclusion that may provide a subject. Then, as in the example, you try to shape the conclusion into a sentence: *Prevent thefts in college lots by adding lights and regular police patrols.* This may not be your final subject (it may not even be close to the final one), but at least it is a beginning.

You will note that we suggest ending a brainstorming session—whether you are doing it alone or with other people—with a sentence that is written down. Writing the sentence is not meant to be a final act in your search for a subject. Rather it is merely a "closure" on the brainstorming session, one that enables you to pick up easily where you left off if you think more work is necessary.

In the pages that follow, we will give more suggestions for finding and shaping subjects. As you read them, keep in the back of your mind what we have said about *brainstorming*—a technique which is useful in combination with other subject-hunting devices.

Freewriting

Freewriting is a form of brainstorming, the difference being that in freewriting you tend to use "running prose"—sentences and parts of sentences that run from margin to margin of the page. Most brainstorming, as we use the term, consists of words and phrases in list form. Most freewriting looks like ordinary writing on the page, although it is somewhat choppier and often rather disconnected.

The advantage of freewriting is that it loosens you up psychologically and allows your brain and hand to coordinate and warm up together (many writers have cold engines). The point of it is to start and keep going: write from the left margin to the right margin and don't stop until you feel like a baseball pitcher after a good warm-up—loose and ready for action. Here's an example of freewriting:

> Here I am, sitting under this tree, half dozing in the sun. Shouting and bellowing; it started almost without warning. One minute, silence on the quad. Long curves of flights of frisbees and oofs of pleasure when the frisbee is caught. Whirl and turn and throw again. "HAVE YOU THOUGHT ABOUT GOD TODAY?" No, and I didn't yesterday, nor the day before nor the day before—tomorrow and tomorrow creeps in . . . what's the rest of that and what's it from? "GOD IS WITH YOU, HE WANTS TO KNOW. . . ." *I* want to know why I can't sit here in the sun without somebody bellowing in my ear. 100 ft. away and he's the noisiest thing in 6 acres of quadrangle. What do preachers want to come here and bother us for anyway? Do they ever get converts? I don't need them—I'm *already* a believer. They are raucous, noisy, tiresome, irrelevant, and a plain bore. UNDERLINE THAT!

The idea that the student told himself to underline suggested a subject for writing. He eventually wrote a paper that described how he felt about the event he freewrote into his notebook: He called his paper: *Godspelling the Quad: One Form of Noise Pollution.*

Keep a Journal

A *journal* is a set of scribbled notes and personal remarks that you put down when something intriguing happens, or when you hear about an idea that you want to remember. A journal is useful because it is full of information, and also of little observations that can trigger the imagination. The entries can consist of a sentence, a phrase, a conversation, a quotation from a magazine article, a line from a movie or story. It can be your reaction to an event. It is also a good warm-up device; write for awhile, and then find an idea.

A JOURNAL ENTRY:

Went to lunch with Lillian, who said that she found the concert last night "sickening." The movie two nights before she said was "sickening." The lunch was "sickening." Lillian is becoming, well, repetitive.

Worked on the report due in Psych until 5:00. Then played a little touch football for a while. Knee still hurts.

Lillian called and said she got a job at the bookstore and would I come over and talk about it with her. She seemed subdued, and didn't say that the thought of 20 hours of work a week would make her sick. As it turned out, she *was* subdued. I can't decide whether she is 12 years old or 22. She can run the range of 10 years in a few seconds. She's not as bad as Duane [his roommate] tho, who acts like he's 12 all the time.

Lillian proofread my psych paper and found six errors that I had missed. "Sickening," she said.

I went home and went to bed.

NEXT DAY: I found an idea! *Discuss the current slang on the campus.*

Look Around You

One of our friends, a professional writer, says: "If it's ideas you're after, get out of your chair *and go look*. Walk around; listen." After the great flood in Corning, N.Y., in 1972, R. N. Hoye wondered: What is a flooded house like after the water is gone? What do people face when they return to their homes? He went to look:

[1]The first problem is just to get in. If the front door has swollen, is blocked by mud, or has something jammed against it, it may be necessary to break a window to gain entry. Inside, the first thing observed is a water-line four or six or ten feet high all around the walls. The floors themselves are warped into unbelievable waves of wood six to ten inches high, very easy to stumble over. Everything in every room is coated with mud between two and four inches deep, and the mud not only is still wet, but has an unforgettable odor. Rugs, sofas, pillows, tables, and chairs are all

soaked, not just sodden or damp. Books have swollen and burst their bindings. Any ashtray or vase you pick up is full of brown, cold water. Everything drips.

²Go into the kitchen. The doors on some cabinets are so swollen that it takes a few hard pulls to get them open. When you do open the cabinets, water runs out. The washing machine is filled with water; there is an ugly waterline on the refrigerator. Now go upstairs. In the bedrooms, the mattresses are soaked and covered with mud. The mattresses are so heavy that two people can barely drag one, and then only a few feet at a time. Everything folded in drawers and hanging in closets is soaked, too. Even the shoes on the floors of the closets have water in them.

³Of course, if you have a basement, it's still full of water; you may be able to see the top of the furnace. There's nothing to do here until the pumpers start making their rounds. In your garage, bikes, sleds, lawnmowers, and tools already have begun to rust.

Nearly every sentence of Hoye's represents an observation — a going-to-look at something which could provide ideas for several papers: (a) A flood causes irreparable damage to a house, clothing, and equipment. (b) A flood leaves a mark on a family's possessions that can never be paid for. (c) Some flood-damaged goods can never be used again.

Surprise Yourself

One problem with looking for material is that you may find more of it than you know what to do with; life is full of surprises. But if surprising ideas won't come easily to you, go to them. Surprise yourself.

A student remarked in class one day: "It seems that every good idea I have about writing is just a twisted version of an ordinary one."

"Meaning what?"

"Well, if you take an ordinary idea and give it a little *twist,* it will come out unordinary — surprising. When I was in high school I read that statement of Admiral Oliver Hazard Perry's: 'We have met the enemy, and they are ours.' When my brother took the SAT test to get into college, he and thousands of others the same year had to write an essay for the SAT based on a statement from the comic strip *Pogo:* 'We have met the enemy, and he is us.' The change in the quote is surprising, and helps to suggest ideas."

Surprise yourself (and your reader) with a *description* one might not normally expect. The scholar Elaine Partnow writes: "Through all this sleuthing I have come to feel that the public regards women in past and current history very much like fine character actors — we recognize them but do not know their names; we need them but do not pay them homage;

we make demands on them but do not document their contributions." Women as character actors: the surprise inherent in the description is itself a "found idea," one which helps find and shape other ideas.

Other Options for Finding Subjects

Another student writes home regularly. Before mailing her letters, she copies them on the photocopier in the library. Into the letters she puts everything she can think of, making her parents happy and also supplying ideas for papers and essays to come. A third student is an annotator of books and magazines. Never lend him a book unless you want it back full of underlinings and remarks in the margin like *This is not true!!* He also keeps a notebook of observations and quoted material from his reading. We would hesitate to use his notebook method by itself. Think of having to read all the way through a notebook to find a remark you were sure you remembered putting down—somewhere. But his notebook works for him.

And that, of course, is the point. If brainstorming, freewriting in books, or keeping a diary, notebook, or journal works for you, do it. Indeed, don't be afraid to try anything that may produce or trap an idea. *Skim* a magazine or book; *watch* a TV channel you seldom watch; *read* a newspaper as if you were from a foreign country; *chat* with a stranger at the laundromat or supermarket. Interview a professor who teaches a course you never heard of: "How did the course come to be taught? What do your students learn in it?"

Hooking an Idea

One cold winter day we were talking to a student who had too many ideas. His father was a high school principal, and he was planning to write about the joys and sorrows of being a school principal in a small town.

The student showed us a dozen pages of false starts. We read them and asked, "How many subjects have you got here?"

"That's the trouble," he said. "I've got so many ideas about being a principal and so much to say that I don't know where to begin. If I could just get started . . ." We pointed to the back of the classroom. Along the wall was a line of coat hooks, and his coat was hanging on one of them. "Look at your coat," we said. "When you came in, you didn't throw your coat at the wall and hope it would miraculously stay up there off the floor. You hung it high and dry on a hook. You are trying to throw your next piece of writing at a rhetorical wall, hoping it will stay there. But your writing keeps falling down in a heap. Try some hooks. For example:

Why school principals *fail.*

The hooks are provided in the words *why* and *fail.* As you plan your paper, keep hanging your ideas on those two words."

We told the student about other possible word-hooks for this paper:

The *successful* principal *listens.*
How a *good* principal *prepares.*
A principal who keeps his job is *lucky.*
A principal and town *politics.*
Should you be a principal? Yes, if you have *patience* and physical *stamina.*

For two reasons, we recommend the hook strongly to writers. First, it dramatizes clearly and simply one of the natural ways the human brain works, and so helps us find and clarify ideas. It is natural for us to characterize and capsulize our experiences in single words (and, sometimes, phrases):

- That course is *boring.*
- For some American citizens, President Reagan was a *teflon* president.
- But I'm not *ready* to get married!
- All he wanted in life was *to act.*
- The Civil War was a *bloody disaster,* the first *modern war.*
- To me, God is a woman, and every thing about Her reminds me of the *female.*
- A partial solution to the apartheid in South Africa is [is not] *disinvestment.*
- The war on poverty *can be won.*

Each italicized word or phrase represents an idea-hook on which you can hang a paper or theme. Note, by the way, that the hook can be more than one device of grammar. In the examples above:

Boring, teflon, and *ready* are adjectives.
Female and *disinvestment* are nouns.
To act is an infinitive.
Bloody disaster and *modern war* are noun phrases.
Can is an auxiliary verb (consider the difference between "*can* be won" and "*may* be won.")

A second reason why we recommend the hook is that it supplies control throughout the writing process, as shown in the drawing on p. 8. No matter where you are in the process—whether in finding ideas, outlining, rewriting—the hook provides a check on what you are doing. If, for instance, you are writing on why principals *fail,* throughout the writing process keep checking the *fail* hook to see that your paper is still hanging on it. For example: You will *fail* as a principal if you are not a good listener, an adept politician, and an organized planner. A student writing about a successful principal might use different hook(s): A principal's job is not an easy one but if you have *patience* and *physical stamina,* you will be successful.

Here, at the stage of finding ideas, we suggest only that you consider hanging your paper on something—or on something*s.* (Some ideas need two, even three, hooks.) Also, in this early stage, it is not important whether your hooks are expressed in a title, a sentence fragment, or a full sentence. The main thing is to get those hooks on scratch paper so you can think about them and get started writing.

MARTIN AND THE NERD: A CASE HISTORY

*T*o demonstrate some ways of finding ideas, we taped an interview with Martin, one of our students. As background, you need to know that students in our community start studying computers in about the seventh grade, and that our university, one of the centers of computer training in the world, has many computers available for practice and study. The italicized questions in the interview are ours. Martin begins:

> Walking home from class, I was thinking about an idea for my paper. As you know, my major interest is in computers, and so it was natural to think about computers as a general subject. I'd recently heard the argument that Computer Science—like many technical-training majors—does not prepare students well for life. This seemed like a line of thought to follow. Should I hang the paper on "preparation for life"?
>
> Later I talked this over with my roommate, and he reminded me of my complaint about "computer nerds"—you know, computer addicts—and that some of them smell bad—they don't wash often enough, and live in squalor.

The computer did it.
Computers can't...
Contains a lot of numbers...
Nerds smell bad.
Addresses like houses.
How often do we consider the human cost...
    nerds are human
Should they be allowed to use computers at all?
They ruined him — all he ever did was sit
    in front of a computer and play games.
There are two main species of computer needs.

So what, I thought, has that got to do with anything? I wandered around the subject some more, and scratched on some paper with a pencil. Here's the paper with my scratches:
I don't know what some of these entries mean now.

It looks as though you were wandering all over the map at this stage.

Well, yes. I'd started with that business about computer training—no, with *technical* training not preparing people well for life. Until my roommate reminded me of what I had said about nerds, I hadn't thought about them at all. (I believe in *talking* to people about papers and paper topics. People should talk more about their ideas anyway, bounce them off some-body else.)

At this point, I started a typical journal entry. I keep these in a spiral notebook—there's not much order or sense in them usually. Here is the way the entry looked, with my own comments on it:

> We all know about the benefits of computers, but how often do we consider the casualties — those who use the machines? I refer to that subspecies of mankind known to those in the computer trade as "computer nerds." Who are these people, and how did they become computer nerds?
>
> In this exposition I will discuss methods of detecting computer nerds, and examine their relations with computers (the role of computers in their lives?)

As you can see, this did have some direction. I was focusing on the idea of the computer nerd; the technical training subject was too big and unmanageable. But after letting this sit for a while, I read it and was bothered by the number of little ideas in the big subject; *benefits of computers, casualties, nerds, how they got to be nerds, detecting them and examining them* . . . all too much, too much.

Where did the term nerd *come from? Is it yours?*

Oh, no, it's the standard term. That's what people call them.

What did you do next?

I tried typing a paragraph. This one had a title.

```
                Computer Addiction

     We are often told of the benefits of computers.

But how often do we hear of the casualties among those

who use the machines?  I refer to those who become

addicted to computers.  In the trade, we call them

"computer nerds."
```

Now here I was trying to do something about all those little ideas I'd had earlier. You know, now I was focusing on the paper, getting some control of it. This paper was going to have as hooks *computer nerds* and how they have become *addicted*. In fact, it was the *addiction* hook that made the paper grow — go, I should say. I was moving toward a thesis: *Computer programming is addictive*. [A *thesis* is the main point of a paper. See p. 25.] But then I realized that a better and more manageable thesis would deal with the *computer nerd* and *his addiction*. Therefore, my thesis became: *A computer nerd is a person who has become addicted to computer programming*.

Here is Martin's paper, the result of his search for ideas and a subject.

COMPUTER NERDS

[1]We are often told of the benefits of computers, but how often do we hear of the casualties among those who use the machines? I refer to those who become addicted to computers, known to the trade as "computer nerds."

[2]There are two main varieties of these people—the day nerd and the night nerd. By choice, most of them choose to be day nerds, but at many computer installations supervisors or teachers allow them to work only at night, thus converting them into night nerds. A less common variety live with a 25- or 26-hour clock, being fixed as neither day nor night nerd.

[3]How do you distinguish computer nerds from the general public? Beginning nerds are recognized by the (programmable) calculator worn on the belt, ready for a quick draw in a financial emergency—such as a restaurant bill that must be split, or a tax return. As nerds gain experience, the calculator is replaced by a punch-card, which is carried in the left front shirt pocket. The punch-card phase is short, however, because considerable status is attached to the acquisition of the ultimate distinguishing sign: "terminal eyes," named after the computer terminal at which the computer nerds spend most of their waking hours.

[4]During development of the fully fledged computer nerd, several behavioral traits are evident. He (*he*, since female nerds at this time do not appear to exist) becomes more withdrawn; he is unwilling to communicate with people, preferring instead communion with the computer; and his health deteriorates as he spends more and more time out of natural light. In the final phases, the nerd develops characteristics common to hunted animals. He knows that his days at the computer are numbered, yet he cannot stop. He prefers developing better and better game programs to doing school work. Eventually, lack of sleep or inadequate course grades bring about his downfall.

[5]There is no doubt that computer programming is addictive, particularly for the nerd. Programs are never free of errors, but the challenge always is to find the final perfect one. Just as that one error is "fixed," another appears. And so on. The principle is the same as those underlying alcoholism and gambling: "One more, and then I'll give up." Aggravating the problem are supervisors or teachers who don't try to distinguish between someone working on a computer assignment and one working on a game program. By the time the problem becomes evident, much time has been lost and another addict has been created.

PRACTICE

Discussion

1. Consider again Martin's paper, pp. 17–18. How effective is it? Can you suggest improvements?

   Suppose that you believe Martin should begin again on his general subject. How might he formulate his ideas or get new ones? Can you suggest a *surprise* in his topic? Different *hooks*?

2. Let us assume that you want something changed. This change may involve better service for your car, different scheduling of classes, more money from home, the highway in front of your house repaired, or improved funding for women's sports at your college, etc.

Look back at the strategies for finding ideas that we have examined. Prepare for class discussion a few specific answers to these questions:

a. What change do you want?

b. How did you decide on the change?

3. Andy Rooney called an essay "Can We Find the Hiding Places We've Lost?" Here are the first three paragraphs from his essay:

> [1]It seems to me it's getting harder and harder to find a place to hide things. Some people are better at hiding things than others, but even the good hiders are having trouble these days. Traditionally, Americans have done their hiding under mattresses, in cookie jars, under the front door mats, behind pictures, on top of shelves, and under underwear. These hiding places are no longer secure and the time may fast be approaching when we will run out of hiding places.
>
> [2]The United States government can't even find a satisfactory place to hide the missiles from the Russians and there's been a big squabble about it in Congress. One of the ideas has been to build a lot of missile sites in Nevada but only put actual missiles in a few of them. The Russians wouldn't know which sites had them and which were dummies. This is a very clever idea but not actual hiding.
>
> [3]One of the biggest hiding problems on a homeowner's level is where to put the silver so burglars won't steal it. In many cities you can't rent a safe deposit vault at the bank because they've all been taken by people who thought of that before you did. All across the country Americans with silver knives, forks, and spoons have hidden them away in the bank and are now eating off dime-store utensils. This way they can leave their silverware to their children, who won't dare leave it around the house to eat off either.

Work backwards from these paragraphs. Make a scratch list of the ideas that might have occurred to Rooney as he prepared to write. What were his surprises? His hooks?

Here is Rooney's eighth paragraph. How do you suppose he got the idea for this paragraph on the garage and other areas in the house?

> [8]Hiding places like our garage, our attic or our cellar are fast disappearing. Houses are being built without attics or cellars, and architects are designing houses with less of what they call "waste space." What all of

us want is more "waste space," not less. That's the best kind of space and it's the kind of space you hide things in. The architecture that provides a place for everything imposes an order on our lives that precludes the haphazard arrangement of the things we own that permits us to hide them so well.

4. Satchel Paige, the great athlete, used to say: "Don't look back; something may be gaining on you." Make up several imitations of this remark, to be used as hooks and titles for papers.

Other quotations as possibilities:
   a. "No man but a blockhead ever wrote except for money." (Sam Johnson)
   b. "Edgar Allan Poe, a drinker with writing problems, . . ." (Clyde Haberman)
   c. "I wish that dog was half mine." *Why?* "I'd kill my half." (anonymous)
   d. "America's grandpas are now mugging their young." (Norman Macrae, an English economist, writing on American Social Security)
   e. "Home owner: one who is always on his way to the hardware store." (anonymous)
   f. "Academic bureaucrats are the cancer cells of this place." (anonymous)

Writing

1. Write a paper based on Practice 2, under *Discussion Questions*.

2. Take a blank sheet of paper and start writing. Don't stop to think —simply begin. If nothing else gets you moving, write "One, two, three, four, get up and bar the door . . ." Write anything that crosses your mind until you get to the bottom of the page.

   Pick up a second sheet. From the first sheet, make a few lists of words and phrases that strike your fancy, like: "I can hear the faucet dripping. I remember Lee left the cap off the toothpaste again. Sloppy roommate." Make a judgment: "He is sloppy but easy to live with." Generalize: "Sloppy roommates are tolerable if they are easy to live with."

   Spend a few minutes working back and forth between your first sheet of paper and your second. Listen for the meanings. On your second sheet, write a column heading: *Hooks*. How many hooks can you find from the first sheet? From the second? Can you find or create any surprises?

CHAPTER 2
THE WRITER'S STANCE

We bumped into one of our former students the other day. Now a junior, he told us he was taking a course in philosophy. "The prof's really strange," he said. "He rambles the whole hour about a philosophical idea while he's looking out the window — never looks at us. And about half the time he uses such odd terms that we don't know what he is talking about. As you used to say, he won't communicate until he improves his stance!"

Stance refers to how you place or position yourself rhetorically in communicating to other people. Our student's professor of philosophy would improve his stance if he talked *to* the students in his class, instead of looking out the window as he talked. He should always be concerned about his audience — How are they responding to his remarks? He should change his role from philosophical specialist to teacher of undergraduates. Finally, he should make at least one major point clearly in each hour, and keep to that point without rambling.

As a writer, you also position yourself. Your *writer's stance* is the position you take in relation to three important elements in a piece of writing:

1. You (your *role* as writer).

2. Your thesis (your *point* or main idea). We will discuss the thesis at length in Chapter 3.

3. Your *reader(s)*.

APPLYING THE PRINCIPLES OF STANCE

So far, we have been discussing *stance* in fairly general terms. Now let's be specific, and apply the principle to some writing problems you may have. Our examples will come from two student writers, Michael and Nancy. Michael's example is brief; Nancy's is longer, and we will follow it from conception to finished paper.

Michael drives a cab part-time. He has an interesting idea for a paper: that cab driving is an unglamorous job. Here is one of the paragraphs in his first draft:

> Traffic can destroy patience faster than threading heavy thread through a needle. City driving sneaks up on your nerves. It doesn't blast you; it just gnaws at your stomach. Cars are death traps. It takes so little to be behind a wheel—almost anyone can get a license. And there's not much money in it. Driving all day I saw them all, wild drivers, incompetent drivers, angry drivers. I made mistakes too and put lives in jeopardy; I came to respect the power of the automobile.

When he talked to us, Michael said that he did not feel comfortable with what he had written. Something, he wasn't sure what, had gone wrong; he was stuck and could not continue with any confidence.

The problem was that he had not yet found an appropriate stance for the essay. What was he trying to say about cab driving? His paragraph rambles, making three or four points without developing any one of them adequately. To improve his work, he needed to specify the three elements of stance:

> *Role:*   I am a student working part-time as a driver for a local cab company. I am nineteen years old.
>
> *Thesis:*   Driving a cab part-time is a poor way for a college student to make money.
>
> *Reader:*   The "general reader," who might be curious about what it's like to drive a cab.

About the general reader we will have more to say later. Michael began to rewrite his paper, getting this result for two paragraphs:

> On an average twelve-hour workday on Saturday or Sunday, I make twenty-five to thirty dollars after paying for half of the gas I use — a company requirement. I start at six o'clock in the morning, and finish at seven in the evening. But since the supper hour is the busiest time of the day, I often have to stay an hour late. The cabs eat gas like luxury cars. Twenty-five percent of my profits are lost in paying for gas. In the winter, between calls, I either turn off the engine or burn up all my profits. Cold, cold.
>
> I receive tips from perhaps one-fifth of the fares. If a person gives me a quarter he smiles benevolently as if he has finally proved to himself that he really has a philanthropic heart. "Well, how much do you get as a tip?" some will ask. Or: "What's the right amount to tip?" A common comment, after a toothy smile: "Well, you got me here safely, didn't you? I think you deserve a tip." An extra dime falls into my hand, and after my word of thanks, I hear a chuckle or two, and a pleasant, "You're welcome, you're quite welcome."

These paragraphs are not perfect, but they're better than Michael's first effort — more interesting, readable, and informative. We know who the writer is, why he wishes to communicate to us, what the point of his communication is.

As a part of a new assignment, Michael tried shifting his stance:

> Your cabs are in terrible condition; some are actually unsafe. The horn did not work on mine all last weekend. The brakes on No. 37 are so badly worn that they will not respond without pumping. Since most of us have to drive fast to get from one place to another to pick up a new fare, we are endangering our lives and other people's — just to do our jobs.

The writer's role here stays the same, but Michael has changed his thesis and his reader, who is now the owner of the cab company.

Let's consider another writer. Nancy was working on a paper for her composition class. But the paper — on her experiences backpacking in Europe last summer — refused to get written. She made several false starts, tried an outline that got nowhere, and filled parts of three pages with neat handwriting that turned into scrawls as she realized that the paper just was not coming out right.

What to do? She remembered her instructor's suggestion: "If you get into trouble on a paper, don't keep fighting it — come see me right away!"

So, bundling up her material (false starts, scrawls, and the outline that went nowhere), off Nancy went to her instructor's office. He looked at what she had written so far and said to her: "Surely we can do something with this. But before we go on, tell me—just how do you feel about your subject?"

"Traveling in Europe? A perfect subject for me," said Nancy. "I just spent over two months living it. I'm following your advice: 'Write about what you know.' I have a lot of concrete materials, so the paper ought to write itself. I don't usually have much trouble writing, but right now each word comes harder than the last one. I feel as if I should tear it all up and start over. But *how* do I get a better start? Talk about frustration!"

The basic solution to Nancy's problem, her instructor told her, may lie in improving her stance. She had forgotten that a successful paper is always written by somebody, to somebody, and for a purpose. Using her material as an example, let's examine the elements of stance—*role, point* (thesis), and *reader.*

The Role

You do not use a role to cover up your true self or to give a false impression to a reader. Nor do you use it to play out a fictional part, as you might if you were acting on stage or in film. Your role as writer is a legitimate part of you and your existence. Who are you and what do you do? How many roles do you adopt as a matter of course in your daily life?

Nancy is eighteen years old. She graduated from high school last spring. She lives in a dormitory and has a part-time job. She is taking a general science course, and hopes eventually to be a hospital technician. She saved her job money during her last year in high school in order to backpack through Europe in the summer with a friend. Here are some of her roles that she mentioned to her instructor:

—babysitter   —owner of a bicycle
—consumer   —stenographer-typist
—taxpayer   —cook
   (five cents on every dollar)   —daughter
—sister   —amateur pottery maker
—U.S. citizen   —environmentalist
—college student   —member of Sierra Club

Her instructor had told her that he could not find Nancy in the first drafts of her paper—that, in effect, he could not see one of her clear roles as a writer in them. "Before you start writing again," he told her, "pick a role and stick to it. What do you want to be?"

"An American traveling in Europe."

"Pretty vague," he said. "Politicians, movie actors, tourists, soldiers, business executives — they can all be 'Americans traveling in Europe.' Can you be more specific?"

"OK, I am a woman; I'm eighteen; I know a little French, but no other foreign languages. I took 2,500 hard-earned dollars out of my bank account — that was all there was in it — and flew off to another part of the world, not knowing any more what I was getting into than if I were flying to the moon. But I was going to see everything!"

"Good enough," he said. "There's a genuine role for you: a young American woman on the loose over there without much money who's going to see every castle and museum on the continent. Now — what is your thesis?"

The Thesis

Her instructor talked to Nancy about several possibilities for a thesis — the point of the paper, *its main idea stated in one specifically written sentence.* She could discuss the language problems she encountered, the difficulties of travel for someone without much money, the sights to see, the problem of communicating with parents and friends thousands of miles away.

But Nancy kept coming back to one idea that she considered important. Too many young Americans, like herself, went off merrily to Europe without being properly prepared for what they would encounter. Her thesis suggested itself. Why not try to warn travelers about three or four problems they might encounter, and suggest how they could go about solving them? At this stage, then, her hooks for the paper were *traveling in Europe* and *problems.* (For a discussion of *hooks,* see Chapter 1, p. 12).

Her instructor agreed that this idea could lead to a sensible thesis. (The final version of her thesis is given below.)

The Reader

Now Nancy needed to specify a reader.

"You already know," said her instructor, "that you seldom (if ever) write anything that is directed to every person who reads English. Most pieces of writing are directed to a special reader or group of readers. Your own composition textbook is directed to one group of readers; an article in *TV Guide* is directed to another; a set of directions on repairing a motor-boat engine to yet another. While these groups of readers may overlap somewhat, they usually do have a certain distinctness. Write for a specific reader, Nancy; aim for a particular target."

Nancy commented that her thoughts about her role and thesis also seemed to suggest a certain group of readers—those young American backpackers with little money who intended to see Europe but wouldn't always know what to expect.

A Completed Stance

Nancy's completed stance now looked like this:

My role:	I am a young American who traveled through Europe this summer. I would like to show how other backpackers can do the same thing, but do it more easily than I did.
My thesis:	In order to make traveling easier and more pleasant in Europe, buy three informative books, learn about Youth Hostels, and be prepared for the "male problem."
My reader:	Young Americans who might want to travel as I did. My essay will be slanted somewhat to women, but men should definitely be interested too.

Here is Nancy's completed paper.

WHAT YOU ALWAYS WANTED TO KNOW ABOUT BACKPACKING IN EUROPE (BUT DIDN'T KNOW ENOUGH TO ASK)

[1]So you're going to hike around Europe! You have saved some money; you have your backpack all ready to go (complete with a box of bandages for the very sore feet you're going to get); and you have pored over your collection of travel folders, looking again at those glamorous canals and castles and mountains that will shortly be in front of your camera.

[2]But have you talked to other young people who have recently been there? Do you know what to look out for and what to expect? I thought I was well prepared in every way, but some problems came up I did not expect. I could have dealt with them much more easily if I had had the information I am giving you here. I'll omit a lot of little things in order to concentrate on three larger ones: certain useful books to buy, the nature of Youth Hostels, and the problem of men in southern Europe. (I assume that, like myself and most of the other young travelers I met, you are traveling light and on a small budget—I got home with twenty-five cents.)*

---

*In order to make your sentences flow smoothly in your introduction, you may have to paraphrase your thesis rather than state it word for word. Note that Nancy's original thesis (p. 25) is paraphrased in paragraph 2.

[3]Before you begin your trip there are two or three books I would recommend you buy and read. One is a budget guide, Frommer-Pasmantier's *Europe on Fifteen Dollars a Day*. This book tells you a great deal about all the major cities in Europe. It has descriptions of the fascinating places to go and often how to get there. It also includes names of inexpensive restaurants and hotels. The book is a reassuring thing to have when you arrive in a big city with no place to sleep. Also, by reading about what is in a city before you go, you can decide in advance if you want to visit it.

[4]Another important book to get is a *Rail Schedule*. It includes train schedules for all of western Europe. If you have a Eurailpass, which is probably the cheapest and fastest way to travel in the free countries on the continent, this book will be a great help. Having a complete *Schedule* allows you to stop in little out-of-the-way places because you know when and where you can get connections *out* of them. It's usually not wise to jump on a train going to a tiny town if you have no idea when you can catch another train to leave. Also, having the *Rail Schedule* will inevitably save you long hours of waiting in train stations. Since many of the southern countries do not post schedules, it is extremely time-consuming to stand (sometimes for hours) in information lines trying to find out when you can leave.

[5]A third book I recommend is the *Youth Hostel Guide*. This book tells you where the hostels are and how far they are located from the train stations. It gives hostel facilities, hours, and (sometimes) prices. I tried to get along without a hostel book some of the time by using the information offices at railway stations. The information clerk could usually tell me if there was a hostel and how to find it. But if you are planning to do any traveling in rural areas, like Normandy in France, as I did, you will definitely need a *Hostel Guide*. The townspeople in such areas often don't even know their hostel exists.

[6]Staying in Youth Hostels can make your living expenses much lower, but sometimes the problems and restrictions of staying in a hostel may make other accommodations more desirable. Hostels are dormitory-type hotels that rent a place to sleep for between $.75 and $2.50 a night. Their quality varies greatly. Some of them are very clean and have all the comforts of home. Others are incredibly dirty and primitive. Before you plan to make a habit of staying in hostels you should know that they have two large drawbacks.

[7]First, hostels are usually located far away from the center of the city, sometimes too far to make staying in one economical. Be prepared either to walk a long way into town or to spend money on subways and buses. Second, the early curfews in most hostels makes staying in them a problem if you want to go out on the town. Most of them have a curfew as early as 10:00 P.M. Although there are a few hostels that will charge a small fine for being late, most of them simply lock the doors at 10:00 so no one can get in *or* out. If you are in a city like Munich or London where you want to stay out late, I would advise staying in a cheap hotel rather than in a hostel.

[8]Hostels are closed during the day between 9:00 and 5:00. This causes some difficulty if you arrive in a new town early in the afternoon and go

straight to the hostel. You will end up wasting a lot of time just waiting for it to open. And you will have plenty of waiting ahead of you in the check-in line. Because hostels are closed all day and because many of them require that you reregister every night, you could end up in some very long lines, especially during the summer months. The fact that the hostels are closed from 9:00 to 5:00 means that you may have to keep walking around all day. In the southern countries like Italy and Spain, where an entire town closes up during the afternoon, you can end up with nothing to do and no place to go.

[9]If you women are planning to spend any time at all in Italy, Greece, or Spain, you should be forewarned about the male population. (This section should be read by you men too because you will undoubtedly be approached by an American girl looking for someone to protect her or just to sit with her until her harassers leave.) The first thing you have to realize when traveling in these countries is that a local woman does not ordinarily walk out on the street without a sister or an older woman with her. So when you go out on the street alone you are automatically taken to be a tourist — and available. Also, the men have some kind of Early Detection device for American girls. It doesn't matter what you look like or what you are wearing. In Italy particularly you will be leered at, jeered at, whispered to, pinched, and generally driven crazy by the men. Don't think you can go unnoticed; the mere fact that you are an American on the street draws attention to you. Being with a man helps sometimes, but not always. My girl friend and I were with eight British and American boys in Rome, and it made absolutely no difference. You can be wearing a potato sack and the men will still bother you — I wouldn't recommend wearing a dress or shorts and halter tops anywhere. Wearing jeans instead will save you a lot of trouble. All of this may sound exaggerated to you, but it isn't. And it's better to expect the worst. If you are bothered less than you expected to be, it's better than entering a country like Italy unprepared for the hassles.

[10]A final point. Don't be discouraged by any of the things I have warned you about. Just know what to expect, and prepare carefully for your trip. Europe is a wonderful place, and I had a wonderful time. I have no regrets, and I would go again. Have a great time — and hang on to your Eurailpass!

PRACTICE

Discussion

Before discussing the following questions, review the summary of Nancy's *writer's stance* (p. 26)

a. In her first two paragraphs, how does Nancy show a concern for her reader? How does she *involve* her reader in her topic?

b. The thesis of the essay is stated, in paraphrased form, at the end of paragraph 2. Given the nature of Nancy's topic, is this a natural place for the thesis? Are there other places where the thesis might comfortably be placed? Why must the reader's reactions be closely considered when you decide on a location for your thesis?

c. Why will the reader appreciate the expression *"Another important book to get . . ."* at the beginning of paragraph 4?

d. Toward the end of paragraph 5, Nancy writes: "But if you are planning to do any traveling in rural areas, like Normandy in France, as I did, you will definitely need a *Hostel Guide.*" How, if at all, does this sentence reinforce Nancy's adopted role in her writer's stance? Do you find other sentences in other paragraphs that remind the reader of her role?

e. What other readers could this paper be directed to? What changes would be necessary in Nancy's role for other readers?

f. What kinds of readers (other than those we have already mentioned) would not find this paper very useful? Explain.

g. In paragraphs 6 and 7, how does Nancy make sure that her reader can follow the organization of her ideas?

h. A well-made paragraph can often be considered as a small "essay." Discuss the effectiveness of paragraph 9 as a little essay. Does it have a stance any different from that of the whole essay?

i. How does Nancy's conclusion fit her stance? Is there any contradiction in her conclusion?

j. The purpose of writing, of course, is to communicate ideas, attitudes, facts, and values. When a reader finishes a piece of writing, he should know more than he did when he started. Using brief phrases, make a list of "new knowledge" you have gained from Nancy's writing. What does this list tell you about a successful paper?

k. As a typical reader, write a note to Nancy making comments or suggestions about her writer's stance and her material. What, for instance, would you wish she had covered in her paper that she did not?

THE WRITER'S STANCE AND YOU

*A*re you wondering whether Nancy's writing problem is typical of most of the problems you will face? It *is* pretty typical. She had started out simply to write a paper on her European experiences, and she specified her stance using that idea as a broad base on which to build. For most assignments (whether you choose a topic or it is given to you by your instructor), you can follow a procedure roughly similar to Nancy's when you specify your own stance.

To help you with your various stances in preparing to write your papers, we suggest that you ask (and answer) certain questions about role, thesis, and reader:

Role: In this paper, who am I? What role can I most reasonably adopt? Will I feel comfortable in this role? What are my purposes in adopting it? Can I maintain it consistently throughout the paper?

Thesis: What main point do I want to explain or prove to my reader? Can I state this point specifically in a single sentence?

Reader: What reader, or group of readers, do I want to inform or convince? Have I identified the most appropriate reader?

Overview: How does my writer's stance look as a whole? Are its three parts logically related?

Your Role and Your Reader

Of course you are limited to some extent by the roles and readers that, in a practical way, are available to you. A readership of middle-aged bankers or Los Angeles cabdrivers would not have been practical for Nancy's essay on traveling in Europe. And if she were given the topic "Defend or Attack Offshore Drilling for Oil," her writer's role would probably be limited because, as she mentioned in her list of possible roles, she is an environmentalist and a member of the Sierra Club, an organization pledged to preserve the coastline against offshore drilling. As to what this specific limitation would amount to, she would have to decide for herself. Each of you will have your own limitations in roles — limitations governed by age, philosophy, political and religious beliefs (or lack of them), experience, knowledge of the subject, and so on. But on most topics, even within the framework of such limitations, there should be several writer's roles you can choose for your papers.

For most topics, there are also several possible audiences. On the offshore drilling topic just mentioned, your readership might be one of these:

— legislators considering an offshore drilling proposal
— drivers of cars who buy gasoline
— other college students of your "type"
— any persons interested in the topic
— any persons uninterested in the topic (a challenge to the writer)

—a writer who has written an argument for or against offshore drilling

Some of these audiences are more general than others. On many topics you may find that it is practical to address these *general readers,* a class of people who vary somewhat in age, occupation, and interests. But you should always specify and describe even your general audience because it will usually have certain characteristics that set it off from the "whole world" of readers. A letter written to your local newspaper on rezoning prime farmland for industrial use should not be directed to all readers of the newspaper because all of them are not equally interested in the subject or able to do anything about it.

To take another example, a critical essay on a novel should not be written for "everybody" but only for those interested in serious fiction generally and in your novel specifically—usually someone who has read the novel. If your group of readers have not read the novel, then that fact affects your thesis and your essay, which in this instance is likely to take the form of a review ("For the following reasons, this book is good—read it").

Too many students believe that their audience consists of one person, the instructor. In some cases, he may be your only reader. But in reality, he is quite often your *teacher-editor,* a trained professional who stands between you and your readers, pointing out where you have gone wrong in your essay, what you have done well, how you can make your work more convincing.

Guidelines for Identifying "The Reader"

Most papers are written for reader*s,* in the plural. To see how we can identify them, lets look in on a brainstorming session (for *brainstorming,* see pp. 7–9). The students in the session are brainstorming the audience for a short paper discussing requirements for the film study major at the college. The paper will argue that the requirements should be *increased.*

> *Arthur:* Audience is all students here.
> *Scott:* Not all are interested.
> *Catherine:* Just majors.
> *Wilda:* No, majors and minors.
> *Francisca:* They are not the ones who make the requirements.
> *Wilda:* Decide on one group.
> *Scott:* Who has the most power? To make changes?
> *Instructor:* Faculty committee on Majors and Minors.

Scott: Tenured professors on the committee, then.

Catherine: Are all professors on the committee tenured?

Wilda: What's the membership like?

Instructor (reading): Two full profs., one in 18th century lit, one in film study; two assistant professors, one in film study, one in composition, one student—five people total. Student's name is Gary Nelson.

Wilda: Anyone know the student?

Francisca: I think that's the Nelson who writes movie reviews for the paper.

Shannon: Three people, then, who care about film; two unknown. Shall we write for the three we are sure of, and guess about the others?

Don: They wouldn't be on the committee unless they were reasonably sympathetic to film study.

Shannon: Assumption: the committee wants the film study courses to succeed. Would not mind increasing hours for the major.

Scott: But another assumption: At least two people on this committee might think doing that would decrease the majors in either rhetoric or "straight" literature. Watch out for *them.*

Catherine: You mean they might be hostile to the proposal in the paper?

Francisca: OK, assume two hostiles in the audience.

We'll break off our account of the brainstorming session here. The group has clearly moved toward a good sense of their audience for an argument that requirements should be increased for the major in film. In essence, their conclusion was that the audience should be taken as mixed in several ways—student and professorial; possible hostile to the argument, and non-hostile; knowledgeable about film study and not knowledgeable. The paper should be written to "spread" to this audience. In other words, no part of the audience should be ignored in certain parts of the argument. If, for example, the writer assumes that all members of the audience know the history of the major in film and why certain requirements have been put in, he or she may miss the student member and possibly the two professors who do not teach in the film program.

We can set up flexible guidelines for considering readership or audience:

1. If possible, list the people in the audience—or, at least, the *types* of people. Know who and what they are.

2. Consider their knowledge; how much do they *know* about your subject and its various parts? (Are they very familiar with one part but not another?)

3. What are their prejudices—or prejudgments? What kind of automatic acceptance or rejection of your ideas are you likely to encounter? Familiar (and controversial) subjects like abortion, capital punishment, and "big"

government touch many nerves in people. But sometimes subjects that are less familiar and controversial can bring strong reactions you never expected. That can be awkward! Think, for example, of the worldwide firestorm of negative reaction caused by President Reagan's decision to lay a wreath in the German military cemetery where SS troops are buried—a case of an audience that was seriously misread.

4. What parts of your argument—or of your material—are they likely to accept? For whatever reason, what parts are they not likely to accept? Shape your paper accordingly.

5. As you write, keep in mind the typical faces of your readers. Imagine, as you write, that you are speaking to them and that they are reacting to your ideas as listeners would. Doing this gives you an immediate imaginative feedback on your ideas as you write them.

Your Thesis

Much of what we have said on the practical limitations of role and reader also applies to the thesis. The thesis, discussed at length in the next chapter, is dependent on role and reader. If you change either of these latter two, your thesis will probably change as well. A thesis is also dependent on what you know about your subject. Nancy said that so far as foreign languages are concerned, she knows only "a little French." Given this fact, it is doubtful that any thesis of hers could easily deal with the Italian language, classical French literature, or modern Greek grammar. But given the knowledge about Europe gained in her travels, she might construct a number of interesting theses, as follows (for the purposes of illustration, we will ignore here the problems of role and reader):

- The average Englishman seems friendlier to the backpacker than the average Frenchman.
- If you want to stay healthy in Europe, stick to simple foods and carry plenty of stomach medicine.
- For an American traveling in Europe, French is the most useful foreign language to know.
- Although France has the reputation of being anti-American, France seems more Americanized than England, Germany, Greece, Italy or Spain.
- The American Youth Hostel Association needs tighter control from its top administration.
- The beauty of Greece is undeniable, but its beauty is unvarying and, after a while, rather boring.

PRACTICE

Discussion

1. Here are two brief essays, both of which try to influence the thinking of the reader. Answer the questions following each essay.

[1]I had thought that, with my age and experience, I was beyond embarrassment, but I was wrong. Having been lured to a drive-in for a showing of the film, *Shampoo,* I found myself embarrassed by the explicitness of the scenes.

[2]But I was embarrassed for the performers, not for myself. That they felt required to do this was a sign of their artistic weakness, not their power. And I remembered a line in Frohman's autobiography, quoting the late great actress, Laurette Taylor: "The most serious, tender, passionate love scenes," she said, "are those that are projected over the footlights through suggestion, without actual contact."

[3]And it is historically true that the greatest love scenes in the world have always been played free from physical contact—not because the authors were Puritans (there is a whole thick dictionary on Shakespeare's bawdy alone), but because they are penetrating observers of human emotions, and know that man's body is meaningful only when it is activated by his spirit.

[4]Shakespeare indeed realized this above all others. This dramatist, whose language was the saltiest on the English-speaking stage, showed a tremendous delicacy and restraint in depicting the overt behavior of his lovers.

[5]In *Romeo and Juliet,* the most tender scene is played with the distance of a balcony between the lovers. In *The Tempest,* Ferdinand and Miranda are shrewdly playing a game of chess. In *Twelfth Night,* Viola's love for the Duke is concealed beneath a boy's disguise. In *As You Like It,* Rosalind and Orlando merely touch hands. Even in the fierce and lustful infatuation of *Antony and Cleopatra,* not a gesture is made that might offend a conclave of bishops.

[6]Yet, in all these cases—as in other Shakespearean plays—we know we are in the presence of two persons who love each other physically as much as emotionally. This is the purpose of art: not to give us a clinical view of a chemical attraction, or to titillate us with sexual gymnastics that are more ludicrous than erotic, but to gain our belief by implication and suggestion.

[7]In fact, it is one of the paradoxical qualities of sex that the more accessible, the less provocative; the more explicit, the less intriguing; a black silk nightgown is far more stimulating than nudity.

[8]Just as a bad composer needs furious crescendos to cover the empti-

ness and banality of his music, so does a bad writer require absurd physical writhings to mask his essential hollowness of spirit. Indecent exposure of the emotions is worse than a moral transgression; it is an artistic crime. — Sidney J. Harris.

a. What is the thesis?

b. What role does Harris assume in the first paragraph? How does he change his role in the second paragraph? In what way does his broader role help to extend his argument to art rather than to a discussion of *Shampoo*?

c. How would the essay have been different if Harris had maintained the role of a man "embarrassed by the explicitness of the scenes"?

d. Why does Harris choose his examples from Shakespeare, rather than from recent movies? How does his use of evidence help to identify his readers? Would his readers be interested in the role he assumed in the first paragraph?

e. In what ways does Harris begin with the specific and move to the general?

f. Is this an essay about only the movie *Shampoo*?

[1]A traveler enters Maine at the very spot where John Paul Jones's *Ranger* slid from the ways in 1777. A flawless thoroughfare of cement has replaced the winding, rutted trail of olden days. . . .

[2]It was a road, not long since, of small white farms nestling in the shadow of brooding barns and sheltering elms; of old square homes built by shipbuilders and shipmasters; of lilac-scented Junes, and meadows rich in the odors of mallow and sweet-grass; of irregular stone walls; ancient taverns; solid, mellow little towns happy in the possession of architecture and tradition and family pride; of long stretches of pine woods, cool and fresh in the heat of summer; of birch-clad hill slopes, forests of oaks and sugar maples, swelling fields and flat salt marshes shimmering mistily in the warm summer sun; of life-giving breezes from the strip of deep blue sea at the far edge of all these things.

[3]It was a beautiful road: a road for health and rest and peace of mind; a priceless possession, to be cherished and forever held in trust for the descendants of those who laid it out and made it possible. It was the essence of Maine; the gateway to the great and beautiful Maine wilderness to the north and east.

[4]Today it is a road of big signs and little signs and medium-sized signs; of cardboard signs tacked to pine trees and wooden fences and dilapidated barns; of homemade signs tilting drunkenly in ragged fields and peering insolently from the yards and walls of furtive-looking houses; of towering signs thrusting garish, mottled faces before forests,

fields, and streams, like fat, white-faced streetwalkers posing obscenely in a country lane; of little indecent litters of overnight camps, crawling at the edges of cliffs and in trampled meadows as though the countryside had erupted with some distressing disease: of windrows of luncheon boxes, beer bottles, paper bags, wrapping paper, discarded newspapers, and the miscellaneous filth of countless thoughtless tourists; of doggeries, crab-meateries, doughnutteries, clammeries; of booths that dispense home cooking on oilcloth and inch-thick china in an aura of kerosene stoves, smothered onions, and stale grease; of roadside stands resembling the results of a *mésalliance* between an overnight camp and an early American outhouse; of forests of telephone and electric light poles entangled in a plexus of wires.

⁵It is a road rich in the effluvia of clams in batter, frying doughnuts, sizzling lard; in tawdriness, cheapness, and bad taste, but in little else.
— Kenneth Roberts, "Roads of Remembrance"

a. What is Roberts' thesis? Has he supported it adequately?
b. Why should Roberts care about a road in Maine? What is his role?
c. For whom is Roberts writing? Do you consider yourself a member of his audience? How are you affected by his essay?
d. Which of the two essays makes a greater impact on you, Harris' or Roberts'? Explain your answer. Is your ability to do anything about the problem described related to your response about impact?

2. One of us received this letter, quoted in its entirety. How do you think the writer viewed the reader? The subject of the letter? The writer himself? Is the letter effective?

> Dear Professor Tibbetts:
> This letter is to inform you of the death of Mr. _____, who is currently enrolled in your English 302, Sec. B. The student's registration will be officially cancelled by the appropriate college office in the near future.
>   Sincerely,
>   _____, Associate Dean

3. Read this extract from a student's research paper. Describe and justify the student's use of *stance*.

> ¹Most authorities agree that *handedness* is the tendency to use a certain hand to perform most tasks. Modern authorities agree that handedness is related neurologically to the brain. One popular theory is that of "cerebral dominance," which means that one side of the brain

dominates the other, this dominance being translated into the preference of one hand over the other.

[2]The researcher encounters difficulty finding good authorities on the subject of handedness. First, the subject itself has no common name. One may have to look in his sources under *left-handedness, right-handedness, laterality,* and *handedness* before he can find information. Many good reference works (for example, the *Collier's Encyclopedia*) have no material on the subject. Those authorities which are available fall roughly into two groups: (1) the medical and (2) the psychological and educational. Since these two groups of authorities often do not agree with each other, one must decide whether to use certain information or to throw it out as being unscientific or unreasonable. In the latter category may be put the theory of Professor _____ in Educational Psychology 280. He told his class that handedness was the result of accident, depending upon which hand a child used in his crib or ate with. If the professor were correct, the laws of probability should require that about half the population be right-handed and half be left-handed.

4. The remarks following are taken from an address delivered by George Plimpton at a Harvard commencement. Plimpton is probably best known for his book *Paper Lion.* His speech was quickly reprinted in several places, most notably the *New York Times.* What is Plimpton's role? Who is his audience? Will his audience accept his advice? How is their acceptance (or lack of acceptance) related to his role? The speech has been reprinted many times. How has Plimpton's use of role and audience helped to make his address popular?

[1]I have been led to understand that tomorrow you are going to graduate. Well, my strong recommendation is that you don't go. Stop! Go on back to your rooms. Unpack! There's not much out here. . . .

[2]The point is we don't want you out here very much. We on the outside see graduation as a terrible event—the opening of an enormous dovecote from which spring into the air tens of thousands of graduates. What is particularly disturbing is that you all come out at the same time—June—hordes, with your dark graduation cloaks darkening the earth. Why is it that you can't be squeezed out one at a time, like peach pits, so that the society can absorb you without feeling suffocated?

[3]My own profession is being swamped with writers coming out of college, despite the condition out here that no one reads. Indeed, my friend Kurt Vonnegut was saying the other day that the only solution to the moribund state of publishing would be to require of all those on welfare that before receiving their welfare checks, they must hand in a book report. . . .

⁴If your parents insist you pack up and come home, there are always measures. If you're a chemistry major, tell them that you've become very attached to something in a vat of formaldehyde. If you're in pre-law, tell them that you're thinking of bringing home a tort. Your parents will probably have forgotten what a tort is, if they ever knew, and it *sounds* unpleasant—something that your Mom wouldn't want to have stepping suddenly out of a hall closet. Surely, there is hardly an academic field of one's choice which does not have a nightmare possibility with which to force one's parents to pony up enough to allow nearly a decade of contemplation in one's room.

⁵You'll remember the King in *Alice in Wonderland*. When asked: "Where shall I begin?" the King says, "Begin at the beginning, and go on until you come to the end; then stop." What I am suggesting is that you stop at the beginning, stop at your commencement. It's not very interesting to stop at the end—I mean *everyone* does that. So stop now. Tell them you won't go. Go back to your rooms. Unpack!

5. The four paragraphs following represent the introduction to a longer article by Nancy Hunt. From these paragraphs, you should be able to describe the author's use of stance in the rest of the article. What is Hunt's role? Who is her audience? Identify her thesis.

¹When I landed at Utica, N.Y., one recent weekend, I had been flying 7½ hours with just one fuel stop at Youngstown, Ohio, to break the journey and wash my hands. Tired, dirty, and hungry, I wanted only to tie down my Piper Tomahawk, find a motel room, and get a drink.

²I spotted the only vacant parking spot on the ramp and was heading for it when a Cherokee taxied past, whipped around directly in front of me, and grabbed my space. I jammed on my brakes and sat there in stupefied indignation. I've seen some pushy people on the ramp at Midway Airport [in Chicago], but not *that* pushy.

³Welcome to the surly East, home of bad manners!

⁴Because I was born in New York City and reared in Connecticut, I consider myself an expert on Eastern manners. Chicagoans often laugh derisively when I say that Midwesterners are kinder and more courteous, but a trip back East confirms my view. . . .

Writing

1. As a writer, some of your first questions are: Who are my readers? How do I want to affect them? That is,

● What do I want them to believe?

● Do I want them to take action? Of what kind? Why?

- How and where should I tell them the point of my paper?

- How can I tell them who *I* am? (I'm not a ghost, after all, but a human being — *writing*.)

> Write two versions of the same essay. For your major you are required to take a course for which you believe there is no practical use.
> a. Write an essay directed to the dean of your college, explaining why you and your fellow majors should not be required to take the course. Be cool and objective.
> b. Write to other students in your major field. Try to get them to support you in your efforts to have the requirement abolished. In this version, your stance and approach to the subject will be more personal.

2. There is a bill before the state legislature that will impose a severe punishment for hitchhiking in your state. (We will assume that the laws now covering hitchhiking are often not enforced and the punishments, if any, are mild.) Consider these roles, along with the suggested readers. You are:
   a. A state trooper writing to your state representative.
   b. A student living 50 miles from campus; you are writing to your campus newspaper.
   c. A trucker writing to the Opinion column of your union's monthly magazine.
   d. A woman student writing to your worried mother who lives in another state.
   Write a paragraph for each of these four situations, filling out your stance with a clear thesis. Let your paragraph be the *introduction* to your letter or article.
   Given the general problem, what other stances are citizens in your state likely to take?

3. Write a paper in which you disagree (a little, a lot, or entirely) with Sidney J. Harris' article (pp. 34–35). But write for a different reader or group of readers. You might write to the local theater, asking that such movies not be shown. Or, defending movies like *Shampoo*, you might write to Harris himself.

4. Here is an exotic writing assignment, one which you should not consider unless your instructor — in his or her unwisdom — insists.
   You are a "Sand Dolphin," a species of intelligent beings (as yet unknown to people) that live mainly in the South Seas. One day you discover a well-preserved 1974 Volkswagen "Bug" lying in ten feet of water. Of course, you don't know it's a VW. One door is

open and swinging slightly in the current. Nothing on the VW is obviously broken. (Where did it come from? You don't know, and neither do we. Perhaps it fell off a ship transporting it.)

The Sand Dolphins have a highly developed culture, complete with an elaborate communication system. It is your responsibility to report the objects you have found to the Ministry for USO's (Unidentified Sunken Objects).

The members of the Ministry — like you — look, feel, and (most important) think like sea creatures. For instance, their idea of measurement is based upon the dimensions and physiology of a fish. They would never describe any object as being so many "feet" long.

Taking a Sand Dolphin's role, write a report to the ministry describing *in detail* the object you have found. You may use or ignore the fact that dolphins are mammals.

CHAPTER 3

MAKING A POINT— YOUR THESIS

After you have worked for a while with the idea of the writer's stance and practiced creating your own stances, you will probably discover that only the thesis gives you any continuing trouble. So let's consider a few practical strategies for arriving at a thesis and making it more useful in planning your essays.

Every written communication must make a point. A letter to your newspaper, a note to the postman, an article on Democrats in the state legislature, a memo to your boss at work, a textbook on the American colonial period, one of your papers—each makes a point about something. The sharper the point, the more successful the communication. In written form, your paper's point is its thesis—*the main idea stated in one specific sentence.* The thesis that you use to guide your early planning does not always appear word for word in the essay itself. Sometimes, in order to fit a thesis into the flow of your writing, you may have to reword it slightly or take two or three sentences to state it. But for the purposes of planning, practice putting each thesis in a single sentence.

Why is a thesis useful? First, it helps you respond to the essay assignment and shape your ideas before you write. Second, the thesis helps you organize your material as you write; it keeps you from wandering away from your topic. Third, after you have completed your essay, you can use your thesis to judge whether you have done what you set out to do. Fourth, in conferences both you and your instructor will refer to your thesis when you discuss your essay's effectiveness—for example, its organization and the relevance of supporting material. And, of course, the thesis as expressed in your essay is a great help to your reader.

PRACTICE

Discussion

1. Read the following essay for class discussion. The student stopped writing toward the end of paragraph 4. Can you guess why? What seems to be the thesis of her essay? Can you give her any advice for rewriting and improving it? Center your comments on the problem of the essay's point.

   [1] I first got interested in horses when our family went to my uncle's farm and he let me ride an old plow horse. He was an old horse and was never used for anything, and he would not go faster than a walk. But I was fascinated by his personality, if that is what you want to call it. He seemed very wise and responsive, as if he were listening to you talk to him. I used to ride him two or three times a day and talk to him and he would act as if he understood me.

   [2] That same year I started taking riding lessons at a stable near home (there is only one in the area). Since we are not particularly well off, I had to work for my lessons. Every Saturday, I would ride my bike—along with several girl friends—to the stable and work out the horses, clean the stall, and do general handyman work. For this I would get a half-hour's lesson which consisted mainly of yells and shouts of "Donna, GET YOUR FEET TURNED IN!!!" and "You got TERRIBLE hands, Donna!"

   [3] My grandmother in Nebraska heard about my working in the stable and wrote me a worried letter saying that the stables were no place for a girl and that I should stay away from them except when taking lessons. She apparently remembers the stable life from her girlhood in Texas, which was probably very different from today's.

   [4] I got to ride in a few shows, and won a ribbon or two, and then I was really hooked. I wanted my own horse, but we could not afford one. The situation got worse at the stables—the instructor yelling at me and telling lies about me to my mother, who insisted that I keep riding

no matter what. I wanted to ride but I hated the instructor, and my mother kept getting in the situation, until finally I didn't know what to do. So I quit for a while. . . . [end of draft]

2. Read the following two paragraphs and prepare to discuss them in class. Considering the two paragraphs as a brief essay, do you think that Plumb has a clear thesis? If you believe that he has, state it. Does Plumb tend to organize his ideas, in relation to his thesis, in any particular way? Explain, giving examples.

[1]How much privacy have great men ever enjoyed? How far has it been possible to separate their public and private lives? Throughout recorded history and discernibly beyond there have been persons and families of distinction who have been known by name and fame and special status to all members of their communities. High priests, kings, Caesars, popes, emperors—all have belonged to the world in a very special sense. The kings of France dressed and undressed in public, were ceremonially fed before their court; they had an audience for their wedding night, and their wives labored in rooms crowded with nobility. Although it is true that the royal bed was railed off, the rest of the chamber would be thronged with courtiers, listening to the queen's groans, peering and peeping, joking and talking bawdily.

[2]For royalty death was no easier than birth. The courtiers of Carlos II of Spain stood about as the doctors tied the warm entrails of a pigeon on his belly. His priests, putting more faith in San Isidro, brought his mummified remains to the bedside. Their prayers and the hushed gossip of the grandees were drowned by the chants of rival priests, who carried round the room the corpse of San Diego of Alcalá sitting in its urn. It was not much better for Queen Caroline of England rolling in agony in her own putrefaction, whilst her husband, distracted with grief, upbraided her for looking like a dying cow. The grossly fat prime minister knelt by her side and could not get up. The Archbishop of Canterbury mumbled his prayers. The queen, still in possession of her wits, sent for the lord chancellor to make absolutely certain that Frederick, Prince of Wales, would not inherit one iota of her possessions. As she said on this deathbed, she wished him in the bottommost pit of hell. And there in the corner was little Lord Hervey, rouged, powdered, flamboyantly epicene, taking it all down and doubtless inventing what he could not quite hear. He knew he was present at a moment of history, that posterity would be wide-eyed and open-mouthed for every gory detail of the queen's death. To be royal was to live even the most intimate moments of one's life before the hostile, loving, or indifferent eyes of one's court.—J. H. Plumb, "The Private Grief of Public Figures"

THE ASSIGNMENT AND THE THESIS

You write because you need to, whether the "need" is imposed from within or without. Ordinarily, in your composition class, you write in response to an instructor's assignment. So let's now turn to the problem of the typical writing assignment and consider how it can lead to a thesis.

There are, roughly, three kinds of assignments. Here are examples, ranging from the general to the specific:

1. A brief general request for written work:
"Write a paper for next Friday."

2. A request for a type of essay or for a particular essay topic:
   a. "Write an essay convincing someone to take up your hobby."
   b. "Write an essay explaining a cause or effect."
   c. "In your essay, discuss the characterization of Willy Loman in *Death of a Salesman.*"

3. A more specific request that tends to control your response as you write:
   a. "Write a paper that supports an idea that some people ordinarily do not agree with — for example, that organized athletic programs do not foster team spirit or group loyalty in the players; that strongly religious persons can be evil; that going to college may be a serious mistake for certain young people."
   b. "If you were to call for a change in any university (or college) policy or practice, what would that change be? Write a letter to someone in authority outlining the policy or practice and stating your reasons for suggesting the change."
   c. "Some persons believe that Willy Loman is not a tragic character. Define the term *tragic character,* and argue that Willy either is or is not tragic. (You may take the position that he is partially tragic.)"

While assignments 1 and 2 give you more freedom than 3 does, they may be harder to prepare. You have to specify most of the elements of the topic yourself, and you may spend as much time finding and limiting a topic as you spend actually writing the paper. But instructors continue to use assignments like 1 and 2 because with them you can choose your own material and create your own stance. You can write essays that you might not otherwise get a chance to write with the more limited assignments.

The Thesis Journal

Journal entries can help you to develop an appropriate thesis in response to an assignment. After Jack's instructor spent two class periods discussing theses, he gave assignment 3a above. Jack thinks about the assignment in his dorm room, wondering what he will write about, when he hears a sharp blast on a car horn. This blast is followed by a howl of locked brakes, a yell from somebody, and then the familiar crashing sound of metal meeting metal. By the time he gets his eyes focused on the street, the accident is over. The two cars are locked together there on the street, one of them at right angles to the other.

Jack watches from his window as the police come, and then he gets a glimmer of an idea for a paper. He writes in his journal:

```
      Auto accidents are something that I know about.  For two years

I've worked as an assistant to the ambulance drivers for the

Pemberton Funeral Home on weekends and during the summer.  As a part

of the ambulance team, I've seen thirty or forty accidents, a few of

them fatal.  Let me jot down a thesis or two for this assignment:

      Auto accidents should be prevented.

(Objection:  Of course they should be prevented; who would argue that

they shouldn't be?)

      There are fewer auto accidents in Tennessee than in Illinois.

(Wait: I don't really know very much about auto accidents in

Tennessee.)


      Maybe I'd better take my instructor's advice and make a list:


autos                               casket?
accidents                           relatives worried
injury                              cost -- expensive!
mothers                             cost of blood - how much?
fathers                             cost of surgery?
worry for them because they're hurt doctors' fees
auto accidents expensive            nurses
new engine -- cost?                 ambulance costs
burial                              ambulance driving


      Look at all those items that have to do with the financial cost

of the accident!  If somebody pays money for accidents, someone earns

it--doctors, nurses, hospitals, morticians, garages, mechanics.

Everybody always talks about the cost of accidents but never about

the profit in them.

      I've found my hook!  There's good money in accidents.
```

> This is something that I know about because I had made good
> money as part of the ambulance team.
>
> Here is my thesis: <u>Contrary to what many people think there is
> a lot of money to be made from automobile accidents.</u>
>
> Now I need to establish my authority: I know the costs and also
> the money to be made from ambulance calls, and I know from being
> around Pemberton Funeral Home how much caskets and funerals cost.
> Other fees--those charged by garages and hospitals--I'm not so sure
> about. I guess I'd better check on that tomorrow.

Entries for the following day:

> I just called two local hospitals and two garages and obtained a
> page of typical charges for typical injuries and damages, from broken
> legs to smashed fenders. I believe that I can write with reasonable
> authority on the subject. Or can I? I'd better check out my thesis
> again:
>
> " . . . a lot of money to be made from auto accidents."
> Where? New York State? Am I implying that auto accidents "cost" the
> same everywhere? I don't have any authority for making a judgment.
>
> Maybe I'd better limit my thesis. How about this? <u>Contrary to
> what many people think, there is a lot of money to be made from
> auto accidents in the Phillipsburg area.</u>

Jack's essay now has a focus. In addition he feels comfortable with the subject because he has available material, most of it taken from memory.

Another example of thesis development may be useful here. The assignment is: "Write an essay convincing someone to take up your hobby." In checking the assignment, you find that the key words or hooks are already in it: *convincing, take up,* and *hobby.* These help in clarifying your subject. You settle quickly on a writer's role (that of a young person who needs to earn money for school expenses) and on a reader (a similar type of person, particularly one who can work with his hands).

Now you start specifying a point:

1. *My hobby* . . . used to be sports, but a compound fracture took care of that . . . spend more time "clocking" now than in any other leisure-time activity. . . .

2. *Hobby is repairing clocks* . . . odd hobby for a kid . . . took it up by accident. . . . money in it . . . tell why money in clock repair. . . .

3. *Good money in repairing clocks* . . . but it's interesting too . . . almost everyone is fascinated by an old clock . . . that's all I work on . . . remember I have to *convince* someone to take up my hobby. . . .

4. **Thesis:** *If you want an interesting and profitable hobby, take up clock repair.*

Since the thesis is clear, narrowed, and specific, it would be a good one to use when organizing and writing the paper.

The Thesis as Answer to a Question

Finding a workable thesis often seems to involve "thinking out loud," as Jack did, picking your way through ideas as they occur to you, selecting and discarding as you go along. Look for key words in an assignment and underline them. If other key words or hooks occur to you, put them down on scratch paper before they get away. As you think out loud, ask yourself the questions in the following list. (The word *something* stands for your subject or an important idea about it.)

—What was the effect of *something*? Its cause?
—Can I break *something* down or analyze its main parts in order to understand it better?
—Can I compare *something* to another thing?
—Can I define *something*?
—Is *something* typical for some persons and not for others?
—Is *something* good or bad, or partly good and partly bad?
—Who knows about *something*? Who would I see or what would I read to find out?
—What class or category of ideas or objects is *something* in?
—What are the facts about *something*? What things aren't known?
—Can I tell a story about *something*?
—Does *something* do any job that is necessary for a group, large or small?

— How is *something* made or created? Destroyed?
— How can one do or perform *something*?
— Can I recommend *something* to other people? Not recommend?
— Should I suggest changes in *something*?

Note: We discuss the development of answers to many of these questions in Part II.

Here are two examples of how a thesis can be an answer to a question:

> *Question:* How can one do *something*?
>   *Thesis:* *Anyone can put up a standard house wall if he buys good-quality, straight studs, can use a level accurately, and makes all measurements carefully.*
>
> *Question:* What is a *word processor*?
>   *Thesis:* A word processor is a piece of computer software that is designed to help someone design, write, and revise a document.

IMPROVING YOUR THESIS

*A*s you work on your thesis, consider these suggestions for making it useful and effective:

1. *Make Your Thesis Authoritative.*

In other words, "Write about what you know"— one of the soundest pieces of advice on student writing. Even though you may not picture yourself as such, you are an authority on a variety of subjects. So write about them: your family; your friends; your hometown; the politicians, doctors, mechanics, plumbers, carpenters, or lawyers you know; the crabgrass on your front lawn; your parents' divorce; your stereo set; your friend's broken arm; your first vote; your failure to pass trigonometry; your *A* in Spanish.

But do not try to write about the United Nations, poverty in America, racial problems in our cities, Lincoln's first administration, the creation of the American Constitution, the writings of Norman Mailer, the movies of Humphrey Bogart, *unless* (1) in the past you have done considerable research on one of these subjects, and have made yourself an amateur "authority" in the field; or (2) you are willing to commit yourself to hours of research in the library or elsewhere to make yourself reasonably authoritative on the subject.

This advice is necessarily somewhat general. Check with your instructor when you have doubts about your subject and your "authority."

2. *Narrow Your Thesis.*

Because most essays are relatively short, you can't adequately support a very broad thesis in 500 words or so. Narrow your thesis to fit your essay's length by testing your tentative theses, as Jack did (see pp. 45–46). You will find certain questions helpful, especially questions beginning with *why, what,* and *who.*

Tentative thesis:	People in my hometown are selfish.
Questions:	Why do you call them selfish? What do they *do*? Who are the *people* you refer to? *All* of them?
Revised thesis:	Some people in my hometown will not give to the United Fund because they do not wish to support some of the agencies that receive money from the Fund.
Tentative thesis:	Computers are a popular form of mass communication.
Questions:	*All* computers? What *kind* of communication do you mean? *Who* uses the computer for communication?
Revised Thesis:	Among some of my friends, notes on the *Plato* computer terminals are so popular that they have replaced the telephone as the chief method of talking to one another.

3. *Unify Your Thesis.*

In your essay, discuss one thing or group of things. You might ask yourself questions like *How many terms do I have in this thesis? Are they separate topics to be dealt with in different papers? Are some of my terms sub-topics of the larger topic?*

Tentative Thesis:	A blind child is often treated badly by other children because he is different from them; consequently they are embarrassed, because they don't realize how talented a blind child can be.
Questions:	If blind children are *talented*, does that still make them *different*? Are other children embarrassed by the blind child's "differences?"
Revised Thesis:	A blind child is sometimes treated badly by other children on the playground because they do not know how to deal with his "differences."
Tentative Thesis:	Motorcycles are fun, providing fast, inexpensive, and dangerous transportation.
Questions:	Is riding a motorcycle *fun* because it is *dangerous*? Is it *dangerous* because it is *fast*? What is the relationship between *inexpensive* and *dangerous*?

Revised Thesis: Motorcycles provide inexpensive but dangerous transportation.

The last tentative thesis would require the writer to juggle four somewhat illogically associated points about motorcycles. The improved thesis reduces these to two easily associated points by saying, in effect: the machine may not cost much but it can kill you.

4. *Specify Your Thesis.*

As you have probably guessed by now, the whole business of improving a thesis is a continuous process. When you make your thesis authoritative, and when you narrow and unify it, you are simply sharpening your essay's point. And the best single way to make that point even sharper is to avoid general words and to use specific ones instead.

You might ask questions like: Can I tie my point to a more specific word than the one I have used here? What evidence do I have? How can that evidence be translated into specific terms?

Tentative Thesis: Sororities are getting better.
Questions: What do I mean by "better?" If they are better, what difference does that make?
Revised Thesis: Because they offer better housing, better food, and better facilities for study than the dorms, sororities at this college are getting more pledges.

Tentative Thesis: America should have more freedom of speech.
Questions: What do I mean by *freedom of speech*? *Where* in America should this happen? What do I propose to *do* in order to get more freedom of speech?
Revised Thesis: The library Board in Paxton should have a strict procedure to follow whenever a citizen objects to one of the books in the library's collection. (Notice the hook in the phrase *strict procedure.*)

PRACTICE

Discussion

1. For class discussion read the following essay. What is its thesis? Where is the thesis stated? Discuss its unity and specificity. In what way has the writer "narrowed" her coverage of the topic?

HUSSIES AND HOLES IN YOUR EARS

[1]In the old neighborhood, piercing the ears of young girls was an exotic ritual.

[2]All the neighborhood noseys would gather around in a kitchen like eager interns as someone's shaky and half-blind grandmother would miraculously become a surgeon, eagle-eyed and steady of hand. The girl's earlobes were anesthetized with an ice cube, and the largest needle in the sewing box would be heated on the stove and dipped in alcohol for the procedure. The patient would wear a loop of thread, then a piece of straw from a broom before getting her first ladylike pair of earrings.

[3]But some of us were never initiated. "Only gypsies and hussies have pierced ears," Mother maintained. A few girlfriends proved Mother right, becoming bonafide hussies by the sixth grade, even wearing lipstick and stockings and unloosening their braids. There were no gypsies on the block, but Mother knew best.

[4]Away from Mother's overprotectiveness, I finally had my ears pierced in my mid-20s. Not by anyone's grandmother, but in a sanitized doctor's office with no spectators. I should have listened to Mother.

[5]One hole was pierced on an angle and began to stretch, nearly splitting the earlobe in two. A fortune in pierced earrings sat idle as I went back to clip-ons. I began to notice other casualties of ear piercing who had split lobes and infections, even some who had gone through the grandmother method. I pondered a malpractice suit, but too much time had passed. I consulted a plastic surgeon, but it was too costly to have the lobe sutured and the ears repierced.

[6]Other friends, of course, had the fashionable two and three holes in their ears with no complications. My childhood desire never waned.

[7]I'd look for free ear-piercing offers in department stores, even stood in line at one, but chickened out. Finally last month I relented on a lunch hour impulse and had both ears repierced above the original holes. No grandmothers, no doctor, just your basic sales clerk.

[8]I wore the training studs for the requisite 24 days, religiously and liberally applied the antiseptic twice a day, twirled the posts to keep the scar tissue from mending around the holes and polished my pierced earrings.

[9]For not listening to Mother, not once but twice, I now have an infection. But I have no regrets. Fortunately, I still have the same two ears. I have four pierced earring holes, three of which are serviceable. And above all—look, Ma, I never became a hussy. —Leanita McClain

2. Discuss and evaluate each of the following tentative theses. How can they be improved?

a. Traffic destroys superhighways.

b. Biking and hitchhiking through Maine are safe.

c. The Berlin Wall is necessary to the Soviet Union.

d. Adopting the metric system is a mistake.

e. Working and eating in a pizza parlor is boring, hard work, and gives me indigestion, plus the boss is a jerk.

f. The earth is getting hotter.

g. Intercollegiate sports cost the university too much money.

h. Nuclear power plants should be shut down.

i. Welfare takes too much of the tax dollar.

Writing

1. You can learn much about writing useful theses by imitating those used in successful essays. Here are six such theses with certain key words and phrases in italics. Imitate them using your own ideas and material. For example, an imitation of **a** might be: "Unlike my sister, who went out for the swimming team because she thought swimming was a challenging sport, I tried out only because I badly needed the exercise." Are any particular writers' stances suggested by the theses?

    a. *Unlike* my uncle, *who* was a compulsive *alcoholic,* my father *drank* too much simply because he *liked* the *comradeship* of other drinkers.

    b. *Racial problems* in Penant High School *existed* for two years *before busing started.*

    c. For good *apples* in September, *spray* the *trees* with dormant oil just before the *buds* open in the spring.

    d. We *lost* eight basketball *games* that year because we didn't *practice* our basic *plays* enough.

    e. To get a natural color on fresh hardwood, use *first* a light *stain* and *then* a quick-drying standard *varnish.*

    f. Since the independents did not *campaign* in all campus areas, *they failed* to reach many students and *lost* the *election.*

2. Here are some typical assignments you may encounter early in the term. For each assignment, (a) underline the important words or phrases; (b) write a narrowed, unified, and specific thesis.

    a. Tell your reader about the most important event in your life. Do not merely relate the event; describe it and explain in detail why you believe it is "important." (Do you need to define *important*? What might your hook be here?)

    b. In the past two or three years, several things probably have happened in your hometown, or area where you have been living, that you do not approve of. Write an essay explaining one of these events—a decision by an authority, a change in local government, and so on. State specifically why you do not approve. *Hint:* Don't spend so much time in description that you are unable to be specific concerning your disapproval.

c. Write an essay about a clash of personalities that you have experienced or closely observed. What effect on friends or relations did this clash have? Explain by giving details and examples.

d. Write a paper about a person—you or someone you know—who has been successful or unsuccessful doing something. Describe the person's success, or lack of it, and explain in detail why he was (or was not) successful.

3. Write a paper, using one of the theses you developed for #2 above.

4. For *two* of the following topics, develop a thesis that will form the basis of a 500-word essay. Be sure that your thesis is reasonably authoritative, narrowed, unified, and specific.

a. seat belts in cars
b. fishing
c. intramural sports programs
d. house plants
e. movies
f. hobbies
g. video games
h. reading

Choose one of the theses and write an essay.

CHAPTER 4
SHAPING AND OUTLINING IDEAS

In this chapter, we will discuss a number of devices for planning a piece of writing. And that is what they are—plans. None of them is a fixed structure that you must follow blindly. Generally speaking, successful writers, whether amateur or professional, use whatever planning devices they need—and use them flexibly. They may go through all the steps of a *shape, support diagram,* or *outline* (all of which will be discussed in this chapter). But writers may also work forward and backward through the process, refining, changing, switching main ideas or moving them about, inserting and deleting details. A writer may often consider, or actually follow, all the steps in the essay-writing process. But no successful writer allows the process to overrule his or her good judgment concerning any part of the final essay and its plan.

For instance, if you can't make your plan fit your thesis exactly, it may be wise not to force a perfect fit. Theses and plans are *tools* for shaping materials, and sometimes materials refuse to be perfectly shaped. If you think it is necessary, try changing the thesis to fit the plan or changing both to fit each other. But don't change them so much that you distort the truths in your subject.

Sometimes you may have trouble following your plan as you write the essay. This may mean that the plan is poorly made—try inspecting it for logic and order. But this may also mean that a "logic of writing" is (legitimately) taking over. A piece of writing often seems to develop an order and a coherence all its own that are determined partly by the subject, your supporting materials, and by the way you choose to organize it. If you like the way your paper is going, and its new direction appears to be appealing and honest, consider changing the plan to fit fresh developments. Plans are helpful and good, but they are not written on tablets of stone.

Let's see how John Jackson Chase, a successful writer of TV plays, used a plan in the form of a drawing. When he planned a new play (he worked on as many as two or three at a time), he worked in a large room at the end of which was a big blackboard. On the blackboard was this drawing in white chalk (Figure 1):

Figure 1

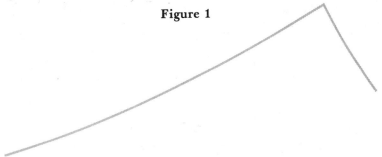

As Chase worked on his play, he scribbled on this white-chalk drawing; the scribblings were in red chalk (Figure 2). What did the drawing mean? (It looks a little like a mountain peak with one steep side.) What were the scribblings in red about? If you questioned Chase, he would gladly tell you what all this meant.

Figure 2

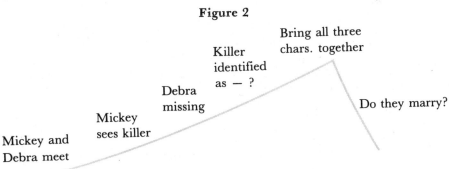

"I start every play with a *shape*," he said. "There on the blackboard in white chalk is my permanent shape for a story. Then I introduce (in red chalk), my characters at the left, give them some conflict to solve as the line moves upward to the right, and finally get to the peak of the shape with the climax of the story, where everything is brought together. The little drop-off after the climax is something almost every story has: a relaxing of tension—like somebody saying, "They lived happily ever after.""

"Sometimes," Chase continued, "I start with the high point, the climax, and write that. Then I move backward to fill in parts of the story."

But why the blackboard with the "shape" on it?

"Oh, it reminds me to fill out the structure of the story. It gives me a feeling of where I'm going and where I've been. Besides, I'm a visual person. I like to see the skeleton of a play, the big bony pieces of it."

GIVE YOUR PAPER A SHAPE (OF ITS OWN)

Chase's idea about the shape of a piece of writing is not new, although perhaps his application of it is. Most of us—at one time or another—have visualized a paper as starting at the top of a page and continuing downwards, the result being the rough geometry of a composition (see Figure 3).

Figure 3

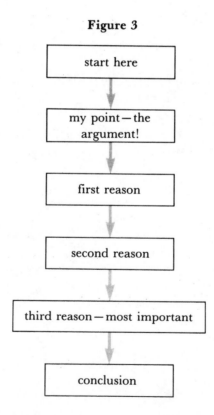

start here

↓

my point—the argument!

↓

first reason

↓

second reason

↓

third reason—most important

↓

conclusion

The total *shape* here is that of the classic argument, the thesis stated first, with the proofs or reasons coming after. The reasons are given in the order of importance, from least to most. The increasing size of the balloons symbolize this order.

Indeed, the shape of a paper is a symbolic outline of your material. Using only the main ideas in your paper, you doodle a shape on a piece of scratch paper until you are satisfied that these main ideas are in the proper order and are given the proper emphasis, which is represented visually. For instance, in the argument we have been discussing you would not want a shape like that in Figure 4.

Figure 4

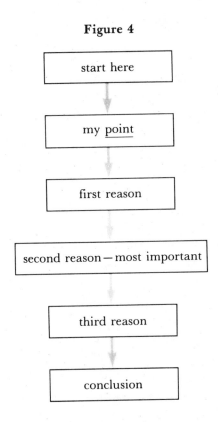

Here the third reason would just be an anticlimax. Nor would you want a shape like that in Figure 5, which shows a fat conclusion that is as long as the rest of the paper — out of proportion.

Figure 5

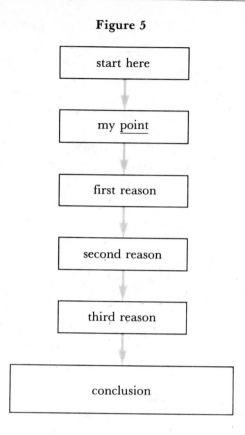

SHAPING A SAMPLE PAPER

In chapter two, we saw several students brainstorming an audience for a paper arguing that the requirements for the film major be increased. When one student (named Arthur) planned this paper, he first started with a list of ideas that he would put in it:

Need more courses in film major
Students don't know much about modern techniques of acting
Students don't know much about modern films
Students don't know much about modern directing
Many things are right with the major

To deal with these logically, Arthur considered several shapes that the paper might take, using sheets of paper to draw on. He finally settled on the basic shape in Figure 6—question and answer. Why? Arthur said he thought that starting with a question would intrigue his readers and make them want to read on.

Figure 6

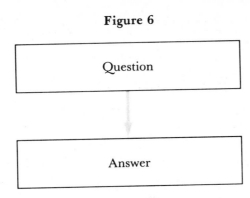

To fill in the shape of his paper, Arthur made the drawing in Figure 7. In this drawing, he tried to illustrate for himself the parts of the argument, especially in the section where he notes that the film major is already being well managed. Arthur does not want to attack the major; he only wants to make it better. The three basic subpoints he wanted to stress equally, so he makes them all the same size in the drawing.

Figure 7

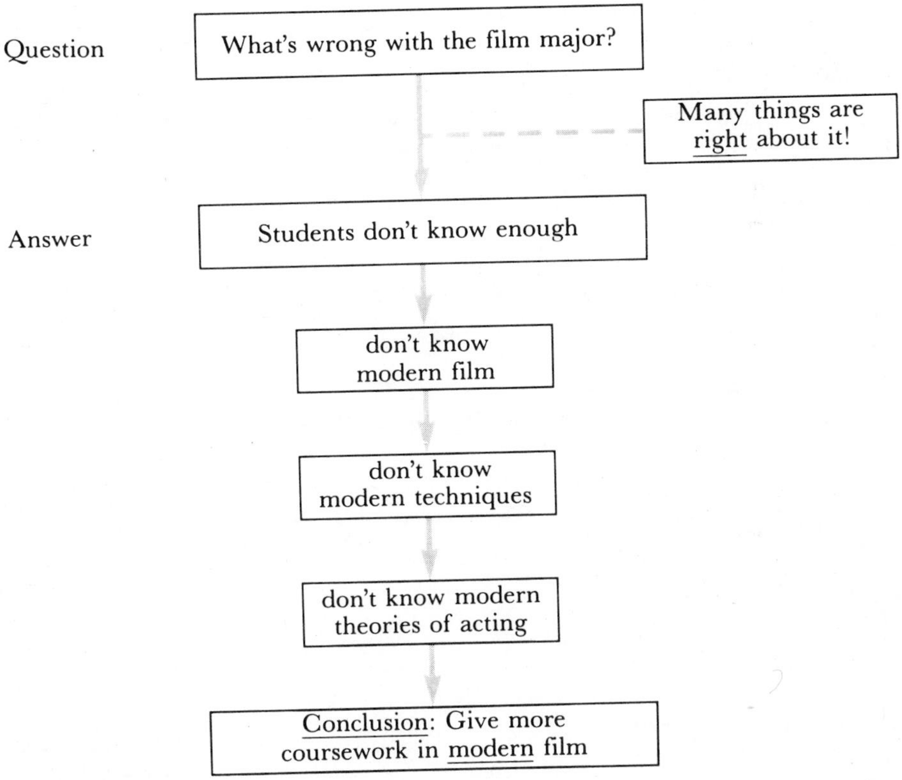

Question   What's wrong with the film major?

Many things are right about it!

Answer   Students don't know enough

don't know modern film

don't know modern techniques

don't know modern theories of acting

Conclusion: Give more coursework in modern film

Advantages and Disadvantages of the Paper "Shape"

The *shape* is a quick way of getting an overall pattern of your paper quickly in mind—and in your eye. It is essentially a big doodle on a large piece of scratch paper, taking only a few minutes to draw. In fact, on many subjects you can draw half a dozen shapes in a short time, each one supplying a different pattern or structure to your paper.

A disadvantage is that the shape gives only the big pieces of the pattern, and if you don't have the smaller ones already in mind you have to search for them.

SUPPORT DIAGRAMS

The *support diagram* is another version of the planning *shape* (see p. 59). Both are "visuals." But there are two basic differences between these types of planning device. First the *shape* is linear; it represents the one-dimensional progress of your paper as it "develops" *down* the page. The support diagram works in two dimensions: up and down, and left and right. Second, the support diagram shows logical relations rather more clearly than the shape does.

Support diagrams typically connect pieces of evidence to your statement or generalization. That is, they show how examples, details, and facts *support* or explain a main point or idea in the paper. For example, see Figure 8, which illustrates how a basic support diagram can be drawn.

Figure 8

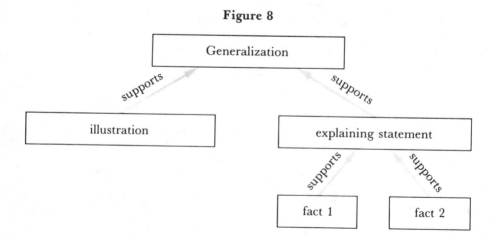

In Figure 9, we put material into the diagram.

Figure 9

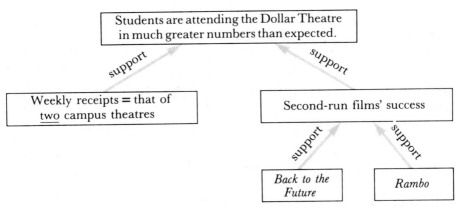

As you add more evidence and specific facts to your main point, the more detailed your support diagram becomes. Consider now the diagram in Figure 10.

Figure 10

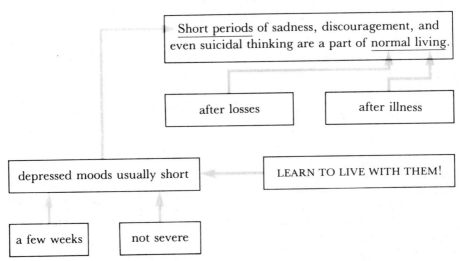

The support diagram *connects* and *explains* relationships. All of the arrows you use should tie ideas logically together, as in Figure 11, which is merely Figure 10 without the writing.

Figure 11

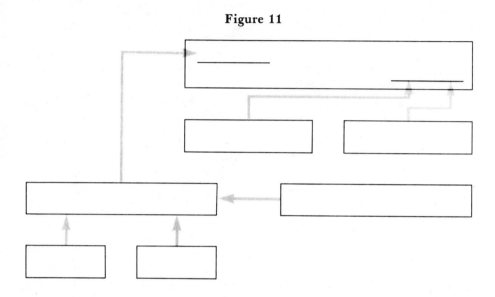

Here is the paragraph we can write from the support diagram on "periods of sadness."

Short periods of sadness, discouragement and even suicidal thinking are a part of normal living, particularly after losses and physical illness. These depressed moods usually last a few days, perhaps a few weeks at the most. They are not severe enough to interrupt the business of everyday life. Most of us learn to live with them. — Anne H. Rosenfeld

THE FORMAL *OUTLINE*

The question of whether to make a formal outline or not depends upon the needs and the requirements of the course. Even professional writers disagree about outlining.

Stephen Jay Gould is Professor of Geology at Harvard University. In 1980 his columns in *Natural History* won the National Magazine Award for Essays and Criticism. In 1981 his book, *The Panda's Thumb,* won the

American Book Award for science. Here is what Gould says about outlines (for his columns in *Natural History* he produces a paragraph-by-paragraph outline):

> I really do believe outlines exist in heaven. I'm a Platonist when it comes to articles. I really believe there is a correct organization for each article. Once you find it, everything fits in.

Jacques Barzun has had a brilliant career as Professor of History, Provost of Columbia University, and writer extraordinary. He has published over two dozen books, several of them on writing and English usage. His opinion of outlines:

> Well, for my taste, outlines are useless, fettering, imbecile. Sometimes, when you get into a state of anarchy, or find yourself writing in circles, it may help to jot down a sketchy outline of the topics (or in a story, of the phases) so far covered. You outline, in short, something that already exists in written form, and this may help to show where you started backstitching.
> — *On Writing, Editing, and Publishing*

To suggest that writers are either outliners or anti-outliners is an oversimplification. One reason is that *outline* is an ambiguous term. It can mean a few jottings on scrap paper, or a detailed piece of formal architecture covering several pages and with every roman numeral, arabic number, and upper- and lower-case letter reverently placed in its assigned niche. So the important thing to remember is that an individual has many options for showing the plan of a paper.

Some writers and teachers have found that a formal outline clearly shows how pieces of evidence (A, B, and C) support the generalizations or main points (I, II, III) of a paper. Even if a writer has used another kind of planning, it is easy to convert such a plan into a *formal outline*. Note how the *support diagram* on p. 61 can be converted into a formal outline, mainly because the writer has a clear notion of how her evidence supports her main idea.

      Thesis: Recognizing that short periods of sadness are natural, psychologists are more concerned about long periods of depression.

I.   Short periods of sadness, discouragement, and even suicidal thinking are a part of normal living.
     A.   They often occur after losses.
     B.   They may occur after physical illness.

    C.   These depressed moods usually last a few days.
        1.   They may last a few weeks at most.
        2.   They are not severe enough to interrupt the business of everyday life.
    D.   Most of us learn to live with these short periods of depression.
II.   . . . (rest of outline omitted)

The Relationship Between "Shapes" and Outline

If a writer chooses one of the *shapes* for organizing a paper, it is possible to translate that shape into an outline. Here is how one girl, named Cathy, came up with some ideas about junk mail (p. 00), and how she translated those ideas into a shape and later into two kinds of formal outlines.

LIST OF IDEAS ABOUT JUNK MAIL

Every day I come home to a mail box full of mail.   INTRO

Mail box won't hold it all. Stuck in door.

Father is woodworker, so gets related catalogs.   why?

I talked to the mailman about the problem. He'd like to stop junk mail.

I go through the mail by throwing out half of it.

I don't know how we get on some lists.

Mother invited to "make a million."   why?

Our hobbies and interests are result of our junk mail.

Some junk mail elegant.

Some of it looks like there's a check inside.   Description

I threw away an airline ticket because it looked like junk mail.

Junk mail is garbage—throw it out.

L. L. Bean stopped sending me a catalog because I didn't order anything else. Only one I can remember. They all keep coming.

Some junk mail comes in plastic covers.   Description

We ordered clothes once. That was a mistake.   why?

Companies must sell their lists.

what we do with it

After grouping her main ideas, Cathy could see that she had a shape for her paper.

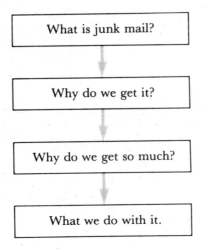

TOPIC OUTLINE

Next, Cathy developed a thesis and a topic outline — an outline that lists topic ideas in the form of phrases or single words in the headings.

> *Thesis:* Because our family has a variety of hobbies and interests, we get a lot of junk mail that we treat like junk.

I. Definition of *junk mail*
   A. Bulk rate postage
   B. Advertising
II. Hobbies and interests of the family
   A. Woodworking
   B. Investing
   C. Gardening and camping
III. Lists sold by companies
   A. Farm, fleet, work clothes catalogs
   B. Financial brochures
   C. Camping, clothing, and gardening catalogs
IV. Junk mail as *junk*
   A. Clutter
   B. Garbage

Cathy decides that the topic outline isn't adequate for her needs because she wants better control of her paragraphing. She makes a sentence outline where she can see every idea in its complete form. She has found that a formal outline is useful when she wants to organize a paragraph deductively, going from the general (topic sentence) to the specific examples and details as she eventually does in her paper on junk mail.

> *Thesis:*   Because our family has a variety of hobbies and interests, we get a lot of junk mail that we treat like junk.

I.   Junk mail is a particular kind of mail. *(paragraph)*
    A.   Junk mail goes for "bulk rate."
    B.   Junk mail consists of advertising or soliciting brochures.
II.   The hobbies and interests of our family reflect the kind of junk mail we receive. *(paragraph)*
    A.   My father is a woodworker, so he gets everything connected with carpentry.
    B.   My mother is an investor in stocks and bonds, so she gets investment brochures.
    C.   I once had a garden, so I get garden catalogs.
    D.   I ordered something from L. L. Bean, so now I get sporting goods catalogs from all over.
III.   The companies we order from have sold their lists of customers. *(paragraph)*
    A.   My father gets farm and fleet catalogs as well as work clothes catalogs.
    B.   My mother gets invitations to "make a million."
    C.   I get every conceivable kind of catalog related to clothing, camping, and gardening.
IV.   We treat the catalogs like junk. *(paragraph)*
    A.   We seldom look at them.
    B.   We throw them in the garbage.

> *Conclusion:*   As a result of all our junk mail, our family has reduced the number of things that they order by mail and have taken to buying from the local stores.

The Form of Outlines

Since Cathy has been well-trained in the conventions of formal outlining, she knows that it is customary to employ numerals and letters in this order, according to the rank of ideas or to the *levels of subordination.*

I. First level (main heading)
    A. Second level
       1. Third level
       2. Third level
          a. Fourth level
          b. Fourth level
    B. Second level
II. First level (main heading)

Headings on the same level of subordination should be roughly parallel—that is, equal in importance and gramatical form. The following example violates this principle in four ways:

I. Definition
    A. Bulk rate
    B. Junk mail is a good way for advertisers to sell their merchandise.
II. The hobbies and interests of our family reflect the kind of junk mail we receive.
    A. Father woodworker

A and B are improperly subordinated to Part I. A and B are not parallel in importance or grammar. Part II is put in sentence form, which violates the form established in Part I. (The rule is this: When for the first time you use a particular form for a heading—a full sentence, a phrase, or a single word, for example—*use the same form in subsequent entries for that level of heading*.) Furthermore, you should avoid single headings like II-A above. When you break a heading into subordinate headings, you must get at least two of these lower-level headings. Often when a single heading hangs out in space, you will find that it really belongs with the previous major heading.

FOUR TYPICAL QUESTIONS ABOUT OUTLINES

1. *What type of outline should I use?*
    The answer to this depends on many factors—the length of your paper and the complexity of your material, to name only two. When preparing to write a long paper which presents a lot of material and complex issues, you might like to make a complete sentence outline that maps out every detail of your argument and its evidence. If you are going to do a short, relatively uncomplicated paper, perhaps a brief topic outline would be sufficient.

Not the least important factor in your choice of outline is your own preference. What type of outline do you feel most comfortable with? For most assignments, which type seems to work best for you?

2. *How specific should an outline be?*

Specific enough to do the job. It should suggest what your paper is going to do—what its thesis is and what its main supporting points are. It should also supply some examples of evidence or detail that you will use in developing your ideas. But the outline is, as we said earlier, just a skeleton; and it can suggest only the bare bones of your completed paper.

If you have any doubts about a particular outline, show it to your instructor.

3. *What can I do if I start an outline, get a point or two down, and then can't continue?*

When this happens, you may be trying to build a house before acquiring concrete, bricks, lumber, and shingles. Before you can build a paper, you need materials for it. Here is where the *shapes* or *support diagrams* can be useful. These forms may help to show you where you need more material.

Some writers find the card system useful: Get some 3 × 5 or 4 × 6 file cards, or small pieces of stiff paper cut to size. Next, write down your thesis on a sheet of paper and place it where you can see it. Start writing your ideas down on your cards, one idea to a card. Note that—*one idea to a card;* preferably, one complete sentence to a card. The point is to separate your ideas so that you can later classify and organize them.

4. *I know I shouldn't do it, but I always make an outline after I write the paper. How can I train myself to make one before writing?*

Writers often check their organization *after* they have written a paper. It is usually a good practice, however, to plan before you write. Consider your outline as a figurative road map—refer to it before you start on your trip so that you won't end up at the seashore when you wanted to go to the mountains.

How a Thesis Suggests an Outline

The phrasing of the thesis often suggests a pattern in the outline. A typical thesis:

I

Since St. James Catholic Church has recently been remodelled, it is a

II   III

more pleasant place to worship, and thus may draw members from other churches in the area.

In creating your stance, you direct your ideas to someone who is not directly familiar with the Catholic churches in your area. After considering the phrasing of the thesis, you can construct an outline like this:

I.   Description of the remodelling.
II. Description of the effect of the remodelling.
III. Why this may bring new members to the church.

THE HOOK AND THE OUTLINE

As you recall, we recommended the hook as a useful device in finding ideas (see p. 12). Like the thesis and the outline, hooks are often valuable throughout the writing process. They provide control, a simple reminder of where you want to go and how effectively you are getting there. Here's an example of their value as related to the outline.

A student wrote a paper that, in its first draft, did not satisfy her. Something was wrong with the fit between the material and her organization. She thought of throwing the paper away, but then decided to make one last attempt to salvage the large amount of work she had put into it. So she wrote her title, hooks, and paragraph topic sentences on an "outline page":

Title: Power to Both Parents

Hooks: *power, both parents*

Topic Sentences:
1. Introduction (thesis): Neither the husband nor the wife should be the dominant figure in the family.
2. Both the husband and wife should share major financial decisions.
3. Both parents are responsible for the discipline of the children, and they should share this responsibility equally.
4. Both should share in the maintenance of the house.
5. The children also have a responsibility to the family unit.
6. *Conclusion:* Cooperation is important between parents if a family is to be successfully maintained.

After inspecting this "outline page," the student saw her own problem immediately. Paragraph 5 was hooked to an idea outside her topic, so she cut it.

HOW TO CHECK AN OUTLINE

If you choose to write from an outline, the following suggestions may be helpful to you.

1. See that all the *parts* of the outline are there — thesis, main headings, and subordinate headings.

2. Use the proper outline *form* (see pp. 66–67). Make particularly sure that your headings are reasonably parallel. There are minor exceptions to this rule. Sometimes you can't quite get your headings parallel; the idiom of the language won't allow it. But you should get as close to complete parallelism as you can.

3. Make your outline reasonably *specific,* particularly in your thesis and the main headings (I, II, III, etc.).

4. Check the outline for *logic.* Do all the parts fit together? Does every supporting point firmly fit your thesis? If necessary, try the subject-predicate test. To make the test, write the major parts of your outline in full-sentence form, using clear subject-predicate patterns:

> I MY CAR MECHANIC *was very thorough.*
>   A. HE *checked the distributor twice.*
>   B. HE *cleaned the carburetor, even though it did not appear to need cleaning.*
> II. But THE MANAGER *did not appreciate the mechanic's work.*
>   A. THE MANAGER *said that the mechanic spent too much time on routine jobs.*
>   B. HE *refused to give the mechanic overtime to complete important repairs.*

If your outline is logical, and all its parts fit together, you can draw connecting arrows (as shown above) from SUBJECT to SUBJECT and from *predicate* to *predicate.* You may also develop a *support diagram* of your ideas to check them for logic (see pp. 60–62).

5. Check the outline for the proper *order*—that is, for a sensible sequence or organization of ideas. Check each level separately—first I, II, III, etc.; and then A, B, C, etc.; and so on. Except for the general rule that important ideas are often placed last, there is no special rule about order. The arrangement of your points should make sense and should not be incongruous. The order of points below, for example, would not be very sensible:

> I. The manager did not appreciate the mechanic's work.
> II. The mechanic was very thorough.

This order would force you to describe the manager's attitude toward the mechanic's work before you had described that work. It's hard to write a paper backwards.

PRACTICE

Writing

1. We borrowed the outlines from two essays and scrambled their main and subordinate points. We also took these theses and combined them into the list of points.

   a. Copy each item from the list below onto a separate card. You may rewrite for the sake of clarity. or consistency. Identify the thesis. Arrange the cards into a logical order. Draw a shape that fits the material. Make a sentence outline.

   Students often do not know or understand the issues in important political campaigns.
   Average student load: 15 to 18 semester hours
   Foreign policy too complicated for students
   Students are immature in their political judgments.
   Local issues usually unfamiliar to students
   Many laws understood only as a personal affair ("how it affects me")
   College students have neither the time, the knowledge, nor the maturity to be politically active outside the university.
   Containment of communism complex historically
   Preparation—two hours for each hour spent in class
   Limited knowledge of national social issues
   The Middle East a complicated issue
   Students too hasty in their judgments
   Many students work 10 to 20 hours a week to make money.
   Students prone to use politics as an exciting drug
   National issues only superficially understood
   60 hours total per week excluding time for relaxation
   Students need all their time for study, classwork, and (in some cases) earning money.

   b. For the following items on the subject of *moving furniture*, make a topic outline.

   A mover's workday can vary from 10 to 18 hours.
   A mover has to work in temperatures that vary greatly.
   Some days it is 95 degrees with 95% humidity.
   Going in and out of air conditioning is hard on the body.
   Moving furniture demands speed because movers must keep a schedule.

A mover is expected to lift at least 100 pounds alone.

When customers live in second- or third-floor apartments, moving furniture is difficult.

Sometimes a crew moves 2 or 3 households in a day.

Apartment buildings often have narrow stairs and landings.

Heavy furniture and appliances sometimes must be lifted over the head to get upstairs or downstairs.

Some furniture has sharp edges which cut into the hands.

Moving furniture, particularly on stairways, demands agility and strength.

A mover must hold onto the furniture to prevent accidents.

The boss-driver, not the furniture mover, sets the pace.

The mover has to please the driver, customer, and management.

Moving furniture in the summer requires stamina to work long hours in hot weather.

2. Pick out the thesis from the list of items in Practice **1a** and respond to it by answering, qualifying, or attacking it. Put your response in a thesis and write an outline of 15 to 20 items. Use whatever outline form you feel comfortable with.

3. Write a paper using the outline you prepared for **2**.

4. After you have decided on a specific thesis, create an outline based on the card system suggested on p. 68 ; and then write the paper from the outline. Do not be afraid to modify your thesis and your outline as you write. Remember that both thesis and outline are only aids to writing. If your essay takes a legitimate turn (in responding to the assignment) that is not represented in your thesis and outline, change them. In your outline, keep at least your major headings in the full-sentence form.

5. Outline the following student-written paper. Pick out the thesis, and write out the main and subordinate points in outline form. What kind of an outline — topic, sentence, or mixed — would be most satisfactory for a paper of this length? What kind of a *shape* would you develop at the planning stage of this paper?

[1]I am writing this in reference to some letters that I have sent to you which were never answered. These letters concerned the possibility of my working full-time at your restaurant during my month-long vacation from college. The fact that you didn't answer any of my many inquiries regarding employment shows much inconsideration in your attitude toward me.

[2]When I left my job at your restaurant at the end of August, you promised me a job any time that I would be home from school — Labor

Day, Thanksgiving vacation, weekends, etc. I was also told that the Christmas season is one of the busiest times of the year at the restaurant. Many people travel by car during this period, and the restaurant is located near the intersection of several main interstate roads. More workers are needed if the restaurant is to be smoothly and efficiently run. Why didn't you keep your promise to me?

³During the time that I worked for you, I worked hard—I did everything that I was told to do, and I did it quickly and efficiently. Besides keeping fifty tables in the cafeteria dining room cleaned off and ready for the customers, I was expected to unload dirty dishes from a cart and stack them on the dishwasher's counter. I was also told to vacuum the dining room carpet every day, clean and dust the booths and furniture, and fill condiment containers on every table. I was ex- pected to do all of this alone, even when busloads of people would stop at the restaurant. I managed to always get all of my work done on time, and you complimented me frequently on the good job I had done.

⁴When you had some other job for me to do, I always did it will- ingly. Several times I did dishes when other workers had too many other things to do or if they didn't come to work. Also, during the Fourth of July holiday period, I worked on the foodline serving customers. Several times, also, I gave up my day off to go in and work for other bus girls who got sick. I was never paid any extra wages for the extra jobs I did.

⁵I am sure that you were satisfied with my work. I realize that I didn't have any experience working in a restaurant when you hired me, but you did give me a raise after I had only worked three days. As I said before, you complimented me often on the job I had done. The customers must have been satisfied with the appearance of the dining room, because many people left tips for me, which is not a common practice in a cafeteria-style restaurant.

⁶I feel that I treated you fairly as my boss. I was never late to work, and I never stopped working early. I took my breaks only when you told me that I could, and I never took any "extra" breaks when a manager wasn't around (like many of the other workers did). Busing tables isn't a very interesting job, but I never complained. I worked every day that I was scheduled to, and never asked for any extra days off.

⁷I hope that you realize, after reading this, how inconsiderate you were by not answering my inquiries. I treated you with fairness and respect, but in this case, you didn't treat me in the same way. If I had been lazy and done a sloppy job while I worked for you, I probably would have expected my letters to be ignored. Because I waited weeks for a reply from you, I was unable to find any other type of work over vacation. I hope that in the future you will be more considerate and fair to the college students who work for you.

PART TWO

DEVELOPING PAPERS

CHAPTER 5

INTRODUCTION—
STRATEGIES OF DEVELOPMENT

In previous chapters, you learned some techniques for finding a subject, thinking about it, and finally shaping it into a plan for a paper. In this chapter, we will introduce you to some other ways that writers think about a subject and how that thinking process influences the organization of paragraphs and papers. We call these processes *strategies of development* because the subject matter often suggests certain ways of developing topics. While at times you will use the strategies for writing at the paragraph level, we will also show you how writers mix the strategies in longer papers.

We will follow Greg, a pre-med student, as he thinks about a very real problem: The college's Board of Trustees has voted to increase tuition at his school by 30% in the next academic year. Then the trustees plan to increase tuition the following year by 10%. Since he is one of five college-age children in a family, he cannot depend on his parents for much financial help. The federal government is cutting its funding for Guaranteed Student Loans (GSL's), so he isn't sure if he will be able to borrow enough to pay his tuition. He is a pre-med major; consequently he cannot transfer to a "cheaper" college because pre-med programs aren't offered in the other state schools. He works summers as a life-guard, and he works 20 hours a week in the college cafeteria during the school year. That income, combined with his GSL, barely covers expenses.

Greg considers the effect that a 40% hike in tuition will have on him. He gets increasingly angry about the prospect of having to go in debt, and this anger is reflected in his comments jotted down quickly on scratch paper:

> Not fair. The debt is going to be impossible to pay back.
> Mom doesn't work.
> Parents proud of me wanting to be a doctor.
> Dad is a self-made man who works hard in his own business. Never took anything from anyone.
> Never any money left over, after paying debts and mortgage.
> Pre-med expensive.
> University charges more tuition for pre-med courses.
> Chose a public university because cheaper.
> Job at cafeteria barely covers room and board — no tuition or books.
> If I leave school to get some money for school, can I pick up my studies again?
> John and Susie barely managing to stay in school, even with loans.
> Takes a lot of persistence to apply for work.
> The total cost for college is increasing twice as fast as the inflation index. Does this make sense?
> The government is decreasing funds for loans. Harder to get in future.
> What could I do if I left school?

Certain observations that Greg has just jotted down can be translated into *the strategies of development* mentioned earlier. Applied to Greg's situation as a pre-med student, the strategies could be used as follows:

1. *Description* — A description of the financial situation of Greg's family: number of children, amount of mortgage, and other debts.

2. *Narration* — A true story narrating his finding and keeping jobs in order to supplement his student loan.

3. *Personal Experience* — A historical account of Greg's single-mindedness in wanting to be a doctor and how it has been a consistent thread influencing his life.

4. *Process* — An accounting of the steps in applying for a student loan.

5. *Cause-effect*—An analysis of the effect of his having to leave school since he may not be able to qualify for a student loan to pay the increased tuition.

6. *Classification*—A breakdown of the kinds of loans available, most of which he is not eligible for.

7. *Illustration*—An account of three friends who will have a difficult time staying in school with increased tuition and reduced student loans.

8. *Definition*—An extended definition of *student loans*.

9. *Comparison-contrast*—An explanation of the kind of program Greg is enrolled in, compared with the program he could get in other colleges.

10. *Analogy*—An extended comparison in which he shows that the rate of tuition increases over a period of years in the college is higher than the rate of inflation. Nationally, college tuitions are increasing at double the rate of inflation, and experts believe that this will be the pattern for years to come.

After thinking about the subject of increased tuition, and after studying his jottings, Greg decides that the best argument he can make is to write to the Board of Trustees and his state legislator, objecting to the tuition increase. He knows that all the points in his jottings won't be relevant because he can't deal with all the possible topics on the subject. Nevertheless, he chooses those points that he believes would be most convincing and those that would perhaps be applicable to other students in his predicament. For instance, using *cause and effect* as a strategy to show that he—and others—might have to leave school (as a result of an increase in tuition) should convince his readers that the increase will cause unnecessary hardship.

After choosing this strategy, Greg outlines his stance.

> *Role:* College sophomore (pre-med) who has relied on part-time jobs and student loans to pay college expenses.
>
> *Audience:* The Board of Trustees and a state legislator.
>
> *Thesis:* The proposal to increase tuition over 40% by the school year 1988 should be reconsidered because restrictions on federally subsidized Guaranteed Student Loans (GSL's), and the inability of most students to get high-paying jobs, will result in many students having to drop out of school.

As the thesis just shown implies, Greg's thesis is one of *cause and effect,* and the developmental strategy of his paper will reflect that fact.

The choice of a strategy depends partly on the nature of the subject and partly on the kind of evidence available to you. Certain subjects seem to encourage a writer to employ specific methods of development.

Below is an example of how one student used all of the strategies of development in a paper on bumper stickers. Read the paper and prepare the questions for class discussion.

STICKING TO BUMPERS

Introduction

[1]Four children in the back of a car can drive vacationing parents crazy. At least our parents told us this often enough. "Shut up, and quit fighting! Look at the scenery!" (The scenery was hot dog stands and Taco Bells.)

[2]Suddenly, right in the middle of Flagstaff, Arizona, my father said "God bless America—and please hurry." A minute later he said: "Become a doctor, and support a lawyer." And then: "You touch-a my car, I break-a you face."

Narration

[3]He was, of course, reading bumper stickers in busy traffic. My mother is smart; she knew that if you can keep four hot, unhappy young people—ranging in age from nine to eighteen—from killing each other for only a short time, you are ahead of the game. The other kids were appointed lookouts, and I was made secretary for the Great Sticker Hunt. I was also appointed Drawer of Conclusions—father is a lawyer.

[4]For the next few days, we saw enough bumper stickers to fill a small notebook, and I outlined my conclusions. First, the bumper sticker appears everywhere. It is glued on old rusty VW's and new Cadillacs—more on the former than the latter, however. Drivers of very expensive cars—foreign or domestic—do not, we think, buy bumper stickers.

Thesis

Definition

[5]The bumper sticker is basically an argument. It may or may not be serious; but it has to be short. It tends to be epigrammatic. It can state a "fact"—SOFT JUDGES MAKE HARDENED CRIMINALS—or a call for action—FIGHT ORGANIZED CRIME: ABOLISH THE IRS. The subject of the argument is seldom much older than last month's newspaper.

Elaboration of thesis

Classification— first large category:

unserious

Illustration—

[6]Bumper stickers seem to fall into seven broad groups. Four groups are relatively unserious, or even represent overt attempts at humor. The first of these is personal. Examples: I'M A TENNIS BUM.
I TRAVEL THE FIFTH ST. BRIDGE. PRAY FOR ME.
In a second group are the determinedly wacky:

two subcategories
of unserious

GET STONED—DRINK WET CEMENT
SURF NAKED
CLEAN AIR SMELLS FUNNY
FIGHT SMOG—RIDE A HORSE
DON'T STARE; I'M DANGEROUSLY ATTRACTIVE

Illustration—
third subcategory
of unserious

[7]In a third group of the relatively unserious stickers are derivations of other messages: HAVE YOU HUGGED YOUR KID TODAY? becomes HAVE YOU HUGGED YOUR HARLEY TODAY? and KEEP ON TRUCKIN' becomes KEEP ON TOLKIEN. Such derivations—or "echoes"—are important to the determined collector. On a dull day of vacationing you can trace eight or ten themes that undergo relatively unsubtle variations. On different bumpers you can be asked whether "today" you have hugged your wife, husband, grandparents, kids, motorcycle, and the defensive line of the Pittsburgh Steelers.

Illustration—
fourth subcategory
of unserious

[8]A fourth group of the unserious stickers makes little sense—at least to me. Examples:
FLOWERS DO IT!
JOHANN'S BACH (printed in gothic script)
CUSTER HAD IT COMING
I FOUND IT!
WOULDN'T YOU RATHER BE RIDING A MULE ON
     MOLOKAI?
I BRAKE FOR UNICORNS AND HOBBITS
SUPPORT ONOMATOPOEIA

Classification—
second large
category: serious

[9]The next three groups are relatively more serious. In the first of these, the driver of the car makes a clear pitch for his or her profession:
FIREMEN STILL MAKE HOUSE CALLS

Illustration—
first subcategory
of serious

LOVE A NURSE
IF YOU CAN READ THIS THANK A TEACHER
ENGINEERS DO IT WITH PRECISION
IF YOU DON'T LIKE HOW WE TAKE CARE OF
     YOUR GARBAGE, WE'LL RETURN IT. (seen on the
     bumper of a garbage truck)

Illustration—
second subcategory
of serious

[10]In the second group of serious stickers, we find arguments that are related to marriage, sex, and the family:
ANOTHER FAMILY FOR ERA
CELEBRATE FAMILY VALUES. THIS IS FAMILY
     YEAR!
WE BELIEVE IN MARRIAGE
A WOMAN WITHOUT A MAN IS LIKE A FISH
     WITHOUT A BICYCLE

SOULS OF GREAT LIFE ARE WAITING TO BE
    BORN: HAVE ONE!
ABORTION NOW!!

Illustration—
third subcategory
of serious

[11]The last group of serious stickers argues a political point, sometimes with an unpleasant edge of meanness or satire:

TAKE A WOLF TO LUNCH. FEED HIM AN
    ENVIRONMENTALIST.
SPLIT WOOD, NOT ATOMS
NUCLEAR POWER PLANTS ARE BUILT BETTER
    THAN JANE FONDA
A BUSHEL OF GRAIN FOR A BARREL OF OIL
CLEAN UP AMERICA—SHOOT A REDNECK

Process

[12]In furthering our attempts to understand the bumper sticker syndrome, we tried writing a few, and in doing so learned a little about how to produce them. What you try for is a short statement that is both pointed and relevant to a recent event which most people are aware of. So first pick such an event. Next, associate it with another thing, idea, or person that is well known. Then, try to use a play on words or a pun. The readers should have "instant recognition" when they read the message, and perhaps be persuaded by the argument, serious or not. You can see the elements of the process working in this sticker: KEEP AIR CLEAN AND SEX DIRTY. (I won't reproduce any of the stickers we made up—they are too awful.)

Cause-effect

[13]Why do thousands of American drivers go to the trouble to buy bumper stickers? They seem like such trivial messages to display to the world. One answer may be that they reflect the triviality of modern "media journalism." News stories on television, for example, are typically short and abbreviated, as are bumper stickers. Only one point is highlighted in both types of messages, so that the viewer gets a dramatic but distorted idea of the complexities involved. When the President spoke in Chicago, the evening TV news account of his long speech showed him speaking only two sentences, both taken out of context. One of them was not even the full sentence as he spoke it.

Comparison
(with other short
communications)

[14]We live in an age of bumper-sticker journalism. The Letters columns in magazines and newspapers often use letters of one sentence. These deliver no more than an opinion without evidence or reasons given. Like the chopped-up TV interview and the one-sentence letter in a national magazine, the bumper sticker gives us a message lacking background,

context, or development. These are messages without authority or anybody standing behind them; and they are as forgettable as today's comic page. They are meant to last only a few seconds in one's consciousness and then disappear.

[15]Given the way we live today, the bumper sticker probably satisfies an American need to make a point quickly, painlessly, and—most of all—anonymously. The car involved may be identified clearly as a Ford, Chevrolet, Plymouth, etc. But when was the last time you saw a signed bumper sticker?

PRACTICE

Discussion

1. Reread the paper on bumper stickers.
   a. Outline the process this writer may have followed in collecting her information about bumper stickers, recording her findings, and creating other thoughts on the subject.
   b. In what ways could you follow a similar process in pre-writing?
   c. How satisfactory and complete is the writer's definition of *bumper stickers*?
   d. Do you agree with the writer's classifications? How would you change them?
   e. Discuss the use of evidence in the writer's support of her thesis.
   f. Describe her stance.
   g. What advice would you give this writer to improve her paper?
   h. Did the writer support her thesis?

2. For class discussion, suggest a strategy for each of the following subjects.
   a. *Subject:* The environment
      Thesis: The plants and streams of the wilderness areas are being destroyed by litter, pollution, and heavy traffic.
      Strategy:

   b. *Subject:* Household pets
      Thesis: Over the years, the pets in our family have been an endless source of amusement and frustration.
      Strategy:

c. *Subject:* Trying out for a play
   Thesis: Even though I study the lines beforehand, whenever I read for a part my voice control is poor because a try-out is an unusual acting situation.

   Strategy:

d. *Subject:* Running for student office
   Thesis: There are three important steps in running for student office: applying, campaigning, and developing a constituency.

   Strategy:

e. *Subject:* Nervous headaches
   Thesis: My headaches are caused by the pressures of having to meet strict course deadlines.

   Strategy:

f. *Subject:* Nonflowering house plants
   Thesis: Of the foliage house plants, succulents and cacti are the easiest to grow in a dry climate.

   Strategy:

g. *Subject:* Camping
   Thesis: Campers who travel in recreational vehicles are typically congenial people who bring their television sets and motor bikes and the like to camp in commercial or park campsites.

   Strategy:

h. *Subject:* "Pass/fail" courses
   Thesis: "Pass/fail" courses are an educational opportunity to study a subject without having to face the pressure of a conventional grading system.

   Strategy:

i. *Subject:* Two science-fiction movies
   Thesis: *The Empire Strikes Back* is a movie with a thin plot, unconvincing characters, and bizarre situations; *Close Encounters of the Third Kind* is a film with a strong plot, realistic characters, and situations based on actual happenings.

   Strategy:

j. *Subject:*   Hand guns
   Thesis: Like automobiles, hand guns are dangerous but controllable mechanisms.
   Strategy:

Writing

Choose one of the 10 subjects above, or a similar one, and write a short paragraph or paper using one strategy.

You may look ahead to chapters 6–9 to get further details on managing the strategy you choose.

CHAPTER 6

DESCRIPTION, NARRATION, PERSONAL EXPERIENCE

DESCRIPTION

*W*hen you describe a thing, you give its qualities, nature, or appearance. The word *describe* comes from the Latin *describere* ("to copy" or "to sketch"), which implies that the thing described has a material existence. Customarily, the words *describe* and *description* have been used to refer to material things, although of course one may describe abstractions such as states of mind or moral attributes.

You will find description useful in either single paragraphs or full papers. It is often necessary when you want to talk about a person or place; but description can be used to support your point in any kind of writing.

Sensory Images

Good descriptions often appeal to one or more of the five senses. The writer tries to make the reader see, hear, feel, smell, or taste the experience being described. These word pictures or sensory images help the reader experience vicariously what the writer has felt. They also help to create the mood that the writer wishes to achieve.

Descriptions usually support a larger purpose. Not only must you be an astute and careful observer, but you also need to relate your observations to a point or a descriptive purpose. Notice how Anaïs Nin, through her description of sights and smells in Fez, Morocco, makes the point about the importance of women's eyes.

SIGHT	Colors seep into your consciousness as never before: a sky-blue jellaba with a black face veil, a pearl-grey jellaba with a yellow veil, a black jellaba with a red veil, a shocking-pink jellaba with a purple veil. The clothes conceal the wearers' figures so that they remain elusive, with all the intensity and expression concentrated in the eyes. The eyes speak for the body, the self, for the age, conveying innumerable messages from their deep and rich existence.
POINT: *Importance* *of eyes*	
SMELL	After color and the graceful sway of robes, the flares, the stance, the swing of loose clothes, come the odors. One stand is devoted to sandalwood from Indonesia and the Philippines. It lies in huge round baskets and is sold by weight, for it is a precious luxury wood for burning as incense. The walls of the cubicle are lined with small bottles containing the essence of flowers—jasmine, rose, honeysuckle, and the rose water that is used to perfume guests. In the same baskets lie the henna leaves that the women distill and use on their hands and feet. For the affluent, the henna comes in liquid form. And there is, too, the famous *kohl,* the dust from antimony that gives the women such a soft, iridescent, smoky radiance around their eyes.
Importance *of eyes*	

Behind every good description there is a point being made: the sunset is *beautiful,* the earthquake was *frightening,* the birth of a baby is *miraculous,* the political ideas of Theodore Roosevelt were *pragmatic.* Consider the point in the passage below, which describes the break-up of Ernest Shackleton's ship during his expedition to the Antarctic in 1915:

Sounds of the ice	[1]There were the sounds of the pack in movement—the basic noises, the grunting and whining of the floes, along with an occasional thud as a heavy block collapsed. But in addition, the pack under compression seemed to have an almost limitless repertoire of other sounds, many of which seemed strangely unrelated to the noise of ice undergoing pressure. Sometimes there was a sound like a gigantic train
Details	with squeaky axles being shunted roughly about with a great deal of bumping and clattering. At the same time a huge

ship's whistle blew, mingling with the crowing of roosters, the roar of a distant surf, the soft throb of an engine far away, and the moaning cries of an old woman. In the rare periods of calm, when the movement of the pack subsided for a moment, the muffled rolling of drums drifted across the air.

Pressure of the ice

²In this universe of ice, nowhere was the movement greater or the pressure more intense than in the floes that were attacking the ship. Nor could her position have been worse. One floe was jammed solidly against her starboard

Details

bow, and another held her on the same side aft. A third floe drove squarely in on her port beam opposite. Thus the ice was working to break her in half, directly amidships. On several occasions she bowed to starboard along her entire length.

Accumulation of ice on bows

³Forward, where the worst of the onslaught was concentrated, the ice was inundating her. It piled higher and higher against her bows as she repelled each new wave, until gradually it mounted to her bulwarks, then crashed across the

Details

deck, overwhelming her with a crushing load that pushed her head down even deeper. Thus held, she was even more at the mercy of the floes driving against her flanks.

Ship's reaction to pressure of ice

⁴The ship reacted to each fresh wave of pressure in a different way. Sometimes she simply quivered briefly as a human being might wince if seized by a single, stabbing pain. Other times she retched in a series of convulsive jerks accompanied by anguished outcries. On these occasions her

Details

three masts whipped violently back and forth as the rigging tightened like harpstrings. But most agonizing for the men were the times when she seemed a huge creature suffocating and gasping for breath, her sides heaving against the strangling pressure.

Comparison: ship like a dying "giant beast"

⁵More than any other single impression in those final hours, all the men were struck, almost to the point of horror, by the way the ship behaved like a giant beast in its death agonies. — Alfred Lansing, *Endurance*

The point behind the description is that the destruction of the ship was terrifying, and the descriptive details contribute to this point.

Point of View

Lansing wrote his description over fifty years after the expedition, a fact which partly controls his point of view. *Point of view* is the angle — psychological or physical (or both) — from which the writer views his subject. Lansing's point of view is that of the researcher, poring over old diaries and accounts of Shackleton's voyage and listening to the stories of the few survivors still alive. To recreate the incident, Lansing blends his point of view with that of the men inside the ship. You—the reader—hear, see, and feel what the trapped sailors heard, saw, and felt. Lansing's ruling principle is the terrifying physical effect of the ice on the ship and the terrifying psychological effect on the crew members. He presents his paragraphs in deductive fashion, following topic sentences with brilliant descriptive detail; we hear the weird sounds ("gigantic train with squeaky axles," "the moaning cries of an old woman"), and we feel the pressure of the ice ("she retched in a series of convulsive jerks," "her three masts whipped violently back and forth as the rigging tightened like harpstrings"). The climax of the passage occurs in paragraph 4, where the ship is described as a huge, dying animal fighting for life. All of these details give the reader an idea of the terror the sailors must have felt.

When writing description, do not lose control of point of view, your physical and psychological "angle." Here is a student's paragraph in which the point of view is fuzzy:

Point of view *implied in* we	As we strode through the alleyways between the houses, we met a few shy, ragged children who were gleefully playing with an equally ragged dog. From the stoop of his front door,
Details	a wrinkled old man with a red bandana wrapped around his head meditatively surveyed the distances beyond the mesa.
Shift from we *to* *impersonal* one	In the distance, one could discern the dim shapes of the farmers in their sparse corn patches. The rhythm of a
Who is "hearing"?	woman grinding corn could be heard along the yellow street from within one of the small apartments.

Although the student uses clear details, his shift in point of view blurs their effect. The reader may wonder how the writer saw "dim shapes in the distance," and heard sounds "along the yellow street," and knew at the same time that the dim shapes were farmers and that the sound came from a "woman grinding corn." This is not just a pedantic objection. Both description and narration demand a sense of reality in handling point of view. The reader should be made to feel that he is observing the scene in a natural way, the way he might observe it if he were there. The writer of this passage would have treated the scene more naturally and convincingly had he first described a dim shape in the distance, and *later* described it as a farmer. Also, the description would have been strengthened had the writer not recognized the noise from the apartment until he asked someone what it was, or until he went into the apartment to find out for himself. (These ideas on point of view can also be applied to the writing of personal experience papers, discussed on pp. 98–108.)

The shifts in point of view in this student's paragraph are not particularly bad. Violent shifts, however, may cause the reader to feel that instead of being led into a scene he is being yanked into it. For instance:

I was driving around that night, not thinking about anything particularly. I was completely unaware that before the evening was over I was going to witness the most horrible experience of my life. It was when I reached the top of the hill overlooking the valley where the accident occurred that I got an empty feeling in the pit of my stomach. It is strange what mixed thoughts run through your head when you see a bad accident.

Besides "telling" his reader too much and not allowing the details of the accident to speak for themselves, the writer shifts from the experience as it unfolded to his later reactions to the experience.

In the following passage from the same paper, the writer uses point of view accurately:

I stepped out of the car and walked toward the ditch. Suddenly I head a man's voice clearly over the muffled sounds of the crowd. The voice said: "Bring a flashlight over here!" A highway patrolman who was standing next to me turned the beam of his big flashlight down between the rows of corn. The voice kept speaking, and I could see by the patrolman's flash that it belonged to the county sheriff.

When the writer walked toward the ditch, he heard a voice. He accurately reports here the series of events as he saw and heard them: an unidentified voice spoke, the patrolman turned his flashlight toward the voice, the speaker turned out to be the sheriff.

PRACTICE

Discussion

Discuss the point of view, use of details and sensory images in the following description of a boy's father:

[1]My father's world was monstrous. He knew places like Corsicana, Waxahachie, Nacogdoches, Wichita Falls, Monahans. His world was more than half the size of Texas. He would come home and tell us about it and expand our boundaries. He knew what the road looked like between Sonora and Eldorado, between Borger and Pampa. He loved roads and the way they looked. We would be driving to

Grandma Hale's farm and come to a place that wasn't characteristic of our immediate world and he would say, "This looks like the road between Cuero and Yoakum."

[2]He brought home the very best kind of gifts. A puppy in a shoe box. A chicken with a bad leg. A 25-pound sack of peanut brittle. Once he brought two milk goats. He had traded the old Ford for a smoking Chevy with the door wired shut on the driver's side. I can see him turning in off the road, grinning behind the cracked windshield, those two goats riding on the back seat with their heads poked out the windows.

[3]Another time he brought an entire stalk of bananas. I wrote a theme about it for school. He brought home the first loaf of sliced bread our neighborhood ever saw. Bread, cooked in a bakery 150 miles away and sliced on a machine, and every slice just perfect. People came from two streets over, to see and taste. It was sure fine having a hero for a father.

[4]The sweetest times of my growing up came when he'd take me with him on the road, beyond my world, to the edges of his own. We'd go smoking along at 35 miles an hour. He'd push the brim of his hat up in front, and he'd brace the wheel between his thin old knees and steer that way. He'd take out his harmonica and play "Red River Valley" and "Coming Around the Mountain," and "Springtime in the Rockies." I am so grateful now for those days, inside my father's world.
—Leon Hall

Writing

1. Observe someone (on a bus, train, elevator, or in a classroom) engaged in some activity, unaware of being watched. Make eye contact and keep it for as long as possible. Write a short description of the person's reaction. For example, here is a description of a child:

> One day, as my bus swerved around a corner, and I was clinging tightly to the edge of my seat to keep from sliding onto the floor, I noticed across from me a young black girl, no more than ten years old. She was singing. Her white hat, perched on her braided hair, bobbed up and down, and her scuffed brown boots tapped on the floor, keeping time to her song. She had a soft, high voice, but she didn't stay in tune. My eyes met hers, and I smiled. Her mouth snapped shut and she quit singing. Her brown eyes turned icy cold, then she slowly and deliberately turned her head to look out the window, her mouth clamped tightly shut for the rest of the ride home.

2. Visit one of the following places. Spend some time there observing the people and taking notes. Try to record the way the place smells

and feels; brainstorm for a possible hook. Then, using your notes, write a description. Before you begin to write, decide on the particular point you intend to make.

a. A college cafeteria at lunch time
b. A clothing store that caters to the well-to-do
c. A warehouse clothing outlet or an army surplus store
d. A boutique
e. A beauty salon

NARRATION

A *narrative* is an account of an incident, or series of closely related incidents, that makes or illustrates a specific point. Since a narrative is a story, a writer can use narration when it is important for the reader to know "what happened." When writing a narrative, you need to ask yourself two questions: (1) Is the narrative relevant to my purpose? (2) Assuming that it is relevant, how can I tell it effectively? The first question you have to answer for yourself, as circumstances arise. To the second question we can suggest some partial answers.

In order to be effective, a narrative must get smoothly and quickly to its point and make that point dramatically. A narrative that dawdles along, introducing unnecessary people and irrelevant detail, is usually a failure. The reader will skip over it to get to something else. In writing vivid and convincing narratives, you should know how to compress certain details and expand others in order to give shape and emphasis to the incident you are relating. Here is how one writer uses narrative to emphasize the general ideas he is conveying:

Compressed description and historical account

From birth, the Fijians are in and out of the jungle. They understand the tangled greenery that covers the South Pacific islands the way a New Yorker understands Times Square. Their senses are sharper than the white man's and their strength and endurance are greater. There is very little left for them to learn about the jungle. Certainly the news, a year or so ago, that they were to be "trained for jungle fighting" by the Allies must have struck them as comical, though none of them ever said so. In fact, I was recently told by a New Zealand captain stationed at the Fiji camp on Bougainville that the men there had been unfailingly deferential and kind to their white tutors. They are a people with an extraordinary sense of humor, but they have an almost pathological

Story

aversion to hurting the feelings of a friend. However, at the end of their training, which took place in the Fijis, they al-

lowed their sense of humor a fairly free hand. The company of white soldiers who had trained them arranged to fight a mock battle with them in the bush. After dark, each side was to try to penetrate as far as possible into the other's lines. The main idea was to see how well the new Fiji scouts had learned their lessons. It turned out that they had learned them pretty well. During the night some of the white scouts worked thirty or forty feet into the Fiji lines, and figured they had the battle won, since they hadn't caught any Fijians behind *their* lines. When they came to check up at daylight, it developed that most of the Fijians had apparently spent the night in the white headquarters. They had chalked huge crosses on the
Climax   tents and the furniture and had left one of the most distinct crosses on the seat of the commanding officer's trousers, which he had thrown over a chair around 4:00 a.m. — Robert Lewis Taylor, "The Nicest Fellows You Ever Met"*

The climax of the story nicely points up the ideas presented in the first part of the passage: that Fijians are at home in the jungle and that they have a sense of humor.

Dialogue in Narration

Dialogue, the written representation of conversation, is often useful when you wish to relate an incident or describe something—a state of mind, an attitude, a belief, etc. In most nonfiction works, writers use dialogue sparingly, compressing or reporting it indirectly when they can. In employing dialogue, you may find these suggestions useful:

1. Where it is possible, avoid unnecessary repetition of the speakers' names or unnecessary description of the way they speak. It is old-fashioned and tiresome to write:

   "I see you in the corner," whispered Baker softly.
   "How did you find me?" inquired Charles curiously.
   "I smelled the pipe you've been smoking," purred Baker evilly.
   "Oh!" exclaimed Charles alarmedly.

---

*Reprinted by permission; © 1944, 1972 The New Yorker Magazine, Inc.

2. Present dialogue simply:

> I'll not forget my first — and last — meeting with that old Texan. He came striding down the line I had just surveyed on his property, pulling up my line stakes and tossing them over his shoulder as he came. When he got up to my surveying truck, he wasn't even out of breath:
> "Get off my land."
> "O.K., I will — in just a minute. If you'll just —"
> "Get off *now*."
> "Yes, sir, right now, just like you say."
> And I did leave, as fast as possible.

3. Above all, remember to compress and shorten your dialogue whenever you can. Harry Crews reports a "conversation" he had as a farm boy in Georgia with his dog Sam:

> [1]The moment I sat down in the shade, I was already wondering how long it would be before they quit to go to the house for dinner because I was already beginning to wish I'd taken two biscuits instead of one and maybe another piece of meat, or else that I hadn't shared with Sam.
> [2]Bored, I looked down at Sam and said: "Sam, if you don't quit eatin my biscuit and meat, I'm gone have to cut you like a shoat hog."
> [3]A black cloud of gnats swarmed around his heavy muzzle, but I clearly heard him say that he didn't think I was man enough to do it. Sam and I talked a lot together, had long involved conversations, mostly about which one of us had done the other one wrong and, if not about that, about which one of us was the better man. It would be a good long time before I started thinking of Sam as a dog instead of a person. But I always came out on top when we talked because Sam could only say what I said he said, think what I thought he thought.
> [4]"If you was any kind of man atall, you wouldn't snap at them gnats and eat them flies the way you do," I said.
> [5]"It ain't a thing in the world the matter with eatin gnats and flies," he said.
> [6]"It's how come people treat you like a dog," I said.

Suggestions for Writing Description and Narration

1. Limit the focus of your description and narration in order to make a single point.

2. Keep a consistent *point of view*.

3. Use sensory images when relevant and suitable.

4. *Show* with vivid language and specific details.

5. Whenever using dialogue, compress and simplify.

PRACTICE

Discussion

1. Discuss the point of the following narrative. How does the author maintain a consistent point of view? (The author, Gerald Durrell, captured animals for zoos.)

> He [Pious, a native] flicked the crocodile with the bag; it opened both eyes, and suddenly came to life with unbelievable speed. It fled through Pious's legs, making him leap in the air with a wild yelp of fright, dashed past the hunter, who made an ineffectual grab at it, and scuttled off across the compound toward the kitchen. Pious, the hunter, and I gave chase. The crocodile, seeing us rapidly closing in on it, decided that to waste time going round the kitchen would be asking for trouble, so it went straight through the palm-leaf wall. The cook and his helpers could not have been more surprised. When we entered the kitchen the crocodile was half through the opposite wall, and it had left havoc behind him. The cook's helper had dropped the frying pan, and the breakfast was all over the floor. The cook, who had been sitting on an empty kerosene tin, overbalanced into a basket containing eggs and some very ripe and soft pawpaw, and in his efforts to regain his feet and vacate the kitchen he had kicked over a large pot of cold curry. The crocodile was now heading for the forest proper, with bits of curry and wood ash adhering to its scaly back. Taking off my dressing gown I launched myself in a flying tackle, throwing the gown over its head, and then winding it round so tight that it could not bite. I was only just in time, for in another few yards it would have reached the thick undergrowth at the edge of the camp. Sitting in the dust, clutching the crocodile to my bosom, I bargained with the man. At last we agreed to a price and the crocodile was placed in the small pond I had built for these reptiles. However, it refused to let go of my dressing gown, of which it had got a good mouthful, and so I was forced to leave it in the pond until such time as it let it go. It was never quite the same again. Some weeks later another crocodile escaped and did precisely the same thing, horrifying the kitchen staff, and completely ruining my lunch. After this, all crocodiles were unpacked within the confines of the pool, and at least three people had to be on hand to head off any attempts at escape. —Gerald Durrell, *The Overloaded Ark*

2. Discuss the effectiveness of the narrative and dialogue in the following passage. How does Roberts achieve the sound of real people talking? Identify his introductions to dialogue. What is Roberts' thesis? What is his point of view?

[1]I rounded a bend [on my recumbent bicycle], and suddenly, through an opening in the trees, saw a great splash of spilt truck on the landscape. Two semis had recently collided, and one was strewn in dramatic disarray down the hill, its cargo a giant splat on the countryside.

[2]As I paused to gaze at the scene, I heard a rustling in the leaves behind me. Turning to look, I saw five of the biggest, meanest-looking characters I have ever seen heading toward me from the nearby Potomac. I nodded in friendly but uneasy greeting.

[3]"What's this?" asked a mountainous black man.

[4]"It's a recumbent bicycle," I replied, "with solar panels to power the electronic equipment. I'm traveling cross-country."

[5]"Where you coming from, buddy?" asked a burly redhead.

[6]"Columbus, Ohio. I'm doing a 14,000-mile loop around the United States that should take about a year," I said, mouthing my standard response.

[7]"Yeah? You crazy, or what?"

[8]"Sorta." I grinned. "What are you guys doing here?"

[9]A white guy with long black hair in a ponytail answered. "We're convicts, man, from the Maryland Correctional Facility over in Hagerstown."

[10]"Hey, is that right?" I chuckled nervously. "Well whaddya know. You escaping?"

[11]"Naw, man," spoke the giant black. "You kiddin' me? We workin', man. We out here to clean up that truck." He gestured over his shoulder.

[12]"Ah, I see," I answered with some relief.

[13]After a bit more banter, I prepared to leave. "Well, I better hit the road," I said, "I'm shootin' for Shepherdstown . . ."

[14]"Whoa!" interrupted the redhead. "We gotta fix you up, man!" He turned on his heel and motioned for me to follow. The others set off in the same direction—toward the truck—laughing.

[15]I apprehensively followed them through the woods, arriving at a couple of yellow state trucks and a few armed guards. Other inmates milled about. We took a turn into another part of the woods and came upon a large bundle under a tarp set back in the bushes. "Our stash, man," explained the huge black guy.

[16]He pulled back the tarp, exposing their private stock of the truck's cargo. Beneath the cover . . . what else but a giant mound of Sara Lee pastry!

[17]He grabbed a box and shoved it into my hands. "Have some walnut cake, my man."

[18]Another spoke up. "Oh, man, you don't want no walnut cake. Cheese danish, man. Cheese danish. *That's* where it's at!" Another box was placed on the first.

[19]The redhead handed over another. "You want some of these apple things, buddy?"

[20]Before long I was standing there in the beautiful Maryland woods amid a jovial crowd of murderers and bank robbers, laughing helplessly as my armload of Sara Lee pastries grew to an absurd height. "I'm on a bicycle," I finally managed to blurt out. "I can't carry all this!"

[21]"C'mon," suggested the giant. We returned to the bike, still sitting in the middle of the towpath with a crowd of decidedly rough characters standing around it. Nothing appeared to be missing.

[22]I started struggling with a box of apple danish, at last securing it under a bungee cord. The giant grabbed the walnut cake. "Gimme that." He stuffed it between the fairing and the electronics package on the front of the machine. "Don't worry, it'll stay." I managed to hang a bit more here and there, then diplomatically declined the rest.

[23]We said our goodbyes and I set off again down the quiet trail, festooned with pastry, laughing for miles. You just never know in an enterprise like this. You just never know. — Steve Roberts, *An Encounter in the Woods*

3. Following is a narrative describing an experience one student had while hiking in the mountains. Read the essay and answer the questions after it.

[1]The Geology Field Camp had one entire day to spend in the Tetons with no lecture or "rock stops." Seven of us women decided to take a 17-mile hike up the Paintbrush Divide. Considering my unfamiliarity with the area and my inexperience climbing on snow, I was hesitant about joining the expedition. However, the leader assured me that we would stay together all the way up to the Divide.

[2]As soon as we started on the trail at 6:30 A.M., I could see that I was going to be the slow one. I wasn't worried about getting too far behind because I had done some hiking. However, at 9:00, I became concerned because I discovered I was alone. By 9:30 the trail the others had traveled couldn't be seen because of heavy snow that began to fall. By 10:30 I was getting pretty lonesome. I felt totally alone in the wilderness. I had fallen several times through the snow where streams had cut away the bottom and made the drift thinner. I was getting scared and a little panicky.

[3]Then I slipped and fell. It took me 10 seconds to slide down to a pile of rocks 200 yards below me. Getting back up to the trail was the problem I had to face. I could take only a few steps before the slope became too steep to walk on. Fortunately, I had my rock hammer with

me, so I cut footholds in the rock to pull myself up. It was exhausting, hard work. I knew that if I missed my footing I could fall all the way to the bottom, either injuring or killing myself on the way down.

⁴After an hour of digging and climbing I reached the trail. Whether out of fear or exhaustion, I was shaking so much when I finally got there, I could hardly stand up.

a. The writer narrating her hiking experience tells us in paragraph 2 that she was first "concerned," then "pretty lonesome," and finally "scared and a little panicky." How could she have used description to *show* how her emotions increased in intensity? How much space would she need to develop her realization that she was in a dangerous situation?

b. In paragraph 3 the writer tells us that she fell 200 yards in 10 seconds. What sensory images might describe her experience in the fall? (Which of her senses would probably have been most affected?)

c. The hiker tells us that she was in a dangerous situation because she could easily fall again. List a few details she could have used to *show* the reader the seriousness of her predicament.

d. Discuss the effectiveness of the conclusion. Is there a point? What advice would you give the writer to help her improve her narrative?

Writing

1. Following is a poignant narrative about a woman's grandmother who became forgetful. Perhaps you have had experiences with relatives who have changed as they retired and grew old. Using Silverman's narrative as a model, write about an experience you have had with a relative, neighbor, or friend. Be sure that your narrative has a point and a point of view. Use dialogue, if it is appropriate.

¹Tonight Grandma is sleeping in an Indiana rest home. Each morning she packs, telling the nurse she is going back to the farm. She says she is going down the road to the bus stop to catch the Greyhound out of Indianapolis back to Coatesville.

²I asked her last spring if she was allowed to keep a bird in the nursing home, remembering the blue parakeet she kept in the farm kitchen.

³"Oh, I reckon I can keep what I want," she said. "You know I live out in the country and can do what I want."

⁴She sits in the maple chair, thin and pale, still wearing a pink flowered dress, as she did when we trailed her into the barn. Her new

companions, more than 100 geriatric patients, silently wait for the Jell-O to be served. Outside, the Indianapolis slaughterhouses, factory smokestacks, and motels have replaced the grainfields. Grandma's hair is white, for winter settled into her mind a decade ago, but tucked in her wheelchair she believes it is a farm spring. — Linda Parker Silverman, "Roots"

2. Think about and list the details of an event that made an impression on you or one that you remember vividly. In particular, try to "relive" any conversations that occurred so that you can write the dialogue with the sound of real people talking.

   Write a narrative about the event, keeping a consistent point of view. For example, if you were to narrate your experience of being locked in a fruit cellar as a child, the point of view would be affected by your being directly involved. However, if you were narrating an event from the viewpoint of a bystander, it would be more objective.

   Suggestions:

- My first visit to a hospital (either as a patient or visitor)
- Walking into a house after a burglary
- The fire that nearly destroyed our house (or neighbor's, or friend's)
- My hardest assignment — giving bad news
- Selling an old car

PERSONAL EXPERIENCE

Writers often use personal experience in the form of anecdotes or examples to give validity and support to their main points. The personal experience essay is an autobiographical slice of a life, written usually to mark a change or to narrate an important event. Because such an essay is a "slice" of life rather than the whole loaf, by nature it must be limited and narrowed. Essentially there are two kinds of this essay.

The first kind deals with a *single thread* of happenings in your life — something that is woven into the fabric of your past and is important to you. Your "thread of happenings" may have to do with a hobby, a personal relationship, an idea, the result of an accident, an ambition, a physical defect. What the thread is does not matter, so long as it can be traced for a period of time and has some significance.

In such a paper, you cover only those events and persons that relate closely to the thread you are discussing. Here is an essay that exemplifies the "thread of happenings." Notice how the writer shows how *not* knowing how to drive has affected his life in the past and how it will affect it in the future.

Can't drive

[1]I have a confession to make. I am 22 years old. *And I don't know how to drive . . .* When I was going to high school in New York, my inability to drive never bothered me, probably because none of my friends knew how to drive. Once I went away to college, however, things changed. Owning a car was not only a social status symbol, but a practical way to get away from the campus on dull weekends. I found myself at the mercy of more mobile friends and roommates. Any suggestion I made about a weekend trip was greeted with a scornful, "Look, Kaufman, you can't even help with the driving. . . ."

[2]I wish I could report that these college experiences chastened me, that they taught me there are indeed places in this world where the New York City subway system does not go. They did no such thing. Despite the scorn of my peers, I was prepared to live out the rest of my life a resolute pedestrian.

Chronology: Then . . . First happening in thread: Father says, learn to drive

[3]Then, in December, while I was home from my senior year in college on Christmas vacation, my father took me aside. In that stern father-to-son tone he reserves for major pronouncements, he said, "Jonny, I think it's time you learned how to drive." Fleetingly, a thought crossed my mind: The old man's going to get me a car for graduation. No such luck. My father's decision that I learn how to drive was prompted by the age-old desire of parents that their children receive the benefits they never had. My father never learned how to drive. My mother can't drive either.

Second happening: Driving lessons

[4]I returned to college and promptly called Phil's Professional Driving School. Phil agreed to take me on and assigned me to Dennis, a recent college graduate and one of his best teachers. On a cold and wintry day in January, Dennis drove up to the entrance of my college dormitory and told me to get into the car—on the driver's side. I panicked. "You don't understand," I sputtered. "I've never driven a car. Never. I can't even drive a golf cart." Dennis smiled reassuringly and pointed to the extra brake on the passenger side of

the car. He coaxed me into the driver's seat and told me to start the ignition. "It's a bit like learning how to swim," he said. "We throw you into the traffic and see how you do."

Continuation of Thread: So . . . *Elaboration on driving lessons*

(⁵So) off we went. *For the next three months* Dennis and I met once a week for our one-hour lessons (at $12 a crack, all paid for by my father). Dennis was very patient. Bit by bit he broke me of all my bad driving habits: my tendency to stop dead in the middle of the road whenever I spotted a car in the rear-view mirror, my tendency to flash the right-turn signal when turning left, my tendency when parking to forget to put the car in reverse or, when I remembered to put it in reverse, forgetting to put it back into drive.

Transition showing change in attitude: Gradually . . .

(⁶Gradually,) I found myself developing not only the skills but the mentality of a driver. I began to hate pedestrians, one-way streets and city traffic. All I wanted was an open road that I could zoom down at 40 miles an hour (I could never get up the courage to go any faster). My parents would have been proud.

Continuation of Thread: Then . . . *Third happening: Refused to take driver's test*

(⁷Then,) just as I was about to enter the mainstream of American life, just as I was about to get my wheels—I developed cold feet. In April, Phil set up a road test for my driver's license. Two hours before the test I called Phil and told him I couldn't make it because I was studying for a final exam (a partial truth—I did have an exam that afternoon but I could have taken an hour off). Phil rescheduled my road test for the first week in July. Twenty-four hours before that test I called him again and told him I had a bad case of sunburn and couldn't move my arms (another half-truth—I did have a sunburn, but it only became acutely painful when I contemplated driving a car).

Effect of Thread— Can't and won't drive (the main point)

⁸Perhaps it's genetic: My parents don't know how to drive, so I will never be able to learn. Perhaps it's political: Automobiles are symbolic of the affluent suburbs that are drawing away jobs and businesses from my beloved New York City. Perhaps it's psychological: The fact remains that I'm scared to death of cars and even if I ever got a driver's license I would never trust myself behind the wheel.

Conclusion

(⁹Then again,) perhaps it's just as well: If God had meant for me to learn how to drive, he would have put me in California. —Jonathan Kaufman

The second kind of personal experience essay is one in which you concentrate on a particular event that has had an influence on your life. But you cannot simply narrate something that happened to you and call the result an essay; the event must be explained and analyzed. In other words, it is not only the event itself that you need to develop but also your later reactions to it. Here is a paper with that kind of emphasis:

Introduction: [1]During the summer between my seventh and eighth grades in junior high, my parents sent me to a YWCA camp at Grass Lake. I was happy to go because I liked all the activities of boating, swimming, and crafts that would be provided. Although I did not know any other girls who were going to that particular camp, I felt confident that I would soon make friends. I imagined that the camp experience would be free and joyous; it was to be my first summer away *Expectation set up:* from home and my expectations of youthful pleasures, happiness, and shared enthusiasms were great. When I arrived I was assigned to a cabin with five other girls. Nothing occurred during the early hours to make me less enthusiastic. Although none of my cabin mates were very friendly, I felt that any reserve would disappear in the camp experience.

First hint of expectation not being met: [2]During the first week the girls in my cabin were polite to me and boisterous and friendly to each other. They all had one common experience—all were members of the same junior-high school and its swim team. It was obvious that they were a tight little clique, and since I did not belong to it, I was only a person who did not really exist for them.

Detail: disliked   [3]I became the minority of one. I could never understand their allusions and jokes; I was made to feel that my presence was tolerated and, finally, even to feel that I was intensely disliked. I have never been wholly sure of what I represented to the girls. In some way I seemed to threaten them, their amusements, their activities. Although they shunned me, they could not seem to forget my presence and I could never be sure of a peaceful hour totally free of annoyance.

Experience introduced: [4]For some reason, witless enough, I continued to hope that at least one of the girls would change their attitude toward me and that I could have one friend. After six weeks, all of my attempts to make friends had been rebuffed. One day one of them took me aside and suggested that all of us sneak out and go swimming from the rowboat while the other campers had their cabin rest period. To say that my heart leaped at the suggestion seems silly now, but that is what happened. I knew that it was against the rules, but I was willing to take the chance because I felt that then the rest of the summer would be golden and warm with friendship.

Detail   [5]On the lake that afternoon, we swam freely around the rowboat, one girl always staying in the boat. Finally, I was the last person still in the water and, as I started to climb back into the boat, one of the girls took off her shoe, a brown loafer, and began hammering at my fingers where I clutched the side of the boat. I tried to hang on; I was terrified and quickly reached a point of hysteria and exhaustion. She beat at my fingers until my hands bled and I cried for help. The others watched passively although with quiet satisfaction. I knew that I would die, that I would drown without any one

Climax   of them attempting to stop it. I pulled my hands away and began the long swim to shore. The girls in the boat rowed after me, their pursuit giving me the strength to swim as fast as I could. When the boat moved along side of me, my instinctive response was to attempt to dive deep into the water, anything to get away from them. One of them caught hold of me by the strap of my bathing suit and pulled me into the boat. I could not look at any of them and when we reached shore we all went silently to our cabin. I walked slightly apart from the rest.

Effect: immediate   ⁶Since we had broken the rules about leaving camp without a counselor, I could not report my experience to anyone. All I could do was hide in my cabin, nursing my injured fingers until I could get my parents to take me home. I had little to say to the counselors or any other girls. In a few days I left with my parents.

Effect: later   ⁷I do not know, looking back, what there was in me, in the projection of my personality, that affected the other girls so that they hated me enough, if hatred it was, to wish me harm. It was my first experience with irrationality and savagery. I dream of it still.

PRACTICE

Discussion

1. As you read the essay above, how did your attitude toward the writer change from the first paragraphs to the last? How do you account for this change?

2. In what way did the writer attempt to analyze the experience she reports? Does she believe that she created the hostility? Do you?

3. How effectively does the writer show that this experience had a profound influence on her life? How would you change the paper?

Suggestions for Writing Personal Experience Papers

You are the best authority about yourself. You know more about your own experiences and their effect on your life than anyone else. If you keep in mind the following advice about personal experience themes, you will find that writing them will give you an opportunity to use some genuinely creative techniques.

1. Choose a "thread" or an event that has a point. At one time or another, each of us has had a friend or acquaintance who goes on and on about his experiences. But his stories never get anywhere. Our reaction to them is, "So what? Why are you telling me all this?" In order for you to avoid this kind of reaction from your reader, narrow your thesis so that your essay has meaning for you *and* your reader.

2. Make your experience come to life. Use dialogue, if you wish, to show an interaction or conflict between people, but don't overuse it so that your essay reads like a film script. Describe the scene or situation with detail, using sensory impressions of touch, smell, sight, hearing, and taste. Try to build some suspense if possible. Use vivid words to show emotional and physical response. (See Chapter 12 for more advice on vivid writing.)

WRITING AND REVISING PERSONAL EXPERIENCE (AN EXAMPLE)

*W*hen Jan set out to write about her grandmother, she had a point that she wanted to make: *Even though my grandmother was stiff, formal, and countrified, I respect her for giving me a sense of pride in my heritage.* However, in her first jottings taken from notes in her journal, Jan has only the bare bones of a paper.

GRANDMA

[1]I remember Grandma all right—but not really as a preferred member of the family. She was Polish and a very rigid person, always preferring the harsh idea or the harsh saying to the warm grandmotherly one.

[2]Actually, I didn't know her very well, although I can remember that she always seemed the same: rather stiff, formal, countrified. It seems odd that she was both countrified and formal, but that is the way she appeared to me. She only understood me if I talked loud to her, which meant that I always talked slowly, pronouncing each word carefully in a formal way.

[3]The only time I can remember when she seemed human and warm was the time when she came down to her basement with a jug full of alcoholic

beverage. We had been hauling firewood and stacking it in the basement, and she said that since we had been working as hard as men we could drink like men. The four of us (my cousins and my sister, and I) drank down the foul stuff and really enjoyed it, just because Grandma had finally noticed us.

⁴When Grandma died, I did not feel anything. I stood by her grave and tried to cry. But the tears would not come. I have never understood why. I respected her but could not grieve for her.

As Jan rereads her journal, she is struck by her use of particular terms to describe her Grandma: *rigid, countrified, formal,* and *stiff.* She also notes that she has given no examples to support those descriptive terms. She searches her memory to find specifics in the form of anecdotes, sensory details, and examples. She remembers:

How Grandma made chicken soup
How she looked in her wedding picture
How she accepted gifts
How her house smelled
How she gave us liquor
How her funeral left us feeling, etc.

With these and other details, Jan fleshes out her paper. After several drafts, the paper, organized by a *thread of happenings,* supports her main point.

GRANDMA (Revised)

¹Some people remember deathdays as naturally as others remember birthdays. Without hesitation my father can recall the exact month, day, and year she died—but I can't. It was June, I think, about six or seven years ago and I was at work with my dad. I didn't cry because I didn't really know her. I had to tell my father that she died. "She" was his mother, but he didn't cry either.

²I referred to her as "Grandma," not using more affectionate names like "Gram," "Granny," or "Grams." Grandma was a rigid, aloof elf of a woman who was foreign by birth and by nature. She spoke Polish to my dad. She called my mom Re VeRand for undeterminable reasons. She preferred the outhouse to the upstairs bathroom. And when she made chicken soup she left both chicken feet adrift in the pot—claws and all. She rarely baked bread; she never baked cookies. Her house wasn't full of the sweet, warm smells that accompany such activities. It smelled of coal dust and time. Much to my dismay our bi-annual family vacations inevitably led to backwoods Pennsylvania and that idiosyncratic immigrant.

³I didn't really know her as a person, much less as a grandmother. In my

entire sixteen years of life she had never taken me on a picnic, or told me a bedtime story, or even tucked me into bed. She never initiated conversation and, on the rare occasions I addressed her, I had to shout. To this day I don't know if she was deaf, or if I just thought she understood shouted English better than spoken English.

[4]Looking back, I can remember her wedding picture on top of the china cabinet in her dining room. She wasn't smiling—her arms were akimbo and her fists were clenched. A look of grim determination overpowered any bridely radiance she might have possessed. Surprisingly, she never changed. I have always envisioned grandmothers as being silver-haired ladies with gentle voices, adoring eyes, and eager smiles. My grandmother didn't possess any of those qualities—in her pictures or in person.

[5]It isn't hard to recall the many incidents that helped me formulate and later strengthen my opinion of Grandma. When I was seven my family spent Christmas with her. I was just learning to crochet, and my first project was a present for her. I remember spending months working on that ugly aquamarine potholder—crocheting, unraveling, starting over, until I was satisfied that it was perfect. I was bursting with pride when I finally finished it. I somehow thought she would appreciate all the work that went into that gift and love me for it, as a grandma should. I don't remember being hugged or thanked. I don't even remember seeing it around the kitchen, ever. I never gave her another gift, and my father never dragged our family back to Pennsylvania for Christmas again.

[6]Several years later, when I was fourteen, my two cousins, my sister, and I spent an entire afternoon hauling firewood and stacking it in Grandma's basement. We had wanted to go shopping in Johnstown, but Grandma hadn't, so no one went anywhere. Grudgingly we stayed home to work instead. That evening Grandma appeared with a dusty old jar filled with a powerful-looking concoction. She declared that if we could work like men we could drink like men too. I think that was a peace offering, because Grandma catered to her sons and grandsons while virtually ignoring her daughters and granddaughters.

[7]Now, at twenty-three, I can remember standing under the canopy at her funeral and honestly trying to cry, to feel some sort of loss. I am one of the few grandchildren that bear the family name and I thought that should have made us closer. I didn't feel anything. Time, experience, and knowledge have made me realize that she had reasons for being different and aloof. She had a hard life: thirteen children, an alcoholic husband, the depression, and war—she had proven that she was a survivor, and that she wasn't obligated to live up to my standards or anyone else's. She may not have fit my definition of what a grandmother should be, but I had no right to place demands on her. She didn't owe me anything. No matter, when I think of her now I'm proud of my heritage. I gladly carry her name. Most importantly, I'm grateful for the priceless gifts she left me . . . a stubborn Polish pride in the family name and the will to be a survivor too.

PRACTICE

Discussion

1. Read the final version of *Grandma,* and answer these discussion questions.
   a. Discuss the effectiveness of the "thread" the writer uses to unify her paper.
   b. Choose specific points that show the reader how important the writer believes her "thread" is.
   c. Why does the writer spend so much time describing the negative or bad qualities of her grandmother?
   d. Discuss the effectiveness of using the past to discuss the present.

2. Study the suggestions for writing personal experience essays. Then analyze the following essay, using the questions at the end.

   [1]When I was fifteen I played on the same baseball team with Joe Haller, who ten years later was the batting champion of the American Association. The year after that he played three games with the parent club before he ruined his knee and had to retire. At fifteen, he was already a brilliant, locally famous shortstop. He was a perfectionist, and would chew out any player who made an error. Since I played second base, my mistakes were right under his nose, and I got the benefit of his advice more than any other player on our team.

   [2]Occasionally an opposing player would steal second base, sliding neatly under my tag—a mistake that made Joe furious. He would shout, "That's not how you do it!" As the baserunner left the bag to retrieve his cap, Joe would straddle second base. He would sweep his glove across the shallow groove the runner had just made in the dirt, crying, "Get your glove *down!* Don't let him slide *under* you!" The umpire watched respectfully. The stands were silent. Joe's father, our coach, nodded in agreement from the dugout. Then Joe would throw the ball to our pitcher, and the runner would take his place on second base, and the game would resume.

   [3]Joe never made a mistake that summer until one night-game late in August. We were winning; we were in the field; the bases were empty; there were two outs. The batter hit a very high pop-up behind the pitcher's mound, and Joe called for it, loudly. But for some reason he didn't move from his position deep at shortstop. The ball went so high that it almost disappeared into the blackness of the sky. I glanced at Joe, who stood still, peering up, searching for the ball. Again, he called out, "I got it!" but he didn't move, and he was at least a dozen yards away from where the ball would land. "He's lost it," I thought, and I

started running as fast as I could toward that spot behind the mound, peering up through the haze of lights. I caught sight of the ball as it descended, like a bullet. I went on running; I had a bead on it. But suddenly I lost my nerve; I was afraid of crashing into another player — and I glanced down. In that instant I saw the rows of white shirts in the stands and beyond them the black impenetrable summer sky; and I saw how brilliantly green was the infield grass: the stadium lights gave it a sort of electric glow. When I looked up again the ball was *there,* an inch above my outstretched, open glove.

⁴Joe trotted toward me, smiling sheepishly. I nodded to him, and turned my back, and, buoyed along by the bleacher-rattling crowd, I went across the gleaming grass to the dugout.

1. How does the writer set up the situation? For instance, how are Joe Haller and the writer contrasted?

2. How does paragraph 2 develop the contrast?

3. In what way does paragraph 3 contradict the first two paragraphs? Discuss the effectiveness of this kind of organization of narrative.

4. What kind of personal experience essay is this one — *single event* or *thread of happenings?*

5. Discuss the effectiveness of the conclusion. What would you recommend to the writer?

6. Dialogue is used sparingly in this selection. Is it sufficient or insufficient for the author's point? What *is* the point?

Writing

1. Here are introductions from personal experience essays that (except for *d*) students have written. Choose one, adapt it to your own experience, and write an essay using the adaptation as your introduction.

   a. I'm the patient, easy-going type, calm in emergencies, afraid of nothing, indifferent to change. In my judgment it would take a lot to get me rattled. That's why I can hardly believe that I could get so irritated with another person's irresponsibility [or some other trait], but I did.

   b. Let's get one thing straight right away: I am not a fighter. I am a peaceful person, who has always enjoyed being a _____.

   c. Fired by a hypersensitive imagination, I was easy prey for the romantic stimuli of my youth: comic books, television, and movies.

   d. "There is perhaps, for all concerned, no period of life so un-

pleasant, so unappealing, so downright unpalatable, as that of
_____."—Fran Liebowitz
e. All my life I hated poetry.
f. Gone are the days when being called a Pollyanna was a form of
compliment.

2. Write a paper describing something you had difficulty learning,
using the "thread of happenings" organization. Your hook might be
based on the fact that you felt *incompetent* because you couldn't succeed in learning a particular skill. As you develop your stance,
try to use a hook that describes your role and limits your thesis
(see pp. 12–14).
    Suggestions:
a. Getting the volleyball (or tennis ball) over the net
b. Hitting a golf ball on the green
c. Learning to sew or cook
d. Learning to swim or surfboard
e. Learning to skate (ice or roller)

3. Review the material on description and narration as developmental
strategies. Then search your memory or your journal for significant
events, or spend some time freewriting about those events. You
may be able to identify a recurring pattern in the form of a *hook.*
Perhaps you'll be reminded of a single event that had a significant
consequence for you. From your notes, develop an organizational
plan and write a single-event paper. Do not merely narrate an
anecdote or a story.

CHAPTER 7
PROCESS, CAUSE AND EFFECT

PROCESS

If you want to tell your reader how something happens, you can use *process,* a writing strategy that describes a series of steps leading to a particular end point. Process is useful because it can be as short as a paragraph or as long as a full paper. It can also be used with other strategies.

One of the two basic kinds of process development is the artificial process, which traces the development of a situation or set of circumstances created by human beings. When you give directions or tell someone how to do something, you explain an artificial process. The manufacture of gasoline is such a process:

Steps in process
1. Heat the raw petroleum.
2. Cool the resulting vapor into liquid.
3. Use further refining processes.

End point
4. Blend liquids and treat chemically to get grades of commercial gasoline.

The second kind of process is *natural,* one which occurs in the real world around us. A natural process, for instance, may be the result of an instinctive reaction to some basic drive. Birds instinctively migrate every year. In this natural process they begin by losing some of their feathers and growing new ones, taking many trial flights, and eating a great deal to store up fat. The steps and end point in this process are:

Steps in process	1.	Molting
	2.	Trial flights
End point	3.	Building a reserve of fat to get ready for migration.

Natural processes are also often dependent upon timing. For instance, birds migrate south in the fall of the year and north in the spring of the year.

PRACTICE

Discussion

Here are examples of both types of process. Read each and answer the questions at the end.

[1]The marriage flight is one of the most important days in the life of an ant colony. Its date varies according to the species but, in the case of the *rufa,* it falls between May and September. On one day—and on only one day in a single season—the reproducers must leave the nest, and workers chase out any reluctant ones.

[2]They fly out on an August morning and, in the air, they mingle with the sexed ants from neighboring nests. A pursuit begins until each female offers herself to a male on a neighboring tree. Then, in turn, the males mate with her and, in so doing, they accomplish the only act for which they were created. The next day, they all will be dead and many of the females as well. Of the surviving females, some may return to their original nests. Others will be adopted by nests in need of a queen or big enough to require more than one.

[3]Finally, others will go out alone and found a new nest. The female digs herself in about five inches below the surface of the earth and carves out a cell for herself with no exit. There she lays her eggs. Some of them will become larvae, but not all—most of them serve for food for their mother and for the larvae which she chooses to raise. If winter falls, the larvae must wait until the following spring before they

become ants. On the other hand, if workers are born before the cold weather sets in, they immediately begin to dig galleries, the beginning of a future nest. They start foraging for food, and the normal life of an ant-nest has been founded. —"Ants," *Realities* magazine

EXTINGUISHING AN OVEN FIRE

[1]The blazing oven is another appliance problem, although it doesn't usually indicate anything is wrong with the appliance. But it calls for a mighty quick remedy. It usually shows up first as smoke trailing out of the oven vent. If, as is usually the case, the broiler is in action, the whole kitchen may be full of smoke. If you open the oven door, all the blazes in hell seem to sail out at you. In this event, try to hang on to your nonchalance and just shut the oven door again. The chances are the big, beautiful sirloin inside isn't ruined, the house won't burn down, and the entire mess isn't as bad as it looks.

[2]First, turn off the broiler. Then yank the top off your biggest salt container. Next open the oven again and slide the broiler rack and the steak out a little with a carving fork or some other long utensil that won't burn and doesn't make you reach in so close you get spattered with fiery fat. (Fiery fat can set your clothing afire.) Then *pile* on the salt by the fistful—at the points the flames are coming from. This salt business is a sort of old wives' tale, but it works if you have plenty of the stuff. It doesn't act chemically by creating some fancy fire-smothering gas. It simply stifles the fire by covering it up and shutting off its air supply—like a load of sand. But it's better than sand from the culinary standpoint because you can wash it off, and if a few grains remain they won't chip your teeth. Whatever you do, *don't* throw water on the fire. This blasts into steam, floats and spatters blazing grease all over the place, and can give you some very nasty burns and possibly set the kitchen on fire.

[3]Actually things cool off surprisingly fast with the broiler turned off and salt piled on the conflagration. Everthing usually is under complete control in a minute or two. But even with the fire out, you're likely to have a case of jitters. Just remember it's not anywhere near as horrible as it looks.

[4]In the rare event that you can't put the fire out (most unlikely), shove the whole works back in the oven and shut the door—also the oven vent if possible. This, at least, keeps your private inferno locked up where it can do the least harm until the fire trucks arrive.
—George Daniels

1. Identify the *steps* and *end point* of each process.

2. Which process is *natural,* which is *artificial*? In what ways are the processes fundamentally different?

3. In a process paper, there are usually certain transitional "signals" *(first, later, after this, before, and so on)* which help the reader discriminate among the various parts of the process. List the signals in the examples. Do most of the signals fall into any particular class or type?

4. Describe the writer's stance in each passage. The two kinds of process ordinarily have different stances. Explain why this should be so.

SUGGESTIONS FOR WRITING PROCESS PAPERS

When you use process strategies of development, you are essentially describing how something is done, how it works, or how it "happens."

Artificial Process

In the artificial process, you often give directions to a specific person or group (people who want to learn how to put out an oven fire, for example), and your writer's stance is clear and precise. You will probably use a time or chronological order because some steps should be done before others. For instance, when showing the process of how detergents work, it is logical to discuss adding the detergent to the water *before* you discuss what happens when water and detergent are combined. You must, therefore, give careful thought to the sequence of steps or stages when describing a process.

Keep in mind that your reader may know little about your subject and may need definitions of terms and clear signals showing how the steps or stages are separated. You may wish to speak directly to the reader and address him or her as *you*. Certain suggestions may help you to use artificial process:

1. Decide if you are giving directions or making an explanation. Then choose the writer's stance that is most appropriate.

2. Determine the end point or purpose of the process.

3. Determine the relevant, main steps of the process that lead to the end point or purpose. *State the steps clearly,* and *use transitions.*

4. If possible, keep to a clear chronological sequence of events in the process, but avoid irrelevancies.

Natural Process

The natural process is somewhat more difficult to write because you have to look carefully at the sequence of steps in order to find them and the end point. Natural processes often involve scientific subjects, so you must be well informed in order to describe the process. However, neither you nor your reader is necessarily *in* that process. You are both standing off from it—watching it and trying to understand how it works. Instead of addressing the reader, try using the *who (or what) does what* formula:

[*Who*] The male [*does what?*] mates and dies.

PRACTICE

Discussion

1. Below is an artificial-process paper that uses process to inform.
   a. How does the student use the *who does what* formula to describe how she adapted to partial deafness?
   b. Note the order of steps. How long a period would you judge this process took?
   c. If you were writing a paper like this how would you change the sequence of steps? How useful are the abstract terms *physical, mental,* and *social?*
   d. Discuss the student's use of definition.
   e. Describe her stance.

Introduction
Definition by
classification and
operation

[1]When I was eight, I had a radical mastoidectomy—a surgical procedure consisting of chiselling out the infected bone (behind the ear) called the *mastoid.* This is a serious operation, often leaving the patient with little hearing in the affected ear. Thanks to miracle drugs, mastoid operations are infrequently done today. However, since I lived in a remote area of North Dakota where the health care was not easily accessible, I developed a mastoid infection before my family realized how seriously ill I was.

Effect

[2]Young people are adaptable, so I didn't realize that being deaf in one ear was anything to worry about. My friends and family didn't treat me any differently. Even though the operation had been very painful and disagreeable, I was so

Introduces the strategy: process

Thesis

First step: physical

Four examples

Second step: mental

Two examples

Third and final step: social

One example

Conclusion

glad to be back in school, doing the things I liked to do, that I really didn't pay much attention to the stages I went through in adapting to partial deafness. As I look back over the years, I can see that I developed a conscious process of adapting to deafness. I made physical, mental, and social adjustments.

[3]The first step in adapting to deafness was physical. I had to position my body so that I could hear my friends and family. Since my right ear was my "bad" ear, I learned to tip my head to the right so that the sound entered my left or "good" ear. Over the years it has become such a habit that all my photographs show me with my head tipped to the right. Another way I found that I could position my body was to get on the right-hand side of people. Even today, when I sit on a couch or ride in the back seat of a car, I always sit on a person's right. When we walk down the street, I always get on the "outside" or right-hand side. This sometimes causes me some problems with men who think they should be on the "outside." I never talk when I drive a car because I can't hear well enough to carry on a conversation, without losing track of my concentration.

[4]I realized early that consciously positioning my body to the situation was not enough, so I progressed to the second step—being alert. I knew that I had to concentrate and listen very carefully to those around me. Other people were not going to go out of their way to help me hear. Besides, I wasn't willing to go around explaining that I heard with only one ear. Who cares! Therefore, I learned that by concentrating I could increase my hearing ability dramatically. By watching faces and lips, I taught myself lip-reading. Today, I can tell what is going on in television shows when the sound is off by reading the actor's lips. I also became alert to body language —unusual gestures, facial expressions and movements— that helped tell me what people were thinking.

[5]My final step was to adjust my social life to partial deafness. I couldn't have much fun at large parties because the commotion created too much "surface noise" for me to carry on conversations. However, when I was forced into large groups, I tried to figure out the general conversation and make suitable noises like "Oh?" "Is that so?" "Well!" and "I agree." I'm afraid there were times when I agreed when I shouldn't have. Occasionally, I received some peculiar looks when my pat answers didn't quite fit the discussion.

[6]I am lucky that I became partially deaf when I was very young. I have since met older people who became deaf late in life. Instead of working on the process of hearing, they have

become lazy and resentful. They make *other* people do the
work. No one wants to shout while conversing. It is better to
answer with an occasional "I agree," even when it doesn't fit,
than to be a demanding, irritable deaf person.

End point implied:
adaptation
successful

2. Here is part of a magazine article written by a doctor describing a process. Is this a natural or artificial process? Identify the steps and the end point.

[1]At 11 p.m. on Dec. 22, 1963 fire broke out aboard the Greek luxury liner *Lakonia* as it cruised the Atlantic near Madeira, and passengers and crew were forced into the water. The air temperature was over 60°, the sea almost 65° and rescue ships were in the area within a few hours. Nevertheless, 125 people died, 113 of these fatalities being attributed to hypothermia, the lowering of the body's inner heat, perhaps no more than 6° from the normal 98.6°. . . .

[2]The moment your body begins to lose heat faster than it produces it, hypothermia threatens. As heat loss continues, the temperature of the body's inner core falls below normal. Hands and arms (the extremities most needed in order to survive) are affected first. When body temperature drops to 95°, dexterity is reduced to the point where you cannot open a jackknife or light a match.

[3]According to recent research by the Mountain Rescue Association, the body reacts in a series of predictable ways when inner-core temperature falls. At 2.5° below normal, shivering begins, an automatic body process to create heat. But it takes energy to shiver — comparable to what is expended sawing wood—and the heat loss continues. The more the core temperature drops, the less efficient the brain becomes. Although you may have a pack on your back with a sleeping bag and food in it, you may not have the sense to use them.

[4]If the core temperature drops to 94°, you will stop shivering but every now and then will experience uncontrollable shaking. Your system, automatically getting rid of carbon dioxide and lactic acid, also releases blood sugar and a little adrenaline, giving you a surge of energy, which causes the violent shaking. This last desperate effort by the body to produce heat utilizes a tremendous amount of energy.

[5]"Now," you think, "I must be getting warmer because I am not shivering anymore." By this time you are pretty irrational. If someone were to ask you your name and telephone number, you probably wouldn't know them, for the brain has become numb.

[6]If nothing is done, death usually occurs within 1½ hours after the shivering starts. In fact, a shivering person can go from fatigue to exhaustion to cooling beyond the recovery point so quickly he may perish before rescuers can build a shelter or get a fire started. —J. Clayton Stewart, "Growing Cold by Degrees"

PLANNING AND WRITING A PROCESS (AN EXAMPLE)

*J*ack has a collection of old comic books that are becoming valuable with age. He belongs to a collector's association, which has invited him to write an article describing his process of storing comics in order to protect them from moisture, acids, and sun. He writes a paragraph on how he will plan his article:

> My comic books don't fall into just one class. I have three different kinds: run-of-the-mill, more valuable, and *very* expensive. They all require particular treatments that overlap. What is the best way to describe the storage process without confusing my audience? Perhaps I should give the basic method of storing the least valuable comics, and then build on that method in a discussion of storing the more expensive ones. My steps in the process might look like this:

	Run-of-the-Mill	*More Valuable*	*Very Expensive*
Step 1:	omit	use Mylar bags	same
Step 2:	use acid-free box	same	use acid-free notebook
Step 3:	use acid-free millboard	omit	omit
Step 4:	store in dry place	same	same

This kind of pattern made writing his process easier than if he hadn't identified the relationships shown above.

KEEPING COMICS

[1]Comic book collectors who are serious (like me) are known as "hard-core" collectors. There are, so one hobby magazine recently stated, tens of thousands of ordinary collectors, but only a few thousand hard-core ones. And for us, the problem is not just collecting—but keeping. Comic books were printed on very cheap paper using terrible techniques of production. Put a valuable comic book in the sun, and it may be ruined in a matter of hours. Store it improperly in a damp place, and it may be ruined in a matter of months or a few years. The answer is to store them properly and thus save your collection.

[2]Like most collectors, you probably have a large number of run-of-the-mill comics. Place these on edge (never flat) in acid-free millboard boxes. When putting them in the box, take special care of the corners. Nothing protects the edges from bending, so put them in carefully. After packing every group of 10 or 15 comics, insert a piece of acid-free millboard. These supports will keep the comics from sagging. Bags are not necessary for these

comics. Stack the boxes in a dark, cool place with relatively low humidity.

³For your more valuable comics, an extra precaution is necessary. Place the valuable ones in three mil Mylar snugs before putting them in an acid-free box. These snugs are inert polyester bags that will last hundreds of years without decomposing. Normal polyethylene bags last only five years. When putting comics in the bags, again be careful of the edges and corners, since the corners bend easily. Mylar is quite stiff and holds the comic in a vise-like grip. This is beneficial if the comic is flat and straight in the bag, but detrimental if the corners are allowed to remain folded. Use a popsicle stick or some other blunt, flat instrument to push the corners down after the comic is in the bag. Also, watch the back cover and see that it is in straight also.

⁴Store these bagged comics in small or large acid-free cartons. The small cartons are a little more expensive, but provide slightly easier access to the comics.

⁵If you have *very* expensive comics costing $100 and up, give them the best treatment. Use a snug especially made for a three-ring binder. This snug, which clamps the comic like the regular snugs, is four mils rather than three mils thick. It also has an edge with punched holes for the binder. The binder, which should be well constructed and sturdy, makes it easy to display your valuable collection. The binders should also be stored in a dark cool place.

⁶Actually, any of the storage schemes for the expensive comics can be used for less expensive varieties. The best methods cost a lot of money though, up to 60 cents per stored comic. The scheme for run-of-the-mill comics costs only four cents per comic. The best rule is: Spend in proportion to what your comics are worth to you.

PRACTICE

Discussion
Read Jack's paper on storing comic books.

1. Outline the stance. How does the writer's *point of view* influence his *role*?

2. Where in each paragraph are the basic steps described? Discuss the applications of the steps to the three divisions (or *classes*) of comic books.

3. Discuss the importance of the materials necessary in the *process*. How is the choice of materials relevant to the *purpose* of the process?

Writing

1. Think about some medical problem you or one of your family has had. Consider *one* of the following:
   a. What was the process your body went through when you had your medical problem?
   b. What kind of process did you develop to adjust to your problem?

   You may want to interview some experts or do research in order to deal with (a) above. (You will develop a process yourself when you deal with one of these topics — search your memory, freewrite everything you can remember, group your material, identify a hook, plan your stance, and write.)

2. Choose one of the following topics. If possible, practice the process, keeping notes on what you do and in what order. Identify a suitable audience, outline your stance, and write a paper.
   a. How to write exams
   b. How to make a house burglar-proof
   c. How to pierce your ear in more than one place
   d. How to talk to an answering machine
   e. How to pack a bag for backpacking

3. Choose one of the following topics and write a process paper. If you have had no experience with any of these processes, identify one of your own.
   a. How to use psychology in dealing with _____
   b. How you defeated computer anxiety
   c. How a shopping mall changes a community
   d. How a coach taught me to _____

CAUSE AND EFFECT (CAUSATION)

Cause and effect (or simply causation) refers to a specific relationship between events in time. If you fail to look both ways before crossing a street and get hit by a car, the *cause* is failing to look and the *effect* is getting hit. If a doctor tells you that you have a broken leg from the accident, the broken leg is the effect of getting hit by the car, which is the cause. An event (in this case, the accident) can be *both* a cause and an effect of other events.

As a strategy of development, *causation* answers the question "Why did it happen?" You will find causation useful not only by itself but also combined with other strategies. It is often used with *process* because *how* something happened (process) is often related to *why* something happened (causation).

For many subjects—particularly those related to social and political matters—causes and effects are ambiguous or indistinct, leaving you unsure about the truth of the situation. Therefore, you must be very careful when you discuss causes and effects. For many subjects you also have the reactions of your reader to worry about because your analysis of a cause-and-effect relationship might be controversial, and your reader may not agree with you. For example, in discussions about causes and effects in certain social issues—such as crime or government spending—some readers may object to your analysis. Therefore, stance is very important in this strategy.

Recognizing the Signs of Causation

In order to identify and determine whether or not a cause-and-effect relationship is logical, you should look for certain signs. Two of the most common are:

The Sign of Association. Suppose you find two events, A and B, in association. Their being together could imply that A causes B, or vice versa. However, B must ordinarily occur whenever A does—otherwise you probably don't have a genuine cause-and-effect relationship. For instance, hair should bleach when a strong solution of peroxide is applied to it; the cook should burn his hand every time he touches a very hot skillet handle.

The Sign of Time-Sequence. If B comes after A in time, this fact may imply a causal relationship. If a student stays up all night studying, the fatigue he suffers the next day is an effect signaled by time. But determining time-sequence is so tricky that a special name has been given to the fallacy of misinterpreting it. The fallacy is called *post hoc* (short for *post hoc, ergo propter hoc*—"after this, therefore because of this"). You create the *post hoc* fallacy if you say that A causes B merely because B comes after A. In other words, if the 8:30 train comes after the 8:15 train, you cannot say that the earlier train "causes" the later one.

In brief, the signs of causation are no more than signs—they are not proofs. To avoid making fallacies in thinking about causation, you must take each sign and investigate it carefully. Never assume that a causal relationship exists until you find proof.

Here are four types of cause-and-effect sequence that you should be aware of. (The examples support the thesis: *Proper gearing and equipment may help a biker avoid leg and knee problems.*)

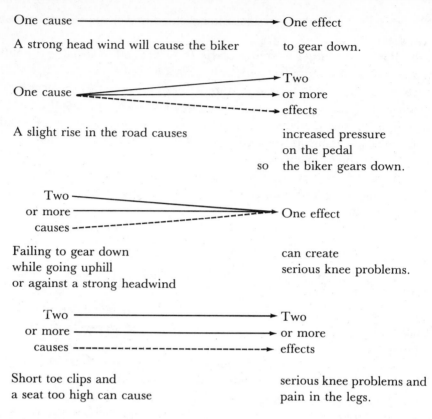

In most situations, more than one cause or effect is involved. Drug addiction, for example, may have several causes, and these causes may have more than a single effect.

Following is an annotated cause-and-effect paper written by a student. Notice the writer's use of transitions, examples, and summary statements, making the cause-and-effect relationship clear.

Definition of term by negation

[1]Student-watchers have long identified a common type on campus—the "Joiner." I don't mean the woman who belongs to the band and the Pi Phis, and maybe in her junior year joins an accounting honorary. Nor do I mean the engineer

Question posed; answered by succeeding pars.

who belongs to a mere three organizations. Nothing so limiting works for the true Joiner, who may belong to six or eight eight organizations, and who may pop up in student government as well. What makes Joiners join?

First cause, supported by three examples

[2]First, Joiners like the limelight. Most of the groups they belong to are visible. On the dorm council they write petitions, or collect the petitions of others. In the marching band they perform before thousands of people. In fraternities,

they are the treasurers who hound people for money and make long reports in meetings on the state of fraternal economy.

Transition, introducing second cause with one example

³As these remarks imply, Joiners like to run things. My sister is a Joiner, and one can be sure that any group she belongs to, she is president or leader of. If the group has no important office to fill, she will run it by indirection, volunteering to do this or that job, writing any necessary letters or memos, being the first one at the meeting and the last to leave. No job is too small for her to take on cheerfully. By the end of the semester, any group she joins discovers that she she has become its chief bottle-washer and major spokesman. She has fulfilled her desire to control events and people.

Summary statement, explaining effect *of* cause

Last cause *with transition,* finally

⁴Finally, Joiners join because they must have something to do with themselves. They are usually hyperactive. Have you ever seen a Joiner sitting alone, perhaps in the Union, just reading a book? Sam, on the men's side of my dorm, is a Joiner; and for all the time I have known him, he has never been alone. People in the dorm say that Sam even goes to the bathroom with somebody. He belongs to eight organizations, and will someday be president of the country — if he can just decide which political party to join.

Example

Surprise ending

Occasionally, it is necessary and rhetorically useful to organize a cause-and-effect essay or paragraph by introducing the effect first, then giving an explanation of the causes. Note how the writer in the following excerpt explains why the poor have more garbage than the rich.

Effect

¹. . . low-income neighborhoods in Tucson discard 86 percent more garbage per week per household than do high-income areas, and 40 percent more waste than medium-income districts. There is a trick to that statistic. There are more people per household in low-income areas. But, even dividing on a per person basis, the poor produce more garbage than the middle class and only slightly less than the rich.

Question: *why?*

²Why? It's not so hard to figure out. The rich buy antiques, the poor buy and throw away cheap or used furniture. The rich give their old clothes to the "Goodwill," the poor buy them there, wear them out and throw them away. And it is the poor and the working people who discard most of the packaging waste. They are the ones who drink soft drinks and beer and eat low-cost canned vegetables and canned stews, fish sticks, pot pies, and T.V. dinners. And, if

Causes   they eat out at all, it is at McDonalds or Burger King or Kentucky Fried Chicken, with the packaging which that entails. It is the rich who have their food flown in fresh daily from Florida or Spain. It is the rich who eat in the fancy French restaurants with all those superb dishes prepared from scratch, sans packaging and sans disposable dinner ware. — Judd Alexander, "Truth and Consequences"

Suggestions For Writing Cause And Effect Papers

When describing causation, remember this advice:

1. *Investigate your subject thoroughly, either from your own firsthand knowledge or from research.* Identifying the causes and effects in a subject that you know firsthand can be easy to do. Your dissatisfaction with your roommate, for instance, may be based on the fact that he won't do his share in keeping the apartment clean. The *cause* is his laziness or carelessness. The *effect* is your anger and frustration. But identifying the causes of pollution in Los Angeles is much more difficult because pollution is a complex problem, and without doing research, you will not know enough to write about the subject.

2. *Qualify your generalizations carefully when you draw cause-and-effect relationships.* Do not hesitate to use qualifiers such as "it seems to me," "it may be," or "the evidence points to." In most cause-and-effect relationships, you deal in probabilities rather than certainties, particularly when you get out of the realm of scientific subjects.

3. *Be sure that your time sequence is accurate and inclusive.* This is especially true when you are explaining scientific causes and effects. You should present the chronology of the steps as they actually occur, and you should include every important link in the chain of events in order to ensure the accuracy of your paper. Here is an effective explanation of why Mexican jumping beans jump:

> [1]A simple examination reveals the secret of the fascinating twisting, turning and jumping of the beans. Inside each bean is a tiny yellow caterpillar, the larvae of a small moth. How does it get there? The moth lays an egg in the flower of the spurge shrub. In time the eggs hatch and the larvae are said to work their way deep into the blossom, where they are eventually encased in the seeds.
>
> [2]The caterpillar devours a large part of the inside of the seed, so that it occupies about one fifth of the interior of its little home. To move the bean, the caterpillar grasps the silken wall of the bean with its legs and vigorously

snaps its body, striking its head against the other end of the bean and sending it this way or that. The bean may actually travel several inches at a time, or leap in the air. Some people call them bronco beans because of the way they jump.

[3]A jumping bean may keep up its antics for as long as six months. Then the caterpillar finally emerges from its house and becomes a moth. — "Why Mexican Jumping Beans Jump," *Awake!*

4. *Separate "sufficient" from "contributory" causes.* An event may contribute to a cause, but it will not be sufficient in itself to create an effect. Failing to add baking powder or soda to biscuit dough is *sufficient* cause for the dough's failure to rise. A *contributory* cause to the flat biscuits might be a distracting phone call you had just when you were about to add the leavening agent. However, it isn't the phone call that caused the biscuits to be flat, but rather your forgetting to add the soda or baking powder. So you separate the phone call (*contributory* cause) from the lack of leavening agent (*sufficient* cause).

5. *Do not ignore immediate effects in a chain of multiple effects.* Note this description of the multiple effects of the cholera organism:

> For centuries, men had known that cholera was a fatal disease, and that it caused severe diarrhea, sometimes producing as many as thirty quarts of fluid a day. Men knew this, but they somehow assumed that the lethal effects of the disease were unrelated to the diarrhea; they searched for something else: an antidote, a drug, a way to kill the organism. It was not until modern times that cholera was recognized as a disease that killed through dehydration primarily; if you could replace a victim's water losses rapidly, he would survive the infection without other drugs or treatment. — Michael Crichton, *The Andromeda Strain*

A diagram of this chain of cause and effect might look like this:

Cholera organism (first cause)
    ↘ diarrhea (first immediate effect)
        ↘ dehydration (second immediate effect)
            ↘ death (ultimate effect)

In this case, the failure to investigate the implications of an important immediate effect led to disastrous consequences.

6. *Much of what we loosely call "cause and effect" is actually "correlation."* In the process of identifying causation, researchers study samples to see if they can

establish a pattern from which a generalization can be drawn about why something occurred. For example, from many medical experiments, researchers have discovered that there is a *correlation* between high cholesterol level and heart disease. They do not conclude that high cholesterol level *causes* heart disease but that a significant *correlation* exists between the two. You may use correlation in an analysis of cause and effect, but do not identify as causes what may only be correlations.

PLANNING AND WRITING CAUSE AND EFFECT (AN EXAMPLE)

*J*ana writes:

```
        Irritationnnn. IIIritatatat . . .irrittt. IRITIATION
what did I do, s  hit the sf shift key?
        This is the most . . . . ok back to electric typewriter.
        The keyboard is unfamiliar.  The screen hurts my eyes.
The printer goes clack, brzzt, clack.  If you punch the wrong
button, the whole thing disappears.  The screen talks back to
me:  ARE YOU SURE YOU WANT TO LOG OUT, JANA?
        I say: Yes, you monster, LOG ME OUT OF THIS THING!!!
        It says dutifully, JANA LOGGED OUT MONDAY OCTOBER 20,
1987, 2:35 PM.
        Phooey.
```

Now Jana has it out of her system. Her mother, a free-lance writer, has a new computer with a word processor and letter-quality printer added on. Jana can log into the computer whenever her mother isn't using it. But as you can see from her brainstorming above, her early experience on the new and unfamiliar equipment was not a pleasant one.

After two days and hours of practice with the computer and word processor, Jana decides to write a cause-effect paper based in part on the brainstorming material quoted above.

What I want to show [she writes in her plan of attack on the paper] is that when you first use the computer and word processor, all the causes lead to one effect: confusion and anger—most of which are UNNECESSARY. That is my hook: *unnecessary*.

Writer: me.

Point: I just said it.

Reader: Anybody just starting out on a word processor.

Here's my order of main ideas:

Makes no sense, partic. keyboard
Machine confusing — commands?
Printer noise

But now they don't seem to bother me as much. (?)

And here I go!

Jana's draft

1. All right monster, I have logged in. And I have named
you. . . ZARKON. (Wasn't Zarkon a villain on STAR TREK?) Well
irregardless, ZARKON, you are now (and forever will be) a villain.

2. The first thing about you, ZARKON, is that you're crazy.
Look at your keyboard. The asterisk is above the 8 where the
apostrophe ought to be; so I keep writing Mother*s Manuscript,
Jack*s foot,etc. On the left side of the keyboard are 10 buttons
numbered F1 through F10. On the right side are buttons called Num
Lock and Scroll Lock, End, Ins, and so on. My favorite button is
nanmed PrtSc. Didn't she win the Derby last year?

3. When I put my fingers on the keys, I inevitably place
them wrong because there are extra keys where no keys should be.
Also the key shift for capitals is one key too far to the left, so

I keep hitting the wrong key when I want to make a capital. The result is I can't type decently and spend too much time correcting.

4. On top of that, ZARKON, you are too hard to use when I try to take the WordPerfect lessons. I log in, punch the buttons your manual tells me to, and then you say WRONG COMMAND. How could it be the wrong command when you told me to do it? Now I just sit there with the cursor flashing at me. My lesson is gone from the screen--how do I get it back? I punch the ESC [escape] button and nothing happens. Listen, ZARKON, If I say escape, I mean escape. Let me out! I called the dealer. He said, write in DIR for directory. Ok, now I am back to the lesson. But how did I get there?

5. Now, ZARKON, a few words about your printer. It goes clack, brzzt, clack; and now and then whirrpp. Your daisy wheel is a real flower, too. It goes in two directions, almost at once. The noise this printer makes is awful, and in Mom's little office it scrapes on my ear like a fingernail noise on a blackboard. Then, ZARKON, you jammed your paper. When I got up to unjam your paper , I tripped over the plug and pulled it out of the wall and ERASED ALL MY WORK.

6. ZARKON, you are an idiot and a bore and noisy. . . two days ago. Now, for some reason you seem docile and even pleasant. Even dare I say it, even a little easy to use? Is it possible you have spiked my diet cola with a little outer-space dumb drug?

7. I am not yet ready to believe that the two ZARKONS are one and the same, that just because I get a little used to you, you are suddenly a pussy cat.

8. ZARKON--are you trying to tell me that all the pain and irritation were unnecessary?

9.. Brrzt, clack.

For questions about Jana's paper, see the Practice, p. 127.

PRACTICE

Discussion

1. Remember that Jana's paper on the computer (and word processor) consists at this point of (a) a short piece of brainstorming, (b) a scratch outline of topics to cover, and (c) a first draft.

   Go back over these three materials and make direct suggestions to Jana for her next draft, which we will assume will be her final one. Consider every part of her writing problem: hook, point of her paper, organization of draft, paragraphing, sentences, words, choice of detail, grammar. Do you recommend that she make many changes in her draft?

   Describe the cause-effect patterns implicit in the paper.

2. Discuss the accuracy and validity of the cause-and-effect relationships in these statements:

   a. The state's experiment in the abolition of capital punishment is going badly. During the first six months of the trial period, murders are up an estimated 20 percent and there has been a rash of sex crimes against children. Two child rapists last week got life imprisonment—which practically means, in this state, parole after twenty years.

   b. *Statistic:* If you change jobs very often, your chance of having a heart attack is two or three times greater than if you stay at one job for a long time.

   c. Why do people who in private talk so pungently often write so pompously? There are many reasons: tradition, the demands of time, carelessness, the conservative influence of the secretary. Above all is the simple matter of status. Theorem: the less established the status of a person, the more his dependence on jargon. Examine the man who has just graduated from pecking out his own letters to declaiming them to a secretary and you are likely to have a man hopelessly intoxicated with the rhythm of businessese. Conversely, if you come across a blunt yes or no in a letter, you don't need to glance further to grasp that the author feels pretty firm in his chair. —William H. Whyte, "The Language of Business," *Fortune* magazine

   d. The dog [as a pet] has advantages in the way of uselessness as well as in special gifts of temperament. He is often spoken of, in an eminent sense, as the friend of man, and his intelligence and fidelity are praised. The meaning of this is that the dog is man's servant and that he has the gift of an unquestioning subservience and a slave's quickness in guessing his master's mood. Coupled with these traits, which fit him well for the relation of status—and which must for the present purpose be set down as serviceable traits—the dog has some characteristics which are of a more equivocal aesthetic value. He is the filthiest of the domestic animals in his person and the nastiest in his habits. For this he makes up in a servile, fawning attitude towards his master, and a readiness to inflict damage and discomfort on all else. The dog, then, commends himself to our favour by affording play to our propensity for mastery, and as he is also an item of expense, and commonly serves no industrial purpose, he holds a well-assured place in men's regard as a thing of good repute. The dog is at the same time associated in our imagination with the chase—a meritorious employment and an expression of the honorable predatory impulse. —Thorstein Veblen, *The Theory of the Leisure Class*

3. Discuss the following research on woodpeckers as an example of cause and effect. How does the research relate the evidence on woodpeckers to human problems? Discuss the effectiveness of this relation.

WHY WOODPECKERS DON'T NEED HELMETS

[1]Do woodpeckers suffer from headaches? Probably not, according to people who worry about the problem. If they did, the birds would presumably stop slamming their beaks into trees hundreds of times a day. Still, researchers from the Brentwood Veterans Administration Hospital in California and the Neuro-psychiatric Institute at UCLA decided to find out why the countryside was not littered with dazed and dying woodpeckers.

[2]Led by psychiatrist Philip May, the research team used high-speed filming techniques to measure the trajectory, impact velocity, and deceleration of an acorn woodpecker's head as it hammered into a tree trunk. The bird, grounded by a wing injury, was living in a ranger's office at a California State Park. May and his colleagues say the clatter of a typewriter was enough to set the woodpecker banging away on a tree trunk in the office.

[3]Analysis of film shot at speeds up to 2,000 frames per second revealed that the woodpecker's beak slammed into the trunk at speeds of 20 to 23 feet a second, about 15 miles per hour. One complete peck took one thousandth of a second or less, creating an impact deceleration on the order of 1,000 G. One G is the acceleration needed to overcome the earth's gravity. An astronaut in a *Saturn V* rocket experiences only 3.5 G during lift-off.

⁴The researchers discovered that woodpeckers blink for a few milliseconds as their beak is about to hit the tree. This may protect the eye from chips or simply keep it in its socket during repeated sharp decelerations. The bird also makes a few practice jabs before really letting go; something like an amateur carpenter lining up a nail.

⁵Several physical factors act to protect the woodpecker brain during all this pounding. The brain is very light, weighing less than an ounce, and it is tightly packed into a brain case of tough spongy bone. Sets of opposed muscles may have a shock absorber effect.

⁶According to the California researchers, the most important element may be the precise trajectory the bird's head follows as it strikes at the wood. The woodpecker pecks in a straight line. This protects the brain from tissue-tearing shearing forces that would set up by rotational or angular motion, such as the arc described by an arm swinging a pick. In addition, May and his colleagues observed that the woodpecker keeps its neck tense at the moment of impact, the way a boxer does when preparing for a punch he knows is coming but cannot block.

⁷The researchers believe their findings have direct implications for the design of safety helmets. Helmets should be thicker and lighter, made of firm shock-absorbing foam with a thin outer layer of a harder material to spread the impact and resist puncture. Ideally, there should be some form of neck brace. The researchers even speculate that the high collars of old-fashioned military uniforms might have had a practical justification in this sense.

⁸In the meantime, they advise the person who discovers that he is about to smash his head into something to tighten the muscles of the neck and hold it flexed in the chin-down position. That is to say, if you find you must bang your head on a tree, try to do it the way a woodpecker does. — James Hansen

4. Discuss the effects that would occur if one of the following were suddenly taken away from you and you had to live for a year without it:
   a. a telephone
   b. a television set
   c. a refrigerator
   d. a typewriter
   e. a bicycle, car, or motorcycle

Writing
1. Choose one of the following hypothetical situations that could be appropriate for you. (If you don't have a car, situation *a* wouldn't fit your life.) If none of the situations suit you, develop one of your own, using the format: "If I . . . then . . ."

Make a list of all the possible effects of your taking such an action. Classify or group the effects, develop a generalization for each class or group, and use the generalizations as paragraph topic leads (or topic sentences) in a discussion of causation.

a. If I decide to sell my car, then . . .

b. If I get married this month, then . . .

c. If I decide to quit school and go to work full-time, then . . .

d. If my parents are unable to help pay my tuition next fall, then . . .

e. If I can move into an apartment, then . . .

f. If I change majors, then . . .

2. Pick a subject concerning your hometown. Write a paper discussing the possible cause-and-effect relationships in the subject. Possible broad subjects: crime, education, religion, prosperity, government, sports, race relations, culture, economics. (Be sure to narrow your topic.)

3. Develop a cause-and-effect essay on one of the following familiar topics:

a. The effect of children on a family, or the effect of not having children.

b. The effect of the change of seasons on your behavior.

c. The effect of paperback books on reading.

d. The effect of compulsory attendance laws on education.

e. The effect of the Beatles on popular music.

f. The effect of moving a child from one community to another.

The following topics are more specialized and may take some research:

g. The effect of salt on automobiles.

h. The effect of extreme cold or extreme heat on a machine or animal.

i. The effect of loss of electricity, due to a storm, on a household.

j. The effect of public opinion polls on the news.

k. The effect of allergies on the body.

You may find a combination of process and cause-effect useful for some of the above. For example, the *process* of salting the streets in the winter has an *effect* on automobiles.

CHAPTER 8

CLASSIFICATION, ILLUSTRATION, DEFINITION

CLASSIFICATION

Classifying or grouping things is a natural way to think. Young children playing with rocks separate large ones from small ones, rough ones from smooth ones. As they grow older, they become more sophisticated in their classifying, and they begin to group their playmates into those they like to play with and those they don't. When they enter school, they separate their school clothes from their play clothes. Then as they learn to use abstractions in their thinking, they identify subjects in school that they are interested or successful in. In every one of these classifications, the grouping is made according to a *ruling principle:* rocks classified according to *size* or *smoothness;* friends classified according to *amiability;* clothes classified according to *use;* school subjects classified according to *success* or, perhaps, *interest.*

Although classifying is a process "natural" to human beings, it is useful to remember that classes as such do not exist in nature itself. We create classes and systems of classification to help us understand our world.

The "Ruling Principle" in Classification

Classifying is the act of grouping things, persons, activities, ideas, and so on, according to their similarities and differences. By the time you are of college age you are so accustomed to classifying and to being classified that you are scarcely aware of the process. Yet classification affects nearly every part of your life. To mention only a few of the possibilities, you may be classified in religion as a believer, nonbeliever, or agnostic; a Christian or non-Christian; a Protestant, Jew, or Catholic; a Methodist, Baptist, or Episcopalian; etc. In politics, you are Republican, Democrat, or Independent. In school, you are a freshman, sophomore, junior, senior (or unclassified). In a university, you may be placed in the College of Arts and Sciences, Engineering, Education, etc. If you are in Arts and Sciences, you may be classified as an English major, math major, or psychology major, etc. (In classifying, the *et cetera* is important. Be sure that all the members of the class are included.)

A *classification,* to define the term more accurately, is a significant and informative grouping of things, persons, activities, ideas, etc. The key words here are *significant* and *informative.* We classify in order to use information, and the most informative classifications are those based upon significant groupings. If, in order to understand them, we separate the students in a particular composition class into two groups, men and women, we have made a classification, but it does not seem significant nor does it satisfy our curiosity about the students.

To make such a classification useful, we must apply a significant *ruling principle,* which is a unifying idea or point of view used in the act of classifying. The division of a composition class into men and women is based upon a ruling principle of *gender,* which is not a particularly significant grouping here, and thus will not prove to be very informative. Other ruling principles of varying significance might be *athletic ability, religion, major field, interest in composition,* etc.

In the following passage, observe that there are two ruling principles, cloud *formation* and *altitude:*

> [1]Clouds are classified according to how they are formed. There are two basic types: (1) Clouds formed by rising air currents. These are piled up and puffy. They are called "cumulus" which means piled up or accumulated. (2) Clouds formed when a layer of air is cooled below the saturation point without vertical movement. These are in sheets or foglike layers. They are called "stratus," meaning sheetlike or layered.
>
> [2]Clouds are further classified by altitude into four families: high clouds, middle clouds, low clouds, and towering clouds. The bases of the latter may be as low as the typical low clouds, but the tops may be at or above 75,000 feet. — Paul E. Lehr, R. Will Burnett, and Herbert S. Zim, *Weather*

As with the other strategies of development, classification is created by the writer *for a specific reason*. In the classification of clouds, the writer's aim was to explain cloud formations to a reader who is not a scientist and who knows very little about clouds.

A diagram of another classification may help you visualize how this strategy works. Note how the following discussion of different types of kisses might be diagrammed.

If one wishes to classify the kiss, then one must consider several principles of classification. One may classify kissing with respect to sound. Here the language is not sufficiently elastic to record all my observations. I do not believe that all the languages in the world have an adequate supply of onomatopoeia to describe the different sounds I have learned to know at my uncle's house. Sometimes it was smacking, sometimes hissing, sometimes sticky, sometimes explosive, sometimes booming, sometimes full, sometimes hollow, sometimes squeaky, and so on forever. One may also classify kissing with regard to contact, as in the close kiss, the kiss *en passant* [in passing], and the clinging kiss. . . . One may classify them with reference to the time element, as the brief and the prolonged. With reference to the time element, there is still another classification, and this is the only one I really care about. One makes a difference between the first kiss and all others. That which is the subject of this reflection is incommensurable with everything which is included in the other classifications; it is indifferent to sound, touch, time in general. The first kiss is, however, qualitatively different from all others. — Soren Kierkegaard, *Either/Or*

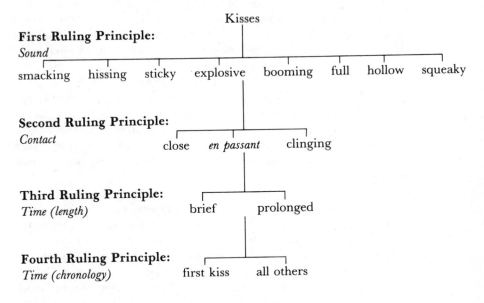

Kisses

First Ruling Principle:
Sound
smacking   hissing   sticky   explosive   booming   full   hollow   squeaky

Second Ruling Principle:
Contact
close   *en passant*   clinging

Third Ruling Principle:
Time (length)
brief   prolonged

Fourth Ruling Principle:
Time (chronology)
first kiss   all others

Point of classification: The first kiss is different.

Below is a classification of *dieting drop-outs* using a clear stance and ruling principle: Dieters drop out for a *reason* (or a rationale).

<table>
<tr>
<td>

Introduction:
Rhetorical
questions posed

</td>
<td>

[1]So if eating is not the most important thing in life, why are you eating again? Why, after all those promises and privations, have you once more become a diet drop-out? Are you morally as well as physically flabby? Are you weak of will, irresolute of purpose? Are you so undisciplined, so infantile, so *greedy,* that you can always be counted upon, sooner or later, to cave in at the sight of a Hershey bar with almonds, a freshly baked loaf of rye bread, a creamy, winy, buttery coquille St. Jacques?

</td>
</tr>
<tr>
<td>

Answer to
questions: ruling
principle

</td>
<td>

[2]The answer, of course, isn't nearly that simple. There are many different kinds of diet drop-outs, each with her own *raison d'eat.* I have divided them into four categories: the alcoholic, the psychologist, the biologist and the out-and-out quitter.

</td>
</tr>
<tr>
<td>

Alcoholic:
first class

</td>
<td>

[3]The alcoholic eater, like her drinking counterpart, is doomed from the moment she first slips off the wagon. Let her munch a single salted peanut and she's got to go on to devour the entire can. Let her nibble the tiniest forkful of cherry cheesecake and within minutes all that's left is a faint pink smudge. In the life of the alcoholic eater there is no such thing as a taste or a sip, a spoonful or a slice. As soon as she succumbs to the seduction of "just one bite," she's had it.

</td>
</tr>
<tr>
<td>

Psychologist:
second class

</td>
<td>

[4]When the psychologist goes off her diet, it's really her mother who's making her do all the eating. Her conversation is full of references to early-childhood traumas and the inexorable forces of the unconscious. "I'm having an anxiety attack," she says from behind her butterscotch sundae. "I'm feeling rejected. I'm searching for love."

</td>
</tr>
<tr>
<td>

Biologist:
third class

</td>
<td>

[5]The biologist who returns to full-time eating talks knowingly about sodium intake and metabolic rates and insists that she is not failing her diet but vice versa. "No matter how little I eat," she observes as she ladles the gravy onto her mashed potatoes, "everything I put in my mouth turns to fat."

</td>
</tr>
<tr>
<td>

Out-and-out
quitter:
fourth class

</td>
<td>

[6]The out-and-out quitter quits her diet because she can no longer endure reaching for a green-pepper ring when what she really wants to reach for is a mousse. She awakens in the night racked with hunger pains that no amount of celery stalks can assuage. She is sick of unpersuasive food substitutes such as mock potato pudding made with cauliflower, mock sour-cream sauce made with cottage cheese, mock

</td>
</tr>
</table>

malteds made with neither malt nor ice cream and mock Bloody Marys made with neither vodka nor gin. The will that has sustained her through lunch after lunch of beef bouillon with cucumber garnish slowly leaks away, and a life without éclairs no longer seems worth living. —Judith Viorst, "A Dieter's Lament"

Stance:

Role: A woman who has had trouble staying on diets. She is herself a *diet drop-out.* She may have used all of the excuses she lists, and be an "out-and-out quitter."

Audience: Any person who has ever tried to stay on a diet.

Thesis: There are four classes of diet drop-outs, each with her own *raison d'eat* (reason to eat!).

Suggestions for Writing a Classification Paper

Here are some suggestions for writing the classification paper that you should find useful.

1. The first step in classifying is to list your evidence. The evidence you collect is from your experience or reading. Your evidence may be the answer to a question such as "What kinds of . . . ?" or "What are the facts about . . . ?" After you have collected the evidence in order to answer the question, you have a list. Once you have your list, you should be able to see relationships, keep the evidence that is pertinent, and ignore the rest. Then you can identify your ruling principle and develop categories.

2. Next, remember to avoid artificial overlapping or illogical classifications. Simply chopping your subject into parts will not necessarily give you a valid classification. If you divide your composition class into (a) men and (b) good students, you have made a classification that is artificial and probably useless.

3. Be consistent with your ruling principle. You may change your principle if, after having investigated your subject thoroughly from one angle, you wish to investigate it from another. Note that the classification of clouds used two ruling principles. If you were studying political systems, for example, you might use several different ruling principles: (a) time-sequence or history, (b) causes and effects, (c) types of systems, (d) philosophies of systems, (e) success of systems, to name just a few.

4. Make sure your classification has a point. Don't try to write a classification paper without a specific stance.

5. Avoid most either-or classifications. For instance:

> Voters are either left-wing or right-wing.
> Financiers are either successful or unsuccessful.
> Rhetoric students are either good writers or poor writers.

By its very structure, each of these either-or classifications probably distorts the truth because it omits certain members of the total group—those who would fall somewhere between the extremes of "left" or "right," "successful" or "unsuccessful," and "good" or "poor." Among a group of rhetoric students, for example, there are likely to be writers who are "excellent," "good," "fair," "poor," and (perhaps) "terrible."

WRITING AND REVISING A CLASSIFICATION PAPER (AN EXAMPLE)

To understand more clearly how the process of classification works in the contexts of thinking and writing, let's follow a student named Tom who wants to understand the *behavior* of the fifteen eight-year-old boys that he supervised in summer camp. His purpose in using classification is to get some ideas for dealing with these boys when he returns to his counselling job next summer. He has made some scratch notes, and from those notes he writes the rough draft of a paragraph.

KIDS AT A SUMMER CAMP

Most campers fall into at least one emotional category that reveals a lot about the way they think about life. Every counselor should expect at least one of the following. *The Homesick Kid* is normally the one in his bunk while everyone else is playing soccer outside. Odds are he's writing home (at least three times a day). This kid has probably never been away from home much before, and normally he wishes that he is anywhere but camp. But at the end of camp, he'll cry even harder because he doesn't want to leave. *The Whiner* complains about everything. At meals, the food is always too gloppy, runny, bland, or spicy. At night, the bed is too hard or too soft, and the games are always too hard or too boring. Some kids are *Non-Existent,* and as their counselor you never meet them until their parents come to pick them up. They tend to be lethargic, hard to find, and exceptionally quiet — meaning that they sometimes end up being a counselor's favorite. *The Jock* is the all-around athlete, able to beat anyone in camp (including his counselors) in tetherball, football, soccer, etc. They're great to have around, though, if you need something heavy (a trunk, bed, or person) lifted. *The Super-Jock* is another story. He thinks he can do anything well, but his prime attribute is normally making excuses (sun too bright, glove too big or small, field too rough, not the way we play at home). Along these same lines is the *Veteran* — the kid who has done it all "many times," and is an expert at absolutely everything. Unfortunately for him, the camp never seems to do anything "his way," and he normally learns some big lessons in humility by the time the summer is over.

After Tom reviews what he has written, he discovers that he has failed to follow the steps for developing a clear classification system: He has no *ruling principle* and no *categories*. Instead, he has treated each boy as a separate class; consequently his grouping overlaps: a *homesick boy* can be a *whiner;* a *veteran camp-goer* can be a *jock*. Tom reconsiders his ruling principle. What each boy "thinks about life" is pretty vague, so he decides that a more important *ruling principle* would be to consider how various classes of boys contribute to the success of the camp, thereby helping the counselor run a better program. Tom believes that the classification system should be useful for the counselors, so he changes his system to include three categories: *leader, follower,* and *obstructionist*. His definitions help him to place the boys in these categories:

> A *leader* is a boy who takes initiative and has certain qualities that make other boys respect and follow him.
> A *follower* is a boy who does what the leader expects, but seldom acts on his own initiative.
> An *obstructionist* is a boy who exerts no positive leadership but hinders the day-by-day progress of the camp with unacceptable behavior.

Keeping these three categories in mind, Tom can now see that whether or not a boy is homesick is irrelevant. It is the way his homesickness keeps him from being a *leader* or causes him to be a *follower* or *obstructionist* that is important. It isn't whether or not a boy is selfish or generous that is the important thing, but how these traits affect his behavior and his leadership qualities.

Next Tom developed a *stance:*

Role: A college freshman who supervised a group of eight-year-old
boys at YMCA summer camp the summer after graduating
from high school.

Audience: Other counselors of the YMCA camp or any other boys'
camp.

Thesis: If you want to succeed as a camp counselor, you should
recognize that eight-year-old boys fall into three categories
— *leaders, followers,* and *obstructionists.* (It will make your life
easier if you know how to get cooperation from the members
of each class.)

Here is Tom's completed paper.

CAN EIGHT-YEAR-OLD BOYS BEHAVE RESPONSIBLY?

[1]When I took a job as counselor at the YMCA camp, I had hoped to
work with older boys because I had experience with a twelve-year-old
brother and his friends. Consequently, I was disappointed to be assigned to
a group of eight-year-olds, an age I considered too child-like to interest me.
I knew, however, that it was my job to understand the boys who come to
the camp with varying backgrounds and personalities. It was apparent that
I would be expected to teach, counsel, and clean up after these boys, so I
had to learn something about them fast. Eight weeks — the length of the
camp — isn't very long.

[2]During the summer I learned that there are three kinds of eight-year-old
boys — *leaders, followers,* and *obstructionists.* I knew that my life would be
easier if I could get the best from each class of boy because I could make use
of their abilities to lead or follow. The *leaders* I define as those boys who take
initiative, and have certain qualities that make other boys respect and
follow them. The *followers* are boys who do what the leader expects but who
show no initiative. A *follower* seldom acts on his own initiative to help make
camp successful. The *obstructionist* is a boy who exerts no positive leadership
but hinders the day-by-day progress of the camp with unacceptable
behavior.

[3]The *leader* class may consist of only one or two boys. If a camp counselor
can find any boy who others will look up to and one who will also support
the counselor, he is lucky. A *leader* is usually self-confident, but not over-
bearing. He may be a good athlete, so he understands what team-work
means. Other boys look up to athletes because they can beat other teams in
tetherball, football, or soccer, making the camp team look good. The boys
in the leader class have usually been to summer camp before, so they know
the procedures and are not likely to be homesick. It is a good idea to identify any leaders in your group early because they can make your life as a

camp counselor infinitely easier. They can cooperate with you by rounding up the followers at the end of a day, and they can get *followers* to cooperate with you.

⁴The next largest class is *followers,* subclassified into *retreating* and *eager* boys. The *retreating boy* is usually homesick. He may stay in his bunk writing home every day. Sometimes he won't eat, so he is lethargic. A *retreater* will usually comply with directions because he is frightened. *Retreaters* are often generous. If a retreater gets a package of cookies from his parents, he shares it with the whole cabin. This kind of sharing helps to form a cohesive group.

⁵*Eager* boys make good followers, particularly if they believe that they are lucky to be at any camp at all. Most boys' camps try to admit each summer a few children from orphanages or foster homes. Their fees are usually paid by the YMCA or a service club like the Kiwanis or Rotary. Since these boys have no family and are used to institutional life, they think the camp food is great, the beds comfortable, and the counselor a good guy.

⁶The largest class — and the biggest problem for a camp counselor — is the *obstructionist.* Perhaps eight-year-olds become *obstructionists* when they are away from home because they have to accommodate to a new environment. Consequently, they are complainers. They whine about the food being too runny, bland, or spicy. Their beds are too hard or too soft. The games are boring. Some boys who fancy themselves good athletes complain when they don't succeed: the sun is too bright, the baseball glove is too small, the field is too rough, and the camp team doesn't play by the rules that they know. Some of the obstructionists are selfish because they are used to having people wait on them. They can't get used to doing the everyday chores of washing dishes, making beds, and sweeping floors. A selfish boy may draw a line around his bunk, padlock his food packages from home, and even steal food from other boys.

⁷A counselor must put a great deal of effort into getting the obstructionists to accept responsibility for the group. One way of dealing with these boys is to be abrupt and order them about. However, this will probably make them even less cooperative than they were before. I have found a better way: Make them feel important. They are usually very insecure and frightened of a new experience, so they show their insecurity by aggressive and selfish behavior. I try to treat obstructionists as I treat my little brother when he displays similar behavior. I pay attention to him and make him think I'm interested in what he does. If I treat *obstructionists* as I treat my brother, by the end of eight weeks they usually become more cooperative — not completely cooperative — but *more* so!

⁸Other counselors may find my classification incomplete, and they may not agree with my solutions. But these are the kinds of boys that I found in the YMCA camp. Knowing what I learned last summer will help me next year when I face another group of boys whose parents happily shipped their kids off to summer camp for me and my friends to civilize.

PRACTICE

Discussion

1. Study Tom's final draft. How well do the details and examples support each of his categories? Discuss the point of the paper. Is it clear enough that another counselor could follow Tom's advice? What suggestions do you have for improvements in the paper? Improvements in the classification system?

2. For class discussion, make a significant classification of the following items. You may need to subdivide to complete your classification. *Hint:* One of the category *names* may be in some of the lists. Give the ruling principle of your classification. Use the heading *Etc.* if an item doesn't fit your classifying system.
   a. *Time,* table, book, chair, magazine, divan, *Sports Illustrated,* newspaper, bookcase, *Fortune.*
   b. Truck, station wagon, automobile, luxury car, "semi," convertible, pickup, sports car, compact, economy car.
   c. Left-winger, Southern Democrat, socialist, communist, right-winger, Democrat, Republican, independent, middle-of-the-roader.
   d. Poet, novelist, journalist, editorial writer, TV commentator, textbook author, social philosopher, newspaper columnist, writer for *The National Enquirer,* writer on college paper, literary critic.
   e. Thugs, robbers, rascals, killers, arsonists, scoundrels, shoplifters, murderers, burglars, assassins, car thieves, rapists, traitors, villains.
   f. Various kinds of *rights:* moral, natural, political, original, acquired, absolute, relative, property, liberty, equality.
   g. Presidents, governors, prime ministers, mayors, kings, princes, queens, despots, princesses, commissars, dictators, rulers, wardens, magistrates.

3. For purposes of research, a major university has classified "human subjects" in the following categories. Discuss the accuracy of the classification. What is the ruling principle? Are all classes represented? Do any of the classes overlap?

TYPE OF SUBJECT:

A. _____ Adult, non-student

_____ University student

———— Minor

———— Other (explain)

B. ———— Normal volunteer

———— In-patient

———— Out-patient

———— Mentally retarded

———— Mentally disabled

———— Individual with limited civil freedom

———— Pregnant women, fetuses, and the dead

4. Discuss the following ideas for classification papers. Identify any flaws in the ruling principle.
   a. In her first classification exercise, a seventh-grader wrote, "I classify my friends by their loyalty, manners, or indifference toward me."
   b. Harp strings are classified according to the materials they are made of—cat gut, springs, or nylon—because the different materials influence the tone of the sound.
   c. When I put my stamp collection in order, I separate the stamps first by country, then by series and date.
   d. From a U.S. government questionnaire: Check your nationality —(a) white, (b) black, (c) Asian, (d) Hispanic, (e) Cuban. (e) Cuban.
   e. People: There are two main categories, significant people and outsiders. Significant people include family, friends and business associates; outsiders may be anyone from the cashiers at the local supermarket to pedestrians on the street. People can be considered significant even when they have a negative impact. Prison guards, for example, would be extremely important to a prisoner. — Shannon Brownlee
   f. Casey Stengel, famous manager of the New York Yankees: "All right you guys, line up alphabetically according to size."
   g. Looters belong to three categories. There are everyday thieves —men and women of no conscience—who would steal wherever and whenever no authority existed to restrain them.

      In the second group are those who feel deprived and frustrated and seize the opportunity to express their grievances at being unemployed, hungry, angry at society, their bosses or spouses, and who feel they have little chance for revenge. These individuals are easily galvanized into action by watching others behave wantonly.

The third category interests psychiatrists the most because any of us could potentially become looters. In the wake of a disaster, impulses usually contained — greed, naked aggression, lust for power, etc. — often flow unchecked. The carnival atmosphere reigns, while the impulses to help and to heal may be given short shrift. — *Wall Street Journal*

Writing

1. Here is a list of ideas about dress shirts. Classify the ideas in a logical system. Be sure to identify your ruling principle. (You may add other ideas you have, or omit those given here that do not fit your ruling principle.)
   a. The dress shirt is like a vestment. (Look up *vestment*.)
   b. The dress shirt is like a shield.
   c. The dress shirt has many connotations.
   d. The dress shirt shows one's orderliness.
   e. The dress shirt differentiates social classes.
   f. Wearing a dress shirt is a gesture of respect.
   g. The dress shirt shows one's social class.
   h. The dress shirt shows one's neatness.
   i. Dress shirts are like girdles.
   j. The dress shirt is a symbol of appropriateness.
   k. The dress shirt is a sign of compliance.
   l. The dress shirt impedes the flow of blood to the brain.
   Now write an essay about the dress shirt, using your classification system. Or, if you don't like the subject, develop your own list, classify, and write an essay on it. Suggestions:

high-heel boots or shoes	automobiles
skirts	bicycles
ties	motorcycles
jeans	umbrellas
designer clothes	cameras

2. Write a paper in which you classify your reactions to "things" around you. Be sure to identify the significance of your classification. Examples:
   a. Things you worry about.
   b. Things you keep secret from your family.
   c. Things you celebrate.
   d. Things you laugh about.
   e. Things you feel guilty about.

3. One of our students brought a first draft to us. She recognized that something was wrong with her system of classification. Write the student a letter, telling her how she can improve her classification of country music songs. You might begin your criticism by applying to the paper the *Suggestions for Writing Classification* (see p. 135). For example, you might identify the writer's *classes* and check for overlapping categories, asking her if a *truckdriving song* can't be both *comical* and *sensitive.*

[1]My mother was born in the hills of Tennessee, and she loved country music. She missed the Grand Ol' Opry, and whenever she had a chance to visit Nashville, she always attended a concert. We grew up in a home where the radio or stereo constantly played country musicians like Johnny Cash, Kenny Rogers, or Loretta Lynn. *Coal Miner's Daughter* was our favorite movie.

[2]After I went away to college, I began to think about my favorite country music. Lately, I have classified the form into three kinds—the saccharine, exaggerated "cheatin' " songs; the truckdriving, comical songs; and the sensitively written, intelligent songs. The three kinds are covered in the order that I find most enjoyable.

[3]Since I rank these classes according to my listening preference, I find the least enjoyable songs are the sloppy, "I-miss-my-country-hearted-man" ballads. These songs are the ones country-music haters use to illustrate how bad country music is. Even though the critics overgeneralize and do not see the true treasures in country music, I'm afraid I have to agree with them in considering this class. These soppy ballads are the least tolerable because they bemoan unrequited love, unfaithful partners, loneliness, and drinking. Conway Twitty whines about "Linda on his miiiiiiind . . . ," Barbara Mandrell drones on about "Burnin' the Midnight Oil," and Dolly Parton bursts into tears when she sings, "I Will Always Love You." I find these songs repetitive and trite.

[4]The truckdrivin' songs are my favorite examples of country humor. They are often charming and witty. C. W. McCall's "Convoy" and "Wolf Creek Pass" are part of this class as are Red Sevine's "Teddy Bear" and Dave Dudley's "Six Days on the Road." The CB radio is an important part of the lyrics in some of the songs in this category. Even though I've never ridden in a truck and I don't find truck stops interesting, I think these songs are fun.

[5]The category I enjoy most is the most difficult to describe. This class contains the beautifully emotional country songs, thoughtful and sensitive without being overwrought. They are intelligently and honestly written. Willie Nelson exemplifies this class with "On the Road Again," and Emmy Lou Harris' rendition of "Beneath Still Waters" is superb. Marty Robbins' "El Paso" is an older example of the kind of song that portrays the best of country songs.

[6]Recently, I heard a song on the radio that caused me to sit through a green light I was laughing so hard. It was a country song spoofing country music in general and supporting my categories. A singer with a strained, emotional southern accent moaned about prison, drinking, trains, mothers, women, cheating, brawls — *etc., etc.* I think you get the idea.

4. Choose a topic that can be classified, and write an essay. Be sure to keep in mind the following: (1) choose the ruling principle(s) by which you plan to classify; (2) identify your purpose in classifying (your reader should not read your classification and say, "So what?"); (3) choose a writer's stance that suits the ruling principle and the purpose of the classification; (4) write the paper.
   Here are some possible topics (modify when necessary):
   a. There are distinct kinds of people who patronize laundromats/ sporting-goods stores/pizzerias/delicatessens; *therefore* . . .
   b. I have encountered many types of people/ideas since coming to college. *My conclusions are* . . .
   c. The subjects in my major field can be divided into several categories; *consequently* . . .
   d. The parents of successful children fall into several categories, but *the most important category is* . . .
   e. The summer and part-time jobs available to a college student have certain characteristics, *so when you look for a job* . . .

ILLUSTRATION

Illustration, as one dictionary says, is the "act of clarifying or explaining." It also refers to the material used to clarify or explain: the details, facts, or examples a writer employs to communicate specifics. Any time you support a generalization with evidence in the form of specific examples and details, you are using *illustration.* You can have a generalization at the paragraph-topic level, or a generalization that acts as your thesis for a paper. In either case, you must support those generalizations. But it isn't *where* you use specifics that is important; rather it is that your evidence should be specific and convincing. As readers, we are often bored and put off by general or abstract statements. We enjoy examples and details because these give us a chance to picture situations for ourselves and to understand quickly what the writer is talking about.

Using Specific Examples and Details

Here are a few statements — written by a student — that give a reader little to understand and nothing to picture:

> I learned very quickly last summer that there was one thing you had to understand immediately when you worked around a waterhole drilling rig: safety was the watchword. Rigs are dangerous. I had to be careful and watch my step. One of the other roustabouts forgot this, and he got badly hurt.

The student gives us a general statement: "Rigs are dangerous." However, he doesn't specify *how* they are dangerous. Why was "safety" the "watchword"? How and why did another roustabout get hurt? Here in a second draft is the passage rewritten for specificity: Notice how the writer states a generalization first, then moves to more specific examples, finally ending with a statement about *one* roustabout.

Generalization During the drilling operation, a *rig* is dangerous at *three times:* when the *head driller* is *breaking out, putting pipe on,* or *drilling hard.* Take *breaking out (removing pipe),* for instance. The driller *signals* when he wants his *helper* to put his *wrench* on the
Specific details pipe. When he is ready, he will *clutch-out* and throw the *rotary table* into *reverse.* After the table begins to turn, if the helper does not take his *hands* off the *wrench* he will get his *fingers cut*
Application to *off* because the wrench *slams* against the *drilling mast* with the
one person — force of 200 *horsepower* behind it. One *roustabout, Billy Lawe,*
Billy Lawe got careless one day and lost *three fingers* on his *left hand.*

Let's look at another example of dull, uninformative writing that lacks specific material:

> The Model T Ford was versatile. It could do lots of things on the farm. It provided necessary power for emergencies and other things farmers needed to do.

By contrast, Reynald M. Wik uses illustrative *specific* detail to describe the versatility of the Model T:

Generalization [1]On the farm the Model T proved extremely versatile. In the fall when sparks from railroad locomotives often set prairie fires, farmers would use a car to pull a walking plow

Specific details   to make a fire guard to control the flames. Model Ts were used as early as 1913 to fight forest fires. In butchering hogs, the power from a car could be utilized to hoist the pig out of the hot water in the scalding barrel. In the fields, Model Ts Ts pulled hay rakes, mowers, grain binders, harrows, and hay loaders. Pick-up trucks stretched woven wire, hauled water to livestock, and distributed supplies where needed. Ford trucks hauled grain to elevators, brought cattle and hogs to market, and returned from town with coal, flour, lumber, and feed.

Specific details   [2]To secure belt power, farmers attached pulleys to the crankshaft, or bolted them to a rear wheel to utilize the 20-horsepower motor for grinding grain, sawing wood, filling silos, churning butter, shearing sheep, pumping water, elevating grain, shelling corn, turning grindstones, and *One fellow*   washing clothes. One ingenious fellow used the spinning rear wheel to knock the shells off walnuts. One farmer said his *One farmer*   Model T would do everything except rock the baby to sleep or make love to the hired girl.

Sometimes, however, specific examples and details alone do not stimulate the reader's interest. The material must also be presented vividly and vigorously so that the reader can identify with the person writing the essay. Consider Richard Wright's account of his early life. Notice how Wright uses a single example to support his paragraph lead: *My first lesson in how to live as a Negro came when I was quite small.*

[1]My first lesson in how to live as a Negro came when I was quite small. We were living in Arkansas. Our house stood behind the railroad tracks. Its skimpy yard was paved with black cinders. Nothing green ever grew in that yard. The only touch of green we could see was far away, beyond the tracks, over where the white folks lived. But cinders were good enough for me and I never missed the green growing things. And anyhow cinders were fine weapons. You could always have a nice hot war with huge black cinders. All you had to do was crouch behind the brick pillars of a house with your hands full of gritty ammunition. And the first woolly black head you saw pop out from behind another row of pillars was your target. You tried your very best to knock it off. It was great fun.

[2]I never fully realized the appalling disadvantages of a cinder environment till one day the gang to which I belonged found itself engaged in a war with the white boys who lived beyond the tracks. As usual we laid down our cinder barrage, thinking that this would wipe the white boys out. But they replied with a steady bombardment of broken bottles. We doubled our cinder barrage, but they hid behind trees, hedges, and the sloping embankments of their lawns. Having no such fortifications, we retreated to the brick pillars of our homes. During the retreat a broken milk bottle caught

ILLUSTRATION 147

me behind the ear, opening a deep gash which bled profusely. The sight of blood pouring over my face completely demoralized our ranks. My fellow-combatants left me standing paralyzed in the center of the yard and scurried for their homes. A kind neighbor saw me and rushed me to a doctor, who took three stitches in my neck.

³I sat brooding on my front steps, nursing my wound and waiting for my mother to come from work. I felt that a grave injustice had been done me. It was all right to throw cinders. The greatest harm a cinder could do was leave a bruise. But broken bottles were dangerous; they left you cut, bleeding, and helpless.

⁴When night fell, my mother came from the white folks' kitchen. I raced down the street to meet her. I could just feel in my bones that she would understand. I knew she would tell me exactly what to do next time. I grabbed her hand and babbled out the whole story. She examined my wound, then slapped me.

⁵"How come yuh didn't hide?" she asked me. "How come yuh awways fightin'?"

⁶I was outraged and bawled. Between sobs I told her that I didn't have any trees or hedges to hide behind. There wasn't a thing I could have used as a trench. And you couldn't throw very far when you were hiding behind the brick pillars of a house. She grabbed a barrel stave, dragged me home, stripped me naked, and beat me till I had a fever of one hundred and two. She would smack my rump with the stave, and while the skin was still smarting, impart to me gems of Jim Crow wisdom. I was never to throw cinders any more. I was never to fight any more wars. I was never, never, under any conditions, to fight *white* folks again. And they were absolutely right in clouting me with the broken milk bottle. Didn't I know she was working hard every day in the hot kitchens of the white folks to make money to take care of me? When was I ever going to learn to be a good boy? She couldn't be bothered with my fights. She finished by telling me that I ought to be thankful to God as long as I lived that they didn't kill me.

⁷All that night I was delirious and could not sleep. Each time I closed my eyes I saw monstrous white faces suspended from the ceiling, leering at me.

⁸From that time on, the charm of my cinder yard was gone. The green trees, the trimmed hedges, the cropped lawns grew very meaningful, became a symbol. Even today when I think of white folks, the hard, sharp outlines of white houses surrounded by trees, lawns, and hedges are present somewhere in the background of my mind. Through the years they grew into an overreaching symbol of fear. —*Black Boy*

The word picture Wright draws of his life as a child is so distinct and strikingly alive that readers get the impression that they are there at the scene hearing the mother's tirade and feeling the boy's pain and frustration.

No writer can create reality. He can only create the illusion of reality by choosing details, examples, and words that are strikingly alive—*vivid*.

As the novelist Joseph Conrad wrote: "My task which I am trying to achieve is, by the power of the written word, to make you hear, to make you feel—it is, before all, to make you *see*."

A basic strategy in writing vividly is: Don't just *tell* your readers—*show* them, too. General statements can explain a great deal, but they are often flat and colorless in comparison to the examples and details that *show* the reader what you have in mind.

The Representative Example

Magazines and newspapers are full of essays with titles like "The Typical College Student of the '80s," "The Workaholic in You," and "The Senior Citizen Today." In these essays, the writer gives a representative picture of a class. The writer understands that no person has all the traits described, but that it is often useful and informative to give the reader a composite picture of a particular group. We like to read such essays to see if we fit the picture. The writer of a representative example must be a keen observer of human behavior; otherwise, the picture will be unrepresentative and faulty. Following is an excerpt from an essay describing the typical workaholic:

Generalization about the class, introducing topic	¹Those who overwork out of compulsion—the work addicts, or workaholics, of this world—are in trouble. Their addiction can lead to dead-end careers, to poor health, even to early death. They are so emotionally dependent on work that without it they start coming unglued. Though the pure-bred workaholic is rare, there is a little of him in almost everyone. It is well to know the warning signals and how to cope with them. . . .
Thesis	
Generalization about the class	²As employees of large corporations, work addicts can have a hard time of it. The staff psychiatrist at a huge national manufacturing firm tells of an executive in the New York headquarters who came to him for help. Discussion brought out that the executive felt best when things were "impossible"—when he was being seriously tested and overworked. Free time made him uneasy and anxious. Many addicts like him end up self-employed so they can have expandable working time. (But even blue-collar workers can manage to become work addicts by taking second jobs or constantly volunteering for overtime.
Example: blue-collar workers	
Generalization about the class	³Wherever he earns his living, the workaholic is likely to work hard not just on the job but off duty too. "When his back is to the wall," says Howard Hess, a Western Electric corporate psychiatrist, "he may cut the lawn with a vengeance or play a murderous game of tennis." A Chicago

Example   psychiatrist, Dr. Saul M. Siegel, recalls a work addict who had an extramarital affair. He kept working as hard as ever, though, and "wound up with both a nagging wife and a nagging mistress."

Generalization about the class   [4]While work addicts work hard, they tend to die easily. Time and again, researchers have found that the compulsively hard-working person is particularly prone to heart

Example   disease in middle age. — Warren Boroson, "The Workaholic in You"

Suggestions for Using Illustration

As you plan an essay using illustration, keep the following suggestions in mind:

1. Make sure that you use specific details and examples in your illustrations.

2. Use appropriate examples. If you are trying to show that student shoplifting exists on your campus, do not use examples of non-students who shoplift. Do not describe shoplifting that occurs off-campus in the downtown stores — unless that is part of your thesis.

3. Use appropriate and varied signals for your examples, but don't over-signal. You do not have to use "for example" or "another example of this is . . ." every time you introduce a new illustration. If you think your reader doesn't realize that another illustration is coming up, use a variety of signals:

> For instance . . .
> Hence . . .
> Thus . . .
> Another case . . .
> Additional evidence . . .

4. Develop some kind of order in your use of illustration.

WRITING AND REVISING ILLUSTRATION (AN EXAMPLE)

One day, when Kathryn was out jogging, she took a rest in an old cemetery close to her college. It was a lovely fall day, so she decided to walk around and read the inscriptions on some of the gravestones and monuments. When she returned to her dormitory, she wrote about her impressions:

[1]Mount Hope Cemetery was a very enjoyable place. I expected the graveyard to be less than pleasing, but I was surprised. Instead of seeing a piece of earth with dead bodies underneath and gravestones lined up like seats in a movie theatre, I found a place that made me think more of life than of death. Each gravestone, or at least each family plot, had its own personality. This gave me a feeling for the people who had died. They didn't seem like generic corpses, but rather people who had lived and done certain, unique things in their lives. This is what I caught myself thinking about as I walked through the cemetery.

[2]There was a lot of life in the cemetery to take notice of. Though the trees screened the cemetery from the outside, out of the corner of my ear I could still hear traffic. Life existed inside the cemetery as well. I saw squirrels, chipmunks, birds, and insects galore. People were there jogging, and even doing their rhetoric assignments for their college course. I wouldn't say that the graveyard was absolutely bustling or anything, but it was more energetic than I expected. The foliage, too, was healthy and alive looking. The grass was green and thick, and the trees were plentiful.

[3]The placement of the bushes, gravel roads, and land slopes gently separated the cemetery into small, semi-private areas. Each family had its own place which was private, yet part of the rest of the graveyard community. Each family's place had its own feeling, its own personality. One spot I remember very well. In a hollow were several graves covered by a large, old maple. The grass grew in long, thin clumps the way it does under large, old trees, and dirt predominated. All the stones in this area were dark charcoal grey, and somewhat old. It made me think of an old, sad family who perhaps had no more children who would ever visit their graves.

[4]The Paro family of tree stumps was one of my favorite groups. The family name was written on a huge stone shaped like a tree trunk with an anchor leaning up against it. Surrounding this was a forest of stubby little tree-stump stones for individual members of the Paro family. The anchor interested me. What seafaring family would live in Illinois?

[5]The Campbell family had a stone shaped like the Eiffel Tower which almost shone. It looked more like a monument than a gravestone. I wondered if this family had anything to do with Campbell Hospital; they seemed to be flaunting their money. Even if they couldn't take it with them, they could still show it off.

[6]Other areas were more touching. A family buried a 29 year old daughter under a Greek temple ruin. The Waters family buried a child, their "darling," under a small stone shaped like a scroll, covered with lichen and discolored. An ornate stone, carved to look like a tree with day lilies, trillium, lily of the valley, and ivy winding around it, covered another grave. It was green with moss, and discolored with time. I found this to be the saddest stone of all. It was small, like a child's grave, and whispered sad

things about death when young. This stone was sad and depressing, and didn't have much to do with life at all, but it had the right to be sad, if someone who died young was buried beneath it. At first I reacted the same way when I saw other stones with "mother" or "father" on them, but then I realized that although I personally would not like to be remembered only as the mother of someone, at least epitaphs like this made each grave different from the others. The epitaphs showed that people had done something that others, at least, considered unique and worthwhile in their lives.

[7]Mount Hope was a cemetery that allowed the people buried there to retain something of their personalities. While death may make everyone equal, in Mount Hope death did not make everyone the same. Pieces of people's lives showed, even if they were very small, making each person different from the rest. I think this made the cemetery less sad. I felt better knowing that people can make a lasting impression on others. It seems to me that one of the saddest things about death is that people and what they did are so easily forgotten.

After reading her draft, Kathryn sees that not all of her paragraphs support her main point — that each gravestone or family plot in the Mount Hope cemetery gives the impression that a person who was unique is buried there.

For example, paragraph 2 is a pleasant description of a cemetery, but it doesn't do much to support her main point. Some of paragraph 3 needs to be better focused. Paragraphs 4–6 are really the only paragraphs that support her point, but they don't support it well.

As a result of her analysis, Kathryn goes back to revise the paper, tying her illustrations to her main point in a more organized, convincing fashion.

[1]I expected a visit to a cemetery to be less than pleasing, but I was surprised. Paradoxically, I discovered that the cemetery made me think more about the people when they lived — in other words, think more about life than death. Each gravestone or family plot had its own "personality," giving me a feeling for the people buried there, that they had been unique in some way.

[2]Mount Hope Cemetery is an attractive, well-kept place. Trees, bushes, and small slopes separate the cemetery into semi-private areas. Each family has its own private place, and each family plot has its own personality. In an older part of the cemetery, a little hollow is covered by a large, old maple tree. The grass grows in long, thin clumps, typical of shady areas. All of the family stones in this area are in old, dark charcoal-grey marble. The plot is not well-kept — weeds grow among the stones, and it is evident that no one has visited for many years. The area has been neglected and makes me think of a sad family made up of two old people with no children to visit their graves.

[3]At another spot in the older area of the cemetery, I saw this simple phrase on a gravestone: "She lived for others." I could imagine a woman who was plump and rosy-cheeked, with many children to care for. Her death must have caused grief for those who had known and loved her.

[4]Family names are important in some areas of the cemetery. Sometimes a grouping of gravestones with the family name make a distinctive display. An example of this is the Paro family plot whose name is written on a huge stone shaped like a tree trunk. However, a peculiar addition to the tree trunk makes the monument most unusual—leaning against the trunk is an anchor. Surrounding the trunk is a forest of stubby little stone tree stumps designating the graves of individual members of the Paro family. I wondered if the anchor was a metaphorical symbol for stability and security of the main trunk of the family.

[5]The Campbell family had a monument shaped like the Eiffel Tower that stood much higher than any other family gravestone in the cemetery. Compared with the other stones it seemed to be an ostentatious flaunting of wealth. One got the impression that the family believed if they couldn't take it with them, they could at least show it off.

[6]One family buried a 29-year-old daughter under a monument that looked like the ruin of a Greek temple. Another family buried their child, called their "darling," under a small scroll-shaped tombstone. A small child was buried under the stone carving of a little tree with day lilies, trillium, lily of the valley, and ivy winding around it.

[7]At first I was sad when I saw stones with "mother" or "father" carved on them. I thought that I wouldn't want to be remembered only as "the mother." However, I realized that designations like these made each grave different from the others, showing that these people had been considered special and worthwhile by their families or loved ones.

[8]Mount Hope Cemetery allows the people buried there to retain something of their uniqueness. While death may make everyone equal, in this cemetery death does not make everyone the same. I felt better knowing that people can make a lasting impression on others. It seems to me that one of the saddest things about death is that it is too easy to forget the specialness of the individual. A gravestone or burial plot may be the last place where people can be made special for those of us left behind.

PRACTICE

Discussion
1. Study the rewritten paper about the cemetery.
   a. Discuss the writer's use of *signals* and *examples*.
   b. Discuss the appropriateness of the examples.

c. In what way(s) could Kathryn's essay be about other cemeteries? How is this cemetery different from others? How do the choice of examples indicate the difference or similarity?

d. How does Kathryn use description as a means of exemplification or illustration?

2. Read the two student papers below. Analyze their content. Which essay is more convincing? Give specific reasons for your judgments, paying particular attention to the writers' use of informative, lively facts and details to support their theses.

A LIFEGUARD'S LIFE

[1]Many people have a stereotyped idea of the lifeguard bravely rescuing a beautiful drowning girl. But this idea of the lifeguard is not always an exact one. In fact, an alert guard at an average-size public pool seldom is forced into the water to save a drowning person, and rarely is the drowning person a beautiful girl. During the two years I worked at a public pool as a lifeguard, only once did I find it necessary to make a swimming rescue, and then the victim wasn't even a girl.

[2]One of the lifeguard's duties, teaching nonswimmers and beginners how to swim, very often takes place in either shallow water or on land where the learning swimmers will not be in any danger of drowning. When the beginners are tested in deep water, they are kept close to shore. The lifeguard has a shepherd's hook (a long pole which is shaped into a hook at one end) which he uses to retrieve exhausted beginners who are floundering in the water. Swimmers who are learning more difficult strokes are usually good enough in the water that they can take care of themselves.

[3]The side of the average pool is usually only several yards away. Even weak swimmers can make this distance with some effort. Also, most of the pool is shallow water where drowning is almost impossible. Around the pool there is lifesaving equipment such as the ring buoy and shepherd's hook, which are used to extend the reach of the life guard. Anyone drowning near the edge of the pool can easily be saved by the hook or the buoy. The only area left for a possible swimming rescue is a small space in the very center of the deep end of the pool. An alert lifeguard can recognize the poor swimmers and restrict them to the shallow water. Sometimes small children in the shallow end find that they are in water over their heads. Their struggles attract attention, and they are usually picked out of the water by some larger person who is swimming nearby before the lifeguard can reach them.

[4]The nature of the average pool makes it practically unnecessary for the lifeguard to make swimming rescues. The stereotyped image of the lifeguard rescuing a drowning person is colorful but not exact. The true picture might be quite different.

[5]The darkly tanned body squirms in the hard, splintery seat of the

lifeguard chair. Sweat trickles from his armpits under the searing heat of the midday sun. The screaming of young children and the splashing of boys dunking their friends echo back and forth in his weary head. A cry for help comes out of the conglomeration of sounds. The victim is only a chubby boy standing waist-deep in the water while two smaller boys splash him. Only the irritating sound of the whistle reminds the swimmers that the lifeguard is high upon his chair watching over them.

HIGH SCHOOLS—LARGE AND SMALL

[1]There are definite advantages in attending a small high school. One of these advantages is the friendliness in a small school. By this I mean that the students know each other by name and usually know some personal information about each other, such as their grades, their activities, and their friends. With this information, one can understand the other students. One knows whether the person has initiative and a mind of his own or if he would rather let someone else do something for him.

[2]Another advantage is that a person in a small high school has a better chance to participate in athletics. For example, a person who is trying out for some athletic team in a large school must have a fairly high degree of natural ability in order to make the team or even to remain on the squad. But in a small school, if a person has a little natural ability and there aren't too many others with a high degree of ability involved in these sports, this person has the chance to train, learn, and participate in these athletic endeavors.

[3]Another advantage of the small school is the various clubs and organizations to which a student can belong. Large schools have these same organizations, but the competition for membership is much greater.

[4]These are the reasons that I am glad that I attended a small high school.

3. Make a list of ten general topics (like dangerous drilling rigs, some family member, or advantageous smallness) with which you are familiar. Then as quickly as you can, jot down ten specific facts, details, or examples for each topic. Variation: Read your list item by item to a classmate and count the number of illustrative details for each one he or she can reel off in thirty seconds. Then try responding to your classmate's list in the same way. Compare totals.

Writing

1. Using the lists you developed for #3 (above under Discussion), choose one that you and your classmates consider the most interesting, and write a short paper using *illustration*.

2. Revise a paper of yours by adding vivid illustration: facts, details, and examples. Insofar as you can, avoid *telling* your readers; *show* them with specific detail—but avoid mere storytelling.

3. Write a paragraph giving a composite picture of the typical yearbook, autograph book, or picture album.

4. Write an essay in which you give at least four specific illustrations to support one of the following topics:
   a. In spite of efforts to abolish cheating, it still occurs on our campus.
   b. Photography is an expensive hobby.
   c. Collecting _____ satisfies my need for accumulating things.
   d. Old descriptions of my family do not reflect the present situation.

5. Using the composite picture of a workaholic (p. 148) as a model, write an essay. Possible topics:

   The typical freshman
   Studyholics
   Partyboys/partygirls
   The typical part-time worker
   The sports nut
   The hobbyist
   The video game addict

6. Write an essay in which you give a representative picture of a typical place or event. Suggestions:

   Amusement parks
   Recreation on campus
   Decorations in my dorm/rooming house/apartment complex
   The use of cosmetics in the 1980s

DEFINITION

*A*ny example of how you intend to use a word or phrase can be called a *definition*. If you clarify a usage which is common or customary, as in dictionary definitions, you give what is called a *reported definition*. The reported definition of *follower* is someone who believes (or follows) another's creed, doctrine, or teachings. If, on the other hand, you give the term a special usage in the context of your own discussion, you have created a *stipulative definition.* Tom, the student who classified boys as *leaders, followers,* and *obstructionists* (see pp. 136–138), stipulated his use of *followers* to mean *those boys attending summer camp who do what the leader expects, but who seldom act on their own initiative.*

It is often necessary to define terms beyond a one-sentence definition. Abstract terms, for example, require more attention. Sometimes you may want to deal with traditional ideas in a different way. Or you may wish to take a special view of a subject — and will then need to clarify your terms. So used, definition becomes one of the major methods of developing a subject, and can even be a full-length paper, if you find that the subject is large enough to warrant that much space. *Definition* can be both a method of developing a subject and a subject itself.

Consider this paragraph:

> Mysteries' are about *understanding;* thrillers are about *winning.* In a mystery you are never really sure who the villain is or what he is up to until the end of the book (and sometimes not even then if you have not read carefully). In a thriller you usually know what the villain wants and how he plans to get it. Often you know perfectly well how the story will end — Germany will lose World War II, de Gaulle will not be assassinated, New York will not be destroyed by the nuclear device in the closet in the Pan Am Building. The tension comes from trying to figure out how the hero will avert disaster and survive. The task of the mystery-writer is to make you share a detective's curiosity, whereas the thriller-writer must make you share a hero's fear. — Ken Follett, "A Moscow Mystery"

In this paragraph, we find many of the typical characteristics and uses of definition:

1. Definition works in a context of an event, situation, problem, etc. Ken Follett, in his book review of a mystery novel, clarifies his position on the differences between a mystery and a thriller in order to make his review more persuasive.

2. Definition clarifies an ambiguous situation by explaining the key term (or terms) your essay is based on. You ordinarily define in order to support a thesis convincingly and to get your reader to see the point you are making. In the article from which the paragraph is taken, Follett adopts the role of a book reviewer who tries to persuade his readers that this book is, indeed, a mystery novel, not a thriller, as the book's publishers have advertised it.

3. Definition explains, limits, and specifies. The rest of this section shows you how this is done.

4. Definition is a part of the writer's attempt to give a truthful account of what a thing, act, or idea is really like. Defining is another strategy for getting at the truth.

Techniques of Defining

Now that you know something about definition, here are five practical techniques for getting the ordinary jobs of defining done. We will keep our discussion of each quite brief. All of them could be expanded by adding more examples and details.

Definition by Classification (Logical Definition)
In defining by classification, you put the term to be defined in its *class* (of things, people, activities, or ideas). Then you explain how the term *differs* from other terms in the same class. Examples:

Term	Class	Differences
Epic [is]	narrative poetry	"of exalted style, celebrating heroic adventures, mythical or historical, in poems of considerable length." — *Oxford Companion to Classical Literature*
Bucket [is]	a domestic carrying utensil	deep and round, with a curved handle that fits into the hand, used for carrying fluids, especially water or milk.
Liberty [is]	a human condition, mainly political and mainly negative	that has to do with those freedoms that are neither social, nor religious, nor private; it consists simply of being let alone by the people who have the temporary powers of government.

For logical definitions to be useful, neither class nor differences should be too broadly stated. The class for epic is *narrative poetry,* not simply *poetry.* The class for bucket is *domestic carrying utensil,* not just *domestic utensil* or *carrying utensil.* The list of differences should be complete enough so that the term is clearly distinguished from other terms.

Definition by Negation
This method of definition explains what something is not. A *bucket* is not a "scoop." *Cool* is not "hot." *Liberty* does not mean "license." *Education* has little to do with "training." Negative definitions are useful because they allow you to narrow your general area of definition. You can use them at the beginning of an extended definition to cut out areas of meaning you do not want to deal with, as the student-writer does in this definition of the slang term *rhubarb:*

Anyone who has ever attended a major league baseball game knows what a *rhubarb* is. For those of you who are not sports fans, you must understand that a rhubarb is not the plant from the buckwheat family. Neither is it the stalk of the pie plant from which your grandmother made sauce or pastries. Instead, it is a term used to describe the heated discussion that occurs between a baseball player (or the manager) and the umpire over a close call in baseball.

Definition by Illustration or Example

You can sometimes employ, implicitly or explicitly, *illustration* or *example* to aid in your definition. That is, you can define a thing by giving an example of it. What is an epic poem? *The Iliad, The Odyssey,* and *Paradise Lost* are examples. What do I mean by "a great baseball player"? I mean someone like Joe DiMaggio or Fernando Valenzuela. Defining by illustration or example gives you a simple but incomplete meaning; consequently, you should use this method with at least one of the others.

Definition by Synonym

There are no perfect synonyms. Every word is at least slightly different from every other word. But it is possible to define a word by using another word that is similar in meaning. Examples: A *herald* is a "forerunner." *Honor,* in various senses, may be "homage," "reverence," or "deference." *Cool* may mean "composed," "collected," "unruffled," "nonchalant," "unfriendly," or "not warm." Like defining by illustration or example, this is a specialized approach that you should ordinarily use with at least one of the other methods.

Definition by Operation

You define by operation when you state what something does or how it works: A bucket is a round, deep container, hung from a curved handle, that is used for carrying water, milk, or other materials. Liberty allows one to say or do what he pleases without injuring others. Education is an attempt to discipline the mind so that it can act intelligently on its own.

If sufficiently detailed, the operational definition is valuable because it gives you a practical check on the reality or truth behind a definition. For example, the word *traitor* has been defined as "someone who deserts his country." This is a limited operational definition. But the definition does not take into account the possibility that one's country might be, like certain dictatorships, deserving of desertion. This last idea gives us an *operational check* on the definition of *traitor* and allows us to add a clause to the definition: A traitor "is someone who deserts his country when his country both needs and deserves his allegiance." Observe that the added clause is itself operational. If someone does not accept our operational check on the definition of *traitor,* we can ask him to provide his own check, and then we can argue the matter with him.

Avoiding Errors in Defining

Many errors are caused by the writer's not limiting a definition sufficiently. Consider this definition, which is both logical and operational: "A belt is a thing that a man wears around his waist to keep his trousers up." As a class, *thing* is not limited enough, for it does not take into account what sort of "thing" a belt may be. One can hold up his pants with rope, but that fact does not make the rope a belt. On the other hand, the rest of the definition is too limited because it does not take into account that women often wear belts to hold up "trousers" and that belts have many other uses. The process of limiting in the logical definition should be done in two steps — first limit the *class,* then limit the *differences.*

Perhaps the commonest errors in defining are made by writers who do not realize that their definitions must fit reality. The final question to ask yourself is: Am I telling the truth about this word? If you define *monarchy* as a "contemporary government ruled by a king for his own selfish purposes," you are in danger of being untruthful; for this definition would fit badly, to give only one example, the English constitutional monarchy. The writer who defined *individualism* as "the need of every person to be honored by others" not only blurred the meaning of *individualism* but also stated an untruth about the nature of an important idea. If a student defines *fraternity* epigrammatically as "a snob co-op," is he really being truthful about the fraternities on his campus and about fraternity life in general? The fraternity man may answer that the definition does not fit fraternity life as he knows it, that the definition is not "true." This does not mean that the point is unarguable; it means rather that the students are going to have to agree on the reality behind their definitions before they can get anywhere with their debate.

Observe how a student used a variety of techniques of defining to help her explain the term *ad-lib:*

Introduction	[1]There is nothing more frightening to the amateur in the theater — at least to me — than to forget my lines. After weeks of rehearsal, with my lines seemingly embedded forever in my subconscious, I cannot conceive of forgetting them. However, all actors occasionally forget a line. Then what
Definition by classification	they do is to think up another one, called an *ad-lib.* An ad-lib is a made-up response to a cue when the actor has forgotten

Definition by negation

the playwright's words. It is not part of the script. Ad-libbing requires instant extemporizing—or improvising. The word comes from the Latin *ad libitum,* which means "as one pleases." An actor usually does not "please" to forget a line, but if one is clever the made-up lines will please the other members of the cast who may be waiting for their cues.

Definition by operation

²When I realize I have forgotten a line, my mind races frantically over the lines I *do* know. If I can't remember, I think of a replacement which fits the context of the scene. All of this activity is carried out in the space of about five seconds, although it may seem ten or twenty times longer to the actor. In the meantime, most of the audience may be totally oblivious to what is going on, especially if the actors are cool about the situation.

³For the amateur, the situation is terrifying. I break out in a cold sweat, the silence is interminable, and the stage lights blinding. I feel dizzy. The other actors are in a panic, also. They try to concentrate on the forgotten line in the hope that they can transmit it by mental telepathy. When the actor finally ad-libs, everyone heaves a sigh of relief and the play continues smoothly until another actor drops a line.

Definition by example

⁴The ad-lib requires a certain amount of creativity. Other actors may interject an ad-lib to cover for the one who has forgotten the line. It may also be used when someone has forgotten to enter. The actor who is on stage alone may say something mundane such as, "I wonder where John is?" or "John must be late," or "Perhaps John didn't receive my invitation."

⁵The ad-lib is an important part of performance. Actors must be trained to make up lines in order to fill those gaps that inevitably will occur when a group of amateurs get on stage to play someone else's speeches.

Some Final Suggestions for Defining

In most instances, you will use definition in one of two ways. In the first way, you define a term at the beginning of a paper and then go on to develop your ideas by different methods. In the second, you devote much of your paper to an extended definition, part of which may actually supply your thesis. Sometimes you will need to combine these two ways.

Common to both of them are certain useful practices you should follow:

1. If a term you use is likely to cause confusion, define it when you first use it. If the term is important to your theme and its thesis, define it in the introduction. Don't make your reader guess at what you mean by a particular word or phrase.

2. Look to your dictionary for help, but don't use it as a crutch. Do not merely quote dictionary definitions because they are easy to copy into a paper. Before using them, make sure that they apply to your paper and to the situation you are discussing.

3. Understand the techniques of defining and how they work. Keep in mind, for example, that defining by negation is particularly useful for cutting out inapplicable areas of word meanings.

4. Make your definitions reasonably complete by using as many techniques of defining as are necessary. Remember that the techniques work very well in combination.

5. Run an "operational check" on your definition. Be sure that the definition fits reality — that it is *true*.

Most of your defining will be rather informal. Perhaps for many papers you will need no more than a few words in the first or second paragraph stating how you are using a particular word or phrase. For example: "By *teachers' union* I mean an organization similar to a trade union in which the workers organize to protect their economic interests."

WRITING AND REVISING A DEFINITION PAPER (AN EXAMPLE)

After she had been studying human behavior in her psychology 101 course, Jenine wrote some comments about *competition* in her journal.

Competition is a common form of aggression. Competitiveness usually exists between two or more people. It is the basis for all of our games and sports. All sports pit one or many persons against one or many other persons. Some sports also produce competition against oneself. Runners, bikers, and swimmers attempt to better their own scores, times, or distances. Competition may also be found in more subtle forms. For example, students strive to better their grades or, more importantly to achieve better grades than their peers. Many students try to "stick" their teachers by getting high grades. This seems to be a healthy outlet for competitive aggression. In general, we all strive to exceed others in our social or age group in whatever way possible. Competitiveness, therefore, while not the most obvious, is the most common form of aggression, because most everything we do is an attempt to know more, have more, or do more in school, business, and sports, respectively.

Therefore, aggression, in these forms, and its many others too numerous to mention here, seems to be the greatest facet of human nature. All of our modern problems, from the arms race to the starving Cambodians, have aggression at their roots. This may be debated, as indeed it will be. But this, I feel is positively fundamental, if I know anything about human nature.

Rereading her journal, Jenine wasn't happy with what she wrote. For one thing, she didn't limit her definition well enough. It is true that she could define *competition* as "a common form of aggression," but she saw that she hadn't distinguished *competitive aggression* and other kinds of *aggression.* So she made some notes:

> *Competition* is *good aggression* unless it gets out of hand. I talk a lot about competition in sports, but I really don't show how the rules of sports dictate a "healthy outlet for competitive aggression." I must get some examples to prove that point.

Jenine continued an analysis of her journal entry, noting how many things she had omitted. When she was through she had two pages of ideas from which she planned and wrote a paper.

DEFINITION OF COMPETITION

[1]Competition is a form of aggression, but aggression controlled and channelled—not antisocial, in other words. We think of pure aggression as being one-sided and anti-social: people band together and attack someone else, who may or may not deserve the attack. The attack itself may be one of several kinds, from the merely verbal to full-scale war.

[2]Unlike pure aggression, competition adds a second (and balancing) side to the human equation, so that the forces of aggression are more or less equalized and each side has rights. These rights are formalized in "rules of play," which may be written down in books or simply agreed on when the competition starts. In vacant lots, you will hear young children shout: "That tree is second base. This bare spot will be home plate." And: "Any ball hit into the street is a double." As play begins, shouts of "NO FAIR!" tell us that the agreed-upon rules of aggressive play have been violated by someone.

[3]In addition, competitions are usually made for a reason apart from mere aggression, especially for a prize. And there are many kinds of prizes. You can win the game, lead the league in batting, get the highest pass-completion average in the conference, become the best chess player north of Division Street, win an encyclopedia, be first in your class and graduate *cum laude.*

⁴Yet despite all this, the competitive person is still driven to a great extent by aggression. Indeed if he is not, he may not be successfully competitive. Something burns within the competitive person. Like tennis star Chris Evert Lloyd, the true competitor never gives up. (Lloyd is a particularly good example because she is so controlled and polite — her aggression, while masked by good manners and tact, is evident in her success; she runs her opponents ragged with well-placed shots.)

⁵What burns most in the competitive person is a fanatical desire to win. I knew a checkers champion who wanted to win so badly that when he lost he threw up. My father was so naturally competitive that if his neighbor was mowing his lawn at the same time Dad was mowing his, Dad would try to finish first — to win at lawn mowing. Dad quit playing softball in his late forties because he could no longer "win" in his own eyes, meaning he thought that he could not play aggressively enough to compete.

⁶It is curious to watch how many competitive people "give off" aggressive signals in almost every direction. When they drive they shout at other drivers. In school, they are the ones who stop you in the hall after a quiz is returned to utter the cliché: "Whatja get?" You tell them. Then they say: "Oh, *I* did better than that!" The expensive car is still a major signal of successful aggression. It means: "I won in the competition of the business world, and this Cadillac (or Mercedes or whatever) is my prize."

⁷Why do we accept competitiveness in men and women? Possibly for the very reason that its aggressiveness is controlled and channelled in fairly positive ways. Competition in business provides opportunity and jobs for workers. Competition in sports and films provides entertainment. Only when the aggressive instinct gets out of hand, when individuals no longer agree to play by certain rules, whether written or not, do we worry about what happens when human beings have that sharp "competitive edge."

PRACTICE

Discussion

1. For class discussion, read the second draft of Jenine's paper, and answer the following questions:
   a. Jenine followed the conventions for good defining by classifying *competition* as a form of *aggression*. Next, she limited her use of the term *aggression* to particular kinds. For instance in paragraph one, she calls *competition* "controlled aggression." Identify other limits she has placed on her use of *aggression* in the context of her definition. Discuss the effectiveness of these limits.
   b. Compare the use of examples in her journal entry and in her final paper.

c. Study the journal entry in relation to the final draft. Make a list of ways she improved her thinking about the term *competition*.

2. Study the following definitions. For class discussion, answer the following questions:

a. Which method(s) of defining was used in each of the definitions below?

b. Evaluate the definition as a subject for an extended paper.

c. Evaluate the use of each definition in relation to another strategy. For example, in what kind of paper would a definition of *sunburn* be necessary or useful?

TAXES

"Tax time" means, basically, "touching time." The word "tax" comes from the Latin *taxare*, "to value by handling," which in turn derives from *tangere*, "to touch." A deceptively gentle etymology, since most of us are likely to feel not so much "touched" as rather roughly handled by the Internal Revenue Service. To add verbal insult to financial injury, we are taxed most heavily upon such things as income from capital, things defined as "intangibles." The word "intangible" also derives from *tangere*, and means "untouchable." Why, then, should our intangible assets be the most heavily taxed, our "untouchables" the most rudely "touched"? A sorry state of affairs, etymologically. — *Henry Steele Commager*

MEETINGS

. . . I define "meeting" as a prearranged, formal gathering of five people or more. I don't count one person dropping into my office. I don't count idle chatter in the hallway. I don't count being summoned to a colleague's desk to clear up a disputed point. — *Bob Greene*

DUNKING

Dunking is the art of dipping some kind of bread (or toast or sweet roll) into a cup of coffee or tea. What makes dunking an art is the finesse that the truly adept dunkers use. They pick up a piece of bread by the tip of the fingers. They lightly dip one end of this bread into the liquid, holding it there until it absorbs some of the liquid. Then they shake the excess liquid off the bread and pop it into their mouths without losing a drop or missing a beat.

SUNBURN

The first sign of damage is sunburn, which dermatologists define as an injury of the blood vessels. — *Barbara Brotman*

TECHNOLOGY

Technology is simply the knack of doing things with objects that are not part of your body. If you try to crack a nut with your teeth, you are being natural. If you hit the nut with a rock, you are employing technology. —*Advertisement,* courtesy of *Gould, Inc.*

GUILT

Guilt is hostility turned inward. Cult members often feel guilty about not having achieved something, or they make others feel guilty about not having helped them achieve their Garden of Edens. Cults provide their members with an opportunity to be hostile in a way they find acceptable. —*Milton Kanter*

DRESSAGE

In French, *dresser* means to teach, school, or to train, and *dressage* is an exacting discipline that harmoniously synchronizes the horse's physical and mental abilities to create an obedient and graceful mount. —*Elizabeth Heilman*

3. Using the classification method of defining, fill in the blanks with the appropriate term in the following chart:

Object or thing	Category or class	Example or instance or specific detail
car		
mausoleum		
mystery		
sentence		
baseball		
gloomy		
computer		
capitalism		

4. For class discussion write a brief analysis of each definition given below. What are the techniques of defining being used? Do you see any errors in defining? How would you improve and rewrite any definition that you consider weak or unrealistic? (You may wish to check your dictionary as you go along.)

a. *Shortening* is something you put in a cake to make it better.

b. *Marriage* is the ceremony of uniting two people in holy wedlock.

c. A *dog* is a canine.

d. *Integration* is the getting of people together for political freedom.

e. A *thermocouple* is a temperature-sensing instrument made of two dissimilar metals.

f. *Tree-skiing* is a dangerous and exciting winter sport. It is not cross-country, slalom, or downhill skiing, and it is not the sport of skiing on two trees. Some people call it *woods winding* or *trailing*.

g. A book is *obscene* if it is totally without redeeming social importance and appeals entirely to the reader's prurient interest.

h. When we come to accurate measurement, we find that the word "hard" has dozens of slightly different meanings. The most usual test of hardness in steels is that of Brinell. A very hard steel ball of 10 millimetres diameter is pressed onto a steel plate for 30 seconds with a load of 3 tons. The hardness number decreases with the depth of the indentation. —J. B. S. Haldane, *A Banned Broadcast and Other Essays*

i. [What is meant by *life*? A thing is *alive* when] it does a minimum of four things: it eats "foreign" substances which differ to a greater or lesser degree from its own body tissue. Then it "digests" these substances, and assimilates them into its body, which produces some waste material that is ejected. Furthermore, it "grows": it increases in size and bulk up to a certain point, which is different for different life forms. Finally, it "propagates": it produces, or reproduces, its own kind. —Willy Ley, "Life on Other Planets"

j. The idea that, since democracy is defective, it ought to be abolished, is an example of the commonest error in political philosophy, which I call "utopianism." By "utopianism" I mean the idea that there is a perfect constitution, and politics could be perfect. The last of our democratic duties which I shall mention is to avoid utopianism. Politics are and always will be a creaking, groaning, lumbering, tottering wagon of wretched make-shifts and sad compromises and anxious guesses; and political maturity consists in knowing this in your bones. —Richard Robinson, *An Atheist's Values*

Writing

1. Below is a statement that contains definitions and a thesis. Write a response to it; agree or disagree with the writer wholly or in part. Include your own thesis and definitions in your response. Use as many of the techniques of defining as you think are necessary.

[1]. . . Our appetite for Getting There First has helped us to greatness as a Nation, but it also tempts us into national habits which threaten to pull us apart.

[2]An everyday example is the desperate quest for TV programs that are "relevant." But what people call "relevance" is not really that at all. What they are talking about most of the time is not the relevant but the topical.

[3]*Topical* (from the Greek word "topos" for place) means that which is special to some particular place or time. "Topics of the Day" are the events which, having just happened, are peculiar to that day. We like to read or hear about them because they remind us that we are alive, that there is something special to our lifetime. The topical reinforces our mood with an exclamation point, but does not enlarge or illuminate. Hear this! See that! That's what we say when we point to something topical. On TV, characteristic statements of the topical are the video-taped clips of the day's events offered staccato on the news. The topical event—an earthquake, an airplane hijacking, a hotel fire of an assassination—is announced and diffused, but seldom explained at the time.

[4]The *relevant* is something quite different. "Relevant" comes from the Latin "relevans," which means lifting or raising. To show the relevance of something is to lift it above the current of daily topics, to connect it with distant events and larger issues. The search for relevance is a search for connections that don't at first meet the eye, that will be just as valid—and even more interesting—tomorrow and the day after.

[5]A topical fact becomes every moment less newsworthy. But a historical event is always growing in historical significance. The American Revolution became more interesting after the French Revolution, and both became still more so after the Russian Revolution and after the Chinese Revolution and after President Nixon's visit to Communist China. . . .

[6]What we need are fewer talk shows, fewer interviews and discussions, fewer odd-ball quizzes, fewer celebrity say-so's. And fewer newscasts.

[7]We need programs that bring us less of the "up-to-the-minute" stuff, which every passing minute makes obsolete, and more knowledge. Fewer "situation comedies" and situation tragedies, but more comedy and more tragedy. Fewer reports of today's catastrophe, fewer clichés of today's "burning issues" and deeper visual documentation.

[8]In a word, what we need are more programs about something, and

fewer programs about everything. More programs about how something really happened, how the world has changed and is changing. More about people who do things and make things, and how they're done and made, and less about people who say the kooky and do the ridiculous.

[9]TV will help bring us together — by shared knowledge and common understanding. TV will then be less a solvent and more a cement in our American community. That is what we have tried to offer in "Getting There First." — Daniel J. Boorstin, "Too Much Too Soon."

2. Below is J. Frank Dobie's operational definition of *bandana*. In it he answers the question: What does a cowboy use a bandana for? Study his techniques, then write a short operational definition of one of the following:

   a. A woman's purse, a student's book pack, or a teacher's briefcase
   b. A gardener's trowel or a backyard chef's apron
   c. A football player's helmet, a catcher's mask, or a bicyclist's headgear
   d. A dancer's shoes, a power weight-lifter's belt, or a gymnast's mat

Many a cowboy has spread his bandana, perhaps none too clean itself, over dirty, muddy water and used it as a strainer to drink through; sometimes he used it as a cup towel, which he called a "drying rag." If the bandana was dirty, it was probably not so dirty as the other apparel of the cowboy, for when he came to a hole of water, he was wont to dismount and wash out his handkerchief, letting it dry while he rode along, holding it in his hand or spread over his hat. Often he wore it under his hat in order to help keep his head cool. At other times, in the face of a fierce gale, he used it to tie down his hat. The bandana made a good sling for a broken arm; it made a good bandage for a blood wound. Early Irish settlers on the Nueces River used to believe that a bandana handkerchief that had been worn by a drowned man would, if cast into a stream above a sunken body, float until it came over the body and then sink, thus locating it. Many a cowboy out on the lonely plains has been buried with a clean bandana spread over his face to keep the dirt, or the coarse blanket on which the dirt was poured, from touching it. The bandana has been used to hang men with. Rustlers used to "wave" strangers around with it, as a warning against nearer approach, though the hat was more commonly used for signaling. Like the Mexican sombrero or the four gallon Stetson, the bandana could not be made too large. When the cowboys of the West make their final parade on the grassy shores of Paradise, the guidon that leads them should be a bandana handkerchief. It deserves to be called the flag of the range country.

3. Definition skills are especially important when you must write a discussion of something that you know well but your reader does not. For instance, if you are writing a proposal for insulating a house, you will have to define *loose-fill, foam,* and *blanket* insulation methods so that the owner will know what the choices are.

   Pick a subject you know fairly well and write a paper on it in which you define terms that the ordinary reader may not be familiar with—your subject can be anything from clarinet playing to fixing engines. Pick a stance, and convince your reader to do or believe something. At the beginning, define any terms necessary to your thesis.

4. Choose one of the following terms (or pick your own). Define the term in as many ways as possible, using the methods described on pp. 157–159. Choose a subject that you have some feelings about or some experience with so that you can define by a long narrative example. You might like to expand on the definitions provided in the discussion question 1, p. 167. Group your definitions, develop a thesis, and write an extended definition paper.

   home
   pond
   anger
   noun
   ingratitude
   tennis
   yellow
   surgeon
   hypnotism

CHAPTER 9

COMPARISON AND CONTRAST, ANALOGY

COMPARISON — CONTRAST

Comparing means "showing likenesses"; *contrasting,* "showing differences." Classification (or grouping) is an important step in comparison and contrast because, when you classify, you usually group pieces of information by the principle of similarity. However, when you compare and contrast you identify those qualities that distinguish members of a class from each other by their individual differences. Therefore, when you make a comparison and contrast, you show *likenesses* and *differences* between two or more (but usually only two) persons, ideas, actions, things, or classes — *for the purpose of making a point.* We emphasize "making a point" because you customarily employ the strategy of comparison and contrast to convince the reader of an idea you have — that A is better than B; more interesting than B; more useful than B; and so on. You may show the likenesses or the differences between two things at the paragraph level or in a longer paper.

Planning a Comparison and Contrast

For several reasons, a comparison and contrast requires particularly strong control of your point and organization. First, you usually have more material to work with—two subject areas instead of the customary one. Consequently, you should rigorously narrow your point—or thesis—for a longer comparison and contrast so that you can cover the subjects in the number of words you have allotted. Next, you have to know a good deal about both subjects. Finally, your comparison and contrast must do more than just show similarities or likenesses. This is a trap that students often fall into. They describe the two subject areas, giving plenty of detail for both but omitting the point, thus leaving the reader wondering why the paper was written in the first place.

Note how a student uses comparison and contrast for the purpose of making a decision, and thereby communicating his *point*. His comparison and contrast is not only useful for himself but also for a reader who might be interested in learning about motorcycles and mopeds.

MOTORCYCLES AND MOPEDS

Purpose for comparison/contrast

[1]When I go back to school next semester, I will need a more reliable means of transportation than buses, bicycles or friends' cars. So I'm going to buy a vehicle which will take me when and where I want to go. After examining the various advantages and disadvantages of cars, buses, taxicabs, airplanes, trains, and submarines, I have found that either a motorcycle or a moped will best suit my need for an inexpensive and convenient means of transportation. The problem is to find out which one is better suited for me.

First consideration: cost

[2]My first problem in considering a means of transportation is its cost, including the initial investment, insurance, and gas. The lowest starting price for a new motorcycle is usually around $600, which is definitely out of my price range at the moment. On the other hand, I find that new mopeds, priced at around $320, are more nearly what I can afford. Since drivers of motorcycles in my state are required to carry liability insurance, I would have to pay an additional $45 to $50 if I bought a motorcycle. In my state mopeds can be driven without liability insurance.

[3]I will have to pay for my own gas, which means that I will need a vehicle that will run on the least amount of gas possible. Motorcycles average 50 to 75 mpg, while a moped can get from 80 to 150 mpg.

*Second
consideration:
speed*

[4]I do not need a vehicle capable of high speeds. What I want is one that can keep up with city traffic, which usually travels (on the streets I wish to use) between 20 and 30 mph. Motorcycles have large motors with complicated transmissions that allow them to travel at speeds of at least 45 to 50 mph. Mopeds run on a simple two-horsepower motor. The state law limits them to a maximum speed of 25 to 35 mph, which is fast enough for me.

*Third
consideration:
parking*

[5]Since parking places are hard to find in the university lots, the motorcycle would be less convenient than a moped because I can park a moped in a bicycle rack. Furthermore, I can ride the moped on the university bicycle paths. For getting to and from classes easily, the moped would definitely be more convenient than the motorcycle. Another convenience of the moped is that in my state I don't need a special license, an automobile license being adequate.

*Result: Moped is
better choice*

[6]After comparing the motorcycle and the moped as a means of inexpensive and convenient transportation, I think that the moped better suits my needs. I would advise any student in my position to buy one instead of a motorcycle.

The writer of the essay on motorcycles and mopeds has strong control of his thesis and organization. He makes the comparison-contrast in order to consider his need for better transportation, and that purpose is made clear. Note that he does not try to include irrelevant items such as bicycles and automobiles. He covers both items under consideration completely so that the paper is not primarily about mopeds even though that vehicle is his final choice. His transitional devices (such as *on the other hand* and *furthermore*) help the reader to follow the organization of the material.

PRACTICE

Discussion
Read the following list of contrasts between highbrows and lowbrows. Then answer the questions for class discussion.

Highbrows vs. lowbrows

It is increasingly difficult to distinguish a highbrow from a lowbrow, but there are a few ways of determining who's who.

A highbrow is someone who:

Calls a movie a *film*.

Reads more than just the cartoons in the *New Yorker*.

Calls spaghetti *pasta*.

Knows that the Lone Ranger's theme is the "William Tell Overture."

Knew Mozart's middle name before it became a movie.

Thinks Perrier tastes good.

Recognizes satire when he or she sees it.

Avoids the sports and leisure category in Trivial Pursuit.

Once wrote a term paper on the symbolism in "Jonathan Livingston Seagull."

Thinks a canopy is a bite-size sandwich without crusts.

Understood "Lucid Moments." (local reference)

Likes to use foreign phrases such as "tete-a-tete" and "menage a trois."

Listens to music without lyrics.

Calls food *cuisine*.

Thinks "chow" means goodbye.

Thinks Bruce Sutter is a line of men's wear.

Needs an owner's manual to change a flat tire.

Cannot understand why everyone doesn't own a computer.

Could once recite the entire Greek alphabet.

Can picture himself or herself in a magazine ad for DeWar's scotch.

A lowbrow is someone who:

Thinks mud wrestling is a sport.

Calls a movie a *flick*.

Reads *People* magazine when not standing in a grocery line.

Has an *Enquir*ing mind.

Believes the letters to *Penthouse* are real.

Thinks Pavarotti comes in a can.

Tunes his car's engine even if he can afford to pay someone else to do it.

Has never heard of Franz Kafka.

Thinks a *canape* is the awning of a mobile home.

Avoids the art and literature category in Trivial Pursuit.

Thinks "Amadeus" was dull.

Watches "Wheel of Fortune."

Gets into arguments over which is better, Ford or Chevy.

Stood in line to see "Rambo."

Calls food *grub*.

Idolizes Clint Eastwood.

Is intimidated by books that double as doorstops.

Thinks TV car-chase scenes are exciting.

Knows 12 ways to open a beer bottle without an opener.

Cannot figure out any reason for owning a computer.

Thinks pickled eggs are a delicacy.

Thinks a crouton is someone with a low IQ.

—Jeff Kunerth

1. Why is "Highbrows vs. Lowbrows" not a "full" contrast and comparison?

2. In the list of differences between *highbrows* and *lowbrows,* you will find that the author has listed their differing attitudes toward *the arts, food, sports,* and *cars.* Using those headings (or other headings that you find in the list), develop meaningful topics to use in a comparison and contrast paper.

3. Define what you believe the author means by *highbrow* and *lowbrow.*

4. Since the list includes only *differences,* how would you go about including *similarities?*

Writing
Using your notes from the *Discussion* questions above, develop a preliminary thesis for a *comparison and contrast* paper. Write the paper. You may wish to use different examples than those listed, particularly if you have your own ideas about *lowbrows* and *highbrows.*

ORGANIZING COMPARISON AND CONTRAST

*T*here are three basic methods of organizing *comparison and contrast*. In the "block" method, you first discuss one item thoroughly, then go on to the second, giving about equal space to each. In the second method, you list all the similarities between the two items, then all the differences. In the third "point-by-point" method, you discuss one point or feature of each item, then go on to the next, and so on. The following lists show how the three methods are organized. A and B stand for the two items being compared.

Block	*Similarities-Differences*	*Point-by-Point*
1. introduce subject	introduce subject	introduce subject
2. discuss A (transition)	discuss similarities between A and B (transition)	discuss point 1 of A and B (transition)
3. discuss B	discuss differences between A and B	discuss point 2 of A and B
4. conclude	conclude	conclude

In the three models on the following pages, you will see how the writers used these methods for organizing their writing. The second and third examples are student essays.

BLOCK METHOD

Introduction [1]I think there's something wrong here, but I can't exactly put my finger on it. I recently bought quantities of two fluids.

Discussion of A
(gasoline) [2]The first fluid was gasoline. Gasoline is derived from crude oil, which is found deep under the ground in remote sections of the earth. Enormous amounts of money are
1. Source risked in the search for oil. Once it's found, a great deal more money is expended to extract it from the earth, to ship it to distant refineries, to refine it, to ship it via pipeline to regional distribution points, to store it, to deliver it to retail outlets and then to make it available to the retail consumer. . . .

2. Supply [3]As far as we know, the earth's supply of crude oil is limited. Once it's gone, it's gone. There may be other substances fermenting under the soil that will prove of value to future civilizations, but for the here and now our oil supplies are finite. . . .

Discussion of B
(soda pop)

[4]The other fluid was sweetened, carbonated water, infused with artificial fruit flavoring. Some call it soda pop. It's made right here in town. As far as we know, the raw materials exist in unlimited supply. Most of it falls from the heavens at regular intervals. . . .

1. Source

2. Supply

[5]Almost all of it, by processes chemical and natural, will recycle back into the system. It will become sewage, will cleanse itself, will evaporate and will rain down again from the heavens at some undetermined time and place. It will come back. We can't really get rid of it. . . .

Conclusion
Thesis

[6]When you further consider that roughly a third of the cost of gasoline is taxes, that means that soda pop costs almost three times as much per gallon as does gasoline.
—Robert Rosefsky, *Chicago Daily News*

SIMILARITIES-DIFFERENCES METHOD

Introduction

[1]What was it like for a girl to be brought up by two bachelors? When I was ten, my mother (a widow) died, and I had no one to look after me except her two brothers, Arthur and Alan. Both were in their early forties at the time. Arthur had been married once, long ago, and his wife had left him; Alan had never married and was, people said, a woman hater. Being brothers, they had several traits in common; but they were also very different. And that fact showed up in their treatment of me.

Thesis implied

Similarities between
A (Alan) and
B (Arthur)

[2]For instance, neither of them wanted me to work while I was going to high school. They were brought up to believe that a woman's place is in the home or, at least, in the trailer at the edge of town where we all lived. When they found out I took a job at a local drive-in, Alan bawled me out and made me quit, while Arthur, the more sociable of the two, made a personal visit to the manager to give him hell for hiring such a young kid. Both of them could not understand why I could not get by on the $5.00 a week they gave me for spending money. And besides, they said that the job was interfering with my "schooling."

1. Attitude toward
work

2. Attitude toward
school

[3]School was another thing they were concerned about, and probably with good reason. They always wanted to see my grade reports, although they were never quite sure when they were issued. And I tried to keep them in the dark about that as much as possible. Arthur, who thought he was better educated than Alan, always wanted to help me with my homework. Just to get him off my back, I sometimes let him. About the only thing he seemed to remember from his school days were the names of the capital cities of all the states, which, of course, did not help me much. Alan was always concerned with long-term results, continually asking, "Are

you going to pass this term?" "Are you going to graduate?" I think he was a little surprised when I did. But, if it had not been for their concern, I probably would not have made it past my junior year.

Differences between A and B

1. Attitude toward dating

[4]But in other matters involving me, they had quite different attitudes. Alan was very protective of me as far as boys and dating were concerned. Arthur, however, encouraged me to date because he wanted me to have a good time while I was young. Alan treated me like a young Farrah Fawcett-Majors who was luring every male for miles around. When male friends would stop by, he would always grill them as if they were sex maniacs, while Arthur offered them a beer and talked sports, always managing to put in a good word for his niece. Alan was so protective that he sometimes would drive me to parties or dances, and sit outside a teen den in his pickup, waiting until I came out after the last song died away.

2. Attitude toward drinking

[5]Their concern for me also showed itself in their attitude toward drinking. Alan did not drink much, but Arthur was an alcoholic. He not only drank, he liked other people drinking. He made me my first salty dog. He taught me that any sort of sweet stuff with bourbon was the devil's idea. Alan disapproved greatly of all this, But he was incapable of attacking his own brother, who could charm people with ease. Alan would, when I was seventeen, take a beer out of my hand if I was drinking one—only one!—with Arthur, and pour it down the sink. After Alan had gone to bed, Arthur would go to the refrigerator and get me another one. I was never more than mildly interested in alcohol, however; the sight of Arthur drunk and sick was enough to make anyone cautious.

Conclusion

(with an ancedote that emphasizes their similarities and differences)

[6]Even though they were alike in some things and different in others, my uncles took care of me. When I graduated from high school last year, they came to the ceremony in the pickup. Alan wore his best and only suit, which had been out of style twenty years ago. Arthur was dressed like a king, and was so drunk he had to be carried out in the middle of "Pomp and Circumstance." A strange "family," but they are all I have—and many times all I need.

POINT-BY-POINT METHOD

Discussion of point 1 (research method)

A (Smith)

[1]Broadly speaking, there are two kinds of scientists—call them, as individuals, Smith and Jones. When they do research, Smith plods along through the data, meticulously noting every fact and every variation. He fills notebooks full of explanations and carefully made hypotheses. If he comes to a dead end, as so often happens to a researcher, he just stops and thinks. And thinks. And looks back over the data

and notebooks until he can find a new avenue or approach.

B (Jones)   [2]Jones, by contrast, rushes headlong into experiments, often starting them near the middle, assuming that untested hypotheses are true or that well known variables just don't matter "in this case." He does not stop to think but to dream; and it is intuition, not fact, that often seems to make him suddenly shift in mid-experiment and try a new device or technique. He will even jump to a scientific conclusion, and then work backwards seeing if the experiments and data point to a conclusion he has already tentatively arrived at.

Discussion of point 2 (writing up results)   [3]Yet when they come to write up their results, Smith and Jones will at times, inexplicably, change roles. The careful, meticulous Smith presents doubtful data as certain, weak evidence as sure. He writes in short, abrupt sentences with

A (Smith)   scarcely a *perhaps* or an *in general, we find that. . . .* Whole notebooks that carried neatly noted negative evidence are summed up in a quick phrase or dismissed as irrelevant to the thrust of his argument.

B (Jones)   [4]Jones, however, having experimented by the method of brilliant intuition, now writes in statements dotted with *it seems* and *in most cases*. In sentences four lines long, he manages to qualify, explain, elaborate. Where two tables of figures would suffice, he gives us four; where three instances of negative evidence would be one too many, he gives us six. His arguments sag after page 12; after page 23 they put one to sleep.

Thesis   [5]Is one type of scientist, in the final analysis, more effective than the other? It is impossible to say. Science is not, in the first place, a matter of certainties, as some persons believe. Rather it deals with anxious probabilities and is not a little influenced by plain luck. No matter how Smith and Jones may differ in their work and how they write it up, they may be equally successful in the end. Only time can tell, and after so much time passes, who remembers exactly how scientists performed their jobs?

WRITING AND REVISING A COMPARISON AND CONTRAST (AN EXAMPLE)

Rachel, a member of the track team, has just returned from a strenuous training session in which the coach told her, "Pain is your friend." She thinks about his statement, wondering if he is really correct. She begins freewriting:

[1]I would say that some kinds of physical pain are good for me. Note that I distinguish *physical* pain from other kinds. There is another kind of pain: mental. Mental pain is much worse than physical pain. It lasts longer, and instead of diminishing in a relatively short time like physical pain, it can eat at you for days, months, or perhaps an entire lifetime. If unresolved, it can build up and drive you mad.

[2]Mental pain hurts. It can come from any number of situations. A friend or relative may have gone, a girlfriend or boyfriend may have broken off a relationship, you may have been under a lot of stress, or a misunderstanding may have come between friends. There is a great difference between mental and physical pain—misunderstandings can cause much mental anguish and grief, but you will never hear of a "misunderstood broken leg."

[3]Coach says, "Pain is your friend." Of course, he means the physical pain caused by running. This pain while running or exercising in other ways can be your friend by telling you that you are really working. This pain should not be confused with injury, which is a definite sign that something is wrong. Injury can be caused by too much physical work, or an accident. Sometimes injury is difficult to distinguish from soreness. Soreness is another kind of pain caused by physical work. It generally occurs when you have not exercised in a while, and have just started. You may then have soreness for a few days.

[4]Mental and physical pain have different effects and are caused by different things. For me, mental pain is much more unpleasant because it can linger on, while physical pain fades relatively quickly.

Later, Rachel studies her freewriting. She is now more critical of what she wrote. She sees two problems that are reflected in her freewriting:

> She notes that she has a problem with her terms. She is satisfied with the term *training pain,* but she knows she can't compare that kind of pain with every kind of *mental pain.* Therefore, she reviews her experiences with runners and other athletes. She decides to limit *mental pain* to the *emotional pain* caused by losing, or from having to stay off the team as a result of injury.

> As a result of thinking about her terms, she sees that she needs clearer definitions of the two kinds of pain because the terms will form the basis for her *comparison and contrast.*

After she has tied down her terms, she develops a preliminary outline in which the coverage of two kinds of pain fall naturally in a block organization (see p. 67).

I.   Training pain helps to condition the body.
    A.   If the athlete trains carefully, the training pain will go away.
    B.   Training pain is not caused by an injury.

II.   Emotional pain connected with athletics affects the spirit.
    A.   Emotional pain lasts longer than training pain.
    B.   Emotional pain is connected with losing and with injury.

Rachel's stance:

> *Role:* A student member of the women's track team.
> *Audience:* Other runners and athletes who might be interested in an analysis of pain.
> *Thesis:* Emotional pain is worse for an athlete than physical pain.

ATHLETES AND PAIN

[1]Recently a few members of the women's track team were comparing notes on their aches and pains. I am not a masochist, but I think that the kind of pain that comes from training is good for me (and for other athletes) because it doesn't last long, and also conditions the body. But athletes sometimes suffer another kind of pain — the emotional pain that is nearly always related to losing or being taken off the team as a result of injury. Emotional pain can last longer than training pain and sometimes affects an athlete's self-esteem.

[2]Our track coach often says, "Pain is your best friend." Of course he means training pain — the pain caused by intense physical conditioning. This pain is my friend because it tells me that I am really working hard and getting better at my sport. For example, the first month of training for long-distance running is the most difficult. In this period, I must establish a vigorous stride that can be maintained without pain. Before I can establish that stride, I must break through a wall of pain — a physical barrier that will finally disappear if I continue to push myself beyond it. Getting over that wall can be gratifying because I know that I am not going to experience quite as much pain in the future. In my first month of training, I was preparing for the three-hundred. As I neared the two-hundred mark, the pain became excruciating. It came from inside as though something had exploded, and my legs required all the energy and concentration I could muster.

[3]However, training pain should not be confused with pain from injury. If runners are not careful to establish a schedule for running, or if they attempt long distances too soon, they will get shin splints, a bone and tendon irritation that disables runners. Any pressure on the ankles, knees, and shins will be so painful that a runner will not be able to run for weeks. Other injuries such as stress fractures, bursitis, and tendonitis will not disappear like training pain but will keep an athlete from running.

[4]Emotional pain hurts too, but it is the spirit, not the body, that suffers. And emotional pain lasts longer than training pain. Emotional pain is dif-

ferent from training pain because the discomfort isn't transmitted through the nervous system. However, emotional pain caused by disappointment or anxiety can cause an athlete anguish and grief that will affect the spirit for weeks, months, or even years.

⁵The desire to win is strong in athletes. Runners, in particular, suffer emotional pain when they lose. They usually don't have people in the stands to cheer them on, so they must depend on their own team members for emotional support. I was in a race when three of us moved neck-and-neck toward the finish tape. As I leaned for the tape, I stumbled. Lying on the track, too exhausted to get up, I learned that I had come in second, not first as I had hoped. My desire had not been enough to win. As a result of my stumble, I believed that I had let my team down because we lost the meet. My friends on the team didn't treat me differently, but I believed that I had not done my best. As a result I was disconsolate for weeks. It was only after I won the next race that my self-esteem was renewed.

⁶Suffering a physical injury which keeps athletes from competing may affect the spirit. A friend of mine broke his collarbone while training for basketball. He told me that the break caused physical pain while doing the most routine tasks: dressing, lying down, or even sneezing. But the emotional pain was the most difficult to bear. The day after he suffered his injury, he watched his team practicing in a full-court scrimmage. He said that watching his friends practice the one sport he loves more than anything else made him feel left out and abandoned. Since basketball is one of the few things he looks forward to during the year, having an injury that locked him out of the team caused him more emotional pain than physical pain.

⁷Athletes are bound to suffer pain, but they hope that it is training pain, not the pain from losing or the pain from staying off the team. An athlete's self-esteem is tied up with being part of a team and any fluctuation in the team as an entity or group influences an athlete's self-esteem.

PRACTICE

Discussion
Read the final version of "Athletes and Pain." Prepare the following questions for class discussion.

1. How well has Rachel supported the main points of her comparison and contrast? What recommendations would you make for improvements in her paper and support of her thesis?

2. List Rachel's transitions. How well do they help to advance her comparison and contrast? Could her use of transitions be improved?

3. You followed Rachel through the process of identifying her terms and developing a thesis. Now review her freewriting. Are there any points in her freewriting that could have been used in her second draft?

Writing

1. Here's the rest of the essay printed back on page 38. In it, the author discusses her experiences piloting a small plane between the East and the Midwest. What method of comparison-contrast does she use? Explain. Respond to the selection by writing a comparison-contrast paper based on similar experiences you have had.

[1]When I landed at Utica, N.Y., one recent weekend, I had been flying 7½ hours with just one fuel stop at Youngstown, Ohio, to break the journey and wash my hands. Tired, dirty, and hungry, I wanted only to tie down my Piper Tomahawk, find a motel room, and get a drink.

[2]I spotted the only vacant parking spot on the ramp and was heading for it when a Cherokee taxied past, whipped around directly in front of me, and grabbed my space. I jammed on my brakes and sat there in stupefied indignation. I've seen some pushy people on the ramp at Midway Airport, but not *that* pushy.

[3]Welcome to the surly East, home of bad manners!

[4]Because I was born in New York City and reared in Connecticut, I consider myself an expert on Eastern manners. Chicagoans often laugh derisively when I say that Midwesterners are kinder and more courteous, but a trip back East confirms my view.

[5]As I'm about to land at Lebanon, N.H., a pilot breaks in on the tower frequency—illegally—to snarl, "Someone ought to tell that Tomahawk on short final how to enter the pattern." I have made an instrument approach, and the tower has called every turn for me. (On returning to Midway after a flight to Connecticut, a friend breaks in on the ground control frequency—illegally—to say, "Welcome home, Nancy!")

[6]At Freeport, Me., home of L. L. Bean's, the mail order house, I see in a store window a T-shirt bearing the legend: "I am not a tourist. I live here, and I don't answer questions." Sometimes back East, simple incivility isn't enough; one must advertise the fact. (At Hartselle, Ala., a pilot and his wife take me in their Piper Warrior for a sight-seeing tour of their home town.)

⁷Often the air traffic controllers reflect the manners of the communities they serve. I wouldn't want to undertake an instrument flight anywhere near New York City, so notorious are the controllers there for rudeness. It can be argued that they're too busy to be polite, but Chicago controllers are just as busy and twice as courteous (a few soreheads notwithstanding).

⁸The Aurora tower people always astonish me with their easygoing competence, though on a busy weekend they may have six or eight student pilots in the pattern simultaneously, shooting touch-and-go's. If there's a pause on the frequency, I sometimes thank them after a practice session there. "You're welcome, Six Eight Gulf Whisky," they say to my departing airplane.

⁹There's a time for brusqueness when the weather is down to minimums and the clouds are full of airplanes.

¹⁰But when you finally get your bird on the ground, there's a time for good manners, too. Midwesterners understand that. Someone should tell the folks back East.

2. Pick two words or phrases that are often used in comparable ways. Write a comparison-contrast in which you show the likenesses and the differences between the meanings of the two. Suggestions:

Fashion — Style
Pathetic — Tragic
Persuasion — Force
Stink — Odor
Civil disobedience — Dissent
Amateur — Professional
Politician — Civil servant
Appetite — Hunger
Pacify — Appease
Practical — Practicable
Exercise — Drill
Movie — TV program
Blocking — Tackling
Housewife — Career woman

3. Choose two people you know well — friends or relatives. Make two separate lists, identifying all the qualities that are distinctive for *each* person. Analyze and group the characteristics that these two people share (or do not share). Draw a generalization about each group of characteristics. Develop a thesis or a point, and choose an organizational method. Write a comparison and contrast, trying to keep an appropriate balance between the two people so that you don't cover one more thoroughly than the other.

ANALOGY

An analogy is basically a comparison — ordinarily an *extended* comparison — between two things usually thought of as unlike. Here is an analogy from a student paper:

> [1]A tank truck usually holds between 4,000 and 6,000 gallons of gasoline. Depending on the tanker and the oil company, there are three to six individual compartments which hold 600 to 900 gallons of gasoline apiece. The tank that contains the compartments is elliptically shaped to distribute the pressure equally and to allow a more complete flow of air when the gasoline is delivered.
>
> [2]Until recently the only way to load a tanker was to climb up on top, where the openings to the compartments are located. You can easily picture this by visualizing six pop bottles lined up in single file on a table. A man wants to fill up bottle three, so he takes the cap off. He then inserts a small hose into the neck of the bottle and turns on a faucet which is connected to the hose.
>
> [3]A gasoline tanker is loaded in a similar way, but on a much larger scale. A man climbs on top of the tanker and opens a particular compartment by removing the cap. He then takes a hose with a four-foot metal pipe extension, about three and a half inches in diameter, and inserts the pipe down into the "bottle" (the compartment hole), which measures four inches in diameter. A pump is then turned on, allowing the gasoline to flow into the compartment.

In this analogy, an engineering student explains something relatively *unknown* (loading a tanker) by using her knowledge of something *known* (filling pop bottles). If you, the reader, think that a tanker consists of one long compartment, then the engineer's analogy is valuable and useful. If, however, you knew before reading the analogy how tankers were constructed and loaded, the analogy might not be particularly informative. That means, of course, that you should base your use of analogy on the knowledge of your audience.

All of us know many things that we can use to help a reader understand an idea better. Here a geology major helps to understand how the oil seismograph works by comparing it to shouting at a cliff wall.

Introduction

[1]For over twenty years, my father has worked on an oil seismograph crew. We all know about the big seismographs that detect and measure earthquakes. The oil seismograph is a small portable electronic instrument that detects and measures artificial earthquakes. The purpose of the instrument is to find geological structures that may contain oil. I have worked for the past two summers on a seismograph crew. In that period of time I have learned that the oil seis-

Definition

mograph instrument is not mysterious because it can be compared to shouting at a cliff wall.

First analogy: Echo, and relationship to distance

[2]Let me begin with an occurrence that should be familiar. Imagine yourself standing near the base of a large cliff. If you shout at the cliff face, you will get an echo because the sound waves bounce back from the so-called "interface" where air meets rock. The sound waves travel at 1100 feet per second. You can find out how far you are standing from the cliff by measuring the time it takes for your shout to travel from you to the cliff and back again, and then by solving a simple formula for distance.

[3]The function of the oil seismograph is to find out how far down in the earth the horizontal layers of rock are. To discover this distance, the oil seismologist digs a deep hole (usually 100–200 feet) in the surface of the ground—the purpose of the hole I will explain later. At the bottom of the hole, he explodes a heavy charge of dynamite. Ground waves travel from the explosion down to the layers of rock. At each major interface between the layers, the waves bounce back to the surface. The explosion is similar to shouting at the cliff. Just as sound travels through the air at a certain speed, ground waves travel through the earth, although much faster. Ground waves bounce from rock interfaces as sound waves bounce from a cliff face. And the seismologist can determine distance just as you can determine the distance between you and the cliff.

Echo analogy applied to seismograph

[4]Why does the seismologist dig a hole to explode the dynamite? Much of the ground surface is covered with what geologists call *weathering,* that relatively loose covering of soil, sand, clay, etc., that usually goes down to the water table. This weathering has a disastrous effect upon seismic waves in the ground; it slows them up and even disperses them. To explode a dynamite charge on top of the ground would be like shouting at a cliff face through a bowl of mush—no matter how loud you shouted, little of your voice would get through. So the seismologist drills through the weathering and plants the dynamite charge below it. Usually the weathering has a bad effect only on the waves at the point of explosion; the *reflected* waves will travel through the weathering to the instruments on the surface.

Second analogy: Weathering of ground like mush

Differences

[5]In the interests of accuracy, I should add that the analogy between air waves and seismic waves is partly literal and partly figurative. The principles are similar but the conditions are different. Air waves are relatively constant in speed because the medium varies little. Seismic waves, by contrast, increase in speed with depth, and the increase is irregular and difficult to measure. Also, seismic reflections vary in

ways that no one completely understands. But the analogy is, in a basic sense, revealing and accurate enough to explain to a beginner how an oil seismograph works.

We can diagram the first basic analogy here as follows:

	Shouting at cliff face		*Using a seismograph*
Point A	shout	⟷	set off dynamite
Point B	creates sound waves in air	⟷	creates seismic waves in earth
Point C	waves travel at set rate	⟷	waves travel at certain rates
Point D	waves bounce back from cliff	⟷	waves bounce back from rock interface
Point E	distance can be measured	⟷	distance can be measured

When you construct an analogy, make sure that the compared points *are* comparable. Cut out or explain any points that cannot be logically compared and be certain that the familiar or known side of the analogy is really familiar and known to your reader. It is useless to explain a mineral's crystal-lattice structure by reference to analytic geometry if your reader knows nothing about analytic geometry. Do not try to stretch an analogy too far. Like the fabeled camel which first put his nose in the man's tent, then his head, and finally his whole body, pushing the man out of the tent, metaphor tends to creep into analogies. What starts out to be literally explanatory can become as unreal and metaphorical as a fairy tale.

You may choose to develop analogies by using figures of speech (see pp. 249–252). Figurative language can help you to clarify, dramatize, or sharpen your comparison. The function of such analogies is not so much to explain one "side" of the extended comparison, but to help the reader see the whole thing in a new and fresh way. We all know what war and cancer are, but observe how Sydney Harris uses metaphor to argue that war is *like* cancer; both must be eradicated to save the species.

Introduction
The term "self-preservation" introduced

[1]We say that the aim of life is self-preservation, if not for the individual, at least for the species. Granted that every organism seeks this end, does every organism know what is best for its self-preservation?

Contrast between cancer cells and normal cells

[2]Consider cancer cells and noncancer cells in the human body. The normal cells are aimed at reproducing and functioning in a way that is beneficial to the body. Cancer cells, on the other hand, spread in a way that threatens and ultimately destroys the whole body. Normal cells work harmoniously, because they "know," in a sense, that their pres-

ervation depends upon the health of the body they inhabit. While they are organisms in themselves, they also act as part of a substructure, directed at the good of the whole body.

Beginning of analogy: "Cancer cells [like warriors] do not know about self-preservation"

³We might say, metaphorically, that cancer cells do not know enough about self-preservation; they are, biologically, more ignorant than normal cells. The aim of cancer cells is to spread throughout the body, to conquer all the normal cells —and when they reach their aim, the body is dead. And so are the cancer cells.

⁴For cancer cells destroy not only all rival cells, in their ruthless biological warfare, but also destroy the large organization—the body itself—signing their own suicide warrant.

Extension of analogy: War and cancer both kill

⁵The same is true of war, especially in the modern world. War is the social cancer of mankind. It is a pernicious form of ignorance, for it destroys not only its "enemies," but also the whole superstructure of which it is a part—and thus eventually it defeats itself. Nations live in a state of anarchy, not in a state of law. And, like cancer cells, nations do not know that their ultimate self-interest lies in preserving the health and harmony of the whole body (that is, the community of man), for if that body is mortally wounded, then no nation can survive and flourish.

Argument stated in an "if . . . then" analogy

⁶If the aim of life is self-preservation—for the species as well as for the individual—we must tame or eradicate the cancer cells of war in the social organism. And this can be done only when nations begin to recognize that what may seem to be "in the national interest" cannot be opposed to the common interest of mankind, or both the nation and mankind will die in this "conquest."

Analogy continued

Conclusion

⁷The life of every organism depends upon the viability of the system of which it is a member. The cancer cells cannot exist without the body to inhabit, and they must be exterminated if they cannot be re-educated to behave like normal cells. At present, their very success dooms them to failure—just as a victorious war in the atomic age would be an unqualified disaster for the dying winner. —Sydney J. Harris, "When Winning Is Losing"

When using metaphor in an analogy, keep in mind C. S. Lewis' advice:

1. The figures [of speech] or metaphors should be well chosen by the writer.

2. The reader must be able to understand the figures.

3. Both writer and reader should understand that figurative language is being used.

WRITING AND REVISING AN ANALOGY (AN EXAMPLE)

Gerry Kinder starts to write an extended analogy. He begins with a title:

Is the Greek Letter Organization Just a Country Club?

This Gerry follows with a scratch outline:

1. Me and the Greeks
   — they're OK
2. Snobbery
   and exclusiveness

3. The great life — in both country club
   and Greek house

4. Business deals
   country club
   frat house

Gerry now begins his first draft:

I'm neither for nor against Greeks. My sister went through rush here two years ago and pledged Tri-Delt. She is now a happy sorority girl. I have shown some interest my first year in going Greek and have visited some of the houses and been involved in some of the entertainments. I've played football against Greeks in Touch League. I know and like many Greeks of both sexes. But something bothers me about them—even though I am not "politically" against their organization. (I am not a devout Independent either.)

There is too much snobbery in the Greek system. They remind me of the people I used to caddy for in the country club at home. Their major idea is to be exclusive. Exclusive. The One and Only. Their motto is: Keep others out. Otherwise, why join either the country club or a fraternity/sorority?

Another advantage of both is that you get to live better. In a Greek house you eat better and have a better place to sleep and have fun. Similarly a country club is the place to eat great dinners, and swim in a luxuri-ous swimming pool. There is something very similar about the people sitting around the pool watching the golfers come in at dusk and their counterpart: the boys sitting on the front steps watching the students com-ing back from their late afternoon classes, the sun shining through the trees. Glamor.

And the deals. How many deals are completed over golf and drinks at the country club? How many friendships are cemented in the fraternity, friendships that later are used in furthering business relationships?

At this point Gerry stops. For him, this has been a "letting loose" draft, one that provides ideas and material, a rambling outline of sorts. Now he needs to think hard about the ordering of ideas and shape the whole paper more carefully. He puts down a new order of elements in the basic analogy:

1. Deals (business, etc.)
2. Live better
3. Exclusiveness: *the whole pt.*

Now he begins on the new draft. He cuts the first paragraph entirely because it starts the paper too slowly, and he wants to see how short a paper he can write that still does the job. How vivid—yet economical—can he be? He chooses a new title and writes two new opening paragraphs that set analogous scenes. Having finished these, he simply keeps writing. You will find his (edited) final version below:

GOLDEN GHETTOES

[1]They sit quietly, handsome wives beside them; drinks in their hands, the setting sun glimmering beautifully on their tanned faces. There are muted sounds of traffic from the highway a mile away and sounds of splashing from the pool a few feet away. "I parred the last one!" says a happy man walking toward the club house. He is about fifty, his fine-looking hair glowing silver in the setting sun.

[2]Two-hundred miles from this scene, their sons and daughters sit quietly, tanned faces turned toward the street. A convertible pulls up in the driveway, and a young man with the arms of a sweater tied around his throat vaults gracefully over the side of the car. A girl drinks from a beer can, tilts it high, drops it carefully into a wastebasket. Another girl strides by on the sidewalk, her long legs carrying her smoothly along. "I aced the geology exam!" she calls out happily. A murmur follows her down the street.

[3]Here are two sides of the good life, American style. In the country club, affluent Americans play and enjoy themselves: this is what life is meant to be. In the fraternity and sorority, their sons and daughters play and enjoy themselves: practicing their skills for the life that will be theirs—some day.

⁴But there is more to the uses of Greek organization and country club besides just the good life. It is well known that thousands of business deals every year are made in country clubs. On the golf course, people agree to buy this or sell that. Plans are made: "Let's talk to old Freddy about his work on the downtown mall." (As a caddy I would stand and listen; they ignored me as if I were a 19th century slave, present but invisible.) At lunch they pull out pens and pencils and draw on napkins and add up figures. "Waiter—more napkins!" The lawyers talk to engineers, who talk to city council members, who shout across the room: "Hey, Sam, are you going to handle the Lions' Antique Show this year?"

⁵In the frats, the same kind of scenes occur. The same names, the same ignoring of waiters, similar deals. But little money is involved usually, except for festive occasions. Jack Windsor chairs the Homecoming program. "Can we get THE FILTHY FIVE this year? I heard they were great at Purdue." A senior, graduating at midterm, tells his roommate: "Listen, next year call up Selkirk in my Dad's office; he may be hiring then." Meanwhile, over in a sorority, two girls plot an attack on a favored law school. "I know what you should write in your Statement on the application," says one. "They *love* to hear that you're big on sports."

⁶All this is real enough, the good life and the business deals. Yet what keeps both country club and Greek organization permanently alive is more deeply psychological. It is a sense of being different by choice and warming your whole self in that choice. Members of both organizations swim happily in exclusivity. Not everybody can get in; they are the chosen few. Both organizations come with a dozen privileges that not even a Phi Beta Kappa key can get for you. The key won't allow you to ignore the slave carrying forty pounds of golf clubs; or to eat de-boned trout and drink champagne with the mayor of the city; or to date the star quarterback who (after graduation) will be worth two million dollars on June 1st. Greek house and country club: the golden ghettoes of American life.

PRACTICE

Discussion
1. Read Gerry's final draft and prepare for discussion the following questions:
   a. Diagram the analogy, following the form on p. 186. Discuss the diagram in relation to the paper's organization.
   b. What is the writer's point? Is there a "known" side of the analogy?
   c. How is the organization similar to one of the *comparison and contrast* patterns?
   d. Discuss the use of dialogue in the paper.

e. Study the discussion of the *representative example* on p. 148. How has Gerry used that kind of illustrative material in his paper?

f. How well does Gerry fulfill his goal: to write a vivid, economical paper that "does the job"?

2. Discuss each of the analogies below. Do any of them depend on figures of speech? Is the extended comparison consistently made? Do the differences between the two elements being compared weaken the analogy? Is the "known side" of the analogy familiar enough to you? How could the analogy be improved (if at all)?

a. For a long time now, since the beginning, in fact, men and women have been sparring and dancing around with each other, each pair trying to get it together and boogie to the tune called Life. For some people, it was always a glide, filled with grace and ease. For most of us, it is a stumble and a struggle, always trying to figure out the next step, until we find a partner whose inconsistencies seem to fit with ours, and the two of us fit into some kind of rhythm. Some couples wind up struggling and pulling at cross purposes; and of course, some people never get out on the floor, just stand alone in the corners, looking hard at the dancers.

   That's the way it's always been, and probably, always will be. The only difference now is that for the past few years a group of noisy people have been standing over next to the band and yelling above it, "Hey, listen everybody! You don't have to dance to the old tune any more! You can make up your own tune! You can make up your dance steps! *The man doesn't even have to lead any more!* Forget the band! This is a whole new movement! It's called *you can make your Life whatever you want!*"—Jay Molishever, "Marriage"

b. In practice, showing "respect" for machines means learning not to look on them simply as slaves. When a slave owner sees that his slaves are stronger, faster, and more efficient than himself, he is likely to fear that someday these slaves will realize their power and revolt. In the same way, so long as human beings see machines as slaves, they will continue to regard any machine that is stronger, faster, or "smarter" than themselves as a potential threat. It is only when the stereotypes are broken and an individual human being makes the effort to become throughly familiar with a particular machine—however complex or powerful it may be—that this fear is overcome and the machine becomes a partner rather than a slave. Just as truckers get to know their "rigs," sailors their ships, and musicians their instruments, so ordinary people in the near future may get to know their computers. —Jennings Lane, "Computer Chess"

c. Our dependence on uncertain energy sources to power our big cars and our recreational vehicles, to heat and cool our over-sized houses and ill-designed office buildings, may be as deadly in the long run as an addict's dependence on dope. — William Raspberry

d. Probably you have to go down several coal mines before you can get much grasp of the processes that are going on around you. This is chiefly because the mere effort of getting from place to place makes it difficult to notice anything else. In some ways it is even disappointing, or at least is unlike what you have expected. You get into the cage, which is a steel box about as wide as a telephone box and two or three times as long. It holds ten men, but they pack it like pilchards in a tin, and a tall man cannot stand upright in it. The steel door shuts upon you, and somebody working the winding gear above drops you into the void. . . . When you crawl out at the bottom you are perhaps four hundred yards under ground. That is to say you have a tolerable-sized mountain on top of you; hundreds of yards of solid rock, bones of extinct beasts, subsoil, flints, roots of growing things, green grass and cows grazing on it — all this suspended over your head and held back only by wooden props as thick as the calf of your leg. — George Orwell, *The Road to Wigan Pier*

e. It would sound ridiculous to ask, "Should robbery be studied in our schools?" Yet, if academic freedom is the sole issue rather than national survival, such a question is consistent and in order. If carpentry, why not burglary? Both are ways and means of getting a living. But carpentry is socially constructive and robbery is socially destructive. Communism is likewise socially destructive for its methods frankly include robbery, murder, arson, lying, and incitement to violence. These it defends and advocates on the basis of its working slogan that the "ends justify the means."

We protect our young people from harmful epidemic diseases of a physical nature such as smallpox, by quarantining them. We expose our young people to harmful epidemic diseases of an ideological nature, such as Communism, by a false suicidal interpretation of academic freedom. What youth does when it reaches maturity is something else again. At that time, in the interest of national security, adults should study Communism to be able to recognize it and fight it for dear life whenever and under whatever disguise it rears its hideous head. — Ruth Alexander, "Should Communism Be Studied in Our Schools?"

Writing

1. Write a paragraph or essay using one of the following theses and the analogy that it suggests; or you may use a thesis and analogy of your own choice. Specify your stance.

   a. *Thesis:* The theater department should produce some older, less contemporary plays.

      Analogy: A theater that produces only new plays is like a library that stocks only new books. — Martin Gottfried

   b. *Thesis:* Man should colonize space.

      Analogy: Saying that man should not colonize space because it is too dangerous is like refusing to leave a sinking ship and board a lifeboat because the open sea is too dangerous.

   c. *Thesis:* Smoking should not be allowed in public buildings.

      Analogy: A person who smokes (or who breathes other people's cigarette smoke) takes in a small dose of poison each day.

   d. *Thesis:* Being able to drive a car makes a young person feel like an adult.

      Analogy: Passing one's first driving test is similar to an initiation rite.

   e. *Thesis:* Every citizen should make an effort to avoid littering the nation's roadsides, parks, and cities.

      Analogy: Destroying the nation's environment is like burning down your house.

2. The powerful and prosperous Roman empire was said to have fallen for the following reasons: (a) the rise of despotic one-man rule; (b) the lowering of the prestige of the government; (c) the devaluing of the currency and increasing taxation; (d) the creation of a welfare state; (e) the rise of military control over civil government; (f) the expansion of bureaucracy; (g) the lowering of public morality; (h) the inability of the military to repulse foreign invaders. Write a paper in which you argue by using analogy that the United States is (or is not, or partly is) going the way of ancient Rome.

3. Write a figurative analogy in which you define a term by comparing it to something else. Suggestions:
   Hysteria is like a fire.
   Human opposites are like two magnets.
   Social welfare multiplies like yeast cells.
   Pets are like children.

PART THREE

IMPROVING AND REVISING PAPERS

CHAPTER 10
THE PRACTICE OF REVISION

If you look at the drawing again on p. 6, you will notice how often as a writer you back up to reconsider (revise) something. For instance, from **Outlining,** you may back up to **Finding a Subject;** from **Writing,** you may back up to **Specifying a Stance;** and so on. Also note that each "backing up" affects other elements in the paper. If you go back to reconsider your stance, this often changes something in the **Outlining** stage, which in turn has its effect on **Writing.**

In this book we talk about revision in two ways. First, in this chapter, we will discuss it as a matter of improving and sharpening your work until you achieve a *working draft.* Second, in chapters eleven through fifteen, we continue this discussion, but in those chapters we also emphasize certain elements of basic design in the typical composition: *organization, word choice,* and *sentence structure.*

So we suggest that you consider all of chapters ten through fifteen as covering pretty much the same rhetorical territory—"how to write it and how to revise it."

Two Questions About Revising

When do I start revising?

Answer: from the very beginning. A *revision* is any change in planning or writing.

When is the best time for revising?

Let's answer that by pointing out that there are *worst times*. For example if, ten minutes before you hand the paper in, you decide to revise it for *audience* you are probably in difficulty. Decisions about audience are usually a part of decisions about *stance,* and in most circumstances they all govern your design of the whole paper so completely you can't revise them late without distorting the paper dramatically. There are exceptions to this, of course. But we wish to emphasize that a piece of writing tends to set like wet concrete. You can work both prose and concrete only up to the point where they begin to harden.

Usually the best time to revise the "preparation parts" of your paper is when you decide on them. If possible, revise these early:

Choice of subject

Hook or angle of attack

Stance: writer's role

       audience

       point or thesis

Shape or outline of paper

So much depends on these areas of preparation that if you don't get them firmly in mind, you may find yourself doing more revising than original writing.

An Example of Revision

Brian has an assignment to write a paper using *process*. His instructor encourages the class to write a light-hearted process, one that might entertain by supplying some description or narrative. As we relate the story of Brian's paper, note where and why he stops to *revise*.

"I didn't really have to hunt for a process subject," Brian said. "When Ms. Carlisle said *entertain*, I thought only one word—'funny.' And the funniest process I ever saw was . . ."

"Wait a minute," we said. "Let our readers see some of your first draft."

"OK," Brian said. "I just started writing, with no plan. You'll see what happened."

THE DAY GRANDPA LOST HIS TEETH

Grandpa takes care of his cars. He has had a manual for every one of them, going back to a 1940 Plymouth. He buys the manual from the manufacturer, who supplies real mechanics' manuals, each one about a thousand pages long. But he never uses the manuals. They are stacked on top of the *World Book*—which he never uses either—and get dusted regularly by Grandma, who always complains that they are in the way and are only good for door stops.

"Where is this headed?" we said.

"Not much of anywhere," said Brian. "The assignment said *process* and *entertain,* and I was not processing or entertaining. I only wanted to write about 2–3 pages, and at the rate I was getting to the point I'd be telling it to the reader on page 14.

"I stopped and considered my audience. Easy—the general reader, no special difficulty there. But I needed a hook to hang the paper on—my process I already had in mind, and you will see it in a minute. I thought of another title:

HOW GRANDPA GOT HIS TEETH AWAY FROM THE AIR CONDITIONER IN A 1971 PONTIAC

Catchy, huh? But not *process:* steps leading to an end point. I had to tell the reader how to do something or how something worked."

"Who would care?" we asked.

"I thought of that right away. Then I thought of starting the first paragraph differently, appealing directly to the reader, and making the process angle clear. I decided to hang the whole theme on this hook: the difficulty of what should be a simple procedure, getting an object out of a hole it has fallen into."

From this point on, Brian will tell you himself how he wrote and revised, and revised yet again. We will number his paragraphs, and show the development of the paper. Following each revision, Brian's comments on it will appear in italics.

Note: the revisions were not always made paragraph by paragraph or at the same time.

HOW TO GET AN OBJECT OUT OF
YOUR CAR'S AIR CONDITIONER

FIRST VERSION

Paragraph 1.   If you are typical, it has happened to you. You are sitting in your car. You put an object in front of you, on top of the dashboard. And then it's gone, dropped down through the vents in the dashboard. This happened to my grandfather's teeth (a two-tooth bridge, actually). Down they went into the bowels of the car, and it took him two days to get them out. If they had been smooth or not drawable by a magnet, he would have never gotten them out. Here's how to do it if it happens to you.

REVISION

Grandpa's Teeth: How to Get an Object Out of Your Car's Defrosting Vents

Paragraph 1.   "Oops," Grandpa said. *Tinkle, tank, tinkle.* Silence.
"What do you mean, *oops*?" Grandma said. And then she knew.
"They went down the $"%$# vent," Grandpa said.
"How many times have I told you, keep them in your mouth." She had him. "She'll never let me forget this one," Grandpa said later. "I had to get 'em out, and quick, right after we got home."

Brian's Comments on the Revision

1. I needed a more accurate title.

2. The first version wasn't bad, but the narrative seemed more interesting. I thought I could put some of the first version later in the essay, once I caught the reader's interest.

3. I rewrote paragraph 1 before going on to paragraph 2.

FIRST VERSION

Paragraph 2.   If my informal sampling is representative, two out five
Americans loose stuff down the vents in the top of a dashboard.
Coins, hairpins, five-dollar bills, pills, aspirins, car keys, marbles,
short pencils — and Grandpa's teeth. Anything small can fall down
there and be gone forever! How to get it back? You can't see it, and
you don't know where it's gone. (If you start the engine, will it be
ground up in there?)

REVISION

Paragraph 2.   If my informal sampling is representative, two out *of* five
Americans *lose* stuff down the air vents in the top of *their car* dashboard. *Car keys,* coins, hairpins, *Lifesavers,* five-dollar bills, aspirins
and other pills — and Grandpa's teeth *(actually a two-tooth bridge).* Anything small can fall down there and be gone forever! *If it's something
important you want to get it back.* But how to get it back? You can't see
it, and you don't know where it's gone. (If you start the engine, will it
be ground up in there?)

Comments on the Revision

I had different kinds of revisions here.

1. Some simple errors: I left out the word **of** *in line 1 and misspelled* **lose** *in
line 2.*

2. I put in **their car** *for specificity in line 2.*

*3. Readers know only what you tell them, and I was afraid that they would
visualize* **false teeth** *in line 4, and they would immediately think I was just making
the whole thing up; false teeth are way too big to go down one of these vents.*

*4. Also for the readers' sake, I added line 6, just to take care of the objection
that most stuff that goes down the vent you don't care if you ever see again.*

5. For the sake of emphasis in line 3, I put **car keys** *first. Obviously, they are
the worst thing you can lose. In the next line, I added* **Lifesavers** *because Joanie
Riggs says she keeps a roll on her dash, and once the package is open the little candies
are always rolling out and disappearing into the vents.*

FIRST VERSION

Paragraph 3.   Here is how to get the object out of the hole. First, determine what the object is. There are only two methods of removal, depending on what you lost. If the object has no hole in it, or if it won't respond to a magnet — say goodbye to it. If it's either one of the above . . .

Paragraph 3 has no second version.

Brian's Comments on the Revision of His Paper

All right, now I have to admit that I didn't write an outline for this paper — or make a **shape** *for it (see pp. 54–60). I am basically lazy. I am also basically lost in this paper. Paragraph 3 is out of sync somehow, and I had lost Grandpa and his teeth as a theme in my story. So I made this scratch outline:*

> *Thesis: Getting an object out of your car's vent is easy if you have the right equipment and know how to use it.*
>
> *Hooks or   Grandpa's teeth*
> *"themes":   Equipment (and knowledge of it)*

    I.   *Introd. — his teeth lost*
   II.   *The kind of stuff lost in a typical car vent*
  III.   *How to get it out*
       A.   Two methods
       B.   Go to hardware store
           1.   Buy wire
           2.   Buy fishing magnet
       C.   Techniques of fishing
  IV.   *Conclusion — How to avoid the entire problem*
       A.   Grandpa loses teeth again
       B.   Grandma's reaction

There's no use chewing me out for not making an outline earlier. I didn't, and that's that.

First I wrote a new **Paragraph 3,** *then I wrote the rest of the paper about as fast as I could type. This gave me a working first draft.*

3. When Grandpa got home, he retrieved his teeth in a matter of five minutes. Five minutes later, he also retrieved two screws, a metal loop that held his car together, pieces of a three-year-old shopping list, and an unidentified piece of metal. In addition to these, he now has a windshield vent that works much better, once the junk is out of its system. Here is how he did it—and how you can do it.

4. First recognize the fact that to get an object out of the vent, you have only two methods available. These depend on the nature of what you have lost. If it doesn't have holes in it or if it cannot be attracted by a magnet, forget it. (Grandpa's teeth bridge has several holes for lightness.)

5. Next, go to the hardware store and buy two feet of soft brass wire about the thickness of the lead in a wooden pencil. Also buy a "fishing" magnet, which is about the size and shape of a wood pencil. The magnet has a head which rotates.

6. Now you are ready to fish for the object in your vent. Grandpa's teeth are made of a metal that magnets do not attract. So he took his piece of brass wire and made a hook in one end. He stuck this end down the vent and wiggled the wire, pushing it gently along until about a foot of it was inside the hole. He wiggled the wire some more until he could hear his teeth bouncing against metal. He then fished for the teeth until he could hear them scraping against the sides of the hole, which meant that he had hooked them. He pulled them out with the wire.

7. After finding his teeth, he drilled a hole in the end of the fishing magnet and looped one end of the brass wire through, twisting it tight. Then he went fishing for metal. After a few minutes of this, he went back to fishing with just the wire, ending with the result already mentioned.

8. The best way to get objects out of your dashboard vents is not to let them in there in the first place. Much to Grandma's satisfaction, Grandpa no longer puts his teeth on the dashboard. He puts them in his pocket. They fell out of his pocket when he put his pants over a chair while undressing for bed. He stepped on them, cutting a hole in his foot—the ends of the hardened metal (which curve over the teeth and hold the bridge in place) are very sharp.

9. Grandma's remarks have not been preserved for posterity.

Brian waited two days and then revised his working draft. As before, we will show you what he did to the paper. His comments are italicized.

Grandpa's Teeth: How to Get an Object

Out of Your Car's Defrosting Vents

1. |←"Oops," Grandpa said. *Tinkle, tank, tinkle.* Silence *in the car.*
|← *They sat there in the gas station, just outside Indianapolis.* ←
"What do you mean, oops?" Grandma said. And then she knew.

The attendant was wiping the windshield.

"They went down the $%&(*)% vent," Grandpa said.

"How many times have I told you, keep them in your mouth!" She had him. "<u>She'll never let me forget this one</u>," Grandpa said later. "<u>I had to get 'em out, and quick, right after we got home</u>."

2.   If my informal sampling is representative, two out of five Americans lose stuff down the ~~air~~ *defrosting* vents in the top of their car dashboard. Car keys, *wedding rings* coins, hairpins, Lifesavers, five-dollar bills, aspirins and other pills — and Grandpa's teeth (actually a two-tooth bridge). Anything small can fall into the vent and be gone forever! If it's something important you want to get it back. But how to get it back? You can't see it, and you don't know where it's gone. (If you start the engine, will it be ground up in there?)

Brian's Comments

In paragraph 1, I added a little explanation to "place" the event. It had to be happening somewhere! And it really happened in a gas station.

In paragraph 2, I wanted the reader to understand what these "vents" were — so added **defrosting.**

While talking about my paper with friends, someone said his mother dropped her wedding ring down a vent when the family went to the beach. Seemed like a good detail.

3.   When Grandpa got home, he retrieved his teeth in a matter of five
minutes. *after he got some equipment,* A half-hour later, he *had* also retrieved two screws, a metal loop that ~~had once~~
held his car *keys* together, pieces of a three-year-old shopping list, and an un-
identified piece of metal. In addition to these, he now has *a* windshield
vent *s* that work *s* much better, once the junk is out of ~~its~~ *the venting* system. Here is
how he did it—and how you can do it *too*.

4.   First, recognize the fact that to get an object out of the *a* vent, you have
only two methods available. These depend on the nature of what you
have lost. If it doesn't have holes in it or if it cannot be attracted by a magnet, forget it. (Grandpa's teeth bridge has several holes for lightness.)

5.   Next, go to the hardware store and buy two feet of soft brass wire
about the thickness of the lead in a wooden pencil. Also buy a "fishing"
magnet, which is about the size and shape of a wood pencil. The magnet
has a head which rotates.

6.   Now you are ready to fish for the object in your vent. Grandpa's
teeth are made of a metal that magnets do not attract. So he took his piece
of brass wire and made a hook in one end. He stuck this end down the
vent and wiggled the wire, p *u* shing it gently along until about a foot of it
was inside the hole. He wiggled the wire some more until he could hear
his teeth bouncing against metal. He then fished for his teeth until he
could hear them scraping against the sides of the hole, which meant that
he had hooked them. He pulled them out with the wire.

Brian's Comments

The revisions here are mainly for clarity and "tightening" loose ends.

7.   After finding his teeth, he drilled a hole in the *non-magnetic* end of the fishing
magnet and looped one end of the brass wire through, twisting it tight.
Then he went fishing for metal. After a few minutes of this, he went back
to fishing with just the wire, ending with the result already mentioned.

8.   The best way to get objects out of your dashboard vents is not to let them in there in the first place. Much to Grandma's satisfaction, Grandpa no longer puts his teeth on the dashboard. He puts them in his pocket. They fell out his pocket when he put his pants over a chair while undressing for bed. He stepped on them, cutting a hole in his foot—the ends of the hardened metal (which curve over the teeth and hold the bridge in place) are very sharp.

9.   Grandma's remarks have not been preserved for posterity.

Brian's Comments

Paragraph 7—I was afraid the reader would visualize this wrong. You can't drill into a magnet without ruining it, and I wanted to explain what the process really required.

Paragraph 8—Fixing typical typing errors.

Revision: An Overview

We have seen Brian work his way through the typical strategies of revision, moving backward and forward in the process as he made changes to improve a particular essay. There are no mysteries about what he did, nor are his techniques unusual with him. Every writer revises — although some writers tend to revise more heavily at certain stages than at others.

It is generally true that experienced writers like to revise early, to get a good "foundation" for their papers before starting on a first draft. This foundation can be an outline or "shape" plus a title and first paragraph. These give a sense of *direction* to a paper that even the experienced writer needs. You will recall that once Brian got a scratch outline, title, and first paragraph he thought might work, he was able to move rapidly through to the end of a satisfactory first draft.

Once you have completed such a draft, you have (broadly speaking) two choices. You can continue to look it over, rewriting and revising. Or you can set it aside for a while. We recommend setting it aside.

Why? Because most of us will tend to half-memorize the paper, mistakes and all. By *mistakes,* we mean anything that might be wrong with it — from lapses in logic, to clumsy sentences, to out-of-order paragraphs. If you put it away out of sight, it will in time become a fresh paper, one whose failures (if any) may become evident. How long should you set it aside? As long as you can, without making it difficult to do a final draft and proofreading *it.* For most writers, this schedule is reasonable:

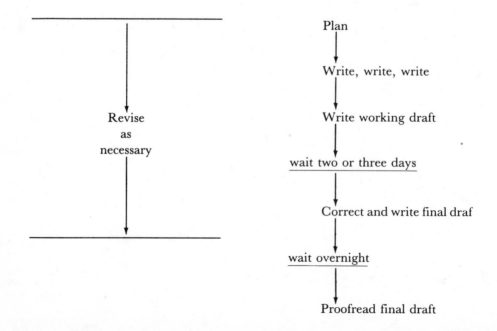

	Plan
	↓
	Write, write, write
	↓
Revise	Write working draft
as	↓
necessary	wait two or three days
	↓
	Correct and write final draf
	↓
	wait overnight
	↓
	Proofread final draft

Final Proofreading

Proofreading is a small but important art. It consists mainly of trying to fool your brain into picking up errors that it either hasn't caught before or has inadvertently memorized. Persons who read proof in publishers' houses usually do the job in pairs. One reads the original manuscript to the other, who has the freshly printed version before him. In this way, each word and punctuation mark are orally checked by two persons. (Despite this system, errors still appear in a great deal of published material.)

A variation on the oral method works quite well for the student writer. Take your cooled-off final draft to a secluded spot and read it aloud *slowly* to yourself, pronouncing each word exactly as you wrote it. Read each paragraph *out of its normal order*. For example, if you have a seven-paragraph essay, read the paragraphs in a sequence like this: 3, 2, 7, 4, 1, 6, 5. In doing this, you can make the whole essay appear odd and unfamiliar, and your ear will pick up errors of several kinds—in logic, for example, as well as in spelling. A faulty generalization may well stand out as you read it aloud, and you can then insert a word or phrase to qualify it. ("Fraternities are dens of iniquity" becomes "Most fraternities at People's College are dens of iniquity.") Some words misspelled sound so odd when pronounced as written that you may catch the mistake (*eariler*, for example, instead of *earlier*).

Even if you take all of these precautions, prepare yourself to accept the fact that errors are going to slip through. But accurate proofreading will cut down their number considerably.

PRACTICE

Discussion

1. Study the following paragraph from a longer essay. Discuss the changes in the revision. In particular, identify the changes that were made because of a shift in role or audience. In what way does the paragraph set the scene for the thesis? How have the changes limited the point of view?

Original

    Thesis: People who are not directly involved in motor accidents seem to be drawn to them.

About a year ago, there was a motorcycle accident near my house. I was on the phone, talking to a friend about an assignment due in school the next day, when I heard a noise like a loud hedge-trimmer on the loose. My mother, who was in the living room with my father and me, ran to the front window. She gave a gasp, gesticulated down the street, and turned around to us and said, "There's a man! There's a man!" and took off out the front door. My father and I, thinking that the strain of her work (she is a teacher) had finally snapped her mind, stayed put, until she came running back in to tell us to "Call the ambulance! Call the Police!" My father got up and ambled out the door to see what the excitement was. My curiosity got the best of me, too, and I told my friend I would call her back later, hung up, and went to the scene of the accident, for indeed it was an accident although I didn't realize what it was until I got nearer. A motorcyclist, zipping through a stop sign, had hit the back of a car and was, at the time I first saw him, lying on the street pavement.

Revision

About a year ago, there was a motorcycle accident near my house, making a noise like a hedge-trimmer on the loose. My mother, who was in the living room, ran to the front window. She gasped, gesticulated down the street and said, "There's a man! There's a man!" and took off out the front door. My father, thinking that the strain of her work had finally snapped her mind, stayed put, until she came running back to tell him to "Call the ambulance! Call the police!" My father called the police and ambled out the door to see what the excitement was. Neither of my parents realized what kind of an accident it was until they got closer. A motorcyclist, zipping through a stop sign, had hit the back of a car and was lying on the street pavement.

2. Read the following paper and use the discussion questions as a means of giving advice to the writer about revising her paper.

Must the Young Be Ignored?

[1]It seems as if there is a gross misconception in our society today. Young people are considered useless and a necessary burden. They are forced to be educated whether they want to or not. They are left with the feeling that they must contribute their share to society, and their remaining years are to be spent thinking of everyone but themselves. There are no activities available and nowhere left to go but into the life of success in business. Here they are destined to sit, waiting patiently for death.

[2]Only after their own children are gone and the great day of retirement comes, have we fulfilled our obligations and have no responsibil-

ity but to ourselves. Considering a lifetime of doing for others and
their many years of hard work, we then have earned the right to plan
for our sole enjoyment. It is our time to sit and wait for our children to
take care of us. In return for all our parents gave us, we can be expected to cater to them, wait on them, and worry about them in the
same manner they had done. Retirement is our time to relax and let
others do for us.

3We see these young people walking the streets, sitting on park
benches, strolling through zoos, and lounging around homes. Winter
months keep us indoors clinging to our TV sets, reading mysteries,
and playing rock and roll records. Visiting is done on many occasions.
After all, we will be putting themselves out for a lifetime; now it is
time for others to make the effort.

4Looking at young people in a different light, we see that with all
the freedom available in our life, he or she still seems to be surrounded
by restrictions. We feel ill at ease with the old, believing that we are
not wanted, are in the way, or are inhibiting their fun. The elderly
want to help run others' lives in the manner they are accustomed to,
but our ideas are most often rejected and labeled outdated. With no
job, no children to raise, and no one listening to their advice, we feel
useless, rejected, and alone. After one of the friends is gone to college,
the joy of doing for each other is lost. Finding a new friend in life is
considered useless or hopeless.

5Socially, we young people often find ourselves completely lost. We
constantly remind ourselves, "I'm too young for this, too young for
that." Fears of making a fool of themselves prevent them from going
out and participating in activities. All ideas of idealism are long gone
and there is no thought of bringing this type of excitement into our
lives. We are frightened at the thought of doing new things, studying
new subjects, investigating new fields, developing new skills, or starting
new hobbies. We consider ourselves too young to begin anything we
have never tried. These people are especially afraid of meeting a failure
if they should try something for the first time.

6It is a sad and irritating circumstance that confines so many young
people to these old attitudes on what to expect during life. Too many
of these people are so wrapped up in their problems that there is no
time left to find a way to make these valuable years count. We are actually the freest group in the population; yet society has conditioned
us to close out every possibility of this freedom with their attitudes
and fears.

7How can the attitudes projected above describe the happy, well-
adjusted young person? There is no way they can. There are thousands
of people today who do not let chronological age keep them young.
These people are living out their lives in a full and complete manner
by waking up and discovering new satisfactions in life. Staying young
is only a matter of thinking young. Happy young citizens are the ones

who are active in societies, have a skilled hobby to be involved in, who teach or work with the old, and who take an active interest in community living. These are the people who give their leisure time to aid others through volunteer service projects. These people are so busy giving themselves to life and others that there is no room for boredom or self-pity.

[8]The young who learn to get outside themselves, and who learn the joy of giving will find a more rewarding purpose in their final years. Their need to create and maintain self-respect is vital and can only be achieved if they will take an interest in the life around them. Finally, the young individual who has an absorbing interest in some phase of recreation or interest possesses a rich asset in his declining years which can help sustain life and make it richer for himself.

a. Check the *stance:*
   (1) What is the writer's *role*? Where in the paper has the writer given any hint about her authority to write on the young?
   (2) Who is the *audience* for this paper?
   (3) What is the paper's *thesis*? Where is it stated?
   What advice would you give the writer for revision of *stance*?
b. List the paragraph leads or topic sentences. Hint: Not all topic sentences appear at the beginning of the paragraph.
c. Make a scratch outline based on the paragraph leads. What kind of an organizational structure did the writer use? What advice would you give the writer for improving her organization? Discuss, in particular, the lack of balance between the negative evidence in paragraphs 1–6 with the more positive evidence in paragraphs 7 and 8.
d. Identify any *hooks* used in the paper. In what way would clear use of *hooks* improve the paper?
e. Study the use of evidence—specific detail and illustration. What advice would you give the writer?

Writing
1. Write a letter to the writer of "Must the Young Be Ignored?", giving some specific suggestions for revision. Deal with *stance, organization,* and *use of examples.*

2. Write a paper based on your experience with the young citizens in our society, refuting the first six paragraphs of "Must the Young Be Ignored?"

3. Choose a paper you have written for this course or another one. Revise the paper, putting to practice what you have learned about revision.

CHAPTER 11

ORGANIZING CLEAR PARAGRAPHS AND PAPERS

THE PROMISE PATTERN

*T*here are many ways to organize a piece of writing. The most frequently used — and for many purposes, probably the best — employs what we call the *promise pattern*. You "promise" your readers at the beginning of your paper that you will tell them certain things, and as you write you fulfill your promise. The promise pattern is most easily seen in a typical paragraph. (This kind of paragraph is often called *deductive* because it begins with a general statement supported by particular details and examples.)

Near the beginning of the following paragraph about surviving in the desert, the author makes a promise (note italics) to his reader:

> These few examples make one thing clear: for anyone who has to survive in the desert, the heat of the day, both cause-and-effect of the lack of water, is the chief danger. *Temperatures reach an amazing height.* In Baghdad the thermometer in the hot summer months often climbs to 150°F., occasionally even to 180° and over (in the sun). In the Sahara near Azizia (Libya) temperatures of 134° in the shade have been recorded, and in July 1913

that was also the temperature in the Great Salt Lake Desert (also in the shade). But if the thermometer is put in the sand there at noon during the summer, the mercury goes up to 176°. On the side of Highway 91, which goes through the Mohave Desert, it has sometimes been 140° in the shade at noon; in the evenings the thermometer sinks to a "low" of 90°. In Libya, Montgomery's and Rommel's soldiers sometimes fried eggs on the armor plate of their tanks. — Cord-Christian Troebst, *The Art of Survival*

In the rest of the paragraph after the italicized sentence, Troebst keeps his promise—to discuss and illustrate amazingly high desert temperatures.

Much of what we say here concerning the organization of paragraphs applies generally to complete papers. For example:

A paper's promise = the paper's *thesis*
A paragraph promise = the paragraph's *topic idea*

The *topic idea* of a paragraph is its main, controlling statement, which is often expressed in a *topic sentence.* The topic idea of Troebst's paragraph is expressed in the italicized topic sentence, *Temperatures reach an amazing height.* Some paragraphs need two or three sentences to express their topic ideas (or promises), while a few paragraphs have no topic ideas at all. A paragraph that contains no topic ideas may fulfill the promise made in a preceding paragraph, or it may provide a transition between paragraphs.

Consider the *promise pattern* in the two paragraphs below. In an earlier section (not given here) the writer promised his reader that he would relate how immigrant Jews lived in a big American city. In the first paragraph, he keeps that promise; in the second he makes and keeps another:

Previous topic   ¹The Jews in Lawndale cut down the trees for firewood
idea developed   and tramped out the grass in the parking strips. They re-
(promise kept)   moved the doorknobs and the light fixtures from the flats
they rented and sold them for junk. They allowed the drains
in their sinks to become clogged with debris, and when you
went into their kitchens, you would see the sink full of water
to the brim with fishtails and other remains of food products
floating in it. I know because my aunt owned her house in
Lawndale for some time after she had moved out of it and
gone to Oak Park, and when I was in my teens I used to go in
and collect the rent for her.

Transition from   ²Obviously this was a situation ideally calculated to in-
previous paragraph   spire racial and religious prejudice. But the dreadful mistake

New topic idea
(promise)

which many persons made was that they supposed that these people were behaving as they did because they were Jews. *The truth of the matter is of course that they were behaving thus because they were peasants. They had not yet learned how to live in an American city.* They, or their fathers, had come from Polish and Russian villages (most of the older members of the community had not even learned to speak English), and when they first came to America they had been herded into slums where it would have been impossible for anybody to live in any other way than they were living. They were now in the first stage of their escape from the slums, but they did not yet

Promise kept

know any better than to take the slums with them. All this was straight sociological conditioning, and it had nothing whatever to do with their being Jews. I am sure that most of us would have been astonished if we had been told that their children and grandchildren would have made their adjustment with complete success and that, long before the date at which I am writing, some of these would have made important contributions to American welfare and become distinguished citizens in music, science, philanthropy, and many other areas of our corporate life. — Edward Wagenknecht, *As Far As Yesterday: Memories and Reflections*

It is important to understand that when you make a promise to your readers you set up an expectation. Suppose you make this statement near the beginning of an essay: *The problem of recreation at Windsor College is not as great as the administration believes.* Immediately your readers expect you to show them in some detail why the problem is not as great as some might think. If you wander off into another subject (like academic achievement, for instance), or do not give details concerning your thesis/promise, you will fail to satisfy the expectations of the readers. They will then say you haven't done your job of communication — and they will be right.

Idealized, the promise pattern for a typical paper appears at the top of p. 214.

PRACTICE

Discussion
1. The following sentences from student papers were written to act as statements of promise. For class discussion, answer these questions: (a) What do these statements promise the reader? (b) Can each promise be reasonably fulfilled by the writer in a paragraph? In a

Promise Pattern

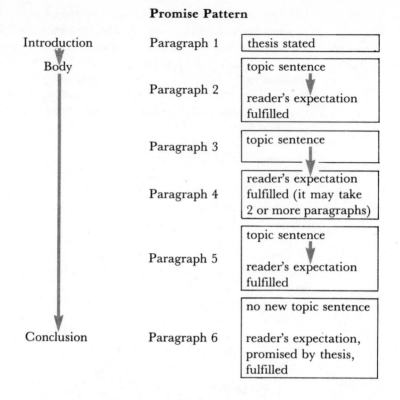

paper of 500–1000 words? (c) If you answered *yes* to either part of (b), explain briefly how *you* might go about fulfilling the reader's expectation for each statement.

   a. Ballet is becoming one of the most popular art forms in America today.

   b. The history of war proves that human beings can never get along.

   c. The American luxury car is less popular now because its snob appeal is gone and it costs too much to repair and operate.

   d. Contrary to what many students think, our chemistry lab has more expensive equipment than the beginning student needs.

   e. There are no good Chinese/French/Italian restaurants in my hometown.

2. June Kronholz, a professional writer, wrote an essay from which we have taken (1) the first two sentences, and (2) selected sentences from paragraph beginnings. Write two or three paragraphs guessing how Kronholz used the promise pattern in the completed essay as published. Her article appeared on the front page of *The Wall*

Street Journal, a newspaper with a highly educated readership. The article was well received and widely praised. Why do you think this was the case?

> [1]This is a story about power, sex, predation and violence in Africa.
> [2]It's about crocodiles.
> [3]First, the power. A crocodile can grow to a length of 20 feet, weigh half a ton and tackle a 900-pound buffalo that wanders past at lunchtime. . . .
> [4]Now for the sex. A crocodile reaches [sexual] maturity when he is 2.5 feet long, which can take anywhere from 10 to 20 years, depending on how well he has been eating. . . .
> [5]Here's where the predation comes in. An adult crocodile has only one predator: a man with a rifle (a Soviet-designed AK-47 is preferred in these parts). . . .
> [6]Now, finally, the violence. Given the choice between a man and a buffalo, a crocodile almost always will opt for a fish. But occasionally a man will happen along the river bank. . . .

3. Using the idealized promise pattern as a guide (see p. 214), read the following essay and look for the writer's employment of the pattern. What is his thesis? His topic sentences? Locate each topic sentence and explain its location in the paragraph. Are the "reader's expectations" fulfilled? Explain specifically why or why not.

> [1]The actual process of riveting is simple enough—in description. Rivets are carried to the job by the rivet boy, a riveter's apprentice whose ambition is to replace one of the members of the gang—which one, he leaves to luck. The rivets are dumped into a keg beside a small coke furnace. The furnace stands on a platform of loose boards roped to steel girders which may or may not have been riveted. If they have not been riveted there will be a certain amount of play in the temporary bolts. The furnace is tended by the heater or passer. He wears heavy clothes and gloves to protect him from the flying sparks and intense heat of his work, and he holds a pair of tongs about a foot-and-a-half long in his right hand. When a rivet is needed, he whirls the furnace blower until the coke is white-hot, picks up a rivet with his tongs, and drives it into the coals. His skill as a heater appears in his knowledge of the exact time necessary to heat the steel. If he overheats it, it will flake, and the flakes will permit the rivet to turn in its hole. And a rivet which gives in its hole is condemned by the inspectors.
> [2]When the heater judges that his rivet is right, he turns to face the catcher, who may be above or below him or fifty or sixty or eighty feet away on the same floor level with the naked girders between. There is no means of handing the rivet over. It must be thrown. And it must be

accurately thrown. And if the floor beams of the floor above have been laid so that a flat trajectory is essential, it must be thrown with considerable force. The catcher is therefore armed with a smallish, battered tin can, called a cup, with which to catch the red-hot steel. Various patented cups have been put on the market from time to time but they have made little headway. Catchers prefer the ancient can.

[3]The catcher's position is not exactly one which a sportsman catching rivets for pleasure would choose. He stands upon a narrow platform of loose planks laid over needle beams and roped to a girder near the connection upon which the gang is at work. There are live coils of pneumatic tubing for the rivet gun around his feet. If he moves more than a step or two in any direction, he is gone, and if he loses his balance backward he is apt to end up at street level without time to walk. And the object is to catch a red-hot iron rivet weighing anywhere from a quarter of a pound to a pound and a half and capable, if he lets it pass, of drilling an automobile radiator or a man's skull 500 feet below as neatly as a shank of shrapnel. Why more rivets do not fall is the great mystery of skyscraper construction. The only reasonable explanation offered to date is the reply of an erector's foreman who was asked what would happen if a catcher on the Forty Wall Street job let a rivet go by him around lunch hour. "Well," said the foreman, "he's not supposed to."

[4]The most curious fact about a riveter's skill is that he is not one man but four: "heater," "catcher," "bucker-up," and "gun-man." The gang is the unit. Riveters are hired and fired as gangs, work in gangs, and learn in gangs. If one member of a gang is absent on a given morning, the entire gang is replaced. A gang may continue to exist after its original members have all succumbed to slippery girders or the business end of a pneumatic hammer or to a foreman's zeal or merely to the temptations of life on earth. And the skill of the gang will continue with it. Men overlap each other in service and teach each other what they know. The difference between a gang which can drive 525 inch-and-an-eighth rivets in a working day and a gang which can drive 250 is a difference of coordination and smoothness. You learn how to heat a rivet and how not to overheat it, how to throw it accurately but not too hard, how to drive it and when to stop driving it, and precisely how much you can drink in a cold wind or a July sun without losing your sense of the width and balance of a wooden plank. And all these things, or most of them, an older hand can tell you. . . . —"Skyscrapers: Builders and Their Tools," *Fortune* magazine

Writing

1. The statements below have been taken from articles, books, or student papers. Does each statement promise the reader to expect cer-

tain material? What kind of material and how much? Write a brief paragraph for each statement answering these questions.

  a. During the many years I have been dissecting sharks, and examining and recording the stomach contents, I have come across many unusual objects. — Theo Brown

  b. What is the brain for? — John Pfeiffer

  c. Everyone in the family must know how gasoline is so *different*. — from a household safety manual

  d. Water skiing is by far the most dangerous summer sport. — student paper

  e. The American wife is finally putting her husband in his place — the kitchen. Also the laundry, the nursery and the supermarket. — first two sentences of a newspaper story

  f. When you approach the eastern front of the Teton Mountain range, you can't help but be awestruck by the abrupt wall of jagged rock shooting thousands of feet above the adjacent land, called Jackson Hole. — geology student

2. Choose a subject that you know something about (or pick one of the suggestions following). Brainstorm everything you know about the subject, keeping a record of your thoughts. Identify clusters of ideas, and develop at least three *promises* that will operate as topic ideas for your paragraphs. From these promises, develop your thesis promise and write a paper, using the promise pattern.

  a. stress

  b. blind date

  c. backyards

  d. junk food

WRITING SUCCESSFUL PARAGRAPHS

Support Your Paper's Promise

A paragraph is a collection of sentences that helps you support your thesis. Itself a small "essay," a paragraph should be clearly written and specific; and it should not wander or make irrelevant remarks. Each paragraph should be related in some way to the thesis or the paper's "promise." Since a paragraph is usually part of a larger piece of writing (essay, research paper, report, etc.), use your *shape, plan,* or *outline* to help you construct paragraphs that support the thesis.

Keep your topic sentence in mind. After you have decided on your paragraph topic sentence, jot down all the facts and details that you have previously collected by brainstorming, freewriting, or thinking about your subject. Arrange these ideas in a logical form and sequence, with your details and *specific* examples fulfilling the paragraph promise.

Consider this ex-smoker's support of his topic sentence:

Topic sentence *(Promise)*	*My body was sicker than I thought it could be.* The joints in my arms and shoulders and the muscles in my chest and my calves hurt so badly the first night I hid in the dark and cried.
Joints, muscles, and calves hurt *General aching*	That pain lasted only one day, but for at least a week I was always aching somewhere. My mouth, nose, throat, stomach, and each tooth were deprived of smoke and nicotine, and their reactions lasted much longer. I kept arching my mouth
Results of deprivation in mouth, throat, nose	wide open as if adjusting cheap store-bought teeth. My throat was sore as if I had smoked too much, perhaps from inhaling too hard on an absent cigarette. I blew my nose needlessly. It is staggering how many parts of me — phalange, organ, membrane, and hair — wanted a smoke, each
Nausea	in its own sore way. For two full weeks I was nauseated. Peanuts and Irish whiskey are as good a way as I found to calm this sick desire of the body for tobacco. The cure, however, is expensive. — Budd Whitebook, "Confessions of an Ex-Smoker"*

Get to the point. Don't waste time or words in stating your topic sentence. Consider this good example of getting to the point — the writer is explaining the ancient Roman's technique for conquering their world:

The technique of expansion was simple. *Divide et impera* [divide and conquer]; enter into solemn treaty with a neighbouring country, foment internal disorder, intervene in support of the weaker side on the pretense that Roman honour was involved, replace the legitimate ruler with a puppet, giving him the status of a subject ally; later, goad him into rebellion, seize and sack the country, burn down the temples, and carry off the captive gods to adorn a triumph. Conquered territories were placed under the control of a provincial governor-general, an ex-commander-in-chief who garrisoned it, levied taxes, set up courts of summary justice, and linked the new frontiers with the old by so-called Roman roads—usually built by Greek engineers and native forced labour. Established social and religious practices were permitted so long as they did not threaten Roman administration or offend against the broad-minded Roman standards of good taste. The new province presently became a springboard for further aggression. —Robert Graves, "It Was a Stable World"

Graves makes his promise in the first nine words, in which he mentions the "simple" technique the Romans had for "dividing" and "conquering" in order to expand their empire. Suppose Graves had started his paragraph this way:

> The technique of expansion was interesting. It was based upon a theory about human nature that the Romans practically invented. This theory had to do with how people reacted to certain political and military devices which . . .

Do you see what is wrong? Since the beginning sentences are so vague, the paragraph never gets going. The writer can't fulfill a promise because he hasn't made one. Here's another example of a poor paragraph beginning:

> The first step involves part of the golf club head. The club head has removable parts, some of which are metal. You must consider these parts when deciding how to repair the club.

Specify the beginning of this paragraph and get to the point quicker:

> Your first step in repairing the club head is to remove the metal plate held on by Phillips screws.

This solid, specific paragraph beginning gives your reader a clear promise which you can fulfill easily without wasting words. (Observe, by the way, that establishing a writer's stance—as we did in the last example—can help you write clearer paragraph beginnings.)

Avoid fragmentary paragraphs. A fragmentary paragraph does not develop its topic or fulfill its promise. A series of fragmentary paragraphs jumps from idea to idea in a jerky and unconvincing fashion.

> [1]My freshman rhetoric class is similar in some ways to my senior English class in high school, but it is also very different.

²In my English class we usually had daily homework assignments that were discussed during the class period. If we were studying grammar, the assignments were to correct grammatical errors in the text. If we were studying literature, we were supposed to read the material and understand its ideas.

³In rhetoric class, we do basically the same things, except that in the readings we are assigned, we look much deeper into the purpose of the author.

⁴In my English class . . .

Fragmentary paragraphs are often the result of a weak stance. In this case, the writer has no clear idea of his role or audience, and so needs to revise his stance.

Keep your thoughts related. Don't allow any paragraph to be a collection of unrelated statements that looks like freewriting or brainstorming. Notice that the following paragraph contains at least six paragraph promises, none of them properly supported.

Paul Schrader's remake of the *Cat People* (1942) has come to the screen as a chilling horror film. The story revolves around a young woman named Irene who believes that making love will cause her to change into a leopard. Irene switches back and forth between cat and human. The actors—Nastassia Kinsky, Malcolm McDowell, and Annette O'Toole—are caught up in this dilemma with anthropological overtones. Nastassia Kinsky, a Russian, is well-known for the Avedon photograph of her with a snake. She is considered one of the most beautiful women in film today. Malcolm McDowell, playing her incestuous brother, is British and married to Mary Steenbergen, who played Marjorie Kinnan Rawlings in *Crosscreek*. In fact, McDowell played the famous editor Maxwell Perkins in the same film.

Avoid irrelevancies in your paragraphs. As with the fragmentary paragraph, the problem of irrelevancies in a paragraph is often the result of a vague *stance.* Notice how the italicized sentence does not fit the development of this paragraph, probably because it does not seem to be written for any particular reader:

We need a better working atmosphere at Restik Tool Company. The workers must feel that they are a working team instead of just individuals. If the men felt they were part of a team, they would not misuse the special machine tools, which now need to be resharpened twice as often as they used to be. *Management's attitude toward the union could be improved too.* The team effort is also being damaged by introduction of new products before their bugs have been worked out. Just when the men are getting used to one routine, a new one is installed, and their carefully created team effort is seriously damaged.

Try Different Organizational Patterns

Experiment with variations on the promise pattern. Read this student's paper in which she uses *time* and *space* as a means of organizing her paragraphs.

A TRIAL

Introduction
(promise)

¹About two years ago, my brother was charged with armed robbery, and I attended all the sessions of the trial. Three days stand out in my memory as being the most difficult of my life—the first day, the day the jury brought in the verdict, and the day my brother was sentenced.

Space and Time

²The first day I became acquainted with the unfamiliar surroundings of the courtroom. When our family entered, it was full of spectators sitting in rows at the back of the court. We sat on two benches near the front. My brother and his lawyer sat on the left side of the room, facing the judge. The prosecuting attorney sat at the right front. The jury sat in a box along the wall on my right. As I sat there, I could feel all the eyes in the courtroom moving back and forth along the row where we were sitting. Whenever I glanced up I saw people smiling at us, but I knew what they thought. If someone laughed, I felt ashamed, and when someone whispered, I was offended.

Time

³On that first day, a young man told the jury that he recognized my brother. He pointed to him and said, "That's the man. That's him!" The girls who worked at the place he supposedly robbed were the next witnesses, and they said they were unsure of his identity. That first day I had to get used to the humiliation of the prosecuting attorney and the witnesses talking about my brother and the robbery.

Time

⁴The day the jury returned and announced the verdict of guilty, I felt a lump in my throat. I did not want to cry in front of all those people. Instead, I cried inside. I could see a tear on my father's face, and that made my agony worse. My mother was shaking her head and tears trickled down her cheeks.

⁵A few days later, my brother was sentenced to a term in the state penitentiary. This time I could not hold back the tears. It seemed that the pool of tears I had cried inside were now rushing up at once. They kept flowing. I tried to wipe them away with my hands, but I couldn't. Crying uncontrollably, I rushed past the people sitting behind us to the restroom to clean my face, but all I could find were rough paper towels that wouldn't absorb the tears. I stayed in the restroom, crying, until they took my brother, handcuffed, downstairs to the jail.

Use the *suspense paragraph* — a class of paragraph that writers organize differently from the promise pattern. We call them *suspense paragraphs* because the writer does not put the topic idea near the beginning, but places it later, near the middle or even the end. This technique allows the writer to concentrate on details and keep the reader in suspense as to what they add up to. The point is held back in order to make the paragraph more dramatic, interesting, or emphatic. This kind of paragraph is often called *inductive,* because it develops from the particular to the general. (It is the reverse of the promise paragraph.) Here is an example.

Details and Observations   My generation of actors were trained to entice our prey. We kept an eye open, a claw sharpened, even when we professed to slumber. However deep the tragedy or shallow the farce, we never forgot to face front. Nowadays, the relation between player and public tends to be more sophisticated. Together they share a mutual experience of pain and sorrow. Sometimes the actor seems able to dispense with his audience — to no longer need them. He may choose or chance to perfect his performance on a wet afternoon in Shrewsbury, with hardly anyone watching, and thereafter the repetition for him may stale. For me this never happens. I never perfect a performance, though obviously I am sometimes better or worse, but I have learned that without a perfect audience, my struggle to the summit is impossible. I am aware as the curtain rises of the texture of the house. Some nights they will appear eager and willing; on others, listless and reluctant to follow the play. Once or twice during the evening they will change course, become willing and cooperative or grow sullen and bored. Suddenly the laughter is stilled, the coughing commences. Is it our fault or theirs? I have long ceased to

Topic idea (point)   wonder. An audience is like the sea, ever changing, never to be taken for granted. — Robert Morley

Here is another suspense paragraph, written by Alistair Cooke, who had been asked to write about the American oil industry, a subject he knew nothing about. He panicked until he found an old man in Texas who knew "more about oil than anybody."

I went to see the old man, and right away he said, "What do you know about oil?" Absolutely nothing, I said. "Fine," was his comment. I sat with him for one day, and went over the fields for another; and in forty-eight hours he took me

Details and examples   step by step over the history and practice of the industry. It was like sitting at the feet of Aristotle and having your mind rinsed out at frequent intervals with such drafts of common sense as "A play has a beginning, a middle, and an end." I went off on many more expeditions after that, and remember with pleasure the tricks of a couple of Irishmen growing spray orchids in an Oregon hothouse, or tramping out at night into the mountains of Arizona with an infrared lamp to spot strategic minerals embedded in the rocks like petrified

Topic idea (point)   tropical fish. *From all these safaris and interviews I came to the tentative, but for me amazing, conclusion that the first-rate businessman in this country is more precise, more imaginative, watchful, and intelligent about his trade than 90 per cent of the writers and academics who despise him.* — Alistair Cooke, *Talk About America*

PRACTICE

Discussion

Prepare some notes for a class discussion of the following paragraphs. Center your analysis of the paragraphs on the *promise pattern*. How well do the paragraphs get to the point and fulfill their promises? Do the authors need a different stance? What suggestions for improvement, if any, would you make? Optional: Rewrite the first paragraph, which is from the middle of a paper on body surfing.

The physical sensations of body surfing are pleasurable. The cold water is invigorating. The churning water is exhilarating. The activity makes me feel more alive and receptive to the sensations I receive. The activity also relieves tension. Besides feeling the power around me working for me, I like to smell and taste the salt water. It reminds me of the difference between the world on land and the ocean world and its vastness. With my experiences in skin diving I can see the beginnings of its vast depths. Standing on the beach I can see its vastness as it disappears over the horizon. It all combines to overwhelm me. I respect the ocean for its vastness and beauty and am somewhat awed by its majesty. Body surfing is a way of escaping the everyday world and entering a more perfect, ideal one. — Student paper

[1]In this confusion, with cigar butts lying about, his large assortment of pipes scattered on whatever would support them, matchboxes everywhere — he was a large consumer of matchboxes, for he struck an incredible number of matches in order to keep a cigar or a pipe alight — and with the air filled with the decaying smell of tobacco, he passed

his working hours in supreme contentment. He enjoyed writing, even though it was always difficult for him, and he enjoyed wrestling with ideas. He could not afford a large and extensive library, and at no time did he possess more than a thousand books. But in a hundred notebooks he preserved the important passages from the books he had read in the British Museum, and the library therefore represented only a part of his available literary resources. He was an inveterate note-taker, and the habit grew even more pronounced as he grew older.

²What Marx did not know was that this mode of life was slowly killing him. It was not only that he smoked too much, but he spent eight or nine hours a day breathing tobacco smoke in a room where, except on calm summer days, the windows were permanently closed. He was taking less and less exercise, and less and less sensible food, for now that he was reasonably affluent he was indulging himself more and more with highly seasoned foods. The only physical exercise came from the Sunday walks on Hampstead Heath, but these were neither so frequent nor so prolonged as in the days when he was younger. Sometimes he would go for a short stroll on Hampstead Heath in the evening. — Robert Payne, *Marx*

Writing

1. Assume that you must get rid of every appliance in your home in order to save electricity. Using *time* organization, write a paragraph in which you describe your decision about which appliances must go first — down to the very last one.

2. Write a paragraph, organized by *space*, on:
   a. The stage as it appeared to you the first time you were in a play.
   b. The college registration procedure the first time you registered.
   c. Your first visit to your dormitory room or apartment.
   d. Your mouth after your dentist applied braces.
   e. Your car after it was wrecked.
   f. Your _____ before/during/after _____ .

3. Write a *suspense* (inductively organized) paragraph on one of the following topics:
   a. A description of a problem, with your solution at the end.
   b. A series of details reporting an event in college life, with a generalizing explanation at the end.
   c. A series of statements or descriptions building up to a prediction.

4. Do a complete rewrite of an old paper, concentrating on paragraph organization.

HOW TO ARRANGE YOUR IDEAS: LEAD YOUR READER BY THE HAND

*I*t is likely that you know more about your subject than your readers do. Much of your material may be unfamiliar to them. A capable writer is often much like a professional guide in a jungle who leads his group of travelers toward an objective by avoiding wild animals, pitfalls, and quicksand traps. It is easier to lose a reader on the page than a fellow-traveler in a jungle. Here are a few suggestions that can help you become a more experienced guide through such dangers.

Start With a Simple or Familiar Idea

If your subject warrants such treatment, you can plan the paper to *lead* the readers from a simple (or familiar) idea to a more complex (or unfamiliar) one. Be sure that they understand each idea before the next is introduced. In the following two examples, each writer uses this strategy.

Familiar detail: beach ball

[1]To help us get a better picture of this solar system let us imagine a model of it reduced some five billion times. In this model, the sun is a beach ball about twelve inches across. Now, how far away would you imagine the planets to be from the sun on this scale? . . .

Familiar details: dust specks and pinhead

[2]Mercury, the closest planet to the sun and as small as a speck of dust in this scale, would be forty-two feet away. Venus, the second speck, about twice as big as Mercury, would be seventy-eight feet away. Earth, about the size of a pinhead next to the twelve-inch beach-ball sun, would be one hundred eight feet away; Mars, fifty-four yards; Jupiter, one hundred eighty yards; Saturn, three hundred forty yards; Neptune, one thousand eighty yards; and more than a mile away, tiny Pluto would move along its slow orbital path around the sun.

Application of familiar detail to scale of solar system

[3]Beyond this model of the solar system, the nearest star, on this same beach-ball scale, would be four thousand miles away. And farther still, the nearest galaxy would be almost four million miles out. —John Rublowsky, *Life and Death of the Sun*

First paragraph of article

[1]Most studies of atmospheric diffusion carried out heretofore have relatively little relevance to air pollution. The theoretical studies have been concerned (with some exceptions) with ideal situations which are sufficiently simple to be

solved, at least approximately, and the experimental investigations have been carried out in situations which approximate the idealizations as nearly as possible in order to test the theory.

Use of familiar detail: cream in coffee

[2]Perhaps I should interrupt myself long enough to explain to nonspecialists just what is meant by *atmospheric diffusion*. In the old days when people took cream in their coffee it was simple to illustrate from their daily experience. If poured into the coffee very slowly and not stirred, the cream would remain a long time where it was poured, and only slowly mix with the dark brown brew. Stirring with a spoon creates an irregular motion we call *mechanical turbulence,* which speeds up the horizontal and vertical spread of the cream and its rapid mingling with the coffee to form a uniform mixture. This spread and mixing is the process known as *diffusion*.

Application of knowns, by analogy, to "atmospheric diffusion"

[3]If the cream were poured first and then the coffee, the tendency of the light cream to rise to the top and the heavy coffee to sink would create convection, which would further tend to mix the two, even in the absence of mechanical stirring. In this case we speak of the stratification as *unstable,* whereas when the heavier fluid is at the bottom we say it is stable. The degree of stability and the amount of mechanical turbulence are the factors which determine the rate of diffusion in the atmosphere. — Morris Neiburger, "Where Is Science Taking Us?"

In the first example, Rublowsky gives his readers a relevant familiar detail (the beach ball) and works from it in order to lead us to a partial understanding of the vast distances in the solar system.

Since the second example is the beginning of Neiburger's article on *atmospheric diffusion,* he explains the term here in his introduction. To do so, he needs to define related terms — *mechanical turbulence, diffusion,* and *stability.* Instead of throwing these words at the reader without explanation, he uses an analogy: the familiar act of putting cream in one's coffee. After the reader has understood how diffusion and turbulence work in familiar liquids, he can better understand how they work in the atmosphere.

Use a Graded Order of Ideas

In a piece of writing you may deal with ideas or actions that vary in interest, importance, usefulness, practicality, or value. For example, there are five ways to leave our college town when vacation starts and one could "grade" them according to:

— How expensive they are
— How fast they are
— How dangerous they are
— How practical they are
— How interesting they are
— How reliable they are

Here is an example of a student's graded order using the organizing principle of *reliability:*

> For you new students who have not yet fought the battle of the student exodus, let me suggest the best way to get out of town before Christmas. Hitchhiking is illegal and dangerous — not very reliable. Planes are fast, but they don't go to enough hometowns, and airports get snowed in this time of year. Somewhat more reliable is the train, but the locals recently have had a nasty habit of running six or seven hours late. A car is better than the train, if you have one or know someone who does — and he happens to be going your way. The most reliable transportation for the average student is the bus. Buses aren't crowded and they are inexpensive. Also they are surprisingly fast, since if you plan ahead you can get an express bus that does not stop at small towns.

It is customary when employing any graded order to go from the "least" to the "most" — for example, from the *least reliable* to the *most reliable,* as in the paragraph above. You should follow this pattern partly because you want to get the less important ideas out of the way quickly so that you can get on with the more important ones. Also, you build up interest if you leave your best point until last. If you give readers your best idea first they may quit reading in the middle of your paper. However, there are exceptions to this convention, as you can see in this example:

Least important
(gas mileage)

[1]A good deal has been written about the values of owning a foreign car, but few people have given much thought to the realities of such ownership. Advertisers bombard us with facts about "fabulous gas mileage," but miles-per-gallon (so far as expense is concerned) is the least important thing to an owner of a foreign car. Of greater importance, since it eats into his mileage "savings" is the high initial cost of an import, which is often four or five hundred dollars more than that of the cheaper American makes. More important still is the fact that parts and repair often cost so much that the import owner finds himself spending more on his car than the owner of a much bigger American automobile.

Most important
(repair costs)

Transition
Most comfortable
(in city)

[2]Similarly, Americans often fool themselves about the comfort of the import, which, it is true, rides and parks like a dream in the city. But the car that gives a comfortable ride in

Least comfortable (in country) town, that parks in a very small space, that turns on a dime, and is easy to get in and out of is a different vehicle on the highway. Anyone who has driven a light foreign car a few miles in a crosswind can sympathize with the Californian who drove his import to Denver and there promptly traded it off for several thousand pounds of power-steered, power-braked metal monster from Detroit before he started his trip home.

PRACTICE

Writing
Write a paper in which you use a *graded order* to explain an unfamiliar process, device, or activity. Where you can, help your reader by moving from simple or familiar ideas to more difficult ones.

Use Signposts

Use Single-Word or Phrase Transitions. Transitions point forward and backward. They are the reader's signposts; without them he or she might easily get lost. The simplest and most obvious transitions are those that count in order: "This is my *first* idea. . . . Now for the *second* idea. . . . *Third,* I think . . ." Less obvious are those transitions that do not so much lead readers by the hand as smooth their way: "*It is certain* that the reactor could not have been shut down so easily if . . . *Nevertheless,* the men in the black suits were blowing up the bridge. . . . *Moreover,* the two physicists could not agree on what to do."

Here are some typical transitional words and phrases:

—To explain or introduce ideas: *for instance, for example, such as, specifically, in particular, to illustrate, thus*
—To count or separate ideas: *first, second, third* (but not *firstly, secondly, thirdly*), *moreover, in addition, another, furthermore, also, again, finally*
—To compare ideas: *likewise, similarly, in the same way*
—To contrast or qualify ideas: *however, on the other hand, on the contrary, but*
—To show cause or effect: *as a result, consequently, therefore, thus*

Such a listing could continue indefinitely, for under special circumstances hundreds of words and phrases that are not ordinarily thought of as being transitional (like pronouns and certain key words) can be used to link words, ideas, or sentences. As an example, here is a brief passage taken from the middle of a magazine article (linking expressions are in italics):

[1]Today it is no secret that our official, prison-threat theory of crime control is an utter failure. Criminologists have known *this* for years. When pocket-picking was punishable by hanging, in England, the crowds that gathered about the gallows to enjoy the spectacle of an execution were particularly likely to have their pockets picked by skillful operators who, to say the least, were not deterred by the exhibition of "justice." We have long known that the perpetrators of most offenses are never detected; *of those detected,* only a fraction are found guilty and still fewer serve a "sentence." *Furthermore,* we are quite certain now that of those who do receive the official punishment of the law, many become firmly committed *thereby* to a continuing life of crime and a continuing feud with law enforcement officers. Finding themselves ostracized from society and blacklisted by industry *they* stick with the crowd they have been introduced to in jail and try to play the game of life according to *this set of rules. In this way* society skillfully converts individuals of borderline self-control into loyal members of the underground fraternity. . . .

[2]What might deter the reader from conduct which his neighbors would not like does not necessarily deter the grown-up child of vastly different background. The *latter's* experiences may have conditioned him to believe that the chances of winning by undetected cheating are vastly greater than the probabilities of fair treatment and opportunity. *He* knows about the official threats and the social disapproval of *such acts.* He knows about the hazards and the risks. *But despite all this "knowledge,"* he becomes involved in waves of discouragement or cupidity or excitement or resentment leading to episodes of social offensiveness.

[3]*These episodes* may prove vastly expensive both to him and to society. *But* sometimes they will have an aura of success. Our periodicals have only recently described the wealth and prominence for a time of a man described as a murderer. Konrad Lorenz, the great psychiatrist and animal psychologist, has beautifully described in geese what he calls a "triumph reaction." *It* is a sticking out of the chest and flapping of the wings after an encounter with a challenge. All of us have seen *this primitive biological triumph reaction*—in some roosters, *for example,* in some businessmen and athletes and others—and in some criminals.—Karl Menninger, "Verdict Guilty—Now What?"

Use Transitional Paragraphs. The transitional paragraph, which usu-'ly acts as a bridge between two other paragraphs, is often found in a fairly long piece of writing. As the short italicized paragraph below illustrates, it can prepare the reader for a plunge into a new topic.

> There was, however, a darker and more sinister side to the Irish character. They are, said a land agent on the eve of the famine, "a very desperate people, with all this degree of courtesy, hospitality, and cleverness amongst them."
>
> *To understand the Irish of the nineteenth century and their blend of courage and evasiveness, tenacity and inertia, loyalty and double-dealing, it is necessary to go back to the Penal Laws.*
>
> The Penal Laws, dating from 1695, and not repealed in their entirety until Catholic emancipation in 1829, aimed at the destruction of Catholicism in Ireland by a series of ferocious enactments. . . . —Cecil Woodham-Smith, *The Great Hunger: Ireland, 1845–1849*

In the longer transition, you may sum up what you have been saying before introducing a new subject, and so give your readers a chance to catch up before you go on to a new topic. Example:

> So far, we have spoken only about that portion of the stellar population that falls within the main sequence. All these stars, as we have seen, are very much the same. They differ mainly in their stages of evolution, which in turn is a result of their mass and the speed at which they use up their original fuel supply. But what happens to a star after it has used up its allotment of hydrogen? Can we find examples of such stars that have reached old age in their life cycle? Or can we find examples of stars that are still in their babyhood as far as the stellar cycle is concerned? —John Rublowsky, *Life and Death of the Sun*

Organize by "Creative Repetition"

Repetition, we are told, is an evil in writing; and it seems that we are told this practically from the time we begin to write. Yet the skillful writer instinctively recognizes that carefully repeating certain key words and phrases can help tie ideas together. The mathematician Norbert Wiener begins his discussion of Brownian motion in this way: "To understand the Brownian motion, let us imagine a *push-ball* in a field in which a *crowd* is milling around. Various people in the *crowd* will run into the *push-ball* and will move it about. Some will *push* in one direction and some in another."

To use repetition creatively, you repeat certain words or phrases in order to keep the reader's mind firmly on the subject. Sometimes you change the grammatical form slightly in order to prevent the repetition from becoming a bore. Here is how one excellent writer of nonfiction employs creative repetition in examining business jargon or *businesese:*

> [1]Its signal characteristic, as the reader and all other critics of businesese will recognize, is its uniformity. Almost invariably, businesese is marked by the heavy use of the passive construction. Nobody ever *does* anything. Things happen—and the author of the action is only barely implied. Thus, one does not refer to something, reference is made to; similarly, while prices may rise, nobody raises them. To be sure, in businesese there is not quite the same anonymity as is found in federal prose, for "I" and "we" do appear often. Except when the news to be relayed is good, however, there is no mistaking that the "I" and "we" are merely a convenient fiction and that the real author isn't a person at all but that great mystic force known as the corporation.
>
> [2]Except for a few special expressions, its vocabulary is everywhere quite the same. Midwesterners are likely to dispute the latter point, but a reading of approximately 500,000 words of business prose indicates no striking differences—in the Midwest or anywhere else. Moreover, in sounding out a hundred executives on the subject, *Fortune* found that their views coincided remarkably, particularly so on the matter of pet peeves (principally: "please be advised," "in reference to yours of . . . ," "we wish to draw attention," "to acknowledge your letter"). The phrases of businesese are everywhere so uniform, in fact, that stenographers have a full set of shorthand symbols for them.
>
> [3]Because of this uniformity, defenders of businesese can argue that it doesn't make for misunderstanding. After all, everybody knows the symbols, and, furthermore, wouldn't a lot of people be offended by the terseness of more concise wording? There is something to this theory. Since businesese generally is twice as wordy as plain English, however, this theory is rather expensive to uphold. By the use of regular English the cost of the average letter—commonly estimated at 75 cents to $1—can be cut by about 20 cents. For a firm transmitting a million letters a year, this could mean an annual savings of $200,000. Probably it would be even greater; for, by the calculations of correspondence specialist Richard Morris, roughly 15 per cent of the letters currently being written wouldn't be necessary at all if the preceding correspondence had been in regular English in the first place. —William H. Whyte, "The Language of Business," *Fortune* magazine

Whyte employs *businesese* as a catchy technical term, and so he doesn't need to vary the word. Every time he refers to the "sameness" of business prose, however, he varies the word or phrase: *uniformity, quite the same, uniform, this uniformity.* Each use of this "word-idea" is just close enough to the last to keep the reader on the track of the essay's main point.

Whyte's article is over thirty years old, but it is still the standard discussion of *businesese,* a fact which says something about the effectiveness of creative repetition.

PRACTICE

Discussion

For discussion prepare some notes on the organization of the following two passages. Describe the writer's stance in each. How well does each writer keep his or her *promise* to the reader and fulfill the reader's expectations? Consider both the paragraph promises (topic ideas) and the essay promise (thesis). Where is the thesis stated? Where are the topic ideas in each paragraph?

Do the writers use any special techniques for arranging their ideas? Discuss their use of transitions, and of organizational devices such as creative repetition.

¹This is something everyone already knows: A well-used city street is apt to be a safe street. A deserted city street is apt to be unsafe. But how does this work, really? And what makes a city street well-used or shunned? Why is the sidewalk mall in Washington Houses, which is supposed to be an attraction, shunned? Why are the sidewalks of the old city just to its west not shunned? What about streets that are busy part of the time and then empty abruptly?

²A city street equipped to handle strangers, and to make a safety net, in itself, out of the presence of strangers, as the streets of successful city neighborhoods always do, must have three main qualities:

³First, there must be a clear demarcation between what is public space and what is private space. Public and private spaces cannot ooze into each other as they do typically in suburban settings or in projects.

⁴Second, there must be eyes upon the street, eyes belonging to those we might call the natural proprietors of the street. The buildings on a street equipped to handle strangers and to insure the safety of both residents and strangers, must be oriented to the street. They cannot turn their backs or blank sides on it and leave it blind.

⁵And third, the sidewalk must have users on it fairly continuously, both to add to the number of effective eyes on the street and to induce the people in buildings along the street to watch the sidewalks in sufficient numbers. Nobody enjoys sitting on a stoop or looking out a window at an empty street. Almost nobody does such a thing. Large numbers of people entertain themselves, off and on, by watching street activity.

⁶In settlements that are smaller and simpler than big cities, controls on acceptable public behavior, if not on crime, seem to operate with greater or lesser success through a web of reputation, gossip, approval, disapproval and sanctions, all of which are powerful if people know each other and word travels. But a city's streets, which must control not only the behavior of the people of the city but also of visitors from suburbs and towns who want to have a big time away from the gossip and sanctions at home, have to operate by more direct, straightforward methods. It is a wonder cities have solved such an inherently difficult problem at all. And yet in many streets they do it magnificently.

⁷It is futile to try to evade the issue of unsafe city streets by attempting to make some other features of a locality, say interior courtyards, or sheltered play spaces, safe instead. By definition again, the streets of a city must do most of the job of handling strangers for this is where strangers come and go. The streets must not only defend the city against predatory strangers, they must protect the many, many peaceable and well-meaning strangers who use them, insuring their safety too as they pass through. Moreover, no normal person can spend his life in some artificial haven, and this includes children. Everyone must use the streets.

⁸On the surface, we seem to have here some simple aims: To try to secure streets where the public space is unequivocally public, physically unmixed with private or with nothing-at-all space, so that the area needing surveillance has clear and practicable limits; and to see that these public street spaces have eyes on them as continuously as possible.

⁹But it is not so simple to achieve these objects, especially the latter. You can't make people use streets they have no reason to use. You can't make people watch streets they do not want to watch. Safety on the streets by surveillance and mutual policing of one another sounds grim, but in real life it is not grim. The safety of the street works best, most casually, and with least frequent taint of hostility or suspicion precisely where people are using and most enjoying the city streets voluntarily and are least conscious, normally, that they are policing.
—Jane Jacobs, *The Death and Life of Great American Cities*

¹Three seconds after you leap from the Golden Gate Bridge, perhaps the most popular location for suicide in the western world, you hit the water 226 feet below at about 75 miles an hour. The trip is nearly always one-way: It's cold down there, fierce crosscurrents pull a body under in seconds, and the water is 300 feet deep. Only 10 out of the more than 500 people who have jumped since the bridge opened in 1937 are around to tell the story.

²Each year more and more people are doing it, or trying to, and the experts agree that an antisuicide barrier is needed at once. It is not about to happen: A special committee studying the question in San Francisco has just voted against the idea, unanimously, after spending

$27,000 on the design and testing of a model. "Much as I hate to say it," sighed Edwin Fraser, bridge district president, "we have to forget it until it's more financially feasible." A barrier would cost between $1 and $2 million and it seems the city has other priorities.

[3]The committee chairman said mail was running strongly against the barrier anyhow. It was not just the expense: The view would be ruined, and besides, folks would only find another place to do it. San Francisco is full of skyscrapers.

[4]"It's nonsense to say that blocking the bridge will merely send suicides elsewhere," says Dr. Richard Seiden, a psychologist at the University of California at Berkeley. "It is the bridge itself that's fatally attractive." The great russet span of the Golden Gate Bridge, with its sweeping, soaring lines poised over the sparkling blue water, is a glamorous place, and nearly all the suicides choose to jump from the landward side, facing the amphitheater-like ring of cities around the bay.

[5]Six survivors of the leap agreed with Dr. Seiden when asked: If they couldn't have used the bridge as backdrop for their attempt, they wouldn't have tried at all. Each of them was in favor of the barrier; none has tried to repeat his act elsewhere. . . .

[6]For thousands, San Francisco is the end of the rainbow, the lovely dream-city where all the rootless, dissatisfied, lonely people come from elsewhere expecting that all their troubles will be cured. It does not work out that way and for some it is the final disappointment. If you cannot make it in this fun city, where can you make it?

[7]At least eight agencies and hospitals here are working to help the suicidal, with "hot lines" and crisis centers. But beyond that, doctors agree, there is a great need for more study, research, clinical investigation and social openness about suicide, and, of course, for that Golden Gate barrier. Says Dr. Seiden, "We really don't have to make it so easy." — Charles Foley, "The Leap from Golden Gate Bridge"

INTRODUCTIONS AND CONCLUSIONS

An effective introduction ordinarily does two things: (1) it catches the readers' interest and makes them want to read on; (2) it tells them what the essay is about, perhaps by stating the thesis or suggesting the main points.

An effective conclusion rounds off the paper. As you will see in the following examples, a conclusion often "matches" its introduction by referring to or restating the writer's early material. If the rest of the paper has been planned carefully, conclusions often seem to write themselves.

Here are two examples of effective introductions and conclusions. Note that the second example delays the main point and puts it in the conclusion.

Introduction

Very few people would sit at the TV for hours to watch a cargo of potatoes take off from planet earth in a spaceship. Yet a single potato orbiting the sun could hold infinitely greater significance for the future of humanity than would the landing of a man on the moon. For a man on the moon can tell us nothing new about injecting happiness into life on *Thesis* earth. *But a potato in solar orbit might lead to the secret of how all growth—hence life itself—is regulated.*

Conclusion

References to material in the article The last of the comments above concern Professor Brown's experiments principally. They convey some sense of the values inherent in orbiting a potato around the sun. NASA has not yet set a date for this expedition, but a "Spud-*Allusion to thesis* nik" has been designed and if the conventional scientific opposition to innovation can be overcome, the chosen potato may take off next year. —John Lear, "The Orbiting Potato"

Introduction

Questions interest the reader Why should any words be called obscene? Don't they all describe natural human functions? Am I trying to tell them, my students demand, that the "strong, earthy, gut-honest"—or, if they are fans of Norman Mailer, the "rich, liberating, existential"—language they use to describe sexual activity isn't preferable to "phony-sounding, middle-class words like 'intercourse' and 'copulate'?" "Cop-you-late!" they say with fancy inflections and gagging grimaces. "Now, what is *that* supposed to mean?"

Conclusion

And yet how eloquently angered, how piously shocked many of these same people become if denigrating language is used about any minority group other than women; if the obscenities are racial or ethnic, that is, rather than sexual. Words like "coon," "kike," "spic," "wop," after all, deform identity, deny individuality and humanness in almost exactly the same way that sexual vulgarisms and obscenities do. No one that I know, least of all my students, would fail to

Thesis stated
as question
question the values of a society whose literature and entertainment rested heavily on racial or ethnic pejoratives. Are
the values of a society whose literature and entertainment
rest as heavily as ours on sexual pejoratives any less questionable? — Barbara Lawrence

There are as many ways to write introductions and conclusions as
ways to write papers. A short, blunt beginning may make an effective
promise: "The amateur productions in the University Playhouse are
poorly directed this year." One-sentence conclusions are occasionally
worth trying, although you should be wary of using conclusions that are
too brief, for they may leave the reader with a feeling of having been
let down.

Here are some ideas for writing introductions. You might start with:

— An apt quotation
— A literary allusion
— A story or an incident relating to your subject
— A statement that shows how interesting your subject is
— A question that limits your subject; the answer to the question is
  your paper
— A statement of a problem that readers should know about
— A simple statement of thesis that limits your subject
— A definition of an important word or phrase relating to your
  subject
— The historical background of your subject (be brief)
— A statement that popular ideas about your subject are wrong and
  that you intend to refute them in a specific way
— A statement that your subject needs new examination; your paper
  is the examination
— Pertinent facts about your subject
— Combinations of some of these methods

For a conclusion, you might end your paper with:

— An allusion to the hook of your introduction
— A reference to the question, definition, statement of thesis,
  historical background, etc., that you started the paper with
— A restatement of your thesis
— A brief answer to the question you raised in the introduction
— A brief statement of the solution to the problem you raised in your
  introduction
— A new question that relates to your paper, a question that gives

the reader something to think about (but be careful not to introduce an undeveloped idea)

— A summary of the main points in your paper (this is often useful if materials are complex, but beware — a summary can be dull and redundant)

— A punchy, single sentence — don't punch too hard

— A new story or incident that relates to your subject

Avoid these errors in writing introductions:

— Writing a vague or ambiguous introduction, leaving the thesis of the paper unclear

— Failing to define terms that the reader is not familiar with; terms should be defined if you are using them in a special sense

— Writing an introduction that is too long; for most short papers, it is a mistake to write more than a one-paragraph (or, at most, a two-paragraph) introduction

And these errors in writing conclusions:

— Failing to fill out a conclusion, leaving the reader hanging

— Adding irrelevant or unnecessary details

— Adding an undeveloped idea; a conclusion is not the place to develop or introduce ideas

PRACTICE

Discussion

For class discussion, review suggestions for writing introductions and conclusions. Then read the pairings below and evaluate how well they fulfill the requirements for introductions and conclusions.

1. Introduction

During my life I've had seven dogs, two snakes, one frog, three turtles, ten fish, four gerbils, four wild baby rabbits, and two guinea pigs. Having so many pets has turned our house into a virtual zoo with all the smells and messes of one. Life is often wild and confusing, but living with all of these animals can also be really fun. One nice aspect of living with pets is that we share a "trade-off" relationship. I feed them, wash them, train them, clean up after them and try to keep them happy. But what have my pets done for me? Owning pets has made me more responsible, relaxed, and outgoing.

Conclusion

Although owning a number of pets can be a very hectic and confusing experience, I would never live without one. Both the responsibilities and pleasures of pet ownership have enriched my life. They have made me a responsible, relaxed and sociable person. I would not care to speculate about how different my life would be without pets.

2. Introduction

Many geologic features of the Midwest define the terrain of that area and indicate to scientists that glaciers once covered this portion of the continent. The effect of glacial activity is evident throughout the Midwest—in moraines, eskers, kettles, and erratics. If a traveller knows about these features and can identify them, driving through the flat agricultural area known as the "bread basket of the world" can be more meaningful and less dull.

Conclusion

The flat but rich and productive topsoil of the Midwest region known as Illinois is not the only result of the former presence of the glaciers. Such features as moraines, eskers, kettles, and erratics are all remnants of a bygone age which help to define the Midwest, at least geologically.

3. Introduction

Last summer my friend Debbie cut her foot on broken glass while playing in a lake. Because the water was murky, she failed to see the glass and accidentally pushed it into her foot when she stepped in the area. This incident illustrates how senseless littering really is. Littering is not only harmful to people (and animals), it causes needless destruction of the environment, destruction which is very hard to undo.

Conclusion

A clean environment is less likely to harm someone than a polluted one. A landscape is much more breathtaking if there aren't any beer bottles to mar it. More important, it is much harder to clean up our environment than it is to contaminate it. And just how hard is it to find a garbage can, anyway?

4. Introduction

Waiting is a kind of suspended animation. Time solidifies: a dead weight. The mind reddens a little with anger and then blanks off into a sort of abstraction and fitfully wanders, but presently it comes up red and writhing again, straining to get loose. Waiting casts one's life into a little dungeon of time. It is a way of being controlled, of being rendered immobile and helpless. One can read a book or sing (odd looks from the others) or chat with strangers if the wait is long enough to begin forming a bond of shared experience, as at a snowed-in airport. But people tend to do their waiting stolidly.

Conclusion

Waiting can seem an interval of nonbeing, the black space between events and the outcomes of desires. It makes time maddeningly elastic: it has a way of seeming to compact eternity into a few hours. Yet its brackets ultimately expand to the largest dimensions. One waits for California to drop into the sea or for "next year in Jerusalem" or for the Messiah or for the Apocalypse. All life is a waiting, and perhaps in that sense one should not be too eager for the wait to end. The region that lies on the other side of waiting is eternity. — Lance Morrow

Writing

1. Choose one of your papers written for this class or another one. Rewrite the introduction and conclusion.

2. After studying the major strategies in organizing paragraphs and papers, you should now be able to use all the skills you have learned in the chapter. Write a paper on a "technical" subject for a reader who knows little or nothing concerning the matter. *Technical* here refers to any subject that may have some mystery or complexity for the layman—for example, putting (in golf), county primary elections, the balancing of tires on a car, the use of shorthand in secretarial work, etc.

    In your paper concentrate on using the promise pattern, writing clear paragraphs, arranging your ideas clearly, and writing a good introduction and conclusion. Use transitions where necessary.

CHAPTER 12

SUCCEEDING WITH WORDS

Words are powerfully alive and powered for manipulation. You can do as much with them as ever painter did with paint, sculptor with stone, or composer with chords. All you need is a little practice and a willingness to bend words and bend to them — and take a certain risk. Try comedy, for instance as in Woody Allen's observation on men and women: "A relationship, I think, is like a shark. It has to constantly move forward or die. And I think what we got on our hands here is a dead shark." So much for *Jaws* and love affairs.

Sign in a store window: INSANITY IS HEREDITARY. YOU GET IT FROM YOUR KIDS. After seeing the following sentence in a newspaper, "Suicide is a viable option," one of our students wrote: "True, but only if you are capable of living." (Look up *viable* to appreciate the wit.) Another student: "On any given Sunday, you can hear the baseball announcers babbling away, batting their clichés from pillar to post." Complaining about his college administration, another student wrote: "The dean will do you a favor one day and do you in the next."

Such bright and light turns of words are not just for the self-consciously literary. The language belongs to us, to you — to everybody. And everybody — if we put his or her or their mind to it — can produce a verbal drink with a twist of lemon in it. Here is singer Bette Midler on her weird audiences in Germany:

> I'm used to attracting some fairly outrageous crowds—in fact, I pride myself on it—but I have never seen anything as extreme as what I got in Germany. I think the women were even more amazing than the men. More severe, and certainly much tougher. With platinum-blond ducktail hairdos, long, long squared-off nails and no expression whatsoever. . . .
>
> The men tended to have a bit more expression, but also a lot more leather. And they came in irons of every variety, from metal-studded chokers to handcuffs. Sitting in my dressing room and listening to the clanking of metal as the audience came in, I throught I was about to perform for a chain-link fence.—*A View From A Broad*

ACCURATE WORDS

The best writing uses accurate wording. One should call things by their right names, and not call a chair a "table"; a student's reasoned difference of opinion with an instructor an "act of rebellion"; a careless piece of writing "artistic" merely because it "expresses the author's personality." Accurate wording begins in clear thinking and in making clear choices about verbal possibilities.

The writer who says, "I know what I mean but I can't put it into words," is forgetting that, so far as writing is concerned, words *are* meanings. Before you can find an accurate word to put on paper, you must first have a clear idea of its meaning. In a paper on the novelist Joseph Conrad, a student wrote that "the plot of *Lord Jim* is unusually diaphanous." When his instructor objected to *diaphanous,* the student replied: "My dictionary says *diaphanous* means 'transparent.' What I meant was that Conrad's plot is clearly outlined in the novel." His instructor pointed out that the full meaning in the dictionary was "transparent as in gauzy cloth." A more accurate word choice, perhaps, for what the student had in mind could be found in what he had said to his instructor: "Conrad's plot is clearly outlined in the novel."

Notice that the change of wording in this example involves more than just a word-for-word substitution. It is a curious fact, and one well worth remembering, that in revising you often cannot pull a "poor" word out of a sentence and replace it with a better one. Many times the "better" ones you try won't fit the context in either meaning or sentence structure. So you may have to back up to the beginning of the sentence—and sometimes to the beginning of the paragraph—and rewrite much of the material.

There is a two-way relationship between words and ideas. In the writing and revising stages, you select some words and discard others. During this process, you are choosing or creating ideas and also, in a sense, evoking emotions and attitudes. In an autobiographical paper, one student explained how this process worked for her:

> What I had written in my first draft was this: "I have been expanding my ideas lately about being crippled." Then I paused because I did not know how to go on. I knew that my attitudes had changed about the accident and what it had done to me, but I could not put it into words. I pondered this problem for a while but couldn't find a solution. So I went to bed.
>
> The next day I looked again at my lonely sentence that began: "I have been expanding . . ." I scratched through the sentence and wrote: "At last I accepted the fact that I am a cripple." For I suddenly realized that something had been happening to me over the past few months. I had been subconsciously learning to *accept* the fact that I will be crippled for life. This was the unformed idea that I had been trying to teach myself to put into words.

Like this student, as you hunt for words to express yourself, you are also thinking. And this thinking process may change the nature and goal of your hunting. But as far as your readers are concerned, it is the *result* of the search that counts. Since readers want to understand, they wish above all for you to be both accurate and clear in your choice of words.

SUITABLE WORDS

When Harry Truman was President, he and his wife Bess visited a horticultural show. As he walked around, Truman kept praising the best plant specimens, saying, "My, you must use good manure on this." After a time, someone asked Mrs. Truman, "Couldn't you get the president to say *fertilizer*?"

"Heavens no," Mrs. Truman said. "It took me twenty-five years to get him to say *manure*."

This anecdote illustrates a second principle of effective wording— that of *propriety,* or the *suitability* of word choice. Slang is suitable in some situations and for certain readers, but not for other situations and readers. Highly formal language is suitable in some circumstances, but not in others. To determine what is suitable, consider your *stance:* your role as writer, your thesis, your reader.

It does not seem suitable to use *orthogeosyncline* in a paper on land forms written for the general reader, *predominant aspirations of our senior citizens* in a newspaper article on the problems of old people, or *I didn't like the damn movie* or *The movie was just great* in a magazine or newspaper review of a new film. Considering the writing situation and the reader, the first example is too specialized, the second too formal, and the third and fourth too casual or slangy.

To use words suitably is to use them responsibly, thinking as you write and revise about your role and subject—and readers. Will they understand what you mean? Will they approve of your verbal "manners"?

PRACTICE

Writing

Consider the italicized words and phrases in the following sentences. Are they *accurate* and *suitable*? (Your dictionary may help you with some of them.) Rewrite each sentence to make the wording more effective.

a. There is just one more *thing she forgot to overlook.*

b. I'm in favor of *letting the status quo stay as it is.*

c. The student should not have his *curriculum of study preplanned* to make him *follow a role,* but rather have it *displayed* to *intensify* his already *inherent capacities.*

d. We were so *enervated* we lost any *moral* we had as a *real good* team.

e. From a letter: Well, the weather here is *crummy,* and the food *putrid.* The social events are too dull *to partake of.*

f. People don't *realize* all the time I spend on the job. I'm *insane* about work.

g. Sam's statement was loud and *formidable.* He *inferred* that no one should *belittle* a referee by throwing bottles of *alcoholic beverage* at him.

h. Can you give a *legible* description of the *highlights* of the *company's economic package?*

i. I can *do* that job of description *up right* if you will let me *discuss on* all the *facets* of the religion.

j. Written for a literary magazine read by students: Since Shakespeare's *optimum interest* was in tragedy, the critic *must of necessity utilize a functional analysis* of symbols *inherent* in the tragic plays.

k. Her accident was a *serious* disaster.

EFFECTIVE WORDS

You know that your words should be accurate and suitable. Here are a few more suggestions for making them so and for increasing the general *effectiveness* of your wording.

Be Specific

According to a recent newspaper story, county supervisors in Stockton, California, put up signs near a landfill where people were supposed to dump their garbage. The signs read "Foothill Sanitary Landfill Facilities," and people passed right by them looking for a place to dump their garbage. But an imaginative official saved the day, or Stockton might now be knee-deep in trash. He put out new signs that read simply: "Dump."

Stocktonians knew what *dump* meant because it was specific—explicit, definite, particular. *Foothill Sanitary Landfill Facilities* was vague, indefinite, and general; and so the expression communicated poorly. If you are in doubt about whether your wording is specific, try placing it on a *specificity ladder:*

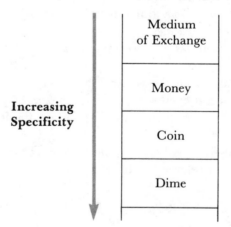

Increasing Specificity

Medium of Exchange

Money

Coin

Dime

As you step down the ladder from the top, you use words that are increasingly specific. Although *money* in the ladder above is a fairly general word, it is more specific than *medium of exchange. Coin* is more specific than *money*, and *dime* more specific than *coin.*

Here is another example of a specificity ladder. This time, we are considering a type of human conduct:

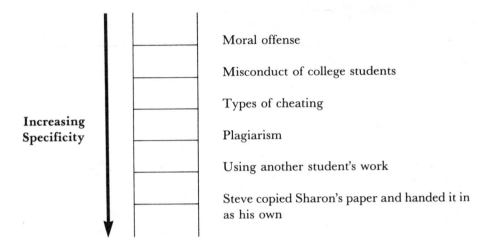

**Increasing
Specificity**

Moral offense

Misconduct of college students

Types of cheating

Plagiarism

Using another student's work

Steve copied Sharon's paper and handed it in
as his own

What happens to your writing when you choose words from the bottom rungs of a specificity ladder? First, you will discover that your ideas seem to flow more smoothly and quickly because you are being definite about them and clarifying them as you go along. "What do I mean by a *moral offense*? I mean, in this instance, that Steve copied Sharon's paper and handed it in as his own." Of course you can mean something else by *moral offense*—a thousand ladders could be constructed starting with that phrase on the top rung. Second, your readers will discover that you are "explaining" things to them as you write. This paragraph is vague and needs explanation:

> Why the student body should continue in this state of apathy is not really understandable. The practice and theory of politics are studied in the classroom but political habits on campus do not seem to benefit from such labor. Many a political figure has been invited to speak, only to discover that the students are not really interested.

The paragraph, made specific, explains the point better:

> Our student body is dull and slack-minded. All students here must take at least one course in history or political science that teaches them something about the theory and practice of American politics. Yet students have no interest in campus elections; only twenty percent voted in the Student Senate elections in October. It may be said that these student elections are not important. Perhaps. But nobody seems to care about national political affairs either. When Senator Rogers spoke here last week, the auditorium was two-thirds empty; and when he called for questions no student cared enough to ask one.

PRACTICE

Discussion

1. Construct specificity ladders using these words or phrases on the top rung. Where necessary, consult your dictionary.

low-income individuals   physically fit
effective leadership   brotherhood
somebody's bad temper   beauty

2. Read the two passages below. Underline the specific words. As a reader, do you consider the passages successful? Why?

[1]Thoroughbred horses eat well, work hard and, after the years and effort that have gone into improving the breed, their digestive tracts work at a truly magnificent pitch of efficiency. Under normal conditions we had 1,350 horses in the stable area at Suffolk Downs. And every morning we had 30 tons of manure to dispose of. Not to give the horses undue credit, it wasn't entirely the pure unadulterated product. The floors of stalls are covered with straw, and what you end up with is a sort of thatchy mixture. For decades mushroom growers bought all this stuff they could get. They came and got it and left their money behind. By the time I came to Suffolk the formerly eager mushroom men were in the process of converting to synthetic fertilizer. They were still willing to take the manure off the track's hands *if* we charged them nothing and shipped it to them. That cost us $100,000 a year.

[2]It's a problem. It really is. The grooms muck out the stalls and pile the manure in front of the barns, and that's where the obligation of the horsemen ends. The track has the job of collecting and delivering it to railroad flatcars, a job we contracted out.

[3]There was one phase of the operation that wasn't contracted out. After my son Mike graduated from high school he came to work at the track, and I handed him a shovel and pointed him in the general direction of the paddock. The thoroughbred is a high-strung animal, and once he is led into the paddock he seems to understand that something is about to happen. Mike's job was to stand there with his shovel and watch carefully. It made for a very active 20 minutes nine or 10 times a day. The boss' son should always start at the bottom, and I couldn't think of anything more bottom than that. — Bill Veeck, "Racing Has Its Dirty Side"

[1]Let us say that you work in an office building with 1,000 people and that every day at least two are hurt on the job. Some suffer such

ghastly wounds—multiple compound fractures, deep cuts severing muscle, sinew and nerve, shattered pelvises—that they may never return to their old posts. And every six months or so, a body is taken to the morgue.

2Almost anywhere, this would be called carnage, and a hue and cry would be raised. But in the big-tree logging woods of the Pacific Northwest, it is simply endured with what logger-writer Stan Hager has called "proud fatalism," and few outside the loggers' trade even know of it. Miners trapped behind a cave-in draw national media attention, but in the dim rain forests men fall singly and suddenly. There aren't any TV cameras. —William Blundell

Writing

1. Write a paragraph or two to a friend asking to borrow his car. Be very specific about your reasons for needing it.

2. Write a short paper supporting or attacking the candidacy of "someone" for "something"—for example, of someone who wants to be a student representative, a member of the tennis team, a teaching assistant, an aide in the admissions office, a secretary, bookkeeper, etc. Designate a reader or readership, and use specific words to describe the strengths or weaknesses of your candidate.

Watch Your Connotations

A word's *connotation* is what the word suggests or implies. Its *denotation* is its literal, neutral, or ordinary meaning.

A writer cannot control the connotations of the words he uses as well as he can control their denotations. But he should try. A reader often reacts to the suggestive coloring of a word more than to its neutral meaning. For example, Philip Morrison (professor of physics at MIT) remarks that "black holes" in space may be more important as verbal connotation than as physical realities:

> The term *black hole* has to do with sleep, death, memory, and also has evocations of the Black Hole of Calcutta. Before you know what it *is,* it's exciting, and a little bit frightening. If they had been called Schwartzschild singularities of the first kind they would have been basically ignored.

Let us consider more examples of connotation, particularly in contrast to denotation:

Word	Denotation	Possible Connotations
Housefly	Small, two-winged insect	Filthiness, uncleanliness, revolting to the senses—"O hideous little bat, the size of snot" —Karl Shapiro, "The Fly"
Prince	Nonreigning male member of a royal family	Wealth, glory, honor, gracefulness, courtesy
Strut	To walk stiffly	Egomania, vanity, swaggering, false pride, pretensions to glory; synchronized movements of a marching band

So long as you are reasonably accurate in your word choice, denotations shouldn't give you much trouble. But connotations, which supply much of the richness and vibrancy of language, may work against you if you fail to take into account what certain words suggest. To begin a critical analysis of a literary work with "The ingredients of this poem" could be a mistake because *ingredients* suggests to many readers flour, sugar, and shortening—the makings of a cake.

Some words—four-letter obscenities, for example—are so furiously connotative that they are ordinarily banned from standard English. Around other words blow the violent emotional winds of social and political controversy. *Communist, reactionary, nigger, whitey, radical, queer* are in most contexts so full of connotative static that their denotative message is lost. Many such expressions are no more than purrs and snarls. For *purr words* and *snarl words,* as S. I. Hayakawa has described them, are not meant to communicate meaning so much as to express emotional approval or disapproval: *filthy, dreamy, bastard, racist, fascist, darling, a great guy, true lover of democracy, authoritarian.*

Unless you are deliberately trying to arouse the passions of your reader, you would be wise to search for less emotionally charged words than ones like these.

PRACTICE

Discussion
1. Used connotatively, what do these words suggest? Can you use any of them in a purely denotative or neutral sense?

red	gripe
redneck	tough
monster	pus
clutch	slob
spider	wormy
ooze	sharp

2. Discuss the uses of connotation in this passage. How effective is the passage? Give reasons for your answer.

> It was a crisp and spicy morning in early October. The lilacs and laburnums, lit with the glory fires of autumn, hung burning and flashing in the upper air, a fairy bridge provided by kind Nature for the wingless wild things that have their home in the tree tops and would visit together; the larch and the pomegranate flung their purple and yellow flames in brilliant broad splashes along the slanting sweep of the woodland; the sensuous fragrance of innumerable deciduous flowers rose upon the swooning atmosphere; far in the empty sky a solitary oesophagus slept upon motionless wing; everywhere brooded stillness, serenity, and the peace of God. — Mark Twain, "A Double-Barrelled Detective Story"

Writing
1. Write three short angry letters, of paragraph length, to your college newspaper. In the first, use highly connotative language. In the second, use as little connotative language as you can. In the third, write a letter that combines or "averages" the connotative qualities of the first two. Which of the three letters is the most successful? The most "accurate"?

2. Write a paragraph to your worst enemy. Use "purr words." (Or write a paragraph to your best friend using "snarl words.") What is the effect of this technique?

Use Figures of Speech Carefully

"I see a *rat*!" she said, pointing to the little furry creature disappearing through a hole in the wall.

"I see a *rat*!" she said, pointing to her ex-husband sitting with a blonde at the next table.

The first rat is real or *literal,* a furry fact with four legs and a tail. The second one is not real or literal but *figurative.*

A figure of speech takes a fresh look at something; it is in effect a *re-perception.* In her novel *Memento Mori,* Muriel Spark looks freshly at the dreariness of old peoples' lives in a hospital. Even when they sleep, their situation is hardly human; and she writes of "a long haunted night when the dim ward lamp made the beds into gray-white lumps like terrible bundles of laundry which muttered and snored occasionally."

Why are figures of speech used so much by writers? Because they give life and vividness to writing. In his novel *McTeague,* Frank Norris describes a little, prissy old lady at a party: "Miss Baker had turned back the overskirt of her dress; a plate of cake was in her lap; from time to time she sipped her wine with the delicacy of a white cat."

Well-chosen figures of speech can turn workaday writing into brilliant prose. The literary critic F. L. Lucas describes in his book *Style* the bitterness and hatred in Jonathan Swift: "It is idle to wish, as Swift trots like a lean grey wolf, with white fangs bared, across his desolate landscape, that he were more like a benevolent Saint Bernard; he would cease to be Swift."

There are several types of figures of speech. Two of the most common are the *metaphor,* which implies or shows a comparison between two things usually considered as unlike ("She was a phantom of delight"); and the *simile,* which states the comparison by the use of *like* or *as* (old people who look "like terrible bundles of laundry"). Another rather common figure of speech is *personification,* which gives human attributes to inanimate objects, thoughts, and emotions ("Death is an amiable man wearing spectacles behind which there are no eyes"). Such distinctions are interesting and valuable for the scholar, but for the writer they ordinarily are not very useful. We have never heard of a writer who has separate stacks of similes and metaphors on his desk to be used, as the physician's prescription runs, "when necessary." Most writers pay no attention to the *type* of figure they are employing. Instead, they concentrate on making their figures of speech genuinely appropriate to their subject.

Suggestions for Using Figures of Speech

1. *Unless a figure of speech genuinely enlivens your prose, stick to a literal statement.* A syndicated sports columnist started a piece on college athletics with this: "The ivy stands out on the red brick walls as if it were varicose veins on a society matron's thigh." What an ugly, ineffective, and inappropriate image! Better he had used a literal statement: "The red brick walls are thickly covered with ivy."

2. *Be sure that your figure of speech is not incongruous or illogical.* "My weight has ballooned somewhat" is illogical—one's weight is a numerical figure and cannot *balloon,* although one's body can. "It is too early for the President to start honing his ulcer." Incongruous—one hones a knife, not a condition in the stomach lining.

3. *Avoid mixed metaphors.* Example: "*Huckleberry Finn's* pivotal literary crescendo lies in the scene in which Huck refuses to turn Jim in." A *pivot* supplies a turning point; a *crescendo* builds to a peak; and a writer can't force the two of them to work together. Another example: "No satire can hold water unless it is salted with wit." First we are asked to believe that a satire can contain a fluid, then that one can put salt in it. These figures might have worked if the writers had dropped the second metaphor. Or perhaps they should have avoided figures entirely.

4. *Picture your figures of speech.* This advice, given by Jacques Barzun and Henry Graff in *The Modern Researcher,* helps you cut out those figures that are incongruous, illogical, mixed—or simply unnecessary. *Picture* these:

> Put your shoulder to the wheel, your nose to the grindstone, and your feet on the ground. ["Now try to work in that position," goes the old joke.]
> This restraint runs through the spectre of Chinese-American relationships. [Ever see a restraint running, much less through a ghost of a relationship?]

If you get a silly mental picture of your figure of speech, during your writing or revising stages, consider changing or dropping it.

5. *Do not use exaggerated figures of speech.* Sometimes writers become so attached to a figure which they think is novel and fresh that they fail to see that it overstates the situation. Let the figure slip up on the reader; don't slap him in the face with it: "The car cornered with the grace of a ballet dancer, its 300 howling horses straining like prize fighters under the hood." "Nonsense," says the reader. A statement like "When he praised her, she grinned like a hungry tiger" is also an exaggeration. Better perhaps: "When he praised her, she purred." (It is possible that some people do grin like tigers; life often triumphs over metaphor. But in writing, as in life, overdoing it can be dangerous.)

A Final Note on Figures

Hard-and-fast rules for the use of figures of speech are difficult to make. No sooner does an authority state that one must not mix metaphors than someone cites Shakespeare's "take arms against a sea of troubles." The figure, which is Hamlet's, is logically impossible, a fact that Shakespeare was surely aware of. Hamlet's allusion is to life, which sometimes is impossible. Use common sense in choosing figures. Every figure presents its own problems. For extraordinary situations, like Hamlet's, use extraordinary figures.

In general, let the figure fit the circumstance and clarify your prose, not fog it up. This is fog: "Professor Elspeth grades papers like an elephant stamping on gnats." The figurative language doesn't communicate. Professor Elspeth may grade peculiarly—but in what way? "When I sit down alone in my room to do my math homework, I feel like Daniel in the lions' den." Why Daniel? Where is the den? Who are the lions?

Perhaps the best practical suggestion for usng figurative language successfully can be stated simply in two parts: (1) Strive for accuracy and a pleasant liveliness (figures should add to the precision of a statement, not detract from it); (2) don't exaggerate too much, or strain for effect.

PRACTICE

Discussion
1. Underline the figures of speech in the following passages. State briefly but specifically how well you think the writers have used the figures.
   a. "[Social] class is like a fur coat—soft and warm to wrap around you if you have it, a constant goad and affront if you're one of those left out in the cold."—Sara Sanborn
   b. At the end of Herman Melville's *Moby Dick,* the lone survivor describes the scene just after his ship has sunk: "Now small fowls flew screaming over the yet yawning gulf; a sullen white surf beat against its steep sides; then all collapsed, and the great shroud of the sea rolled on as it rolled five thousand years ago."
   c. "The society which scorns excellence in plumbing because plumbing is a humble activity and tolerates shoddiness in philosophy because it is an exalted activity will have neither good plumbing nor good philosophy. Neither its pipes nor its theories will hold water."—John Gardner
   d. Quotes from three U.S. senators:
   "It seems that many times when we want to change the water,

we wind up throwing out the baby." — Mike Gravel

"I do not agree with those here or elsewhere that favor throwing out the baby because of dirty water." — Frank Denholm

"I say today, let us not throw out the baby with the bath water, let us not lose sight of the forest for the trees, let us not trade off the orchard for an apple." — John Pastore

e. He is pretty good at unravelling a complex issue or, as Seth Nicholson once said, "unscrewing the inscrutable."

f. A reporter on the 1975 Ali-Frazier fight: "Now, Frazier's face began to lose definition; like lost islands re-emerging from the sea, massive bumps rose suddenly around each eye. . . ."

g. The fans' hopes anchored on the fullback were knocked out from under them, and the road looked bleak for the team.

h. A young and frightened soldier in battle views nature: "The red sun was pasted in the sky like a wafer." — Stephen Crane, *The Red Badge of Courage*

i. The American dream has shed its cocoon and revealed itself for what it is.

j. We played the pinball machines in those days with a lover's passion — so much energy we wasted on a clucking machine.

k. "If a man does not keep pace with his companions, perhaps it is because he hears a different drummer. Let him step to the music which he hears, however measured or far away." — Henry Thoreau, *Walden*

l. "Everything was coming up roses for a young west suburban married couple as long as two paychecks — his and hers — were rolling in. Then came the first of five children. And the cozy little two-paycheck dream world of Donald B. and his wife, Phyllis, collapsed into a rat race — slowly at first. Then the vicious circle of debt accumulation began to close in. When its grip was total, it embraced the young couple in $5,000 worth of debts." — *Chicago Daily News*

2. For class discussion, create a figure of speech for each of the following words. Example: "*Dictionaries* are like watches: the worst is better than none, and the best cannot be expected to go quite true." — Samuel Johnson

art	rack	eternity
rock	pain	temperance
justice	chance	bump

What is the main difficulty you find in making your own figures?

Writing

1. Write a paragraph on a rather dull subject (eating breakfast, for example). Use many vivid figures of speech. Is your paragraph any better because of the figurative language? Do you detect a strain in your writing? How, if at all, can this be prevented?

2. Write a paper evaluating the figurative language of advertising in magazines that you commonly read. What types of figures are used most? Do the figures blur or clarify the ideas in the ads?

3. Write an essay on the use of figures of speech in a short story by a major writer, for example, "Figurative Language in Faulkner's 'A Rose for Emily.' " How does the author use figures to support the theme and characterization of his story?

Use Standard English

By *standard English,* we mean the language that educated people generally accept as proper and suitable. It is the language used in technical reports, scientific documents, and business letters. It is found in reputable newspapers, magazines, and books—the words that you have just read are an example of standard English.

You should avoid two major deviations from standard English. In the first the writer picks words (usually polysyllabic ones) that are too heavy, abstract, or dignified—too formal. Example:

> Where the [primitive man's] shadow is regarded as so intimately bound up with the life of the man that its loss entails debility or death, it is natural to expect that its diminution should be regarded with solicitude and apprehension, as betokening a corresponding decrease in the vital energy of its owner. — Sir James Frazer, *The Golden Bough*

This sounds as if it were written by a man permanently dressed in a top hat and tails.

In the second deviation from standard English, the writer is excessively casual, slangy, or informal, as in these expressions:

enthused	figured (thought)	bad vibes
turkey	hype	real great
aced it	ivory-tower types	the pits
screwed up	got to me	sit on it
fouled up	klutz	dot your eye
a drag	mega- [— —]	out of his gourd

Your reader probably won't object to the suitability of your word choice unless you startle him with something that seems inappropriate. As long as you stay more or less in the broad area of standard usage, you should be safe enough. Don't be too formal or too informal. When you check your paper for word choice, don't address your reader as if you were delivering a sermon in St. Patrick's Cathedral, or take him familiarly by the hand as if he were a bosom buddy, which he probably isn't.

PRACTICE

Discussion
Prepare for class discussion a few notes on any deviations from standard English in this passage from a student's paper. Prepare to defend or attack the writer's choice of words.

> From watching the painters who used to come to my father's studio during my high school years, I have learned to distinguish between the real painter and the ungifted phony who likes to call himself "creative." The real painter usually has a sane and balanced attitude toward his work. But the phony is often unstable and uptight about little personal problems which show up in his work and ruin it. Also the real painter has the courage to be independent as an artist, for he is sure of his art and his technique. If he makes a mistake, there is always tomorrow and another piece of work; to him art *is* work. To the phony, however, art is not so much a definite piece of work with definite demands in craftsmanship as it is his awesome thing, his bag. "Get your kicks, man," is the cry of the "creative" phony, whose only subject is himself and whose only technique is to imitate the real painter's work.

Writing
Read over an issue of your college paper carefully, marking any wording that deviates from standard English. Write a letter to the editor, giving your evidence and your conclusions concerning the quality of usage in the paper.

Be Idiomatic

The term *idiom* has two meanings, both having to do with what is natural in language. In its first meaning, idiom is the "language peculiar to a people or to a district, community, or class." Thus we speak of the effect of Spanish idiom on the speech of Texans; of the difference between American idiom and British idiom; of French idiomatic use of adjectives (they typically come after the noun instead of before). This first meaning of *idiom* refers to the natural way a language works.

In its second, more limited, meaning *idiom* refers to particular expressions that are natural to the language but not ordinarily explainable by grammatical analysis. Examples:

drink your coffee up	take to [someone]
act your age	beat up [a person]
make do	keep house

Arguments about idiom are mainly useless; you simply have to go along with the particular idiom in its context. "Carl *is coming* to visit me, and he *is going* to stay a week." How can he be coming and going at the same time? One dictionary gives fifty-two meanings of the idiom *take up*—as in "He will *take up* bridge when he gets old." Do such usages make sense? Idiom merely smiles and says: "I don't *have* to make sense."

Idioms are found in every part of the language, but they are particularly evident in prepositional constructions, in which they influence the meaning at will (*from* will? *to* will?). Try changing the prepositions in the movie title, *The Sailor Who Fell from Grace with the Sea:*

The Sailor Who Fell *with* Grace *from* the Sea
The Sailor Who Fell *by* Grace *into* the Sea
The Sailor Who Fell *for* Grace *by* the Sea

English idioms are usually hard for foreign speakers to learn. A bridge player we know had as a partner an excellent player who was young, pretty, and French. After he made a terrible mistake and trumped her ace, he was astonished to hear her say in low, elegant tones—"I am mad about you!" Idiom reversed her meaning, for as it turned out she was mad as the devil *at* him.

To "be idiomatic," as our heading says, is to use the natural forms of the language. When in doubt about an idiom, speak it aloud and listen to the sound. Reading your early drafts aloud will help because what sounds right will usually be right. If you are still in doubt, see if your dictionary can help you. Most dictionaries have usage notes on common problems of idiom. Another good source is Theodore M. Bernstein's *The Careful Writer,* which has an alphabetical list of idioms that give trouble. Bernstein's book should be in your library's reference room.

PRACTICE

Discussion

1. Each line in the poem below (and even the title) contains at least one idiom. Underline the idiom, and paraphrase it in a few words. Are your paraphrases generally longer than the originals? What does this tell you about the nature of idioms?

On Meddling With Idioms

At any rate they take heed
Although every now and then they don't.
Most set about to take notes
But some look down on such and won't.
A few fight shy of hearing
When I set about to speak —
By and large at least it seems so.
Of and on they say my points are weak.
I explain they'll not come in handy
But my pleadings don't catch fire.
And they all appear to watch out
In any event not to be inspired.
They make no bones about it
That it's I who set up the friction
When I mull over their papers
And meddle with their idiomatic diction.

           — Richard J. Marince

2. For class discussion, correct any faulty idioms in the sentences below.
   a. He simply had a passion over oysters.
   b. Judge Poofenverber cleared his throat and handed up the verdict.
   c. The second danger of the job is that we work under extreme heat.
   d. The young doctor's education was being frustrated because he couldn't practice in cadavers.
   e. People are not declining from building homes in our town because we have no sewage system.
   f. It was the most diverse information they had ever published.
   g. A Japanese highway official writing for Americans driving in Japan: "When a passenger on the hoof hove in sight, tootle the

horn, trumpet to him melodiously at first. If he still obstackle your passage, tootle him with vigor and express by word of mouth the warning, 'Hi! Hi!' "

h. He walked forth and back across the room.

i. "Amazing English idiom," said the German. "You make down a bed, make with your face, make over your mind, and make forward a story to keep us all happy."

j. "What do you choose that book to be read to out of for?"

—quoted by Sir Ernest Gowers in his *Plain Words: Their ABC*

INEFFECTIVE WORDS

*T*here are many causes of ineffective wording—lack of specificity, misleading connotations, distracting or exaggerated figurative language, nonstandard usage, unidiomatic choice of words. But ineffective word choice can be more than just a negative thing—a failure, say, to write specifically. Its causes are often rooted in carelessness; and, in fact, carelessness breeds carelessness. One inaccurate or unsuitable word on page two seems to lead inevitably to a rash of imprecise expressions on page three. Don't let the first ineffective word out of your mind and onto the page; and if it does get there, scratch it out before the infection spreads.

You also might try, as you edit your own prose, what a friend of ours calls his "editorial comedy routine." When he reads his work aloud, if he comes to a doubtful or inappropriate expression he tries to make fun of it.

Optimum ("That's an optimistic mother.")
Counterproductive ("We make an awful lot of counters in our factory.")
-wise ("OK dollar-wise but not a good idea wisdom-wise.")

Types of Ineffective Wording

Watch for the following types of bad wording when you write or revise:

Vagueness:

The second phase of the operation involves a new concept and a different attitude.

Phase, operation, involves, concept, and *attitude* are all so vague that the reader doesn't know what the writer is talking about.

A basketball team revolves around its center.

Vague—what is the exact relationship of the center to the team?

This part functions in the engine.

But what does the part *do* in the engine?

Wordiness:

The child's surgical past history in terms of her spinal condition showed a failure in correction.

Cut this to:

Surgery has not helped her spine.

And:

All the huts, square in shape and few in number, had actually been blown away by the incredibly strong wind.

Cut this to:

All of the few square huts had been blown away by the strong wind.

Redundancy:
A redundancy has an implied repetition built into it:

continue to remain	projected forecast
final outcome	first time ever
complete master	unite together
regularly consistent	more preferable
hot water heater	new beginner
original source	all-time record
protrude out	necessary requirement
habitual custom	

Unnecessary Exaggeration:

The honest truth

The truth is "honest" by definition. Just say "the truth."

Tom was literally a fireball in class.

Poor Tom must be pretty burned up. Say something like, "Tom knew all the answers."

An all-inclusive survey

Inclusive means "including everything." Write "an inclusive survey."

She was very furious.

It is hard to be more furious than furious; omit *very*.

The vice-president is very unique.

One can't be more unique than unique—"one of a kind."

Clichés:
Clichés are trite, tired, worn-out expressions. Cut them out, or rewrite. Here are a few:

hate with a passion	the die is cast
raining cats and dogs	the scales of Justice
pretty as a picture	straight from the shoulder
slick as ice	chip off the old block
poetry in motion	beat around the bush
hard as a rock	hot under the collar

PRACTICE

Writing
In these sentences, identify the vagueness, wordiness, redundancy, unnecessary exaggeration, and clichés. Rewrite each sentence, making it specific and clear. Guess at its meaning if you have to.
a. The fact that the group of children has accomplished some worthwhile endeavor gives each member, in terms of the accomplishment, a happy sensation.
b. A good cooperative is a cooperating joint operation.
c. Social scientists have intimated that some of the personal reac-

tions that penetrate into happiness college-studentwise are: satisfaction, achievement, affection, and belief.

d. Here at Wilson Motors, we are proud to say that much labor and concentration is poured into accomplishing a very superb product.

e. As we look down the avenues of life experience, what, ladies and gentlemen, do we see ahead for us living in this day and age?

f. Sanitation is a very important premium in a dormitory, personnelwise.

g. We must unite together to stop this false perversion of the undergraduate student.

h. The upsurges in the Gross National Product were caused by very ideal governing factors in the fields of railways, merchant marines, and canals.

i. Hamlet has been seen to be a neurotically disturbed personality who was all-consumed by hate.

j. First, in the youth, normally the happier segment of our populace, there seemed to be a very wonderful glow, as if smugly possessing an insight of the wondrous events in store for the anxious world.

Avoid Jargon and Shoptalk

The worst misuses of language today are not in bad grammar, unsuitable wording, vulgarisms, "colloquialisms," or the like. They are in the growing employment of *jargon* like this:

> Improved administration and management of the intervals in work related to the personnel coffee periods must be a constant aim in order that maximum utilization of labor from the minimum number of personnel may be achieved.

A possible translation: "Take shorter coffee breaks, and do more work."

Jargon is the opposite of plain English, which tends to employ the short, specific words: *take, break, work.* Nor is jargon the language of ordinary speech, which says things directly: "Do the best you can." Instead jargon puts such an idea into abstract polysyllables: "The maximum quality of your endeavors should be achieved."

The writer of jargon uses the worst possible writer's stance. Writer and reader and thesis all disappear in a babble of colorless words — *operation, implemented, in terms of, personnel, minimum* — dead words seemingly not written by or for living human beings.

Much jargon has its origins in *shoptalk,* the special language or terminology of a profession. *Interface, software, chip, memory, boot,* and *menu* are the shoptalk of computer buffs; *wheel, arbor, pivot, mainspring* the shoptalk of the watchmaker; *motif, symbol, archetype, protagonist* the shoptalk of the literary critic.

In defense of shoptalk, its users have long claimed that they cannot communicate in their businesses or professions without it, that a geologist, for example, could not talk to other geologists without saying *stratigraphic* eight times a day. This defense is not always convincing. As one geologist at the top of his profession wrote us:

> You can always tell an incompetent in geology by his language. The less he knows the more he throws in big words. He'll write "Pennsylvanian limestone strata" when all he needs is "Pennsylvanian rocks." He'll write *anticline* and *syncline* when *high* and *low* say the same thing.
>
> The main characteristic of the genuine expert in science is that in choosing words he writes both for other experts and for the nonspecialist, the man in the street. He knows that if he hits the man in the street, he will hit nearly everybody else he is writing for. Besides—and this is the important thing—*big words can hide a bad idea.* If you don't put your scientific notion in simple language, you may not know if it's any good. And we can't waste money and time on bad ideas.
>
> I have hanging on my office wall the motto:

> # kiss!
>
> (Keep It Simple, Stupid!)

Avoid jargon and shoptalk when you can.

PRACTICE

Discussion
G. K. Chesterton wrote:

> It is good exercise to try for once in a while to express any opinion one holds in words of one syllable. If you say "The social utility of the

indeterminate sentence is recognized by all criminologists as part of our sociological evolution towards a more humane and scientific view of punishment," you can go on talking like that for hours with hardly a movement of the gray matter inside your skull. But if you begin "I wish Jones to go to gaol [jail] and Brown to say when Jones shall come out," you will discover, with a thrill of horror, that you are obliged to think. The long words are not the hard words, it is the short words that are hard. There is much more metaphysical subtlety in the word "damn" than in the word "degeneration." — *Orthodoxy*

Try "thinking" the sentences below into a clear and simple English that the person in the street would understand and appreciate. Use as many one-syllable words as possible, and check your dictionary when necessary.

a. Sinistrality is a developmental anomaly of preferred laterality, and represents a mishap to the normal development of dextrality.

b. The social-management concept of the disadvantaged necessitates our raising them above the poverty level.

c. Mrs. Smith, in regard to your child's adenoids, our operation decision is one of contraindication.

d. Menu-driven services and flashy color graphics have yet to demonstrate a compelling appeal. The coming of the microcomputer has made obsolete visions of vast networks of dumb terminals tapping into a mainframe. Yet the microcomputer is also creating a demand for interactive information service, not just online databases, but also electronic messaging and other interactive communication services . . . *Computers and Electronics*

e. When industrial or commercial fraud and calculated complexity reach epidemic proportions, non-volitional expenditures are incurred to a level which often spur into being a mini-trade that counsels, for a price, consumers about avoidance techniques. These "cures," as with some debt-counsellors, are often as exploitative as the disease. — Ralph Nader, "Involuntary Economy"

f. "Now, Mr. Barlow, what had you in mind? Embalmment of course, and after that incineration or not, according to taste. Our crematory is on scientific principles, the heat is so intense that all inessentials are volatilized. Some people did not like the thought that ashes of the casket and clothing were mixed with the Loved One's. Normal disposal is by inhumement, entombment, inurnment or immurement, but many people just lately prefer insarcophagusment. That is *very* individual. The casket is placed inside a sealed sarcophagus, marble or bronze, and rests permanently above the ground in a niche in the mausoleum, with or without a personal stained-glass window above. That, of course, is for those with whom price is not a primary consideration."—Evelyn Waugh, *The Loved One*

g. As a nurse, I work with patients within a therapeutic milieu structure.

h. We have escalated the interface in the demilitarized zone.

Writing

Rewrite the following passage in plain English, free of jargon and clichés.

[1]Triteburg and its million residents invite you to a glorious convention and vacation in its crystal-clear and cool mountain air. With one foot in its colorful past and the other in its bright future, Triteburg is proud of its rich heritage and its reputation as a fast-growing and progressive metropolitan center . . . a modern city with an ever-changing skyline set against the magnificent backdrop of the ageless mountains in the romantic atmosphere of Indians and pioneer miners.

[2]In Triteburg you will find an infinite variety of first-class accommodations—hotels, motels, highway hotels. In the nearby mountains are luxurious resorts, rustic cottages, and modern campgrounds. Dozens of fine restaurants offer menus to appeal to the most discriminating taste. Our convention facilities, available for groups of any size, are second to none.

[3]Triteburg's unique Hospitality Center can answer your questions about every vacation or convention need: Where to stay and eat . . . what to see and do . . . information about fishing, hunting, boating, or skiing . . . everything you need for the vacation of a lifetime or for a convention that you will long remember.

CHAPTER 13

SENTENCES (I) — EFFECTIVE STRUCTURE*

Ideas ricochet around in our heads, unruly as children at play, ignoring our attempts to keep them in order. One would think that, when ideas are reduced to written form, they would become more manageable. After all, we've got them down on paper and squeezed into a small narrow space we call a *sentence,* which in size is ordinarily only a few inches long and less than a quarter-inch high:

> This is an English sentence.

*About the sources for the material and techniques in this chapter: We started experimenting with a new system for teaching the sentence in 1954. Some years later, from 1959 to 1961, we started testing the material on non-student adult writers. In this period, we learned a great deal from the editors at the Extension Course Institute, Air University. For the next dozen years we taught the sentence material to students ranging in age from 12 to 21. It also appeared in the second and third editions of this textbook, and we have learned much from teachers who taught it. Finally, on certain questions of syntactic theory, we owe a debt to the scholar Francis Christensen and his important book, *Notes Toward a New Rhetoric* (New York: Harper and Row, 1967).

Yet, if anything, ideas are more troublesome in the narrow space of the written sentence than they are in one's mouth as speech. Who doesn't have more trouble writing than talking?

You can, however, turn to your own advantage the fact that sentences are written in small, narrow spaces. The ideas thus recorded can be manipulated — combined, separated, switched, taken out, put in. The sentence-space keeps its basic outer form, but *you* control almost everything else about it. You can write (note punctuation, which separates the units):

a. One unit

> One of the first things I do when I get up is put on my shoes.

b. Two units

> When I get up , the first thing I do is put on my shoes.

c. Three units

> When I get up , I put on my shoes — the first thing I do.

Or you can change the contents of the sentence-space:

d. When I get up in the morning , I walk around barefoot.

e. What business is it of yours what I do when I get up?

f. Drop dead.

As you can see, you have many choices in writing a sentence. Of course, you must always take into account the existence of the sentence-space itself. But you can fill — or empty — the space almost any way you wish. And you can partition it into *units,* as we did with punctuation marks in *b, c,* and *d* above. Employing such units in typical sentences, as a matter of fact, is of major importance. You have a good chance of succeeding as a writer of sentences *if you can handle their units.*

UNITS IN THE TYPICAL SENTENCE

*F*undamentally, you write a sentence by setting down clearly separated *units* so that the sentence "accumulates" through the addition of parts.

Before he learned to cook soup and stew, Mike always threw leftovers away
—a habit which cost him money in wasted food.

Unit	Type of Unit
Before he learned to cook soup and stew,	opener
Mike always threw leftovers away—	*sentence base*
a habit which cost him money in wasted food.	

We will discuss *openers, sentence bases,* and *closers* in the pages that follow. For the moment, it is enough to point out that readers can easily understand each of the units of information about Mike as they move their eyes rapidly along the masses of wording in the sentence. The units themselves *are separated by punctuation,* which helps to indicate where they start and stop. The sentence also has a useful signal in the word *before,* which implies that a time relation will be expressed in the units to follow.

Our main purpose in this chapter is not to teach you how to analyze sentences, although we will perform a few simple analyses. Instead it is to show you how to write better prose by following certain basic rules for creating firm structure in your sentences.

As you read the material, also bear in mind that we are showing you how to write *and* punctuate at the same time. This is the easiest way to learn the basic rules of punctuation.

SENTENCE BASES

A sentence base, as the term implies, is the fundamental unit of a sentence. The sentence bases in the following examples are in heavy type:

a. Because I startled it, **the cow mooed and ran away.**
b. **Cheryl and Sue danced and sang.**
c. **The girl in the long blue skirt standing by the bandstand sang a few bars of one of the earliest songs written by Paul McCartney after he left the Beatles.**
d. **Ronald Reagan won the 1984 election,** a fact which did not surprise many people.
e. **The shrub,** which was overfertilized, **is dying in the backyard.**

Here are the major characteristics of the typical sentence base:

1. A sentence base makes a complete statement. A base usually has no punctuation inside it. We will explain certain exceptions later. These statements are not sentence bases because they are not complete:

   Because I startled it. . . .
   . . . a fact which did not surprise many people.
   . . . which was overfertilized. . . .

2. A sentence base can have something added: (1) to the front of it—an *opener,* as in *a* above; (2) to the end of it—a *closer,* as in *d;* (3) to the middle of it—an *interrupter,* as in *e.*

Here is a piece of professional writing that shows how sentence bases work; the bases are in heavy type:

> ***The octopus has a remarkable trace of adaptability. Dumas determined that,*** by patiently playing with them until he met some response. Usually, ***octopi were most submissive when very tired. Dumas would release an exhausted octopus and let it jet away with its legs trailing. The octopus has two distinct means of locomotion. It can crawl efficiently on hard surfaces.*** (Guy ***Gilpatric once saw an octopus let loose in a library. It raced up and down the stacks,*** hurling books on the floor, possibly a belated revenge on authors.) ***Its method of swimming consists of inflating the head,*** or valva, ***with water and jetting the fluid to achieve moderate speed. Dumas could easily overtake the animal. The octopus discharged several ink bombs and then resorted to its last defense,*** a sudden plunge to immobility on the bottom, where it instantly assumed the local color and pattern. Keeping a sharp eye out for this camouflage stunt, ***Didi confronted the creature again.*** At the exhaustion of its psychological warfare effects, ***the octopus sprang hopelessly from the bottom, fanned its legs and dribbled back to the floor.*** —Jacques Cousteau, with Frédéric Dumas, *The Silent World*

Since a sentence base gives your reader a unit, it is usually unpunctuated. Why break up a unit unnecessarily? Yet punctuation is sometimes needed in a base to explain certain ideas you want to present *inside* the unit—for example, a listing of two or three elements. In each of these examples, every part of the list is a part of the total base unit:

> *Don't you loathe this <u>wretched, evil man?</u>*
> *I was <u>nervous, angry, and irritated.</u>*
> *The President <u>ordered out the Marines, sent two carriers to the island, and defied Congress to interfere.</u>*
> *The <u>Dodge, Chevy, and Ford</u> all crashed at the far turn by the wall.*
> *The <u>cold, congealed</u> porridge is not fit to eat.*

FREE UNITS IN THE SENTENCE

If your writing contains sentence bases only, after a while you will bore yourself and your reader. Your prose will be choppy, and you will discover that some of your ideas lack coherence or necessary information. For the sentence-base pattern tends to act like a stylistic cookie-cutter, producing "assembly-line" sentences that state ideas flatly without providing transitions or necessary explanation.

Therefore, to fill out many sentences, you will need to supply free units. A *free unit* has three characteristics: (1) it is incomplete and cannot stand by itself, as a sentence base can; (2) it is placed *before, inside,* or *after* the base it goes with; (3) it is usually punctuated at the "joint" where it fits the base. Such units are called *free* because they are "removable." (When removed, the base can still stand as a complete statement.) Of course, when you remove a free unit from its base, you usually change the meaning of the entire sentence. There are three kinds of free units (note punctuation):

1. *Openers* (placed before the base)

> After he got his $2.00 raise, *Wright yelled with joy.*
> In inspecting the car, *we discovered that it was powered by electricity.*

Openers add detail and provide transitions from sentence to sentence:

> For instance, *Belle Meade Hospital is now using only 65 percent of its available beds.*
> After the optometrist charged him $150 for his new glasses, *Jefferson swore he would never go back to him.*
> Lying there on the ground in the sun, its metal seeming a dull gray, *the .45 did not look dangerous.*

As in the last example, you can use two or more openers if they are necessary.

2. *Interrupters* (placed inside the base)

> *My roommate,* frustrated by my inability to manage our food budget, *began to scream at me.*
> *The work I enjoyed most* — I am speaking of part-time work — *was pruning trees for the city.*
> *Mr. McClean thought that his seven wives* (or some of them) *had married him just for his money.*

Interrupters explain and add detail to the ideas in a base:

> *My aunt,* who was the best friend I ever had, *died last week.*
> *Johansen's serve* — which was different from any I had faced before — *had a weird bounce on concrete.*
> *Mom* (being unsympathetic to my views on sex) *got up and left.*

3. *Closers* (placed after the base)

> *The owners said nothing about trading their aging quarterback,* probably because the team thought of the "old" man as their leader.
> *That pig is pretty agile*—considering how fat he is.
> *We left the apartment early* (making sure to leave a note for Roger).

Closers perform about the same job as interrupters. But because of their position, they can also supply afterthoughts, as in the last two examples. Or they can provide explanations:

> *The captain pulled on the bell rope,* which suddenly broke off in his hands.
> *The weight of most of the trucks ran 15,000 pounds,* less than the weight specified in the contracts.
> *You had better leave the door unlocked*—just in case Jeanne returns tonight.
> *This has been a lovely birthday* (much nicer than I had hoped for).

PRACTICE

In the following exercises, practice getting a "feel" for the sentence units—both *base* and *free*. In each blank, create and write an appropriate unit, or part of one. Pay particular attention to the punctuation marks.

a. *The table had been badly stained by an acid compound,* one which ____(closer)____ .

b. Since the flag ____(opener)____ , *we assumed that the wind had changed.*

c. *My roommates' objection,* which ____(interrupter)____ , *was easy to respond to.*

d. *The work experience I enjoyed most*—____(interrupter)____—*taught me to be very careful in high places.*

e. *Perhaps it was a good thing* (considering ____(interrupter)____) *that we decided not to get married.*

f. *We left the apartment early,* ____(closer)____ .

g. Although ____(opener)____ , *my math text has good material in algebra.*

h. Like me, *she* ____(base)____ .

i. They believe in gun control; *they* ____(base)____ .

j . *Fill the tank* _____*(base)*_____; *park the* _____*(base)*_____.

k. _____*(opener)*_____, *the old couple across the hall* _____*(base)*_____.

l . Because _____*(opener)*_____, _____*(base)*_____.

m. _____*(opener)*_____, _____*(base)*_____.

n . _____*(base)*_____; _____*(base)*_____.

o . _____*(base)*_____, _____(closer)_____.

p . _____*(base)*_____ (_____(interrupter)_____) _____*(base continued)*_____.

SENTENCE SIGNALS

A sentence signal is a word placed at the beginning of a sentence. It helps the reader anticipate the direction your sentence will take. There are four general types of signals:

1. Signals of *time:*

> *While* spraying the plant, he discovered mites on its leaves.
> *Before* lighting the pilot light, be sure that the heat exchanger is clean.

2. Signals of *logical relation:*

> *Thus* inflation continues to be a major problem in the Western democracies.
> *Because* the ice was over two inches thick on the telephone poles, repair crews were unable to work in Sapulpa.

3. Signals of *similarity* and *contrast:*

> *Like* the other teachers, she went on strike.
> *But* the school board refused to grant pay raises.
> *Yet* the Supreme Court seems determined to stay out of obscenity questions as long as possible.

4. Signals that *count* or *differentiate:*

> *First,* let us define the term correctly.
> *Then,* at this point, it is possible to see the precipitate in the tube.
> *Finally,* all passengers should observe the no-smoking rule.

Sentence signals are small but important aids for the reader. Use them whenever they are appropriate.

THE SENTENCE BASE RULE

The sentence base rule is an important part of this chapter. It summarizes the techniques of sentence construction that we have been explaining and points forward to the discussion of revising in the next chapter. Based on the work of competent writers, the rule makes three suggestions.

1. Break up your ideas into clear, *specific* units — sentence bases and free units (openers, interrupters, and closers).

2. Use punctuation to show where the units start and stop.

3. Where necessary, use sentence signals (*but, and, also, so,* etc.) to help your reader anticipate the direction your sentence will be taking.

Sentence units, of course, tell us something — give us information. In fact, they could be called *units of information*. Bases give us a complete idea; free units often explain, give reasons, identify people or things.

For good effect, units can't be too long or too short. They must be long enough to supply their information, short enough to be easily read and understood. You have probably already noticed that in ordinary prose there are more *units* than *sentences* — sometimes many more. In the last two small paragraphs you have just read, there are seven sentences, but 16 units.

An effective writer will produce more units than sentences. What does this fact mean to you? First, in a practical way, it means that ordinarily you should not write long, strung-out sentence bases. Rather, you should break them up into readable sections. Second, you should try to make the structure of a sentence work *for* you:

● Put complete ideas in bases.

● Put incomplete ideas in free units.

● Use free units to give explanation, detail, reasons; and to supply transitions. Openers are particularly good for transitions.

● Keep units as short as you reasonably can, and still supply necessary information. A very long unit may not be readable or clear.

Here are examples of sentences that illustrate the sentence base rule:

1. *Sentence base by itself*

> **The Constitution does not provide for first- and second-class citizens.**
> — Wendell Willkie

2. *Opener* (with a sentence signal), *followed by a base*

> *When* we Americans are through with the English language, *it will look as if it had been run over by a musical comedy.* — Finley Peter Dunne

3. *Base with two interrupters*

> ***Perhaps Brand and Cooke,*** lacking interests that could absorb them, fuming like children over trifles, *simply invented their hate of each other in order to have something to feel deeply about.* — Richard Wright

4. *Base with a closer*

> ***There's a shipment of human parts come in downstairs*** — hearts and kidneys and brains and the like. — Ken Kesey

Writers employ free units to break up a sentence in order to give it shape and clarity. For the reader's sake, they carefully signal the beginning and end of the units with punctuation marks. But punctuation is an art rather than a science, and a writer has choices about where to put punctuation marks. The great American historian Carl Becker wrote this sentence as a base unit:

> *The best-known and the most valiant defender of the freedom of mind was Voltaire.*

Since this has two ideas in it, Becker might have shortened the base unit and emphasized *and the most valiant* as an interrupting free unit:

> *The best-known* — and the most valiant — *defender of the freedom of mind was Voltaire.*

Is one version of the sentence better than the other? Probably not; however, they do create different emphases in the ideas expressed.

PRACTICE

1. Identify by name (*opener, base,* etc.) each of the units in the following sentences. Circle the punctuation marks that separate the units. Underline the sentence signals. How does each unit help the reader understand the ideas expressed?

a. In science, the credit goes to the man who convinces the world, not to the man to whom the idea first occurs. —William Osler

b. Before I leave the dorm for vacation, I lock my stereo in the closet (a useless gesture, considering that the lock is breakable).

c. Obviously, a stationary population—one in which the birth rate matches the death rate—is out of the question for many years to come. —David E. Lilienthal

d. Dean McIntyre (he's the one who has been calling you long-distance) has also written a letter of congratulation about your award.

e. Drug addiction is *not* increasing; in all probability, it has declined since the turn of the century. —William McCord

f. She disagrees with you, but she respects your opinion.

g. She disagrees with you; she respects your opinion, however.

h. In the summer before the French Revolution, all of France was, it seems, gripped by a deep malaise, an underlying panic to which contemporaries gave the name of *la grande Peur*—the great Fear. —Adlai Stevenson

i. He struggled in a wild frenzy of fury and terror, almost mad terror. —D. H. Lawrence

j. The storm took the helicopter ten miles from the airport.

k. Ten miles from the airport, the storm overtook the helicopter.

l. For instance, violence—accidents, suicides, and homicides—accounts for fully three out of four deaths among males age 15 to 24, making the American death rate for this age group 62 percent higher than the Swedish rate.

m. I was raised to farm work, which I continued till I was twenty-two. —Abraham Lincoln

2. For class discussion and writing practice, consider again the sentences in Practice **1**. Pick out half a dozen of the sentences and write imitations of them. Use your own ideas, and modify or switch the units around if you wish. For instance, for *e*, you could write:

> Highway accidents are not increasing; in all probability, they have declined since 1984.
>
> Since 1984, highway accidents probably have not increased.
>
> Highway accidents—judging from the evidence—have not increased since 1984.
>
> Highway accidents seem to have decreased recently (since 1984, to be exact).

3. In each of these sentences, either the base or the free unit is missing. Supply the missing unit and write out the whole sentence.

a. After I finished my car payments, _____.
b. _____, although they could not dance easily on the sticky floor.
c. _____ (who was leaning against the instructor's desk) _____.
d. Because the stapler had run out of staples, _____.
e. _____ — leaving mud and silt six inches deep on Main Street.
f. _____, which had been seen stalking a rabbit last Tuesday, _____.
g. After _____, Henry can finish weeding the garden.
h. The angry homeowner, who _____, yelled at the students when they were a block away.
i. Margie will never graduate from college, no matter _____.
j. To run for president of a sorority demands stamina, particularly _____.
k. Ducks don't usually bite — except _____.
l. That textbook (which _____) is the dullest I ever read.

PARALLELISM

*A*n expert in expository writing was asked, "If you could pick one sentence device that is more important to clear sentence construction than any other, which would it be?"

He thought a long moment and answered: "If I had to pick one — and mind you, there isn't just one — I'd have to say *parallelism.* It's impossible to talk sensibly about anything, from cardboard boxes to democracy to why people buy certain automobiles, without employing parallelism. You can't even make a laundry list without it. But parallelism is not only a clarifying device, it also makes for more interesting and effective prose. Imagine where Lincoln would have been without it: '. . . that this government *of the people, by the people, for the people,* shall not perish from the earth.' "

Using Parallelism

Parallelism refers to a listing of sentence elements which are: (a) roughly equal in importance or emphasis, and (b) written in the same grammatical form. Example:

Parallelism is *interesting, practical,* and *effective.*

Equal in importance and using the same form, the three italicized words in the list are parallel. We could make the list *un*parallel by changing the form of one of the words:

. . . interest, practical, and effective.
. . . interesting, practicality, and effective.
. . . interesting, practical, and to be effective.
. . . interesting, practical, and effectiveness.

As you look at the following examples of parallelism, observe three things: (a) that a parallelism of two items is ordinarily joined by the words *and* or *or* and has no punctuation; (b) that a parallelism of three or more items ordinarily has *and* or *or* before the last item; and (c) that in a parallelism of *three* or more items, commas separate the items.

Parallel Items	*Non-Parallel Items*
Marge and Mary	Marge and pretty
Marge, Jim, or I	Marge, strong, or Jim
to study, learn, and memorize	to study, learning, and memorize
dusty, old, rickety, or messy	dust, old, rickety, or messy
light or dark	light or darkened
I came, I saw, I conquered.	I came, I saw, I will have conquered.

Parallel items can be anything from single words to full sentences. The items can be short:

rod and *reel*
rod, reel, and *bait*
I need a rod, I need a reel, and *I must have some bait.*

The items can be relatively long:

a new steel rod and *a rusty old reel*
a new steel rod, a rusty old reel, and *fresh wriggling bait*
I need a new steel rod with plenty of flexibility, I would like to replace the rusty old reel,
    and *I want the best possible bait for trout fishing in cool weather.*

In order to use parallelism well, you should know where it begins and ends in a sentence. In the examples below, we have shown the beginning and ending of each parallel construction with [   ]. (Note punctuation.)

a. [*You* and *Jim*]
b. [*You* and *Jim*] are hungry.
c. [*Jim, Mary,* and *I*] are as wet as drowned rats.
d. Like us, the others were [*hungry, cold, wet,* and *tired*] — although they had already rested for an hour.
e. The [*hunter, fisherman,* and *game warden*] were [*warm, cozy,* and *drunk*].
f. She hated to [*study, memorize,* and *learn*].
g. [*we stopped, we listened,* and *we trembled*].
h. My son, [*cutting across lawns* and *avoiding the sidewalks*], got to school early.

Parallelism allows you to state ideas easily, quickly, and economically. That sentence itself is an example of the generalization: ". . . to state ideas *easily, quickly,* and *economically.*"

Using parallelism helps you write sentences that are more interesting and specific. It also gives your prose a pleasant strength and a musical rhythm. Many memorable sentences depend on parallelism:

a. [*Four score and seven*] years ago our fathers brought forth upon this continent a new nation, [*conceived in liberty* and *dedicated to the proposition*] that all men are created equal. — Abraham Lincoln
b. The Lord is [*my strength* and *my shield*]. — Bible, King James Version
c. A sudden violent jolt of corn likker has been known to [*stop the victim's watch, snap his suspenders,* and *crack his glass eye right across*]. — Irvin S. Cobb
d. We hold these truths to be self evident: [*that all men are created equal; that they are endowed by their creator with certain unalienable rights*]; that among these are [*life, liberty,* and the *pursuit of happiness*]. . . . — Thomas Jefferson
e. [*The energy, the faith, the devotion*] which we bring to this endeavor will light [*our country* and *all who serve it*] — and the glow from that fire can truly light the world. — John Kennedy

PRACTICE

Underline the parallel constructions in these sentences. Use [ ] to mark the constructions. For each sentence, ask yourself: Why is the parallelism interesting? What would the sentence be like without it? Why would the use of a different device possibly weaken the sentence?

a. Even when he was 43, ancient quarterback George Blanda could still pass, kick, and run.

b. And the Lord went before them by day in a pillar of a cloud, to lead them the way; and by night in a pillar of fire.
   —Exod. 13:21

c.   Last scene of all,
That ends this strange eventful history,
Is second childishness and mere oblivion
Sans [without] teeth, sans eyes, sans taste, sans everything.
                    —Shakespeare, *As You Like It*

d. Feeling miserable, tired, and run-down, he reached for his jar of wheat germ.

e. Darting through the traffic—one foot on the gas, one foot on the brake, my hand jabbing the horn—I came suddenly on the repair crew blocking the road.

f. It was beautiful and simple as all truly great swindles are.
   —O. Henry

g.   Down to Gehenna or up to the Throne,
           He travels the fastest who travels alone.
                    —Rudyard Kipling

h. The greatest of evils and the worst of crimes is poverty.
   —George Bernard Shaw

i. Any well-established village in New England or the northern Middle West could afford a town drunkard, a town atheist, and a few Democrats. —D. W. Brogan

j. I am tired and sick of war. Its glory is all moonshine. It is only those who have neither fired a shot nor heard the shrieks and groans of the wounded who cry aloud for blood, more vengeance, more desolation. War is hell. —William Tecumseh Sherman

Avoid Faulty Parallelism

Note how the faulty constructions below are improved by putting parallel ideas in parallel form:

Faulty: A good hunting dog can [*find* the bird, as well as *bringing* him back to the hunter].

Improved: A good hunting dog can [*find* the bird and *bring* him back to the hunter].

Faulty: I think his report should be regarded as [*of poor construction* and *inconclusive*].

Improved: I think his report is [*poorly constructed* and *inconclusive*].

Faulty: In cooking the frozen hot dogs, [*the tongs were used* and *I also built a very hot fire*].

Improved: In cooking the frozen hot dogs, I used [*tongs* and *a very hot fire*].

Many examples of faulty parallelism are created by the writer's trying to jam too much into one sentence.

Faulty: Also predominant on a boy's mind during his high school years are the desire for sexual activity, the want for a car, experimenting with smoking and drinking, and the testing of authority.

Improved: During high school some boys can think only of [*smoking, drinking, sex,* and *rebellion*].

Faulty: The church group voted on invitations to parents to meetings, decided why there was a necessity for the formation of a Youth Committee, and a Youth Sunday.

Improved: The group decided [*to form* a Youth Committee and *to establish* a Youth Sunday]. They also voted *to invite* parents to meetings. (*Two sentences.*)

PRACTICE

Underline the faulty parallelism in the sentences below. (a) Place [ ] around each faulty parallelism. (b) Rewrite the sentence, using correct parallelism and two or more sentences if necessary. (c) Put [ ] around your improved parallelism. (Don't be afraid to recast a sentence thoroughly, but do try to keep its basic meaning.)

a. The quality of a comic strip exists in relation to the drawings, the language as well as the situations involved. (*Hint:* Employ a new subject for the sentence; for example: "A comic strip is only as good as its drawings. . . .")

b. Let's start to plan the recreation program, describe the advisor's job, and the budgeting for the playground equipment.

c. With information from the library, and experiencing my accounting major, I can help explain course requirements to students who plan to major in accounting.

d. Maryanne says that her qualifications for the position are good and is excellent at dealing with the public.

e. The old Ford was creaky, cranky, and the starting of it was hard.

f. My friend said that he wanted an accomplished woman and lovable, and who makes a lot of money.

g. The politician said he was honest, of considerable legislative experience, was chairman of three important committees in Congress, and his ability to pay attention to his state's problems made his election necessary.

h. Because I dislike violent movies and also being a peaceful person, I refused to see *Dressed to Kill*.

i. My experience shows the value of love perfectly by contrasting sex with spiritual.

j. The American worker's greatest flaw and possibly the most outstanding reason for his boredom is his too high expectations regarding his job.

SUBORDINATION

Subordination, as the term implies, makes sentence elements *unequal* in grammar or emphasis. Subordinated elements are not bases or main clauses; they can never stand alone as a sentence:

Jack Reiss, *who quit his job last week,* believed his boss was taking advantage of him.

The interrupter in italics is subordinated to the main part of the sentence, which can stand alone. The subordination here could be reversed:

Jack Reiss, *who believed his boss was taking advantage of him,* quit his job last week.

Subordination covers a large number of possible variations in ranking the parts of sentences. Here are typical variations, with the subordinated elements in italics (note how many subordinate elements are *free* units):

1. Using a *clause:* See examples above.

2. Using an -*ing* phrase:

Jack, *believing that his boss was taking advantage of him,* quit his job last week.

3. Using an -*ed* phrase:

Abandoned by his crew, the captain of the ship stuck to his post.

4. Using an *appositive* or "explainer":

> Carol, *our treasurer,* bought a new motorcycle.

5. Using a *descriptive phrase:*

> The children, *obviously anxious about their dog,* dashed into the street.
> *Before breakfast,* they swim for thirty minutes and jog a mile.

Subordination is often signaled by punctuation, but many subordinate clauses do not require punctuation:

> The house *that Jack built* is falling down.
> The woman *you saw* lives upstairs.

Subordination strengthens your prose by cutting unnecessary expressions, making relationships clear, and smoothing the flow of words.

> *Weak:*　　He came into the office. It was after lunch. He looked flustered.
>
> *Improved:*　*Looking flustered,* he came into the office *after lunch.*
>
> *Weak:*　　They were disturbed by the laughter at the movie. They complained to the usher.
>
> *Improved:*　*Because they were disturbed by the laughter at the movie,* they complained to the usher.
>
> *Improved:*　*Disturbed by the laughter,* they complained to the usher.
>
> *Weak:*　　The student said that he had lost his research paper. This happened on Tuesday.
>
> *Improved:*　The student said that he had lost his research paper *on Tuesday.*

PRACTICE

1. One way to get a feel for the art of subordination is to take sentences that use it and recast them into short, choppy ones. Pick a sentence with a fair amount of subordination:

> He suggested instead that the Philosophical Society, after filling its glasses, should invite Mr. Freak of the senior class to give his imitation of two cats quarreling on a roof. —Stephen Leacock

Rewrite, omit the subordination, and chop into small sentences:

> He suggested something. The Society should fill its glasses. Then it should invite Mr. Freak. He is a member of the senior class. He should be asked to do something. It is to give an imitation. His imitation should be of two cats. They are quarreling on a roof.

Work backwards, and create choppy sentences from these smooth ones:

a. "It is useless to go to bed to save the light, if the result is twins."
   — Chinese proverb
b. "I believe it stupid to torment [students] to write on topics that they know and care nothing about."— F. L. Lucas
c. "Our grandfathers, particularly those living in and around Boston, were of the opinion that the English spoken in Boston was the 'purest' in the whole country."— Bergen and Cornelia Evans

2. Now that you have done Practice **1**, work "forward"— revise these choppy sentences for proper subordination. You may need more than one sentence in your rewritten versions.

a. The pilot was experienced. He had 1000 hours flying time. He brought the crippled plane into the airport. It did not have a scratch.
b. This is the painting that Smith sold. It is very rare. Smith had wanted it for years. He paid $20,000 for it.
c. She joined the company. Then we knew her better. We learned to like her. Her shortness of temper did not seem to matter.
d. The snow got too deep. They could not drive in it. It stopped about midnight. They slept in the car. The engine was left running to keep them warm. They ignored the danger.
e. The football fans are middle-aged. They are having a picnic. The food is on the tailgate of a hundred station wagons. The martinis are ice-cold. Some fans will not see this game.

VARIATIONS ON
THE TYPICAL SENTENCE

*H*ere are some interesting sentences:

> Among those whom I like or admire, I can find no common denominator, but among those whom I love, I can: all of them make me laugh. — W. H. Auden

These are the times that try men's souls: The summer soldier and the sunshine patriot will in this crisis, shrink from the service of his country; but he that stands it Now, deserves the love and thanks of man and woman. Tyranny, like hell, is not easily conquered; yet we have this consolation with us, that the harder the conflict, the more glorious the triumph. . . .
— Thomas Paine

The afternoons were long; sunsets were sad glories: allegorical wars between dark heroes and the lords of light. — Jack Vance

I had not known my father very well. We had got on badly, partly because we shared, in our different fashions, the vice of stubborn pride. When he was dead I realized that I had hardly ever spoken to him. When he had been dead a long time I began to wish I had. It seems to be typical of life in America, where opportunities, real and fancied, are thicker than anywhere else on the globe, that the second generation has no time to talk to the first.
— James Baldwin, *Notes of a Native Son*

Sentences like these provide variety and drama. The techniques for writing them are relatively simple, and you might like to try them out yourself. Write a few sentences every day in which you imitate the sentence patterns and techniques discussed in the rest of this chapter. Create your own variations. Take off and fly a little. But don't worry about crashes — nobody ever got hurt from falling off a sentence.

Try Different Beginnings

By changing the way your sentences begin, you can add variety to your writing almost automatically. Here is a sentence that follows the subject-verb-object pattern:

She has a new sports car.

By using various kinds of beginnings, you can work variations on this:

With object as subject:	Her new sports car is easy to drive.
With change of subject:	Her prized possession is a sports car.
With -*ing* subject:	Driving a sports car is a sign of status in a university community.
With infinitive subject:	To drive a sports car is a sign of affluence.
With subordinate clause:	After her grandfather's estate was settled, she bought a sports car.
With -*ing* phrase:	Having received her inheritance, she bought a sports car.
With prepositional phrase:	After the model change, she bought a sports car.

With *it/there*: There is nothing more fun than a sports car.
With *that/what*: That she spent her money on a new sports car is obvious. What she wanted more than anything else was a new sports car.
With a question: A new sports car? She just bought one.

Employ Inversion

Most sentences are written using this normal word order: "They did not say a word." In creating an *inversion,* or *inverted order,* you shift a sentence element into an *earlier* position in the arrangement of words: "*Not a word* did they say." An occasional inversion makes your writing more interesting and dramatic:

Normal order: He slid down the slope, scraping skin from his elbows.
Inversion: *Down the slope he slid,* scraping skin from his elbows.
Normal order: The vampire stalked through the castle, his eyes glowing.
Inversion: *Through the castle stalked the vampire,* his eyes glowing. (a double inversion)

Precisely because inverted sentences are dramatic, they should be used sparingly.

Try a Periodic Sentence

For richness and suspense, use an occasional *periodic sentence,* which keeps your main thought suspended until the end, a position of emphasis. The periodic sentence has two virtues: (1) you can pile many ideas into its versatile and flexible structure; and (2) it holds the reader's interest like a detective story. How, the reader wonders while reading through a periodic sentence, will it all turn out? Here are some examples (italics added):

At that great moment in history, ranking with the moment in the long ago when man first put fire to work for him and started on his march to civilization, *the vast energy locked within the hearts of the atoms of matter was released for the first time in a burst of flame such as had never before been seen on this planet.* —W. L. Laurence

Cleanliness is a great virtue; but when it is carried to such an extent that you cannot find your books and papers which you left carefully arranged on your table — when it gets to be a monomania with man or woman — *it becomes a bore.* — C. B. Fairbanks

There is a homely adage which runs, "Speak softly and carry a big stick; you will go far." If the American nation will speak softly and yet build and keep at a pitch of the highest training a thoroughly efficient navy, *the Monroe Doctrine will go far.* — Theodore Roosevelt

Use Qualifying and Balancing Devices

In your writing you will sometimes need to qualify your statements. That is, you will need to limit the range of an assertion or include an exception to an idea expressed in the base. Suppose you write: "I like Wagner's music, even though some of it is excessively dramatic." Here you qualify the idea in the sentence base ("I like Wagner's music") with an idea in a closer that is introduced by the phrase *even though.*

In balancing ideas, you can use certain *signs of correlation* to indicate that the ideas are equal in importance and emphasis. Here are some typical signs:

Either-or:	Sandy wants *either* strawberry *or* vanilla ice cream.
Neither-nor:	We wanted to go swimming, but *neither* Judy *nor* Alice was able to go.
Both-and:	We went to Hawk Beach because the water there was *both* safe *and* warm.
Not only-but also:	Howells should be admired *not only* for his vivid storytelling *but also* for his knowledge of human beings.

Sometimes you will need to express *opposing* ideas that are equal in importance. So you should use a special kind of balancing structure known as *antithesis:* "Linda likes swimming but not baseball." Antithesis is an art beloved of satirists, preachers, and politicians: "Woolworth was not brave; he was a coward. He was not fair; he played favorites. He was not moral, but righteous; not honest, but slyly dutiful; not skillful, but lucky; not . . ." Poor Woolworth. It is easy to get carried away by this sort of thing.

Let Meaning Determine Your Structure

Surely, the most important suggestion of all is: *Let meaning determine the structure of your sentences.* If your meaning demands a certain type of sentence or a certain construction, use that sentence or construction. A sentence expresses an idea. If your idea is one of cause and effect, for example, your sentence construction in some way must show cause and effect: "Since all children should be able to read, we must build schools to teach them." The *since* tied to the opener, which is in turn tied to the sentence base, helps give the reader a sentence that moves clearly from opener to period and that also neatly marries structure and sense. Of course there are other ways to state this idea: "We must build schools because all children should be able to read." Here, *because* signals the cause-and-effect relation. (Many cause-and-effect sentences have either a *since* or *because* in them.)

As you allow the meaning to determine the structure of your sentences, you will combine several of the structures discussed in this chapter. For example, Tom dislikes baseball. Perhaps he dislikes football and tennis too. And he loathes swimming. To express these ideas accurately, you write something like: "Tom dislikes football, tennis, and baseball—but swimming he actually loathes." To express a rather simple set of ideas you have created a complex and interlocked set of constructions:

Sentence base:	Tom dislikes football, tennis, and baseball
Parallel elements:	football, tennis, and baseball
Signal:	but
Inversion:	swimming he actually loathes.

All these guidelines end with a bit of practical and general advice: Use different sentence structures and lengths. Occasionally sneak up on your readers with a sentence they do not expect. Don't plod along writing one *subject-verb-object* sentence after another. Make your sentences show a little sparkle and life—but remember that too much sparkle, like too much champagne, will only make your readers dizzy. Here is a sparkling bit of prose that illustrates many of the variations we've been talking about:

> It is curious to be awake and watch a sleeper. Seldom, when he awakes, can he remember anything of his sleep. It is a dead part of his life. But watching him, we know he was alive, and part of his life was thought. His body moved. His eyelids fluttered, as his eyes saw moving visions in the darkness. His limbs sketched tiny motions, because his sleeping fancy was guiding him through a crowd, or making him imagine a race, a fight, a hunt, a dance. . . . he sweated. He felt the passage of time and was making himself ready for the morning with its light and noise. And all that time he was thinking—vaguely and emotionally if he was intellectually untrained, in symbols, animals, and divinities if he was a primitive man, often in memories, sometimes in anticipations of the future, and far oftener than he himself would believe, forming intricate and firm decisions on difficult problems carried over from his waking life. —Gilbert Highet, *Man's Unconquerable Mind*

PRACTICE

1. Identify the sentence structures of the following sentences. Look for parallelism, inversions, periodic sentences, and qualifying and balancing devices.

   a. All animals are equal, but some animals are more equal than others. — George Orwell

   b. Though I speak with the tongues of men and of angels, and have not charity, I am become as sounding brass, or a tinkling cymbal. — 1 Cor. 13:1

   c. In some sort of crude sense which no vulgarity, no humor, no overstatement can quite extinguish, the physicists have known sin; and this is a knowledge which they cannot lose. — J. R. Oppenheimer

   d. All in green went my love riding/on a great horse of gold/into the silver dawn. — E. E. Cummings

   e. We must conquer war, or war will conquer us. — Ely Culbertson

   f. In the free billowing fender [of the automobile], in the blinding chromium grilles, in the fluid control, in the ever-widening front seat, we see the flowering of the America that we know. — E. B. White

   g. Through all his life one idea runs — "Avoid the intelligent men and embrace the mediocre."

   h. A man may be old, he may be ugly, he may be burdened with grave responsibilities to the nation, and that nation be at a crisis of its history; but none of these considerations, nor all of them together, will deter him from sitting for his portrait. — Max Beerbohm

2. Discuss these two passages. How are they similar and different in their use of the sentence variations discussed on pp. 282–286?

   > [1]Here is what we know about the state of poverty: its boundaries do not appear on any map; it has no flag or official song, but once you are there it is difficult to get your zip code changed; as a character-building experience it is overrated by the rich and overpopulated by the poor; and it's a place where nobody goes for the weekend.
   >
   > [2]Earl Campbell had never given much thought to being poor, had never really realized how deprived his family had been, until — in the space of a single year — he won the Heisman Trophy, signed a contract worth $1.4 million to play for the Houston Oilers and became the hottest thing to hit the NFL since *Monday Night Football*. When the full weight of his family's privation hit him, Campbell decided to take some

of his NFL greenbacks and build a spacious new house for his mother and then turn the rundown plank shack where he had grown up into a museum where other underprivileged kids could come see firsthand that the NFL was, indeed, the land of opportunity.

[3]And so, as Campbell's fortunes soared on football fields across America last season, his mama's new house went up. And lest the contrast between his past and his present would be too subtle to grasp, Campbell had the new house built about 25 feet from the old one, with only a large gray septic tank between them. —Bruce Newman, "The Roots of Greatness"

[1]Dogs fare ill in proverbs. They are greedy, fierce, filthy, and servile. They defile cisterns, return to their vomit, drive the patient ox from the manger, bark at their own fleas, eat each other, bay the moon, suffer under a bad name, get themselves hanged and beaten, and whine, snarl, cringe, fawn, and slaver in a myriad dangerous and disgusting ways. Dogs are mentioned many times in the Bible, but only with abhorrence. That they licked Lazarus' sores was intended not as an indication of their pity but of his degradation. They fare even worse in Shakespeare than in the Scriptures; their combined servility, ferocity, and filthiness seems to have fascinated the poet with revulsion.

[2]Until fairly recently the dog was a scavenger. His food consisted exclusively of garbage and his residence was the kennel or channel, the loathsome trickle down the center of the street into which refuse was thrown. Great houses, having much garbage, had many dogs, and there was a regular functionary, the dog whipper, to keep them in subjection. Blows and kicks were the rule and for the slightest offense dogs were hanged. Sometimes just for the fun of it.

[3]In such an atmosphere and under such a regime *a dog's life* was, no doubt, a wretched one to lead. *To go to the dogs* was to descend low indeed, and *to die like a dog* to make a miserable end. The sayings might be trite, even then, but at least they had meaning. —Bergen and Cornelia Evans, *A Dictionary of Contemporary American Usage*

3. Using the ideas supplied in the sentences below, create new sentences that employ the variations suggested in this chapter. Omit any sentences or sentence parts that seem irrelevant in your new sentences. But try to use as much of the detail as possible.
   a. I read *Dracula*. It frightened me. I did not understand some of it. After reading it, I dreamed of blood and castles. I did not understand much of the story.
   b. Darwin College needs a new rugby field. The players are unhappy. The trustees will not vote the funds for it. The players are thinking of trying to raise money by charging people to watch the games for the rest of the season. The field is very bumpy and rough. It has a shallow irrigation ditch running through it.

c. The desert is full of killers. The desert seems empty. The desert is hot, but the heat does not kill all life. Many forms of life live off other forms. Many inhabitants of the desert look like bugs from another planet.

d. His mother screamed when she first saw it. Spiders did not frighten him. He got a big black spider as a pet. He kept it in a coffee can. He was curious, not fearful. The spider was more afraid of him than he of it.

e. Censorship is wrong. Censorship at times is necessary. Society has certain rights. Individuals should be able to read or view what they please without censorship. Books that show pictures of people being tortured are an evil.

f. The child was bored. The professor was angry at being interrupted. The mother stayed in class with her child. The child ran out of paper and crayons. The student brought her five-year-old child to class.

g. She wanted to experiment with the new. She did not care for tales of failure in the past. She liked chemistry most of all. Tales of dusty kings bored her. She enjoyed working with figures and test tubes and chemical unknowns.

CHAPTER 14
SENTENCES (II) —
HOW MEANING MATCHES STRUCTURE

In *Centennial,* James Michener tells what happened to an independent cowman who tried to bring his cattle on the land of a major ranch — *he became shot:* "In eleven such incidents no one ever saw who did the shooting, nor were there even suspicions. But eleven would-be intruders became shot."

There is an example of how sentences "mean"! In most statements about a shooting, one is forced to build in at least a hint of responsibility. *The cowman was shot.* (Who shot him?) *Lassiter shot the cowman.* (We know who shot him.) Even *There was a cowman shot* implies that somebody or other pulled the trigger. But *He became shot* is like *He became ill.* Nobody did it; it was an act of God or of bad luck, like getting the measles or stepping on a rattlesnake.

Of course, the ironic ambiguity of *becoming shot* was, in the rancher's view, intentional. Such examples prove again how meaning and structure must be matched — or deliberately mismatched — if writers are to get the effect they wish. Ordinarily, if you want an action effect, use an action verb. To express nonaction (or "*is*-ness"), use a form of *is,* like *are, am, be, been,* etc. "To *be,* or not to *be:* that *is* the question," said Hamlet. Oddly enough, even today some authorities condemn *is* verbs, saying that they are not lively enough—but we haven't noticed anybody rewriting Shakespeare lately.

The English sentence communicates thought or meaning in four fundamental ways. So it follows that you need only four types of sentence base in order to express almost any idea. The system we are describing works for subordinate clauses too, but to save space we will ignore such clauses here.

Types of Sentence Base	Example
Action—Subject *does* [something]	My wolf *howls* at the moon.
	The wolf *bit* my ear.
Passive—Subject *is done* [by something]	The wolf *will be punished.*
	My ear *was treated* by the doctor.
Is—Subject *is* [something]	The wolf's name *is* Ferdinand.
	Ferdinand *was* happy.
It/There—it/there *is* [Subject]	It *was* fun owning a wolf.
	There *is* no life like a wolf's.

As you examine these bases, observe that they are created by four different kinds of relationship between the *subject* and *verb* of a sentence. Verb tense and number, by the way, do not matter when describing the four types of base. (My wolf *howls,* My wolf *will howl,* and My wolf *might have been howling* are all action bases. The wolf's name *is* Ferdinand and The two wolves *are* angry are both *is* bases.)

Now let's look at each of these four bases in detail.

THE ACTION BASE

In writing the *action* base, you say: *SUBJECT does [something]:*

a. My *father-in-law works* for a living.   (*SUBJECT does*)
b. *Sherry cries* when she watches sad movies.   (*SUBJECT does*)
c. My *father-in-law shoots pool* for a living. (*SUBJECT does something*)
d. *Sherry cries* real *tears* when she watches   (*SUBJECT does something*)
   sad movies.

In every instance, the action base is made with a subject and its own action verb. If you need an object for the action, as the writer did in *c.* and *d.,* you insert it after the verb.

THE PASSIVE BASE

The passive base can be thought of as a reversal of the action base. Take an action base:

Mrs. Parker heard the bell.   *(SUBJECT does something)*

Reverse the action, and make a subject out of the object:

The bell was heard by Mrs. Parker.   *(SUBJECT is done by something)*

Here *bell,* now the subject, is being acted upon (is "passive").

The typical relationship between action and passive statements looks like this (the agent does the acting):

Action

Passive

[agent]

a. The *wind* blew the flowers.   The flowers were blown by the *wind.*

[agent]

b. *Explorers* found the cave.   The cave was found by the *explorers.*

[agent]

c. The *saw* cut my arm.   My arm was cut by the *saw.*

These examples show the *complete* form of the passive, and every complete form will have all the parts mentioned. The shortened form of the *passive* (what we will here call the *short passive*) omits *by* and the *agent*:

a. My arm will be cut.
b. The cave has been found.
c. The job was completed.
d. The worker should be fired from his job.

Each of these four short passives can be made into a complete passive—if you know the agents. The *complete passive* of *d.* might read:

[agent]

The worker should be fired from his job by the *supervisor.*

PRACTICE

1. Indicate whether the action bases below are *Subject does* or *Subject does something.*
   a. The crowd stood up, making a loud noise.
   b. They sang "The Star-Spangled Banner" and "America."
   c. The water leaked into the house.
   d. It warped and cracked the walls and floors.
   e. When my folks arrive, they will want to eat right away.

f. Traveling makes me hungry too, so I always carry some crackers and jelly along on a trip.

2. Locate each *action base* in these sentences. Identify the statements as *Subject does* or *Subject does something*.
   a. Whales eat very small pieces of food.
   b. His aunt will whip him when she catches him, for she hates him when he skips school.
   c. The flowers are blowing in the wind.
   d. Miss Enright should have taken enormous pains with her work.
   e. She should have been much more careful.
   f. In truth, peace makes strange bedfellows.
   g. Before starting to work on the bridge, the engineer made many careful plans, some of which actually worked.
   h. The king delivered a statement to his subjects, hoping that they would believe him.

3. Pick 2 sentences from Practice 1 and 3 from Practice 2. Turn them into passive bases, using both *Subject is done* and *Subject is done by something*.

4. For the sentence bases below, state whether the passive construction is *complete* or *short*.
   a. The best theme in the class was written by Mary Parkhurst.
   b. The job of repairing the tile in the men's room will be completed by the Standish tile company next week.
   c. The exhaust gases are not completely burned in this engine.
   d. A complete search of the premises should have been made by the FBI.
   e. The mirror on the vanity has been broken.
   f. My typewriter was dropped, and now it will not work.
   g. The situation was corrected last week when Mr. Standbey made his statement.
   h. President Juan Lavero was toppled from power this morning by a group of colonels who said they favored a less oppressive regime.
   i. Her article on prairie dogs was accepted by *The Pan-Handle Gazette.*

THE IS *BASE*

The *is* base expresses a state of being ("*is*-ness") in the past, present, or future. By *state of being,* we also mean "possible" or "probable" being. The *is* base says that *Subject is something:*

SUBJECT +	*is* verb	+ something
_____	is/are	_____
_____	were	_____
_____	will be	_____
_____	should be	_____
_____	should have been	_____
_____	can be	_____
_____	could be	_____
_____	etc.	_____

Examples of the *is base:*

> Progress *is* our most important product.
> He *might have been* guilty of murder.
> The Cave *will be* dangerous when we enter it.
> The orange juice in the refrigerator *is* very sour.
> Using this 30 amp fuse, my furnace *should have been* safe from power failure.
> That *might be* the best reason for dropping the course.
> Alaska *was* the last new frontier.
> We *are* happy.

Note: A few verbs besides *is* appear in *is bases:*

The milk seems warm.	Your car *sounds* good.
The dog *smells* bad.	Her hairdo *looks* peculiar.
My drink *tastes* funny.	You *will become* a millionaire.
I *feel* sick.	He *became* dead.

PRACTICE

Examine the sentences below and identify each *is base.*
a. Wolves are irritable when tired.
b. I am a great believer in the four-day work week.
c. This will have been the first day she's been absent.
d. They asked Wilson to provide the evidence.
e. The box contains aspirin. But it is not an aspirin box.
f. The judge was entirely consistent. He made trouble for the defendant by every one of his judgments on the case.
g. He waved his hand and whistled a song. He seemed happy.
h. I am now a pauper, having put all my money into repairs on my car's engine.
i. He dropped the sandbag on his foot. He is pretty unhappy about that.

THE IT/THERE *BASE*

*T*he *it/there* base has two main characteristics: (1) It begins with a meaningless "filler" phrase *(it is, there is, there are)* that does no more than get the sentence started. For example: *There is* more fighting in Ireland this week. (2) The subject of the sentence is delayed and does not appear until after the *it/there*: There's more *fighting* in Ireland.

> The *it/there* base says: It/there is Subject.

> *There's* snow on the ground.   (Snow *is* on the ground.)
> *There will be* apples on the trees.   (Apples *will be* on the trees.)
> *It's* hard to understand.   (To understand *is* hard.)
> *It was* terrible that he didn't win.   (That he didn't win *was* terrible.)

It/there bases are easy to manage if you remember that they employ meaningless fillers to start with. If an *it* or *there* at the beginning has meaning, it is not part of an *it/there base*. *It* can stand for other words, and *there* can indicate a certain place. Note the distinctions below:

> *There's* snow on the ground *(it/there)*.
> *It* (the snow) is melting (not an *it/there* because *it* refers to *snow*).

> *There is* a fight going on on the field *(it/there)*.
> There (on the field) is the injured player (not an *it/there* because *there* refers
> to a place).

Note: Verbs like *seem* or *appear* sometimes are used to help form *it/there* bases:

> *It seems to be* raining.
> *There appeared to be* no one in the building.

PRACTICE

---

1. Pick out the *it/there* bases in the sentences below. Explain why each base belongs (or does not belong) in the *it/there* category.
   a. There's a storm warning just being announced on the radio.
   b. There is the lightning, just above those trees!
   c. The fox ate my chickens. It broke through the wire fence to get at them.
   d. It's a shame that you caught the flu and missed so many classes.

    e. There will be a number of important ideas covered in the next two weeks.

    f. It appeared that Mike had lost his way on the trail.

    g. There is my belt, hanging on the wall in the basement.

    h. If you borrow it, bring it back. It is the best belt I have.

    i. Suddenly, there were a dozen horses surrounding the stagecoach.

    j. I certainly remember that Friday. It was the unluckiest day I had ever spent.

    k. "Medicine," said the doctor. "It's a rough profession. But there are tougher ones, and I have never been sorry I became a doctor."

    l. It seems that Louisa isn't pregnant after all.

2. In the paragraphs below you see several good examples of how the modern writer uses the four types of base that we have been discussing. Identify the types of bases used in the starred sentences. Prepare for class discussion some notes on the effectiveness of the types of bases used.

    1*It is curious that wine-making in North America had to wait until the developing of California. By that time, the Eastern States had been settled and civilized for two hundred years. Their climate was equally suited to the vine. *Their people were good wine-drinkers. Why did Virginian wine not grow up in the seventeenth century at the same time as the wine of the Cape?

    2*The answer lies in the terrible little beetle-like creature called the *phylloxera*, a native of the eastern United States. *Nothing was known about him until about a hundred years ago, but he had meanwhile been preventing the growing of grapes for wine anywhere in his domain. All that the farmers knew was that the European vines they planted withered and died. *There is a kind of vine which is native to North America; it grew profusely — giving really terrible wine where anybody tried to tame it — and was immune to the attacks of the phylloxera. *But the imported vines of Europe were no sooner planted than their roots were eaten up and they died.

    3The importance of this for Europe was not realized until too late. *The little beetle found its way to France in the 1860s, probably on an American vine being imported for experimental grafting purposes. *Its progeny swept through the country like the plague, doing the most appalling damage. *Within twenty years, they had killed virtually every vine in France — in Bordeaux, Burgundy, Champagne: nowhere was spared. *The rest of Europe suffered the same fate. For a while it looked like the end of European wine. But it was discovered that the roots of the American vines were immune to phylloxera. There was nothing else for it but to bring in millions of American vine-stocks and graft on to them the remaining cuttings of the old European vines. *To everybody's infinite relief, it worked. *The roots resisted the scourge; the branches bore their old fruit. There will always be arguments about whether the wine is quite as good as it was before the disaster. *But it was saved; that was the great thing. And to this day, every vine in Europe, with a handful of exceptions, is grafted, before it is planted, on to an American root. — Hugh Johnson, *Wine*

THE FOUR SENTENCE BASES — WHEN TO USE THEM

In the past, some rather doubtful rules on this subject have been stated. The commonest goes something like this: "Avoid sentences using *is, was, are, am,* etc. because they are 'weak' rhetorically. Instead, use strong action verbs." But the fact is that none of the bases is inferior to the others. There is nothing inherently weak about *is* verbs, for example. Otherwise the cartoon hero Popeye, as he goes about massacring his opponents with spinach-inspired fists, would never sing:

> I·*am* what I *am,*
> And that's what I *am*
> I *am* Popeye the sailor man!

Nor — if the construction were inherently faulty — would Ernest Hemingway employ the *it/there* form ten times in the first two pages of his novel *A Farewell to Arms.*

It is true that, statistically speaking, the four bases are not equally used. Good writers use the *action* and *is* bases much more often than the other two types, probably because the world reflected in most prose is full of action and states of being. The *passive* and *it/there* bases are employed less, partly because they can be easily misused (as we will show in a moment), but mainly because they don't seem to be needed as much.

As our last comment implies, the four bases are a part of the writer's tools. And as tools, they should be used when necessary, each having its special function at a particular time.

Action Bases

Use *Action Bases* to express an action. Example (italics added):

[1]Although the Indian traders may not have been as glamorous as the explorers or soldiers or lawmen or cattle barons, their influence remains strong and enduring. . . .

[2]*Traders opened the West* for colonists. *They awakened* the *world* to the rich promise of the North American continent. *They sold* the Indians *tools* they needed to make a hard existence easier. When the Indians lost the battle for their homeland, the *traders moved* with them to the reservations the government allowed them to live on. When Indian people began their new lives, the *traders sold* them white men's *clothing, saddles* and *harnesses, grain, utensils, food* and *tools.* Often, the *traders settled disputes* between them, *buried* their *dead, attended* their *ceremonies, ministered* to their sick, *filled out* endless *forms,* and *helped them* adjust to a new, inverted way of life.

[3]In most cases, the *Indians trusted* the *trader* more than they did the men from Washington, or the starched preachers who threatened them with a hell they did not believe in, or the single-minded school teachers who refused to learn the Indian ways. The *Indians trusted* the *traders* because they could understand what it was the traders wanted from them, and because they admired men who made a good trade.

[4]The good *traders spoke* the *language* of the Indians. *They ate* and *smoked* with them, *married* their *women, respected* their *customs. They treated Indians* as business men treat their customers, not as inferiors, or as wards, or as savages, or worse, as downtrodden unfortunates. *They befriended* and *argued* and *bargained* with them. The traders' survival depended on the Indians' need for them.

[5]Juan Lorenzo Hubbel, a trader to the Navajos, wrote: "Out here in this country, the trader is everything from merchant to father confessor, justice of the peace, judge, jury, court of appeals, chief medicine man and *de facto czar* of the domain over which he presides."—Jo Brown "Indian Traders of North America"

Passive Bases

Use *Passive Bases:*

a. *For variety:*

Just as I drove up, Mrs. Sheehan appeared at her front door screaming like a banshee. She *was heard* by the neighbors living a block away.

After the attack on Pearl Harbor, the President spoke to Congress; and within a few hours war *was declared* against the Japanese.

b. *To emphasize a word or an idea:*

The Smith house, not the Jones house, *was insured* by Acme.

The furniture in your room *should be* more sensibly *arranged.*

c. *When you don't know who or what the agent is:*

My books *were removed* from the library desk where I had left them.

This valve *has been taken* out of the gas line leading to the kitchen stove.

d. *When you need to explain something about the agent:*

                            [agent]   [explanation]

The valve *was removed* by the plumber, *who has gone to the shop.*

                                [agent]   [explanation]

The Smith house *was insured* by a company *that no longer writes fire insurance.*

                                                  [agent]

Some of the corn crop this year *was ruined* by heavy rains, *which did*

                [explanation]

great damage in the northern counties.

Bad Uses of the Passive

If misused, the passive can be wordy, awkward, or unemphatic:

A picnic table *was located* by Jim.
A sonata *was played by* the orchestra.
The banquet *was held* during which speeches *were made* and songs *were sung.*

One of the most common (and serious) misuses of the passive is the gobbledygook passive, in which the writer uses vague or polysyllabic words (and usually omits the agent). Examples of gobbledygook passive:

The experimental rationale *was explained* in the Foreword and *was* more fully *detailed* in Chapter 3.
Psychological characterization *will be considered* a major factor in the present analysis of *Huck Finn.*

Improving a Bad Passive

For a bad passive—whether it is wordy, awkward, unemphatic, or so gobbledygooky that a reader simply cannot understand it—there is one major strategy for improvement: *Turn the statement into an action base.*

a. *Poor:* A picnic table was located by Jim. (7 words)
   Improved (action base): Jim located a picnic table. (5 words)

b. *Poor:* The banquet was held during which speeches were made and songs were sung. (13 words)
   Improved (action base): During the banquet, we heard speeches and sang songs. (9 words)

The solution to the gobbledygook passive is *never* to write a sentence like this in the first place:

> It has been decided that to maintain optimum learning conditions in the library, evening hours will be extended to 2:00 A.M.

But if a sentence like this sneaks up on you in a first draft, identify the agent(s) in the situation, and put the idea into one or more specific action bases:

> The library has announced that its evening hours will be extended to 2:00 A.M.
> Mr. Harlan Smith, Director of the Library, has announced that . . .
> Mr. Smith announced today that starting Sunday the library will close at 2:00 A.M. Smith claimed that closing the library later will allow more students to use it.
> So that more students can use the library, it will close at 2:00 A.M. from now on.

Is Bases

Use *Is Bases* to express a quality, characteristic, or condition. Example (italics added):

> But perhaps we should not altogether despise soap opera. *It is* the one really original narrative *form* thus far contributed to art by broadcasting, and one fine day it may even produce its masterpieces. Now, the *secrets* of soap opera *are these: It* must *be* about family life (threatened family life, motivated especially by sex, money, power, and challenged loyalty), and *it* must *be endless.* Ordinarily, narrative structure anticipates its own end; for the artist, *knowing where to end* (on the kiss, the climax, the killing, the revenge) *is everything.* The *opposite is true* of soap opera. *It* must *be interminable* and terminate in more or less the same way life is and does. Theoretically, a *soap opera is* the great *art form* of the reaction shot. And merely reacting, rather than concluding, the characters live their lives chewed up by time. A *soap opera is* not a *narrative form* defined by the beginning, middle, and end of an action or an event. On the contrary, its basic *unit* of imagined time *is* the *span* of the generations. —Stephen Koch, "Intrigue and the Wringing of Hands"

A Bad Use of the "Is" Base

When you have *nouns* (naming words) on both sides of the *is* verb, you have, in effect, an equation: noun = noun.

noun = noun
The man *is* Tom.
(man = Tom)

The problems *are* bad ones.
(problems = bad ones)

But if the nouns in the *is* base do not "equal" each other (noun ≠ noun), you may get a seriously illogical equation, as in this sentence: *The first difficulty was a lack of boys to pick from for the debate team.* Here *difficulty* does not "equal" *lack* (difficulty ≠ lack). Improve the sentence by changing the "equation" and making it more specific: *The first difficulty was that few boys wanted to try out for the debate team.*

Poor: The main problem of an accountant is his reputation. (problem ≠ reputation)
Improved: An accountant's main problem is that of keeping his reputation untarnished.
Improved: What is an accountant's main problem? It is how to maintain a good reputation.

Poor: One of the most important reasons for supporting the union is stable employment. (*One* [reason] ≠ *employment*)
Improved: Let's support the union so that we workers can have stable employment.
Improved: You should support the union—it helps you to keep your job.

In another kind of bad noun ≠ noun construction, there is no naming word or expression in one side of the "equation":

Poor: Love is where you have a very strong liking for someone. (*Love* ≠ *where*)
Improved: Love is having a very strong liking for someone.

Poor: My greatest happiness is when I am alone. (*happiness* ≠ *when*)
Improved: I am most happy when I am alone.
Improved: My greatest happiness is in being alone.

It/There Bases

Use *It/There Bases:*
a. *To make a beginning:*
Once upon a time, *there was* a fair princess who loved a frog.

There are three ways to catch trout, but only one of them works very well.

b. *To state a condition or circumstance:*
   It's a beautiful day.
   It is raining.
   There were reasons for my resignation.

c. *To give an opinion or judgment:*
   There's no business like show business!
   It is easy to write clear sentences, once you know how.

d. *To introduce a fact:*
   It is true that the Dean promised me I could take 20 hours.
   There was a broken window in my dorm room last week.
   There will be no good young quarterbacks on the Bears' roster next year (a "future fact" or guess).

As these sentences demonstrate, the *it/there* is both normal and pleasant when properly used. But when it occurs in wordy or awkward constructions like the following, you should revise the sentence:

Poor:	For those who wish more heat, *there is* a heater switch on the dashboard.
Improved:	If you want more heat, turn the switch on the dashboard.
Poor:	At the feet of the corpse *it was* found that *there were* five empty jewel cases from three different robberies.
Improved:	At the feet of the corpse, the police found five empty jewel cases from three different robberies.

In both these examples, we improved the weak sentences by shifting to active constructions. A lot of sentence improvement works exactly like this: You look at the sick sentence, ask "What is happening here?"; and answer the question with an active construction.

PRACTICE

Discussion
Prepare the following passage for a class discussion of well-shaped sentences.

[1]Sibelius's identification with his people was so complete that his music, even at its most personal, bore the stamp of their spirit. Such nationalism goes deeper than the quotation of folk tunes. "There is a mistaken impression among the press abroad," he wrote, "that my themes are often folk melodies. So far I have never used a theme that was not of my own invention." The important point is that some of them could have been folk melodies, and at least one of them—the chorale from *Finlandia*—became one.

[2]Sibelius, like Grieg before him, revealed the northern landscape. The more fanciful of his listeners like to discover in his music the brooding forests and lakes of his native land or the legendary heroes of its sagas. Sibelius's rugged strength and his command of the large forms enabled him to win and to hold the attention of the world—or at least part of it. England and the United States became the centers of his cult, where he was acclaimed as enthusiastically as in his homeland. Neither in Paris, Berlin, Vienna, nor Rome has he achieved a comparable eminence.

[3]Sibelius's reputation in serious music circles rests upon his seven symphonies. The first two are in the romantic tradition and pose no special problems. Their successors show a steady development toward refinement of style, conciseness of thought, and tightness of structure. In these works Sibelius discourses upon the great themes of nineteenth-century music—nature, man, destiny. His idiom is sparse and avoids sensuous brilliance. He exploits the somber colors and low registers of the orchestra. He uses short incisive motives that lend themselves to symphonic expansion and development. His speech is direct, abrupt, pithy.

[4]It is in the orchestral and choral works of his first period that Sibelius is most explicitly national. The bardic *En Saga* (1892) was followed by the orchestral legends *The Swan of Tuonela* (1893) and *Lemminkainen's Homefaring* (1895), and the symphonic fantasy *Pohjola's Daughter* (1906). These appeared during the years of tsarist oppression when to be patriotic was tantamount to being a revolutionary. Conceived in epic mood, they accorded with the temper of the liberation movement and brought Finnish culture to the attention of the world.
—Joseph Machlis, "Jan Sibelius, a National Artist"

Writing

1. For each of these sentences, add an explanation to the agent. Example: *The bicycle had been borrowed by Rolfe.* Explanation added: *The bicycle had been borrowed by Rolfe, whose car had broken down the night before.*

   a. The check will be mailed by my husband. . . .

b. He was rescued by friendly Indians. . . .
c. The table was badly stained by an acid compound. . . .
d. The house trailer was flipped over by the tornado. . . .
e. My excuse was accepted by the coach. . . .

2. Identify the passive bases in the sentences below, and explain why the sentences are bad. Rewrite each of the bad passives. Invent agents for each passive construction, and make each sentence as specific as possible. You may keep the passive base or change it to an action base. (Use more than one sentence, if necessary.)
   a. The bill was passed and the senators were praised.
   b. Our street light was knocked out, paint was thrown on the porch, and a note was attached to the door.
   c. Paintings on the walls of the Psychology Building are seen as beautiful.
   d. It has been decided that security regulations should be reintroduced in planning repair functions.
   e. Time-sharing proposals in the College of Engineering should be implemented before Tuesday.

3. Identify each base shown below. Then rewrite the sentence into each of the three other bases. For example:

	Gina likes milk.	*Action* base
	Gina is a milk-liker.	*Is* base
Rewrites	Milk is liked by Gina.	*Passive* base
	Then there's Gina the milk-liker.	*It/there* base

(What does this exercise tell you about the relative "rigidity" of the sentence bases?)
   a. There's hardly any truth to your statement.
   b. Smith is right about that.
   c. The criminal was caught.
   d. The criminal was caught by the police.
   e. My dream was wonderful.
   f. I love you!
   g. His name is Larry.
   h. It's impossible for me to do that.
   i. It's snowing.
   j. Sam slashed his personal budget.

4. Rewrite these faulty *is bases,* in which either a *noun does not "equal" a noun,* or there is no noun on one side of the "equation." Identify the nouns in both the bad "equation" and in your rewritten sentence.

a. Another good quality of our employees is their absentee record.
b. Democracy is where people vote for their leaders.
c. The feasibility of installing the carpet, we think, is a big problem.
d. Because the Dodgers lost their second baseman was the reason they lost the pennant.
e. My main wish is Dad will get to retire early.
f. My high salary was since I was needed by the company.
g. Marrying is when you take a woman for your lawful, wedded wife.
h. The main reason I passed the exam is good studying.
i. Another reason is because my teacher likes me.
j. Graduation is where you are finally finished forever with learning.

5. We listed above four uses of the *it/there base* (pp. 301–302). For each of the four uses, create two *it/there bases* of your own.

6. In a paragraph or two, describe specifically a close member of your family. Use as many *is bases* as necessary. Why do you need them for your description to be relatively complete?

7. Think of a situation that needs correcting; for example, a hazardous traffic condition in your town; an overcrowded lecture hall in a freshman course; a faulty procedure in your part-time job. In two or three paragraphs, write an account of the situation to someone in authority. Use clear *action bases* where you can.

8. Rewrite an old theme. Concentrate on improving the statements in the paper. If necessary, redefine your stance and completely rewrite the theme.

CHAPTER 15
SENTENCES (III)— REVISING AND EDITING

Only a genius gets a sentence right the first time. Most of us write . . . rewrite . . . and then write again—trying to get the proper match between meaning and structure. Revision usually improves this match; but with revision, as with other techniques in composition, you need a plan—or a set of suggestions—in order to make it more purposeful. After writing a "bad" sentence, how do you fix it? In this chapter we will offer a number of suggestions for revision, all of them based on the following premise: As you inspect your own sentences, imagine that you are a cool, objective, and slightly negative editor who does not mind telling himself to rearrange, cut, and reword.

SUGGESTIONS FOR REVISING AND EDITING*

1. *Think about what you've said.* Many bad sentences are a result of the writer's failure to think about and visualize what he has written. Leo Rosten

---

Editors and instructors often hear this complaint from writers after they have rewritten a sentence: "But you changed my meaning!" The objection has some validity, but the response to it has more: "One cannot usually make a significant improvement in a weak sentence without changing the meaning." In fact, when writers revise or edit a sentence, they try to make *meaning* more exact at the same time that they improve *structure* and *word choice*. In the sentence, everything works (or does not work) together.

found a sentence in the *New York Times* that shows how such a failure can result in unintentional comedy.

> There is Mr. Burton growling and grousing and endlessly chewing the lips, ears, and neck of Elizabeth Taylor as the faithless wife of a dull ambassador with whom he is having a clandestine affair.

Rosten commented: "I am glad, in a way, that Mr. Burton was endlessly chewing the neck of Miss Taylor as the faithless wife of a dull ambassador, because it probably wouldn't be fun to chew her neck as anyone else; but who is the ambassador with whom Burton, it says here, is having a clandestine affair?" Rosten quoted another sentence from the *Times:*

> Among her biggest gambles was during their tempestuous courtship.

Said Rosten: "I hate to be a spoilsport, gentlemen, but you just can't 'was' during anything."

2. *Check your stance.* Is a weak writer's stance hurting your sentence? A student wrote about a class project:

> The availability of time is an important factor in the project choice.

The stance is vague here—no writer, reader, or clear point. Clarify the stance and rewrite completely:

> In choosing a problem for our project, we must remember that we have only three weeks' time.

3. *Make your subject-verb relationship as clear and specific as possible.* A vague relationship helped make a mess of this sentence:

> Parental *endeavors* (subject) in regard to education *suggest* (verb) that . . .

How can endeavors *suggest*? Specify the subject and verb; then clarify the rest of the sentence:

> *Parents* at Elm School now *insist* that their children be taught to read.

Here is another example of vague subject and verb:

> *One* of the most important reasons for going to graduate school *is* more training.

Edit this by changing both the stance and the subject-verb relationship:

Students who want more training *should go* to graduate school.

Or:

Do you want more training? Then [*you should*] *go* to graduate school.

4. *Read your sentences aloud.*

Pedalling hard, she reached top of the hill.

That is a sentence one of us wrote several years ago. It went through our hands and the hands of an editor before the omission was found—by a proofreader reading the sentence aloud:

Pedalling hard, she reached *the* top of the hill.

Since people read hundreds of words a minute, it is easy to miss all kinds of errors—dangling modifiers, misspellings, illogicalities, vague usage, careless punctuation, omissions. *The ear will catch what the eye will not.* Human beings spoke and heard language a million years before they wrote it, which is why the best editing often combines the talents of ear and eye and voice.

5. *Use the sentence base rule.* Check back to pp. 272–273 for a full explanation of the rule. Also see **6** below.

6. *Make sure your sentence openers logically fit the bases that follow.*

> *Faulty:* Like many specialities in engineering, you must learn . . .
> *(dangling modifier)*
> *Improved:* Like many kinds of engineers, you must learn . . .
>
> *Faulty:* To be considered for the debate team, the voice must be trained.
> *Improved:* To be considered for the debate team, you must first train your voice.

7. *Avoid "nouniness" and "preposition piling."* Good sentences use no more nouns than are absolutely necessary. Abstract nouns are particularly troublesome. This sentence is "nouny":

> *Personality analysis* is the *determination* of *function defects* and *utilization* of their *cures.*

The sentence contains seven nouns — two of them used as clumsy modifiers: "*personality* analysis" and "*function* defects." This sentence is so bad it can't be edited; who knows what it means?

In a sentence, prepositions can multiply like rabbits. Such "preposition piling" occurs with nouniness and is a sign of it:

> English teachers agree that personal ownership and use *of* a good dictionary is a prime necessity *for* every student *in* obtaining the maximum results *from* the study of English.

Rewrite, cutting some of the nouns and altering others; for example, make *ownership* and *use* into verbs. Then the prepositions can be reduced from five to zero, the nouns from ten to three:

> English teachers agree that students should own and use a good desk dictionary.

Here is a portion of a satiric essay on nouniness in modern prose:

> Have you noticed the new look in the English language? Everybody's using nouns as adjectives. Or to put that in the current argot, there's a modifier noun proliferation. More exactly, since the matter is getting out of hand, a modifier noun proliferation increase. In fact, every time I open a magazine these days or listen to the radio, I am struck by the modifier noun proliferation increase phenomenon. So, I decided to write — you guessed it — a modifier noun proliferation increase phenomenon article. . . .
>
> Abstraction is the enemy both of clear expression and easy understanding. And abstract is what these strings of nouns become. And very quickly the reader or listener doesn't know what the actual relationship is. Take "Reality Therapy," the name of a new book. Do you gather that the author uses reality as a means of therapy or that the goal of his treatment is facing reality or that he has worked out some sort of therapy which he applies to reality? Take a phrase puzzled over in *Newsweek:* "antenna television systems operation." Manufacture? broadcasting? consulting? The article said that somebody was going into that field and I still don't know where he's going. I suspect that the people who turn out these phrases might insist that they are seeking greater precision, as though each new noun pinned down the matter a bit more. Wrong. Another article like this one and we'll have a modifier noun proliferation increase phenomenon article protest campaign, but will you know what you've got? — Bruce Price, "An Inquiry into Modifier Noun Proliferation"

8. *Cut out deadwood—words and phrases that are not doing enough work in the sentence.* The sample sentence in **7**, on using the dictionary, illustrates how to cut out deadwood. Here are more examples:

> *Poor:* A woman who was present there saw the break-in.
> *Improved:* A woman there saw the break-in.

> *Poor:* We are in receipt of your memo of August 14 making reference to football tickets sold by some of the players.
> *Improved:* We received your letter of August 14 about football tickets sold by some of the players.

> *Poor:* In relation to his idea, it does not seem to me to be a workable one.
> *Improved:* I doubt that his idea will work.

> *Poor:* A second area in which Jane should have a better knowledge involves rules of attendance.
> *Improved:* Second, Jane should know more about rules of attendance.

9. *Rewrite to avoid monotony or lack of emphasis.*

> *Poor:* Many favorable comments are beginning to be made about fantasy movies by the critics. These comments are long overdue and welcome to students of film.
> *Improved:* Recently many critics have made favorable comments about fantasy movies. To students of film, these comments are welcome—and long overdue.

> *Poor:* I took the job happily when the head of the company offered me more money because of my long experience and also technical school training in the field.
> *Improved:* When he found out that I had both technical training and experience, the head of the company offered me the job with a higher salary. I accepted his offer happily.

The last two improved versions work well partly because they follow the three suggestions offered by the sentence base rule (p. 272).

A FINAL NOTE ON EDITING

*R*ecently, a student came in to see one of us about his writing problems, particularly about his weak sentences. We talked over several of them, bringing out ideas and possibilities hidden inside (or behind) them.

In effect, we were "co-editors," identifying, analyzing, rethinking, and rewriting some of the troublesome constructions. You can do the same job by "talking" over your own sentences with yourself. Here are two of the student's sentences, with comments about their weaknesses:

Poor sentence: The students were accused of plagiarism, and they were told in terms of their careers in academia that they should not be too hopeful.

Comments: Stance and viewpoint are weak—*who* told the students? The two passive constructions are vague. Deadwood: *in terms of. Their careers* and *in academia* are not doing much work in the sentence either. Vague: *They should not be too hopeful.*

Edited sentence: After she accused the students of plagiarism, the Assistant Dean told them that they might be expelled.

Together, we created a clearer stance, cut out the deadwood, employed an opener, changed the vague passives to active constructions, and made the whole sentence more specific.

Poor sentence: The misuse of the environment must be improved in regard to the liquor industry.

Comments: Read the sentence aloud—we must *improve* our *misuse?* This says exactly the opposite of what the writer intended. He was probably thrown off the track by several weaknesses: the poor stance, the vagueness and deadwood *in regard to the liquor industry;* the passive *misuse . . . must be improved.*

Edited sentence: Let's pass a law in this state abolishing throwaway beer bottles.

We changed the stance. Now the writer is addressing a more specific group of readers. We cut unnecessary words, changed the bad passive to an active verb, and substituted the more specific phrase *beer bottles* for the vague phrase *liquor industry.*

PRACTICE

Edit and rewrite these sentences. Don't be afraid to change them when necessary. The point is to write a *better* sentence.
a. The assassination of Lincoln had much speculation to it.
b. The fact that the new trainees at first do not get to do much work on the actual engines should not give them a feeling of demotion.

c. It must be considered a possibility that the student nurse must be able to face physical damage, broken bones, crainial disorders, pregnancy, or even death.

d. It happened at the hour of three when there is much relaxing during the coffee break.

e. The nerve center of the oboe lies in its reed, and in its bore is its soul; the need of a good reed is the bane of the player's life.

f. Mr. Coleman announced his resignation this morning. He would have liked to have stayed a while longer.

g. "Don't expire before your license do." — from the Illinois State License Bureau

h. He only dislikes action pictures and neither does his brother.

i. The next point to make about idiom differences is one of the most difficult problems for many foreigners.

j. It is not believed that the critics show complete rationality in their judgments when they criticize the Fall Frolic.

k. After explaining my job to me, there was a car sent by the Head Ranger to take me to the office.

l. Our family has been really having huge difficulties with hard-core resentment on the girls' part, who have been claiming that we play favorites for the one boy.

m. Thus the continual success, interest, and the test of endurance are reasons why marathon bicycle racing is an important topic.

n. Although these statistics may look suspicious, it is because there is not a more specific breakdown of them.

o. In response to the attack on my report on Adventure Playgrounds, I will prove to you, the newspapers, radio, and TV its validity.

p. Perched prettily on the branches, we watched the first robin of spring.

q. Invariably the problem of the car breaking down will sometimes arise.

r. The exploration of student differences in response to the instructor's stimulus questions cause the students to return to the textbook seeking justification for their opinions and ultimately encourage the articulation of their personal views.

s. The loss of professors' credibility represents an indispensable foundation upon which authority structures are undermined.

t. The nation's domestic ills may keep, although there is a risk in deferring them.

u. Last year the campus had a great increase in narcotics arrests, most of them on a marijuana possession charge or for smoking marijuana.

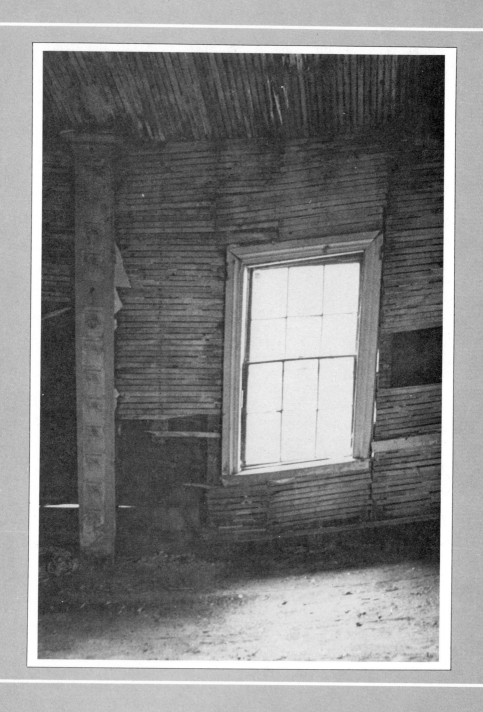

PART FOUR

HANDLING SPECIAL ASSIGNMENTS

CHAPTER 16

WRITING A PERSUASIVE ARGUMENT

Situation One:

"I got gas for my car today—those *prices*! The big oil companies are sure out to get all they can out of the consumer."

"Well, it's not the oil companies' fault. They can't get enough oil for their refineries."

"I bet they've got *plenty* of oil! They just know they have the consumer where they want him. We've got to have fuel for our cars and houses, and they'll jack up the prices in this fake shortage, and then keep them there after the shortage is over."

"How do you know it's a fake shortage—are you an expert on the oil business or something?"

Situation Two:

Dear Sir:

I read your recent editorial in which you attacked the patriotic organization "Freedom Ringers" that calls people on the telephone and tells them how bad communism is.

I don't understand your point at all. Isn't telephoning a voluntary act? Who pays for the call? Not the man who owns the phone. Who is forced to listen? Any man has a recognized right of not listening to a Freedom Ringer.

Why does the telephone company yield to pressure? Is freedom of speech coming to an end in America?

Very truly yours,

Each of these situations involves *argument,* which is an attempt to convince or persuade. But neither situation represents a *formal argument,* as we use the phrase here. A *formal argument* is an orderly arrangement of carefully defined terms and properly qualified statements (backed by evidence) which support a single thesis. A formal argument is a written attempt to *convince* or *persuade* the reader that he should *believe* something or *do* something (or both).

It is possible to argue two or three theses in a long formal argument. But in practice, a well-made formal argument tends to have its own unity, so that even if you are arguing two or three theses, you will find that there is an implicit single thesis underlying or supporting them. It is important that a formal argument have evidence. Formally speaking, assertions such as these are not arguments:

"The big oil companies are sure out to get all they can out of the consumer."
"Any person has a recognized right of not listening to a Freedom Ringer."

The formal argument requires you to manage your stance with unusual care. When such an argument is successful, both you and your reader feel that you have arrived at a conclusion more or less together, having agreed to believe in the thesis of the argument. As the writer, you *lead* your reader to agree with you not by force or deception but by the legitimate power of your persuasion.

What makes a formal argument *persuasive?* In most genuinely persuasive arguments there are five elements. We will discuss each of these elements in the pages that follow.

1. *A human approach.* The writer strikes the reader as an honest, believable person who has a genuine interest in his material and in his reader.

2. *Solid evidence.* The writer does not rely on mere assertion; he uses pertinent facts, details, statistics, or testimony from authorities to back up his statements.

3. *Good logic.* The writer makes the right *connections* between his pieces of evidence; he creates accurate generalizations and draws proper conclu-

sions. If the evidence warrants, the writer makes use of the thinking and organizational strategies of *cause and effect, comparison and contrast, analogy,* etc.

4. *An avoidance of fallacy.* The writer not only avoids logical errors, he also avoids irrelevancies, false appeals to emotion, or question begging. (These and other fallacies are explained in this chapter.)

5. *A clear argumentative organization.* The writer organizes his argument so that his reader can understand all its parts and how the parts relate to each other and to the thesis.

USE A HUMAN APPROACH

*T*he *human approach* in argument involves a special adaptation of the writer's stance, particularly the relationship between the writer and reader. The human approach has two basic aspects, closely interrelated. The first deals with the writer's *character* (his "ethical proof"), the second with the writer's *feeling for his reader* (his "you-attitude").

Ethical Proof

From the time of the ancient Greeks, authorities in rhetoric have pointed out that the arguer's character is very important. The Greek word for "character" was *ethos,* and a writer (or speaker, in ancient times) whose work showed him to be honest, fair, and reasonable was said to be employing *ethical proof.* As Cato, a Roman, put it, an orator should be "a good man skilled in speaking."

When your good character appears in a written formal argument to your advantage, you too are employing the very old device of ethical proof. But such proof is not to be artificially displayed in an argument. Rather, you should emphasize your natrual good qualities, and at the same time suppress any qualities — such as a tendency to jump to conclusions — that might injure your character or your believability in the eyes of your reader. Such suppression is not dishonest if it improves the truth and effectiveness of your argument.

As an example of ethical proof, consider these paragraphs from the end of John Kennedy's inaugural address:

Modesty and   [1]In your hands, my fellow citizens, more than mine, will
patriotism   rest the final success or failure of our course. Since this coun-

try was founded, each generation of Americans has been summoned to give testimony to its national loyalty. The graves of young Americans who answered the call to service surround the globe.

²Now the trumpet summons us again—not as a call to bear arms, though arms we need—not as a call to battle, though embattled we are—but a call to bear the burden of a long twilight struggle, year in and year out, "rejoicing in hope, patient in tribulation"—a struggle against the common enemies of man: tyranny, poverty, disease and war itself.

Concern for others   ³Can we forge against these enemies a grand and global alliance, North and South, East and West, that can assure a more fruitful life for all mankind? Will you join in that historic effort?

⁴In the long history of the world, only a few generations have been granted the role of defending freedom in its hour *Courage* of maximum danger. I do not shrink from this responsibility —I welcome it. I do not believe that any of us would ex-*Selfless dedication* change places with any other people or any other generation. The energy, the faith, the devotion which we bring to this endeavor will light our country and all who serve it—and the glow from that fire can truly light the world.

⁵And so, my fellow Americans: Ask not what your country can do for you—ask what you can do for your country.

⁶My fellow citizens of the world: Ask not what America will do for you, but what together we can do for the freedom of man.

High religious and moral standards   ⁷Finally, whether you are citizens of America or citizens of the world, ask of us here the same high standards of strength and sacrifice which we ask of you. With a good conscience our only sure reward, with history the final judge of our deeds, let us go forth to lead the land we love, asking His blessing and His help, but knowing that here on earth God's work must truly be our own.

In this brief passage, the admirable qualities of President Kennedy's character shine through *as an integral part of the argument.* This ethical proof, which really cannot be precisely described in the marginal notes, is woven into the texture of honest, clear arguments.

The "You-Attitude"

The *you-attitude* can be summed up like this: "As a writer, I am as interested in you [my reader] as I am in myself or my subject." *Example:* Joe Smith writes a brief argument addressed to his neighborhood Advisory

Board, a group that acts as a go-between for the citizens of Valley Road subdivision and the City Council. He wants the two-way stop on Valley Road and Race Street to be replaced by a four-way stop. He writes this draft:

> The two-way stop at Valley and Race is at present a real danger to both pedestrians and drivers. Two accidents have occurred there within the last month. Valley feeds into the highway south, and drivers pick up speed two blocks north of the intersection. By the time they arrive at that point they are going quite fast. Race Street drivers or pedestrians (not to mention bike riders) often find it difficult to get across Valley Road safely.
>
> Let's ask the City Council to put a four-way stop at Race and Valley.

This is a decent enough draft, but there is no particular feeling for the readers or their problems. So, after receiving a bit of advice, Joe rewrites his draft, and creates a stronger you-attitude:

> Have you, as members of the Advisory Board, thought about making a recommendation to the City Council about the stop at Valley and Race? Most of you are my friends and neighbors, and I've heard you complain about that stop more than once. Rod and Sue Jensen's boy Greg nearly got run over on his bike the other day trying to get across Valley during the rush hour to deliver his papers.
>
> Do you think a four-way stop at Valley and Race might solve our problems? If you believe this might be the best solution, would you mind if I presented a more detailed plan for the stop (including costs) at the August 4th meeting? The City Council would probably be happier with an Advisory proposal if it came with a cost analysis.

Observe that ethical proof and an agreeable you-attitude support each other in evolving an effective *human approach* to an argumentative question. When Joe Smith refers (honestly and accurately enough) to the fact that his friends and neighbors are involved in the traffic problem and that Greg Jensen nearly got run over, he creates interest in the situation. He asks for the Board's judgment concerning the four-way stop instead of bluntly telling them that the stop is necessary. He gives them the impression (again honestly) that he has thought the matter through; he knows what the costs will be, and he will present the figures to the Advisory Board at the next meeting.

A common objection to the idea of using ethical proof and a you-attitude to support a human approach is that "they can be easily faked." Practically speaking, this doesn't seem to be the case. For one thing, the human approach does not ask you to create any aspect of your personality that is not already there; most writers have good sides and certain kinds of genuine interests in other human beings. The approach merely suggests that you make use of all possible avenues of rapport between you and the readers and that you try to show them the proofs of your character that truly exist, along with your genuine interest in them and their welfare.

PRACTICE

Discussion

The following passage is a clear example of the use of ethical proof; the employment of the you-attitude is somewhat more subtle. The passage is taken from an argument against racial discrimination made by Henry Gonzales, U.S. Representative from Texas. Obviously Gonzales is addressing a wide and varied audience. Explain how he uses both ethical proof and the you-attitude.

[1]No man ought to either practice or condone racism; every man ought to condemn it. Neither should any man practice or condone reverse racism.

[2]Those who would divide our country along racial lines because they are fearful and filled with hatred are wrong, but those who would divide the races out of desire for revenge, or out of some hidden fear, are equally wrong. Any man, regardless of his ambitions, regardless of his aims, is committing an error and a crime against humanity if he resorts to the tactics of racism. If Bilbo's racism was wrong—and I believe that it was—then so are the brown Bilbos of today.

[3]Fifteen years ago as a member of the City Council of the city of San Antonio, Texas, I asked my fellow Council members to strike down ordinances and regulations that segregated the public facilities of the city, so as to end an evil that ought never to have existed to begin with. That Council complied, because it agreed with me that it was time for reason to at long last have its day. Eleven years ago I stood almost alone in the Senate of the State of Texas to ask my colleagues to vote against a series of bills that were designed to perpetuate segregation, contrary to the law of the land. I saw the beginnings then of a powerful reaction to racist politics, and I begged my colleagues to remember: "If we fear long enough, we hate. And if we hate long enough, we fight." I still believe this to be true. Since then there has been vast progress in Texas. I did not know how to describe to you the oppression that I felt then; but I can tell you that the atmosphere today is like a different world. Injustices we still have aplenty, but no longer is there a spirit of blatant resistance to just redress of just grievance.

Yet despite this change in the general atmosphere, despite the far healthier tenor of public debate and public action today, I felt compelled almost exactly a year ago to address the United States House of Representatives on the continuing and alarming practice of race politics, and what I chose to call the politics of desperation.

GIVE SOLID EVIDENCE

Deep in the seventh tier of our university library, we were hunting for an elusive quotation in a book that didn't seem to exist. After about an hour, we decided to give up and headed for the stairs, which happened to be close to the study carrel of a friend. "Hey," he said, "Are you going home? You're going to get wet!"

"But it couldn't be raining — the sun was shining only an hour ago."

Our friend said nothing but merely pointed to a coat rack on which hung his dripping raincoat.

Factual Evidence

Appropriate cliché: "The evidence [a wet raincoat, for example] speaks for itself." But to allow it to speak for itself in your papers you must put it there in the first place. Always support your arguments with *evidence* — facts, figures, results of experiments, statements from authorities. As you write, check each important statement by asking: "Do I have *evidence* for what I am saying?" Of course, you will seldom, if ever, have perfect evidence, whatever that might be. Argument deals with the *probable,* not with the perfectly true. But to be persuasive, your statements — and your evidence — should be as factual (as "probably true") as you can make them. But how do you know that a thing, idea, or happening is "true," that it represents what we agree to call a *fact? Facts* are those statements which we can *validate, corroborate,* or *verify. Nonfacts* cannot be validated, corroborated, or verified. William James, in his essay "Pragmatism," commented:

> Truth lives . . . for the most part on a credit system. Our thoughts and beliefs "pass," so long as nothing challenges them, just as banknotes pass so long as nobody refuses them. But this all points to direct face-to-face verifications somewhere, without which the fabric of truth collapses like a financial system with no cash basis whatever. You accept my verification of one thing, I yours of another. We trade on each other's truth. But beliefs verified concretely by *somebody* are the posts of the whole superstructure.

A fact is a piece of truth, then, that exists because "somebody" has *verified* it—has read up on it, asked about it, looked at it (even heard, tasted, felt, or smelled it). Here is a list of facts expressed in short sentences:

> Blood is running from a cut on my face.
> The king is on his throne.
> This is a football.
> A leaf fell.
> I am holding a smelly tomato.
> The Common Market was a free-trade idea.
> Babies often get the croup.
> This piece of paper is clean.

Each of these might be considered a statement of "fact" if it has been verified. Genuine facts should be verifiable by more than one reasonable person or authority. If only one person sees a particular flying saucer, the saucer is for all practical purposes not a fact. If no one besides you sees a leaf fall, or sees the leaf on the ground, the leaf and its falling have not been verified. If people around you can't smell the tomato you are holding, never have heard of babies getting the croup, and can't agree that "this piece of paper is *clean*" then these statements are not to be considered factual.

Let's not argue about "people around you" having no sense of smell, being ignorant of both babies and childhood diseases, or never having seen a "clean" piece of paper. These are all possibilities, and should be taken reasonably into account for individual situations; they are a part of the process of verification. One does not ask a color-blind person, however "reasonable" he may be, to give an authoritative opinion on the distinction between a red dress and a green one. And of course one should always consult genuine authorities on a particular subject. Ask a pediatrician how often babies get the croup. Then it is likely that you will obtain the facts.

General and Particular Facts

A *generalization* (or a *general statement*) is a remark about a class or group of things, actions, or ideas:

> California produces more tennis stars than any other state.
> Most stunt pilots use biplanes.
> Dictators rule by fear.
> Babies often get the croup.

As these statements suggest, the generalization itself can be a *broad* fact concerning a number of *particular,* individual facts. An important relationship between the particular and the general can be illustrated by this inverted pyramid.

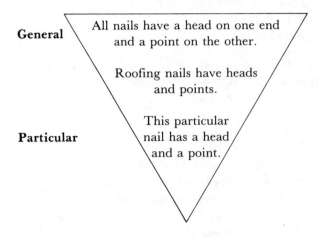

General

All nails have a head on one end and a point on the other.

Roofing nails have heads and points.

This particular nail has a head and a point.

Particular

As the diagram shows, the ideas of the general and the particular are relative. "Roofing nails have heads and points" is less general than "All nails have a head on one end and a point on the other," but more general than "This particular nail has a head and a point." Here is another example, working from the particular to the general, that uses single words instead of statements: "John" (referring to an actual young man, age ten) is a particular. "Boys" is more general. "Human males" is more general still.

General Statements and Value Judgments

General statements based on facts are usually more difficult to verify than particulars are.

"The English have produced great poets" can be considered a decent factual generalization based upon an examination of many particulars: the great English poets, from Chaucer on. Since the statement is also a *value judgment* — a statement of opinion about the worth of something — it is open to simple contradiction by someone using a different standard of judgment: "I don't think the English poets are as great as you say; I don't like Chaucer, for instance. The Italians have produced greater poets than the English have."

The value judgment is necessary in expressing opinions or preferences: "The wine was excellent last night"; "Harding was a poor president"; "I prefer stick shifts." It is often hard, however, to prove that a value judgment has any factual basis unless a standard for judgment has been established.

Even general statements that are relatively free of value judgment can be troublesome when one tries to show that they are factual. The truth of "Babies often get the croup" hinges, according to one physician, on what *often* means. "Many babies do get croup," says he, "but *often* to me implies a majority. *Most* babies don't get the croup." "The Common Market was a free-trade idea" seems to be a clear-cut fact until one realizes that the idea of the Common Market was and is open to various interpretations and that definitions of *free trade* vary according to experts' views of political and economic history.

Inferences

When we draw a conclusion from one or more facts, we make an inference. General and particular statements of fact are often based upon inferences:

Yellow fever is transmitted by the mosquito. *(Beginning with the work of Walter Reed in 1900–1901, scientists have repeatedly shown that the mosquito carries yellow fever, a fact that we infer from repeated experiments.)*

Sally is allergic to penicillin. *(Every time she takes the drug, she breaks out in a rash. We infer a factual cause-and-effect relation between the drug and the rash.)*

Mexico is friendly to the United States. *(We infer this general fact after investigating many specific incidents concerning Mexico and the United States. In nearly every incident, either the government or the people of Mexico or both have indicated friendliness to us.)*

The man next door is laughing loudly. *(The voice is that of a man. The noise sounds like laughing. The noise is not soft or moderate, but loud.)*

Facts: A Summary

The difficulty of obtaining facts can be overdramatized. Don't fall into the trap of believing that factual material on most subjects is impossible to come by, even though it is true that some areas of human investigation — like the nature of political influence or of artistic inspiration — seem to produce very few facts indeed. The main thing to bear in mind is that facts exist because responsible persons (accountable, rational, and ethical persons) *say* they do, which is what we mean by "verifying" and "validating." When, in a certain area of investigation, the methods of verifying and validating change, or when responsible persons change their opinions, the facts may change also.

A generalization may be (or may imply) a decision, a summary, an interpretation, an opinion, or a value judgment. A generalization may also combine two or more of these. For the purposes of essay writing, we will assume that you will make your generalizations *after* you have inspected the facts available on your subject and *that your generalizations are based on the facts*. If you cannot find facts, you cannot generalize accurately.

PRACTICE

Discussion

1. Making inferences is basic to argumentation. You can play games with them, as Robert Fuerst does here:

> At any large convention of psychologists, you may hear some speaker tell the story about a psychologist who trained a cockroach to jump at a verbal command. After a period of conditioning, the roach invariably jumped when the psychologist said, "Jump." One day, the psychologist pulled a leg off the roach and then said, "Jump," and the roach jumped. He pulled another leg off the roach and again the roach jumped at the verbal command "Jump." The process was continued until the last leg was removed from the roach, and this time when the psychologist commanded, "Jump," the roach did not budge. In reporting this experimental work, the psychologist wrote, "When a cockroach loses all of its legs, it becomes stone deaf." — Robert Fuerst, "Inference Peddling"

   Make up three or four stories about inferences like this, the sillier the better.

2. Draw inferences (seriously) from these facts:
   a. The 1970 census showed that Ann Arbor, Michigan—the home of the University of Michigan—had per capita (1) more dentists and (2) more robberies than any other sizable American community.
   b. More people die of respiratory diseases in Arizona than in any other state.

c. Students who take driver's training as an elective have fewer accidents later in life than those who take it as a requirement.

d. In a recent survey, the U.S. Fish and Wildlife Service
discovered:

> . . . that there were 20.6 million hunters; that the ratio of hunters, by
> sex, to total population was 21 out of 100 men and 2 out of 100
> women; that the hunter's average household income was $14,700; that
> 56 percent reside in urban areas; that deer hunting accounted for the
> greatest number of days of participation in a single year (103 million),
> followed by rabbit hunting (88 million days), squirrel hunting (69 mil-
> lion days), and quail hunting (47 million days); and that hunters in the
> year of the survey and in the course of hunting spent $1.2 billion on
> food and drink, $1.8 billion on equipment, and $2.1 billion on trans-
> portation. — John Mitchell, *The Hunt*

3. Taken from a longer essay, the following passage shows how
evidence is ordinarily used to bolster an argument. The writer
argues that many persons are wrong in their belief that the
American worker is a robot victimized by the assembly line. Read
the argument and prepare the discussion questions at the end.
Although this essay was written in 1973, its argument is still
cogent, supported as it is by solid evidence.

> [1]In this [the widespread notion that a majority of American laborers
> work on assembly lines], as in so many other respects, undue attention
> to Detroit and the automobile industry makes for gross distortion.
> General Motors is a huge corporation which fascinates our social
> critics. But GM, which has about one-third of its 550,000 employees
> on the assembly line, is not a typical firm and the automobile industry
> is not a typical industry. A much more accurate picture of what is fast
> becoming the typical manufacturing firm is provided by the Bendix
> Corporation, which has less than 10% of its 57,000 employees on the
> assembly line, while 50% are white-collared workers and 30% are pro-
> fessional and technical staff.
>   [2]And even this picture, taken by itself, is skewed, since the average
> American worker does not work for a manufacturing firm. Indeed, a
> majority of blue-collar workers are not outside manufacturing — they
> are in transportation, construction, utilities, trade, etc.
>   [3]More and more, as the American economy becomes a "post-
> industrial," service-oriented economy, fewer and fewer people are
> engaged in blue-collar factory work, in blue-collar work of any kind, in
> manufacturing altogether. The factory is following the farm as *yesterday's*
> typical place of employment. Today, there are more insurance sales-

men than blue-collar steelworkers in America, and the insurance "industry" as a whole probably employs more people than does automobile manufacturing. There are more white-collar than blue-collar workers in the American labor force, and by 1980 the ratio will reach an overwhelming 5:3. Moreover, by 1980, some 25% of these white-collar workers will be either in the "professional-technical" category (teachers, engineers, scientists, etc.) or in the "managerial" (public and private) category. — Irving Kristol, "Is the American Worker 'Alienated'?"

a. Irving Kristol was Henry Luce, Professor of Urban Values at New York University and co-editor of the scholarly journal, *The Public Interest.* How are these facts important in your evaluation of his use of evidence?

b. How many separate pieces of evidence are there in the passage? List them.

c. Why does Kristol object to General Motors as a *sample* of American industry?

d. In paragraph 1, why does Kristol write "10% of its 57,000 employees" instead of "a small number of its large employee force"?

e. What is the purpose of paragraph 2? What does *skewed* mean?

f. There is an analogy in the first two sentences of paragraph 3. What is it? Can it be called evidence? Of what?

g. Is the evidence in paragraph 1 more, or less, specific than that in paragraph 3? Is paragraph 3 more, or less, convincing than paragraph 1?

h. Summarize Kristol's argument.

Writing

1. Write a brief, clearly reasoned argument responding to Kristol's statements. You may use or ignore the fact that Kristol was writing in 1973. You may agree, partly agree, or disagree with him. Or you may make a different argument entirely. (What you write can depend largely on your work experience.) Choose an appropriate reader for your writer's stance. You may wish to address Kristol directly or to write for his typical reader, an educated American who requires more information about the subject.

2. The Spanish philosopher Ortega y Gassett wrote, ". . . one does not hunt in order to kill; on the contrary, one kills in order to have hunted." Study the data from the U.S. Fish and Wildlife Service (under 2. d. *Discussion* above), and relate the data to the quotation from Ortega y Gassett. Write an essay in which you draw some

conclusions (or inferences) about hunting, based on the data and the quotation. (You may also wish to evaluate the data and the quotation in light of your experience. For example, is the quotation a value judgment or factual?)

Authoritative Evidence

For our purposes, an *authority* is a person who knows what he is talking about. He can be a theoretical expert in his special area of knowledge, someone who has had practical experience in the field, or both. As a former professor of urban studies at a major university and an editor of a scholarly journal, Irving Kristol might reasonably be considered a theoretical authority on the American blue-collar worker. A man (let's call him Jim West) who has worked for a few years in a blue-collar job could be a "practical" expert on his type of job.

Kristol will know more theory and have a broader range of knowledge about the blue-collar worker than West, but West will know more detail concerning his particular job than Kristol. If you were writing a paper on the American worker, you might read Kristol to obtain theoretical knowledge and go to a man like West for practical information on, for example, operating a punch press. Of course, both of these authorities would know something about the other's "area" of knowledge. If you were writing on the alienation of workers, you could certainly take into account West's firsthand knowledge of blue-collar work. Your decisions about which authorities to use depend on the nature of your thesis.

It is wise to remember that all authorities, whether theoretical or practical, are limited to some extent in the type and quality of their knowledge. Furthermore, they may be limited simply by being forgetful, prejudiced, out-of-date on the evidence, or plainly dishonest.

As a writer, you can use authoritative evidence in two ways: (1) you can quote authorities to bolster your own argument; (2) you can act as your own expert or practical authority. From your reading and experience, you should have considerable knowledge that you can use authoritatively. Whether you use your own or others' ideas, consider the following questions as you evaluate the *quality* of authoritative opinion:

1. *Is the person an authority on the subject?* We tend to associate the idea of authority with well-known people in special fields, whether their opinions are authoritative or not. It is wise to accept the artistic evaluations of a good actor on acting, but when that same person gives advice on political matters, we should be wary. The opinions of glamorous or popular per-

sons, like movie stars and sports figures, are seldom authoritative except in their own fields.

2. *Is the authority unprejudiced and sensible?* Just being an authority does not make one free from prejudice or egomania. The pathologist Sydney Smith has written of a world-famous authority on pathology: "Spilsbury, like the rest of us, could make mistakes. He was unique, I think, in that he never admitted a mistake. Once he had committed himself to an opinion he would never change it." An expert can be as prejudiced or obstinate as anyone else.

3. *Is the authority up-to-date in his specialty?* In many fields, last year's knowledge is unreliable. The authority should demonstrate that he knows the latest information in his field.

4. *Does the authority have evidence on the question being discussed?* Unless the expert has seen and examined the evidence for himself, it is unlikely that his opinion is valuable. A psychiatrist recently diagnosed the mental ailment of a political agitator without ever seeing the man. Under these circumstances, the psychiatrist's opinion was probably not authoritative.

PRACTICE

Discussion
The first passage below is part of a letter written by a physician to the science editor of *Saturday Review;* the second is part of a memo written by a college student. Prepare some notes for class discussion on how each writer uses authoritative evidence. Also discuss the writer's stance of each excerpt.

[1]In "Fluoridation vs. the Constitution" Professor Arthur Selwyn Miller stated that the case for holding fluoridation unconstitutional would be strengthened if there existed soundly documented medical evidence that flouridation threatened the health of the population. My own research, as well as the research of others, strongly suggests that fluoridation constitutes a hazard to the health of a significant portion of the population.

[2]I have been engaged in the diagnosis and treatment of allergy since the inception of this specialty in the early 1920s and have contributed to development of the discipline through clinical research. I established and directed allergy clinics in five Detroit hospitals. Currently, I am

consultant in allergy at Harper Hospital, Detroit, and attending physician at Woman's Hospital, Detroit. I am a Fellow of the American Academy of Allergy, the American College of Allergists, and the American College of Physicians.

[3]In 1953 I was first to report, in the *Journal of the American Medical Association* (vol. 151, page 1398), a new disease caused by smoking. This disease, which I termed "smoker's respiratory syndrome," simulates asthma and eventually leads to emphysema. I would not have recognized the illness in my patients had I not by chance suffered from it myself. Because I recovered upon ceasing to smoke, I began to take a closer look at some of my patients who, presumably suffering from allergic asthma, had failed to respond to the conventional treatment for that ailment. A large percentage of these patients recovered without treatment when they stopped smoking. Since publication of my article in *JAMA,* numerous physicians have corroborated my observation and have thus prevented chronic emphysema in their patients. — George Waldbott, M.D.

To:	Director of Personnel, Cleardale Corporation
From:	Bob Cooper, Part-time Summer Worker
Subject:	The Problems with Morale and Productivity at Cleardale Corporation and How They Can Be Solved

[1]Recently, you asked me to respond to a questionnaire dealing with employee morale and productivity. The questions were short-answer and allowed only for a minimum of detail. I felt that I could not do justice to the importance of the problems by answering the questionnaire, so I decided to write this report. I will deal exclusively with those problems which lower employee on-the-job morale and productivity. Because I am here with the company only for the summer months, I feel that I can give an unbiased appraisal of the problems affecting employee morale and productivity — I do not work long enough every year to become either pro-management or pro-employee.

[2]My qualifications for pointing out those problems include three summers' experience at Cleardale. During this time, I worked in all departments of the plant and performed many unskilled jobs; also, I worked for three months as a quality control inspector. So, I believe that I have a good idea of the working conditions of the plant and a first-hand knowledge of the problems affecting them. My other experience includes several business courses in college dealing with employee motivation and productivity. I believe that this background provides me with the theory and the analytical techniques necessary to identify problems in the area of morale and productivity.

Writing

An authority is "a person who knows what he is talking about," someone who is either a practical or theoretical expert. We have never known a student who was not at least partially authoritative in *some* subject or area. Any job you have had, for example, gives you a degree of authority in writing an argument concerning it.

Write an argument in which you explain carefully why you are reasonably authoritative on a subject, and why your evidence should be considered valid. Create a specific writer's stance for your paper.

USE GOOD LOGIC

*T*here is nothing complicated about the basic logic of rhetoric or composition. Such logic simply represents the operation of common sense, which interrelates two activities: (1) finding the *connections* between things; (2) *concluding* what, if anything, these connections mean.

Avoid Loose Generalizations

You often hear the remark, "Oh, that's just a generalization." This is a misleading comment, for it implies that generalizations are by nature untrustworthy or somehow inferior to other types of statements. As we ordinarily use the term, a fact is "true" by definition; but a generalization is "true" only if the facts have first been found and properly used in making *connections* — in drawing the general conclusion from them. A generalization, therefore, may be *un*true, a *little* true, *partly* true, *mainly* true, or *entirely* true.

In order to make your statements as true as possible, you must avoid making careless or loose generalizations. A loose generalization is a faulty, or partly faulty, statement about a group or class of ideas, occurrences, things, persons, etc. Most loose generalizations are created by thinking carelessly about the subject and the available evidence. Here are some examples:

City children don't get enough sunshine.

Who says so? What city children? All over the world? What is meant by "city"? How much is "enough"? Who is an authority on *enough sunshine*? How does the writer know this? How many cities has he been in?

College students are working too hard and have no time for play or private thought.

Where? In the United States? In what sort of "college"? Ivy League? Big Ten? Small state college? Large junior college? All colleges in the United States? Could one person be an authority on this subject? What would he have to do to be an authority? What is meant by "working too hard"? By "no time for play or private thought"?

In France, people accept religion for what it is.

Has this writer been in France? When, and for how long? What sample of the population did he see? Did he talk to them about religion? What is meant by "religion"? By "people"? Eighty-year-old men? Young children? The clergy? (Catholic, Jewish, Protestant?) What does "for what it is" mean?

How to Qualify a Generalization

You do not have to get *all* the facts before you can make connections and draw a reasonably truthful conclusion. Although some subjects require more facts than others for valid generalizing, for many subjects you can draw *tentative* or *qualified* generalizations. To *qualify* means to modify or to limit according to the evidence that is available. Take the three loose generalizations given above. Carefully qualified, they might read:

> Along Parsons Avenue in Chicago, where I lived for ten years, I saw a number of children who didn't get enough sunshine because they usually played indoors.
> The engineering students I know at Collins College have to take so many credit hours that they have only three or four hours a week for relaxation.
> When I was in Paris for three months last summer, I knew several young workingmen who were rather casual about observing the laws of their church.

It is wise to acquire the habit of using qualifying words and phrases where necessary, particularly when you are writing about people and their activities. But be wary of words that state an absolute condition, words like *always, never, continually, every.* Also be wary of implying these words in sentences like ["*All*] people love freedom," or ["*All*] women dislike men who smoke cigars." Here is a list of qualifying words and phrases that you can use with some assurance:

usually	often	a lot	customarily
nearly	occasionally	many	a little bit
some	sometimes	a great deal	ordinarily
generally	a few	most	almost all

To sum up: A generalization is an attempt to find out the truth about something—or a lot of somethings—and to state the truth in short-hand form. Imagine, for example, that we are trying to make a general, true statement about the total assets of the wealthy Mr. Jordan. We discover that he owns stocks and bonds, cash, houses, five automobiles, and two racing horses, with a total value of $300,000. He also keeps in a bank vault a number of gold bars worth about $285,000. We may generalize roughly that *half of Mr. Jordan's fortune consists of bar-gold.* If Mr. Jordan should be a vigorous buyer and seller of bar-gold, we might from time to time have to change our qualifying statements about his fortune, as follows:

(100%)   Mr. Jordan's fortune consists *wholly* of bar-gold.
 (99%)   *Practically all* of his fortune consists of bar-gold.
 (95%)   His fortune consists *almost entirely* of bar-gold.
 (90%)   *Nearly all* his fortune consists of bar-gold.
 (80%)   *By far the greater part* of his fortune . . .
 (70%)   *The greater part* of his fortune . . .
 (60%)   *More than half* his fortune . . .
 (55%)   *Rather more than half* his fortune . . .
 (50%)   *Half* his fortune . . .
 (45%)   *Nearly half* his fortune . . .
 (40%)   *A large part* of his fortune . . .
 (35%)   *Quite a large part* of his fortune . . .
 (30%)   *A considerable part* of his fortune . . .
 (25%)   *Part* of his fortune . . .
 (15%)   *A small part* of his fortune . . .
 (10%)   *Not much* of his fortune . . .
  (5%)   *A very small* part of his fortune . . .
  (1%)   *An inconsiderable part* of his fortune . . .
  (0%)   *None* of his fortune . . .

This ingenious example involving Mr. Jordan's fortune has been taken from *The Reader Over Your Shoulder* by Robert Graves and Alan Hodge. Try as they might, Graves and Hodge could not make the qualifying phrases very precise. Phrases like *the greater part* and *a large part* are rather ambiguous even when they are presented in a "qualifying scale" like theirs. But the example does show that qualifying can be done with words and that a writer can qualify with a fair degree of accuracy.

PRACTICE

Discussion

The statements below have been represented as satisfactory generalizations in student essays. Which statements make proper "connections"? Upon what kind of authority? Which are loose generalizations? How can these be effectively qualified?

a. In the history of censorship, no book has been banned oftener than the Bible.
b. Sharks do not eat people.
c. The motives of the United States in the Vietnam war were not imperialistic.
d. Football players are good students.
e. A window screen keeps all the flies out.
f. Sonic booms don't hurt you or your property.
g. By the year 2025, the human race will reproduce by cross-pollination.
h. The moon is a military base of great importance.
i. Evolution is true.
j. Humans evolved from apes.
k. Teenage dance steps are immoral.
l. The Wolverine 8s are not selling because people think they are American cars, and American cars are not as popular as they used to be.
m. Freudians have silly theories about sex.
n. If lightning strikes your house, open a window in your basement so that the lightning will find its way out.
o. The cause of juvenile delinquency is parents.

Induction and Deduction: A Definition

There are two kinds of logic, *inductive* and *deductive*. Whether you are conscious of doing so or not, you use them both a great deal, even when you do something as ordinary as bake bread, replace a defective fuel pump in your car, or put a cut rose in water to preserve it.

Suppose a man says to his wife: "Gee, honey, I hope the Pinkhams' old dog doesn't get loose and bite one of the kids." Hidden in this remark is a fair amount of logic whose *connections* and *conclusions* we can outline by showing you the processes of induction and deduction.

Induction moves from facts to a generalization:

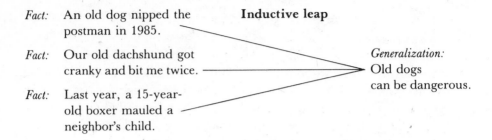

Fact: An old dog nipped the postman in 1985.

Inductive leap

Fact: Our old dachshund got cranky and bit me twice.

Fact: Last year, a 15-year-old boxer mauled a neighbor's child.

Generalization: Old dogs can be dangerous.

Deduction moves from a generalization to a conclusion. (This process can be illustrated by what is known as a *syllogism.*)

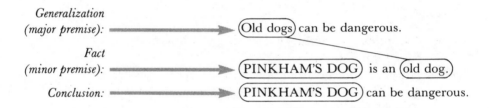

Generalization (major premise): Old dogs can be dangerous.

Fact (minor premise): PINKHAM'S DOG is an old dog.

Conclusion: PINKHAM'S DOG can be dangerous.

"Old dog" is the *middle term*—it connects the major premise to the minor premise. "PINKHAM'S DOG" is the *subject*—it connects the minor premise to the conclusion.

Refer to these examples as we explain inductive and deductive logic more thoroughly.

Induction is a logical process in which you make connections between particulars or facts in order to come to a generalization about them. Practically speaking, every induction has an *inductive leap*—the jump you have to make from a limited number of facts (of varying authoritative quality) to your generalization. If you see three old dogs, and they are all mean and cranky and bite, you can leap to the generalization that "Old dogs can be dangerous," which is not too long a leap—particularly if you don't want to get bitten.

The length of your inductive leap depends on the nature of the subject and how many "facts" you've got. The more old dogs that bite you can find, the smaller the leap to your generalization. If, in a period of twenty years, you hear of only two old dogs that bite, your leap is pretty large, and you may never make a good connection to your generalization. If you step off thirty bridges over streams and fall into the water each time, your inductive leap to "People who step off bridges fall into the water" is pretty small and can be easily made. But the leap, no matter how many "facts" you can muster, always exists. After all, it is always possible that someday you may step off bridge number 1,000,001 and just hang there in space.

Deduction is a logical process in which you make connections between a generalization (*major premise*), a fact (*minor premise*), and a conclusion.

Deductive reasoning can be most clearly seen in the *syllogism,* which is a three-sentence chain of reasoning. The classic syllogism in its full form has a broad major premise, a relatively narrow minor premise, and a conclusion drawn from these two premises. The *middle term* and the *subject* connect the parts of the syllogism.

In ordinary writing, deductive reasoning is most often expressed in the *enthymeme,* which is a compressed syllogism. Examples:

> An old dog like Pinkham's can be dangerous.
> Of course, Mike will die eventually; he's human, just like all of us.

Expanded into a full syllogism, the second enthymeme becomes:

Major premise:	All *persons* die.	*person* = middle term
Minor premise:	MIKE is a *person.*	MIKE = subject
Conclusion:	MIKE will die.	

Here is another example of an enthymeme:

> Since he is an elephant, Herbert eats peanuts.

And its full syllogistic form:

Major premise:	All *elephants* eat peanuts.	*elephant* = middle term
Minor premise:	HERBERT is an *elephant.*	HERBERT = subject
Conclusion:	HERBERT eats peanuts.	

Using Induction and Deduction

Since induction moves from facts to a generalization, and deduction moves from a generalization to a conclusion, these types of logic have often been discussed as if they were two separate things. But actually they are interrelated, as this example shows.

At a social gathering, a Frenchman remarked to a friend that all the long-haired men he had observed in the United States were political leftists.

"Oh?" said the friend. "What about Jones over there — his hair is so long he's wearing it in a ponytail."

"Of a certainty," said the Frenchman, "Mr. Jones is also a leftist."

The chain of reasoning the Frenchman created looks like this:

Induction

Fact: A long-haired man is observed to be a leftist.
Fact: Another long-haired man is observed to be a leftist.
Fact: Yet another . . .

[INDUCTIVE LEAP]

Generalization: All long-haired men are leftists.

Deduction (a Syllogism)

Major premise: All long-haired men are leftists.
Minor premise: Jones is a long-haired man.
Conclusion: Jones is a leftist.

Observe that the major premise of the syllogism is itself a conclusion inductively arrived at. As it turned out, Jones was not a leftist, leaving the Frenchman in a logical error. How can such errors be avoided in your handling of logic? The answer lies mainly in carefully managing logical *connections, generalizations,* and *conclusions:*

1. Make sure your inductive generalization is based on a sufficient number of reliable and authoritative facts. *Keep your inductive leap as small as possible.*

2. Check your deductive reasoning in the following ways: (a) Make sure that each premise is as accurate as you can make it. "All long-haired men are leftists" is a faulty major premise because it states a generalization that simply is untrue. You remember the minor premise in our sample syllogism on p. 336 — "Pinkham's dog is an old dog." As it happened (this is a real-life example), Pinkham's dog was not old; he merely looked old because of his gray, mangy fur. (b) Expand each enthymeme into the full three-sentence syllogism to see if the connections and conclusions are properly made. (c) Do not shift your middle term. Examples of illogical shifts:

All football players are *strong*.
John weighs *225 pounds*.
John is *strong*.

Those who commit murder should be severely punished.
That police officer just killed a *fleeing bank robber*.
That police officer *should be severely punished*.

In both examples, the writer has shifted the middle term. Weighing 225 pounds is not the same as being *strong*. A police officer who kills a fleeing bank robber is not ordinarily considered by the law to have committed murder.

PRACTICE

Writing

1. After crash-landing on the planet Vark II, Captain Foubar of the Space Service found that he had plenty of water but no food. Raging with hunger, he explored the area near his ship, finding an abundance of small black flowers about six inches high. After eating two of the petals, he got rather sick and saw strange visions. His sickness passed in a few minutes, but he was still hungry and continued to explore the strange planet. He discovered a yellow weed that resembled a dandelion. He ate a little and found it reasonably good—at least it did not make him sick. He gathered about a pound of the yellow weed and took it back to his ship.

   The next day, he decided to try more of the black flower. After eating about a dozen petals, he became violently ill, and the visions this time were terrifying. In a desperate attempt to counteract the effect of the flower, he ate two yellow weeds. Almost immediately the sickness and the visions left him.

   Captain Foubar wrote down his experiences in the ship's log, using the classic inductive and deductive forms. He expanded each of his enthymemes into a syllogism. What did the captain write in his log?

2. Expand the following enthymemes below into the three-sentence form of the syllogism. Identify the subject and the middle term. If you can, rewrite the enthymeme to make it more reasonable.

a. Phil shouldn't have married a girl with a personality so different from his; pluses and minuses cancel each other, you know.

b. Any businesswoman who makes as much money as Lenora does must be very competent.

c. Judging from his antisocial behavior last night (talking against the government), Judson must have been either drunk or crazy.

d. Old Mr. Roberts can't be rich because he's signed up for Medicare.

e. A typically modern, sexy novelist, Smith has written an evil book.

f. Paley, make up your mind which side you're going to be on—people have to be either for us or against us. You sound like you don't believe in our position.

g. As a college student, Joe should enlist because the army needs superior minds.

h. Holden, you've got to get a job; no patriotic American should live on welfare.

i. *Cheers* is not educational at all; why should it be on television?

j. Since Barber was definitely at the scene of the crime, he must have committed the murder.

k. Richard is too ignorant to have gone to college.

l. Only those who do valuable work for America should be elected to public office. I was in the Air Force for five years.

m. Yond Cassius has a lean and hungry look; He thinks too much: such men are dangerous. —Shakespeare, *Julius Caesar*

n. Jorgenson took the Fifth Amendment in a congressional investigation; therefore, he is one of those undermining American democracy.

o. Since Professor Bunner does not publish, she must be a good teacher.

A VOID FALLACIES

A fallacy is a weakness or an error in thinking or arguing. Fallacies are ordinarily caused by one or more of six basic human errors:

Oversimplifying
Jumping to a conclusion
Being irrelevant
Being too emotional
Deceiving oneself
Being dishonest

Of course, these human errors can never be totally eradicated from even the best-reasoned argument. However, by being aware of such pitfalls, you can eliminate a great number of them from your thinking, thus making your arguments more persuasive and forceful.

Recognizing and Correcting Fallacies

Here are descriptions of twelve major fallacies; for each one we suggest a method of improving the thinking or the argument. (The term *question,* when used in connection with fallacies, usually refers either to an argument's thesis or to one of its main points.)

Begging the Question

This fallacy is the mistake of assuming that some or all of a question or thesis is already proved—before the writer has proved it. To say that "Any person in the neighborhood who refuses to keep up his property should be prosecuted" begs two questions: first, whether refusing to keep up one's property is a bad thing for the neighborhood; second, whether failing to keep up property is covered by statute or is in any way illegal.

The statement that "The mistakes of teachers are buried on the welfare rolls" begs these questions: whether teachers make "mistakes," and whether there is a necessary relationship between teachers' "mistakes" and persons' ending up on welfare. Either of these questions or propositions might profitably be argued, and that is the point—they would have to be argued and *proved.* They cannot merely be assumed. Begging the question is an important fallacy because it often occurs at the starting point of an argument and thus renders the whole argument invalid.

Correction: Find the begged question and omit or prove it.

Rhetorical Question

The rhetorical question is usually a form of indirect attack. The attacker asks a loaded question to which he does not really want an answer. Such questions are inherently argumentative and often question-begging: "Mr. Webb, when are you going to stop being so bad-tempered?" Rhetorical questions are sometimes filled with emotion: "Is our do-nothing police force ever going to stop vicious murderers from roaming our streets at will?"

Correction: Customarily, omit the rhetorical question unless you have already proved the question. If you have satisfactorily proved that Webb is bad-tempered, you might inquire if he contemplates controlling his anger—but then the question is perhaps no longer rhetorical. It is worth adding that rhetorical questions are great fun, and it would be a pity to avoid them altogether.

Ad Hominem ("To the Man")

In this fallacy, instead of attacking the argument, the writer attacks the person who made it. Examples: "You can't trust any statement made by that notorious socialist, Kurt Bleil." Or: "I won't work on the committee's proposal as long as there are psychologists on it. If Professor Ratmaze leaves, I will discuss the proposal."

Correction: Drop the attack on the person and consider the question, argument, or proposal at hand. Ask yourself: Are you discrediting the person who made the proposal in the hope that his or her argument will also be discredited? Is your primary aim to evaluate the evidence or to criticize the personalities involved? Evaluating your motives may keep you from committing the *ad hominem* fallacy.

Stereotyping

In stereotyping, instead of describing persons as they actually are, the writer resorts to a trite description of cliché—every football player is big and stupid, every politician hypocritical and crooked, every movie star frivolous and shallow.

Correction: Check your description or generalization for accuracy. Have you, for instance, taken one attribute of a class and applied it to *everyone* in the class? Have you generalized from too few instances and then applied your generalization to the entire class?

Either-Or Fallacy

Writers commit this fallacy when they oversimplify a complex issue by assuming that there are only two sides to it. Either-or is one of the commonest fallacies, perhaps because all of us naturally think in either-or patterns: "You are either for or against me"; "She loves me, she loves me not"; "We should win the war or get out." Sometimes called the *black-or-white fallacy,* this error in logic is unusually dangerous because it is so easy to fall into and also because it gives no chance for alternatives.

Correction: Recognize any other possibilities or alternatives that may exist besides the two stated.

False Dilemma

Related to the either-or fallacy, the false dilemma presents two (or sometimes three) firm courses of action, and then demands that the reader choose one. Examples: "Which are you going to buy, a new house or one that has been lived in?" (Maybe you don't want to buy a house at all.) "You can either come to my party or stay home." (Maybe you want to go to a movie.)

Correction: Point out that there may be other choices or actions than the ones offered.

Statistical Fallacy

Any misuse of figures, numbers, percentages, graphs, and so forth may involve a statistical fallacy. Most of these fallacies are created when a writer forgets this all-important fact: *In themselves, statistics prove nothing.* It is the writer who proves by using statistics. But statistics are not always meaningful. What, for example, is the meaning of the statistic that at age 24 engineers make an average of $7,500 per year more than high-school English teachers? Such a statistic must be related to something and to somebody for it to have meaning.

Correction: Ask questions like, "Is the statistic accurate?" "Who says so?" "What does the statistic mean?" One might ask about the previous example: In what part of the country do English teachers and engineers make these salaries, and what are the living expenses there? What is the authority behind these statistics? What is the basis for comparison (nine-months' salary vs. twelve-months' salary)? How sure is one of receiving this salary? (Are teachers laid off as often as engineers?) Is the comparison at age 24 significant? How do salaries compare at age 40? What have salaries to do with student interest in a profession? With working conditions? In other words, what is the question being argued? Is it the *right* question? Statistics have a way of distorting issues and propositions. "There are," Disraeli said, "three kinds of lies: lies, damned lies, and statistics."

Faulty Sampling

The flaw in many samples is that they are not representative of the group about which a generalization is made. A classic case of faulty sampling occurred in 1936 when the *Literary Digest* asked people in various parts of the United States whom they were going to vote for (Landon or Roosevelt) in the presidential election. The results of the poll said that Landon would win—but Roosevelt won by a landslide. The flaw in the sampling occurred because the *Digest* polled only persons whose names appeared in telephone directories. Taken in the middle of the Depression, this sampling omitted large numbers of people who did not have a telephone and voted Democratic.

Correction: Make sure that your sample is representative of the group under discussion.

Loose Generalization

A loose generalization is a faulty, or partly faulty, statement about a group or class of ideas, occurrences, things, persons, and so forth. Examples: "Large families make for happy children"; "All small automobiles save gas." In both examples, the writer has made careless and excessively broad statements about a group. Upon examining the evidence, it becomes obvious that some small cars are not "gas savers" — the phrase needs definition too. And one finds unhappy children in some "large families" (again a phrase needs definition).

Correction: Reason carefully from the evidence available. Examine broad statements for possible inaccuracy. When necessary, qualify your generalizations. (See pp. 333–334 for further discussion.)

Causal Fallacy

Three kinds of causal fallacy are important: (a) Mistaking the nature of a cause. Example: A boss believes that an employee does poor work because he is lazy, but the real reason is that he has difficult personal problems. (b) Failing to see that there is more than one cause. Example: "Barbara is a fine violinist because she has great natural talent." Since Barbara's parents required her to practice two or three hours a day for five years, there are probably at least two causes for her fine playing — talent and hard work. (c) Being misled by the order of events. If event B comes after event A, one should not automatically jump to the conclusion that A *caused* B. Example: John started dressing neatly after his mother scolded him for being sloppy. His mother congratulated herself, but the real reason for John's neatness was a new girlfriend who did not like sloppy boys. As you have seen in the discussion of cause and effect in Chapter 7, this common fallacy is called *post hoc* (short for *post hoc, ergo propter hoc* — "after this, therefore because of this").

Correction: Identify the true cause or causes in a situation, checking for the nature of the cause, multiple causes, and proper time-sequence.

False Analogy

In the false analogy, the writer tries to compare two things that are not comparable or fails to understand the nature of the analogy. Example: "The most successful public service in our town is the garbage collection which is managed entirely by three private firms. If we want to improve our other public services, like police work and fire prevention, we should consider using a number of small firms that compete in the same way that the garbage collection companies do." The analogy is doubtful because the "services" involved are not really comparable. For instance, garbage collection is a regular service that is fairly constant, while the police department and the fire department provide services on a less regular and emergency basis. Emergency services tend to be distinctly different from non-emergency ones.

Here is another example: "It does not hurt to cut up your education by stopping to work for a year. Like those animals that grow a new leg or tail, you can re-learn what you have forgotten when you return to school." The comparison is metaphorical, but the writer is taking it literally. He has misunderstood the nature of his own analogy and so has rendered his conclusion invalid.

Correction: Check your analogy to see whether the two things being compared are comparable and in what sense they are comparable. Be very careful with figurative analogies. They are useful for explanation, but not as proof. (See pp. 187 – 188 for further discussion.)

Ignoring the Question

Almost any form of irrelevancy can be identified as ignoring the question — the fallacy of failing to stick to the thesis of an argument or of wandering away from an important point of the argument. Accordingly, this fallacy often seems to be the result of other fallacies. For example, if one starts out refuting an argument by Jones but slides into a personal attack on him, the writer falls into both *ad hominem* and ignoring the question. Many cases of ignoring the question are created by carelessly forgetting one's thesis. If a writer begins to argue that all auto mechanics in the United States should be federally licensed, and then breaks into a condemnation of the Pinto as an unsafe car, he is ignoring the question.

Correction: Identify the question and rewrite, sticking to the question and omitting irrelevancies.

PRACTICE

Discussion

In the following examples, identify the fallacy *by name* in two steps. First, determine which of the six basic human errors (p. 340) the writer made. Second, name the specific fallacy. In some examples, you may find more than one fallacy.

Note: You may be surprised by the amount of truth in many statements that also include fallacies. Why do truth and fallacy

often live happily side by side? One reason is that truths are
seldom absolutes but rather mixtures of the true and false. Another
reason is that half-truths can, superficially, be more convincing
than "whole" truths. As Stephen Leacock ironically remarked, "A
half-truth in argument, like a half-brick, carries better."

a. The basic physics courses here at the university are bad. My
   physics instructor is a weak teacher; he does not know his
   material and is not interested in his students.

b. Juvenile crime in America is increasing. Over 1,000,000 youths
   are arrested every year. More than 55,000 youths are in jails.
   One-fifth of all youth is delinquent. Half the auto thefts, a third
   of the robberies, and a tenth of homicides and assaults in the
   United States are committed by youths. What is the cause?
   Society is to blame.

c. Grades are arbitrary. Students are in college to learn, not to get
   grades.

d. Making the sale of drugs a crime just makes using drugs more
   tempting. It is a fact that doctors have the money to satisfy this
   temptation and it is also a fact that doctors have a higher rate of
   addiction than people in any other profession.

e. I may or may not concede that some cops honestly try to maintain law and order. I will concede part of this, or all of this
   partly. If an old lady in respectable clothes falls down on the
   street, the cop will heroically try to help her, but the sight of an
   old bum on the same street brings out some atavistic desire in
   the cop with the cop mentality. The fakery of his charity reveals
   itself. He loves the old lady? Maybe; but, if so, only because it
   gives him a justification to beat up the old bum. — Nelson
   Algren, "Down with Cops"

f. A professor is like a tradesman. Like a plumber or electrician,
   the professor serves an apprenticeship so that he can learn a
   skill. Therefore, as the customer judges the worth of a tradesman's skill, we students should be able to judge the worth of a
   professor's teaching.

g. What are the other candidates afraid of? Mr. Bostwick says we
   cannot educate *all* of the children "because by definition not all
   children are educable." What kind of Nazi remark is that? Is he
   going to tell us which of our children can be educated and
   which cannot be? Of course all children are educable; they are
   human, aren't they? Mr. Bostwick should put on his black arm-
   band and parade around like the Nazi he is — why (and we demand that he answer this question) is he afraid to educate *all*
   American children?

h. Our neighbor says about the new divorce law: "Divorce is only a symptom, and you don't cure a disease by treating its symptoms."

i. Before the end of the present century, unless something quite unforeseeable occurs, one of three possibilities will have been realized. These three are: The end of human life, perhaps of all life on our planet. A reversion to barbarism after a catastrophic diminution of the population of the globe. A unification of the world under a single government, possessing a monopoly of all the major weapons of war.

I do not pretend to know which of these will happen, or even which is the most likely. What I do contend is that the kind of system to which we have been accustomed cannot possibly continue. — Bertrand Russell, "The Future of Man"

j. From letters to the editor on the causes of alcoholism:
Alcoholism is caused by alcohol just as surely as tuberculosis is caused by the tubercle bacillus. — a doctor
Alcoholism is an act of the will; thus it is a sin, not a disease.
The real cause of alcoholism is in advertising. — the president of a County Beverage Board
The manufacturers and distributors of alcoholic beverages are almost entirely responsible for the problem.
The cause of alcoholism? People. — a clergyman

k. The bourgeois [middle-class] clap-trap about the family and education, about the hallowed co-relation of parent and child, becomes all the more disgusting, the more, by the action of Modern Industry, all family ties among the proletarians [the workers] are torn asunder, and their children transformed into simple articles of commerce and instruments of labor. . . .

Our bourgeois, not content with having the wives and daughters of their proletarians at their disposal, not to speak of common prostitutes, take the greatest pleasure in seducing each others' wives. — Karl Marx and Frederick Engels, *Communist Manifesto*,

l. "Sexual permissiveness among America's college women hasn't changed much since 1930," a Stanford University researcher said Tuesday.

But the four-year study of 49 students at an unidentified Eastern women's college also showed "that American college students have evolved patterns of sexual behavior that will remain stable for some time to come," said Mervin B. Freedman.

Freedman, assistant dean of undergraduate education and a

research associate at the Institute for the Study of Human Problems, reported his findings in the *Merrill-Palmer Quarterly*.

— Associated Press news release

m. In the modern world we have no choice but to be atheists.

USE A CLEAR ARGUMENTATIVE ORGANIZATION

For your argument to be persuasive, its organization must be clear enough so that your reader will have no doubts about what direction your thoughts are taking. There are basically three major kinds of organization in formal argumentation:

1. The *organization of fact* — in which you argue the truth (or reality) of an idea, opinion, occurrence, and so on;

2. The *organization of action* — in which you argue that something should be done, that an action should be taken;

3. The *organization of refutation* — in which you argue that another person's argument is wrong, invalid, or fallacious.

In practice, these three argumentative organizations often do not appear as distinct and separate forms. You may find yourself combining, for example, fact and refutation organizations in a single essay because you need them both to support your thesis. But the organizations can be most clearly understood if we discuss them separately. An argumentative organization is built around a thesis; accordingly, we will begin our discussion by distinguishing between the thesis of fact and the thesis of action. We will take up refutation later.

Theses of Fact and of Action

The *thesis of fact* states that something is (or is not) true, or was (or was not) true. Of course the thesis may be qualified by stating that something is or was partly true. Any type of necessary qualification may be made. Examples of fact theses:

Capital punishment is an uncivilized practice.
Although it was tried only on a relatively small sample of the population, fluoridation seemed to prevent tooth decay in Sweetbrush, Indiana.

The thesis of fact is ordinarily a statement about the present, the past, or both.

The *thesis of action* states that a change must be made. Examples of action theses:

> We must do away with capital punishment in the United States because it is an uncivilized practice.
>
> Since fluoridation of drinking water prevents decay in children's teeth, the citizens of Sweetbrush, Indiana, should add fluoride to their drinking water.

The thesis of action is a statement about the future that is based upon a statement of truth, sometimes implied, about the present or past. The thesis of action must be based on a thesis of fact. In other words, you cannot argue for any kind of change in human affairs until after you have proved that there is a *need* for the change. As you will shortly learn, *fact* arguments and *action* arguments differ in both purpose and organization.

Organization of Fact Arguments

An organization of fact is simply a clear presentation and elaboration of a thesis of fact. You set down your ideas straightforwardly:

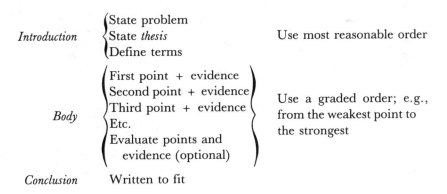

For a short paper, an introduction of one or two paragraphs is sufficient. In the introduction, be sure you tell your readers all they need to know, especially about the thesis and definition of terms. In the body, separate the main points clearly so that your readers can tell them apart. Use any graded order that seems appropriate; a common one is suggested in the diagram above. (See pp. 226–228 for a further discussion of graded order.) It is natural and more convincing to save your strongest point until last. Evaluating the points and evidence may be unnecessary, unless you are trying to prove something important about them. Write the conclusion to fit the whole argument. Don't try to argue a new point in the conclusion—this is usually unconvincing.

The following letter to a college newspaper is an example of a fact organization:

Introduction: one paragraph *Problem and thesis stated* *Issues stated*	[1]When I was accepted by Ivy, I was very proud. This is a great private university, with a fine reputation all over the United States. But since coming to school, I have discovered one thing about the university that is injuring its educational program—its attempt to compete in big-time college football. I have heard students, and also the administration, claim that football is necessary because the alumni want it, or because Ivy needs it for prestige. None of these is a major issue; none of these issues is relevant to the educational problems created when Ivy tries to compete in football against state schools with large enrollments and low entrance standards. This competition is what I mean by *big-time football.*
Term defined	What I mean by *injuring our educational program* I will explain in the rest of this letter.
First point + *evidence*	[2]Contrary to popular belief, football players are not always more ethical than ordinary students. At Ivy, freshmen players cause more than their share of the cheating problems. In two of my classes I have seen players cheat, but I have never seen other students cheat. Admittedly, this is a small sample. But it is an accepted fact that more players than non-players in the past four years have been brought before the Honor Council for plagiarism. This situation occurred despite the fact that players are outnumbered more than twenty to one by nonplayers.
Second point + *evidence*	[3]Cheating on this scale by a small group of students lowers both the moral and intellectual tone of the university. In order to limit cheating, instructors in some freshman courses have been forced to monitor exams more closely than ever. And freshman composition teachers are giving a large number of in-class themes, a practice that reduces the course to the level of a high school offering.
Strongest point left until last (note transition) *Evidence*	[4]But however irritating and high schoolish these practices may be, they do not weaken our educational program as much as tutoring, the special attention that many instructors give to football players both in the classroom and in their offices. Time and again, the instructor in my introductory literature class has had to stop to explain a simple literary interpretation to a hulking tackle. There are four such

"students" in my class; they are noisy and disruptive; and my instructor, who is a tolerant man, has been forced to lower his teaching to fit them while the rest of us squirm with boredom. Moreover, when we go to his office — this has happened to me twice — there is the tackle, getting free advice on commas and semicolons, things he should have learned in freshman comp.

Conclusion   [5]It is hard to believe that a small group of athletes could injure the educational process in a major university. But that is what these players are doing. Many of them cannot meet our academic standards, but they are here anyway. This situation can only further weaken the fine educational program that Ivy has established and maintained for so many years.

Very truly yours,
John Cate

Organization of Action Arguments

As we explained earlier, an action argument must be based on a fact argument. This relationship determines an important part of the action organization. If you have not proved to your reader that there is a *need* for a change (fact argument), then you probably have to provide the argument of fact before going on to the argument of action. This would mean, practically speaking, that you would have to write two separate but related arguments. But we will assume here that the need for a change is evident, so that you have only to explain it briefly before beginning your argument of action. For this type of argument, here is a typical organization:

Introduction   State *need* for action (the problem)   Use most
State *thesis* (proposed action)   reasonable order
Define *terms*

Body   Give as much *fact* argument as necessary
Give details of proposed *action*: expand as necessary
State why action is *practical*
State why action is *beneficial*
State why action is *better* than other proposed or possible actions (optional)

Conclusion   Written to fit (many writers state here why their proposed action will satisfy the need introduced at the beginning)

Here is an example of an organization of action: a letter to the same college paper, answering the preceding letter.

Introduction: one paragraph

Problem (need for action) stated

Thesis of action

Definition of term

[1]John Cate's recent letter about football players lowering the academic standards of Ivy centers on a small group of athletes who cause trouble in class, lower academic standards, and cheat. It is true that some of them were brought before the Honor Council this year. Yet there were only four athletes — all football players — involved in this group. They are the ones causing the trouble Mr. Cate is so disturbed about. To take care of only four players, he recommends that Ivy "get rid of big-time football. . . ." To put the case in the classic terms of argument, he has identified a need, but he has not suggested a practical solution. Ivy cannot condemn the whole football program because of four players. I suggest an effective solution to the problem. Ivy should apply the same entrance requirements to athletes as to other freshmen. By *entrance requirements,* I refer to the required College Board scores, high-school grades, recommendations from teachers, and interviews.

Paragraphs 2 and 3 give an argument of fact; the student must argue fact before he can argue action

[2]It is well known at the university that many freshmen players are recruited directly by the coaches or alumni. Such players are often athletes first and students second. In many instances, they had given no thought to coming to Ivy before a coach or an alum talked to them. Three of the four players Mr. Cate is so unhappy about are in this category. None of these three had good College Board scores or high-school grades. Their teachers did not recommend them for Ivy, and they should not have come here. But the Admissions Committee — manned almost entirely by instructors — voted to let these students in as special cases. This is not unusual. A number of students, and not just athletes, are let in as special cases. Some, for example, have high College Board scores but weak high-school grades.

[3]Mr. Cate mentions that over the past four years more football players than nonplayers have been brought before the Honor Council for cheating. He is right, but what he does not state is that in all but two of these cases the players involved were those that were admitted as special cases by the Admissions Committee. In other words, the players causing most of the trouble are not "students" at all; they are sort of athletic appointees.

Why proposed action is practical and beneficial

[4]The action to be taken seems obvious: Judge all of our proposed freshmen as *students.* Require all of them to pass our high entrance standards and ignore whether they are athletes. This is a practical solution because the Admissions

Committee will only have to do what it has been supposed to do all along. Moreover, this solution will take care of Mr. Cate's problem; there will be few, if any, football bums infesting his classes and taking up his instructors' office hours. Also, my solution has the special attractiveness of allowing Ivy to continue its football program, which I think is a benefit to both the university and its students.

Conclusion

[5]One final point: I play football. I also have a B+ average. Only three of our varsity players are as of now in academic trouble. The fact that most of us do pretty well in our studies indicates that the need is not to get rid of football players but to get rid of certain students (who happen to be players) who should not have been allowed to enter Ivy in the first place.

Very truly yours,
Doug Cleary

PRACTICE

Writing

This writing assignment is designed to give you experience in shaping fact and action arguments. It is based on the following argumentative letter written to the American Association of University Professors (AAUP), a major professional association of college and university professors. The letter was published in the AAUP magazine, *Academe.*

[1]I read with great interest your recent "Evaluating Teachers" issue (*Academe,* October, 1979). I always read articles about teacher evaluation with great interest. I keep waiting for someone to point out that the open-ended "comments" students are usually urged to write about their instructors are, in effect, anonymous letters. Since these forms, with their odious collection of blind quotes, are taken very seriously these days, we college teachers find that we are the only professionals whose performance is at least partially judged on the basis of anonymous letters. No matter what the charges, we can never confront our accusers. We have no idea who they are.

[2]It might be interesting for the civil libertarians among us to consider the legal and ethical implications of a system whereby certain members of the academic community are regularly invited to comment

on other members, with the heartening assurance in advance that they can cloak their comments in anonymity.

³Let us also consider the outcry on America's campuses if we were encouraged to submit, along with our grades, anonymous comments on our students, which comments would be part of their permanent record and would be forwarded to their potential employers—just as our teaching evaluations are usually preserved in departmental files, forwarded to personnel committees, and even mailed to other schools where we might be seeking an appointment.

⁴I have often wondered why the AAUP, in its laudable solicitude for our professional welfare, has never—as far as I know—questioned a system that regularly subjects its members to anonymous letters. Would *Academe* print an anonymous letter? Accept an anonymous article?—Howard Clarke

Your writing assignment, which can be shaped further by your instructor, includes:

a. Agree or disagree with Professor Clarke. (You may agree or disagree in part, of course.) The broad subject is *teacher evaluation*.
b. Create a *thesis of fact,* based on your experience as a student, on the issues in the letter. (What facts do you have?) After you have created this thesis, consider its possible weaknesses. Rewrite it, if necessary.
c. Create a *thesis of action* on the same subject. Again, consider its possible weaknesses.
d. Write:
   1. An argument based on your fact thesis. Pick a reader or type of reader: Professor Clarke, the readers of *Academe,* your college dean, other students.
   2. An argument of action. Again, consider possible readers.
   3. A combination of (1) and (2).

Organization of Refutation Arguments

In the argument of refutation, you take someone else's argument and prove that it is, to some degree, wrong, invalid, or fallacious. An argument is like a tower made of rocks. If you pull out one of the rocks near the bottom, the whole tower is likely to fall. If you show that one important part of an opponent's argument is weak, his whole case may topple. Thus before you write a refutation you need to examine your opponent's argument to see if you can find any weak spots in it. Here are some possible weak points to look for:

1. *Faulty premises.* A premise is a basic idea, stated or assumed, on which an arguer builds his argument (or a part of it), or from which he reaches a conclusion. If you can show that your opponent's premises are faulty, you can probably refute his entire argument. Refuting his major premise is likely to cut him down on the spot. Even refuting one of his minor premises is a victory. Here is a premise from the first student letter:

> Cheating on this scale by a small group of students lowers both the moral and the intellectual tone of the university.

If you can show that cheating by a small group of students does not "lower both the moral and the intellectual tone of the university," you have weakened his argument considerably. Sydney J. Harris wrote: "There is nothing more dangerous than a person with a good mind who begins to reason, logically and coolly, from insufficient premises: for his answers will always be valid, justified, rational — and wrong."

2. *Faulty definitions.* A *definition* is itself a kind of premise, a part of an argument's foundation. If your opponent has been careless in defining, you can answer as follows:

> Mr. Cate says that by *big-time football* he means competition against "state schools with large enrollments and low entrance standards." His definition is meaningless because Ivy does not compete against such schools. B_____ University, it is true, has 30,000 students but it also has high entrance standards — it admits only those from the top quarter of the high-school class. W_____ University has low standards but only 6500 students. We compete against only four state schools, two of which I have mentioned. The other two (J_____ College and M_____ University) do not fit his definition either. Mr. Cate's carelessness in defining throws doubt on his whole argument.

3. *Fallacies in logic or in presenting the argument.* See pp. 340–345 for a complete discussion of fallacies.

4. *Faulty use of evidence and authority.* Mistakes here are usually either those of using insufficient or irrelevant evidence, or using a wrong or doubtful authority. (For further discussion, see pp. 329–330.)

5. *Impractical or undesirable action (applicable only to action arguments).* In many areas of argument, there is general agreement by everyone concerned that something must be done — a definite need for action does exist. But your opponent's suggested action may be impractical, undesirable, or irrelevant. It may bring about greater evils than now exist in the situation. If you believe that your opponent's suggested action is wrong, it is your job to point out *specifically* what is wrong with it. You may also give your own

argument of action. But strictly speaking, a refutation states only the flaws in an opponent's argument.

Before writing a refutation, analyze your opponent's argument. Isolate its parts, from the thesis to the premises to the evidence used. If you can show that his thesis is badly worded, vague, or perhaps not stated at all, you can shoot down his argument with a paragraph. You do not have to waste much time on an opponent who does not even know the main point he is supposed to be arguing.

In organization, your refutation might look like this:

Introduction	State errors in opponent's thesis or main argument
	Admit when opponent's argument is strong; this is both sensible and honest
Body	State flaws in opponent's argument; arrange flaws in graded order, leaving greatest till last
	State your own argument of fact or action (optional)
Conclusion	Written to fit

PRACTICE

Discussion
1. Of the following theses, which are of fact and which of action? For each action thesis, state the thesis of fact (the *need,* in other words) which would have to be proved before one could argue the action thesis. In each thesis, what terms need definition?
   a. The press should not be allowed to cover in great detail any important murder trials.
   b. Alcohol is a dangerous drug.
   c. The individual states in the Union should be allowed to determine their own educational policies.
   d. Poverty is a cause of crime.
   e. Help abolish poverty.
   f. Scientists should refuse to work on any type of nuclear weapon.
   g. Swimming is the best form of general exercise.
   h. Robert E. Lee was a more capable tactician than Ulysses S. Grant.
   i. Undergraduates planning to go to law school should not have to take a foreign language.
   j. I don't care whether you believe me or not; he's got four people on that motorcycle with him!

2. Analyze the organization of the following student argument. How
   successful is the argument? What is the writer's stance?

   [1]Resident Advisors (RA's) are a tradition at almost every college in
   this country, and ours is no exception. You can find at least one RA
   living on every floor of every residence hall ("dorm") on this campus. I
   myself am an RA for this semester; and if my experience is any indication, the college should abolish the RA system as soon as possible.

   [2]RA's are people selected by the Housing Division to perform many
   duties and services for an overwhelmingly ungrateful group of students
   each year. The basic "duties" of an RA are fourfold:
   a. To keep peace and harmony among the residents on the floor;
   b. To provide the residents with an atmosphere in which learning, in
      all forms, is a way of living.
   c. To provide para-professional counseling if and when required;
   d. To enforce college regulations if and when necessary.

   [3]But what the residents really expect and want from their RA's are
   things like:
   a. Being allowed to wake up their RA any time of the day or night
      just to talk or to let them into their room when they're locked out;
   b. Having their RA pretend she didn't see the residents smoking dope
      or drinking beer.
   c. Having their RA tell their roommate or neighbor to turn their
      stereo down when they're too scared to do it themselves;
   d. Giving them light bulbs when theirs burn out;
   e. Filling out maintenance forms when their air conditioning fails.

   [4]And if an RA is not around 24 hours a day just in case somebody
   wants her services, then she's labeled a bad advisor who's "never
   around when you need her." On the other hand, if an RA is always on
   the floor and ready to help, then she's called "nosy." So an RA can't
   win. And it's frustrating.

   [5]But the worst part of the job is the fact that the student residents
   themselves don't want RA's, and they're very vocal about it. Residents
   are defensive about their privacy and they don't want any member of
   the college staff living among them. To them, RA's are unnecessary
   additions to college housing. And I think the students are probably
   right. *Any* responsible student on the floor could be assigned to supply
   light bulbs, maintenance reports, and spare keys. And with the current
   attitude of the residents, RA's don't usually get very many students
   coming in just to talk or get advice.

   [6]As for enforcing regulations—it's more than a one-person job
   anyway. Residents generally work together to create and maintain the
   type of atmosphere they want to live in. No individual RA can create
   or destroy the style of a living unit.

   [7]As it stands right now, each RA receives free room and board, tuition and fees, and a monthly stipend of $50. That amounts to approx-
   imately $2200 per RA per academic year. With about 170 RA's on
   campus, the total cost comes to $374,000. I truly think that in the

future we should use this money to give the students something they need and want. Resident Advisors are not needed or wanted. Is it worth $374,000 per academic year merely to keep a tradition?

3. The following letter, by David T. Lykken, professor of psychiatry and psychology at the University of Minnesota, was sent to the editors of *Discover* magazine. Analyze its refutation argument. How effective is it in refuting the "myths" it discusses?

[1]That there is a machine or a "test" that can detect lying is one of the great American myths. For nearly ten years I have been trying to explode this myth. In 1980 alone, a million of my countrymen had to submit to lie tests. Thousands of them were refused employment, many others lost their jobs and reputations. Some went to prison convicted of crimes they did not commit.

[2]I have enjoyed the edifying essays of Lewis Thomas, a man of science, culture, and manifest good sense. What, then, am I to do when I find Thomas ruminating on the sociobiological implications of the lie detector myth [December], which he treats as fact, "propped up," he says, "by genuine, hard scientific data"? To tell a lie, "even a small one," he reports, sets off "a highly reproducible cascade of changes in the electrical conductivity of the skin, the heart rate, and the manner of breathing . . . and now we have a neat machine to record it as well."

[3]One is dismayed to see the very essence of the myth thus dignified by the elegant prose of a respected scientist-philosopher. I had assumed that we Americans were uniquely vulnerable to this myth because we are such suckers for technology and what masquerades as scientific; I had supposed that scientists would be less easily taken in. I see now that the problem goes deeper; Americans are suckers, period.

[4]There is no such thing as a lie detector. Lying does not produce a "reproducible cascade" of distinctive physiological changes. There is no specific response that everyone emits when lying but never when telling the truth. When we lie about something serious, most of us experience some sort of inner turmoil, what Daniel Defoe described 250 years ago as "a tremor in the blood." No doubt we remember thinking that, if the target of our falsehood could only see that turmoil within us, the jig would be up. When the polygrapher adjusts the chest belt that measures breathing movements, attaches the electrodes that will record sweating of the palms, and then pumps up the blood pressure cuff on our arm, we readily believe the jig *is* up.

[5]What we forget is that a false accusation can elicit an inner turmoil also—and the lie detector cannot tell the difference! The polygraph pens do no special dance when we are lying. Many polygraphers think that they can see "deception" in the choreography but they are mistaken. Most of the thousands of polygraph examiners in the U.S.

are ex-cops, graduates of a six-week course that covers psychology, physiology, electronics, and "the art and science of the polygraph technique," a course using a syllabus that would make Dr. Thomas blush. If we really want to understand the lie detector, we would do better to consult Floyd Fay, a young man who was recently released from prison after serving more than two years of a life sentence for a murder he did not commit (they finally found the real killers).

[6]Fay was arrested at home at 4 o'clock one morning and hauled off to the Toledo jail to be grilled about the murder of his friend Fred. Because he was innocent, Fay agreed to take a lie detector test. He was asked a short list of questions repeated several times. There were three relevant, or "Did you do it?" questions, such as "Did you kill Fred?" interspersed with three control questions, such as "Before you were twenty-four, did you ever think of doing bodily harm to someone for revenge?" If Fay had been consistently more aroused or disturbed by the control questions, he would have passed the test and been set free. But, not surprisingly, Fay's pulse was stronger and his palms were more moist when he was asked the relevant questions, no doubt because he was sensible enough to realize that "Did you shoot Fred on March 28th?" was considered more "relevant" to his immediate prospects than those so-called control questions about his thoughts and actions years earlier.

[7]This type of lie test has become standard in the industry precisely because the polygraph measures only relative disturbance or arousal and cannot detect lying *per se*. But because the control questions are not controls at all in the scientific sense of that term, the polygraph test is strongly biased against the truthful respondent. Put yourself in Fay's place: you didn't kill anyone, your denials are truthful. But the authorities suspect you may be guilty; that is why you are being given the test. When the man asks, "Did you kill Fred?" what would happen to the surging of your pulse, the sweating of your palms?

[8]Fay wound up in a prison where they use the polygraph on inmates who have violated prison rules. Those who fail the test are usually transferred to the maximum security prison, a dangerous and punishing place. Because of what had happened to him, Fay began a study of the law and the lie detector. From an article of mine, he learned how the control question test is supposed to work—and also how it can be beaten. It is not easy to inhibit one's reactions to the accusatory relevant questions. It is quite easy, however, to augment artificially one's reactions to the control questions, and, if the pens dance harder after the control than the relevant questions, you must pass the test. Fay contacted 27 inmates who were scheduled to undergo such a trial by polygraph. He explained the technique to them, showed them how to bite their tongues or secrete a nail in one of their shoes and press on the sharp edge of the nailhead when the control questions were asked. Although all 27 admitted to him that they were guilty of the offenses

charged, mostly involving drugs, 23 of the 27 managed to beat the lie test in this manner.

[9]The "hard scientific data" that Dr. Thomas refers to are, I fear, also mythological. For 50 years the lie detector wormed its way into our confidence largely on the basis of extreme and unsubstantiated claims of 95 per cent and 99 per cent accuracy. There are some hard data now, two studies published since 1976, that prove what Fay and thousands of other victims have discovered to their cost: submitting to the lie detector to prove one's innocence is a hazardous expedient. In both these recent investigations, of the suspects who were determined later to have been innocent, *half* of them failed the lie test!

4. Make a few notes for a class discussion of the following argument, taken from a magazine advertisement.

For Every Right There is an Obligation

[1]If you kept telling a child about his rights and never about his duties, you'd soon have a spoiled brat on your hands. We're doing the same thing in this country but on a vastly more dangerous scale.

[2]The "right" of unions to strike for more pay but no obligation to earn it.

[3]The "rights" of new nations to independence but no obligation to prove they deserve it, no obligation to use freedom for the good of mankind.

[4]The "right" of young people to education but no obligation to pay their own way to get it.

[5]The "rights" of criminals and communists to flout the laws of our land, without any obligation to contribute to its worth and its freedom.

[6]Spoiled children grow into adult criminals, who have to be punished by the decent society they defy. Why wait? — advertisement by Warner & Swasey in *Newsweek*

Writing

Write an argument using an organization of fact or action that is based on some of the ideas in the ad printed above. Sample thesis: *A majority of students at _____ College apparently feel an "obligation" to pay their own way, since over 55 percent of us are working our way through college.* Pick a specific writer's stance for your argument; for example, you might want to address Warner & Swasey directly.

CHAPTER 17
*LIBRARY RESEARCH**

In writing the research paper, you will go outside your own experience and use mainly the ideas of others, usually authorities on the subject you have chosen. In most cases, the research paper is based on library sources (books, periodicals, and newspapers), but you may also consult authoritative living persons. The research paper should not be for you a new or unusual rhetorical problem. You find and limit your subject, as you have always done. You evaluate and organize your materials and evidence and create a stance, as you have learned to do. For most students, the only difficulty is how to mesh these activities with library research. How do you get into the maze of a library and safely get out, several days later, armed with dozens of neatly written note cards which can be turned into a documented paper?

Following a series of steps in your library research will help:

Step 1: Choose your subject, ask a question, and write a narrative.
Step 2: Follow a search strategy.
Step 3: Make a working bibliography.
Step 4: Read, take notes, and evaluate the evidence.

---

*Caroline Tibbetts, Reference Librarian, University of Delaware, Newark, acted as consultant for these research chapters.

STEP 1: CHOOSE YOUR SUBJECT, ASK A QUESTION, AND WRITE A NARRATIVE

Choose Your Subject

If your instructor has not assigned subjects for the research paper, you should choose a subject that has interested you and that you will enjoy working with. The following suggestions may help:

1. Consider your own special interest or academic major. Look through some of the dictionaries and encyclopedias in your major field. See "Special Reference Works" (pp. 387–392) for a list of some of the more important titles. For example, if you are a music major, you might like to look at the *New Grove Dictionary of Music and Musicians.* This book's discussion of folk music might suggest a subject dealing with one aspect of that form.

   Do not choose highly technical subjects, particularly those that require a technical terminology. You may have to spend so much time explaining the terms that you will not be able to develop your points.

2. Look through current magazines and newspapers. What kinds of subjects are being discussed? Do any of them interest you? Keep a file of photocopied or clipped newspaper and magazine articles on two or three topics that you think might be of use later.

   Be wary of subjects so current that there may be little or nothing in the library about them. Also, be wary of subjects that you feel strongly about. If you are emotionally involved in an issue, you may find it difficult to be objective and fair.

3. Choose a subject that you will enjoy over a period of time. If your subject bores you, you may have trouble convincing your reader that you believe in your thesis. Also, be prepared to change your mind about a subject in the process of researching it. The facts may be different from what you imagined them to be. For instance, Judy Goldsmith, who wrote the model research paper (p. 410), believed at first that women politicians were more powerful than they turned out to be. This fact influenced the way Judy developed her thesis and shaped her paper. (*Note:* We will be using her work throughout this chapter to show examples of research techniques.)

4. Choose a subject for which you can prove a point. A research paper that merely explains or surveys the situation isn't very meaningful. Since you

are in the business of convincing your reader, you should take a stand on your subject, proving that your position is valid and reasonable.

Ask a Question You Hope to Answer

Frame a question about your subject that interests you and that you hope to answer. The answer to that question may lead you to a thesis. The question will help you to narrow your topic and provide a focus for your research. Judy Goldsmith asked: *What do women have to be and do to succeed in politics?*

Write a Narrative Describing Your Research

Write a narrative explaining to yourself—and to anyone else who might be in a position to help you—what you want to know. In your narrative describe your *role,* and your *audience* (see stance, pp. 21–22). (You are not quite ready to develop your thesis, but you should state your question.) In your narrative, use specific terms to describe the research you are about to do.

Judy Goldsmith wrote the following:

Role	I'm a freshman in college, majoring in political science. I have always assumed that political science would prepare me
Subject Terms	for a career in politics. However, I don't know how *women politicians* in the *United States* have succeeded. For instance, I
Subject Terms	don't know how *women senators* or *representatives* differ in their pursuit of a career. I don't know what women did to become
Subject Term	*political candidates*—what they experienced in the process, how much support they received, or how they were treated.
Subject Term	Consequently, I'd like to learn something more about *women in politics,* how they decided to run, and how effective they have been. I am certainly interested in the kind of education that successful *women political candidates* have. As a result of my research, I might change my mind about politics as a career or political science as a major.
Question Posed	My question is: *What do women have to be and do to succeed in politics?*
Audience	My audience will be the young men and women in my class and my friends in the dormitory who would read my paper. Perhaps my political science instructor would be interested in it also.

Writing a narrative has provided several key words or subject terms that may be useful to Judy when she uses reference works, periodical indexes, and the card catalog. In addition, she has identified two important elements of her *stance—role* and *audience*. Later she will be able to answer her question with a *thesis,* completing her *stance.*

STEP 2: FOLLOW A
SEARCH STRATEGY

*B*efore you go further with the subject, you should see whether your library has material on it. Keeping in mind your subject headings or key terms identified in your narrative, run a brief check on three sources: (1) *reference books* (particularly encyclopedias); (2) the *card catalog*; and (3) a *major periodical index.* You want to know whether material on your subject exists.

This diagram gives a visual image of what the *search strategy* consists of:

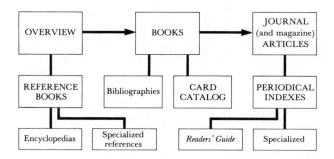

Search in Reference Books

Encyclopedias

The most efficient way to use a multivolume encyclopedia is to turn first to the index, which is contained in a separate volume. There you may find the main entry for your subject. If you can't find it, you will need to look for related subjects. For example, Judy discovered that encyclopedias do not have an index entry for *Women Political Candidates*. But when she looked under *Political Parties* and under *Women,* she found references such as *Women, Legal Rights of; Women's Liberation;* and *Women, Status of.* These articles gave her historical information that was useful, but she didn't find anything very specific about *Women Political Candidates.* She did check *see* and *see-also* entries, a process that sometimes will give additional information, but nothing new turned up for her on her subject.

You shouldn't be discouraged if an encyclopedia doesn't cover your subject in the way that you had expected.

Special Reference Works

Check any reference books in your subject to see if they give general information that might be useful. Be sure to examine the indexes and tables of contents of these books for ideas that might help you narrow your subject to a workable topic. (See the list of reference works arranged according to discipline at the end of this chapter.)

Judy found a helpful reference of a special kind in the *Women's Rights Almanac.* In checking the *Table of Contents,* she discovered an article entitled, "Politics and Government: The Nearly Invisible Women." The statistics in the book were dated, but they gave her some ideas about what to look for. More important, the title piqued her interest — why *nearly invisible?* (These terms led her to a particular emphasis in her *thesis.*)

Search the Card Catalog

The card catalog is an alphabetized collection of index cards that carry information on every book your library contains. For each book, you will find three types of cards: (1) author or main entry card; (2) title card; and (3) subject card. When using the card catalog for a preliminary investigation of your subject, check the subject cards first. If you do not find your subject listed, you should try a more general classification, as you did with the encyclopedia indexes.

Judy couldn't find *Women — Political Candidates* as a subject in her library's card catalog, so she tried *Women in Politics — U.S.* and *Women — Civil Rights.* She analyzed her subject from different angles and considered closely related terms which referred to it, such as *Women — Political Roles.*

Here is the kind of card Judy found under *Women in Politics — U.S.*

WOMEN IN POLITICS — UNITED STATES.
HQ
1391   Mandel, Ruth B.
.U5   In the running : the new woman
M36   candidate / by Ruth B. Mandel. — New
           Haven : Ticknor & Fields, 1981.
              xxi, 280 p. ; 24 cm.

              1. Women in politics — United States.
              2. Women — United States.   3. Feminism —
              United States.   4. Electioneering —
              United States.   I. Title

GU   TTL#6343482, gasp   GUAAsc   80-24190

Note particularly the subject entries listed at the bottom of the card. They will be useful to you in the same way the *See* and *See-also* references were when using the encyclopedia indexes.

When librarians assign subject headings, they use as a guide either *Sears List of Subject Headings* or *The Library of Congress Subject Headings,* one of which may be shelved near the card catalog. Skim these reference books, looking for different headings, to see if you can find information on your subject.

During this process, keep a list of the terms that yield results, so that you can use them again when using indexes and other references.

Another way to find out what books on your subject the library contains is to check the *shelf list,* a listing of all the books in call-number order. After getting the call number of one book that deals with your subject, you can check the shelf list for books with similar numbers. If you are not allowed to go into your library's stacks, the shelf list can be a valuable way of finding other material on your subject.

On-Line Computer Catalog

Your library may have its more recent acquisitions on a computer card catalog. If so, you will be able to do an *author/title, author,* or *title* search. If you know the call number of the book, you can do a *call number* search.

If you are fortunate enough to have a library with a bibliographic display, you might be able to get from the computer a list of books written recently on your subject. With the help of a librarian and the *Library of Congress Subject Headings,* Judy found some of the books in her library by entering into the computer *Women in Politics — United States — History — 20th Century.* This process was a great time saver for her, once she knew the key to the computer's subject descriptor.

Check Out the Books

Now is the time to see if the important books on your subject are actually in the stacks. If they are, check them out; if not, put a hold on them. If your library has open stacks, browse through all the books shelved together on your subject. Sometimes you will find valuable books this way that you have missed in the card catalog. Check the tables of contents and indexes. Also check for bibliographies at the end of chapters or the end of books. You may find pertinent or interesting material that can give you a new answer to your question or, perhaps, steer you to a different question.

PRACTICE

Where in your library's card catalog would you go to find the following information? (Indicate the drawer numbers in your answer.)
1. Books by Isaac Asimov
2. Information about cats
3. A history of Africa
4. The *Koran*
5. A biography of Ernest Hemingway
6. Twentieth-century American poetry

Periodical and Newspaper Indexes

Most of the major newspapers in the United States publish their own indexes. You will also find one for the London *Times.* If your topic is one of current interest, you may find valuable information in newspapers. Because Judy's subject was current, she found useful articles in the *Wall Street Journal* and the *Chicago Tribune.*

Periodical indexes for specific academic disciplines are available also (see pp. 387–392). You may find the *Readers' Guide to Periodical Literature* most useful. The *Readers' Guide,* as it is most often called, lists recent articles published in 198 popular magazines. It is published twice a month, combined every three months into a larger volume, and then published yearly in one bound volume.

Most periodical indexes contain roughly the same format. To use an index efficiently, you need to be aware of the information presented in the front of each issue: (1) suggestions for using the index; (2) abbreviations of the periodicals indexed; (3) a list of the periodicals indexed; and (4) the key to other abbreviations. This information will tell you how to read references and abbreviations such as *Bull Atom Sci, jt, Ja, il, por,* and give you other important help in using the index.

To look up your subject, again start with a specific term. If you can't find it, move to a broader subject. Periodical indexes use cross references in the same way encyclopedia indexes and card catalogs do.

On p. 369 there are some of the entries for *Women — Political Activities,* all useful for the topic *Women in Politics.*

After you have identified the items in the *Readers' Guide* that may contain information on your subject, check the card catalog to see if your library has the magazines in bound form. Current magazines, as well as older bound issues, may be listed in a Kardex file. Many librarians now have magazines on microfilm, in which case the microfilm number appears over the call number on the catalog card.

Microforms

The print explosion in the last few years has created so much paper that libraries have been forced to take magazines and other periodicals out of circulation and photograph them. They are stored on reels (microfilm) or in small pieces in separate envelopes (microfiche). The library provides machines that enlarge the film so that you can read or photocopy the page you wish to use in your research.

Government Publications

Government documents are important enough that they are housed in regional libraries called Government Documents Depositories. If your library has such a Depository, you will have access to most of the documents printed by the United States Government. If your library isn't a Depository, someone in your reference department will know where it is and help you get the documents from inter-library loan. The government also provides indexes such as *American Statistics Index* and the *Monthly*

Subject heading ———————— **Women**—Employment—*cont.*
Working women. J. L. Norwood. *Mon Labor Rev* 107:2
Jl '84
Anecdotes, facetiae, satire, etc.
How to sneak out of work [excerpt from Powermom]
H. Mundis. il *Glamour* 82:182+ Jl '84
Bibliography
Through the career-book maze. S. S. Fader. *Work Woman*
9:83-4+ N '84
Psychological aspects
See reference ————————— *See* Psychology, Industrial
Equal rights
See also reference ——————— *See also*
Equal pay for equal work
National Organization for Women
Woman suffrage
Women—Employment
Braving scorn and threats. O. Friedrich. il *Time* 124:36-7
Date ——————————— Jl 23 '84
Cutting sexism to the *coeur* [France] M. Bogin. il *Ms*
13:26 O '84
Title of article ——————— Equality spells change in other nations. P. M. Jones.
il *Sch Update* 117:12-13 N 2 '84
Here she is: Ms. America. L. D. Kratcoski. il *USA Today*
113:98 N '84
J.S. Mill on the subjection of women. S. Collini. bibl
f il por *Hist Today* 34:34-9 D '84
Turning back the clock on women and minority rights:
the Reagan record. M. F. Berry. por *Negro Hist Bull*
46:82-4 Jl/Ag/S '83
The winding road to equality [special issue] il *Sch Update*
116:2-8+ My 11 '84
Subdivision of subject ——————————— **Health and hygiene**
See also
Beauty, Personal
Black women—Health and hygiene
Feminine hygiene products
Gynecologic examinations
Gynecologists and patients
Menopause
Menstruation
Pregnancy
Young women—Health and hygiene
100 drugs doctors prescribe most for women. D. R.
Title of magazine ——————— Zimmerman. il *Good Housekeep* 198:118-19+ Mr '84
African women blaze a trail [participants in health develop-
ment] V. Mojekwu and others. il *World Health* p24-6
Ap '84
The anti-aging lifestyle [special section] S. Reice. il *Ladies
Home J* 101:115-22 S '84
Beauty & health report. C. R. Corcoran. See issues of
Glamour
Beauty: a new spirit, new freedom [special section] il
Vogue 174:600-21+ O '84
Beauty briefs. A. Brooks. See issues of Glamour
The beauty of health [special issue] il *Ms* 12:51-3+ My
'84
Body shop. See issues of McCall's beginning January
1984
The bottom line [susceptibility to decompression sickness]
Author ——————————— E. De Man. il *Women's Sports* 6:49 My '84
Feeling good. See issues of Mademoiselle
Fitness protects women against heart disease, too.
Prevention 36:93 Je '84
Health style. See issues of Vogue
Is the weight you gain all water? M. Oppenheim. *Redbook*
163:24 Je '84

Catalog of United States Government Publications to help you identify useful
material for your research topic. Judy would find *Congressional Information
Index* and *Index to U.S. Government Periodicals* useful if she wanted to do
more in-depth research.

PRACTICE

In a recent issue of the *Readers' Guide,* look up one of these subjects: *Occupations, Publishers and Publishing,* or *Medicine.*

1. Is the subject subdivided? If so, what are the subdivisions? (See the sample on the preceding page.)

2. Are there *See-also* references? List them.

3. What do the following abbreviations mean? *Ja, My, D, il, Good H.*

4. Look up one of the articles printed on your subject. Describe the process you went through to find the article in your library.

(Optional): Make an On-Line Data Base Computer Search

Many libraries offer an on-line bibliographic search of literature indexed in a variety of data bases. A *data base* can be thought of as the on-line equivalent of an index or abstract publication. Depending upon the kind of subject you choose, you may find an on-line computer search useful. You must pay for the service, and you probably will need the help of a librarian. Here is where your narrative describing your research will come in handy. By reading your narrative, your librarian will know if an on-line search will provide useful information on your subject.

Librarians

Throughout this process, you should be aware that every library has a staff of trained professionals who are ready to help you. After you have made every effort to do your own research, you may find that you need help. It would be foolish for you to spend hours looking for something when a librarian can help you find it in a few minutes. However, before asking a librarian for assistance, be sure that you have followed all the leads you know about.

After you have surveyed your library's resources, you should be able to say whether you have chosen a workable subject. After checking the reference books, the card catalog, and a periodical index, you may discover that little has been written on your subject or that much of what has been written is not available in your library. In that case, you will have to change your subject.

But let us be hopeful and assume that your search strategy has turned out to be successful, so that you intend to research your first choice of subject. Therefore, you will be ready for Step 3, *making a working bibliography.*

STEP 3: MAKE A WORKING BIBLIOGRAPHY

*A*t this point, many students start using shortcuts, some of which may actually work. But unless students have done a lot of research and writing, shortcuts can lead only to errors and frustration. The best researchers are usually both careful and lazy, careful in taking all the steps but lazy in not wanting to repeat any of them unnecessarily. For instance, if you don't make your working bibliography cards accurate the first time, you may not be able to find some of your sources in the library. Or you may have to go back to look up a source before typing your final bibliography. The best rule is to do everything right — *once.*

Study the MLA form for *List of Works Cited* (p. 401). Notice that the following bibliographic card gives all the material necessary for such a list; therefore, if you have done this step properly, all you need to do is to alphabetize your bibliography cards and type them for your final draft.

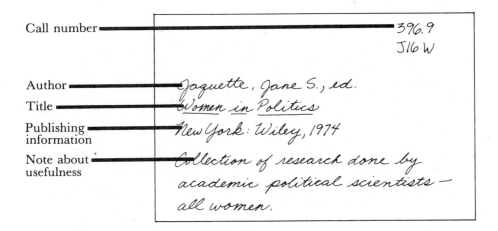

Call number	396.9 J16 W
Author	Jaquette, Jane S., ed.
Title	Women in Politics
Publishing information	New York: Wiley, 1974
Note about usefulness	Collection of research done by academic political scientists — all women.

Go slowly through those encyclopedias, other reference works, periodicals, and books that looked promising when you were searching for a workable subject. Take brief notes on the bibliography cards, indicating what you feel to be the particular usefulness of each source. If a source doesn't look helpful, abandon it.

In other words, even at this early stage, it is wise to anticipate Step 4 and start evaluating your sources and evidence. Begin with the most informative and most interesting sources. Skim through them and look for aspects of your subject that are repeatedly emphasized. This repetition often gives a clue to important developments in your subject. Don't get lost in a blind alley—a small part of a subject which one source treats voluminously but which the others ignore.

Check Other Bibliographies

To be sure that you haven't missed any important books or articles on your subject, you might see if anyone has developed an annotated bibliography on your topic. The *Bibliographic Index* may be useful at this point.

Interviews

You may discover that research on your topic is presently being done. If so, you might like to interview some authorities in your community. If the person you interview will give permission, tape the interview. Transcribing a tape is much easier than trying to listen and take notes. Since you have a fairly good grasp of your topic by now, you will know some appropriate questions to ask.

Sometimes it is possible to over-research a topic. You will be the judge of whether you have enough material for the paper. If you are satisfied with the material you have found, and you believe that you will be able to answer your question, go on to the next step. You can always go back to the library to find additional material, if necessary.

STEP 4: READ, TAKE NOTES, AND EVALUATE THE EVIDENCE

You may believe that the three elements in step 4 are distinct operations that must be tackled separately. Actually, you can do several of them at nearly the same time if you are careful. By now, you should have some idea of what is the best source material available on your subject. If you aren't sure, the following guidelines should help you to evaluate your sources.

1. *Check the date.* If your topic needs up-to-date information, a book or article written before the last decade or even in the last five years may be too old. On the other hand, a source that is older than a decade may be useful, particularly if you need a historical perspective on your topic. Needless to say, statistics and other quantitative data must be recent.

2. *Check the viewpoint.* Does the author take a particular position on the topic that would bias his or her objectivity?

3. *Skim the table of contents, introduction and index.* See if the content of the book deals with the sort of question you need to answer.

4. *Check the author's authority.* See pp. 329–330 for a discussion of *authoritative evidence.*

The Form of Notes

As you take notes, you should consider both their form and how they may be used in your paper.

Take notes on four-by-six cards, not on sheets of regular notebook paper, for they are too large to handle. Do not use three-by-five cards because you might mix them with your bibliography cards. *Put only one idea* — a paraphrase, summary fact or quotation — on each card.

> quote, p.157
>
> Women who succeeded in politics
> They didn't let their family situation interfere.
>
> "The women in our study who became politically active (1) waited until their husbands died, (2) had husbands who strongly supported their efforts, or (3) did not get into any long-term involvement with men at all."
>
> Kelly and Boutilier, *The Making of Political Women*

The two-part title in the upper-left corner is useful because it tells you what is on the card without your having to read it. When you come to arrange the note cards before outlining your paper, such careful labeling will pay off. In the upper-right corner is a reminder that this material is quoted (a good way to avoid accidental plagiarism) and that it was taken from page 157. At the bottom, the card provides the author's name and the title of the book or article.

Always give the complete citation on at least one note card. That way, if you lose your bibliography cards, you will have the reference without having to backtrack.

It is often convenient to make photocopies of magazines and reference-work articles, especially when you cannot check them out of the library. Some researchers have come to depend on photocopies for notes, sometimes clipping the passage needed and pasting it on a four-by-six card. Others have started using larger pages for notes so that they can use photocopies. Since you are learning a process for conducting library research, you should consider photocopying an addition to but not a replacement for notetaking. Your instructor will advise you *how* or *if* to use photocopies as part of your collection of notes.

Here is one pitfall you should watch for. It is easy to be complacent when you leave the library clutching a copy of an article or a single photocopied page from a reference work. You may think you have all the information that you need, but you may have failed to get the necessary bibliographic information. Therefore, you must always make a bibliographic card for every source, including those that you photocopy.

Taking Notes

This may seem like an odd place to discuss the *use* of notes — even before you have started to outline your paper. But we have discovered that students often go wrong later because they went wrong earlier. If you have a clear idea of what quotations and paraphrases are for, and how they should be eventually worked into your writing, you will be able to take notes more purposefully and avoid some common errors.

The quotations and paraphrases on your note cards provide much of the content — the material and the evidence — of your research paper. Such content comes from the work of other people who have written the articles and books you read. A note card is no more than a piece of paper on which you reduce the ideas of another person to manageable form.

As you take notes, bear this fact in mind: Students often use too much of others' work. Some research papers turn out to be no more than a loose sewing together of other writers' thoughts. A good general rule can be stated in two parts:

1. Use the materials and opinions of others mainly *as support* for your ideas, not in place of them.

2. When using sources, paraphrase as much as possible. A *paraphrase* restates a passage, using words *different* from those in the original. A *quotation* uses the *original* words of the passage. Quote only when the writer says something better or more vividly than you can, or when for the sake of evidence you choose to present the author's own words. Keep paraphrases and quotations short.

Accurate Paraphrasing

To illustrate paraphrasing, we will use this sample selection from Fletcher Pratt's *A Short History of the Civil War*:

In 1862 Abraham Lincoln was only the spokesman of an angry people, and no one realized more clearly than he that he did not have *carte blanche* from the nation — a fact which has been obscured by the halo that has since surrounded his name. To the majority he was at that time still the low, cunning clown, the President by hazard, and Chase, Stanton or Seward (according to whether one lived in the West, the Atlantic states or New England) the frequently thwarted brain of the administration. It must be remembered that the arrangement was then the normal one in American politics; the last seven Presidents had all been Merovingians ruled by some Mayor of the Palace. Lincoln's shambling gait, awkward movements, and low jokes made him appear as the most inept of all the presidential ventriloquist's dummies. Beside him Zachary Taylor looked like a drawing-room fop and Franklin Pierce like a courtier. When he leaned over and patted the leg of a Congressman who was urging some unfeasible scheme and threw him off balance with the remark "My, my, what big calves you do have," the discomfited legislator could see nothing in it but a piece of *gaucherie*. Even the skill with which the President charmed Kentucky, Maryland and Missouri out of the rebels' lap made no impression. His part in the intrigues was largely secret and both Southerners and Northerners regarded the series of events as fortuitous. The surprising thing in the North was not that the border states remained in the Union but that so many of the others left it.

Here are two paraphrases of the passage:

Paraphrase 1

Abraham Lincoln did not have *carte blanche* from the nation. Even so, he was a very effective president who charmed many southern states out of the rebel's lap. He was the first president in many years to act on his own without being another powerful politician's mouthpiece; he was never just a political ventriloquist's dummy.

Paraphrase 2

According to Fletcher Pratt's *A Short History of the Civil War,* Abraham Lincoln's political skill during the early years of the war was a study in contrasts. While appearing to be a buffoon who made irrelevant remarks at the wrong times, a politician who became president only by accident, he was actually involved in partly successful attempts to save the border states. Since the power given him by the country was incomplete (in Pratt's phrase, "he did not have *carte blanche* from the nation"), he had no choice but to move slyly and by indirection.

You can see that Paraphrase 1 is not a paraphrase at all but rather a careless mixture of summary and unmarked quotation. A paraphrase like it is considered a form of *plagiarism.* Paraphrase 2 fairly states Pratt's ideas and honestly places words in quotation marks that the writer has taken directly from Pratt.

Plagiarism

Plagiarism is using the words or ideas of another writer without giving proper credit. The plagiarist usually intends to pass off his paper as being an original creation when it is not. Borrowing other people's ideas and their wording without giving due credit will create problems for you as a student because teachers can take severe action against the writer of a plagiarized paper.

Plagiarism takes many forms:

1. *Word-for-word copying without using quotation marks or crediting the writer's source.*
2. *Using another student's work but turning it in under your own name.*
3. *Using a catchy or clever phrase or comment without giving credit.*
4. *Taking material from a variety of sources and tying it together to make it look original.*

Most colleges and universities define "plagiarism" in their student codes. If you wish further information, check the rules on written work in your own institution. Your instructor undoubtedly will give you more complete advice on this problem, which proves vexing to students and teachers alike.

Proper Techniques For Quoting

Short Quotations

Always quote accurately. Short prose quotations (those of fewer than five lines) should be worked into your own material smoothly and coherently. Note how the writer of the following sentences has varied the way *Fletcher Pratt* has been identified as the source.

> *As Fletcher Pratt states,* "the skill with which the President [had] charmed Kentucky, Maryland and Missouri out of the rebels' lap made no impression" (15).

> In light of our admiration of Lincoln, *Fletcher Pratt's comment* concerning the President's "shambling gait, awkward movements and low jokes" (15) may seem oddly inappropriate.

(The numbers in parentheses are page numbers, an appropriate use of parenthetical documentation form described in detail on pp. 404–405.)

In the first quotation, the brackets indicate *editorial insertion*—words or phrases put into the quotation for the sake of grammar or explanation.

You must copy a quotation *exactly as it is printed.* You may show your reader that a grammatical error or a misspelling in the text is not yours by inserting [sic] immediately after the error.

Long Quotations

Prose quotations of more than four lines are usually put in *block form* and indented five spaces from the left-hand margin. And quotation marks are *not* used to set off the entire quotation. Here is an example of how a block quotation is set up in relationship to the regular text of a paper.

> It is very easy to forget that during much of his administration, Lincoln was an unpopular president. For one thing, as Fletcher Pratt points out, he did not look or act much like a president:

> > Lincoln's shambling gait, awkward movements and low jokes made him ap-
> >
> > pear as the most inept of all the presidential ventriloquist's dummies. Beside

him Zachary Taylor looked like a drawing-room fop and Franklin Pierce like a courtier. When he leaned over and patted the leg of a Congressman who was urging some unfeasible scheme and threw him off balance with the remark, "My, my, what big calves you do have," the discomfited legislator could see nothing in it but a piece of *gaucherie* (15).

Ellipsis Marks

An *ellipsis* is an omitted portion of a quotation. *Ellipsis marks* (three or four spaced periods) indicate the place in the quoted material from which the words were removed. *Ellipses* are usually made in the middle or at the end of the quotation. Here are two examples:

> Pratt's comment on the political history of the time was: "It must be remembered that . . . the last seven Presidents had all been Merovingians ruled by some Mayor of the Palace" (15).

> As Fletcher Pratt states, "To the majority he was at that time still the low, cunning clown, the President by hazard. . . ." (15).

The three periods in the first example indicate that a phrase has been removed from the middle of Pratt's sentence. The four periods in the second example indicate that material from the end of the quoted sentence has been omitted.

Four ellipsis marks are also used when a *full sentence or more* is removed from a quotation. The four periods in the following example represent the omission of a full sentence:

> "Lincoln's shambling gait, awkward movements and iow jokes made him appear as the most inept of all the presidential ventriloquist's dummies. . . . Even the skill with which the President charmed Kentucky, Maryland and Missouri out of the rebels' lap made no impression" (15).

Ordinarily, you do not use ellipsis marks at the beginning of a quotation; that is, you do not write:

> Pratt's opinion is that Lincoln was ". . . at that time still the low, cunning clown. . . ."

Instead you fit the beginning of the quotation smoothly into your own sentence without the ellipsis marks:

> Pratt's opinion is that Lincoln was "at that time still the low, cunning clown. . . ." (15).

PRACTICE

Writing

1. Read the following passage describing women politicians. Then, on five separate note cards, put down: (1) a quotation from the passage that is worked into your own sentence(s); (2) a longer quotation to be used as a block quote in a paper; (3) a one-sentence paraphrase of the entire passage; (4) a quotation using an ellipsis inside one sentence; (5) a quotation using an ellipsis that "bridges" two or three sentences.

> [1]Women [politicians] acknowledge the tactical value in staying cool and smiling. In addition, some women seeking votes have plucked the sting from negative images by confronting them directly, and even using them to make other people smile. For those candidates with the talent and flair to employ it, humor serves as a powerful tool for dealing with stereotypes. It was a valuable asset for Barbara Sigmund, a county commissioner in New Jersey, when a political opponent referred to her in public as a "witch." Shunning a direct counterattack, Sigmund donned a tall, black, pointed hat and carried a broomstick when she appeared in the state capital the next day. In a statement to a bevy of journalists, she laughed and noted that it was October and her opponent apparently was celebrating Halloween a bit early in the month. Sigmund's press coverage on that occasion more than compensated for any negative publicity his remark had generated.
>
> [2]In Maryland's 1976 congressional campaign Barbara Mikulski chose a direct, good-humored approach for undercutting potential negative reactions to her image as an outspoken woman. Mikulski specifically aimed her door-to-door campaigning at areas of the congressional district she ran in which were not part of the district she served on the Baltimore city council. The people in her council district liked her and knew her personally. But in the rest of the congressional district she felt

she had to prove she was not a "loud-mouthed broad" or a "six-foot, two-hundred-pound truck driver." When such epithets were hurled at her specifically, she turned them to her advantage by using a talent for public speaking. During her campaign she told the Civic Democratic Club: "My opponent is going around calling me a big mouth. Well, when they call me a big mouth, they're right. When I fought against putting massage parlors to keep the sleazos off Eastern Avenue, I was a big mouth. When I fought to keep the prison ship off our neighborhood, I was a big mouth. . . . And when I go to Congress and tell the President of the United States not to turn his back on the MIAs, they can call me a big mouth. That's okay, I'm proud of it."

[3]Yet sometimes it does seem as if women searching out the right posture for public life confront a choice between the pit and the pendulum. While finding good-humored ways to avoid being judged as offensive or stamped a "Bella Abzug," a "witch," or a "loudmouth," women cannot afford reticence. They must appear confident and outspoken to disabuse the public of another negative image—a widespread notion that women are political novices, thus unqualified for public leadership. In addition to deciding how feminine to look and sound, how assertive and outspoken to appear, and whether or not to move on the opponent with an attacking stance, women more than men must convince people that they know what public business is all about and that they are equipped to conduct it. Because she is assumed to be ill experienced outside the domestic sphere and her circle of personal relationships, a woman must consciously construct a public image which exudes competence. Female candidates for all levels of office feel pressure to prove themselves by spending a good deal of campaign time discussing complicated issues and asserting their ability to handle difficult problems. Despite the fact that election analyses have shown the public rarely deciding on the basis of issue expertise, female candidates are selecting competency as the most critical tool to hone for their success. It is gospel among them that a woman has to be twice as good and work twice as hard as a man to go half as far.

[4]Barbara Sigmund and Barbara Mikulski eschewed defensive responses to attacks on their public personalities. Since an angry reaction is more likely to confirm rather than to counteract a negative image, astute women like these are discovering other means for winning votes short of shaping their personal identities to fit an idealized cardboard cutout of political woman. They keep cool; they use humor to reverse a stereotype to their advantage; and most of all, they strive to make personal contact with the greatest possible number of voters because they are confident that once people know them, negative stereotypes will fade in the light of a more complex and more positive reality. —Ruth Mandel, *In the Running*

2. In her book *Women Winning,* Barbara Trafton reports that state representatives Barbara Roberts (Oregon) and Elizabeth Mitchell (Maine) advise new women officeholders to do eight things. Read the passage and answer the questions after it.

¹Be perceived early on as strong. Women who make it into elective office are usually the cream of the crop. We quickly earn respect among colleagues for our ability to grasp the issues, to work hard, and to maintain close contact with our constituents. So show your strengths: speak up at caucus meetings and committee sessions.

Discourage the perception that women know little about finance, business, and other "men's issues." "Women are expected to know about education and human resources," says Roberts, "but we're not supposed to know about taxation, bonding, trucking, agriculture, and timber management. So when we do know about these latter areas, we're twice as impressive." The committees in these areas tend to be powerful, since many of their decisions involve large sums of money. And they are often looking for token female members. By accepting an appointment to one of these committees, working hard at it, and making tough political decisions, you may find a short cut into the political power base. . . .

²Develop an expertise. Try to emerge as the star of your committee. Learn the issues, and learn which members of your body are most interested in each of them. If you become a resource person for your caucus on the complicated issues, you will be sought out to play a role in decision making.

Get to know your colleagues. Take an interest in caucus members from both conservative and liberal camps. Don't spend all your time working on issues, recommends James Tierney, former majority floor leader in Maine; you have to spend time working with people if you want to become a leader among them. "You have to make sure all the members of your caucus feel you care about them and their particular problems, such as replacing the fire station that just burned down in one district. If you come into the body with a narrow agenda—to push for day care centers and flex-time, for example—you may succeed on your issues, but your long-term relationship with your colleagues may suffer." Respect your colleagues' views, and tap their expertise whenever possible. Never impugn their integrity or motivations.

³Volunteer to help strengthen the caucus; earn a reputation as a hard-working member. When your race is easy, assist other candidates with their campaigns.

⁴Keep your perspective on your work. Many of us who entered politics in the mid-seventies were burning to solve the world's problems in our first terms, and we wore our emotions on our shirtsleeves. I

recall the majority floor leader of the Maine Senate telling me floor debate had doubled since I and two women colleagues had joined the body. It's fine to disagree, but do so without being disagreeable. Don't let yourself be labeled argumentative. Remember that today's opponents may well be tomorrow's allies.

⁵Keep your sense of humor. The double standards you encountered in your campaign won't vanish when you enter office, and it does no good to rail when your colleagues call you Mrs. and each other Senator, when you take a tough stand and are accused of being bitchy, or when you are referred to as "the pretty lady mayor." It may take many gentle but firm reminders to convince both colleagues and constituents that your looks and your housekeeping skills are irrelevant to the job at hand. In the meantime, hang on to your ability to laugh.

⁶Always assume your turn for a position of power is next. You can never be sure who will be around next session; a plum position may unexpectedly open up. Should an opportunity appear, be ready to move. But be patient—moving into a position of leadership takes time, whether you're a man or a woman.

Using the passage just quoted, a student made this note card:

> Trafton, Barbara M. _Women Winning_, p. 151
> Trafton gives the following rules for succeeding in politics:
> 1. Be perceived early on as strong.
> 2. Learn about the issues.
> 3. Develop an expertise.
> 4. Get to know your colleagues.
> 5. Volunteer.
> 6. Keep a perspective on your work.
> 7. Be humorous.
> 8. You'll get your turn at power.

a. What mistake(s) has the student made in the note card?
b. Write the card and correct the mistake(s) made.
c. If the student had used the material as it appears on the card in a paper, what would the student be guilty of?

3. Read these paragraphs from Jeane Kirkpatrick's book describing her study of women legislators. Answer the questions at the end.

On Winning and Losing

[1]Obviously the women in this study eventually won a seat in the legislature. But, as we have seen, not all won the first time they ran. About one-fourth have at some time lost a legislative election. Two lost their initial elections, two lost when they tried to move to the Senate, several lost a race after winning, then ran again. Losing holds no terror for them. The same high self-esteem which gives them a generalized expectation of success armors them against failure. Frequently, it is reinforced by "avoidance" defenses which block out awareness-threatening interpretations of events.

[2]All these women are achievement oriented, and some are explicitly competitive; none like to lose, but they are not terrified by the prospect nor destroyed by the experience. The ability to lose is a key characteristic of politicians as is the capacity to bear conflict. The capacity to lose without being psychologically destroyed or crippled requires, above all, *a high opinion of the self which is not basically vulnerable to the response of voters.*

[3]This does not necessarily imply self-esteem invulnerable to the opinion of others, only that the fundamental evaluation of the self is not at stake in all interpersonal relations. The attitudes of husband, children, or others related by ties of intimacy may be very important — even crucial — to the self-confidence of these women. But the reactions of constituents are not threatening to their self-esteem. The capacity to have positive, pleasant relations with others without a large (and therefore dangerous) psychological investment is a fundamental requisite for participation in democratic politics. . . .

[4]Responses to the questionnaire indicate self-consciousness about the ability to risk losing and failure. Almost three-fourths say they do not get very upset when they fail at something they try. Four-fifths deny that it is difficult for them to overcome disappointment. Most indicate that they have ready interpretations of loss which define it as irrelevant to basic self-estimates.

[5]Losing is bearable but winning is better. The women in this study enjoy winning, but they do not enjoy it too much. Two of them probably get intrinsic pleasure from conflict. The remainder participate in the competition that campaigns entail as means to ends other than winning. After a hard, often grueling campaign, victory seems to most just reward for hard work.

[6]There is no evidence either that winning per se enhances self esteem, it seems to be interpreted as proof of skill and industry, not of loveableness.

PRACTICE

Writing

1. a. Write a one-sentence paraphrase of each paragraph.
   b. Write a quotation card in which you quote the words *avoidance* and *self-esteem*.
   c. Write a note card in which you introduce Jeane Kirkpatrick as the author of the study from which this selection is taken.
   d. Write a note card in which you incorporate material into the following sentence: *Even though these women report that they like to win an election . . .*
   e. How would brackets improve the use of this quotation? "There is no evidence either that winning *per se* enhances self-esteem, it seems to be interpreted as proof of skill and industry, not of loveableness."

2. The Mandel book was published in 1981, Trafton in 1984, and Kirkpatrick in 1974. Reread the three selections (pp. 379–383).
   a. How important is the date of publication?
   b. Based on the short selection provided for you in this chapter how would you evaluate the usefulness of each?
   c. Look up at least one of the authors in a bibliographical reference book. Evaluate the author's credibility as an expert on the subject. (See pp. 329–330, argument chapter.)

3. Write a progress report, using at least 3 footnotes, describing your research thus far. You may find the following questions helpful.
   a. What is your "research question"? Do you have an answer? If not, why?
   b. Have you found an authority or quotation that has helped you narrow and focus your topic?
   c. Describe the kind and number of sources you have found. Did you have difficulty finding material?
   d. Have you had to change your topic? If so, why?
   e. When will you be ready to start writing?

A LIST OF REFERENCE WORKS

General Reference Works

Encyclopedias

Chambers's Encyclopedia, 4th ed. 15 vols. Elmsford, N.Y.: Maxwell Science International, 1973.

Collier's Encyclopedia. 24 vols. New York: Collier, 1949–1951. (Continuous revision). Yearbooks.

Concise Columbia Encyclopedia. 1 vol. New York: Columbia UP, 1983.

Encyclopedia Americana. International Edition. 30 vols. Danbury, CT: Grolier, 1985. Yearbooks.

The New Columbia Encyclopedia. 4th ed. 1 vol. New York: Columbia UP, 1975.

The New Encyclopaedia Britannica. 15th ed. 30 vols. (3 parts). Chicago: Britannica, 1985. Yearbooks.

Biographical Dictionaries and Indexes

Biography and Genealogy Index. 2nd ed. Detroit: Gale, 1980. Supplements.

Biography Index: A Cumulative Index to Biographical Material In Books and Magazines. New York: Wilson, 1946–date.

Current Biography. New York: Wilson, 1940–date.

Dictionary of American Biography. 22 vols. New York: Scribner's, 1928–1937. Supplements to 1960.

Dictionary of National Biography. Ed. Leslie Stephen and Sidney Lee. London: Oxford UP, 1908–1909. Supplements to 1960.

International Who's Who. London: Europa, 1935–date.

Webster's Biographical Dictionary. Rev. ed. Springfield, Mass.: Merriam, 1972.

Who's Who in America. Chicago: Marquis, 1899–date.

World Authors. Ed. John Wakeman. New York: Wilson, 1975. With supplements to 1975.

Almanacs

Facts on File. New York: Facts on File, 1940–date.

Information Please Almanac. New York: Simon, 1947–date.

The World Almanac and Book of Facts. New York: Newspaper Enterprise, 1868–date.

Atlases and Gazetteers

Atlas of American History. Rev. ed. New York: Scribner's, 1978.

Columbia-Lippincott Gazetteer of the World. Ed. Leon E. Seltzer. New York: Columbia UP, 1962.

Goode's World Atlas. Ed. Edward B. Espenshade, Jr. 16th ed. Chicago: Rand, 1982.

The Times Atlas of the World. 7th Comprehensive Edition. New York: Times, 1985.

Periodical Indexes

Humanities Index. New York: Wilson, June 1974–date.

Magazine Index. Los Altos, CA: Information Access, 1976–date. (Microfilm).

Nineteenth Century Readers' Guide to Periodical Literature, 1890–1899. 2 vols. New York: Wilson, 1944. With supplements to 1922.

Poole's Index to Periodical Literature, 1802–1881. Rev. ed. Boston: Houghton, 1891. Supplements to 1907.

Readers' Guide to Periodical Literature. New York: Wilson, 1900–date.

Social Sciences and Humanities Index (formerly titled *International Index,* now in two parts: *Humanities Index* and the *Social Sciences Index*). New York: Wilson, 1916–1974.

Social Sciences Index. New York: Wilson, June, 1974–date.

Newspaper Indexes

National Newspaper Index. Los Altos, CA: Information Access, 1979–date (Microfilm).

New York Times Index. Times, 1913–date.

Official Index to the (London) Times. London: Times, 1906–date.

Pamphlet Indexes

Vertical File Index: Subject and Title Index to Selected Pamphlet Material. New York: Wilson, 1935–date.

Book Review Indexes

Book Review Digest. Minneapolis: Wilson, 1905–date.

Book Review Index. Detroit: Gale, 1965–date.

Bibliographies

World Bibliography of Bibliographies, 1964–1974. 2 vols. Totowa, N.J.: Rowman, 1977. (Updates Besterman, Theodore.)

Bibliographic Index: A Cumulative Bibliography of Bibliographies. New York: Wilson, 1938–date.

Guide to Reference Books. Ed. by Eugene P. Sheehy. 9th ed. Chicago: ALA, 1980. Supplements.

Subject Guide to Books in Print. New York: Bowker, 1957–date.

Special Reference Works

Art and Architecture

The Art Index. New York: Wilson, 1929–date.

Chamberlin, Mary W. *Guide to Art Reference Books.* Chicago: ALA, 1959.

Contemporary Architects. Ed. Muriel Emanual. New York: St. Martin's, 1980.

Ehresmann, Donald L. *Fine Arts: A Bibliographic Guide to Basic Reference Works, Histories and Handbooks.* 2nd ed. Littleton, CO: Libraries Unlimited, 1979.

Encyclopedia of World Art. 15 vols. New York: McGraw, 1959–1968.

Naylor, Colin and Genesis P-Orridge, eds. *Contemporary Artists.* New York: St. Martin's, 1977.

Osborne, Harold, ed. *Oxford Companion to Twentieth Century Art.* New York: Oxford UP, 1981.

———, ed. *Oxford Companion to the Decorative Arts.* Oxford: Clarendon, 1975.

Sir Banister Fletcher's History of Architecture. Rev. J.C. Palmes. 18th ed. New York: Scribner's, 1975.

Businesses

Ammer, Christine, ed. *Dictionary of Business and Economics.* New York: Free, 1984.

Business Index. Menlo Park, CA: Information Access, 1979–date (Microfilm).

Business Periodicals Index. New York: Wilson, 1958–date.

Brusaw, Charles T., et al. *Business Writers Handbook.* 2nd ed. New York: St. Martin's, 1982.

Dow Jones-Irwin Business and Investment Almanac. Ed. Sumner N. Levine. Homewood, IL: Dow Jones-Irwin, 1985.

Encyclopedia of Business Information Sources. Ed. Paul Wasserman. Detroit: Gale, 1983.

McGraw-Hill Dictionary of Modern Economics: A Handbook of Terms and Organization. 3rd ed. Ed. Douglas Greenwald, et al. New York: McGraw, 1983.

Drama

Dramatic Criticism Index. Detroit: Gale, 1972.

Hartnoll, Phyllis, ed. *The Oxford Companion to the Theatre,* 3rd ed. London: Oxford UP, 1967.

McGraw-Hill Encyclopedia of World Drama. 2nd ed. 5 vols. Ed. Stanley Hochman. New York: McGraw, 1984.

New York Times Theatre Reviews. 15 vols. to date. New York: Times, 1971–1980.

Ottemiller's Index to Plays in Collections. 6th ed. rev. by John M. Connor and Billie M. Connor. Metuchen, N.J.: Scarecrow, 1976.

Play Index. 5 vols. New York: Wilson, 1949–1982.

Education

Current Index to Journals in Education. New York: Macmillan, 1969–date.

Education Index. New York: Wilson, 1929–date.

Education in the United States: A Documentary History. 5 vols. Ed. Sol Cohen. New York: Random, 1974.

Encyclopedia of Education. 10 vols. Ed. Lee C. Deighton. New York: Macmillan, 1971.

Encyclopedia of Educational Research. 5th ed. Ed. Harold E. Mitzel, New York: Free, 1982.

Dejnozka, Edward L., and David E. Kapel eds. *American Educator's Encyclopedia.* Westport, CT: Greenwood, 1982.

UNESCO. *World Survey of Education.* 5 vols. Paris: UNESCO, 1955–1971.

Film

Bawden, Liz-Anne, ed. *The Oxford Companion to Film.* London: Oxford UP, 1976.

Beaver, Frank E., ed. *Dictionary of Film Terms.* New York: McGraw, 1983.

Film Literature Index. Albany, N.Y.: Filmdex, 1974–date.

Halliwell, Leslie. *The Filmgoer's Companion.* 7th ed. New York: Hill and Wang, 1980.

Magill, Frank N. *Magill's Survey of Cinema: English Language Films.* First Series, 4 vols. Englewood Cliffs, N.J.: Salem, 1980.

———, ed. *Magill's Survey of Cinema: English Language Films.* Second Series, 6 vols. Englewood Cliffs, N.J.: Salem, 1981.

———, ed. *Magill's Survey of Cinema: Silent Films.* 3 vols. Englewood Cliffs: Salem, 1982.

New York Times Encyclopedia of Film. 13 vols. to date. New York: Times, 1984.

New York Times Film Reviews. 13 vols. to date. New York: Times, 1970–1982.

History

Adams, James Truslow. *Dictionary of American History.* 2nd rev. ed. 6 vols. and Index. New York: Scribner's, 1942–1976.

American History and Life. Santa Barbara: ABC-Clio, 1964–date.

The Cambridge Ancient History. 3rd ed. 12 vols. Cambridge: Cambridge UP, 1923–1939. 1970–1973.

The Cambridge Medieval History. 8 vols. New York: Macmillan, 1911–1936.

The Cambridge Modern History. 13 vols. Cambridge: Cambridge UP, 1902–1926.

Freidel, Frank, ed. *Harvard Guide to American History.* Rev. ed. 2 vols. Cambridge, Mass.: Belknap, Harvard UP, 1974.

Historical Abstracts. Parts A & B. Ed. Eric H. Boehm. Santa Barbara: ABC-Clio, 1955–date.

Langer, William L., Ed. *American Encyclopedia of World History: Ancient, Medieval and Modern Chronologically Arranged.* 5th ed. Boston: Houghton, 1972.

The New Cambridge Modern History. 14 vols. Cambridge: Cambridge UP, 1957–1970.

Literature

Abstracts of English Studies. Ed. William H. Magee, Canada: U of Calgary P, 1958–date.

Cambridge History of American Literature. 4 vols. Ed. William Peterfield Trent, New York: Putnam. 1917–1921.

Cambridge History of English Literature. 15 vols. Eds. A. W. Ward and A. R. Waller. Cambridge: Cambridge UP. 1908–1927.

Contemporary Literary Criticism: Excerpts from Criticism of the Works of Today's Novelists, Poets, Playwrights and Other Creative Writers. 31 vols. Ed. Carolyn Riley. Detroit: Gale, 1973–date.

Cook, Dorothy and Esebel S. Monro. *Short Story Index.* New York: Wilson, 1953. Supplements to 1983.

Essay and General Literature Index. New York: Wilson, 1934–date.

Granger's Index to Poetry. 7th ed. New York: Columbia UP, 1982.

Hart, James D. *The Oxford Companion to American Literature.* 4th ed. Rev. Dorothy Eagle. Oxford UP, 1983.

Holman, C. Hugh. *A Handbook to Literature.* 4th ed. (Based on original by William F. Thrall and Addison Hibbard.) Indianapolis: Bobbs, 1980.

Kunitz, Stanley J. and Howard Harcraft. *American Authors, 1600–1900.* New York: Wilson, 1938.

MLA International Bibliography of Books and Articles in the Modern Languages and Literature. New York: MLA, 1921–date.

The New Cambridge Bibliography of English Literature. 5 vols. Cambridge: Cambridge UP, 1969–1977.

Spiller, Robert, ed. *Literary History of the United States.* 4th rev. ed. 2 vols. New York: Macmillan, 1974.

Steinberg, S. H., ed. *Cassell's Encyclopedia of World Literature.* 3rd rev. ed. Ed. J. Buchanan Brown. New York: Morrow, 1973.

Twentieth Century Short Story Explication. 3rd ed. Hamden, CT: Shoestring, 1977. Supplements to 1981.

Music

Baker's Biographical Dictionary of Musicians. 7th ed. Rev. by Nicolas Slonimsky. New York: Schirmer, 1984.

Diamond, Harold, ed. *Music Criticism: An Annotated Guide to the Literature.* Metuchen: Scarecrow, 1978.

Green, Stanley. *Encyclopaedia of the Musical Theatre.* New York: Oxford UP, 1981.

Music Index. Detroit: Information Service, 1949–date.

New Grove Dictionary of Music and Musicians. 20 vols. Ed. Stanley Sadie. London: Macmillan, 1980.

New Grove Dictionary of Musical Instruments. 3 vols. Ed. Stanley Sadie. New York: Macmillan, 1984.

The New Oxford Companion to Music. Ed. Denis Arnold. New York: Oxford UP, 1983.

New Oxford History of Music. 10 vols. London: Oxford UP, 1954–1975.

Thompson, Oscar. *The International Cyclopedia of Music and Musicians.* 10th ed. Ed. Bruce Bohle. New York: Dodd, 1975.

Philosophy

Baldwin, James Mark. *Dictionary of Philosophy and Psychology.* 4 vols. Gloucester, MA: Peter Smith, 1960.

Dictionary of the History of Ideas. 5 vols. Ed. Philip P. Wiener. New York: Scribner's, 1973–74.

Encyclopedia of Philosophy. Ed. Paul Edwards. 4 vols. New York: Macmillan, 1973.

Philosopher's Index. Bowling Green, OH: Philosophy Documentation, 1967–date.

World Philosophy: Essay-Reviews of 225 Major Works. Ed. Frank N. Magill. Englewood Cliffs: Salem, 1982.

Political Science

Congress and the Nation. 5 vols. Washington: Congressional Quarterly, 1965–1981.

Cyclopedia of American Government. 3 vols. Eds. Andrew McLaughlin and Albert Bushnell Hart. New York: Appleton, 1914.

The Guide to American Law: Everyone's Legal Encyclopedia. 10 vols. St. Paul: West, 1983–1984.

History of U.S. Political Parties. 4 vols. Ed. Arthur M. Schlesinger, Jr. New York: Chelsea, 1973.

International Political Science Abstracts. Oxford: Blackwell, 1951–date.

Laqueur, Walter, ed. *A Dictionary of Politics.* Rev. ed. New York: Free, 1974.

Plano, Jack C., and Milton Greenberg. *The American Political Dictionary.* 6th ed. New York: Holt, 1982.

Public Affairs Information Service Bulletin. New York: Public Office Information, 1915–date.

Psychology

Baldwin, James Mark. (See *Philosophy*.)

Encyclopedia of Psychology. 4 vols. Ed. Raymond J. Corsini. New York: Wiley, 1984.

The Encyclopedic Dictionary of Psychology. Eds. Rom Harré and Roger Lamb. Cambridge: MIT P, 1983.

The Great Psychologists. 4th ed. Philadelphia: Lippincott, 1978.

Psychological Abstracts. Arlington: American Psychological, 1927–date.

Religion

Encyclopedia Judaica. 16 vols. New York: Macmillan, 1972. Supplement 1982.

Encyclopedia of Religion and Ethics. 2nd ed. 12 vols. Ed. James Hastings. New York: Scribner's, 1908–1927.

Hastings, James. *Dictionary of the Bible.* Rev. ed. Eds. F. C. Grant and H. H. Rowley. New York: Scribner's, 1977.

Interpreter's Bible. 12 vols. New York: Abington, 1952–1957.

The Interpreter's Dictionary of the Bible. 5 vols. New York: Abington, 1976. Supplement, 1976.

The Jerome Biblical Commentary. Ed. Raymond E. Brown, et al. Englewood Cliffs: Prentice-Hall, 1968.

New Catholic Encyclopedia. 17 vols. New York: McGraw, 1967–1979.

The Oxford Dictionary of the Christian Church. 2nd ed. Eds. F. L. Cross and E. A. Livingstone. London: Oxford UP, 1974.

Religion Index One. Chicago: American Theological Library, 1953–date.

Science

Applied Science and Technology Index. New York: Wilson, 1913–date. (Before 1958, see *Industrial Arts Index.*)

Biological and Agricultural Index. New York: Wilson, 1916–date. (Formerly *Agricultural Index.*)

Encyclopedia of Computer Science and Engineering. 2nd ed. Eds. Anthony Ralson and Edwin E. Reilly, Jr. Cincinnati: Van Nostrand, 1983.

The Environment Index. New York: Environment Information Access, 1971–date.

Fishbein's Illustrated Medical and Health Encyclopedia. 22 vols. Westport, CT: Stuttman, 1981.

History of Technology. 8 vols. Ed. Charles Singer, et al. Oxford: Clarendon, 1954–1984.

McGraw-Hill Dictionary of Scientific and Technical Terms. 3rd edition. Ed. Sybil P. Parker. New York: McGraw, 1984.

McGraw-Hill Encyclopedia of Science and Technology. 5th ed. 15 vols. New York: McGraw, 1982.

Science and Engineering Literature: A Guide to Sources. 3rd ed. Ed. Robert Malenowsky. Littleton, CO: Libraries Unlimited, 1980.

Van Nostrand's Scientific Encyclopedia. 6th ed. Cincinnati: Van Nostrand, 1983.

Social Sciences and Sociology

Abstracts in Anthropology. New York: Baywood, 1970–date.

The Combined Retrospective Index Set to Journals in Sociology, 1895–1974. 6 vols. Eds. Annadel N. Wile and Arnold Jaffe. Washington: Carollton, 1978.

Encyclopedia of the Social Sciences. 15 vols. Eds. Edwin R. A. Seligman and Alvin Johnson. New York: Macmillan, 1930–1935.

Encyclopedia of Sociology. Rev. ed. Guilford, CT: DPG Reference, 1981.

Gallup, George H. *The Gallup Poll, 1935–1971.* 3 vols. New York: Random, 1972.

———, *The Gallup Poll.* 1972–1977. 2 vols. Delaware: Scholarly Resources, 1978.

International Encyclopedia of the Social Sciences. 18 vols. Ed. David L. Sills. New York: Macmillan, 1968. Supplement 1978.

Larousse Encyclopedia of World Geography. London: Westbook, 1964.

Sociological Abstracts. San Diego: Sociological Abstracts, 1953–date.

Worldmark Encyclopedia of the Nations. 6th ed. 5 vols. New York: Worldmark, 1984.

CHAPTER 18
WRITING THE RESEARCH PAPER

After doing your research carefully and before beginning the step of classifying your evidence, you should have three kinds of information: (1) bibliography cards that give accurate and brief descriptions of all your sources; (2) note cards, keyed to the bibliography cards that contain paraphrases and quotations of important material; (3) bits of information that you have retained from reading. (In a general way, this last kind of information is of subtle but considerable help in writing your paper.)

Now set aside your bibliography cards and follow these steps:

Step 1: Classify evidence: develop a preliminary plan and thesis.
Step 2: Study documentation, make a list of *Works Cited,* and write a rough draft.
Step 3: Revise the rough draft.
Step 4: Write the final draft and proofread.

STEP 1: CLASSIFY EVIDENCE: DEVELOP A PRELIMINARY PLAN AND THESIS

Group your note cards by title and subtitle. In such groupings, you have the beginning of a preliminary plan and thesis. You may make one or two other plans before you are finally satisfied with your organization. This first step may indicate any gaps in your research, perhaps requiring you to re-read your notes and survey your sources again, or even to make another trip to the library. Your first or second plan may show you where you can use your own experience and knowledge *(role)* to tie up various aspects of your research. It may also show you how to make your paper more interesting for your *audience*.

After Judy Goldsmith made her first plan from a grouping of note cards, she discovered that she had to make adjustments *twice* before she was satisfied with her final outline and thesis. Her classification of note cards fell into groups like the following:

Women Politicians

lack power at all levels
family cooperation important
need to be strong, not afraid of losing
must fight stereotypes held about women
law and business good professions for politics
must be knowledgeable on many issues
need to be aggressive and work hard
must take initiative and run for office
volunteerism — good training

Since Judy knew that she had to narrow her topic, she wouldn't be able to use the material in all her groupings. Therefore, she chose groups of cards that seemed to be logically related and would answer her question (see p. 363). Then she diagrammed a rough plan from which she would test her preliminary thesis: (See *suport diagrams,* pp. 60–61 and p. 395.)

> *Preliminary*   In order to succeed in politics, women must take the initia-
> *Thesis:*   tive and run for office, fight the stereotype of women, and be
>   knowledgeable on many issues.

In looking over her rough plan and preliminary thesis, Judy realized that her points were neither interesting nor persuasive. In addition, the thesis didn't answer the question of what political candidates should *be*. Her first point was out of date for the young college women of 1986 who

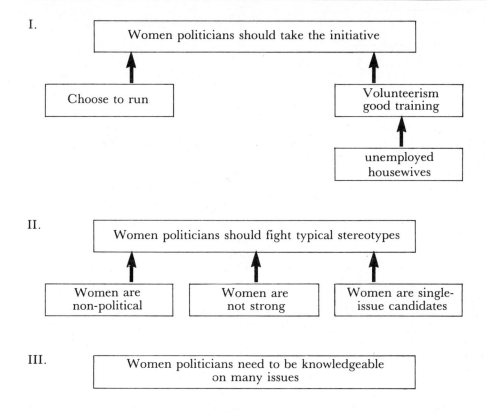

I.

Women politicians should take the initiative

Choose to run

Volunteerism
good training

unemployed
housewives

II.

Women politicians should fight typical stereotypes

Women are
non-political

Women are
not strong

Women are single-
issue candidates

III.

Women politicians need to be knowledgeable
on many issues

might find the volunteer route an unacceptable way to enter politics.
Then Judy decided to test her preliminary plan and thesis against her
stance (see p. 363). In her narrative she had described her role as a political
science major who wanted a career in politics. Her preliminary thesis and
plan had nothing to do with *education,* a point that she had identified as being important. She decided that the direction her paper was taking in the
first plan didn't fit her role or her purpose in choosing the subject.

Her audience was her instructor and students in the composition
class and, perhaps, her political science teachers. But her handling of the
subject did not accurately describe the picture of the future of the woman
political candidate in the next decades, so her paper written from this plan
would probably not interest them. Judy then decided to go back to her
sources and note cards.

In the second analysis of her subject, she decided to give more emphasis to the point she had neglected in her first plan—*women politicians
lack power.* She also decided to deal with *volunteerism* as history. Since she
had found studies showing that law and business provide training and a
quick entry into politics, she revised her plan:

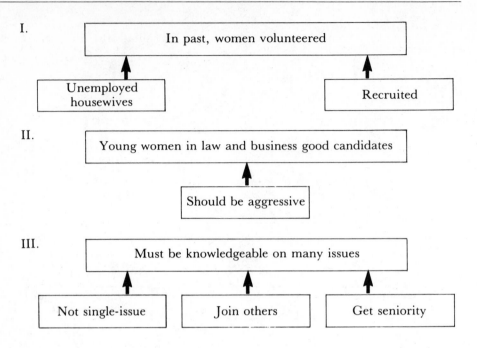

I.

In past, women volunteered

Unemployed housewives

Recruited

II.

Young women in law and business good candidates

Should be aggressive

III.

Must be knowledgeable on many issues

Not single-issue

Join others

Get seniority

From this plan, Judy developed her final thesis:

> *Thesis:*   If women want to consider politics as a career, they should aggressively seek office and achieve seniority and power by being knowledgeable in many fields. (*Note:* This is the thesis of the model research paper, pp. 410 – 421.)

From this second plan, Judy developed an outline with her sub-points more logically tied to her main points. See p. 411 for Judy's final outline. Also see Chapter 4 for more information about writing an outline.

STEP 2: STUDY DOCUMENTATION, MAKE A LIST OF WORKS CITED, AND WRITE A ROUGH DRAFT

You are now ready to write your rough draft, using your outline (or plan) to guide you and keep you on track. However, before you start to write, study the MLA documentation forms (pp. 404–408). You will note that three forms of documentation are discussed: parenthetical, footnote, and endnote. Your instructor will tell you which form is required. (The model research paper uses the parenthetical form.)

In this chapter we will cover the conventions and rules in the following order:

(1) Rules for a list of *Works Cited* (or *Bibliography*)
(2) Rules for parenthetical documentation
(3) Rules for endnote documentation
(4) Rules for footnote documentation

We have arranged the systems of documentation in this order so that we can show you how the parenthetical form relies on the list of *Works Cited.* Therefore, as you study the parenthetical form, check back to our *Works Cited* section so that you can see why it is so important to compile your list *before* you write your rough draft. We suggest that you follow this plan as you go through your bibliography and note cards.

1. Alphabetize your bibliography cards, the works you cite in your paper.

2. Make a list (alphabetized) from your cards, leaving plenty of white space between items. This will help you to add new items in case you find a reference you had previously missed, but one that you want to quote. (This process will also be useful if you choose the endnote or footnote form because you will have a cross-check on your references.)

3. Whenever you draw on material from a note card—direct quotation, paraphrase, or summary—put a number in your rough draft where you have used the material. Put that same number on the note card. Do this even if you choose the parenthetical form; otherwise you may lose track of where your references were used in the text. If your rough draft uses twenty separate references, you should have twenty cards numbered consecutively in the same way that you use them in your paper.

After you have listed your sources in your preliminary *Works Cited,* start to write from your plan or outline. Do not begin with the introduction, but start with the body of your paper. It is very easy to get so tied up with your introduction that you fail to get a good start on your main points. As you write, do not look back and do not revise until you have written a complete section, such as the first main point. Some writers find that keeping *paragraphs* on separate *sheets of paper* will allow them to edit parts of the paper before putting them all together. Writing a little piece at a time may be a less onerous task than facing the entire paper, particularly if your blocks of time are limited to an hour or two. After all the pieces are put together, you can edit and revise (see chapters 10 and 15.)

STEP 3: REVISE THE ROUGH DRAFT

*A*fter you have written your rough draft from your outline or plan, use the following checklist to see if your material is as logically organized, clear, and accurate as you can make it.

Check List for the Rough Draft

Outline

1. Is your thesis placed at the top of the outline page so that it can be checked against the outline?
2. Do each of your first-level points (I, II, III, etc.) support the thesis?
3. Do your second-level points (A, B, C, etc.) support your first-level ones?
4. Are the items in the outline parallel in content and in form? Did you use complete sentences for all first- and second-level points? (The sentence outline is preferred for research papers, but your instructor may want you to use another form.)

Introduction

1. Is your thesis clearly stated?
2. Have you shown why the topic is important enough to interest your reader?
3. Have you defined any terms that the reader should clearly understand?

Body

1. Have you checked your reasoning in the paper?
   a. Are your generalizations supported by well-chosen evidence?
   b. Are your causal relationships logical?
   c. Have you checked your facts? Your sources?
2. Are your paragraphs unified and logical?
3. Have you used your sources properly?
   a. Do your sources support your ideas and points?
   b. Are your quotations integrated with your own ideas?
4. Have you reviewed the material on paraphrasing and quoting (pp. 375–379)?

5. Have you used correct quotation, note, parenthetical, and bibliography forms?
    a. Did you give a complete note reference for the first time you used a source in the paper?
    b. Did you check the bibliography against your notes to see that you have included all sources?

Conclusion

1. Do you have a concluding paragraph which restates the thesis and rounds off the paper?
2. Have you introduced any new and significant ideas in the conclusion (usually a poor idea)?

Proofreading

1. Have you read the paper aloud at least once, listening and watching for anything that doesn't sound and look right?
2. Did you avoid shifts in tense and person?
3. Are your parallel ideas stated in parallel form?
4. Have you overused the passive voice?
5. Are your signals and transitions clear so that your reader can follow your organization?
6. Have you used words precisely and accurately?
7. Have you avoided errors in spelling, grammar, and punctuation?
8. Have you proofread for typographical errors?

See chapter 10 (p. 196) on revision to guide you further. Most of the same rules apply to the research paper that you have used for revising other forms of writing.

STEP 4: WRITE THE FINAL DRAFT AND PROOFREAD

The final draft of your paper should be typed, double-spaced, on 8½ × 11-inch sheets. (If you are lucky enough to have the use of a word processor, check to see if your instructor will accept a computer print-out, particularly if you have a letter-quality printer.) Write on one side of the paper, leaving top, bottom, and left margins of an inch. Except for the title page, number all pages consecutively in the upper-right corner, beginning with page one, one-half inch from the top. Starting with page two, type your last name just before the page number, but without any punctuation marks, or p's for *page*.

Research Paper Without a Title Page

On the first page, keeping a margin of one inch from the top, type your name, instructor's name, course number and date on separate lines, double-spaced, and flush with the left margin. Center the title, and double-space twice between the title and the text.

```
Judy Goldsmith

Mr. Jones

Rhetoric 102

May 3,1986
                    Tough, Strong Women:   Politics as a Career


Ever since women . . .
```

Research Paper With a Title Page

The same kind of information is provided on a title page, but arranged differently. (See title page of model research paper, p. 410).

Before handing in the paper, proofread it one last time, following instructions on pp. 207 and 399.

Be sure to photocopy your research paper and keep it in a safe place in case you wish to refer to it at a later date.

THE LIST OF WORKS CITED (BIBLIOGRAPHY)

The *Works Cited (bibliography)* provides your reader with an alphabetized list of sources you used in the paper — those you cited in notes or in parentheses. Your instructor may also want you to list all the sources you have read or consulted. If that is the case, you may add another section entitled *"Works Consulted."*

Arrange the entries in your *Works Cited* in alphabetical order by the surname of the author. When no author is given, use the first word of the title; when the title begins with an article (*a, an,* or *the*) or with a preposition, use the second word. If you have two sources written by the same author, it is not necessary to repeat the author's name in the second entry. Instead, type 3 hyphens, follow with a period, skip two spaces, and give the title:

> Kirkpatrick, Jeane. *The New Presidential Elite: Women in National Politics.*
>   New York: Basic Books, 1976.
> - - -. *Political Woman.* New York: Basic Books, 1974.

Be aware of the slight difference between the use of commas and periods here and in the notes; also note that parentheses are not used to set off the place of publication, publisher, and date. In addition, the *first* line of each bibliography entry is flush to the left margin, while subsequent ones are indented about five spaces.

Books

The general rule is: Give author (last name first), title of book, place of publication, publisher, and date.

One Author:
>   Sapiro, Virginia. *The Political Integration of Women: Roles, Socializa-*
>   *tion, and Politics.* Urbana: U of Illinois P, 1983.

Two or More Authors:
>   Gelb, Joyce and Marian Lief Palley. *Women and Public Policies.*
>   Princeton, NJ: Princeton UP, 1982.

No Author:
Note: If the book cited has no author, give name of the book first.

Editor or Translator:
> Stewart, Debra W., ed. *Women in Local Politics.* Metuchen, NJ: Scarecrow, 1980.

Note: The name of the translator would come after the title of the book: Trans. _____. If there is more than one editor, use *eds.*, after giving both names as you have done with two authors (see above).

Government Publication or Corporate Author:
> Center for the American Woman and Politics. *Women Appointed to State Boards and Commissions.* New Brunswick, NJ: Rutgers U, 1975.

Edition or Revision:
> Baxter, Sandra and Marjorie Lansing. *Women and Politics: The Visible Majority.* Rev. ed. Ann Arbor: U of Michigan P, 1983.

Article Reprinted in a Collection:
> Mezey, Susan Gluck. "Perceptions of Women's Roles on Local Councils in Connecticut," *Women in Local Politics.* Ed. Debra W. Stewart. Metuchen, NJ: Scarecrow, 1980.

Note: If you cite more than one article in a collection, give complete bibliographic information for the collection (see Stewart reference under *Editor or Translator*). Rather than citing the entire bibliographic information for the Stewart collection every time you use an article from the book, give only the last name of the editor as given below:

> Mezey, Susan Gluck. "Perceptions of Women's Roles on Local Councils in Connecticut," Stewart 177–197.

Introduction, preface, forward, or afterward of a book:
> Perry, Lewis. Forward. *Freedom, Feminism and the State.* Ed. Wendy McElroy. Washington, DC: Cato Institute, 1982.

Reference Works

If the reference is well known:
> "Women, Status of," *Encyclopedia Americana,* 1983 ed.

Note: If the article has an author, give author first.

Note: If the reference is unfamiliar, give complete bibliographic information:

> Gager, Nancy, ed. *Women's Rights Almanac.* New York: Harper and Row, 1974.
> *Guide to American Law: Everyone's Legal Encyclopedia,* 10 vols. St. Paul: West, 1983–1984.

Periodicals and Newspapers

Because you will need volume or series number when you deal with scholarly journals, follow this order: author's name, title of the article, name of the periodical, series number or name, volume number, date of publication, and page numbers. If the periodical is published daily, weekly, or monthly, omit volume and issue numbers.

> Caudle, Sheila. "Geraldine Ferraro: A Woman for This Political Season?" *Ms.* July 1984: 61–65.
>
> Dold, R. Bruce. "Women in Politics Grow in Influence." *Chicago Tribune* 21 September 1984 sec. 1:6.
>
> Jennings, M. Kent. "Gender Roles and Inequalities in Political Participation: Results from an Eight-Nation Study." *The Western Political Quarterly* 36 (1983): 364–85.

Interviews

Give the name of the person interviewed, form of interview, and date. If the person interviewed is not well known to your reader, give his or her title in parentheses.

> Sattherthwaite, Helen. Representative (Illinois State Legislature). Personal interview. 8 June 1987.

PRACTICE

Listed below in a scrambled fashion are four sources:

> Wasson, Kyle: *Journal of Psychiatry;* (October 1954); pp. 201–215; vol. 22; "Notes on Insanity."
>
> V. R. Belle; 1965; Harper & Row; *What is Sanity?*; New York.
>
> Rivers, Karen; pp. 10–15; "Craziness"; ed. J. B. Goode; Boston; *Psychoanalytical Interpretations of Fundamental Behavior:* Houghton Mifflin; 1955.
>
> Falk, Peter and J. Q. Stuart; Chicago; 1961; *Stanislavsky and the Normal Mind;* Univ. of Chicago Press.

Using proper bibliographical form, unscramble each of the items and put them in alphabetical order. Be sure your punctuation matches that in the models provided on pages 401–402.

DOCUMENTATION: PARENTHETICAL FORM, ENDNOTES, AND FOOTNOTES

*T*he forms used in documenting papers vary considerably from discipline to discipline. A note in a biology journal may not look very much like a note in a journal devoted to geology. Nor would a note in a journal of literary criticism necessarily look like either of these two. And there are even variations within disciplines. Many book and journal publishers that produce material on English literature and composition use the note and bibliography forms authorized by the Modern Language Association. These are the forms we recommend.*

Documentation gives the reader the source of the fact, paraphrase, or quotation you use in your paper. It says to the reader: "Here is where I found this information in case you are interested in pursuing the subject further."

Parenthetical Documentation

Parenthetical documentation has certain advantages over endnotes or footnotes. First, your readers have the reference in the text so that they can tell immediately where you found your material. With the source in the text, the reader doesn't have to look down at a footnote or turn pages to look for your list of endnotes. If readers want the complete citation, they can look at your alphabetized *Works Cited* to find the complete reference.

In order for these advantages to work, however, all parenthetical references must be clear enough so that an exact match in the *Works Cited* is possible. If you keep your readers in mind, you can give them information in the text itself or in parentheses so they know exactly who or what you are quoting. For example, if you use the author's name in the text, you do not have to give it again in the parenthetical documentation (unless you are using two works by the same author). If you don't give the author's name in the text, then you provide it in the parentheses. Using the books referred to in our *Works Cited* (pp. 420–421), we will show you how the parenthetical documentation system works.

---

*There are several excellent paperbacks available which deal comprehensively with the problems of footnoting, bibliography, and the research paper generally. Two of the best are James D. Lester's *Writing Research Papers: A Complete Guide,* Fifth Edition (Glenview, IL: Scott, Foresman, 1987), and Kate Turabian's *A Manual for Writers of Term Papers, Theses, and Dissertations,* 4th Edition (Chicago: U of Chicago Press, 1982).

Author not named in the text:

Single mothers are not as active in politics as married mothers (Sapiro 124).

The author named in the text:

Sapiro found that single mothers are not as active in politics as married mothers (124).

Citing a work listed by title:

Geraldine Ferraro claims to have caused some of her own misery during her campaign for Vice President ("Ferraro").

Citing a multi-volume work:

The Women's Equity Action League has sent up a tax-deductible fund which lobbies for enforcement of equal opportunity and pays for legal activities connected with enforcement of civil rights legislation (Guide, 10: 403)

Citing a work when the *Works Cited* contains two or more works by the same author:

Since law school has only recently been open to large numbers of women, few women previously held the necessary professional qualifications for politics (Kirkpatrick, *Political Woman* 60).

Citing an indirect source:

Kanter defines *tokenism* as "the means by which the dominant group advertises a promise of mobility between the dominant and excluded classes" (qtd. in Mezey 178).

Note Forms

When note forms are used in documentation, the notes are numbered consecutively, just as you number them in your paper. In the paper itself the number is placed after the punctuation mark.

Content Notes in Parenthetical Documentation

Sometimes you will have reason to give your reader information that is too bulky or inappropriate for the text itself. Or perhaps you will need to cite several sources that would interfere with the readability of your paper if you listed all of them parenthetically. In these two cases, use notes, number them consecutively and place them at the bottom of each page (where the citation occurs) or, better yet, at the end of the paper before the *Works Cited.* See notes #1 and #2 in the model research paper, p. 419.

Endnotes

Sample First-Note References

Books

The general rule is: Give author, title, place of publication, publisher, date, and page number, in that order. *Note:* In providing the source in either endnotes or footnotes, as well as in the bibliography, be most careful in your placement of parentheses, commas, and other punctuation marks.

One Author:

¹Jean J. Kirkpatrick, *Political Woman* (New York: Basic Books, 1976) 48.

Two or More Authors:

²Joyce Gelb and Marian Lief Palley, *Women and Public Policies* (Princeton, NJ: Princeton UP, 1982) 76.

No Author:

³"Women's Equity Action League and Fund," *Guide to American Law* (St. Paul: West, 1983–84) 10, 403.

Editor:

⁴Debra W. Stewart, ed., *Women in Local Politics* (Metuchen, NJ: Scarecrow, 1980) 3.

Editors:

⁵Marianne Githens and Jewel L. Prestage, eds., *A Portrait of Marginality: The Political Behavior of American Women* (New York: Longman, 1977) 7.

Government Document or Corporate Author:

⁶Center for the American Woman and Politics, *Women Appointed to State Boards* (New Brunswick, NJ: Rutgers U, 1975) 13.

Edition or Revision:

⁷Sandra Baxter and Marjorie Lansing, *Women and Politics: The Visible Majority,* Rev. ed. (Ann Arbor: U of Michigan P, 1983) 25.

Article Reprinted in a Collection:

⁸Elizabeth G. King, "Women in Iowa Legislative Politics," *A Portrait of Marginality: The Political Behavior of the American Woman,* eds., Marianne Githens and Jewel L. Prestage (New York: Longman, 1977) 297.

Reference Works

Although they are books, reference works that are alphabetically arranged do not need the publisher or page and volume number if they are well known. The general rule is: Give author, title of article, title of reference work, and year of publication. If the work is not well known, give complete bibliographic information.

⁹"Women, Status of," *Encyclopedia Americana* 1983 ed.
¹⁰Nancy Gager, *Women's Rights Almanac* (New York: Harper & Row, 1974) 394.

Periodicals

The general rule: Give author, title of article, title of periodical date, page number. Scholarly publications with continuous pagination, use volume number, year, and date.

¹¹Sheila Caudle, "Geraldine Ferraro: A Woman for This Political Season?" *Ms.* July 1984: 63.
¹²M. Kent Jennings, "Gender Roles and Inequalities in Political Participation: Results from an Eight-Nation Study." *The Western Political Quarterly* 36 (1983): 365.

Newspapers

Use the same format as you would with a periodical that is paged anew with each issue; in addition indicate the edition, if known, and the section before the page number.

[13]R. Bruce Dold, "Women in Politics Grow in Influence," *Chicago Tribune* 21 September 1984 sec. 1: 6.

Interviews

Give the name of the person interviewed, title and affiliation, the place, date, and kind (personal or telephone) of interview.

[14]Helen Satterthwaite, personal interview, 8 June 1985.

Endnotes as They Might Appear in a Paper

The first time you cite a source in your paper, put down all the information about the source in the endnote. Subsequent references usually require only the name of the author and the relevant page number(s). A word of caution: if you have two or more works by the same author, you will need to add the title (or a shortened version of it) so your reader knows which work provided the information. If there is no author, use the abbreviated title and page number instead. Here is a list of endnotes to illustrate the procedure.

One book by the author:

[5]Peggy Lamson, *In the Vanguard: Six American Women in Public Life* (Boston: Houghton Mifflin, 1979) 15.
[6]Lamson, 46–47.

If you also cited another book by Lamson in your paper you would have to do it this way:

[6]Lamson, *Vanguard,* 46–47.
[7]Lamson, *Changing Politics,* 79

When no author is given:

[9]"Ferraro", *Chicago Tribune* 1 January 1985 sec. 1: 4.
[10]"Ferraro", sec. 1: 4.

Footnotes

Footnotes follow the same format as endnotes, except that they appear on the same page as do the note numbers in the text. Separate the footnotes from the text by two double-spaces. Single-space the footnotes, indent each as a paragraph, and double-space between each note.

SAMPLE RESEARCH PAPER

*T*he sample research paper and outline written on the subject of women in politics will show you the culmination of one student's efforts. The paper contains many of the techniques and forms discussed in this chapter so that you can see how they work together in an actual situation. Here are a few things you should note about the format of the paper:

1. The body is double-spaced, with block quotations indented ten spaces and also double-spaced.

2. The outline, notes, and *Works Cited* are double-spaced both within and between each entry.

3. The numbers preceding each paragraph have been added so that you can refer to specific paragraphs when discussing the paper. (You should *not* use such numbers in your own paper.)

The Practice (p. 423) not only should give you a better understanding of the principles and conventions illustrated in the paper; it should also help you apply them to your own efforts.

Note: If your paper does not begin with an outline or abstract, it does not require a title page. See instructions (p. 400).

Tough, Strong Women: Politics as a Career

by

Judy Goldsmith

Rhetoric 102,   Section A-4

Instructor: Mr. Jones

May 3, 1986

1

Thesis: If women want to consider politics as a career, they should aggressively
seek office and achieve seniority and power by being knowledgeable in many
fields.

I. In the past, women have entered politics late in life through

    volunteerism.

    A. Many were unemployed housewives who worked as volunteers in the local and

       state levels.

    B. They were generally recruited to run for office.

    C. They failed to get seniority and power because they entered politics late.

    D. The exceptions were women trained in law and business who entered

       politics without the long apprenticeship of volunteerism.

II. Young women trained in the professions should consider politics

    as a career.

    A. Law and business are ideally suited to politics.

       1. They provide good training in bargaining and compromise.

       2. They allow for flexibility.

    B. Women should gain visibility by aggressively seeking office.

       1. Move out of solitary positions in government service.

       2. Go door to door in the community.

    C. They need to be tough.

III. Women will have to be knowledgeable about many issues.

     A. They should not be single-issue candidates.

     B. They should join other women to get power and influence.

     C. They should build a power base and gain seniority.

Goldsmith 2

Ever since women got the vote in 1920, there has been a slow but steady
increase in the number of women voting, of women in positions of leadership,
and of women representatives in Congress and the country's legislatures.
However, women haven't achieved the power and seniority that they hoped for.
Generally they do not hold key positions of influence in our legislative
assemblies. To make up for this lack of political power, they have demanded
equal rights, particularly in education and the work place. Professions that
had previously been male-dominated and closed to women have opened up as a

1.
result of universities and colleges being forced to admit women into their
professional programs. Two of those professions--law and business--provide
practical training for a career in politics. As more young women establish
themselves in law and business, they should consider politics as a career,
using their legal and business knowledge to help women gain power at the state
and national levels. If they do decide to consider politics as a career, they
should aggressively seek office and achieve seniority and power by being
knowledgeable in many fields.

Our political system, particularly at the state and local levels, has
depended heavily on the volunteer efforts of married women. It isn't
surprising, then, that most women legislators have moved through the ranks of
public service and volunteerism to political office. Jeane Kirkpatrick's study
of forty-six women state legislators (serving in 1971), showed that almost all

2.
of the women who were successful candidates for political office fifteen years
ⓐ ago, moved from housewife to volunteer worker to legislator (61). Elizabeth
King found a similar pattern in her study of thirty-three Iowa women
legislators who were serving in 1972. Most of these women were unemployed
housewives who moved from volunteer to candidate (288). Most of the women in
both studies did not actively seek election, but were recruited by friends or

Goldsmith 3

party members. None of the women in the King study decided to run on their own
(289). But forty-percent of the Kirkpatrick sample decided to run without
"being approached, or sounded out, or persuaded by anyone" (71).

Extrapolating from these two studies, we might conclude that in the decade
of 1960-70, few women volunteered to run for political office or chose politics
as a career. Even Mildred Fenwick, a successful congresswoman of the ninety-
fourth Congress, says that she did not consciously head for a career in
politics, but "was sort of gliding in by the unpaid volunteer backdoor route"
(qtd. in Lamson 15).

The women who have gone the route of housewife to volunteer to legislator
have made valuable contributions to our political system. However, since many
of them waited until their children were grown before entering politics, their
median age was usually between forty-five to fifty, a fact that Frieda L.
Gehlen found in her study of women in Congress (307). This means that most of
these women have been in politics too short a time to build a power base and
gain seniority. As a result, many women legislators have been ineffective.
Marianne Githens describes their dilemma:

> . . . women desire to run for and get themselves elected to public
> office. They achieve this objective too late, however, and without
> the "specialist" training that permits them to entertain further
> political ambition. The low status they enjoy because of their prior
> occupations limits them in their activities in the legislature once
> they get there. . . . ("Spectators" 208)

The exceptions to the situation described by Githens are the women lawyers
who move into politics without a long apprenticeship of volunteerism and who
have the "specialist" training necessary. The six lawyers in Kirkpatrick's
study ran for office and were elected without going through the long

apprenticeship of volunteer work that was necessary for other women.
Furthermore, the women lawyers were younger when elected, giving them more time
(F) to be re-elected and to establish seniority (83).

      The time has come for young women trained in business and law to choose
(G) politics as a second career and move into positions of power. Many studies
point to law and business as professions giving experience and training in
bargaining and compromising--political skills that seem necessary for success
in government (Mezey 71). The professions of law and business also give a
6.   legislator flexibility. It is possible for men and women practicing these
professions to be gone for periods of time whereas teachers, social workers,
and other professionals cannot leave their desks to be legislators. It is also
(H) in the best interests of both women and men in law and business to be active in
politics because most legislation affects business and legal interests
(Githens, "Spectators" 197).

      Positions of power and influence are held by men and women in law and
business. A study of the Maryland legislature (1971-73) shows that even though
lawyers made up less than half of the total legislature, of the six standing
7.   committee chairpersons four were lawyers, the fifth was a businessman with a
(I) law degree, and the sixth was in business.[1] The only woman lawyer in the
legislature was a standing committee chairperson (Githens, "Spectators" 198).

(J)   However, just being trained in law or business doesn't necessarily get a
woman candidate elected. She must aggressively seek office and be visible in
her district. In the past, many women have been almost invisible in their
8.   political activities, allowing men to take the best positions so that the men
were noticed, not the women. Diane Margolis reports in her study of women's
activities in local poloitics: "Women's activities tended to take place in
situations where they would not be widely observed; the reverse was true of

Goldsmith 5

men's activities" (26). Women candidates who wish to succeed must get involved

in large-group political activities, working with many people rather than in

isolation in order to get visibility. Another way to get visibility is to go

out into the community, where one can seek volunteers to support a campaign and

solicit votes and contributions by door-to-door visits. Minette Dodere, who

ran for the Iowa legislature in 1980, spent two hours every evening ringing

doorbells. She also attended as many public meetings in her district as

possible (qtd. in Trafton 110).

(K)   Women have an advantage in door-to-door solicitation. They will be

admitted to homes more readily than men, particularly in the evening hours

after dusk. Consequently, they will be able to use the evening hours to their

9.   advantage. Since a woman usually opens the door in the evening hours, women

candidates will be invited into the home more often than men (Trafton 128).

Women should take advantage of the trust and receptiveness that families have

toward a female candidate.

      But it isn't enough to be trained in the two most popular professions for

politics, and it isn't enough to be an aggressive candidate. A woman running

for office must be tough, tough enough to withstand personal attacks. Women

candidates are often the victims of false allegations because they are not

staying home or doing typical female jobs.[2] So their male opponents sometimes

believe that they can attack a woman's private life. As early as 1978,

10.   Geraldine Ferraro while running for Congress, had to fight against "allegations

that her marriage was in trouble, rumors that she was having sexual affairs

with several men, and accusations that she was a lesbian" (qtd. in Mandel 64).

After her defeat as vice-presidential candidate in 1984, she said that her

(L)   campaign taught her that she is a "tough broad" ("Ferraro"). One can believe

that she is tough because she has survived in American politics.

Harassment can occur at the state level also. Maxine Waters, a black
California state legislator reports that when she first entered the California
state legislature, "all kinds of roadblocks (were) put in my way simply because
11.
of this perception they had of this black woman coming from Los Angeles who
needed to be taught a lesson." She prevailed over the "roadblocks" and became
Assembly majority whip (Marshall 58).

In addition to being tough, a woman candidate must be informed on many
issues. She must acknowledge her interest in the home and family, but she
cannot be a single-issue candidate. During a politician's career, she will
have opportunities to vote on a variety of issues, not just those that interest
her the most. Barbara M. Trafton, a Democratic National Committee woman and
for six years a member of the Maine state legislature, warns potential women
office-seekers:
12.

(M)

But don't limit your discussions to your issues. You must take care
to avoid appearing as a one-issue candidate ("Mrs. Smith is interested
only in day care and therefore wouldn't work for more economic
development") . . . To win widespread support--among men as well as
women--you must research traditional male issues such as finance,
public works, and business regulation, and show you're as well versed
in these matters as in others (72).

One way that women legislators have made their influence felt is
through the organization of women's caucuses. Women in ten states have formed
bipartisan caucuses whose purpose is to check legislation for its effect on
13.   women. As a result, women in state legislatures are gaining power, partly
because they have learned to deal with all the issues, and because their power
and influence are felt on women's issues. Marilyn Goldwater, a Maryland
Democrat, gives credit to her success and selection as the House of Delegates'

Goldsmith 7

deputy majority whip because she was president of the women's caucus. Men are

learning to work with the women's caucus in trade-offs on major issues

(Lublin).

(N)   Ruth Mandel, director of Rutger's Center for the American Woman and

Politics, succinctly defines the role of women in American politics:

Recognizing that rigid adherence to nonnegotiable ideologies sows

dissension and reaps defeat, effective political women operate as

14.   realists. They know that politics at its best is a matter of

compromise; that no one wins nominations and elections, stays in

office, and moves on to positions of influence and power on the basis

of one set of issues and one group of supporters. They know the value

of teams, coalitions, and diversified support (229).

Women holding political office are growing in number, particularly at the

state level, holding 13.3% of the legislative seats. Unfortunately, even though

their numbers have increased, women lack power in the major committees at both

15.   the state and federal level. In 1984, only 3 of 37 standing committees in the

Illinois legislature were chaired by women (Dold). At the national level,

women are doing much worse. No women were chairs of any standing committees in

(O)   either the house or senate for the 97th or 98th Congresses (World Almanac 82).

(P)   According to Ms. magazine, Geraldine Ferraro is a model of the "consummate

feminist politician"--one who keeps women's issues as a priority but who

achieves power by becoming part of the system. She attributes her success at

16.   being elected to the Democratic Party's platform chair to the fact that "You

pay your dues for a leadership position. You do your work, you do it well, and

you don't step on anybody else in the process of doing it" (Caudle 62).

      In the present generation, young professional women are good candidates for political office. Because many of them are trained in business and law, they will not have to go through the long period of volunteer work to learn the

17.   political ropes. Consequently, they can enter the field of politics earlier than their predecessors did. If they enter the field while young, they may have the toughness to weather political storms and achieve seniority to become a force at both the state and federal levels of politics.

Notes (Content)

1
    June Mank, a city councilwoman from Champaign, IL says that having a law or business background may not enhance a candidate at the city or county level because he or she serves too small an area. The constituents want representatives who are like them and have the same concerns, mainly those at the neighborhood or local ward level. Having a law or business degree might set a city councilwoman apart, consequently making her less effective.

2
    Many authorities comment on the importance of a woman emphasizing her maternal and family roles when she campaigns for office. Stoper says that women who don't emphasize their roles as members of a family can't "put across an image to the voters as normal, warmhearted, responsible" (334). Mandel reports that women candidates are expected by the voters to fulfill all the "domestic, spousal, and maternal duties" (65) in order to come across as a candidate they want to support. In her list of requirements for running for office, Barbara Trafton lists as second and third the importance of support from husband and family (16). Kirkpatrick found that all of the married state legislators in her study considered having a cooperative husband the most important requirement for running for public office. (231).

Goldsmith 10

Works Cited

Caudle, Sheila. "Geraldine Ferraro: A Woman for This Political Season?" <u>Ms.</u>
    July 1984: 61-65.

Dold, R. Bruce. "Women in Politics Grow in Influence." <u>Chicago</u>
    <u>Tribune</u> 21 September 1984, sec. 1:6.

"Ferraro." <u>Chicago Tribune</u> 1 January 1985, sec. 1:4.

Gehlen, Frieda L. "Women Members of Congress: A Distinctive Role."
    Githens and Prestage 304-319.

Githens, Marianne and Jewel L. Prestage, eds. <u>A Portrait of</u>
    <u>Marginality: The Political Behavior of The American Woman.</u> New York:
    Longmans, 1977.

Githens, Marianne. "Spectators, Agitators, or Lawmakers: Women in
    State Legislatures." Githens and Prestage 196-209.

King, Elizabeth G. "Women in Iowa Legislative Politics." Githens and
    Prestage 284-303

Kirkpatrick, Jeane J. <u>Political Woman</u>. New York: Basic Books, 1974.

Lamson, Peggy. <u>In the Vanguard: Six American Women in Public Life</u>.
    Boston: Houghton Mifflin, 1979.

Lublin, Joann S. "Seats of Power: Women Gain Statehouse Roles." <u>Wall</u>
    <u>Street Journal</u>. 31 December 1984: 30

Mandel, Ruth B. <u>In the Running: The New Woman Candidate</u>. New Haven:
    Tichnor and Fields, 1981.

Mark, June. Personal interview. 7 June 1985.

Margolis, Diane. "The Invisible Hands: Sex Roles and the Division of Labor in
    Two Political Parties." Stewart 22-41.

Marshall, Marilyn. "Maxine Waters: America's Most Influential Black
    Woman Politician." <u>Ebony</u> Aug. 1984: 56,58, 60.

Mezey, Susan Gluck. "The Effects of Sex on Recruitment: Connecticut
    Local Offices." Stewart 61-85.

Stewart, Debra W. ed. Women in Local Politics. Metuchen, NJ:
    Scarecrow, 1980.

Stoper, Emily. "Wife and Politician: Role Strain Among Women in Public
    Office." Githens and Prestage 334.

Trafton, Barbara M. Women Winning: How to Run for Office. Boston:
    Harvard Common Press, 1984.

World Almanac and Book of Facts. Newspaper Enterprise Association,
    Inc. 1985: 82.

Annotations for Sample Research Paper

(A) Kirkpatrick's and King's names are in the text, so the parenthetical notation uses only the page number. Note the period placed after the parenthesis.

(B) Transition from paragraph 2 to paragraph 3.

(C) Since Lamson quotes Fenwick, the documentation includes *qtd.* for *quoted.*

(D) Judy blocked the quotation in paragraph 4 because it is longer than 4 lines. Notice that no quotation marks are necessary around block quotations. Since the block is part of a paragraph, three dots are necessary to show ellipses.

(E) Since Githens is both an editor of and contributor to the book *A Portrait of Marginality,* "Spectators" (a shortened title) must be cited in the parenthetical documentation.

(F) Note that the shift to the Kirkpatrick study requires only a page reference.

(G) There is a shift in the paper here, with paragraph 6 moving from history to a proposition for the present and the future.

(H) Mezey and Githens are not mentioned in the paragraph, so their names must appear in the parenthetical documentation.

(I) The note appears after the period, not punctuated by another period.

(J) Note the transition word at the beginning of paragraph 8 — it introduces the paragraph's promise: *She must aggressively seek office and be visible in her district.*

(K) Specific examples are used in paragraphs 8 and 9 — examples that appeal to the reader by supporting and illustrating general statements.

(L) Since the last quotation in paragraph 10 has one page number and comes from a newspaper article, only the name of the article is necessary for documentation.

(M) Three dots in block quotation show that something has been deleted.

(N) Ruth Mandel's position as director of Rutger's Center enhances the authority of the quoted material.

(O) *World Almanac,* even though it is book length, does not need to be italicized in parenthetical documentation.

(P) *Ms.* magazine enhances the writer's ethical appeal because *Ms.* has been very aggressive in promoting women's issues, political and otherwise.

PRACTICE

1. Check the student's outline against the body of her paper by putting outline symbols (I, A, B, C; II, A, etc.) in the margin of the paper where the various topics and subtopics are discussed. How well does the student follow her outline?

2. Why does the title page include so much information?

3. Explain the purpose of the first three paragraphs. Are all three necessary?

4. Where is the thesis stated?

5. What is the writer's stance? Who in particular is she writing to?

6. In paragraph 15, why is *(Dold)* placed after *women* rather than after *seats*?

7. Discuss the rhetorical effect of the Fenwick quotation in paragraph 3, particularly in its relation to paragraph 2.

8. What is the purpose of the lead into paragraph 4? What relationship does the lead have to the information provided in paragraphs 2 and 3?

9. Point out three transitional devices in the paper.

10. What is the rhetorical pattern used in paragraph 8?

11. Why is the information in paragraphs 2 and 3 necessary for the content of paragraph 4?

12. Here is the card for the Lamson quotation in paragraph 3. How did the writer integrate the material into her paper?

Volunteerism   Quote p. 15

In answer to the question; did you
consciously head for a career in politics,
Fenwick answered, "No," she said, "I
think I was sort of gliding in by the
unpaid volunteer backdoor route."

Lamson, *In the Vanguard*

---

13. Here is the card for the Margolis quotation in paragraph 8. The writer chose to omit the statistics supporting the quotation. Discuss the wisdom of her choice.

> *Women's volunteer work unnoticed   Quote, p. 26*
>
> *"Women's activities tended to take place in situations where they would not be widely observed; the reverse was true of men's activities."*
>
> *Solitary work: 43% women, 35% men*
> *Work noticed by others: 43% men, 34% women*
>
> *Margolis, "The Invisible Hands" in Stewart*

PRACTICE

If the sample research paper in this chapter had been written in either *footnote* or *endnote* form, the *Notes* given below show how they would have appeared. Study the forms for endnotes given on pp. 406–408, study the notes given here, and answer the questions that follow.

Notes

[1] Jeane J. Kirkpatrick, *Political Woman* (New York: Basic Books, 1974) 61.

[2] Elizabeth King, "Women in Iowa Legislative Politics," *A Portrait of Marginality: The Political Behavior of The American Woman,* ed. by Marianne Githens and Jewel L. Prestage (New York: Longman, 1977) 288.

[3] King 289.

[4] Kirkpatrick 71.

[5] Peggy Lamson, *In the Vanguard: Six American Women in Public Life,* (Boston: Houghton Mifflin, 1979) 15.

[6] Frieda L. Gehlen, "Women Members of Congress: A Distinctive Role," Githens and Prestage 307.

[7] Marianne Githens, "Spectators, Agitators, or Lawmakers: Women in State Legislatures," Githens and Prestage 208.

[8]Kirkpatrick 83.

[9]Susan Gluck Mezey, "The Effects of Sex on Recruitment: Connecticut Local Offices," *Women in Local Politics,* ed. by Debra W. Stewart (Metuchen, NJ: Scarecrow, 1980) 71.

[10]Githens 197.

[11]Having a law or business background may not enhance a candidate at the city or county level because of the limited area covered. The constituents want representatives who are like them and have the same concerns, mainly those at the neighborhood or local ward level. Having a law or business degree might set a city councilwoman apart, consequently making her less effective. June Mank, personal interview, 7 June 1985.

[12]Githens 198.

[13]Diane Margolis, "The Invisible Hands: Sex Roles and the Division of Labor in Two Local Political Parties," Stewart 26.

[14]Barbara Trafton, reported in *Women Winning: How to Run for Office* (Boston: Harvard Common Press, 1984) 110.

[15]Trafton 128.

[16]Many authorities comment on the importance of a woman emphasizing her maternal and family roles when she campaigns for office. Stoper says that women who don't emphasize their roles as members of a family can't "put across an image to the voters as normal, warm-hearted, responsible." Emily Stoper, "Wife and Politician: Role Strain Among Women in Public Office," Githens and Prestage 334. Mandel (see note 17) reports that women candidates are expected by the voters to fulfill all the "domestic, spousal, and maternal duties" in order to come across as a candidate they want to support. In her list of requirements for running for office, Barbara Trafton lists as second and third the importance of support from husband and family (16). Kirkpatrick found that all of the married state legislators in her study considered having a cooperative husband the most important requirement for running for public office (231).

[17]Ruth B. Mandel, *In the Running: The New Woman Candidate* (New Haven: Tichnor and Fields, 1981) 64.

[18]"Ferraro," *Chicago Tribune* 1 January 1985, sec. 1:4.

[19]Marilyn Marshall, "Maxine Waters: America's Most Influential Black Woman Politician," *Ebony* Aug. 1984: 58.

[20]Trafton 72.

[21]Joann S. Lublin, "Seats of Power: Women Gain Statehouse Roles," *The Wall Street Journal* 31 December 1984: 30.

[22]Mandel 229.

[23]R. Bruce Dold, "Women in Politics Grow in Influence," *Chicago Tribune* 21 September 1984: 6.

[24]*World Almanac and Book of Facts,* (New York: Newspapers Enterprise Association, Inc. 1985) 82.

[25]Sheila Caudle, "Geraldine Ferraro: A Woman For This Political Season?" *Ms.* July 1984: 62.

1. In endnotes 3, 4, 8 and 10 only the name of the author and a page number are given. Why?

2. Compare *endnote* 11 with *content* note 1 at the end of the model research paper. Also compare *endnote* 16 with *content* note 2. What is the purpose of a *content* note in parenthetical documentation? Is that purpose the same in *endnote* documentation? Which form seems most efficient?

3. Compare *endnote* 14 with the parenthetical documentation reference at the end of paragraph 8 in the paper, both citing Trafton. If you were the reader of a research paper, which form would you prefer? Why?

4. Notice that endnotes give the surname after the first name, but in *Works Cited* the surname appears first. Why?

CHAPTER 19

THE LITERARY PAPER

WHAT IS A LITERARY PAPER?

A literary paper may be written on a single work (a play, short story, novel, or poem) or on several related ones. If you write on several works, they will probably have something in common — for example, all written by the same person or published in the same period. They may express similar themes or belong to a certain class of literature such as science fiction, nature poems, or antiwar plays.

Ordinarily, the point you make in a literary paper (the thesis you support) is made about the work itself rather than about the author, the historical period, the *genre* (the class or type of work), the literary background, or yourself. While these may be brought within the broad area of your subject, they are usually not emphasized in a purely literary paper. Of course, with your instructor's approval and assistance, and by working carefully from a thesis, you could write on one or a combination of these. Papers concentrating on author, period, genre, and background customarily require secondary sources and are therefore literary research papers, which may be outside the scope of your course or take more work than you are prepared to do. However, when assigned, the literary research paper often proves to be a stimulating and worthwhile project.

PRACTICE

To give you an example of a literary paper written about a single work, we have reprinted a story by Stephen Crane and one writer's analysis of the story.

The Bride Comes to Yellow Sky

I

The great Pullman was whirling onward with such dignity of motion that a glance from the window seemed simply to prove that the plains of Texas were pouring eastward. Vast flats of green grass, dull-hued spaces of mesquite and cactus, little groups of frame houses, woods of light and tender trees, all were sweeping into the east, sweeping over the horizon, a precipice.

A newly married pair had boarded this coach at San Antonio. The man's face was reddened from many days in the wind and sun, and a direct result of his new black clothes was that his brick-colored hands were constantly performing in a most conscious fashion. From time to time he looked down respectfully at his attire. He sat with a hand on each knee, like a man waiting in a barber's shop. The glances he devoted to other passengers were furtive and shy.

The bride was not pretty, nor was she very young. She wore a dress of blue cashmere, with small reservations of velvet here and there, and with steel buttons abounding. She continually twisted her head to regard her puff sleeves, very stiff, straight, and high. They embarrassed her. It was quite apparent that she had cooked, and that she expected to cook, dutifully. The blushes caused by the careless scrutiny of some passengers as she had entered the car were strange to see upon this plain, underclass countenance, which was drawn in placid, almost emotionless lines.

They were evidently very happy. "Ever been in a parlor car before?" he asked, smiling with delight.

"No," she answered. "I never was. It's fine, ain't it?"

"Great! And then after a while we'll go forward to the diner, and get a big layout. Finest meal in the world. Charge a dollar."

"Oh, do they?" cried the bride. "Charge a dollar? Why, that's too much—for us—ain't it, Jack?"

"Not this trip, anyhow," he answered bravely. "We're going to go the whole thing."

Later, he explained to her about the trains. "You see, it's a thousand miles from one end of Texas to the other; and this train runs right across it, and never stops but four times." He had the pride of an owner. He pointed out to her the dazzling fittings of the coach; and in truth her eyes opened wider as she contemplated the sea-green figured velvet, the shining brass, silver, and glass, the wood that gleamed as darkly brilliant as the surface of a pool of oil. At one end a bronze figure sturdily held a support for a separated chamber, and at convenient places on the ceiling were frescoes in olive and silver.

To the minds of the pair, their surroundings reflected the glory of their marriage that morning in San Antonio. This was the environment of their new estate, and the man's face in particular beamed with an elation that made him appear ridiculous to the negro porter. This individual at times surveyed them from afar with an amused and superior grin. On other occasions he bullied them with skill in ways that did not make it exactly plain to them that they were being bullied. He subtly used all the manners of the most unconquerable kind of snobbery. He oppressed them; but of this oppression they had small knowledge, and they speedily forgot that infrequently a number of travelers covered them with stares of derisive enjoyment. Historically there was supposed to be something infinitely humorous in their situation.

"We are due in Yellow Sky at 3:42," he said, looking tenderly into her eyes.

"Oh, are we?" she said, as if she had not been aware of it. To evince surprise at her husband's statement was part of her wifely amiability. She took from a pocket a little silver watch; and as she held it before her, and stared at it with a frown of attention, the new husband's face shone.

"I bought it in San Anton' from a friend of mine," he told her gleefully.

"It's seventeen minutes past twelve," she said, looking up at him with a kind of shy and clumsy coquetry. A passenger, noting this play, grew excessively sardonic, and winked at himself in one of the numerous mirrors.

At last they went to the dining car. Two rows of negro waiters, in glowing white suits, surveyed their entrance with the interest, and also the equanimity, of men who had been forewarned. The pair fell to the lot of a waiter who happened to feel pleasure in steering them through their meal. He viewed them with the manner of a fatherly pilot, his countenance radiant with benevolence. The patronage, entwined with the ordinary deference, was not plain to them. And yet, as they returned to their coach, they showed in their faces a sense of escape.

To the left, miles down a long purple slope, was a little ribbon of mist where moved the keening Rio Grande. The train was approaching it at an angle, and the apex was Yellow Sky. Presently it was apparent that, as the distance from Yellow Sky grew shorter, the husband became commensurately restless. His brick-red hands were more insistent in their prominence. Occasionally he was even rather absent-minded and faraway when the bride leaned forward and addressed him.

As a matter of truth, Jack Potter was beginning to find the shadow of a deed weigh upon him like a leaden slab. He, the town marshal of Yellow Sky, a man known, liked, and feared in his corner, a prominent person, had gone to San Antonio to meet a girl he believed he loved, and there, after the usual prayers, had actually induced her to marry him, without consulting Yellow Sky for any part of the transaction. He was now bringing his bride before an innocent and unsuspecting community.

Of course people in Yellow Sky married as it pleased them, in accordance with a general custom; but such was Potter's thought of his duty to his friends, or of their idea of his duty, or of an unspoken form which does not control men in these matters, that he felt he was heinous. He had committed an extraordinary crime. Face to face with this girl in San Antonio, and spurred by his sharp impulse, he had gone headlong over all the social hedges. At San Antonio he was like a man hidden in the dark. A knife to sever any friendly duty, any form, was easy to his hand in that remote city. But the hour of Yellow Sky—the hour of daylight—was approaching.

He knew full well that his marriage was an important thing to his town. It could only be exceeded by the burning of the new hotel. His friends could not forgive him. Frequently he had reflected on the advisability of telling them by telegraph, but a new cowardice had been upon him. He feared to do it. And now the train was hurrying him toward a scene of amazement, glee, and reproach. He glanced out of the window at the line of haze swinging slowly in toward the train.

Yellow Sky had a kind of brass band, which played painfully, to the delight of the populace. He laughed without heart as he thought of it. If the citizens could dream of his prospective arrival with his bride, they would parade the band at the station and escort them, amid cheers and laughing congratulations, to his adobe home.

He resolved that he would use all the devices of speed and plainscraft in making the journey from the station to his house. Once within that safe citadel, he could issue some sort of a vocal bulletin, and then not go among the citizens until they had time to wear off a little of their enthusiasm.

The bride looked anxiously at him. "What's worrying you, Jack?"

He laughed again. "I'm not worrying, girl. I'm only thinking of Yellow Sky."

She flushed in comprehension.

A sense of mutual guilt invaded their minds and developed a finer tenderness. They looked at each other with eyes softly aglow. But Potter often laughed the same nervous laugh. The flush upon the bride's face seemed quite permanent.

The traitor to the feelings of Yellow Sky narrowly watched the speeding landscape. "We're nearly there," he said.

Presently the porter came and announced the proximity of Potter's home. He held a brush in his hand, and, with all his airy superiority gone, he brushed Potter's new clothes as the latter slowly turned this way and that way. Potter fumbled out a coin and gave it to the porter, as he had seen others do. It was a heavy and muscle-bound business, as that of a man shoeing his first horse.

The porter took their bag, and as the train began to slow they moved forward to the hooded platform of the car. Presently the two engines and their long string of coaches rushed into the station of Yellow Sky.

"They have to take water here," said Potter, from a constricted throat and in mournful cadence, as one announcing death. Before the train stopped, his eye had swept the length of the platform, and he was glad and astonished to see there was none upon it but the station-agent, who, with a slightly hurried and anxious air, was walking toward the water tanks. When the train had halted, the porter alighted first, and placed in position a little temporary step.

"Come on, girl," said Potter, hoarsely. As he helped her down they each laughed on a false note. He took the bag from the negro, and bade his wife cling to his arm. As they slunk rapidly away, his hangdog glance perceived that they were unloading the two trunks, and also that the station-agent, far ahead near the baggage car, had turned and was running toward him, making gestures. He laughed, and groaned as he laughed, when he noted the first effect of his marital bliss upon Yellow Sky. He gripped his wife's arm firmly to his side, and they fled. Behind them the porter stood, chuckling fatuously.

II

The California express on the Southern Railway was due at Yellow Sky in twenty-one minutes. There were six men at the bar of the Weary Gentleman saloon. One was a drummer who talked a great deal and rapidly; three were Texans who did not care to talk at that time; and two were Mexican sheepherders, who did not talk as a general practice in the Weary Gentleman saloon. The barkeeper's dog lay on the boardwalk that crossed in front of the door. His head was on his paws, and he glanced drowsily here and there with the constant vigilance of a dog that is kicked on occasion. Across the sandy street were some vivid green grass-plots, so wonderful in appearance, amid the sands that burned near them in a blazing sun, that they caused a doubt in the mind. They exactly resembled the grass mats used to represent lawns on the stage. At the cooler end of the railway station, a man without a coat sat in a tilted chair and smoked his pipe. The fresh-cut bank of the Rio Grande circled near the town, and there could be seen beyond it a great plum-colored plain of mesquite.

Save for the busy drummer and his companions in the saloon, Yellow Sky was dozing. The newcomer leaned gracefully upon the bar, and recited many tales with the confidence of a bard who has come upon a new field.

"—and at the moment that the old man fell downstairs with the bureau in his arms, the old woman was coming up with two scuttles of coal, and of course—"

The drummer's tale was interrupted by a young man who suddenly appeared in the open door. He cried: "Scratchy Wilson's drunk, and has turned loose with both hands." The two Mexicans at once set down their glasses and faded out of the rear entrance of the saloon.

The drummer, innocent and jocular, answered: "All right, old man. S'pose he has? Come in and have a drink, anyhow."

But the information had made such an obvious cleft in every skull in the room that the drummer was obliged to see its importance. All had become instantly solemn. "Say," said he, mystified, "what is this?" His three companions made the introductory gesture of eloquent speech, but the young man at the door forestalled them.

"It means, my friend," he answered, as he came into the saloon, "that for the next two hours this town won't be a health resort."

The barkeeper went to the door and locked and barred it. Reaching out of the window, he pulled in heavy wooden shutters and barred them. Immediately a solemn, chapel-like gloom was upon the place. The drummer was lookng from one to another.

"But say," he cried, "what is this, anyhow? You don't mean there is going to be a gunfight?"

"Don't know whether there'll be a fight or not," answered one man, grimly. "But there'll be some shootin'—some good shootin'."

The young man who had warned them waved his hand. "Oh, there'll be a fight fast enough, if any one wants it. Anybody can get a fight out there in the street. There's a fight just waiting."

The drummer seemed to be swayed between the interest of a foreigner and a perception of personal danger.

"What did you say his name was?" he asked.

"Scratchy Wilson," they answered in chorus.

"And will he kill anybody? What are you going to do? Does this happen often? Does he rampage around like this once a week or so? Can he break in that door?"

"No, he can't break down that door," replied the barkeeper. "He's tried it three times. But when he comes you'd better lay down on the floor, stranger. He's dead sure to shoot at it, and a bullet may come through."

Thereafter the drummer kept a strict eye upon the door. The time had not yet been called for him to hug the floor, but, as a minor precaution, he sidled near to the wall. "Will he kill anybody?" he said again.

The men laughed low and scornfully at the question.

"He's out to shoot, and he's out for trouble. Don't see any good in experimentin' with him."

"But what do you do in a case like this? What do you do?"

A man responded: "Why, he and Jack Potter—"

"But," in chorus the other men interrupted, "Jack Potter's in San Anton'."

"Well, who is he? What's he got to do with it?"

"Oh, he's the town marshal. He goes out and fights Scratchy when he gets on one of these tears."

"Wow!" said the drummer, mopping his brow. "Nice job he's got."

The voices had toned away to mere whisperings. The drummer wished to ask further questions, which were born of an increasing anxiety and bewilderment; but when he attempted them, the men merely looked at him in irritation and motioned him to remain silent. A tense waiting hush was upon them. In the deep shadows of the room their eyes shone as they listened for sounds from the street. One man made three gestures at the barkeeper; and the latter, moving like a ghost, handed him a glass and a bottle. The man poured a full glass of whiskey, and set down the bottle noiselessly. He gulped the whiskey in a swallow, and turned again toward the door in immovable silence. The drummer saw that the barkeeper, without a sound, had taken a Winchester from beneath the bar. Later he saw this individual beckoning to him, so he tiptoed across the room.

"You better come with me back of the bar."

"No, thanks," said the drummer, perspiring. "I'd rather be where I can make a break for the back door."

Whereupon the man of bottles made a kindly but peremptory gesture. The drummer obeyed it, and finding himself seated on a box with his head below the level of the bar, balm was laid upon his soul at sight of various zinc and copper fittings that bore a resemblance to armor plate. The barkeeper took a seat comfortably upon an adjacent box.

"You see," he whispered, "this here Scratchy Wilson is a wonder with a gun—a perfect wonder—and when he goes on the war trail, we hunt our holes—naturally. He's about the last one of the old gang that used to hang out along the river here. He's a terror when he's drunk. When he's sober he's all right—kind of simple—wouldn't hurt a fly—nicest fellow in town. But when he's drunk—whoo!"

There were periods of stillness. "I wish Jack Potter was back from San Anton'," said the barkeeper. "He shot Wilson up once—in the leg—and he would sail in and pull out the kinks in this thing."

Presently they heard from a distance the sound of a shot, followed by three wild yowls. It instantly removed a bond from the men in the darkened saloon. There was a shuffling of feet. They looked at each other. "Here he comes," they said.

III

A man in a maroon-colored flannel shirt, which had been purchased for purposes of decoration, and made principally by some Jewish women on the East Side of New York, rounded a corner and walked into the middle of the main street of Yellow Sky. In either hand the man held a long, heavy, blue-black revolver. Often he yelled, and these cries rang through a semblance of a deserted village, shrilly flying over the roofs in a volume that seemed to have no relation to the ordinary vocal strength of a man. It was as if the surrounding stillness formed the arch of a tomb over him. These cries of ferocious challenge rang against walls of silence. And his boots had red tops with gilded imprints, of the kind beloved in winter by little sledding boys on the hillsides of New England.

The man's face flamed in a rage begot of whiskey. His eyes, rolling, and yet keen for ambush, hunted the still doorways and windows. He walked with the creeping movement of the midnight cat. As it occurred to him, he roared menacing information. The long revolvers in his hands were as easy as straws; they were moved with an electric swiftness. The little fingers of each hand played sometimes in a musician's way. Plain from the low collar of the shirt, the cords of his neck straightened and sank, straightened and sank, as passion moved him. The only sounds were his terrible invitations. The calm adobes preserved their demeanor at the passing of this small thing in the middle of the street.

There was no offer of fight—no offer of fight. The man called to the sky. There were no attractions. He bellowed and fumed and swayed his revolvers here and everywhere.

The dog of the barkeeper of the Weary Gentleman saloon had not appreciated the advance of events. He yet lay dozing in front of his master's door. At sight of the dog, the man paused and raised his revolver humorously. At sight of the man, the dog sprang up and walked diagonally away, with a sullen head, and growling. The man yelled, and the dog broke into a gallop. As it was about to enter an alley, there was a loud noise, a whistling, and something spat the ground directly before it. The dog screamed, and, wheeling in terror, galloped headlong in a new direction. Again there was a noise, a whistling, and sand was kicked viciously before it. Fear-stricken, the dog turned and flurried like an animal in a pen. The man stood laughing, his weapons at his hips.

Ultimately the man was attracted by the closed door of the Weary Gentleman saloon. He went to it and, hammering with a revolver, demanded drink.

The door remaining imperturbable, he picked a bit of paper from the walk, and nailed it to the framework with a knife. He then turned his back contemptuously upon this popular resort and, walking to the opposite side of the street and spinning there on his heel quickly and lithely, fired at the bit of paper. He missed it by a half-inch. He swore at himself, and went away. Later, he comfortably fusilladed the windows of his most intimate friend. The man was playing with this town. It was a toy for him.

But still there was no offer of fight. The name of Jack Potter, his ancient antagonist, entered his mind, and he concluded that it would be a glad thing if he should go to Potter's house, and by bombardment induce him to come out and fight. He moved in the direction of his desire, chanting Apache scalp-music.

When he arrived at it, Potter's house presented the same still front as had the other adobes. Taking up a strategic position, the man howled a challenge. But this house regarded him as might a great stone god. It gave no sign. After a decent wait, the man howled further challenges, mingling with them wonderful epithets.

Presently there came the spectacle of a man churning himself into deepest rage over the immobility of a house. He fumed at it as the winter wind attacks a prairie cabin in the North. To the distance there should have gone the sound of a tumult like the fighting of two hundred Mexicans. As necessity bade him, he paused for breath or to reload his revolvers.

<h1 style="text-align:center">IV</h1>

Potter and his bride walked sheepishly and with speed. Sometimes they laughed together shamefacedly and low.

"Next corner, dear," he said finally.

They put forth the efforts of a pair walking bowed against a strong wind. Potter was about to raise a finger to point the first appearance of the new home when, as they circled the corner, they came face to face with a man in a maroon-colored shirt, who was feverishly pushing cartridges into a large revolver. Upon the instant the man dropped his revolver to the ground, and, like lightning, whipped another from its holster. The second weapon was aimed at the bridegroom's chest.

There was a silence. Potter's mouth seemed to be merely a grave for his tongue. He exhibited an instinct to at once loosen his arm from the woman's grip, and he dropped the bag to the sand. As for the bride, her face had gone as yellow as old cloth. She was a slave to hideous rites, gazing at the apparitional snake.

The two men faced each other at a distance of three paces. He of the revolver smiled with a new and quiet ferocity.

"Tried to sneak up on me," he said. "Tried to sneak up on me!" His eyes grew more baleful. As Potter made a slight movement, the man thrust his revolver venomously forward. "No; don't you do it, Jack Potter. Don't you move a finger toward a gun just yet. Don't you move an eyelash. The time has come for me to settle with you, and I'm goin' to do it my own way, and loaf along with no interferin'. So if you don't want a gun bent on you, just mind what I tell you."

Potter looked at his enemy. "I ain't got a gun on me, Scratchy," he said. "Honest, I ain't." He was stiffening and steadying, but yet somewhere at the back of his mind a vision of the Pullman floated: the sea-green figured velvet, the shining brass, silver and glass, the wood that gleamed as darkly brilliant as the surface of a pool of oil — all the glory of the marriage, the environment of the new estate. "You know I fight when it comes to fighting, Scratchy Wilson; but I ain't got a gun on me. You'll have to do all the shootin' yourself."

His enemy's face went livid. He stepped forward, and lashed his weapon to and fro before Potter's chest. "Don't you tell me you ain't got no gun on you, you whelp. Don't tell me no lie like that. There ain't a man in Texas ever seen you without no gun. Don't take me for no kid." His eyes blazed with light, and his throat worked like a pump.

"I ain't takin' you for no kid," answered Potter. His heels had not moved an inch backward. "I'm takin' you for a damn fool. I tell you I ain't got a gun, and I ain't. If you're goin' to shoot me up, you better begin now. You'll never get a chance like this again."

So much enforced reasoning had told on Wilson's rage. He was calmer. "If you ain't got a gun, why ain't you got a gun?" he sneered. "Been to Sunday school?"

"I ain't got a gun because I've just come from San Anton' with my wife. I'm married," said Potter. "And if I'd thought there was going to be any galoots like you prowling around when I brought my wife home, I'd had a gun, and don't you forget it."

"Married!" said Scratchy, not at all comprehending

"Yes, married. I'm married," said Potter, distinctly.

"Married?" said Scratchy. Seemingly for the first time, he saw the drooping, drowning woman at the other man's side. "No!" he said. He was like a creature allowed a glimpse of another world. He moved a pace backward, and his arm, with the revolver, dropped to his side. "Is this the lady?" he asked.

"Yes; this is the lady," answered Potter.

There was another period of silence.

"Well," said Wilson at last, slowly, "I s'pose it's all off now."

"It's all off if you say so, Scratchy. You know I didn't make the trouble." Potter lifted his valise.

"Well, I 'low it's off, Jack," said Wilson. He was looking at the ground. "Married!" He was not a student of chivalry; it was merely that in the presence of this foreign condition he was a simple child of the earlier plains. He picked up his starboard revolver, and, placing both weapons in their holsters, he went away. His feet made funnel-shaped tracks in the heavy sand.

The Analysis

"The Bride Comes to Yellow Sky" Is a Comedy

[1]Most of our class discussion of Stephen Crane's "The Bride Comes to Yellow Sky" centered on its allegorical meaning. Several students

believed that the story is full of symbols showing a conflict between the values of America's West and East, the Eastern values being evil and treacherous. It seems to me that this interpretation takes the story far too seriously. It also ignores the basic qualities and occurrences in the story, all of which point not to deep, serious meaning but to light comedy.

[2]The plot of "The Bride" is, in construction, like those of other Crane stories we have read, "The Blue Hotel" and "The Open Boat." It is carefully divided into dramatic scenes, and it could easily be staged as a play. The first scene presents the town marshal of Yellow Sky, Jack Potter, and his bride as they sit in the train waiting for its arrival at the marshal's town, Yellow Sky. They are honest and simple persons, not young, but too inexperienced to play the part of newlyweds without great awkwardness.

[3]The second scene is a partial flashback; it begins in time at the same moment as the first scene and its function is exposition: the men in the Weary Gentleman Saloon tell a drummer from out of town about the ancient gunman Scratchy Wilson, who is a superb shot but harmless except when he is drinking. "When he's sober," explains the barkeeper, "he's all right—kind of simple—wouldn't hurt a fly—nicest fellow in town. But when he's drunk—whoo!" Scratchy intends to shoot up the town, and the barkeeper boards up his place to ride out the storm.

[4]Crane shows us Scratchy for the first time in the third scene. The old gunman, drunk and blazing away with two six-shooters at various targets, including the saloon, is looking for a fight but cannot find one. He remembers his old enemy, the marshal, and staggers away to the marshal's house, where he yells for Potter to come out. In the fourth and last scene, the paths of the two men meet as Potter and his bride round the corner heading for their new home and come upon Scratchy loading one of his pistols. The gunman waves his weapon angrily at them until Potter introduces his new wife. At the sight of the two together and at the knowledge of their marriage, Scratchy's rage is gone, and he walks sorrowfully away dragging his feet. The comedy is ended.

[5]It is true that the language (in particular, Crane's metaphor and imagery) appears to be serious and symbolic, as it is in his other stories. When they first see Scratchy, Potter and his wife are afraid: "Potter's mouth seemed to be merely a grave for his tongue. . . . As for the bride, her face had gone as yellow as old cloth. She was a slave to hideous rites, gazing at the apparitional snake." In Crane's description of the couple's reaction to the Pullman, he employs one of his most significant images: "He pointed out to her the dazzling fittings of the coach; and in truth her eyes opened wider as she contemplated the sea-green figured velvet, the shining brass, silver, and glass, the wood that gleamed as darkly brilliant as the surface of a pool of oil."

[6]However, Crane's customary dramatic, ironic, and poetic techniques in this story are generally either overridden by comic effects or

shaped for the ends of comedy. The marshal and his bride are more
than faintly ludicrous on the train. The fear of the men in the saloon is
comic, as is the sudden deflation of the bragging drummer who, after
ducking behind the bar, has "balm . . . laid upon his soul at sight of
various zinc and copper fittings that bore a resemblance to armor
plate." Scratchy is made out to be a holy terror, but his actions and appearance imply otherwise. He accurately and purposefully shoots in
front of a dog instead of at it, and his major targets consist of pieces of
paper and adobe walls. Dressed like a child's idea of a cowboy, in a
maroon shirt and red-topped boots "of the kind beloved in winter by
little sledding boys on the hillsides of New England," the old gunman is
obviously a comic figure playing a childishly attractive game. Even
when he faces Potter and his bride, Scratchy avoids shooting him; he
merely talks about it, and although Potter is doubtful of his antagonist's
harmlessness, the reader is convinced that the marshal is safe.

    [7]Throughout "The Bride" Crane uses comic devices with great
sureness. There is tongue-in-cheek understatement in his catalogue of
the men drinking in the saloon: "One was a drummer who talked a
great deal and rapidly; three were Texans who did not care to talk at
that time; and two were Mexican sheep-herders, who did not talk as a
general practice in the Weary Gentleman Saloon." Crane's favorite
device is comic overstatement. The marshal's marriage is called an "extraordinary crime" that was "an important thing to his town. It could
only be exceeeded by the burning of the new hotel." Scratchy's drunken
bellowing is called the "chanting [of] Apache scalp-music." In describing the action of his characters, Crane uses echoes of and allusions to
the epic to attain comic overstatement. The barkeeper becomes "the
man of bottles." Jack Potter is not merely Scratchy's enemy; he is "his
ancient antagonist." And when no one answers his challenges, Scratchy
addresses the universe and calls "to the sky" like a hero out of Homer.

    [8]Occasionally Crane employs a sort of visual comedy that is close to
slapstick. The marshal and his wife in the Pullman are little better than
two hayseeds, the butt of joking throughout the car. They are terribly
embarrassed and self-conscious. The black porter looks down on and
bullies them, laughing at them as they leave the train. Potter's trying to
tip the porter without drawing attention to himself is perfectly constructed rustic slapstick comedy: "Potter fumbled out a coin and gave it
to the porter, as he had seen others do. It was a heavy and muscle-
bound business, as that of a man shoeing his first horse."

    [9]All of these devices and scenes either anticipate or support the
comedy of the confrontation of the "ancient antagonists" who have been
involved in a burlesque of the Western feud. Holding a gun on the
brave marshal, who is afraid to face the town when it finds out about
his marriage, and who has just been caught skulking around back
streets trying to get home without being seen, Scratchy works himself
into a rage that disappears like a pricked bubble when the bride is
mentioned. "No!" he says. And then in a splendid anticlimax he asks:
"Is this the lady?"

[10]The feud that Scratchy has enjoyed so much is over. "I s'pose it's all off now," he says, and like a child who has lost something forever he walks away dragging his feet, making "funnel-shaped tracks in the heavy sand." But "The Bride Comes to Yellow Sky" is a comedy that implies a happy ending. Surely the marshal and his bride will live happily ever after; Scratchy Wilson, now that the object of his feuding attentions is no longer available, will undoubtedly reform and get religion; and even the dreadful wedding reception by the town that Potter was so frightened of will probably turn out to be no worse than an ice cream social at the Baptist church.

PRACTICE

Discussion

1. What is the thesis of this paper?

2. Does the writer appear in the paper? Where and why?

3. What does the reader know *before* starting to read the body of the paper?

4. How much plot summary does the paper contain? Where does the summary start and stop? (See p. 445 for a definition of *plot.*)

5. Why is some plot summary necessary in many literary papers? Can you give a rule of thumb about how much summary might be necessary in the "average" paper?

6. Analyze carefully the sixth paragraph. How does each of its sentences support the thesis stated in the topic sentence?

7. Write down the thesis of each paragraph. What does this list tell you about the writer's organization of the paper? Is there any paragraph that should have been left out?

8. What is the purpose of the final paragraph?

9. Why does the writer use so many quotations?

10. Explain the *form* of the quotations in the two sentences below. How are the quotations fitted into the sentences? (Before answering, you may want to read the discussion of quoting and paraphrasing, pp. 375–379.)

    a. The fear of the men in the saloon is comic, as is the sudden deflation of the bragging drummer who, after ducking behind the bar, has "balm . . . laid upon his soul at sight of various zinc and copper fittings that bore a resemblance to armor plate."

b. Scratchy's drunken bellowing is called the "chanting [of] Apache scalp-music."

11. Explain the use of verb tenses in the sixth paragraph.

12. Does the writer make any general statements about Crane's story that leave you puzzled or unsatisfied?

13. The literary paper is a form of argumentation. In what ways is this paper an argument? Are you convinced by it? Why or why not?

The Assignment

Essays and longer papers about literature usually fall into two types: those for which your instructor gives you the assignment, and those for which you create your own topic. In either case, you will find that certain techniques for responding to an assignment will be useful.

Let's assume, for a moment, that your assignment says no more than "Write on a literary work."

First, decide how large your *focus* should be on the work. In a large focus you consider a broad aspect of the whole work — its theme, for instance, and how the author develops and supports it. Or you might focus more narrowly on a smaller aspect — plot, character, style, imagery, or point of view. Even more narrowly, you could focus your paper on a single part of the work: an important scene in a play, a short significant passage in a story, or a grouping of six or eight lines in a poem.

You should then examine the theme, the fundamental meaning that the author is trying to express (mainly by indirection) through characterization, action, description, symbolism, imagery, and so on. You will discover that your own writing on a work will have deepest significance if you relate your discussion to its theme. If you decide to focus narrowly on the climax of a novel, consider relating it to the theme of the work. If you wish to focus on the structure of a work, ask yourself: "Why did the author choose *this* structure over the many others available? Does the structure fit well the theme he is trying to convey to his reader?"

These suggestions for broad assignments also apply well to more limited ones, because even though the limited ones will require you to narrow your focus on the work, you still must consider its theme directly or indirectly. It is particularly important to read carefully the assignments using limited topics. You should have a good idea of what your instructor expects. Words in the assignment such as *discuss, explain, analyze, define, compare, classify,* and *describe* give you direct clues to the kind of strategy you should choose before you write the paper. If the assignment begins with *why, how,* or *what* you have a hint that *causation, process,* or *definition* is important in answering the question. As you read, use such clues.

Knowing the Work

You must understand the work thoroughly. *Read it carefully. Know what the work says.* Do not draw conclusions about it unless you can support them with specific evidence from the work. (See the paper on "The Bride Comes to Yellow Sky" for examples of the use of evidence.)

Take notes on the work as you read. Mark important passages that you can refer to when writing the paper—for instance, those passages that present the theme, show a particular trait of a character, reveal the author's point of view, or exemplify a stylistic device.

Below is an annotated poem, showing you how to mark relevant passages. Following the poem are suggestions for analyzing a literary work, poetry in particular.

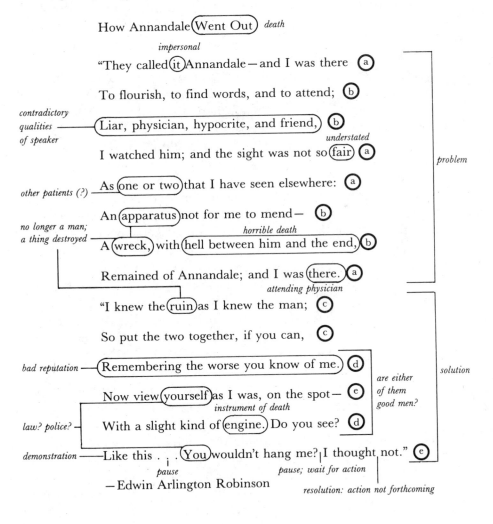

We carefully read the poem several times (at least once out loud), to look for clues. Note these elements: the title (what does it mean?); the fact that it is a speech; the two-part structure; the rhyme scheme; any significant or unusual wording (like *engine,* or *apparatus* for "man"). After we have inspected these and looked up *engine* in the dictionary, we are ready to analyze the poem.

In the poem a man is speaking, without interruption, to the police — or perhaps to other representatives of the law. He is telling them how Annandale died. He was Annandale's friend and doctor and was with him in his last moments. But the doctor makes a startling confession, particularly startling for a physician. He used an "engine," which our dictionary says can be "any mechanical appliance, instrument or tool," to kill Annandale. Perhaps the instrument was a scalpel (he apparently holds it up for the police to see) that he used to put Annandale out of his misery. "Surely you would not punish me for doing such a thing, would you?" asks the doctor. The answer seems to be negative, and you believe the doctor will go free.

Baldly stated, that is the "plot" of the poem. Yet Robinson has the doctor say so much more than this brief summary implies. Annandale, it would appear, is not just a dying man; there is something different about him. He is a "ruin"; the sign of him is not "fair"; he is a "wreck, with hell between him and the end." He is not even a human being any more — "They called *it* Annandale" who is "an *apparatus* not for me to mend." And what of the doctor, who is, we can guess, the only one left to attend Annandale? He calls himself a "liar" and a "hypocrite," one who can make the proper noises (and "flourishes") at the death of a friend. His listeners in the poem know that he has a bad reputation ("Remembering the *worst* you know of me").

The poem tells us in a fairly direct way that what might be called "a mercy killing" was performed by a physician capable of evil. But the poem indirectly tells us a different story. Annandale may be no better than the doctor. Most of the words that describe him have moral as well as physical connotations; we can guess that he is both a moral and a physical "wreck" and that his death is not one to weep over. Besides, what sort of man would have *this* doctor, who confesses that he is a liar and hypocrite, for a friend? And for a friend, the doctor is strangely objective, even coolly ironic: the dying Annandale was a "sight . . . not so fair/As one or two that I have seen elsewhere." Do not these men deserve each other?

The point or theme of this small dramatic poem is ambiguous. As a drama showing people in action, it tells us something about human beings. In the poem, a man who is no better than he should be, alone with a dying friend of similar character who is suffering greatly, takes the risk of committing a mercy killing. Yet there are hints that the dying man deserved to die for other reasons (the listeners do not seem to mind much that he was killed), and there is in the killing as much a feeling of retribution as mercy. Moreover, the doctor has no intention of paying for his crime: "You wouldn't hang me? I thought not." So the theme is a mixed one, a comment on the ambiguousness of friendship and retribution, and on the character of the speaker himself, who contains terrible moral opposites. The poem implies that a human being, like this physician, can be both good and evil and can balance such opposite characteristics with surprising grace and irony.

How is the story of the poem formed and shaped? First, and most obviously, it is a speech; technically speaking, a dramatic monologue. A man talks, revealing himself to others who themselves do not speak but who react "between the lines":

"Do you see? [*reaction*]
Like this . . . You wouldn't hang me? [*reaction*) I thought not."

The poet also shapes his story by putting it into the traditional pattern of the Italian sonnet, which is customarily made of two stanzas, the first asking a question or stating a problem, and the second answering the question or solving the problem. Robinson's poem uses a typical rhyme scheme for stanza one (*abbaabba*), but a somewhat unusual one for stanza two (*ccdede*). The complete structure (organization) of the story, then, is shaped by two basic elements: the dramatic monologue arranged into the pattern of the Italian sonnet.

It is typical of most literary works that, while the author wrote or created them, he is not necessarily in them. Edwin Arlington Robinson is neither the physician nor Annandale; and neither of them, so far as we can tell in this poem, speaks for the poet. We can infer, if we like, that the view of human beings implied in the poem (in its theme) is also Robinson's view; but we cannot infer that opinion directly from the poem. What Robinson "says" is the poem itself, there on the page. For what he believes about the Annandales of the world and their doctors we would have to turn to biographical materials. A literary work can tell us only so much.

How successful is "How Annandale Went Out"? Observe that we don't ask: "Do we like this poem?" A work can be successful but not very likable, or likable but not particularly successful. Our main interest is expressed in the questions: "In this literary work, did the author succeed in what he intended to do? If so, why? If he didn't, why not?"

We believe that it is successful. Robinson took a difficult, ambiguous narrative theme and shaped it carefully and dramatically, using two literary forms, the dramatic monologue and the sonnet. Form and content seem to work naturally together, without any feeling of strain. Ultimately, we *believe* in the poem. We believe that these men and their situation can exist, in all their moral ambiguity and dramatic irony.

READING AND UNDERSTANDING THE LITERARY WORK

After reading the discussions so far and learning something about the nature of literary papers, you should also learn a few things about literary works themselves.* A literary work of any merit says something significant and says it in a significant way. As you read a work, look for this "something" and "way"—the *content* and the *form* that, properly inter-related, create a work of literature.

Over the years, readers and critics have developed a set of terms that they use to help them read and understand the work. As you read this chapter, refer to the following Glossary, which explains only those terms that you will use most often when you analyze a work.

BRIEF GLOSSARY OF LITERARY TERMS

Allusion—an indirect reference to a person, thing, idea, or action outside the literary work. For example, the title of John Steinbeck's novel *Of Mice and Men* is an allusion to Robert Burns' lines in his poem "To a Mouse":

> The best laid schemes o' mice and men
>   Gang aft a-gley;
> An' lea'e us nought but grief and pain,
>   For promis'd joy.

Character—a person in a story, poem, or play.

---

*Of necessity, our discussion in this chapter concerning literary forms and devices is brief and limited. For more detailed information on these subjects, see a text like Bernard Cohen's *Writing About Literature,* Revised Edition, Scott, Foresman, 1973, or Edgar Roberts' *Writing Themes About Literature,* 5th Edition, Prentice-Hall, 1983.

Characterization—the technique of making a fictional person seem "real." Characterization is created by (1) the actions of the person; (2) the person's comments about himself; (3) comments on the person by other characters; (4) authorial comments.

Climax—the major "high point" near the end of the plot, in which the conflict is usually resolved.

Conflict—a struggle between people or forces in a story. (Without conflict, there is no story.) Typical conflicts can be between two people; between a person and his society or his environment (man against "machine," for example, or man against "nature"); between man and God (or the fates); between man and himself.

Exposition—that part of a story that introduces the characters, the setting, and (usually) the conflict. Exposition gives the background details necessary to the plot.

Image—a description, often poetic, which appeals powerfully to the physical senses. Example (from Tennyson's poem "The Eagle"): "The wrinkled sea beneath him crawls."

Irony—a literary device that expresses a discrepancy between appearance and reality. *Verbal irony* says one thing but means another. *Irony of situation* expresses an incongruity between what happens on the surface of a situation and what is actually taking place.

Narrative—a literary work or mode that describes an incident (or a series of closely related incidents), usually in chronological order.

Plot—the whole "story" of a play, novel, poem, or short story. *Plot* includes *exposition, conflict,* and *climax.*

Point of view—the angle from which the author presents a story. Point of view can be *omniscient* (all-knowing), *limited omniscient, first-person,* or *objective.*

Satire—a form of literary argument or attack that ridicules persons, ideas, or institutions in a scornful, ironic, and usually witty fashion.

Structure—the total form of a work. A literary structure is created by the interrelationship among devices such as plot, point of view, imagery, symbol, statement, and theme.

Symbol—a literary device which acts as itself while suggesting another thing (or many things). The American flag, for instance, can *symbolize* many different attitudes and ideas to different people.

Theme—the main point, idea, or statement of a literary work.

Questions to Ask About a Work

To help you understand a literary work, read it carefully with certain questions in mind, and remember to refer to the Glossary on pp. 571–599.

1. What *happens* in the work?

If it is a story, who are the *characters*? What motivates them? (Why do they act as they do?) What is the *plot*? The events of the plot usually progress through a series of *conflicts* until a high point (the *climax* of the plot) is reached, in which the conflicts are resolved. There may be only one major conflict, or there may be several, with one usually predominating. A conflict can be physical or psychological, or both. In most stories, the climax does not come right at the end; time and space are needed at the conclusion to "tie up the loose threads" of the story.

Many literary works (poems, in particular) make statements rather than tell stories. Frost's "Nothing Gold Can Stay" is an example.

2. How is the work organized? What is its *structure*?

What gives it shape or form? If it is a story in the form of a play, does it have acts, and divisions and scenes within the acts? If it is a story, who tells it? (Some long stories are told by different persons, each giving his idea of the action and his views of the other characters.) If it is a poem, are meter and rhyme used to give it shape? Is there a stanzaic pattern? What special symbols, images, ideas, arrangements, or plot devices can help organize the work? A poem can ask a question, and then answer it. A short story can be filled with images of a particular color that symbolize certain attitudes or beliefs. A novel can refer time and again to an idea (like freedom, for instance). Stories within a story can be arranged, as in Chaucer's *Canterbury Tales.* Many works have several organizational devices that work together in a complicated fashion. In *The Scarlet Letter* Nathaniel Hawthorne organizes his story in several ways, chief among them the use of the three important scaffold scenes and the symbol of adultery (the scarlet *A*) that Hester Prynne is forced to wear on her bosom.

All of the elements that go to organize or shape a work create its structure, its total framework. A successful work tends to have its own, unique structure.

3. What does the work *say*?

What is its *theme* (its main point)? Authors tend to state their themes somewhat indirectly through symbol, imagery, allusion, action, characterization, irony, or satire. A symbol like Hester's scarlet *A* may tell the reader much about a work's theme. The important thing about this particular symbol, for instance, is not merely that Hester is forced to wear it because she committed adultery, but that it becomes for *her* a symbol of her rich, defiant nature. She decorates and embroiders it, and wears it proudly. To take another instance, through characterization Crane indirectly creates his comic theme in "The Bride Comes to Yellow Sky" (see pp. 436–439). Scratchy, the old gunman, wears clothes that little boys love to wear while at play, and when the feud he enjoyed so much is over, he walks away like a little boy, dragging his feet.

So, as you read, watch for the author's indirect statements that help you interpret the meaning of the work. For example, the title "How Annandale Went Out" probably contains an allusion to Macbeth's lines on the meaninglessness of life that begin: "Out, out, brief candle. . . . it [life] is a tale/Told by an idiot, full of sound and fury,/Signifying nothing." Is it possible that Annandale's doctor is telling his listeners, with bitter irony, that the momentous events he recounted really meant nothing after all, that human life means nothing?

Themes are often expressed through the indirection of irony. In an ironic statement, the doctor says that the sight of Annandale "was not so fair" as others he had seen. What he means is that the sight of Annandale was horrible, although it does not seem to fill him with horror, a fact which contributes to the poem's theme. In an ironic situation, events point two ways (appearance vs. reality): a beautiful girl graduates from college with high honors and with a shining future—but she is killed in a freak accident as she drives to her first job. It is an irony of *situation* that Annandale's doctor, who should be a saver of lives, deliberately takes one.

Satire is irony sharpened, pointed, and (usually) directed at people or ideas the author believes need reform or scornful instruction. One may consider it an irony of situation that people who are satirically attacked are occasionally quite lovable, but this fact merely reflects the truth that a successful work in any medium seldom presents an issue that is totally black or white. The better the work, as a matter of fact, the more complex its theme appears to the reader. But the reverse is not necessarily true; a complex work is not always well-made or convincing. Perhaps the best literary complexity tends to mirror the real complexities of human life, rather than those of the author.

4. Where is the *author* in the work?

What is the author's *point of view*? If the work is fiction, from what angle is the story presented? Is the author *omniscient* (all-knowing), able to present all the actions and speech of the characters, as well as their thoughts and feelings? Does he use the *limited omniscient* point of view, mainly sticking to one character and seeing events through his eyes? Does he employ the *first-person* viewpoint? Does he present events as they happen but without comment, as if they were simply crossing his range of vision? This kind of perspective, called the *objective* point of view, is most often used in plays but it also can be found in novels, short stories, and poems. Robinson's point of view in "How Annandale Went Out" is objective.

In nonfictional works, authors may take a variety of viewpoints or "positions," which often combine the physical and psychological. To describe a city, a poet may imagine himself on a hill, a point of view that will color and shape his statements about the city. In Tennyson's line, "The wrinkled sea beneath him crawls," the poet's point of view is physically the same as the eagle's; and that is why *wrinkled* and *crawls* seem so effective as images. The possible roles and viewpoints the poet, dramatist, or story writer may adopt are so many that you should consider each work as unique, and describe carefully the point of view of the author in that particular work.

5. Finally, how *successful* is the work?

Does the author accomplish what he set out to do? Why or why not?

WRITING THE LITERARY PAPER

When your instructor asks you to write on a poem, play, novel, or short story, the assignment may well be related to one or more of these elements of literary study:

ELEMENT	POSSIBLE ASSIGNMENT
1. *Character*	What is the cause of Hamlet's madness? (Not only is this a question of character analysis, but as the question is stated it also implies a cause-and-effect strategy of development.)
2. *Theme*	Defend or attack Golding's view of society in *Lord of the Flies*.
3. *Setting*	How does the setting of Conrad's *Heart of Darkness* influence the action?
4. *Structure*	Discuss how the two climaxes of Fitzgerald's *The Great Gatsby* support the novel's theme.
5. *Imagery*	Explain Frost's use of imagery in "The Road Not Taken."
6. *Symbolism*	What are the fertility symbols in Faulkner's *Light in August*? In what ways are the symbols used? How are they related to the theme?

7. *Style* Defend the "repetitiousness" of stylistic patterns in Hemingway's *A Farewell to Arms.*

8. *Genre* What is "The Bride Comes to Yellow Sky"? Is it a tragedy, a tragicomedy, a comedy? Give reasons for your answer.

9. *Point of View* Is Leggett a reliable narrator in Conrad's *The Secret Sharer*? Does it make any difference whether he is reliable?

Assignments on literary topics may implicitly or explicitly ask you to use some of the ten strategies of development. Here are some examples:

1. *Comparison-Contrast* How are the characters Carol and Vida alike and different in Sinclair Lewis' *Main Street*?

2. *Definition* Define Albert Camus' existentialist position (as presented through Meursault) in *The Stranger.*

3. *Cause and Effect* What are the causes of Willy Loman's tragic end in Arthur Miller's *Death of a Salesman*?

4. *Classification* What different uses does Poe make of sound in "The Raven"?

The Writer's Stance

The stance for the literary paper is somewhat limited and unusual. In such a paper you should consider the reader as someone who knows the work fairly well. You might sum up your relationship with your reader as follows:

> I have read a work (that you also have read), and I have an idea about it that may have not occurred to you. I am going to explain this idea, giving you examples from the work to prove my point, and I hope when I am through that you will agree with me.

However, you will never state your intention as explicitly as this. Such a stance is essentially an argumentative one, and the literary paper is fundamentally a form of argumentation that depends for its success on a clear, specific thesis and strong proof taken from the work. For example, when you state that the scenes of violence in a novel are contrived and unbelievable, you should be prepared to prove that point, with specific examples from the text. After reading your paper, your reader should be able to say—"You have not only read the work carefully but have also made a solid, intelligent point about it. And your evidence taken from the work convinces me that you are right."

What to Avoid in Writing the Literary Paper

As an interpretation of literature, your paper must be more than a summary of what goes on in the work. A summary of what a poet says (or seems to say) in a poem, of the action in a play, or of the plot of a novel or short story is often necessary to your interpretation and your argument. But such a summary is only the beginning, a foundation on which to build. Unless they specifically request them, instructors will not accept mere summaries as literary papers. Also be aware of the "chronology trap." It is difficult to write a successful paper on fiction by using a chronological strategy of development because it is so easy to fall into plot summary. If the outline of your proposed essay shows its development to be mainly chronological, start over and get a new focus on the work.

Do not push your interpretations of literature too far. It is often tempting, for example, to explain a character's motivation by writing down something that seems obvious to you at the time but is not based solidly on the evidence in the work. Is there, as has been argued, a homosexual relationship between Huck Finn and Jim in Mark Twain's novel? Read the novel with care and see if the *evidence* points to such a relationship. It has been claimed that some of the description at the beginning of "The Bride Comes to Yellow Sky" points to a theme about the conflict between the values of the decadent East and the innocent West:

> The great Pullman was whirling onward with such dignity of motion that a glance from the window seemed simply to prove that the plains of Texas were pouring eastward. Vast flats of green grass, dull-hued spaces of mesquit and cactus, little groups of frame houses, woods of light and tender trees, all were sweepng into the east, sweeping over the horizon, a precipice.

To argue that this descriptive passage implies a conflict of East-West values is probably pushing an interpretation too far.

Do not assume that there is one, fixed, "right" interpretation of a literary work. Professor Arra Garab comments: "Far too many readers labor under the delusion that there is a magical key to a poem or story, and if they could just find this key, the 'real meaning' would suddenly be revealed to them." As a reader, you should try for a *reasonable* interpretation, one that is firmly based on the evidence in the work. And a reasonable interpretation is not just a matter of opinion ("my reading is as good as yours because my opinion is as good as yours"). Any opinion stated about a work must be based on the facts in the work.

Do not suggest in your paper that the literary work represents literal fact. Hawthorne's Hester Prynne, Marvell's Coy Mistress, Shakespeare's Macbeth, Robert Penn Warren's Willie Stark, the people and situations in T. S. Eliot's *The Waste Land,* Big Brother in George Orwell's *1984* — none of these has ever literally existed in the real world. It may be a temptation to write that "Holden Caulfield shows us what American life was like in the 1950s for a sensitive boy who hated hypocrisy." While it is true that Holden, the leading character of J. D. Salinger's *Catcher in the Rye,* may for many readers illuminate life in a way that sociological treatises never can, he and his experiences are not *literally* true. Although one may reasonably argue that great literature is more "real" than real life, that assertion does not make them the same thing.

Finally, trust your instincts about a work. All literature is about people and written for people. Make use of your experience as you read. Mark passages and descriptions that seem particularly realistic or pertinent to your life and interests. Respond to the work as you read.

PRACTICE

Discussion

We would like you to act as a reader for two literary papers written by students. Each can be considered a successful example of student writing, although you (as a reader) might have a few suggestions for the writers. Discussing the paper in class might be a good idea, particularly after you have looked at the questions at the end of each paper.

The first paper was written in response to an informal assignment given by the student's instructor. The student had idly commented in the hall after class that she had just seen the movie *M*A*S*H* and that in some ways it seemed surprisingly different from the TV series. Her instructor said: "I've never seen the movie, but I've read the book, which is different from the TV show. For your next assignment, why don't you write your paper on *M*A*S*H*? I'd like to know more about the three versions. And it doesn't have to be a heavily 'literary' paper."

The second paper was written in response to a formal assignment: "In a *brief* paper, analyze Ursula Brangwen's real motives regarding love and marriage in D. H. Lawrence's *Women in Love.* Use specific evidence from the novel to support your answer."

*M*A*S*H — Will the Real Swampmen Please Stand Up?*

[1]*M*A*S*H,* by Richard Hooker, has had an unusual life for a war novel. The book was made into a very successful movie, which was later turned into a popular TV series. Even though the paperback book has over "1,500,000 copies in print," to most people *M*A*S*H* is not a novel but a TV series that has been adapted from a movie.

[2]After encountering the three versions of the story, set in an American field hospital during the Korean War, I am a little puzzled — not by the success of each of the versions but by their differences. The book, movie, and TV show differ significantly from each other, yet each has been acclaimed by the public, which apparently does not mind (or is not aware) that it is being exposed to three different treatments of the same story.

[3]The novel centers on three Army surgeons (Hawkeye, Duke, and Trapper — the Swampmen). They are not regular army personnel, and they have little use for anybody in the regular army. They live in a hut they call "the Swamp." When they are not in the Swamp they are engaged in one of two activities: operating on wounded soldiers or giving the authorities fits. The book abounds in outrageous comedy: the Swampmen encourage the dentist to commit "suicide" because he believes he is impotent; they beat another service football team through trickery and guile; they talk back to a regular army colonel after he catches them putting golf balls on his office carpet: "You men are under arrest," the colonel boomed, when he stormed onto the scene. "Quiet!" Trapper said. "Can't you see I'm putting?"

[4]Yet the real theme of the novel has little to do with military service or with the endless conflict between draftees and the regular army. Rather the theme is that trained surgeons are dedicated to saving lives, no matter where they are working or under what conditions they are forced to operate. Medicine is not only the Swampmen's profession but their religion as well. The comedy in the book is secondary and often even perfunctory, sometimes barely funny. Hooker's style is flat; he tells every joke and relates each comic scene in a stylistic monotone. The reader can pass right over a punch line because his comic scenes lack emphasis, energy, and pacing.

[5]But when Hooker (who is himself a doctor) brings the Swampmen face to face with death in their profession, the writing takes on life and passion. Their suffering and concern for their wounded patients are real and moving. Moreover, the descriptions of the operations are very vivid:

> Hawkeye donned a pair of gloves, accepted a syringe of Novocain from a corpsman, infiltrated the skin and the space between the ribs

and shoved the needle into the pleural cavity. Pulling back on the plunger he got air, knew he was in the right place, noted the angle of the needle, withdrew it, took a scalpel, incised the skin for one-half inch and plunged the scalpel into the pleural cavity. Bubbles of air appeared at the incision. Then he grasped the tip of a Foley catheter with a Kelly clamp and shoved the tube through the hole. A nurse attached the other end to the drainage bottle on the floor, a corpsman blew up the balloon on the catheter and now bubbles began to rise to the surface of the water in the bottle. Hawkeye dropped to his knees on the sand floor and as he began to suck on the rubber tube attached to the shorter of the two tubes in the bottle, the upward flow of bubbles increased as the lung was, indeed, expanding.

"Crude, ain't it?" said Hawkeye.

The reader believes that these men are dedicated doctors, and that the author is basing his description on operations he actually witnessed.

[6]The movie is a different story—*literally*. From the unmotivated fight at the beginning between two soldiers to the last comic scene, the movie concentrates on comedy and burlesque. Scenes not in the book are given great emphasis, and they are wildly funny—the "unveiling" of Hot Lips in the shower, for example, or the still-life parody of the Last Supper at the dentist's "suicide" banquet. The movie is basically a comedy that happens to have a field hospital as a setting. Although the Swampmen are still dedicated doctors, their dedication is deemphasized while their antics and brawls fill up the plot. The book's comedy occurs only outside the operating room, but a great deal of the comedy in the movie occurs during the operations; horrendously, red blood spurts and spatters while the quips fly fast. The medical theme almost disappears under the weight of burlesque.

[7]The kind of medical dedication described in the book is seldom matched in the movie. In the book Dago Red tells the Swampmen, "But you people in the Swamp have got to get over the idea that you can save everyone who comes into this hospital. Man is mortal. The wounded can stand only so much, and the surgeon can do only so much." It would be ludicrous for Dago Red to say this in the movie because the seriousness of the situation is not emphasized to that great a degree. But statements of this kind are made quite often in the TV version.

[8]The TV series appears to "average" thematically the book and movie. Certain episodes of the television show focus only on the humor and antics of the doctors while other episodes focus solely on the doctors' dedication to their profession. Like the movie, it sometimes mixes comedy and medicine in the operating room. Like the book, it takes medicine very seriously; the TV Swampmen desperately want to save lives, and they will move mountains to do so. Statements like Dago Red's quoted above are made quite often in the television series.

⁹Why are these versions of *M*A*S*H* different? One answer may be that they were written for different purposes and audiences. The foreword to the novel stresses the surgeons' work and the terrible strain they endure. When Hawkeye, Duke, and Trapper engage in crazy stunts in the book, it is in their spare time—to relieve them from the pressures of their grim life. In the movie, the comedy is its own excuse for being. I understand that when it first came out, people thought *M*A*S*H* was an antiwar movie, but the student audience I saw it with the other night just seemed to think it was hilarious. The TV version takes advantage of both antiwar sentiment and the viewer's simple desire to be amused. Of course the TV shows are much "cleaner" than the other productions; television morality prohibits some of the racier scenes and dialogue that are found in the book and movie.

¹⁰Of the three versions of *M*A*S*H,* I believe that the television version is the most successful and consistent. But I still wonder if war can ever be truly funny.

1. In the first two paragraphs of the paper, the author implies that she will use a particular rhetorical strategy. Does she successfully organize the paper according to this strategy?

2. Is the writer using a large or small focus in discussing the three versions of *M*A*S*H*? Explain.

3. How does the author bring herself into her paper? Describe her stance, using the form: "I am a _____ who _____."

4. What facts or information does the writer assume the reader already has?

5. How important is the plot summary in discussing the three forms of *M*A*S*H*?

6. In paragraph 3, the writer says that the "book abounds in outrageous comedy." Discuss the evidence used to support this statement. Consider paragraph 4 also. Are there any contradictions between paragraphs 3 and 4?

7. Analyze the long quote in paragraph 5 in relation to the statements in the rest of the paragraph.

8. How does the writer use the promise pattern (see pp. 211–213) in paragraph 6?

9. Does the last line of the paper fit the paper's thesis?

10. Do you consider the paper a success? Why, or why not? (Be specific in your answer.)

Ursula: Dominated or Domineering?

[1]Ursula Brangwen, the leading female character in D. H.
Lawrence's *Women in Love,* is a fiercely independent, self-possessed
woman. She is contemptuous of men and marriage because she
believes men try to control and possess her—she thinks marriage
represents total submission. Ursula feels so strongly about her freedom
that she interprets everything that affects her negatively as being an affront to her right to independence as a woman. She construes the
words and actions of those around her in a way that enables her to
become self-righteous and to assume the role of the persecuted woman.
As Lawrence says of her: "She had a maddening faculty of assuming a
light of her own, which exhausted the reality, and within which she
looked radiant as if in sunshine."

[2]When Ursula sees Gerald Crich forcing his horse, a "lovely, sensitive" mare, to stand still at a noisy railway crossing, she criticizes him
for it. After Gerald explains his actions, Ursula's fiery response concerning the mistreatment of animals sounds as if she were actually
referring to the abuse of women:

> "I have to use her," he replied. "And if I'm going to be sure of
> her at *all,* she'll have to learn to stand noises."
> "Why should she?" cried Ursula in a passion. "She is a living
> creature, why should she stand anything, just because you choose to
> make her? She has as much right to her own being, as you have to
> yours."

[3]Ursula reacts in a similar manner when she sees Mino,
Mrs. Birkin's male cat, box his mate with his paws. " 'Mino,' said
Ursula, 'I don't like you. You are a bully like all males.' " When Birkin
tries to explain the female cat's submission, Ursula says, " 'Oh, it
makes me so cross, this assumption of male superiority! And it is such
a lie! One wouldn't mind if there were any justification for it.' "

[4]After seeing Ursula become so self-righteous and defensive in these
two situations, it is easy to understand how she is able to misinterpret
everything Birkin says and does to mean that he wants to control her.
For example, when Birkin says, " 'Adam kept Eve in the indestructible
paradise when he kept her single with himself, like a star in its orbit,' "
Ursula immediately interprets this as an expression of his desire to control a woman. " 'Yes—yes—' cried Ursula, pointing her finger at him.
'There you are—a star in its orbit! A satellite—a satellite of
Mars—that's what she is to be!' "

[5]Ursula even takes Birkin's marriage proposal as another effort to
make her concede to him. When, in her father's presence, he asks her
to marry him, she refuses even to answer him. Finally, she says,
" 'Why should I say anything? You do this off your *own* bat, it has

nothing to do with me. Why do you both want to bully me?' " Ursula feels elated after she has rejected Birkin and embarrassed her father. She relishes the power she has over both men: "Ursula's face closed, she completed herself against them all. . . . She was bright and invulnerable, quite free and happy, perfectly liberated in her self-possession."

[6]Ursula continues to believe that Birkin's idea of marriage is her total submission to him. She says at one point to Hermione: " 'I don't want to give the sort of *submission* he insists on. He wants me to give myself up—and I simply don't feel that I *can* do it.' " Actually, Birkin never does expect Ursula to do any such thing. But she continues to deceive herself into believing this for one reason. She wants to control and possess Birkin in the way that she claims he wants to control and possess her. Because she knows he will never submit to her, she continues to believe it is he who wishes to dominate her. Birkin is perfectly justified in thinking that Ursula

> was the awful, arrogant queen of life, as if she were a queen bee on whom all the rest depended. . . . She was only too ready to knock her head on the ground before a man. But this was only when she was so certain of her man, that she could worship him as a woman worships her own infant, with a worship of perfect possession.

[7]Ursula says she could not bear to surrender herself to Birkin. Yet, "She wanted to have him, utterly, finally to have him as her own, oh, so unspeakably, in intimacy. To drink him down—ah, like a life-draught." Because she is unable to do so, she accuses Birkin of doing to her exactly what she wants to do to him. Birkin says, " 'I tell you, you want love to administer to your egoism, to subserve you. Love is a process of subservience with you. . . .' "

[8]Ursula's intense pride and desire for freedom carry her to the point of wanting to control others. When she sees she cannot succeed, she transfers her motives to Birkin and acts on the defensive. Her constant self-righteousness turns out to be a self-serving act. Everything that she says Birkin is trying to do to her, she is actually doing to him!

1. What does the reader need to know in order to understand this paper? Would you, as a reader, recommend a plot summary for it?

2. Why doesn't the writer discuss the theme of *Women in Love*? Would the paper have been improved if it had been done?

3. Prepare a brief outline of the paper. Concentrate on topic ideas and transitions. Are the transitions of a particular kind? Do they help or hinder the reader's understanding of the paper? Describe specifically the organization of the paper. Should the writer have organized the paper in a different way? Why?

4. Discuss the paper as an argument. For example, are you convinced by the evidence presented that Ursula "construes the words and actions of those around her in a way that enables her to become self-righteous and to assume the role of the persecuted woman"?

5. Block quotations are usually not surrounded by quotation marks (see p. 377). Why are there quotation marks in the block quotation in paragraph 2? Discuss the convention of using double and single quotation marks in paragraphs 3, 4, 5, and 6.

6. Why does the writer use *four* periods in the quotation in paragraph 6 to show a deletion? Discuss the use of ellipsis marks (p. 378) at the end of paragraph 7. Why couldn't the writer just end the quote with a period and quotation mark?

7. Does the writer quote "too much"? Give reasons for your answer.

8. In planning their papers, the writers on *M*A*S*H* and *Women in Love* obviously used different focuses. Compare and discuss each focus. Which paper would be easier to write? Why? Is one paper more convincing than the other? Give your reasons.

Writing

1. By applying the questions (pp. 446–448) to the following poem, annotate it in preparation for writing a literary paper.

> *Because I Could Not Stop for Death* .
>
> Because I could not stop for Death,
> He kindly stopped for me;
> The carriage held but just ourselves
> And Immortality.
>
> 5 We slowly drove, he knew no haste,
> And I had put away
> My labor, and my leisure too,
> For his civility.
>
> We passed the school where children played,
> 10 Their lessons scarcely done;
> We passed the fields of gazing grain,
> We passed the setting sun.
>
> We paused before a house that seemed
> A swelling on the ground;
> 15 The roof was scarcely visible,
> The cornice but a mound.

Since then 'tis centuries; but each
Feels shorter than the day
I first surmised the horses' heads
20   Were toward eternity.

—Emily Dickinson

2. Read the following story, and write a paper on one of its outstanding features—for example, its use of dialogue to build character, or the point of view of the story.

I Worry About You

[1] There were stacks of silver bowls that gleamed in the light, piles of wicker trays and wicker baskets, all sorts of mixers and grinders standing as straight as soldiers in a row, and above hung wooden ladles and forks, metal spatulas and rubber ones—a field of kitchenware that rolled into the distance, into the women's clothes department.

[2] "Look at this," said Mrs. Hankley, picking up a coffeemaker. "You could use one."

[3] "I don't need a coffeemaker," said her daughter, Sarah. "I drink instant."

[4] "You don't want a coffeemaker?"

[5] "No."

[6] Mrs. Hankley was pensive for a moment, looking around. Sarah felt a twinge of pity for her mother, but she ignored it. There was a principle involved here; she had to stand firm.

[7] Mrs. Hankley moved deeper into the center of the kitchenware department, but her way was blocked from the really nice stuff, the microwave ovens, by two fat women who stood side by side in the aisle. Sarah stayed obstinately right where she was. When her mother finally squeezed past the fat women she looked back for Sarah with that worried, almost desperate expression she often wore these days around her youngest child.

[8] How can you fight her? Sarah wondered. "Coming, coming," Sarah called past the two fat women. I will be kind, she thought, but I will not be bought. She worked her way past the two women to her mother's side.

[9] "You need a crockpot," Mrs. Hankley said.

[10] "I don't want a crockpot."

[11] "Don't want a crockpot?"

[12] "Please, don't bribe me."

[13] Pain went through Mrs. Hankley's face. "I'm not trying to bribe you."

[14] "Maybe bribe is the wrong word," Sarah said quickly. Be strong, she thought. "But you can't buy me something to make up for last night."

¹⁵"I'm not trying to make up for anything," Mrs. Hankley said with dignity.

¹⁶"All right." Sarah felt foolish and beaten. How did she manage to lose these arguments even when her mother was in the wrong? "But don't try to help me anymore. *Please?*" She realized that she had suddenly shouted, and she glanced around—the two fat women were looking at her.

¹⁷"Maybe you'd like one of these wicker bowls," her mother suggested, crossing the aisle. "You could put fruit in it. Don't you think that would look nice on your kitchen table?"

¹⁸"Sure, sure."

¹⁹"Or would you like one of these baskets? You could serve bread in it if you have a dinner party."

²⁰"Anything, buy me anything."

²¹But her mother was unfazed by her sarcasm.

²²"Why not both?" Mrs. Hankley said, and gripped one of each kind and held them up cheerfully, her smile turning into the benevolent grin of a victor.

²³The night before, Mrs. Hankley had sent a young man named Paul Winfred to take a look at Sarah, who was waitressing at Papa's Restaurant on Riverside Drive.

²⁴When Sarah saw Paul Winfred, she knew exactly what he had come for. In the last several months Mrs. Hankley had sent five young men—sons and nephews of friends and strangers—to Papa's, all of the men very neat, well-dressed and dull-looking. (Mrs. Hankley liked a well-groomed man; her two older daughters had good taste, too, and married well.) Even one of Mrs. Hankley's old friends had directed an eligible man to Papa's. Mrs. Hankley was so wrapped up in her worries about Sarah that everyone within earshot knew all the details: Sarah being twenty-six, a college graduate, so intelligent and talented (you ought to hear her play the piano: a sweet touch); a girl who could succeed at anything; instead she was stuck waitressing at a crummy Italian restaurant; and such a solitary girl.

²⁵So Sarah spotted Paul Winfred immediately, but she was nice to him anyway. It wasn't his fault: her mother had, of course, given him the impression that it was all right to spy on her. Besides, this one looked a little more intelligent than the other men her mother had sent. After Paul Winfred introduced himself, Sarah just smiled wryly and tried to make him as comfortable as possible. When he offered to drive her home from work she accepted; it was cold out, and there was a fifteen-minute wait for the bus. In his car they chatted politely, and when he stopped in front of her house, he asked her for a date. She had expected this, but she panicked anyway. "I'm busy," she said quickly, opening the car door. "Sorry, thank you so much, thank you, thank you," and she slammed the door and ran toward her apartment building. When she got inside she felt terrible; she had been so rude.

She phoned her mother and said: "How could you do this to me again?"

[26]"He's nice, isn't he?"

[27]"That has nothing to do with it."

[28]"Would you like to go shopping tomorrow? Only seven shopping days left until Christmas."

[29]Sarah and her mother were hurrying through the cold wind that sliced down the corridors between the tall buildings.

[30]"Let's go in here," Sarah said. "Got a good chef salad."

[31]"Let's go on to the Peking."

[32]"Why? That's two more blocks and I'm freezing."

[33]"I want to go to the Peking."

[34]"I'm *freezing*, Mother. Have you no interest in my health?"

[35]Mrs. Hankley smiled, her teeth chattering. "Oh, you sissy. It's only two more blocks."

[36]"I'll be an ice cube by then."

[37]"Who's paying for lunch?"

[38]"Oh, God."

[39]The Peking was blissfully warm. As Sarah followed the hostess through the restaurant she saw a familiar man. He had a plump, smooth face with a double chin, which his tight collar dented, blonde hair that was perfectly parted in the middle, fluffed up and combed back, and a preposterous little moustache. He seemed to know her too, and gave her a quick little smile. When she sat down with her mother at a table, she glanced over at him, and this time recognized him. "Of course!" she said out loud. It was the new hair-do and moustache that had fooled her.

[40]"What?" said her mother, looking up from her menu.

[41]At that moment the man got up, smoothing out the bulging vest of his suit, and started toward them.

[42]"Mother!" Sarah said.

[43]"What?"

[44]"How could you do this—?"

[45]The man was standing over them now. "Hello," he said genially.

[46]Sarah jumped to her feet. "No!"

[47]People at nearby tables sat up and took notice.

[48]Sarah grabbed her coat and purse. "I'm going!"

[49]The man stepped back, startled in a sluggish way.

[50]"What?" said Mrs. Hankley.

[51]"Goodbye!" Sarah said, turned and strode through the restaurant and burst out into the icy street. Then she started to run. After half a block, she heard her mother call out, "Saaaarah!" as if she were seven years old again and late for supper. "Saaaaarah!" But she kept running.

[52]A bus was waiting for a red light on the corner and she ran ahead of it to see if this one would take her home. Yes, it would; she banged

on the door, and the driver let her in. She stood panting, out of breath in front of the bus, searching through her purse for the correct change. After a minute she gave up and stuck a dollar bill in the coin slot.

[53]The bus was only half full and she found a seat to herself. She was sweating—the bus was stifling—and she took her coat off and then her sweater. She put her hand on her heart, which was thumping dangerously.

[54]She thought of the way her mother had looked when that silly peacock came over to the table, and she ground her teeth in disgust. Why should she like the sort of man her mother liked? And if she didn't like men altogether, if she gave up men for good, was it any of her mother's business? And if she wanted to work as a waitress instead of finding a "real" job, must her mother constantly badger her about it? She just wanted time to figure things out.

[55]She had an image of herself sometimes as a kind of small forest animal that blends into the background and watches the world go by. She must be very still and quiet. If you waited long enough you would begin to see a pattern; you would know the safe time to move. Now she had to watch carefully to understand the world better; how to avoid the mistakes she made before.

[56]Paul had been a mistake.

[57]"Men are not all alike," her mother said. "There are some good ones and some bad ones. Don't let a bad one ruin you for the good ones."

[58]But how can you tell them apart?

[59]Her stop was coming up, and she pulled the bell. The bus wheezed to the corner and she went to the front to get off. She was thinking furiously about her mother when she stepped down the stairs, almost running into a bundled-up middle-aged man. She was not aware of how stern and ferocious she appeared until the man looked into her face and then stepped back in a hurry. As she walked away she chuckled to herself over the man's reaction. Her face could get her respect, she thought, even if it might not get her love.

[60]But after a moment this thought threw her into a spasm of worry. She walked along telling herself that this last year was only a respite to gather herself again; it wasn't permanent. All men were not like Paul.

[61]She was sitting in her favorite chair, sipping hot tea when there was a knock at her door.

[62]She asked who it was and she heard her mother say, "Me!" Sarah opened the door and standing there was her mother and the man from the restaurant.

[63]In one quick breath, her mother blurted: "I brought Jim along to prove I didn't set up anything this afternoon." Then she exhaled, looking panicky.

[64]Jim smiled, in what he must have thought was a gracious way. "Really," he said cheerfully, "I haven't seen your mother in ages."

⁶⁵They all stood there in an awkward silence until Sarah finally invited them in. Her mother bustled through the doorway, shivering, her head moving quickly and nervously from side to side, looking around the place as if she had never seen it before. Whenever she was upset she seemed to be a complete stranger to her environment, even if it was her daughter's apartment.

⁶⁶"I haven't seen *you* in ages, either," Jim said to Sarah.

⁶⁷"That's right," Sarah said. "Would you like something to drink? Brandy or whiskey or something?"

⁶⁸"Brandy would be perfect," Jim said. "Just perfect."

⁶⁹"Mother?" Sarah said.

⁷⁰"Brandy, yes," Mrs. Hankley said, distracted. She was looking around at Sarah's apartment with a frustrated, pained expression.

⁷¹Sarah went into the kitchen and Mrs. Hankley followed right behind her.

⁷²"I didn't set it up," said Mrs. Hankley.

⁷³"All *right,* already."

⁷⁴"You don't mind that I brought him? He's not a bad sort. You aren't mad?"

⁷⁵"No, I'm not mad. I'm sorry about this afternoon."

⁷⁶Mrs. Hankley was looking around the kitchen. "If you lived with another girl you could get a bigger place with a bigger kitchen."

⁷⁷"I like living here," Sarah said, pouring a brandy. "I like living alone."

⁷⁸"Do you really?"

⁷⁹Her mother always made her doubt things that she had not really doubted before. "I don't know. I just do it. Jim is out there all alone."

⁸⁰Her mother gave her a long anxious look and went back to the living room.

⁸¹". . . My own firm, doing quite well," Jim was saying when Sarah brought the brandies in. "Ah, here she is. Doesn't she just look perfect? Sarah, you're looking perfect."

⁸²"I'm glad you think so."

⁸³Mrs. Hankley watched her warily.

⁸⁴"And this place," he said. "It's just right, too, so cozy, it's perfect. I imagined you lived in a place like this: spare, hardly any furniture, just a few paintings on the wall." He was sitting up, looking around with an expression of growing astonishment. "It fits you, it really does, like a glove."

⁸⁵"Glad you think so."

⁸⁶Mrs. Hankley shifted worriedly on the couch.

⁸⁷"Do you have a perfect place too?" asked Sarah.

⁸⁸He studied for a second. "Perfect in a different way. I own a house," he said apologetically.

⁸⁹Sarah wondered why some men were attracted to women who disliked them. Jim seemed to savor her scorn, as if it were the exhilaration of danger. Mrs. Hankley watched them both.

[90]Jim chuckled mirthlessly and said: "Did I ever tell you what she said to me when I first met her at that restaurant, what is it, Mama's?"

[91]"Papa's," Sarah said.

[92]Mrs. Hankley sat suddenly rigid and blushed violently. "Sarah loves to kid."

[93]"She looked me right in the eye—" he began.

[94]"Never mind that," Mrs. Hankley said quickly, "tell me how your mother is doing. She got over her operation all right?"

[95]"Looks great, really does," he said. "You ought to give her a call."

[96]"I will. I will," said Mrs. Hankley.

[97]Jim looked at Sarah for a long moment. Holding his glass delicately between his thumb and forefinger, he slowly sipped the brandy. His round face beamed with good health. He set his glass down and leaned toward her. "I feel really lucky that I ran into you today. I've been thinking about you lately. Remember the time I came into the restaurant and the stories you told about the cook? Delightful." He shook his head, chuckling.

[98]Sarah regretted having been pleasant to him that time. Such things always catch up to you eventually, she thought.

[99]Jim glanced at Mrs. Hankley, bringing her generously into the young peoples' intimacy, neatly picked up his glass, and said, "Delightfully caustic stories," and chuckled again.

[100]Mrs. Hankley sat very still, watching.

[101]"Sarah," he said, "I've been waiting for your mother to call me and tell me about you. She always used to call when—"

[102]"I didn't set it up!" Mrs. Hankley cried. She turned to Sarah. "Really, I didn't set it up. I won't do anything like that again. I've decided that you have to live your own life. I can't keep being a mother forever."

[103]"Amen," Sarah said.

[104]"It's a big city," Jim said seriously. "It can be hard to meet the right sort of people. Sometimes it's a very good thing to throw two people of the same type together."

[105]"No more," said Mrs. Hankley. "I'm done with all that. It just doesn't work."

[106]"It worked in its own way," Jim said. He leaned further toward Sarah and smiled. "After all, I met Sarah."

[107]Mrs. Hankley suddenly finished off her brandy and said: "Jim, we ought to go. Sarah is getting tired, aren't you, honey?"

[108]Jim looked at Sarah, then at Mrs. Hankley. He frowned. He opened his mouth, about to object and then closed it. Finally, he nodded decisively. "Yes, we must be going." It was his own idea now. "Finally, I know where you live, Sarah. I'll have to come and see how you're getting along. Hmmm?"

[109]Sarah put on a sour face, and said nothing.

[110]Her coat on now, Mrs. Hankley said goodbye and opened the door.

[111]Jim looked around one last time and sighed: "Perfect place you have. Just perfect."

[112]"Goodbye," said Sarah.

[113]"Goodbye," said Jim. "See you soon."

[114]Sarah was back in her favorite chair minutes later with a cup of tea when there was another knock on the door. Her mother called, "Me again!" and swept in. "He's not a bad sort," she said uncertainly.

[115]"No, I guess not," Sarah said.

[116]"Am I keeping you from anything?"

[117]"No, not at all."

[118]"Any more brandy?"

[119]"Half a bottle."

[120]The bottle sat between them on the coffee table. At first they chatted about whether or not Sarah needed a crockpot, and when that topic was exhausted, they were left with silence. The longer they were silent the more difficult it became to break it, so they pretended that they were perfectly comfortable, giving one another brittle encouraging little smiles. Mrs. Hankley sat on the very edge of the sofa, as though trying to touch as little of the furniture as possible, and Sarah wondered if she might the next moment slide off the couch altogether. But for once Sarah was not irritated with her mother; she was worried about her. Sarah noticed the harried look in her eyes, the tightness around her mouth.

[121]Suddenly, Mrs. Hankley broke the silence with: "I wish you didn't live here. It's so awfully small and drab."

[122]It made Sarah's heart ache to see her mother so unhappy. She got up and put a comforting arm around her shoulders. "I'll move one of these days," Sarah said. What was wrong with a little white lie, she asked herself, if it would for the moment make her mother feel better?

[123]Mrs. Hankley looked skeptical; but willing to be comforted, she said: "Really? Will you move soon?"

[124]Why not? Sarah asked herself. She was very tired of this conflict. Besides, maybe she needed a change. "Sure," Sarah said. "Here, let's finish the last of the brandy. It's been sitting around here too long, gathering dust."

—Richard Maclean

CHAPTER 20
WRITING FOR
THE BUSINESS WORLD

"What sort of writing are you doing these days?" This was a question asked more or less at random of people working in business and government, many of them still in their twenties. Here is a shortened list of the writing jobs they mentioned:

announcements	long-range planning reports
procedures manuals	program reports
proposals	appraisals
requests for action	identifications of problems
instructions	activity reports
reports of meetings	budget reports
grievance reports	scientific papers

And: memos, memos, memos!
       letters, letters, letters!

Thanks are due to Professor Francis Weeks, Director Emeritus of the Division of Business and Technical Writing, University of Illinois. Professor Weeks designed the course that we have been teaching and gave us much useful information on the problems of business writing. Professor Robert Gieselman, Director of the same Division, read and criticized the chapter, and we thank him for his help.

BUSINESS WRITING: FIVE EMPHASES

So far as this book is concerned, the writing jobs listed above *do not represent new types of writing.* In writing for business, you are not going to learn five or ten new kinds of exposition or argument. From first to last, the items on the list simply represent adaptations of rhetorical problems and strategies that have already been discussed in the first 15 chapters. But some of these strategies are more strongly emphasized, or more widely used, than others in "business writing," as the subject is often called. In such writing, you should place particular emphasis on:

1. *A specific stance.* Before you start writing a letter, memo, or report, you must be very sure of your role, thesis, and reader. If you are both a technician and an administrator, for example, you may be shifting roles almost hourly as you write memos, instructions, technical reports, budget proposals, or requests for action to readers as diverse as maintenance workers, stock clerks, or company vice-presidents. If you don't "shift the proper gears" as you adapt your stance, you may transmit the right information to the wrong reader. Even though they may be in similar income brackets and social levels, you don't often use the same stance in writing to a vice-president and a stockholder. It is likely, for instance, that the stockholder won't understand certain technical information that the vice-president would consider obvious.

2. *Clear word choice and sentence structure.* The bane of business writing is the jargonized sentence: "Pursuant to our agreement of the 12th in terms of clarification of repair data. . . ." Says one expert, "If we could just convince our people to avoid big words and empty jargon ['Pursuant to . . . in terms of clarification'], we could cut costs by *thousands of dollars a year* in typing time alone!" (The estimated average cost of dictating, typing, and sending a business letter in the United States today is between $6 and $7, and we have seen estimates as high as $15.) An insurance company in the Midwest recently hired a writing expert to spend one day a week in its home office just to go over company letters and talk to writers. The expert spends much time on the same problems of word choice and sentence structure that you studied in Chapters 12–15.

3. *An organization that is easy to follow.* The most common organizational device in business writing is the promise pattern, which we explained at length in Chapter 11. If you do not remember this pattern in detail, review pp. 211–213 before reading further. Busy executives, managers, scientists, and technicians prefer a "stripped-down" promise pattern, in which all inessentials are cut. "Get it on one page" is a typical order, one which we ourselves heard many times as we worked in various organizations.

4. *Use of the "who does what" formula.* Most letters, memos, and reports tell the reader to believe something, to do something, or to believe *and* do something. The "who does what" formula is short for:

Who does what	Who should do what
Who did what	What did what
Who will do what	What might do what

This formula reminds you that you are discussing conditions and actions, and that you should make these clear to yourself *before* you write. Then, *as* you write, keep telling your readers *who does what* so they won't be confused. Suppose, for example, you are tempted to write this sentence:

> The cost of work which had been accomplished in the Assembly Section before the last inspection date would be difficult to determine due to faulty records for June.

Wordy, vague, and unemphatic, the sentence should be recast using the formula:

Who (what)	*Does (did)*	*What*
Assembly Section	lost	the records for June
I [the accountant]	cannot determine	the cost of work

And the revised sentence reads:

> Since the Assembly Section lost its records for June, I cannot determine the cost of work done before the last inspection date.

The *who does what* formula provides a simple method for making points clear. For instance, we used it in the first few lines of the last paragraph:

Who (what)	*Does (did)*	*What*
This formula	reminds	you
you	should make	these [clear]
[you]	keep telling	your readers
you	are tempted to write	this sentence

5. *A readable format.* "We are after total readability," wrote the chief engineer of a large company. "Readability means more than just using clear words, punctuation, and sentence structure. Our technical and business people should know how to use white space on the page, employ headings, use numbered lists, and so on."

As this comment implies, the *whole page* is a unit of communication in business writing. Readers need to be able to glance at a page and "place" themselves in the flow of the material. Here is how you help them do this:

a. Use as much white space as possible. Keep relatively wide margins. Where you can, break up paragraphs and indent. Of course, you should not use illogical breaks.

b. Use parallelism when you can. Many discussions can be easily broken down into parallel lists or outlines—for example, the parts of a technical process or the explanation of operational costs in a business. Even brief numbered lists like this one are helpful to your reader:
  1. Use headings
  2. Use numbered lists

You should also note our use of numbered headings and lists in this chapter—and in other sections of the book, for that matter.

These five "emphases" apply to almost all kinds of business papers or reports. Bear them in mind as we explain the specific forms that such communications ordinarily take.

PRACTICE

Discussion

1. The three paragraphs below are the first and last two of a scientific report written by an internationally known botanist. From these paragraphs, can you describe the writer's stance? In particular, how limited is the writer's audience? Does the author use much technical language? Nontechnical language? How do you think he would defend his word choice?

> [1]Physiology is the study of vital, or "living," processes. From this definition it can be reasoned that the physiology of corn production is the study of vital processes underlying the growth and reproduction of corn plants. Production enters from the agricultural concern for maximizing growth and reproduction. What we need to understand are the vital processes involved, and then use this knowledge to secure increased yields.
>
> [2]There may be other economic benefits in the offing from basic physiological research, but I cannot identify them now. I am certain however that there are 3 basic levels of regulating plant growth—the

environment, the genetic code, and the hormonal regulation of differ-
entiation. Another generation of research will provide us with a better
understanding of how to manipulate these controls. Already we are experienced in manipulating the environment by irrigating, draining,
plowing, fertilizing, etc. There are sound empirical practices in
breeding and hybridization which expand yearly as we learn more
about the genetic apparatus. The controls to be revealed when we solve
the hormone mystery can only be estimated, but will surely be
considerable.

[3]I'll end by going out on a limb. At the present rate of progress the
corn belt should be averaging 150 bushels of corn per acre in the year
2000. The better farmers will be disappointed with less than 200
bushels. —J. B. Hanson, "The Physiology of Corn Production"

2. In New York City, officers of the First National City Bank believed
that they had to make their messages clearer. Here is an example
of how they rewrote a provision in their personal-loan policy:

Old Provision

In the event of default in the
payment of this or any other Obligation or the performance or
observance of any term or cove-
nant contained herein or in any
note or other contract or agreement evidencing or relating to
any Obligation or any Collateral
on the Borrower's part to be performed or observed, or the
undersigned Borrower shall die,
or any of the undersigned
become insolvent or make an
assignment for the benefit of
creditors, or a petition shall be
filed by or against any of the
undersigned under any provision
of the Bankruptcy Act, or any
money, securities or property of
the undersigned now or hereafter
on deposit with or in the possession of or under the control of
the Bank shall be attached or
become subject to distraint pro-
ceedings or any order or process
of any court.

New Provision

I'll be in default:
1. If I don't pay an installment
   on time; or
2. If any other creditor tries by
   legal process to take any
   money of mine in your
   possession.

Explain in detail how the officers used any of the "five emphases" of business writing to make their provisions more understandable.

3. A typical problem in business writing is that of giving clear, easy-to-read instructions or directions. The following directions are from an instruction sheet that each student at a certain college who registers a car receives from the Campus Police.

   Prepare a *specific* critique of the instructions, showing how they violate each of the five emphases of business writing we have discussed. Then reorganize and rewrite the instructions.

Utilizing Permits and Stickers

This sticker must be properly displayed on the automobile for which it was issued, as indicated below (improper display may result in a monetary penalty).

1. On vehicles not equipped with a fixed rear window (e.g., convertibles, station wagons with retractable rear windows, or others), the sticker must be displayed in the lower left portion of the front windshield (driver's side).

2. On vehicles equipped with a fixed rear window (not retractable), the sticker must be displayed in the lower center portion of that window. THESE STICKERS ARE PRINTED ON THE GUMMED SIDE. THEREFORE, THEY MUST BE AFFIXED FROM THE INSIDE.

Permits are not transferable. When a permit holder changes cars, he must obtain a new permit, by making application to this Division *and surrendering the pieces of the old sticker.* (There is no charge.)

Permit holders who also are parking space renters should display the rental space sticker immediately adjacent to the registration sticker.

Only current stickers may be displayed on your vehicle.

THE LETTER

The letter, the jack-of-all-trades of business communication, performs a wide variety of duties. It can be a request for action, a set of instructions, an appraisal of a farm property, a cover letter for a scientific paper, an announcement, and so on.

A letter is ordinarily written in response to a specific situation or problem—you want a person to do something, to perform a job in a certain way, to give you an idea of what your farm is worth. Perhaps you wish to explain what your scientific paper covers and why you are sending it to a particular journal, or to announce to a group of business executives that you are starting a new service they might be interested in using.

Since letters can do so many different things, it is unwise to insist that you should use specific types of development or a particular rhetorical strategy when you write them. While it is true that a letter may define, compare and contrast, narrate an event, or illustrate a cause-and-effect relationship, in most cases you will not force a strategy on the material in the letter. The *situation* to which you are responding determines the choice and development of the approach you take. For example, if you wish your reader to take a particular action on a problem, you might write a brief argument that contains both a thesis of fact, with a cause-and-effect relationship explained, and a thesis of action explaining exactly how you think the problem could be solved. (See pp. 348–353.)

Form of the Letter

The *form* of the business letter is pretty well standardized now. In the example on the following page, note that the headings give complete information on addresses. Don't leave anything out of these addresses because information like street names and accurate zip codes is often vital for maintaining a correspondence.

Psychology of the Letter

Authorities on business writing have long agreed that successful letters require more than just good ideas and proper form, although these are certainly not to be sniffed at. A letter is usually a miniature piece of persuasion, with its own *ethical proof* and *you-attitude*. You remember that these elements of persuasion, discussed in Chapter 16, help make your ideas more acceptable to your readers. Your ethical proof is the persuasive side of your character, as you present it to your readers. And your you-attitude is the impression that you give the readers that you are genuinely interested in them and their welfare, not just in yourself. You should, for example, think twice before writing an abrupt, unfriendly letter like the one below from a bank executive:

Dear _____:

Concerning your overdraft. That was not our fault, as you state. Our records show that we never received the $500 you say you deposited. Please remit $374.33 to cover the amount of your overdraft.

Instead, the writer should have used a little common-sense psychology, making the bank look better and its customer feel better (*and* increasing the chances of retaining the customer):

```
                                              1001 Calhoun Avenue
                                              Columbus, Ohio 43215
                                              January 7, 1987

          Mr. Weston Sharpe
          Customer Services
          Imperial Manufacturing Company
          4207 Disston Avenue
          Westville, Kentucky 40881

          Subject: (optional)

          Dear Mr. Sharpe:


             _____
             _____
             _____
             _____
             _____
             _____
             _____
             _____
             _____
             _____
             _____
             _____
             _____
             _____
             _____



                                              Sincerely yours,


                                              Mrs. Verdeen Smith
```

Dear _____:

We are sorry that you were inconvenienced when your account was over-drawn recently by mistake. After receiving your letter, we checked immediately to see if we had failed to enter the $500 you mentioned. But we have no record here of having received your deposit. Since, as you say, the $500 was a check from your father, you might ask him to stop payment on his check until you discover what happened to it.

Since you have written no more checks on your account, your overdraft remains $374.33.

We are sorry this problem arose and hope that the matter can be cleared up soon.

The second version is an improvement for several reasons. The writer shows ethical proof by precisely reviewing the details of the transaction and by suggesting to the customer a clear and convenient course of action. The you-attitude is apparent throughout, especially when the writer clarifies the situation ("Since, as *you* say, the $500 was a check from your father") and suggests how the customer can remedy the problem without embarrassment ("*you* might ask him to stop payment on his check until *you* discover what happened to it"). And nowhere in the letter is a harsh word uttered.

Two Sample Letters

When she got her spring grade report, Susan Langford was amazed to find that she had failed a course, one that she *knew* she had done well in. In order to take care of her problem, she defined it carefully, picked a precise stance, organized her material, and wrote the letter on the following page.

In her letter, Susan carefully observed the five emphases of business writing listed at the beginning of this chapter. She takes a specific and clear stance, writing directly to a particular person, the one who can most quickly take care of her problem. Her point or thesis is clear: a mistake was made on her grade and she requests that the grade be changed. Her wording is accurate, and her organization is easy to follow, the three paragraphs forming a pattern that is logical and visually pleasant. The letter has a readable format and plenty of white space. Note especially her use of the "who does what" formula:

> . . . report indicates that I failed I.S. 100. . . .
> I took the course. . . .
> I did four papers. . . .
> I received B's. . . .
> I should have received a "Pass."
> I have my four papers. . . .

As we stated earlier, the "who does what" formula tells the reader what the situation is by making every action specific and clear. Susan does not write: "Written work was accomplished in the course." Instead, she gives the precise *action*: "I did four papers."

102 Sand Road
Green, Alabama 36110
June 11, 1987

Professor J.T. Barkdale
Chairman, Independent Studies
Magnolia Junior College
Arlington, Alabama 36109

Dear Professor Barkdale:

My spring grade indicates that I failed I.S. 100, the Independent
Study course I took on the pass-fail system last spring semester. I
took the course from Mr. Winchell, who resigned at the end of the
term to return to graduate school. I am writing to you because I
presume you can take care of my problem.

I did four papers for Mr. Winchell, three short and one long. I
recieved B's for the three short papers and an A- on the long one.
There were no tests or exams for the course. Given the grades on the
papers, I should have recieved a "Pass."

It seems likely that someone at Magnolia made a clerical error.
Would you please check on this for me and see if my grade can be
changed to a "Pass"? I enclose photocopies of the four papers. Thank
you.

                         Sincerely yours,

                         Susan Langford

It is also worth mentioning that Susan uses good psychology in her
letter. Although she might justifiably be hurt and upset about receiving a
"Fail" when she clearly deserved a "Pass," she does not let her feelings
show or attack the administration of the college. The ethical proof and
you-attitude implicit in the letter will make Professor Barksdale want to
solve her problem as quickly as possible—and to solve it in her favor.

November 8, 1987

Mr. Robert Marker
Assistant to Board of Directors
American Metal-Press Corporation
Winthrop, South Carolina 29730

Subject: Proposed Plan to Decrease Press Down-time

Problem:

      The excessive amount of press down-time we have been
experiencing at our Jefferson Street Plant needs immediate
attention. I estimate that the down-time is costing the company
about $24,000 a week, which cannot be considered a normal production
cost. At the present time, we have no scheduled maintenance program
for keeping the presses in working order. While studying production
reports, I found that poor maintenance is the cause of most press
down-time. The most troublesome areas are:

      1. Gripper Settings
      2. Damper Systems
      3. Fountain Water-Acid Systems
      4. Folder Problems

Solution:

I propose that a Saturday and Sunday maintenance program be
established. On Saturday, two crews of four men could change dampers
and set grippers on all the sheet-fed presses. On Sunday, another
two crews would clean the fountain water-acid systems and make all
the necessary adjustments on the web-press folder. The crews would
alternate weekends to avoid conflicts concerning distribution of
overtime.

Benefits of Program:

      By having a maintenance program we will save many hours of
press-time. With the repairs made on weekends, the presses would be
able to start up on Monday mornings without any difficulty. This
program would cut our production costs, allowing our company to
increase its profits. The cost of the program and the savings that
will be realized follow:

2 crews Saturday	$560
2 crews Sunday	$560
Total	$1,120
Present down-time loss	$24,000
Estimated Savings	$22,780

Sincerely,

Thomas Staff, Press
Supervisor

    Our second sample letter is also a request for action to be taken, but
the situation is different, and the standard format of the letter has been
altered slightly.

    We will leave most of the discussion of Thomas's letter to the Prac-
tice that follows. But, in passing, we should observe something important
about the wording of his letter, and also the wording of Susan's. Both let-

ters use standard English. Neither one of the writers uses formal language or business jargon, or tries to put things in a fancy way. There is only one style in modern letter writing: the natural and informal style that makes its point without unnecessary words or rhetorical flourishes.

PRACTICE

Writing

1. The *five emphases* of business communication stress the use of: (1) a specific stance; (2) clear word choice and sentence structure; (3) an easy-to-follow organization; (4) the "who does what" formula; and (5) a readable format. Using these emphases and our discussion of the psychology of letter writing, prepare notes for a critique of Thomas Staff's letter above. Be specific in your comments.

2. You own a new Glitter 4, a $9,000 car, which is still under warranty. In the past six months, you have had the following "new-car" problems: bad front-end alignment; leaks around the rear window; faulty engine tuning; a side window that won't close. (These are apparently "factory assembly" problems.) You have taken the car to Grump Motors, where you bought it, a total of seven times. The alignment is satisfactory now; the rear window still leaks, but not as badly as it did; the tuning, if anything, appears worse than before; the side window worked for a while, but now refuses to move. Every time you take the car to Grump Motors, somebody gets grease all over the upholstery. You know the shop manager personally. He is a capable, hardworking man, who seems to do the best job he can.

   Using the five emphases of business communication, write a persuasive letter to the Glitter Motor Corporation in Detroit requesting a specific solution to your problems.

3. Imagine that your school expenses are paid by the Warbucks Foundation. The Foundation, in effect, pays you $4,000 a year to go to school. There are no strings on this money, except that you must take a normal class load nine months of the year and maintain at least a B average each semester. You can have a part-time job if you wish.

   At the end of the school year, you must write to Mr. Gawain Buck, Director of the Foundation, explaining to him (1) how you spent the $4,000, and (2) why you deserve a similar grant for the next year.

Write the letter.

THE JOB APPLICATION LETTER

To get a job, you will often write a letter of application. But don't start off writing blindly to any company or employer that comes to mind. Make a plan—consider your ambitions, compile a list of your assets as a prospective employee, and try to find an employer you want to work for, one who needs a person with your qualifications. Your college or university placement office can give you much up-to-date information on companies, schools, governmental agencies on all levels, and other organizations that are hiring; you can also find more information in the library and in professional magazines. Skim the available material and decide which organizations you want to apply to; narrow your list down to those you are genuinely interested in.

When you have decided on a reasonable list of your ambitions and professional assets, and have picked a group of prospective employers, you are ready to plan a letter of application. Such a letter ordinarily has two parts, the résumé and the letter itself.

The Résumé

In the *résumé,* you give all the factual material about yourself and your history that can be easily listed: education (including degrees and certificates), extracurricular activities, experience, and references. Some students like to put their grade-point averages on the sheet, but this information is optional.

In the résumé, you should not only give prospective employers specific details about yourself, you should also save them reading time. So be brief, factual, and clear.

It is unwise to overload your résumé with unnecessary information. Put yourself in an employer's place and ask: "What would I like to know about this person? What could he or she tell me that would suggest a qualified candidate for a job?" A small point—do not abbreviate names, places, or titles any more than you can help; such practice makes you look careless and lazy.

Keep your résumé clean, airy, with sufficient white space, and *perfectly typed.* See the sample résumés, pp. 479–480.

The Application Letter

Since your résumé lists a great deal of specific information about you, the application letter tells the rest — what job you are seeking, why you want it, and what you have to offer the company. Again, put yourself in the employers' place: what do you have in the way of experience, training, or know-how that they might like to have in an employee?

The application letter is a selling device, and it should "sell" *you* — your abilities and your personality. But it should not sell too hard! We mention this because we have seen application letters which have had an effect opposite from what their authors intended. Consider this paragraph from an unsuccessful letter:

> The job description that your company has sent out fits me exactly; it calls for someone who can handle responsibility right away. My ability to take responsibility is something I have always been proud of. An example of this is my being president of the student body for last year. [And so on.]

The trouble with this approach is that the writer tries to force a favorable opinion of himself on the employer — he presents far too much of a "me-attitude." The successful application letter will sell you by (1) being *specific* about your good points, and (2) mentioning them *modestly* and *quietly*. For example, the writer of the unsuccessful letter could have expressed his skill in assuming responsibility by saying something like the following:

> Your company's job description states that you "wish to hire a person who can handle responsibility right away." I was president of the student body here at Collins College last year, and was responsible for appointing students to committees, delegating authority to the committee chairs, and suggesting allocations for student funds to the student council. While I realize that these responsibilities may not be comparable to those in your company, the fact that I took them on may indicate to you that I am capable of assuming a good deal of responsibility in a job with your company.

Choosing the proper stance will go far to help you achieve the right attitude and tone. You can use the same résumé to apply for many different jobs, but each letter should be individually designed for the employer you are going to send it to. Employers are generally *not* alike;

John D. White
221 North Huff Drive
Urbana, IL 61801
Phone: (217) 367-2145

Education:

1979-1983: Mondale High School, Mondale, Illinois

1983-1985: attended Mondale junior college, Mondale
Illinois

1985-1987: attended Winston College, Winston,
Illinois; will graduate May 25, 1987, with
a B.S. degree

Major: Business Administration

Minor: Economics

Extracurricular Activities:

1985-1987: member, Tau Phi Tau social fraternity
(vice-president, 1986-1987)

Winston College Marching Band

Men's GLee Club

Experience:

1980-1981: fry cook, McTavish Hamburger Unit 18

1981-1984: stock boy, Independent Grocery Company

1984-   : Assistant Manager, McTavish Hamburger Unit 11

References (by permission)

Dr. John R. Webster, Professor of Management, Winston
College, Winston, Illinois 61801

Dr. Lucille Carter, Associate Professor of Business
Administration, Winston College, Winston
Illinois 61801

Mr. Dilney Harder, District Supervisor, McTavish
Hamburger Company, 224 East Lake Avenue,
Chicaga, Illinois 60621

ALICIA JAMES RAMIREZ

Applicant for Housing Supervisor
Wilson AFB, Wilson, Texas

Address: 805 N. Cartworth Street, Wilson, Texas 78712

Telephone: 512-655-3322

Professional Objective: To administer housing units and staff
                        on a military base

Education: B.S. in Management, University of Texas (1987)
           (Includes three graduate courses in management)

           Grade average: 4.68 on five-point scale

Experiences related to office management:

          Trainee, Austin Realty Company. Did all kinds of general
          office work, included light bookkeeping. (1980-1981)

          Assistant Manager, Southern Loan Office. Responsible for
          all general office functions, including payroll and
          correspondance with branch offices. Wrote weekly and
          monthly progress reports. Supervised five employees, two
          of whom were part-time. (1981-1983)

          Supervisor, General Office Machines, Inc. Administered
          all general office functions, including Payroll, Repair,
          Sales (clerical only). Supervised ten employees in day-
          to-day work related to the head office.

          All three companies are located in Wilson, Texas.

          These experiences have taught me how to work with many
          kinds of people -- from office workers to repairmen. I
          have been very succesful in my "people skills."

SPECIAL SKILL: I am familiar with the major brands of word
                processor and can use them in every facet of general office
                work.

                In addition, I have trained new office workers in office
                procedure, including all phases of word processing.

Personal Information: Wilson, Texas is my home. I own a house
           here and intend to stay in this community.

References: Will be supplied on request.

they have different needs for different kinds of employees. And as a matter of fact, the employer might be flattered that you have taken the time and trouble to create a letter just for him and his organization. Observe how this letter (which was written to support the résumé on p. 479) acts as a persuasive sales device for John White:

```
                                        221 North Huff Drive
                                        Urbana, Illinois 61801
                                        April 1, 1987

Ms. Judy Chase
Chief, Personnel Division
Great Midwestern Grocery Company
Minneapolis, Minnesota 55456

Dear Ms. Chase:

Our Director of Student Employment here at Winston College told me
that you are looking for a trainee for your store-management program.

I have seven years of part-time experience in food retailing work.
My three years as a stock boy and four years as an Assistant Manager
for the McTavish Hamburger Company have allowed me to view food
retailing and management from widely different perspectives.  My
ability to deal succesfully with the kinds of problems I encountered
in both jobs should prove beneficial to my future work.

My college training has also prepared me for a career in retailing
and management.  I have taken six courses in retailing and four in
management, and have and average of 3.4 (B+) in them.

Considering my experience and training, I believe I could be of
service to your company and would be glad to enter your training
program at whatever level you might place me.

I am available for an interview at your convinience.  Please call or
write if you have any questions about my qualifications.  My resume
is enclosed.

                             Sincerely,


                             John D. White
```

PRACTICE

Discussion

1. Analyze carefully the résumé and the letter in John White's application to the Great Midwestern Grocery Company. What is his writer's stance? Make a detailed list of all the facts and statements in the résumé and the letter to which you (if you were an executive of Great Midwestern) would react positively. Are there any facts and statements to which you might react negatively? Would *you* consider hiring John White?

2. Carol Weinstein saw this ad in a local paper:

Management Trainees

3 positions open. BA or MA in Business Administration desirable. Some experience very desirable. Training will lead to management appointment in health-care facilities. Excellent opportunity. Send résumé to Box 988 c/o the *Courier,* Champaign, Ill. 61820. An Equal Opportunity Employer.

She then wrote this letter:

```
                                        March 5, 1987
                                        405 Wardell Hall
                                        Urbana, Illinois 61801

Box 988
c/o the Champaign-Urbana Courier
110 W. University Avenue
Champaign, Illinois 61820

Dear Sir or Madam:

I am answering the ad which was in the Champaign-Urbana Courier on
Thursday, March 7, 1987.  I am very interested in health care
administration, and would like to go into this field when I get my
degree.  Although I realize that your ad is for positions that are
available now, I will not receive my degree until May 1988.  However,
I hope you will give me a chance to present my qualifications now,
and that you will think them good enough to keep me in mind for
possible positions in the next year or so.

In addition to working toward my Bachelor of Science degree in
Business Administration, which gives me academic knowledge of
business theory and practices, I also have practical experience
working in an intermediate-care nursing home.
```

As you can see from my enclosed resume, I have been the administrator's immediate assistant at Abbott Nursing Home since 1983. This has been mainly a part-time job. However, in the past four years I have worked in several areas of administration and management there. My duties have ranged from general secretarial functions to preparatory work for monthly audits.

Equally important, I have developed an ability to work with and relate well to older people. This is something I think a nursing home administrator must be able to do in order to understand and solve the problems associated with running a good home. I am also taking several courses in social work which focus on the aged. These give me more exposure to the problems that older people face in society.

My interest in this field, combined with further training, makes me feel I could be a competent administrator. As I said before, I realize you need applicants who are available now; but I hope you will keep me in mind for future openings. Thank you for your time.

                                   Sincerely,

                                   Carol L. Weinstein

Carol's letter received a very favorable reply from the employer. Why? Discuss in detail.

Writing
Assume that you need a job next summer. Pick out one specific job that is part-time or full-time. Research the job market and write a full job application (résumé and letter) to a specific employer.

THE MEMO

*H*ow is the *memo* (short for *memorandum*) different from the letter? First, the memo is designed to be read inside your organizational unit — your company, school, governmental division, and so on. The outsider ordinarily does not see such memos, which communicate much of the day-to-day detail needed to run the unit. Second, the memo tends to be shorter and more informal than the letter. Because in most cases the writer knows the person (or persons) he is writing to, he communicates his message to them simply and quickly, but still courteously.

Form of the Memo

A typical memo *form* looks like this:

```
                                        DATE:

   TO:

   FROM:

   SUBJECT:


   _____
   _____MESSAGE_____
   _____
   _____
   _____
   _____
   _____
```

Two Sample Memos

Joanne Larson will be showing a film on plant safety to eighty-three employees next week. Since the projection room will hold only fifty people comfortably, she writes this memo to the four chief supervisors of the plant:

```
                                    DATE:   March 17, 1987

   TO:   Stan Clark, Carla Fowler, Mark McFall, Jim Thomas

   FROM:   Joanne Larson

   SUBJECT:   Scheduling the safety film

        As you know, we are showing the safety film, Keep Your
        Eyes Open, next week in the projection room, which
        holds only fifty people comfortably without
        overcrowding.  I suggest we show the film to the
        forty-one people in the Assembly Section on Tuesday
        at 3:00 p.m., and to the remaining forty-two from the
        other sections on Thursday at the same time.

        If there's any problem about this arrangement, please
        let me know.
```

Don Kildren of the Drafting Division has been asked to organize the flow of map copying so that fewer jam-ups occur in Photo Services. When Don has finished planning the reorganization, he writes his ten fellow draftsmen:

DATE: May 10, 1987

TO: "The Inkmen"

FROM: Don Kildren

SUBJECT: Breaking up the jam in Photo Services

Mr. Durkheim asked me to suggest a way to keep work from piling up for the two photocopy machines. Apparently, nobody can get to them when we have a busy day copying maps. So, how is this for a suggested schedule?

1. Mary, Anne, and Matt -- Monday and Wednesday mornings
2. Tom, Shirl, and Rich -- Monday and Wednesday afternoons
3. Liz, Nat, Paul, and I -- Tuesday and Thursday mornings

If you have an emergency need for photocopying, take the map down to Photo Services anyway -- but please don't make a habit of it.

Thanks. If you have any ideas on the subject, let me know.

Both memos follow pretty well the five emphases of business writing and both effectively use ethical proof and the you-attitude. Readers of both memos would be happy with what they are asked to do and how they are asked to do it.

Consider the memo as a little piece of "frozen talk." Write it as if you were speaking courteously to a friend who happens to work with you. Make it as short as possible without being abrupt.

PRACTICE

Writing

1. Here is the first draft of a memo from a college librarian to her student "stackers." Considering (a) the five emphases of business writing, (b) the proper form of the memo, and (c) the psychology of memos and letters, prepare an analysis of the memo for class discussion. Then rewrite it for greater clarity and brevity.

Referring to my memo about a year ago concerning the method of stacking books in the stack area before the shelvers put them into the shelves in their proper places. At the time of my memo there were three shelvers but now we have only two because the third kept coming into the job drunk. This still occurred, so we fired him — as you remember the other two shelvers are still ok and are working as fast as they can getting the books properly on the shelves. But we need a better system of dividing the books in the stack area before the shelvers get to them because now they are just thrown on the floor in any order and the shelvers have to separate them in the various categories before they start to shelve. Something must be accomplished so that the separation is done before the shelvers get to them, so please see that before the books are put into the shelvers' area they are already divided into the main categories (fiction, nonfiction, biography) and this way the shelvers can simply pick them up and put them in their proper places. Another shelver will be hired as soon as money can be located or special allocating by the Library Board.

2. On p. 487, in scratch form, is a budget breakdown prepared for Rho Rho Rho fraternity. A member of the fraternity drew it up to help him write a memo to the group's finance committee. Using the breakdown in the tables, the student has to (a) explain the meaning of the figures, and (b) make a short statement about the fraternity's financial situation. Prepare the student's memo for him.

NEGATIVE MESSAGES

Since we occasionally act as consultants to firms that wish to improve their written communications, we are always interested in what their problems are. Lately, we have been hearing more of this kind of comment: "Right now we have so many *bad* things to tell people. Somebody's got to tell the vice-president we lost a contract; tell a customer the part for his ten-year-old washer is not available; tell a woman we can't hire her because the budget we thought we had we don't have; tell the paving inspector we are going to be six weeks late getting our entry to Vine Avenue finished. We've got an endless number of things like these going out."

The so-called *negative message* — one which the receiver would prefer not to read, and may be greatly disappointed or even enraged to read — has become one of the commonest problems in modern business communication. To solve that problem, authorities in business writing have suggested six techniques for shaping the typical negative message, which is usually a letter. As you consider these techniques, remember that such a letter is going to provide a shock, sometimes a big one, to its reader. In most forms, it is some kind of *turn-down*. It tells the reader that he won't get the job, the loan, the application for gas heat approved, the delivery of his new car on time. Although there is little you can do to avoid disappointing the reader, you should try to make your message as courteous as possible.

RHO RHO RHO SOCIAL FRATERNITY
COMPARATIVE BUDGET REPORT
For the Semester Ending January 21, 198__

	Actual Results	Budget	Variance
CASH RECEIPTS:			
Room and board	$23,750	$25,000	($1,250)
Miscellaneous cash receipts (Parking revenue, cigarettes, pop, laundry)	1,780	1,600	180
Total cash receipts	$25,530	$26,600	($1,070)
CASH EXPENDITURES:			
Commissary (includes cook's salary)	$20,150	$19,500	($ 650)
Utilities	870	1,000	130
Repairs	1,395	500	(895)
Telephone	75	200	125
Entertainment	355	500	145
Communications (other than telephone)	125	100	(25)
Maintenance	715	1,000	285
Miscellaneous expenditures	950	1,000	50
Total cash expenditures	$24,635	$23,800	($ 835)
TOTAL CASH RECEIPTS:	$25,530	$26,600	($1,070)
– TOTAL CASH EXPENDITURES:	24,635	23,800	(835)
= EXCESS OF CASH RECEIPTS OVER CASH EXPENDITURES:	$ 895	$ 2,800	($1,905)
+ BEGINNING CASH BALANCE:	2,070	2,070	--------
= CASH BALANCE, 1/20/8__	**$ 2,965**	**$ 4,870**	**($1,905)**

1. *Consider using a "buffer" at the beginning of the letter.* The *buffer* absorbs the shock of the turn-down; or, to describe it another way, provides a touch of human sympathy at the outset. These are typical buffers as they appear in letters:

> We have carefully read your application, and are impressed by your qualifications. . . . However. . . .
> I have talked with all committee members about your situation, but. . . .

Authorities on business writing disagree about the use of a buffer. Some even argue against using it at all, believing that it tends to be an unthinking cliché. And sometimes it is. Yet we have often noticed the unhappiness of readers about a negative message that starts out too bluntly—they feel hurt, resentful, or put off. When they do, bluntness *is* a mistake. We believe that you should try (in your own way, using your own words) to provide a "shock absorber" in the negative message—assuming always that the message in question calls for one. It is true that some do not, and in those a buffer just gets in the way.

2. *Make your turn-down early.* Put it immediately after the beginning, whether the beginning contains a buffer or just a general introductory sentence or two. Here's an argument against a long buffer. It makes the reader wait for the turn-down, and waiting may make the reader quite angry. We once saw a businessman rip up a long letter and throw it on his office floor. What angered him was a two-paragraph buffer that made him think he was going to get something, when actually it was just the preparation for a turn-down.

3. *Make your turn-down clear.* Don't mince words, and don't be ambiguous. Your reader wants to know the worst, and he should know the worst in the clearest way possible. You should be as polite as you can, but don't be so diplomatic that the effect of your turn-down is lost on the reader. There is no getting around the fact that your message is essentially a negative one.

4. *Be factual.* After the turn-down, explain in reasonable detail why you cannot give the person what he wants. A reasonable and factual explanation will make him feel better because it indicates that you took the time to deal with his problem. Also, by giving the facts you may open the way to more negotiation of the problem.

5. *If possible or practical, leave hope for the future* at the end of the message.

> . . . Ms. Ryan, although the Recreation Committee did not accept your proposal at this time, why not submit it again in January? As you know, the company will have another $2,000 in the Recreation budget after the first of the year. . . .

Or:

> . . . We are sorry your router motor burned out. But, as a hobby model, it was not made for the sort of heavy work you tried to do. If you would try our Carpenter's Model, you will find that it can do that work easily; and we can guarantee the motor for heavy use.

Warning: Don't leave hope if there isn't any!

6. *Use a friendly tone throughout.* But don't be flippant, too casual, or humorous. Attempting to soften the impact of a negative message by a light-hearted tone and attitude can infuriate the receiver more than the turn-down itself.

PRACTICE

Discuss the effectiveness of this negative message:

Longchamps Apartments

April 8, 1987

Mr. John Garst
505 N. First
Ross, Illinois 61880

Dear Mr. Garst:

I am very glad you have decided that Longchamps Apartments would be the ideal place for you to live. We are proud of the building and the reputation that it has earned over the years.

This year has been rather unusual because we are only midway through our renting season, and yet we are already full and have been forced to turn people away for the past two weeks. As a rule, we seldom have all twelve of our apartments available for renting since we always give priority to our present tenants and allow them the option of staying on before we even consider new ones. Many of them do stay — in fact, next year half of the apartments will be occupied by tenants who will be staying on, leaving only six apartments to be rented. In addition, the large number of students who are always interested in living at Longchamps contributes to our high occupancy rate so early in the season.

I wish you good luck in your search for housing for next year. I'm sure there are still many other apartments available. If you think you would possibly be interested in living here the following year, feel free to drop by our apartment any Saturday afternoon, when we would be happy to answer any questions you might have. Next spring, then, you should see us in mid-February to assure yourself of an apartment. You can stop by in person or write. As before, we can be reached by phone at 344-7996.

I hope you will keep us in mind. We are always ready to welcome students who will contribute to a graduate study atmosphere.

Very truly yours,

Jacqueline Tracy, Manager

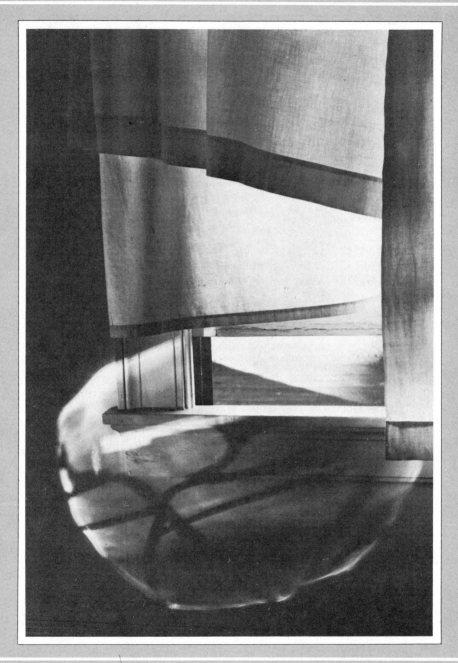

WHITE, Minor.
Windowsill Daydreaming. (1958)
Gelatin-Silver print, 11–15/16 x 8–13/16."
Collection, The Museum of Modern Art, New York. Purchase.

PART FIVE

HANDBOOK

"I always choose the grammatical form unless it sounds affected," said the poet Marianne Moore. This is sensible advice for you as a writer, but first you must know what the grammatical form is. To find the correct form, or simply to polish your skills in grammar, usage, and mechanics, you should use this *Handbook*. We begin with the "small" building blocks of the language, the parts of speech. If, at any point, you need to look up unfamiliar terms, turn to the Glossary beginning on p. 571.

A POINT OF VIEW ON GRAMMAR AND USAGE

*M*uch of what we say or write requires no grammatical discussion, creates no argument. Only a fraction of "normal" English statements contain mistakes or debatable usages. Such are the expressions below. They are questionable (at least, they are questioned by many people):

Do it *like* I say.
I wouldn't do that if I *was* you.
The committee *are* meeting tomorrow.
To badly do that job is a mistake.
It's *me*.

Why do such problems exist at all? A major reason can be found in the imperfections of the language itself. As is generally the case with languages, English has developed inconsistently and irregularly. Many of its patterns of grammar and usage are inconsistent or irregular. One great authority, Edward Sapir, remarked that "all grammars leak." By this he meant — among other things — that the grammars we have invented to describe language are imperfect. Indeed we sometimes expect too much of our grammatical explanations, which often contain contradictions and exceptions. It should be added that not everybody can be — or should be — a grammarian. What most people need are not perfect grammatical answers, but ones that work reasonably well to questions that arise when they write: answers which won't tie their brains in knots.

PREMISES

*T*o answer your questions about grammar and usage, then, we oversimplify, just as all other textbook authors do. But, like most other authors, we work from a set of premises that experts in English have generally agreed upon. We suggest that they be your premises also. On most questions of grammar and usage, then, you should:

1. Consider the practice of good writers.

2. Consider the opinions of authorities. See the list of authorities on p. 495.

3. Consult your own wish for common sense and order in the language. "For all who speak or write," says Wilson Follett in *Modern English Usage,* "the road to effective language is thinking straight."

4. Remember that there are often several ways to solve a problem in grammar and usage, not just one.

Let's discuss the last premise for a moment. Writers often say: "I have a question in grammar [or usage]. Give me the answer." But there may be two answers, or three or four; why be satisfied with one and limit your options? We are commonly asked, for example: "What word can I use to put in the place of this 'bad' one?" The question may be wrongly stated. Many sentences are like brick walls. You usually can't grasp a "bad" brick from the middle of a wall, slide it out, and stick another one in. The whole structure is too firm. Instead, to replace the brick you may have to tear down the wall, and then rebuild it in one of several ways.

ALTERNATIVE SOLUTIONS

*W*hen you can, consider several solutions to a linguistic problem. As an example, consider the familiar problem of agreement with *either-or* and *neither-nor*. It is not hard to remember that with singular nouns in the subject, these pairs take singular verbs. You simply memorize this fact and apply it when necessary:

> *Neither* the car *nor* the truck *was* stolen.

But what do you use when there is one car and two trucks?

> *Neither* the car *nor* the trucks *was (?) were (?)* stolen.

Neither *was* nor *were* sounds right, although the grammatical rule says that *were* is the proper choice—"the verb should agree with the nearer of its subjects."

It is often possible to avoid such a problem (and the possibility of error) by using one of several different constructions that will say pretty much the same thing. Here are a few:

> *Problem:*   Neither the car nor the trucks *was (?) were (?)* stolen.
> *Solutions:*   The car *was* not stolen. Neither *were* the trucks.
> The trucks *were* not stolen. Nor *was* the car.
> The trucks and the car *were* not stolen.
> The car and the trucks *were* still there.
> The car *was* not stolen, and the trucks *weren't* either.
> The trucks and the car *have not been* stolen.
> The thieves *left* the car and the trucks.

BOOKS TO CONSULT

*T*his is not a book on usage alone, so in the following pages we cannot devote much space to the many irksome questions that inevitably arise in a writer's work. But help is available. When you want more information than we have space for, consult one or more of the following:

Bernstein, Theodore, *The Careful Writer: A Modern Guide to English Usage.* New York: Atheneum, 1965.

_____, *Dos, Don'ts and Maybes of English Usage,* New York: New York Times Books, 1977.

Copperud, Roy. *American Usage and Style: the Consensus.* New York: Van Nostrand Reinhold, 1980.

Ebbitt, Wilma R. and David R. Ebbitt, *Writer's Guide and Index to English,* 7th ed. Glenview, Ill.: Scott, Foresman, 1982.

Evans, Bergen and Cornelia Evans, *A Dictionary of Contemporary American Usage.* New York: Random House, 1957.

Follett, Wilson, *Modern American Usage.* New York: Hill and Wang, 1966.

Fowler, H. W., *Modern English Usage,* 2nd ed. Oxford University Press, 1965.

Morris, William and Mary Morris, *Harper Dictionary of Contemporary Usage.* Second Ed. New York: Harper and Row, 1985.

GA
GRAMMATICAL ANALYSIS

GA 1 Learn the Parts of Speech

The parts of speech are classified by the jobs they perform in a sentence. Memorize this table:

nouns
pronouns } *name.*   (Nothing else *names.*)

verbs *state.*   (Nothing else *states.*)

adjectives
adverbs } *modify.*   (Nothing else *modifies.*)

prepositions
conjunctions } *join.*   (Nothing else *joins.*)

To explain how the parts of speech "perform their jobs" in a sentence, let's begin by considering some typical nouns and verbs.

Typical nouns:
The **draw** you made on the last poker hand was pure luck.

His was a great **run**.
The story started in a **place** called Shenandoah.

Typical verbs:
You will never **draw** another hand like that.
He had **run** that race before.
She could not **place** Jim, although she vaguely recognized him.

Draw, run, and *place* are nouns in the first group of sentences because they are *naming words.* But since they are acting as *stating words* in the second group, *draw, run,* and *place* are verbs there. (The verb phrases are *will draw, had run,* and *could place,* but we will ignore such phrases for the time being.)

In the half-mad sentence below (perhaps uttered by a crazy sea captain who had dosed himself on too much rum and grammar), what parts of speech is *forward* acting as?

    1   2   3   4   5
Forward the *forward* sail *forward* the *forward forwardly!*

1. *Forward* is a verb in the "command position," as in "*Do* a good job," or "*Pick* up my books." Military order: "*Forward,* march!"

2. *Forward* is an adjective, meaning "near the front," modifying *sail.*

3. *Forward* is a preposition, meaning "near to" and implying placement, as in "*by* the bridge," "*over* the hill," "*around* the house."

4. *Forward* is a noun, designating the front end of the ship.

5. *Forwardly* is an adverb (note the *-ly*), showing how something is done; it means "boldly and eagerly."

To explain further how the parts of speech work, let's expand the information given in the table at the beginning of this section.

1. **Nouns** are naming words. They fit in the slot in this sentence: "The _____ did it." Here are some examples:

    The *dog* did it.
    The *vandals* did it.
    The *Smiths* did it.
    The *running* did it.

Note that even though *running* appears to be a verb, it is acting as a noun, as the subject of the sentence. Therefore we call it a noun.

We can put two or more words together to make compound nouns: *truck driver, tenderfoot, like-mindedness, lady-in-waiting.*

2. Pronouns are noun substitutes. They are naming words that stand for nouns (*pro* means "for"). Examples:

> *We* did *that* for *you.*
> *This* is *what* *she* did for *her.*
> *What* is *it*?
> Are *they* coming to the party? *Some* are.

3. Verbs state. They can fit in the slot: "The thing(s) _____ it." (*Thing* here stands for any noun acting as a subject.) Examples:

> The thing *wanted* it.
> The things *were* happy.
> The *thing seems to be* a rat.
> The thing *will bake* a pie.
> The thing *should have been allowed to win it.*

As the last three examples indicate, words used as verbs can be combined to make verb phrases.

4. Adjectives modify (describe, qualify, or limit) nouns and pronouns. Examples:

> A *big* house, a *bigger* house, the *biggest* house
> The *sharp* stick, a *sharper* stick, the *sharpest* stick
> They were *young.*
> Truly *able* people are usually *happy.*
> It was *better.*
> *Middle-aged* executives make the *best* managers.

Note: When attached to nouns, words like *the, a, an, this, those, my, her, our,* and so on can be considered as adjectives (they describe, qualify, or limit): *the* market, *my* habit, *their* lives, *a* Pontiac, *that* diamond, *those* people, *one's* dormouse.

5. Adverbs modify a verb, adjective, or another adverb. They often end in *-ly.* Usually they tell *how, why, when, where,* or *how much.* Examples:

> The duck quacked *loudly.*
> It was a *very* old duck.
> Drive *slow(ly).*
> Put the chair *there.*
> I'll be home *early.*

6. Prepositions join nouns and pronouns to other elements in a sentence. The noun or pronoun is considered the *object of the preposition.*

In "before the war," *before* is the preposition, and *war* the object of the preposition; in "in regard to it," *in* and *to* are prepositions, and *regard* and *it* are their objects.

Prepositions can also appear at the end of the sentence:

Which person did you give it *to?*
I am giving the whole thing *up.*
What did you do that *for?*

7. **Conjunctions** join. But unlike prepositions, they do not employ nouns or pronouns as objects.
   a.   **Coordinating conjunctions** connect word units of equal rank:

You *and* I
Tired *but* happy
Cubs *or* White Sox
Help us, *or* we will fail.
I saw you, *so* I knew you were there.

   b.   **Subordinating conjunctions** connect subordinate clauses to main clauses (see the next section for more on clauses). Examples:

When the doorknob fell off, they were trapped in the room.
If it is raining, call a cab to get home.
The tests were postponed, *even though* all the students were ready to take them.
The angel lost its wings *because* it was careless.

PRACTICE

Identify the parts of speech of the italicized words in the following sentences.

1. *Many* colleges *suffer from* high *expenses and low* enrollments.

2. When *one* sees his life *pass before him, he is* not *necessarily ready for* death *or* the grave.

3. *The law* is *what* we *make it, in fact* as well as *action.*

4. *Running, jumping,* and *breathing* are *surely* all verbs. Is that *true?*

5. *All* women are *equal* to *men* (*say the feminists, who* are determined to shatter *many stereotypes* based *on* sex).

6. If *you believe this,* will *you* act *accordingly?*

7. It is *time to play* baseball *because spring* is *here.*

8. *Concerning your* raise *see* Mr. *Partin, the general assistant* manager.

9. *"I dreamed* I *was dreaming,* and of course I had to wake up from my *dream dream,* and that woke me out of my *dream* too."—Dwight Bolinger, *Aspects of Language*

10. *After dreaming, but* before being *entirely awake,* he *began* to snore *fast* and *loud.*

GA 2   Learn to Identify Clauses

A **clause** is a statement created by joining a noun-subject to its own verb. Without such joining, the clause cannot exist.

1. **Main clauses** make complete statements. A main clause can be a full sentence. In the following sentences, the subjects and verbs of the main clauses are italicized:

>   S   V
> Mrs. *Canaday will be* at home on Wednesday.

>   S V
> Two *cars came* down the block to the two-story house.

>   S   V
> The *beer froze* on the back porch.

>   S   S   V
> *Asthma* and *pneumonia are* related conditions.

>   S V
> *Dogs bark.*

2. **Subordinate clauses** are also created by joining noun-subjects to their own verbs. But these clauses differ in two ways from main clauses: (1) they do not make complete statements; and (2) they are usually signaled by what we call here a *subordinating sign.* Here are some examples, with the subordinating signs capitalized:

>   S   V
> IF Mrs. *Canaday will be* at home on Wednesday. . . .

>   S   V
> . . . WHEN two *cars came* down the block.

        S   V
AFTER the *beer froze* on the back porch. . . .

                    S   V
. . . EVEN THOUGH the *beer froze* on the back porch.

           S   V
WHAT *man has put* asunder. . . .

    . . . WHO *has been* usually accurate. . . .

The spaced periods indicate that subordinate clauses cannot stand alone as complete sentences.

Many words can act as subordinating signs. They give readers a signal about what lies ahead in the grammar of the sentence. Here is a partial list (units of two or three words may function as one sign):

after	since	when
although	so that	whenever
as though	that	which
because	until	while
before	what	who
no matter what	whatever	whosoever

That as a subordinating sign may be omitted from its clause, but it should always be understood:

> Car-makers agree [THAT] their products use too much gasoline.
> The good [THAT] a person does never lasts.

Putting subordinating signs and main clauses together, we can write sentences like these (subordinating signs are capitalized):

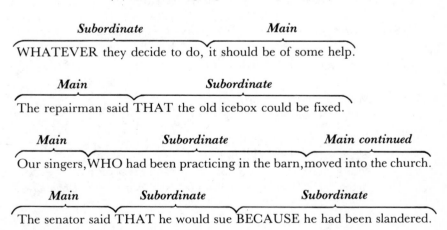

Subordinate   *Main*
WHATEVER they decide to do, it should be of some help.

Main   *Subordinate*
The repairman said THAT the old icebox could be fixed.

Main   *Subordinate*   *Main continued*
Our singers, WHO had been practicing in the barn, moved into the church.

Main   *Subordinate*   *Subordinate*
The senator said THAT he would sue BECAUSE he had been slandered.

Main

THAT the major is honest is obvious.

Subordinate

(The subject of the main clause is "That the major is honest.")

PRACTICE

In each of the following sentences, insert a brace (‿) over the main and subordinate clauses. Underline any subordinating signs, and insert any that are understood.

1. Annihilation is a risk we must not take.

2. A basic principle writers should follow is brevity.

3. "It is useless to go to bed to save the light, if the result is twins." — Chinese proverb.

4. Bacon was right when he said reading makes a full man.

5. The rhetoric teacher is an academic gravedigger who always has his shovel ready.

6. How one writes reflects how one feels.

7. If you are caught between despair and misery, the only way is up.

8. "When you are nine, you know that there are things that you don't know, but you know that when you know something you know it." — Robert Penn Warren, "Blackberry Winter"

Subordinate clauses act in three ways — as *nouns, adjectives,* or *adverbs.*

a.   A **noun clause** substitutes for a noun or pronoun.

Noun:	*Work* is a bore.
Clause:	*What we do* is a bore.
Pronoun:	I approve of *her.*
Clause:	I approve of *how she works.*
Noun:	His parents do not understand his *politics.*
Clause:	His parents do not understand *why he votes Democratic.*

b. An **adjective clause** modifies a noun or pronoun.

A woman *who has a good job* can afford some luxuries.

Americans *who speak Japanese* are rare.

The table, *which had been recently painted,* got wet in the rain.

Any drug *that can cure cancer* may have dangerous side effects.

She *who raises children* should be respected.

c. Some **adverb clauses** modify adjectives or other adverbs. A large number of adverb clauses answer questions such as *how, when, where, how much, why, to what extent.* In the years that we have been teaching grammar, however, it has become plain that these questions alone often do not help identify adverb clauses. In addition to the questions, we suggest a simple "negative formula": An adverb clause is any clause that is *not* nounal or adjectival. In other words, the adverb clause *does not* replace or modify a noun or pronoun.

She is sure *that she will get the job.* (Modifies an *adjective*—"sure.")
So that you can get home easily, I'll lend you my car. (Tells *why.*)
She came *as soon as she got your note.* (Tells *when.*)
They play tennis more *than I do.* (Tells *how much.*)
I knew you stole a cookie *because you had a guilty expression.* (Tells *why.*)

PRACTICE

Identify the italicized subordinate clauses as *noun, adjective,* or *adverb.*

1. They wondered *who he could be.*

2. The fact *that America is a great country* is beside the point.

3. Mr. Smith, *who is a medical technician,* can help us.

4. *If I were you,* I would ask him to call us.

5. She said *that more women would be having children in the next decade.*

6. *When we were in New York,* we stayed at the Biltmore.

7. I go *where I want to.*

8. He will do *what you tell him.*

9. *Whose fault it is* is a serious question.

10. Is this the book *which you had studied?*

GA 3   *Learn to Identify Phrases*

A **phrase** is a grammatical unit "larger" than a single part of speech but "smaller" than a clause. A phrase must have at least two words in it. Unlike a clause, a phrase does not make a statement using a combination of noun-subject and its own verb. Here are five phrases that, taken together, form a complete sentence:

The black horse   with the long mane   by the corral   will be ridden   by an expert cowboy.

Phrases care classified as follows:

1. **Noun phrases:**

Puppy love strikes *many sensible people* as *a pain* in the neck.

2. **Prepositional phrases:**

On the whole, it is not a bad pain *in the neck.*

3. **Verb phrases:**

Mr. Winchell *has been biting* into every peach in the store.
The store owner *will consider* legal action.
Have you *found* any whole peaches?

4. **Verbal phrases** (phrases made from verbs) are not main verbs or verb phrases; they cannot help to make statements in clause or sentence form.
   a.   Participial phrases act as adjectives:

The wart *growing on my finger* was not painful.
The child *hurt by shrapnel* did recover.
Relinquishing their rights, they surrendered.
Born in San Antonio, he grew up with a taste for hot weather.

b.   **Infinitive phrases** use the "to _____" form:

> *To act well* in this life is sometimes impossible.
> She wanted *to replace the astronaut.*
> That work is yet *to be done.*

c.   **Gerund phrases** act as nouns:

> *Raising roses* in this heat is impossible.
> They considered *rearing children,* but later thought better of it.

Here are some typical phrases, along with the jobs they are performing:

Phrase	Name of Phrase	Job Performed (Noun, Adjective, Adverb, Verb)
To be a cop is dangerous.	infinitive	noun (*To be a cop* is the subject of the sentence.)
Her desire *to be a cop* is commendable.	infinitive	adjective (*To be a cop* modifies the noun *desire.*)
Their hurrying through the job was a mistake.	gerund	noun (*Their hurrying* is the subject of the sentence.)
They were people *of integrity.*	prepositional	adjective (*Of integrity* modifies the noun *people.*)
Locking the house, they ran to the car.	participial	adjective (*Locking the house* modifies *they.*)
The persons *locking the house* were the owners.	participial	adjective (*Locking the house* modifies *persons.*)
They protected the house by *locking it up.*	gerund	noun (*Locking it up* is the object of the preposition *by.*)
Before Sunday is soon enough.	prepositional	noun (*Before Sunday* is the subject of the sentence.)
If you must chew tobacco, do it *with style.*	prepositional	adverb (*With style* modifies the verb *do.*)
She was unhappy *to see him leave.*	infinitive	adverb (*To see him leave* modifies the adjective *unhappy.*)
The bad man is my uncle.	noun	noun
This job *is being done.*	verb	verb

PRACTICE

1. First identify the italicized phrases by name: *noun, prepositional, verb.* Then describe the job (*noun, adjective, verb*) that the phrase is performing. (The numeral following each sentence indicates the number of phrases contained in it.)

a. The fur *of the cat was rising.* (2)
b. *By the chair* was where we found her alternately purring and snarling. (1)
c. You *should sit* here *by me on the bench.* (3)
d. *Light bulbs can light our dark cellar.* (3)
e. *The comic strip* "Doonesbury" teaches *by indirection.* (2)
f. *Megaforce* [a movie] *will be forgotten with considerable ease.* (2)

2. Identify the verbal phrases (*participial, infinitive,* and *gerund*) in the following sentences. Then state the job that each phrase is performing (*noun, adjective, adverb*).
a. *Riding a bicycle* is dangerous in this city. (1)
b. *Even double-locked,* her bike was stolen. (1)
c. She was eager *to get it back, calling the police* three times. (2)
d. *By warning the residents,* they prevented more injury. (1)
e. *Warning the residents* was a good idea. (1)
f. *To run away, leaving the area quickly,* was their only concern. (2)
g. Off went the residents, *leaving the area quickly.* (1)

G

FORMS
OF GRAMMAR

G 1   Possessive with Gerund

A *gerund* is a verbal noun that ends in *-ing*:

Pitch*ing* is fun.
Learn*ing* is hard.
His ly*ing* is hard to take.

When the emphasis is on the activity, use the *possessive form* with the *-ing* noun.

> *Problem:*   She did not object to *me hugging* her.
> *Solution:*   She did not object to *my hugging* her.
>
> *Problem:*   The *officer commanding* me to pull over was a surprise.
> *Solution:*   The *officer's commanding* me to pull over was a surprise.

If the emphasis is not on the activity, you may write:

> She did not object to *me* hugging her. (But she might have objected to any
> other person who hugged her.)

I prefer *John* pitching. (The emphasis is on John, rather than on his activity, pitching.)

PRACTICE

Correct the following sentences for faulty possessives; then explain your correction in a sentence or two. If you think that a sentence is correct as it stands, explain why.

1. Hal Johnson writing was the best I had ever read.

2. No one appreciates Elizabeth modeling more than I do.

3. He said that he wished you had stopped him joking about our mistakes so much.

4. The oxen in the zoo were disturbed by the lion roaring.

5. We heard them roaring.

6. Father objected to him dating Susie.

7. He insists on me chaperoning poor Susie on every date.

8. She hated him interfering with her private life.

G 2   *Vague or Ambiguous Pronoun Reference*

Make your pronoun references clear.

Problem: The dresser had glue blocks over the screw holes so that one had to remove the screws before removing the drawer supports. *This* required me to get help from my shop instructor. (What does *this* refer to?)

Solution: Since the dresser had glue blocks over the screw holes, I asked my shop instructor to help me remove the blocks without damaging the drawer supports.

Problem: Our dog knocked two lamps on the floor and broke several glasses on the lamp table. We found *them* smashed the next morning. (Does *them* refer to lamps, to glasses, or to lamps *and* glasses?)

Solution: Our dog knocked . . . We found the glasses smashed the next morning.

> *Problem:*   In discussing the language requirements, *it* made us feel that we had the wrong idea about the usefulness of a foreign language. (What does *it* refer to?)
>
> *Solution:*   As we were discussing the language requirements, we began to realize that we had the wrong idea about the usefulness of a foreign language.

> *Problem:*   I won a lot of money, *which* made me very happy. (It was the occurrence, not the money, which made me happy.)
>
> *Solution:*   Winning a lot of money made me happy.

G 3   Wrong Form of Pronoun

To correct most errors in pronoun form, isolate (or set apart) the construction. Such isolation will help you to discover whether you need the *subject* or the *object* form of the pronoun.

> Subject forms fit in the slot: "_____ did it."
>
> *She* did it.
> *They* did it.
> *He* did it.
>
> Object forms fit in the slot: "They pushed _____."
>
> They pushed *him.*
> They pushed *her.*
> They pushed *them.*
>
> Prepositions, of course, fit in this pattern: "They did it to _____."
>
> They did it to *him.*
> They did it for *her.*
> They did it with *them.*

If you isolate (or set apart) the construction, you can tell whether the pronoun should go in the *subject* or *object* slot.

> *Problem:*   Would you call Jack and *he* on the phone?
> *Isolation:* Would you call *he*? (*He* should be *him*).
> *Solution:*   Would you call Jack and *him* on the phone?

> *Problem:*   Phyllis and *me* will walk to the library with you.
> *Isolation:* *Me* will walk to the library with you. (*Me* should be *I*).
> *Solution:*   Phyllis and *I* will walk to the library with you.

> *Problem:*   The movie program was specially designed for *we* college students.

Isolation: The movie program was specially designed for *we.* (*We* should be *us.*)

Solution: The movie program was specially designed for *us* college students.

Note: The following advice is the subject of debate by many language experts. But it is practical advice and firmly based on modern English usage.

Who vs. *whom.* Use *whom* when it is the object of a preposition: "for whom," "to whom," "beside whom." Use *who* with everything else.

I vs. *me; they* vs. *them;* etc. At the end of an expression, use the *object* form (*me, her, him, them*):

It is *me.*
That is *them* over there.
This is *him* now.

PRACTICE

Find any vague or ambiguous pronoun references, or wrong pronoun forms, in the following sentences. Then correct each error.

1. In Tent City they now have the largest city in the country.

2. Margaret told Helen she was the wisest girl she ever knew.

3. It said in the manual that the car never needs an oil change.

4. Tell the Dean and he about the secret contract with the CIA.

5. Us faculty members knew all about the teaching award.

6. Mark and me were told from the beginning.

7. The money was supposed to have gone to we team members.

8. Carter is an airline pilot, and that is the profession his son wants to follow.

9. He can't see well. This is because he did not get glasses as a child.

10. Miles held on to the cat's paw, which bit him.

11. Mrs. Smith gave a talk on the antique business—in particular on the method of financing it and making a proper report to the IRS. It is a complicated affair.

12. Susie yelled at the owner of the new house on the corner that was watering his roses.

G 4   *Appropriate Verb Tense*

Tense refers to how the verb expresses *time.*

Present tense:	She *wishes* for money.
Past tense:	She *wished* for money.
Future tense:	She *will wish* for money.
Present perfect:	She *has wished* for money.
Past perfect:	She *had wished* for money.
Future perfect:	She *will have wished* for money.

Most questions of tense involve thinking through the logic of the time(s) you intend to put your statements in.

Problem: Then the judge *recalled* that the prosecution *stated* its objections two weeks earlier.

Solution: Then the judge *recalled* that the prosecution *had stated* its objections two weeks earlier. (The verbs logically belong in two different "times.")

Problem: He *was* a handsome man before he *became* a vampire.

Solution: He *had been* a handsome man before be *became* a vampire.

Note: The present tense is customarily used in literary criticism and reviews when describing action and psychological states in the literary work. But it is not used when making statements about the author or his background.

Problem: Shakespeare *sees* Hamlet as a man who *believed* in the supernatural.

Solution: Shakespeare *saw* Hamlet as a man who *believes* in the supernatural.

Problem: In *The Catcher in the Rye,* Holden Caulfield *was* a tiresome adolescent. Perhaps the author, J. D. Salinger, *does* not *understand* his own creation.

Solution: In *The Catcher in the Rye,* Holden Caulfield *is* a troublesome adolescent. Perhaps the author, J. D. Salinger, *did* not *understand* his own creation.

PRACTICE

Where necessary, change the tense of the verbs.

1. At first, Huck Finn believes that blacks are different; later he came to recognize that all human beings will share the same faults and virtues.

2. Here she was, staring angrily at me from the stage. So I say to her: "I can't hear you from the back row!"

3. Mrs. McMinn claimed that the Imperial Valley was the hottest place in California.

4. After Mr. McMinn went to California, his wife was concerned that he could be finding the heat unbearable, so she was writing him to rent an air conditioner.

5. Charles Dickens is a great writer; his *David Copperfield* is a story that every young person will be able to enjoy.

6. Mark Twain writes *Huckleberry Finn* on the top floor of his Hartford home, which he believes to be the best place to work.

7. Sandra remembers that the TV had blown a fuse on the night when we would have been watching a rerun of *Star Trek*.

G 5   Faulty Principal Part of the Verb

The so-called *principal parts* of the verb form this familiar pattern:

Present Tense	Past Tense	Past Participle
ask	asked	asked
ring	rang	rung
bring	brought	brought

In its past tense and past participle, *ask* does not change much, adding only *-ed* (*ask, asked, asked*). *Ring* changes form twice, but *bring* changes only once. A verb like *ask* is called *regular*; verbs like *ring* and *bring* are said to be *irregular*. Through constant usage, most of us "know" most of these forms; but when we come to something like *lie* and *dive,* memory often fails. Should we write "I had *lain* there for an hour"? (One of us can never remember and so—when pushed—says, "I *had been* there for an hour.") Is it "The child *dived* in the pool"? Or *dove*?

The answers to such questions can be found in your standard desk dictionary under the present form of the verb (*lie* and *dive*). And there's your choice: memorize the forms; or avoid the verb; or look it up.

PRACTICE

In your dictionary, look up the principal parts of these verbs:

bid (command)	hang (execute)	sink
bid (offer)	lie	sit
burst	seek	spring
dive	set	swing
forget	shrink	weave
get		

G 6   Proper Use of the Subjunctive

The subjunctive is a verb form used mainly in *contrary-to-fact* statements and after *wishes*. The verb form may be *were, be,* or the verb without the final *s*.

Contrary-to-fact statements:
I would not do that if I *were* you. (I am not you.)
If she *were* true to me she would not go out with other men. (She is not true to me.)
If this *be* patriotism, I am not a patriot. (This is not patriotism.)
After wishes:
I wish I *were* rich.
Let him *live.*
My father requested that his body *be* cremated.
I demand that Smith *be* reinstated. (A demand is a strong wish.)

PRACTICE

In the following sentences, correct the faulty forms of the subjunctive.

1. If he was to live a thousand years, he would not be able to support me adequately.

2. I wish this wasn't Tuesday.

3. I'd drop that gun if I was you.

4. If he was here, we would all leave.

5. Major Burns demands that he is given a transfer to another unit.

6. I would go to Monterey if I was given the opportunity.

G 7   Piling Up Verbs

The English verb system is complex and flexible, made so in part by the rich array of *auxiliaries* (or *helping verbs*): "*had been* kept," "*should have been* doing," "*will have* performed." Yet helping verbs can work against a writer if they are piled up in a sentence so that verb phrases are long and awkward:

> *Problem:*   He *would have liked to have seen* the movie.
> *Solution:*   He *wanted to see* the movie.

> *Problem:*   We *did* not *desire to have become required* as participants by the coach.
> *Solution:*   We *did* not *want* the coach to make us participate.

> *Problem:*   They *had meant to have stopped* the murder.
> *Solution:*   They *had meant to stop* the murder.

G 8   Confusion of Adjectives and Adverbs

Errors with adjectives and adverbs are sometimes created when you confuse the two. For instance, if you wanted to say that someone had body odor, it would be silly to write that he smelled *badly*, for *badly* would imply that his nose wasn't working properly. Follow these suggestions for distinguishing between adjectives and adverbs:

1. Know that adjectives modify nouns and that adverbs modify verbs, adjectives, and other adverbs. (See pp. 515–516 for more discussion of adjectives and adverbs. See also p. 498.)

2. Use your dictionary to check whether a word is an adjective or an adverb.

3. Substitute the word you are in doubt about into one of these patterns:

Subject-verb-*adjective*-object:
You injured a *well* person.
You did a *good* job.

Subject-verb-object *adverb*:
You did the job *well.*
You did it *happily.*

Subject-is-*adjective*:
She is *good.*
She is *happy.*

The substitution should tell you whether the word is an adjective or adverb.

G 9   Degrees of Comparison for Adjectives and Adverbs

The degrees of comparison for adjectives and adverbs are *positive, comparative,* and *superlative*; for example:

Positive	*Comparative*	*Superlative*
cold	colder	coldest
big	bigger	biggest
good	better	best
much	more	most
easily	more easily	most easily
often	more often	most often

The shorter adjectives (and a small number of adverbs) form the degrees of comparison as *cold* does: cold, cold*er*, cold*est.* A few are irregular: *bad, worse, worst.*

Many adjectives of two syllables and all of three or more syllables form the degrees of comparison with the use of *more* and *most:* beautiful, *more* beautiful, *most* beautiful. And most adverbs are formed the same way: curiously, *more* curiously, *most* curiously.

It is often claimed that certain adjectives — such as *unique, round,* and *dead* — have only one degree and logically cannot be compared. Does *dead, deader, deadest* appear logical? When used figuratively or light-heartedly, it probably does. "That was the deadest party I ever went to" expresses the idea perfectly. But in most cases, *dead,* like *pregnant,* expresses an absolute condition — you either are or you aren't. Similarly, *unique* cannot be qualified in expressions like *more unique*—the word means "one of a kind," and you can't get "one-er" than "one." Yet you might reasonably write *almost unique*—almost "one of a kind."

G 10   Misuse of Noun as Adjective

Many nouns make poor adjectives: *liability* action, *validity* record, *believability* reasons, *plot* circumstances. The solution for most of these is to change the wording or the construction.

> Problem: I will now relate the *plot circumstances.*
> Solution: I will now relate the *circumstances of the plot.*
>
> Problem: His experiments have a poor *validity record.*
> Solution: His experiments *seldom work out.*

As you may have guessed, such problems are usually closely related to the use of jargon. See pp. 308–309 for more discussion of "nouny" writing.

PRACTICE

Correct these sentences for: (1) confusion of adjectives with adverbs, (2) the proper use of degrees of comparison, and (3) the misuse of nouns as adjectives.

1. The Maremont Corporation Harvey, Illinois research was conducted by three chemists.

2. The research was done as careful as any technician research in the lab, and it turned out to be the more useful of all the projects started there.

3. She looked beautifully and sweet in her new Levis. But she acted recklesser than she looked.

4. I run every day for endurance reasons. It is good exercise and makes me feel good.

5. Johanna's plane was built strong enough to carry an extra load of fuel easy.

6. "Hold tight to your religion beliefs," his elderly father had said.

7. Her position qualifications are most perfect for the supervisor job.

8. My high grade was the inevitably result of having a kindly teacher.

9. His ambition is the less good thing about him.

G 11   *Faulty Verb Agreement*

Verbs must ordinarily agree with their subjects:

Dogs are popular pets.
A *clue was* discovered.
Each of the female bears *was* found with its cub.
These *people were* innocent.

However, when in doubt let your meaning determine subject-verb agreement.

Problem:	A *number* of these cures *was (?) were (?)* rejected.
Solution (1):	A *number* of these cures *were* rejected. (Obviously, *number* designates more than one cure.)
Solution (2):	*Several* of these cures *were* rejected.
Solution (3):	A *few* of these cures *were* rejected.
Solution (4):	The doctors rejected some of the cures.

Six typical errors in agreement.

1. With clumsy joiners (*as well as, along with, in addition to,* etc.)

Problem:	My *baby, together with three other babies* in the maternity ward, *was (?) were (?)* saved by the nurse.
Solution (1):	My *baby,* together with three other babies in the maternity ward, *was* saved by the nurse. (The general rule is that a singular subject, immediately followed by clumsy joiners or other interrupters, takes a singular verb.)
Solution (2):	My *baby and* three other *babies* in the maternity ward *were* saved by the nurse. (Where you can, use *and* instead of clumsy joiners.)

2. With pronouns.

Problem:	She is one of those *girls who is (?) are (?)* always well dressed.
Solution (1):	She is one of those *girls who are* always well dressed. (Make

the verb agree with the noun [*girls*] that the pronoun [*who*] stands for.)

Solution (2): She is the kind of *girl who is* always well dressed. (Put the whole thing in the singular.)

3. With "subject-*is*-noun" statements.

Problem: The main *issue is (?) are (?)* high prices.
Solution (1): The main *issue is* high prices. (Make the verb agree with the subject.)
Solution (2): The main *issue is that prices are too high.* (Change subject-*is*-noun to subject-*is*-clause.)

4. With collective nouns ("group" nouns).

Problem: The *team is (?) are (?)* happy about their victory.
Solution (1): The *team is* happy about its victory. (Consider the team as one group or unit.)
Solution (2): The *members* of the team *are* happy about their victory. (Use a plural subject.)

Problem: *A hundred feet* of electrical wire *is (?) are (?)* too much for this room.
Solution (1): *A hundred feet* of electrical wire *is* too much for this room. (Consider *a hundred feet* as a unit.)
Solution (2): We don't need a hundred feet of electrical wire for this room.

5. With statements that start with *there*.

Those that begin with a non-adverb or "filler" *there*:
There are TREES in my yard. (*TREES* is the subject.)

Those that begin with an adverb of place:
There [pointing] are the TREES I want cut down. (*TREES* is the subject.)

In both kinds of statement, the subject is delayed. But the subject still controls the number of the verb:

There is no WAY I can accept that. (filler *there*)
There [pointing] are the ROADS you should take (adverb *there*)

Problem: There's *things* to be done today.
Solution: There *are things* to be done today.

Problem: *There is (?) are (?)* happy *cowboys* in Texas.

Solution (1):   *There are* happy *cowboys* in Texas. (Make the verb agree with the subject *cowboys*.)

Solution (2):   *Some cowboys are* happy in Texas.

6. With "either-or" and "neither-nor" statements.

Problem: *Either* the butler *or* the maid *was (?) were (?)* the murderer.

Solution: *Either* the butler *or* the maid *was* the murderer. (In such constructions, pairs of singular subjects take singular verbs.)

Problem: *Neither* the car *nor* the trucks *was (?) were (?)* stolen.

Solution (1):   *Neither* the car *nor* the trucks *were* stolen. (The verb should agree with the nearer of its subjects.)

Solution (2):   The car and the trucks *were* not stolen. (Revise the construction to avoid the "neither-nor" problem.)

PRACTICE

Correct these sentences. If you believe that a sentence is correct as it stands, state why.

1. There's lights on in my house.

2. Was any of his rabbits killed by the weasel?

3. Neither the puppy nor the kittens were responsible for making such a mess.

4. My biggest problem is C grades on papers.

5. I have heard that an army march on their stomachs.

6. There seem to be a great deal of noise coming from the next room.

7. The stadium is one of those structures that surprises you when you first see it.

8. His use of wallpaper, as well as his painting, make the living room quite pleasant.

9. My list of supplies were so long that Mr. Fenwick refused to buy them.

10. The advice of both counselors, which I heard from the next room, are that you go back to the dorm and talk to the resident advisor.

11. Their main complaint is loud stereos and people partying after midnight.

12. These are many of the kinds of reasoning that is mentioned in the Bill of Rights.

G 12   Faulty Pronoun Agreement

Here is an example of faulty pronoun agreement: "*Everyone* was told to pick up *their* books and leave." Since *everyone* is singular, the pronoun *their* does not "agree" with it.

> *Problem:*   I told *each girl* coming to the party to bring *their* own food.
> *Solution (1):* I told *each girl* coming to the party to bring *her* own food.
> *Solution (2):* I told *all the girls* coming to the party to bring *their* own food. (Instead of forcing the pronoun to agree with the expression appearing earlier in the sentence, try starting the sentence with a plural.

Note: See also the discussion of the generic pronoun, p. 595. Observe the typical choices in the following agreement problem:

> *Problem:*   If you want *an employee* to work hard for you, always give *them* plenty of praise for good work.
> *Solution (1):* If you want *an employee* to work hard for you, always give *him* . . .
> *Solution (2):* If you want *employees* to work hard for you, always give *them* . . .

Problems in pronoun agreement can often be avoided by going back to the beginning of the paragraph and deciding whether you want to be in the singular or the plural throughout your discussion. Decide early, for instance, whether you want to discuss *employees* in general, or the *employee* as an individual. Then simply be consistent in choosing pronouns.

PRACTICE

Correct the faulty pronoun agreement in these sentences.

1. Each person rented their own costume for the dance.

2. If someone tries to ride their bike through campus, they'll run over you every time.

3. The university is proud of their lawns and parks.

4. If anyone writes to Charlotte, have them tell her she left her skis here.

5. Each of the rules for the house can be considered practical only when they are enforced.

6. Everyone likes to have more freedom for themselves than they do for others.

7. After one retires, they like to have a hobby to keep them busy.

8. When a nursing student applies for her first job after graduation, they like to know how much money they are going to make.

S

SENTENCE STRUCTURE

S 1   Unnecessary Shifts

In avoiding unnecessary shifts in various sentence elements, follow the "rule of consistency," which is actually only a matter of common sense: In any rhetorical unit (particularly in the sentence), continue as you began.

1. If you began in the past tense, continue in it:

> *Problem:*   Louise *stated* that the papers were filed a year ago, while her attorney *says* they were never filed.
>
> *Solution:*   Louise *stated* . . . her attorney *said.* . . .

2. If you started with indirect discourse, stay with it:

> *Problem:*   Mrs. McMinn said she was thirsty and would I get her some water from the cooler?
>
> *Solution:*   Mrs. McMinn said she was thirsty and asked me to get her some water from the cooler.

3. If you started with one form of the pronoun, stick with it.

> *Problem:*   *One* cannot understand when *you* are young that marriage is full of both pains and pleasures.
>
> *Solution:* When *you* are young, *you* cannot understand. . . .

Pronouns are slippery, shifty beasts:

> *Problem:*   If traveling makes *one* sick, the airline provides paper bags for *you.*
>
> *Solution:* If traveling makes *one* sick, the airline provides paper bags for *him.*

This solution throws both pronouns into the third person and is, at least, grammatical. You could write ". . . makes *one* sick . . . paper bags for *one.*" But this sounds like a British aristocrat at his most pompous. The best policy is to pick out your first pronoun (or noun) and then continue in the same person:

> If traveling makes *you* sick . . . bags for *you.*
> If traveling makes *people* sick . . . bags for *them.*

Or simply avoid the slippery beast in the second clause:

> For anyone who gets sick, the airline provides a paper bag.

4. Don't make awkward shifts in the subject-verb pattern in a series of sentences. Here's an example of an awkward shift:

> After considering the situation at the West End store, the students decided to support the strike there. They refused to cross the picket line, and encouraged others not to pass it. *A notice* about their action *was put* in the school paper and *was paid for* by them. Finally, they sent a delegation to the management of West End. . . .

As they shift from active to passive, the italicized subject-verb patterns break the flow of development in the paragraph and disrupt its unity. The paragraph improved:

> After considering the situation at the West End store, the students decided to support the strike there. They refused to cross the picket line, and encouraged others not to pass it. The school paper published a notice about their action, a notice the students paid for. Finally, they sent a delegation to the management of West End. . . .

An awkward shift of the subject-verb pattern can be particularly noticeable if it appears inside a sentence:

Awkward: Ever since *they saw* the volcano erupt, there *has been a great fear* of Mt. St. Helens in the people who live nearby.

Improved: Ever since *they saw* the volcano erupt, the *people* who live near Mt. St. Helens *have been* afraid. . . .

(See pp. 508–510 for more discussion of consistent pronoun use.)

PRACTICE

Correct these sentences for consistency.

1. The airplane swooped close to the ground, and he blinked his landing lights twice.

2. As they were walking, Harley remarked that most of the elms were dying, but Sheridan explains that there is a new scientific method of saving them.

3. If the elms were all alive, and the method is easily available, we could protect thousands of them in this city alone.

4. The general ordered that the flags be lowered to half-mast on Tuesday and blow taps for the men who were lost.

5. The vice-president had to recognize Mrs. Carlin's ability, but this was not done gracefully by him.

6. A legislature does not like to tax its citizens, and they will usually try to get money some other way.

7. If you want to make a sailor happy, just give them plenty of shore leave.

8. First, mark down the suits, and then you should put "50%-Off" tags on the shirts.

9. Macbeth has trouble with his conscience, but after a time he managed to kill it completely.

10. In a small town, one is never lonely; indeed, you usually feel that you know too many people.

S 2   *Omissions and Incomplete Constructions*

Omissions and incomplete constructions are often accidental; the writer leaves out a word on the page that his mind easily supplies for him—but not for the reader:

Don't leave out a word on ∧ page.   *the*
Many have wondered what happened ∧ Marilyn Monroe.   *to*

Other omissions are created by what might be called a "grammatical hiccup":

Wilma saw the bartender was watering the bourbon.

Obviously, the object of *saw* should not be *bartender* but the whole noun clause:

Wilma saw *that the bartender was watering the bourbon.*

Another example of a hiccup:

Problem: Since he's working here, he's been watering the stock.
Solution: Since he's *been* working here, he's been watering the stock.

Certain idioms seem to be particularly susceptible to incompleteness:

Problem: He was interested but undisturbed by her revelation.
Solution (1):   He was interested *in* but undisturbed by her revelation.
Solution (2):   He was interested in her revelation but undisturbed by it.

Problem: You must learn obedience and respect for the coach.
Solution: You must learn obedience *to* and respect for the coach.

PRACTICE

Supply the missing parts in these sentences. Rewrite as necessary.

1. Playing classical trumpet has and always will be a poorly paid profession.

2. Whenever I see the Statue of Liberty, I get impression power and glory.

3. They agree with Mrs. Kane's interpretation but object Mr. Kane's.

4. Winnie did a good job and earned a great deal money from the Ace Housebuilding Company.

5. The fat old dog was barking, and the puppies regarding him with wonder.

6. We promised the old dog would not bothering the neighbors any more.

7. I remember a dog had a bark like that.

8. He never has and undoubtedly never will speak confidently before an audience.

S 3   Faulty Comparison

Comparisons should be logical and complete. Here is a faulty comparison:

Walcott's beliefs were different from Clark.

The writer is comparing the wrong things — *beliefs* and *Clark.*

Solution (1):	Walcott's beliefs were different from Clark's.
Solution (2):	Walcott's beliefs were different from those expressed by Clark.
Problem:	We are as industrious, if not more industrious, than the East Germans. (This says that we are "as industrious . . . *than* the East Germans.")
Solution:	We are as industrious as the East Germans, if not more so.
Problem:	Our family's house cost more than Smith.
Solution (1):	Our family's house cost more than Smith's.
Solution (2):	Our family's house cost more than the Smiths' did.
Problem:	New York City is bigger than any city in the country. (This means that it is bigger than itself, since it is one of the cities "in the country.")
Solution (1):	New York is bigger than any *other* city in the country.
Solution (2):	New York is the biggest city in the country.

As these examples imply, faulty comparisons seem to be created when the writer does not think this through: "*What (a)* am I comparing with *what (b)*?"

PRACTICE

Correct the faulty comparisons in these sentences. Rewrite as necessary.

1. Baseball talk makes Barb every bit as angry as those persons who talk endlessly of ballet and Bach.

2. My boyfriend says that his writing is easier to read than his teacher.

3. Fewer people went to the movies; more and more they bought their own TV sets instead of watching their neighbors.

4. In *Catch-22*, the plot is easier to follow than the other war novels.

5. This year's Chevrolet is smaller and more expensive.

6. The Swiss make more watches and other timepieces than England or France.

7. This fat goldfish is obviously more greedy than any fish in the tank.

8. Using contractions made Miss Wimm angrier even than when she caught anybody reading comic books in class.

S 4   Split or "Separated" Constructions

English grammar does its job in several ways. One of these can be described by the "rule of nearness": expressions that belong together are put near each other. Here are a few instances:

1. Objects are placed near their verbs, verbs near their subjects.

> *Problem:*   She *sent* to her senator a *letter.*
> *Solution:*   She *sent* a *letter* to her senator.

> *Problem:*   *He as it turned out when we found him was* not lost at all.
> *Solution:*   As it turned out when we found him, *he was* not lost at all.

2. Adjective clauses are placed near the expression they modify:

> *Problem:*   Anders lost his *knife* on the seacoast *which his mother had bought for him.*
> *Solution:*   On the seacoast, Anders lost the *knife which his mother had bought for him.*

3. The sign of the infinitive *(to)* immediately precedes its verb:

> *Problem:*   They wanted *to* immediately and completely *pay back* the loan.
>
> *Solution:*   They wanted *to pay back* the loan immediately and completely.

Note: It is fashionable to say that good writers occasionally split infinitives. One excellent textbook (the first edition of which we used as freshmen back in the Middle Ages) says that "many times" infinitive splitting is "not only natural but also desirable." The authors use this example: "For her *to never complain* seems unreal." Is that better than *"never to complain"*?

It is interesting to note that for every infinitive split by an accomplished writer, there will be a hundred that he won't split. The rule of nearness is not made of granite, but it is not made of Jello either. If you glance over the problems in S 5, S 6, and S 7 on the following pages, you will discover that violating the rule can lead to some pretty comical sentences.

PRACTICE

In the following sentences, repair the split or "separation."

1. Mrs. McMinn told Mike when he went to the grocery store on the corner of First and Main to pick up some eggs.

2. Mike promised to quickly and faithfully carry out her request.

3. We may, if there is no objection, see a double-header this afternoon.

4. The second baseman, dismayed by the spikes of the two-hundred-pound runner bearing grimly down upon him, threw wildly to first.

5. We agreed as soon as the game was over and the noise of the crowd had abated that she would speak to me again.

6. The argument that beer makes one tipsy loses at a raucous major-league ball game all possible force.

7. When you watch people drink and sweat in 115-degree heat, it is impossible to even partly believe that any alcohol reaches the brain.

S 5   *Misplaced Modifiers*

A *modifier* is a sentence element that describes, qualifies, or limits an expression. If a modifier is wrongly placed, the resulting construction may seem illogical. Examples:

Problem: I departed for Europe on a freighter 3,000 miles away.
Solution (1): I departed on a freighter for Europe — 3,000 miles away.
Solution (2): I got on a freighter bound for Europe, which was 3,000 miles away.

Problem: He nearly tried to make all of his teachers happy.
Solution: He tried to make nearly all of his teachers happy.

Problem: We discovered the old well in the north corner of Marston's backyard, which was full of green, brackish water. (The *yard* was full of water?)
Solution: The old well that we discovered in the north corner of Marston's backyard was full of green, brackish water.

PRACTICE

Correct the misplaced modifiers in these sentences. Because some of these errors cannot be satisfactorily corrected by moving the modifier to another position, you may have to rewrite some of the sentences.

1. Her stomach felt better after drinkng the orange juice.

2. The fraternities voted for the Homecoming Queen as a body.

3. Men and women walked down the aisle to receive diplomas — not youngsters.

4. The final thrill came in eating the fish he caught with fried potatoes, sliced tomatoes, and a can of beer.

5. Look carefully at that old man with a beard about a block behind.

6. The Ratched Motel is fixing an early breakfast for campers who are leaving the area at 5:00 a.m. (Assume that the campers are leaving at 7:30.)

7. I'll investigate the crime when you finish with the body for possible clues.

S 6   Squinting Modifiers

The *"squinting" modifier* ambiguously points in two directions at once. Example:

Running away *occasionally* makes Sam feel better.

The reader wonders whether the writer means occasionally *running away* or occasionally *makes Sam feel better.* Such problems can be solved by tying the modifier firmly to what it modifies:

Occasionally, Sam runs away, after which he feels better.

PRACTICE

Correct these squinting constructions by rewriting the sentences.

1. The umpire claimed during the game that Detroit's manager spat in his direction.

2. The manager told us before we sportswriters left to apologize to him.

3. The lawyer who represents himself in most instances is his own "foolish client."

4. They promised after the end of the term to change her grade.

5. He wrote a treatise on mountaineering in the Gobi Desert.

S 7   Dangling Modifiers

The typical *dangling modifier* is an introductory expression that is not "tied" logically to the main clause that follows:

Problem: Having eaten his lunch, the steamboat departed.

The "dangler" implies an action in the opening modifier, but supplies the wrong *actor* for it in the main clause. Such errors are easily corrected by creating a logical tie between both parts of the sentence. This correction can usually be made by changing the opening modifier or the main clause that follows. Sometimes it may be best to rewrite the sentence without the opener.

Solution (1):	After lunch, the steamboat departed.
Solution (2):	Having eaten his lunch, he boarded the departing steamboat.
Problem:	Coming too fast to the stop sign, the brake was applied quickly. (The *brake* was coming too fast?)
Solution (1):	Coming too fast to the stop sign, he applied the brake quickly.
Solution (2):	He applied the brake quickly when he realized he was coming too fast to the stop sign.

Some danglers have no action stated (as such) in the opener, which is an elliptical expression:

Problem:	Upon graduation, my family gave me a hundred dollars and a ticket to Hollywood (The *family* graduated?)
Solution (1):	When I graduated, my family gave me a hundred dollars and a ticket to Hollywood.
Solution (2):	Upon graduation, I got a hundred dollars and a ticket to Hollywood from my family.

PRACTICE

Correct the dangling modifiers in these sentences:

1. Getting up from the typewriter when the water cooler exploded, my news story was completely forgotten.

2. Astonished at the intrusion, her hands fluttered wildly.

3. Inflated to an enormous size, I rode the rubber raft around the pool.

4. By stopping smoking, there was a belief that he could cure his asthma.

5. After snuggling warm on the couch all night, the dawn finally came.

6. Concentrating my orderly mind, the paper was written quickly.

7. After working all summer on the road gang, the tan that Melvin got was the envy of his friends.

8. When only a second grader, my mother was told that I was obviously nearsighted.

S 8   Faulty Parallelism

Parallel elements in a sentence should be (a) roughly equal in importance, and (b) written in the same grammatical form. Examples:

Roger and *Tom* were terrible at ballroom dancing.
Ballroom dancing and *square dancing* are not activities for sissies.
Some small nations preferred to *watch, listen,* and *wait.*

Faulty parallelism fails to put parallel *ideas* in parallel *form*:

Problem: She *believes* in him, as well as *having* faith in him.
Solution: She *believes* in him and *has* faith in him.

Problem: That movie had too much *sex, violence,* and the *language was bad.*
Solution: That movie had too much *sex, violence,* and *profanity.*

Use *correlative conjunctions* properly. These conjunctions are:

either . . . or
neither . . . nor
not only . . . but also
both . . . and

Put correlative conjunctions just before the parallel expressions (and make sure the expressions are really parallel):

The riddle of the Sphinx is not only *unknown* but also *unknowable.*

Not this: To earn money for college they worked *both* for the state highway program in the summer *and* janitoring part-time at night.
But this: To earn money for college they worked for *both* the state highway program in the summer *and* the local janitor service.

Not this: The movie critic *not only* dislikes the violence *but also* the obvious acting.

But this: The movie critic dislikes *not only* the violence *but also* the obvious acting.

See pp. 275–277 for more discussion of *parallelism.*

PRACTICE

Correct the faulty parallelism in the following sentences. For more exercises on parallelism, see pp. 277–280.

1. Her mother could always depend on Trish for going to class and to be making good grades.

2. When he owned that car, he never put in oil, checked the tires, and even the windshield was never washed.

3. In the race, a Porsche came in first, a Ferrari came in second, in addition to a Lotus having come in third.

4. I neither have the money nor the time to go to the game tonight.

5. Politicians are ruining this country, as well as its being destroyed by lenient judges.

6. Making the Dean's list and his captaincy of the football team made Strawbridge very popular.

7. The new seats in Howes Stadium are wide, comfortable, and of well-built quality.

8. Not only when they live on campus but also off, they prefer a private room.

9. Ask your roommate whether she wants to go to the party besides going to the picnic.

S 9   *Proper Subordination*

Subordination allows you to shift the emphasis from one part of a sentence to another, thus making your prose smoother and more logical. An important reason for subordinating one clause to another is to show a logical relationship: *"Because we got cold, wet, and hungry,* we left the stadium at half-time." The following subordinate elements are in italics:

> Callie Marshall was unable to reach Denver, *even though she rode all night through the snow.*
>
> John Frye, *who was one of the most energetic small men we had ever known,* climbed Slew Mountain by himself.
>
> *Although he was small,* John Frye energetically climbed Slew Mountain by himself.

Note that a subordinate element can be put at the beginning, middle, or end of a sentence.

Use subordination to improve choppy or unemphatic sentences:

> *Problem:*   His name was Bellmon. He was black. He was married in his sophomore year. He had two jobs that year.
>
> *Solution:*   Bellmon, *the black married student,* had two jobs his sophomore year.
>
> *Problem:*   They were hungry, but there was a drought, and they lost their farms, so they decided to go to California.
>
> *Solution:*   They lost their farms *after the drought came. Later, driven by hunger,* they decided to go to California.

(Also see pp. 280–281 and 500–502.)

PRACTICE

Use subordination to improve these sentences.

1. He is poor, and he has an old Chevy pickup, but it uses too much oil, and it will eventually have to be sold.

2. The members of the first team could not understand the coach. The misunderstanding became an issue with the Athletic Council.

3. Friendship is of first importance. It helps to create harmony in human relationships.

4. He earned a great deal of money in business. He never worked hard. He paid little attention to conventions of manners and dress.

5. She wanted to major in computer science. She did not have many courses in science or math.

6. Accidents keep occurring on this busy corner. Two extra policemen have been stationed to warn motorists of the danger.

7. The manufacturer gave us a new air conditioner. This occurred before we could complain to the state Consumer's Protection Bureau. He wanted to improve his relationship with customers.

S 10   Faulty Subordination

In subordinating one part of a sentence to another, the writer makes the sentence elements *unequal*. Unlike a main clause, a subordinated element can never stand alone. The relationship between the main and subordinated elements is both grammatical and logical. In these two sentences, note the subordinated elements (in italics):

The old lady, *who had just put on her nightgown,* would not answer the doorbell.

The old lady, *who would not answer the doorbell,* had just put on her nightgown.

The subordination in the second sentence seems illogical. Here are other examples of faulty subordination.

Problem: Just last week I used that pay phone, *which was bombed this morning.*

Solution: This morning, someone bombed the pay phone *that I used last week.*

Problem: Barksdale is a former FBI agent *who was made president of the university today.*

Solution: Barksdale, *a former FBI agent,* was made president of the university today.

Problem: The Houndogs have lost 20 games in a row, *believing that they have no ability.*

Solution: Because they believe they have no ability, the Houndogs keep losing — 20 games in a row.

Problem: The old biplane burst into flames, *when the pilot dived out of the cockpit.*

Solution: *Just as the pilot dived out of the cockpit,* the old biplane burst into flames.

(Also see pp. 280–281 and 500–502.)

PRACTICE

Rewrite these examples of faulty subordination.

1. We are all hoping to move to a better neighborhood, believing that we now have enough money for a new house.

2. Although the grades for his papers stayed the same, most of the class did better on their papers.

3. My father was a poor man because he believed in democracy.

4. The agreement was not signed today, the workers believing it would be.

5. Cancer is related to cigarette smoking, although millions smoke.

6. Farwell, who knows how to act, has directed many plays successfully.

7. Because he had worked very hard for it, Mike was supported by most students for the Council.

8. I got my new teeth when I took Mrs. Farquhar to the theatre.

S 11   Faulty Coordination

Coordinate elements in a sentence should be balanced against each other so that they seem "equal" in emphasis and logic. When "unequal" elements are joined, usually by a coordinating conjunction, an illogical (or faulty) coordination is the result. To correct the problem, subordinate one of the elements at the beginning, middle, or end of the sentence.

Problem: I had a lot of work to do, *and* I had a cup of coffee.
Solution: *Even though I had a lot of work to do,* I had a cup of coffee.

Problem: Liza was an excellent worker, *and* she got the best student job the college had.
Solution: Liza, *who was an excellent worker,* got the best student job the college had.

Problem: The new shingles have been nailed on the roof, *and* the men have not gone on lunch break.
Solution: The men have not gone to lunch, *although they have finished nailing the shingles on the roof.*

PRACTICE

Clarify the relationship between the coordinate elements in these sentences. When you can, subordinate an element at the beginning, middle, or end of the sentence.

1. Friends say that they go to Chicago as often as they used to, and it is a fairly safe city.

2. He was a handsome man and he had a short haircut.

3. There have been many students who have seen the play, and I think it is a good one.

4. The university had a poor debate team this year, and the debaters usually used incoherent arguments.

5. Tennessee is pretty, and we will visit many parts of the state on our vacation.

6. In botany, we learned about the permeability of cell walls, and surprising chemicals can pass through such walls.

7. Susan's husband has a Ph.D., and he shared the household duties with her, not without grumbling.

S 12   Faulty Complements

Certain statements complete their idea with a linking verb (usually a form of *be*) and a noun element. This use of *complements* (or *completers*) supplies a logical equation:

Subject	"be" form (=)	Complement
Miss *Haversham*	*is* (=)	the *Woman* of the Year.
The *material* for the seminar	*will be* (=)	the first *topic* for the committee.

If the noun elements on either side of the sentence do not "equal" each other, you will get an illogical equation, as in these sentences:

Problem: The main problem of an accountant is his reputation. (*problem ≠ reputation*)

Solution (1):   An accountant's main problem is that of keeping his reputation untarnished.

Solution (2):   What is an accountant's main problem? It is how to maintain a good reputation.

Problem: One of the most important reasons for supporting the union is stable employment. (*One* [reason] ≠ *employment*)

Solution (1):   Let's support the union so that we workers can have stable employment.

Solution (2):   You should support the union—it helps you to keep your job.

In another kind of faulty complement, there is no noun element on the right side of the "equation":

Problem: Love is where you have a very strong liking for someone. (*Love* ≠ *where*)

Solution: Love is having a very strong liking for someone.

Problem: My greatest happiness is when I am alone. (*happiness* ≠ *when*)

Solution (1):   I am most happy when I am alone.

Solution (2):   My greatest happiness is in being alone.

PRACTICE

Change the faulty complements in these sentences. Rewrite as necessary.

1. Another good quality of our employees is their absentee record.

2. Democracy is where people vote for their leaders.

3. The feasibility of installing the carpet, we think, is a big problem.

4. Because the Dodgers lost their second baseman was the reason they lost the pennant.

5. My main wish is Dad will get to retire early.

6. My high salary was since I was needed by the company.

7. Marrying is when you take a woman for your lawful, wedded wife.

8. The main reason I passed the exam is good studying.

9. Another reason is because my teacher likes me.

10. Graduation is where you are finally finished forever with learning.

S 13   *Sentence Fragments*

"The umpire called him out. Although he had already crossed the plate." The second statement is incomplete—a *sentence fragment*. Essentially, fragments are pieces of a sentence that cannot stand alone. They are not independent:

> The dead squirrel on the ground.
> Melissa having a good time.
> Waiting for us to come along.

By adding material, you can turn these sentence fragments into independent statements:

> The cat avoided the dead squirrel on the ground.
> I saw Melissa having a good time.
> There was the angry bus driver, waiting for us to come along.

Many fragments can be corrected by combining them with the previous sentence:

> *Problem:*   I refused the job. Because it was not interesting.
> *Solution:*   I refused the job because it was not interesting.
>
> *Problem:*   Virginia did not like the proposal. Even after her friends in the club had completely approved of it.
> *Solution:*   Virginia did not like the proposal, even after her friends in the club had completely approved of it.
>
> *Problem:*   James Earl Ray escaped from prison. A prison that was supposed to be escape-proof.
> *Solution:*   James Earl Ray escaped from a prison that was supposed to be escape-proof.
>
> *Problem:*   The administration believes that it must carry the matter through. Having come this far.
> *Solution:*   Having come this far, the administration believes that it must carry the matter through.
>
> *Problem:*   That group of citizens has finally given Congress an ultimatum. To limit the sale of handguns.
> *Solution:*   That group of citizens has finally given Congress an ultimatum—to limit the sale of handguns.

Note: In professional writing, the fragment is often used for emphasis or stylistic variation:

> "Of course, there's not much in it [the movie *Bonnie and Clyde*] about the nameless, faceless dead men. *Or the orphans and widows and the never-healing scar of a man who never knew his father.*" — Mike Royko

Your instructor will probably object to fragments if (1) you don't know you are using them (unconscious use is a sign that you do not know what a sentence is), or (2) you overwork them. Be sure you know his or her opinions on the matter.

PRACTICE

Revise each of the following constructions so that the sentence fragment is removed.

1. Taxes should be lowered. Because citizens pay too much to the government already.

2. Furnace tape can be used to repair cloth. And many other household items.

3. What happened to the student revolutionaries? The ones who were so evident during the sixties?

4. Some Germans practiced civil disobedience during the Nazi regime. A very small number.

5. That was the final question. Which I did not know the answer to.

6. Earlier she could remember the answer. That had been emphasized in the text.

7. I do not believe in that idea of God. An angry old man with a long beard.

S 14   Comma Splices

Here is a *comma splice*: "I am fond of you, he is fond of you too." The error is that of "splicing" two main clauses or sentences with a comma instead of separating them properly — usually with a period or semicolon. Another example:

> A word processor is actually a "computer-typewriter," it can type the same page a thousand times without the operator's touching the keys.

Sometimes a coordinating conjunction can be inserted between the two clauses spliced by a comma. Sometimes one main clause can be subordinated to the other:

A word processor is actually a "computer-typewriter," *and* it can type the same. . . .

A word processor, *which is actually a "computer-typewriter,"* can type the same. . . .

Here are more examples of the comma splice:

Problem: The garden was full of beans, I ate most of them that summer.

Solution (1):   The garden was full of beans; I ate most of them that summer.

Solution (2):   The garden was full of beans, so I ate most of them that summer. (The first clause is subordinated to the second.)

Problem: I am in no way responsible for your good fortune, you earned everything you have.

Solution (1):   I am in no way responsible for your good fortune. You earned everything you have.

Solution (2):   I am in no way responsible for your good fortune because you earned everything you have. (The second clause is subordinated to the first.)

PRACTICE

Find the comma splice in these sentences. Repunctuate (or rewrite) the sentences.

1. We went to see an unusual play last night, it was about Gertrude Stein, it had only one character, Ms. Stein herself.

2. They enjoy living in that apartment, their landlord supplies more services for them than for the other tenants.

3. I heard what the professor said, however, I did not write it down in my notes.

4. When he was editor of *Fortune,* Henry Luce said that he wanted to hire poets, at least poets knew the language, he said.

5. Luce believed that he could teach poets to write about economics, this was easier than teaching economists to write clear English.

6. The comic book has lost its appeal for many children, television has taken its place.

7. The word *prithee* is archaic, I will not use it any more.

8. First we had dust storms all over the state, then came torrential rains.

9. My horse went lame, consequently I will have to ride a stable horse in Friday's show.

10. "I've been working on a road crew for three summers now," she said, "I'm tired of that kind of work."

S 15 Fused Sentences

"I stopped and opened my car door the pickup behind me hit it." This construction is called a *fused sentence*. It is actually made up of two sentences joined together without any punctuation or capitalization to indicate where the first sentence ends and the second begins. The problem can be solved in several ways.

Solution (1):   I stopped and opened my car door. The pickup behind me hit it.

Solution (2):   When I stopped and opened my car door, the pickup behind me hit it.

Problem: Try not to write fused sentences they are hard to understand.

Solution (1):   Try not to write fused sentences; they are hard to understand.

Solution (2):   Your reader will find fused sentences hard to understand.

Problem: Where are you going when are you coming back?

Solution (1):   Where are you going? When are you coming back?

Solution (2):   Tell me where you are going and when you are coming back.

PRACTICE

In order to improve these fused sentences, repunctuate or rewrite them.

1. She discovered when she was young that she had musical talent later she was sorry she had not taken advantage of it.

2. I know that the period of the 1960s was a period of social change what kind of change was most important?

3. Librarians are now under attack for buying "dirty" books they even have to defend the circulation of certain modern classics like *The Catcher in the Rye.*

4. There was no breeze on the lake this afternoon we just sat there in the boat becalmed.

5. Scientists and creationists can sometimes agree they should not always assume that they are philosophical enemies.

6. Is the crime rate increasing perhaps we don't understand the situation perhaps we are merely getting better statistics.

7. We found Manuel building a set for the play he said he did not have time to help us with the calculus problems.

S 16   Run-On Sentences

The *run-on sentence* has a "stringy," unemphatic effect; it is usually created by a series of main clauses tied together with *or, and, but,* or *so:*

> Punishment is a good idea, and I believe that criminals should be punished, but they should not be put to death, for capital punishment is wrong.

Most sentences of this kind can be rewritten by using subordination and a change of emphasis:

> I believe that criminals should be punished. But since capital punishment is wrong, they should not be put to death.

> *Problem:*   Jim flew to New York, and his plane was late, so he was not able to get to the meeting on time, but his boss did not get angry with him.
>
> *Solution:*   When Jim flew to New York, his plane was late and he missed the meeting. His boss, however, did not get angry with him.

PRACTICE

1. Correct these run-on sentences.
    a. You can make beer much cheaper than you can buy it, and you need a container and a few ingredients, but you have to be sure that all materials are perfectly clean.

    b. Most readers read too slowly, and they miss the overall picture of the essay or book, so they tend to misunderstand the writer's point after they finish.

    c. I am afraid of flying, and I usually take two sleeping pills when I have to fly, but the pills don't work as well as they should, so I just stay awake and shake with fear.

    d. Jigsaw puzzles are fun to work, but they take more time than our family usually has, and the puzzles just sit there on the table half-done for days.

    e. The scientists reported that there will be a new earthquake in California, but it will be further away from San Francisco this time, and it will be lower on the Richter scale, so houses and property should not be greatly damaged.

    f. A fire department gets many strange calls, and some of them are from people who are lonely, and they just want to talk to someone, but they do not want to give their names or addresses.

2. These sentences are fused or run-on, or contain a comma splice. Identify the error, and correct the sentence. Rewrite where necessary.

    a. George Orwell wrote a famous essay called "A Hanging," and in this essay he showed how cruel peole could be, but in truth Orwell had never seen a hanging, for he told a friend that he had manufactured the whole story.

    b. Reasonable debate in a college class is possible, we should encourage it.

    c. Some scientists lie others lie part of the time, a few try always to tell the truth.

    d. Suicide is available to every person not every thinking person should consider it seriously.

    e. Romance shouts defiance at tradition, and tradition answers with a sneer, but the latter usually wins, for most people in the end become traditionalists in their own culture.

    f. She walked the length of the street in front of the great Miami hotels, she saw rows of the living dead propped up in their chairs.

    g. The young wisely ignore the old they think them to be prejudiced, this is not true they are merely tired of hearing the same old questions why don't you ask some new ones?

P

PUNCTUATION

Punctuation marks show the "joints" or joining places in your sentences. In addition to signaling sentence structure or indicating how words, phrases and sentences are put together these marks also tell the reader many small things for example that a string of words is a book title italics that something belongs to somebody apostrophe that a speech is coming comma and quotation marks

Did you have trouble reading that last sentence? No wonder—we didn't punctuate it. Now read it with the punctuation marks added (in *sixteen* places):

In addition to "signaling" sentence structure or indicating how words, phrases, and sentences are put together, these marks also tell the reader many small things—for example, that a string of words is a book title (italics); that something belongs to somebody (apostrophe); that a speech is coming (comma and quotation marks).

PUNCTUATION AND
SENTENCE UNITS

*O*ur research indicates that punctuation is learned most easily in the context of *writing a sentence.* In other words, you write and punctuate at the same time. Generally, it is unwise to write and then punctuate later; those little marks (particularly commas) are too much a part of the sentence and its structure. Punctuating after the fact is rather like putting up a house wall — and then hammering in the nails.

We recommend that before you read pp. 546–561, you look carefully at pp. 265–287. This will give you an idea of the tight relationship between the marks and how they separate and "signal" structures.

Know where you are in a sentence. As the discussion on pp. 267–270 tells you, at any specific point in the words of a sentence you will be inside either a *base unit* or a *free unit.* Example:

Before reading *Mad,* he was sure he recognized satire — now he wasn't sure.

This sentence breaks down into three units (note punctuation):

A	B	C
opener	base	closer

At point A, you are in an *opening* unit; at point B, in a *base* unit; at point C, in a *closing* unit. *The punctuation marks show where the units start and stop.*

Here are more examples; can you identify each unit?

1. He thought she was right; the others agreed.
2. I made a mistake that time. But I won't next time.
3. Family reunions (even the best organized of them) are usually a bore.
4. When we had our last reunion, I refused to go.
5. There was the dusty old book, an ancient tome full of speeches by former governors of Idaho.

Here are the units in those sentences identified:

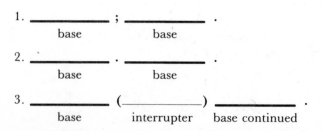

1. _____ ; _____ .
     base   base

2. _____ . _____ .
     base   base

3. _____ (_____) _____ .
     base   interrupter   base continued

4. _____ , _____ .
     opener   base

5. _____ , _____ .
     base   closer

Now we will show you how to use the various punctuation marks.

P 1   Use a Period When . . .

a. You end a sentence:

> Thomas Jefferson was both philosopher and politician.
> I don't know when I'll be back from the movies.

b. You abbreviate:

> M.A. degree   etc.   10:00 p.m.   Sept.   Calif.   Mr.

P 2   Use a Question Mark When . . .

You ask a question:

> What did the senator do then?
> What time is it?
> How can I do better on the next test?

P 3   Use an Exclamation Mark When . . .

You exclaim:

> Fight fiercely, Harvard!
> Never say die, say damn!
> That's the ugliest sports coat I ever saw!

Note: Don't exclaim very often or very loud.

P 4   Use a Comma When . . .

a. You join two main clauses with a coordinating conjunction (*and, or, but, so, for*):

The grass is bright green, *and* all the trees are beginning to bud.
The river is flooding, *but* Dad won't be there to see it.
It is extremely rainy here this season, *so* be sure to bring your raincoat.

b. You join an opening, interrupting, or closing unit to a main clause:

Since Clarice was bored in the second grade, her parents decided to let her skip a
   grade.
We could not shake our pursuers, *although we tried to lose them several times
   that day.*
That's what I want to do, *join the Army.*
Our dachshund, *who was dozing near the fire,* suddenly began to bark loudly.
You grabbed my foot, *not my hand!*

c. You use a parallel construction of three or more elements:

griffins, dragons, and *elves*
Were there *green, yellow,* or *orange* colors in the painting?
We lay on the ground, we stared at the stars, and *we thought deep thoughts.*

d. You place "equal" descriptive words before a noun:

new, nice-looking table

New and *nice-looking* describe *table,* a noun. They are "equal" because you
can put *and* logically between them—"new *and* nice-looking." In the
phrase "new coffee table," *new* and *coffee* are not equal: You wouldn't say
"new *and* coffee table."

honest, wonderful man (honest *and* wonderful man)
hot, dark night (hot *and* dark night)
But: *last spring* semester (not last *and* spring semester)

e. You employ direct address:

John, please wash the car.
Mrs. Rosenthal, would you sit over there?

f. You supply the dates and places:

Chicago, Illinois
January 15, 1986
On May 14, 1916, in Houston, Texas
He died in Nashville, Tennessee, on October 14, 1943.

g. You identify speakers in dialogue:

>   James said, "Where can I find my umbrella?"
>   "It's in the hall closet," Mom said.
>   "If that's the way you're faithful," said Marie angrily, "we're through!"

h. You want to prevent misreading or ambiguity:

>   By speaking of the dead, Lincoln in his Gettysburg Address appealed to. . . .

If you write, "By speaking of the dead Lincoln . . ." your reader may be confused and have to re-read the sentence.

>   The deductions allowed, the taxpayer is able to. . . .

"The deductions allowed the taxpayer. . . ." may be confusing.

PRACTICE

Punctuate the sentences below. *Note:* There are more exercises on the comma on p. 560. You also might like to look at the exericses on pp. 270–273.

1. I do not care for life has other attractions besides fame.

2. A mile above the mountain shook and trembled.

3. The governor of Texas said "San Antonio is the birthplace of at least one great man!"

4. "So?" said the governor of Nebraska. "Kearney is the birthplace of three great women and they are all from the same family!"

5. Ms. Crane our instructor just fainted.

6. On that hot fateful day (October 15 1943) the city of North Platte almost blew away causing many a family to flee for safety.

7. The North Platte River is the finest example of a *braiding* river in this hemisphere a geological observation I have spent 30 years trying to forget.

8. He was tiresome but honest careful but boring.

9. My roommate who has red hair is going to dye it green for St. Patrick's Day.

10. Eddie Murphy is young talented and controversial.

11. My aunt the sister of my stepmother used to play pinochle in the afternoon a strange occupation for someone trained in the law.

12. Small children according to linguists learn to speak in a more organized more predictable way than we used to believe.

P 5   Use a Semicolon When . . .

a. You want to join two main clauses without using a coordinating conjunction:

> The snows of yesterday have all gone; they have melted away.
> His technique on the guitar is sloppy; he doesn't seem to care whether he hits the right notes or not.

b. You want to join two main clauses with conjunctive adverbs. (Note the comma that follows the conjunctive adverb.)

> I caught you red-handed; *therefore,* you will go to jail.
> Sam and Rena went to the church; *however,* they didn't get married.
> The company cheated on its income tax; *consequently,* the Internal Revenue Service demanded back payment of tax.

Note: A *conjunctive adverb* is essentially a "sentence modifier." It says something about a sentence, and it relates the idea in the sentence to an idea expressed just before:

> Solar heating equipment is very expensive; *thus,* homeowners are still choosing more conventional methods of heating their homes.

A list of typical conjunctive adverbs:

Implies Addition	Implies Results or Reason	Implies Contrast	Implies Similarity
also	consequently	however	equally
besides	therefore	nevertheless	likewise
furthermore	thus	still	similarly
moreover	otherwise	yet	
	indeed		

c. You need to clarify a parallel series:

    Unclarified: At the meeting were Smithers the captain, Jones the first mate, and Watterson the bosun.

    Clarified: At the meeting were Smithers, the captain; Jones, the first mate; and Watterson, the bosun.

    Unclarified: My landlady tells my wife what kind of floor wax to use, the same as she uses, when to use it, the same time she does, where to set the refrigerator, the same place as hers, and, most helpful of all, when to get her husband up in the morning.

    Clarified: My landlady tells my wife what kind of floor wax to use, the same as she uses; when to use it, the same time she does; where to set the refrigerator, the same place as hers; and, most helpful of all, when to get her husband up in the morning.

d. You wish to "strengthen" a comma. Note the difference between these sentences:

    The Prime Minister was right, *but* he should have been more careful in making his appeal.

    In calling for devotion to duty, the Prime Minister was right; *but* he should have been more careful in making his appeal.

Because the second sentence already has a comma in it and is more complex than the first, the writer decided to strengthen the joint between the two clauses with a semicolon. In each of the following examples, the comma ordinarily used between rather long sentence units joined by a conjunction has been strengthened to a semicolon.

    These rules may seem rather harsh; *but* if you will stop to consider them carefully, you will understand that they are for the good of everybody.

    Unfortunately, we don't know very much about what goes on inside the brain; *and* many surgeons, indeed some of the best ones, will refuse to operate without careful diagnosis of this condition.

    Before deciding which house to buy, look very carefully at all the listings that the Multiple Service carries; *but* don't ignore other sources like newspaper ads and notices on bulletin boards.

P 6   Use a Colon When . . .

a. You introduce a list:

    Please buy the following: butter, cheese, and bread.

It is often simpler to omit the colon and write: "Please buy butter, cheese, and bread."

b. You introduce quotations:

> Toward the end of his life, Smith wrote to his son, making this plea: "Whatever you decide to do with the old property as a whole, never sell the north woods, for they meant everything to your mother."

c. You punctuate the salutation in a business letter:

> Dear Dean Winkleboom:
> Dear Sir:
> Dear Mr. Ryan:
> Dear Ms. Perez:

P 7   Use Parentheses When . . .

You wish to set off a word or an expression firmly from the rest of the sentence:

> The man I am referring to (Jenkins) is not necessary to our plans.
> There are not enough women doctors and lawyers (this is what the girl said).
> When it was over the ship, the winch (which was holding up the boom) suddenly collapsed.

Parentheses *always* come in pairs. See *Note* in P 8 below.

P 8   Use a Dash When . . .

You need to show a strong break in thought:

> She became president only four years later—the youngest woman ever in the post.
> I never want to get married—not under any circumstances.
> Is there—listen to me—is there any hope for the survivors?

Note: Parentheses and dashes are quite helpful when you want to clarify a sentence that is loaded with too many commas. Observe how one writer, having already used commas around one interrupter, chooses to employ dashes around a second:

Edward Cole, an engineer who owned one of the first 300 Corvettes produced in 1953, remembers that on his first long ride in the rain—from
suburban Detroit 150 miles to Kalamazoo—the water rising in the cockpit
compelled him to take off his shoes and roll up his pants.—Coles Phinizy,
"The Marque of Zora"

Of course, the writer could have used parentheses around either one of his
interrupters. Don't rely too heavily on parentheses or dashes.

P 9   Use an Apostrophe When . . .

a. You use a possessive form:

the *trailer's* wheel (one trailer)
the *trailers'* wheels (more than one trailer)
Peter's arm
Persius' style

Note: Do not use the apostrophe with personal pronouns: "*his* car,"
"these are *hers*"
        If you have trouble remembering whether the apostrophe goes inside
or outside the *s,* simply think of this example. Take the word *dog,* add an
apostrophe and the *s: dog's.* If the word already has an *s,* do the same—but
drop the second *s.* And so *dogs* becomes *dog's* becomes *dogs'.* Here are a few
additional examples:

"The water supply of the town" becomes "the *town's* water supply."
"The water supply of the towns" becomes "the *towns'* water supply."

"The house belonging to Roger" becomes "*Roger's* house."
"The house belonging to the Rogers family" becomes "the *Rogers'* house."

b. You form plurals using numbers or letters:

Last semester, she got three *A's* two *B's,* and a *C.*
There are four *3's* in the winning lottery number.

c. You form a contraction:

He'll be there.
I *can't* be at home today.
It's the thing to do.

Note: Do not confuse *it's* and *its* (without the apostrophe). *Its* is a possessive pronoun like *theirs, hers, his, ours* — and does not take an apostrophe.

P 10   Use a Hyphen When . . .

a. You need a syllable break at the end of a line:

> *real-ization*   *stereo-phonic*   *incor-porate*

(For more information on correct syllable breaks, see p. 565.)

b. You use a prefix before a syllable starting with *e*:

> *pre-empt*   *de-emphasize*   *re-enforce*

c. You make a compound word:

> *self-analysis*   *cease-fire* (noun)   *mother-in-law*

d. You make a compound modifier:

> a *one-year* clause   a *big-time* actor   a *blue-eyed* rabbit

When in doubt about the use of a hyphen, particularly for prefixes and syllable breaks, check your dictionary.

P 11   Use Quotation Marks When . . .

a. You quote the exact spoken or written words of someone else:

> "No country on earth," shouted Senator Blanksley, "is richer than ours!"
> It was John Donne who first said that "no man is an island."

b. You refer to titles of songs, paintings, and short literary works:

> Faulkner wrote that short story, "A Rose for Emily."
> The song is called "Stardust."
> Picasso's "Guernica" is one of the most famous paintings of the twentieth
>   century.

There is always some confusion about where quotation marks are placed in relation to other punctuation marks. The "rules" for such placement are actually quite simple:

1. Commas and periods that end a sentence unit always go inside the quotation marks:

> He remarked, "My house is haunted."
> "My house," she said, "is not haunted."

2. Colons and semicolons, when they divide the quoted material from the rest of the text, always go outside the quotation marks:

> The editorial gave three reasons why Maltby would be "by far the best candidate": his experience, honesty, and fiscal conservatism.
> He remarked, "My house is haunted"; he didn't say anything else.

3. Question marks and exclamation marks go inside or outside the quotation marks according to how the quoted material is being used:

> Did he say, "My house is haunted"? (The question mark is placed *outside* the quotation marks because the entire sentence is the question.)
> He asked, "Is my house haunted?" (The question mark goes *inside* the quotation marks because the quotation, not the entire sentence, is the question.)
> Were you frightened when the ghost said "Boo!"? (The exclamation mark is part of the quotation, while the question mark indicates that the entire sentence is a question.)

Note: Occasionally, you may need to use a "quote within a quote." For the quote inside the quote, you use single marks:

> Marie said, "I would prefer that you do not refer to me as 'that sweet little girl.' "

P 12   Use Italics (Underlining) When . . .

a. You refer to specific words or phrases:

> The word *fragrance* is euphonious.
> I do not understand what Marx meant by *democracy*.

b. You emphasize a word or phrase:

> Do the job *right.*
> I was referring to John *Adams,* not John Addison.

c. You refer to the titles of novels, stage productions, magazines, and newspapers:

> *Moby Dick* (novel) *The Color Purple* (movie)
> *Hamlet* (play) *Sports Illustrated* (magazine)
> *La Traviata* (opera) St. Louis *Post-Dispatch* (newspaper)

The relative length of works determines whether you use quotation marks or italics. Faulkner's short story, "A Rose for Emily," is put in quotation marks, but his novels (like *Sanctuary*) are italicized. Milton's "L'Allegro" is a short poem; his *Paradise Lost* is long—interminable.

PRACTICE

1. Punctuate the sentences below. Many of them can be punctuated in different ways—for example, students have suggested ten or so different solutions to *i.* For each sentence use the punctuation marks that seem to make it read most easily and clearly.
   a. The instructor said Read the chapter called Monopolies in Hansens book Economic Power.
   b. Burns opinion is that the word rapport is French.
   c. The boys lives are in danger so is yours.
   d. The car was new shiny and very pretty but it cost twelve thousand dollars.
   e. Lindbergh flew his airplane a high wing monoplane across the Atlantic.
   f. Before I come back you should have eaten your beans rice and honey.
   g. At the end of the semester however ones work gets easier.
   h. In the musical play Oklahoma there is a well known song called Oklahoma.
   i. At the end of Act II I stabbed him John pulled out the blood red knife and we laid his body on the floor.
   j. Its over taxed heart failing the racehorse dropped before the peoples eyes.

k. Smith who had been there before looked around the house and moving swiftly we all searched the place.

l. Jones father was a small time thug and politician in San Francisco in addition he was on drugs.

m. In spite of the never ending rain however they pushed on and they finally came to the cave.

n. Dickens wrote books for instance he wrote David Copperfield.

o. Dean Woof said his secretary the Admissions Office called and wants to know what to do with the student program requests for preregistration.

p. Steinbeck who wrote The Grapes of Wrath was a self made writer.

q. The dogs forelegs were scratched bruised and broken its eyes were perfectly all right.

r. You must return the child you must keep out of sight and you must above all not call the police.

2. In the following passage, we have numbered each space where the author originally placed a punctuation mark inside a sentence. After you have punctuated the sentences, explain or defend in a brief phrase each punctuation mark you used.

[1]There are some students who can't remember how to spell a word even after they have looked it up in a dictionary. There are others who don't have much luck looking words up in a dictionary because they can't come close enough to guessing the spelling to have much chance of finding the words. Both kinds of students deserve a very limited amount of sympathy (1) especially from themselves. It is true that the English spelling system is the worst in the world (2) but it really wasn't invented out of pure malice (3) and the rules are the same for everybody. Resentment and alibis make the job of learning to spell enormously more difficult. The job does not require unusual intelligence (4) but it does require close attention and a long and patient effort. You may not think it is worth the effort (5) but on the whole the country does. Some kinds of ignorance can be concealed for years (6) but bad spelling can show up every time you write a sentence (7) and it can cost jobs and promotions as well as bad marks on English papers. Few people can afford not to learn to spell at least reasonably well.

[2]If you are a really poor speller (8) the first step is to find out what method of learning a new word works best for you. Some people do best by spelling a word out loud a number of times (9) others by writing it down repeatedly (10) and still others by tracing it with a pencil after it has been correctly written. Find out whether your eyes (11) your ears (12) or your muscles help you most in this particular job. As you try each method (13) be sure you give your full attention to what

you are doing. It is a pure waste of time to use any of them while you are thinking about something else. Five minutes of *real* work on spelling is worth much more than an hour of semiconscious droning or purely mechanical copying.

³The next step is the critical one. Learn three new words a day every day for the next month (14) just everyday words that have been giving you trouble. Anybody bright enough to be in college can do this if he wants to. Most poor spellers give it up and find a new alibi before the first week is over. At first the results are slow and don't seem worth the effort (15) and if you figure that at this rate it would take you the rest of your life to learn a third of the words in your dictionary (16) the whole prospect seems pretty gloomy. But if you really work at the problem consistently and *alertly* for a month you will find that you have made real progress (17) and the ninety new words you know will be the smallest part of it. For one thing (18) you will find that you are seeing words more clearly (19) the new ones are easier to learn. For another (20) you'll have something to build on. You'll be ready to learn a good many words in groups instead of individually. This group method is so attractive that many people want to begin with it (21) but it seldom works well until a good foundation has been laid by the simple but unpopular one at a time (22) method. — L. M. Myers, *Guide to American English*

3. From a textbook, magazine, or other source, find a good short section of nonfiction prose. Copy two paragraphs, leaving out the punctuation, and set your copied page aside for a few hours. Then go back over it and put in your own punctuation marks. How well does your punctuation agree with that of the original? Can you defend any of your variations?

P 13   *Rhetoric of Punctuation*

So far, we have been explaining the "mechanics" of punctuation. *Mechanics* refers to those more or less firm rules that govern how you punctuate most sentences. But in addition to using punctuation marks in a mechanical way, you can use them for effect, to help create certain patterns of emotion and logic in the reader's mind. This *rhetoric* of puctuation allows you to make choices on the basis of stylistic effectiveness and interest. In order to see how rhetorical punctuation works, consider the following scene. When Mr. Smith went to his garage to finish cleaning his Mercedes, he found a terrible and bloody scene inside the trunk, which he had left open the night before. To his ten-year-old son, he said:

> The cat dragged a dead rabbit into the Mercedes trunk last night / get a shovel / put the rabbit in the garbage / and clean up that mess out there.

These sentence structures, not to mention Mr. Smith's fatherly instructions, are clear as glass. But the structures can be punctuated differently, according to how you wish to create certain pauses, emphases, and effects:

> The cat dragged a dead rabbit into the Mercedes trunk last night. Get a shovel, put the rabbit in the garbage, and clean up that mess out there.

This is a calm father, even a dull one. He's obviously not very upset about the rabbit, for he plops down his commas and periods with bland regularity and precision. Here is another version:

> The cat dragged a dead rabbit into the Mercedes trunk last night—get a shovel. Put the rabbit in the garbage and clean up that mess out there!

In the first clause, this father has just seen the rabbit. He's a little sleepy, but by the time he gets out the first few words he's been pretty well awakened by the sight. It takes him a punctuational dash of time to think of the solution ("get a shovel"), after which he excitedly runs his words together in the following two main clauses and omits the comma before "and clean up."

Our third father is angry. He coldly bites off each sentence and stomps on it with a period:

> The cat dragged a dead rabbit into the Mercedes trunk last night. Get a shovel. Put the rabbit in the garbage. And clean up that mess out there.

The cat is going to catch it. So is the son, although he is as innocent as a lamb.

The fourth father is edging on hysteria: the rabbit is bloody, and it smells:

> The *cat* dragged a *dead rabbit* into the Mercedes *trunk* last night! Get a shovel, put the rabbit in the garbage—and *clean up* that *mess* out there!

Punctuation works best when it achieves both mechanical and rhetorical effects. When you separate clauses with commas or enclose a phrase between a pair of parentheses, you do so according to precise mechanical rules of grammar and sentence structure. But when you build on these rules to help write sentences that are particularly interesting or effective, you are using a punctuational rhetoric that varies according to the situation. Consider these situations:

Simple fact; two things happen:
He looked at her, and she blushed.
Not-so-simple fact; cause-and-effect:
He looked at her; she blushed.
The same, with a little drama added:
He looked at her — she blushed.
Rapid cause-and-effect:
He looked at her, she blushed. (The comma splice may be considered acceptable here because the clauses are so brief.)
A reported afterthought:
He looked at her (and she blushed).
Deep, dark dramatic emphasis:
He looked at her and she blushed.

At this point, let's remind ourselves that like all the other forms and devices of rhetoric, punctuation can get out of hand. You can get too flashy with it. You don't want your reader to take special notice of your commas, periods, and dashes or to remark, "My, how clever this person is with the semicolon." Ideally, the main job of your punctuation marks should be to support your ideas and make easy the transmission of your thoughts to the reader. Sir Ernest Gowers, in his *Plain Words: Their ABC,* tells of a writer of a training manual for pilots who ended his comments with, "Pilots, whose minds are dull, do not usually live long." This writer's mispunctuation transmitted a thought he certainly did not intend and, as Sir Ernest commented, converted "a truism into an insult."

Good punctuation should separate with perfect clarity the parts of your sentences. In the long run of writing, such punctuation is the most effective kind there is.

PRACTICE

Here is Lincoln's Gettysburg Address — unpunctuated. If you were Lincoln, how would you punctuate it?

[1]Fourscore and seven years ago our fathers brought forth on this continent a new nation conceived in liberty and dedicated to the proposition that all men are created equal

[2]Now we are engaged in a great civil war testing whether that nation or any nation so conceived and so dedicated can long endure we are met on a great battlefield of that war we have come to dedicate a portion of that field as a final resting place for those who here gave their lives that that nation might live it is altogether fitting and proper that we should do this

[3]But in a larger sense we cannot dedicate we cannot consecrate we cannot hallow this ground the brave men living and dead who struggled here have consecrated it far above our poor power to add or detract the world will little note nor long remember what we say here but it can never forget what they did here it is for us the living rather to be dedicated here to the unfinished work which they who fought here have thus far so nobly advanced it is rather for us to be here dedicated to the great task remaining before us that from these honored dead we take increased devotion to that cause for which they gave the last full measure of devotion that we here highly resolve that these dead shall not have died in vain that this nation under God shall have a new birth of freedom and that government of the people by the people and for the people shall not perish from the earth

562

M
MECHANICS

M 1   *Abbreviations*

Although abbreviations are a useful form of shorthand in some kinds of writing, you should avoid them whenever possible. Write the full form: *university,* not *univ.* or *u.*; *August,* not *Aug.*; *New York,* not *N.Y.*

There are, however, certain abbreviations that have become the standard form: *a.m.* and *p.m.* to indicate time; *e.g.* (the abbreviation of the Latin phrase for "for example"); *Dr.* for *Doctor*; and so on. (Note that *Dr.* should be used only with the person's surname or full name—*Dr. Smith* or *Dr. Jane Smith.*)

When in doubt concerning an abbreviation, first take into account its context. Considering your subject and reader, would an abbreviation be proper? Then check your dictionary for the correct form and spelling. *Ect.,* for example, is a popular mistake for *etc.* (*et cetera*—"and so forth").

M 2   *Capitalization*

Capital letters are used to designate the following items:

a. The first word of a sentence:

Revision is important for the writer.
Encourage them to do better.

b. Proper nouns:

Spain	Atlanta, Georgia
Mary Ann	Korean War
Chrysler Corporation	House of Representatives

c. Proper adjectives:

Shakespearean sonnet	Freudian psychology
Colombian coffee	Buddhist temple

d. Titles of articles, poems, books, magazines, stage productions, etc.

"Ten Ways to Help Cut Inflation" (article)
"Dover Beach" (poem)
A Grammar of Modern English (book)
Good Housekeeping (magazine)
Waiting for Godot (play)

Capitalize all words in a title except *a, an,* and *the,* and except those coordinating conjunctions and prepositions that contain fewer than five letters. If these come first or list in the title, they must be capitalized:

A Farewell to Arms
To Have and Have Not
"A Place to Return To"

e. The first word of a line in "regular" poetry:

Good friend, for Jesus' sake forbear
To dig the dust enclosed here;
Blest be the man that spares these stones,
And curst be he that moves my bones.
        —William Shakespeare

M 3   Manuscript Form

a. Writing material:
Always use standard-size paper, 8½ × 11 inches. Write on *one side* of the paper only. Use a ball-point pen with black, blue, or blue-black ink. If you type, use white typing paper that is thick enough so that writing on a second page does not show through the first.

b. Spacing and margins:
Use double spaces between lines unless you are setting off long quotations. (For more on the format for long quotations, see p. 377.) When typing, allow about 1 ½ inches of space on the left side, and about one inch on all the others. When writing in longhand, use lined paper that has a vertical rule on the left-hand side.

c. Indentation:
Indent the first line of each paragraph about one inch in handwritten papers, five spaces in typewritten ones.

d. Titles:
Put your title on the first page of the paper, about two inches below the top. Leave about one inch between the title and the first line of the essay. Do not use quotation marks or underlining for the title. If your instructor wants you to use a title page, see the sample on p. 410.

e. Numbering pages:
Whether or not you have a separate title page, number the page on which your essay begins with *1*, and the rest of the pages in sequence.

f. Appearance:
The appearance of your final draft subtly influences the reader's impression of your efforts. A sloppy paper often indicates sloppy thinking; so always be neat. When proofreading, you can line through an error or insert a small revision if you do it carefully and then check the correction. When typing, do not strike over an error unless you first erase it—neatly. If your draft contains numerous corrections, redo it.

M 4   Numbers

There are several general rules for the use of numbers that you should be aware of.

a. Spell out in full the following numbers:

1. Those from *one* to *ninety-nine: two, seventeen, twenty-three,* etc.

2. Those used as adjectives: *first, second, seventeenth, twenty-third,* etc. (not *1st, 2nd, 17th, 23rd*).

A street address, however, can be written with the endings *nd, rd, st, th:* East *75th* Street, 187 North *3rd* Street.

b. Use numerals for:

1. Numbers of more than two words:

   1979   2,170 $4,560,000

2. Dates, times, addresses:

August 14, 1982	6:30 a.m.	1311 Locust Avenue
December 25, 1859	10:00 p.m. (but	631 West 93rd Street
	ten o'clock)	

c. Hyphenate compound numbers:

1. From *twenty-one* to *ninety-nine:*

   thirty-seven   *fifty-eight*   *seventy-two*

2. Used as adjectival fractions:

   a *one-fourth* minority   a *two-thirds'* vote

d. Do not begin a sentence with a numeral:

> *Not: 107* people survived.
> *But: One hundred and seven* people survived.

When spelling out the number at the beginning of a sentence is awkward, revise the construction:

> *Not: Forty-five thousand, one hundred and eighty-six* voters are registered.
> *But:* The total number of registered voters is *45,186.*

M 5   Syllabication

To keep an even margin on the right side of your paper, you will occasionally have to divide a word at the end of a line and run it over into the next. When you are in doubt about a word's syllabication, check your dictionary. Here are some general rules to keep in mind.

1. Never divide one-syllable words: *moist, hound, great, Tom, see.*

2. Divide a word with double consonants between the consonants: *wit-ty, refer-ral, com-mand.*

3. Never divide a word so that only one letter remains on a line. Try to get two—and preferably three—letters on a line:

Not:	e-bullient	intrica-cy
But:	ebul-lient	intri-cacy

For words that have prefixes and suffixes, divide where either joins the root: *cast-ing, pre-registration, manage-ment, dis-appear.*

DY
USING THE
DICTIONARY

A good dictionary is important to you in many ways. But it is of special importance to you as a writer. It is a useful source for various kinds of information about words that you may need to know as you work toward improving your papers. At one time or another, you may wish to know such things as:

- the exact meaning of *ecology*
- the spelling of *capital* (*capitol?*)
- whether *overridden* should be hyphenated (*over-ridden?*)
- a synonym for *complete*
- the part of speech of *than* (is it a preposition or a conjunction?)
- when you may use *contact* as a verb
- whether you may write: "*Plus* I wanted more money for college."

Consider for a moment the last problem in the list. On p. 271, we discuss the employment of clear "word signals"—such as *before, but, also, since, then*—in opening positions in your sentences. There are so many possible signals that we could not mention them all, and you will have to depend on your dictionary for help when considering the use of certain signals. Should you, for instance, use *plus* as you might use *and* or *also* to signal the addition of a second or third reason for doing something? The major dictionaries will indicate that in standard written English *plus* can be used as a preposition, adjective, or noun, but not as a conjunction or adverb. Grammatically speaking, dictionaries allow these usages: "X *plus* Y," "on the *plus* side," or "a definite *plus*." But not: "*Plus* I wanted more money for college."

The following desk dictionaries have proved to be the most popular and reliable in regard to grammar, pronunciation, basic definitions, and usage. If you don't have one, you should buy one.

> *The American Heritage Dictionary of the English Language: New College Edition,* 1982
> *Funk and Wagnalls Standard College Dictionary,* 1977
> *The Random House Dictionary of the English Language, College Edition,* 1979
> *Webster's Ninth New Collegiate Dictionary,* 1985
> *Webster's New World Dictionary of the American Language, Second College Edition,* 1983

What does a typical dictionary entry tell you? Let's look at the entry for one of the most discussed words in modern English, *contact*. The source is *The American Heritage Dictionary*.

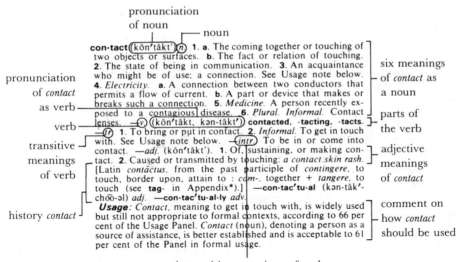

Here you learn that *contact* may be used as a noun, verb, or adjective. You are given different pronunciations of the word and its various meanings. You also learn the major parts of the verb form of *contact* (note the boldface **contacted, -tacting, -tacts**). The usage note at the bottom of the entry tells you that two-thirds of the *American Heritage Dictionary*'s Usage Panel disapproves of the formal use of *contact* as a verb (meaning "to get in touch with"), an observation that may be helpful if you want to know whether to use that form of the word in a paper.

For most words, the standard desk dictionaries give similar information about grammar, pronunciation, and basic meanings. You'll find that dictionaries differ in regard to usage. As you've seen, the *Heritage* pretty much disapproves of *contact* in statements like "Contact your doctor before leaving work this afternoon." By contrast, the *Standard College Dictionary* remarks: "This informal usage, regarded with disfavor by some, is widely used." *Webster's New Collegiate Dictionary* and *The Random House Dictionary* give definitions of *contact* in this sense but make no comment about its proper use.

Dictionaries also supply you with synonyms for many words. Suppose you are having difficulty choosing a word for a paper. You are writing about a certain pleasant emotion you've had recently. Words come into your mind — *happiness, joy, pleasure* — but none seems quite right. Remembering that dictionaries give synonyms, you look up *pleasure* in *The Random House Dictionary* and find at the end of the entry:

> —Syn. 1. happiness, gladness, delectation. PLEASURE, ENJOYMENT, DELIGHT, JOY refer to the feeling of being pleased and happy. PLEASURE is the general term: *to take pleasure in beautiful scenery.* ENJOYMENT is a quiet sense of well-being and pleasurable satisfaction: *enjoyment at sitting in the shade on a warm day.* DELIGHT is a high degree of pleasure usually leading to active expression of it: *delight at receiving a hoped-for letter.* JOY is a feeling of delight so deep and lasting that a person radiates happiness and expresses it spontaneously: *joy at unexpected good news.* 4. luxury, voluptuousness. 7. preference, wish, inclination.

At least one of these words should work reasonably well in your sentence, and having used it you can get on with the rest of your writing.

Indeed, the dictionary is a special tool for "getting on with your writing." It not only supplies you with the kinds of knowledge that we have already mentioned, but it can also act as a small encyclopedia. Without leaving your room for the library, you can ascertain or verify many isolated facts: Who was *Pliny?* He was a Roman scholar who wrote the *Historia Naturalis.* He died in A.D. 79. What is *scrip?* It is paper money issued for temporary or emergency use. What is a *boycott?* Where did the word come from? It is an act of refusing to buy or use something; the word comes from the name of Charles Boycott, an English land agent in Ireland who was ostracized by his tenants for refusing to reduce rents. What is an *arroyo*? It is a deep, dry gulley or gulch cut out by floods or heavy rains.

As you can see, your desk dictionary is good for many things.

PRACTICE

1. Read the introductory material in your desk dictionary. Since dictionaries vary somewhat, you should know exactly what pieces of information your dictionary has and how it is organized.

2. What do *liberal* and *conservative* mean? What is their etymology or history? (*Etymology* is discussed in the introduction to your dictionary.) Should you write, for example: "He has managed to avoid crashes for twenty-five years because he is a *liberal* [or *conservative*] pilot"?

   What is the etymology of:

rape	rapture	Christian	tuxedo	noun
pencil	muscle	chivalrous	Dixie	agnostic

3. In writing essays, should you use, in their contexts, the italicized words below? In each case, give your reasons.
   a. My roommate, *yclept* Sandy, turned out to be a very friendly person.
   b. She *toted* her knapsack wherever she went, even carrying the *bloody* thing to basketball games.
   c. After *jazzing* up the engine a few times, Tinkham was satisfied with its *tune* and *killed* it.
   d. *Whither* the *paly* moon, I wondered, as I *jogged* back to the dorm in the *pitch* dark.

4. Consider this statement: "That word is not *fitting* in this context." How many synonyms can you find for *fitting* as it is used in that statement? Give synonyms for the italicized words as they are used in these contexts:

   I have a *need* for a beer.
   We *command* you to release your prisoners.
   Why did the epidemic *happen*?

5. What is an *antonym*? After checking your dictionary, give antonyms for:

like (*verb*)   viciously   morose   light   raw
  disinterested   creature   classy   sweetly   ignominious

6. Give the part of speech of the words below. If the word is a *noun*, state whether it is singular or plural; if a *verb*, give its tense.

criteria   rung (*verb*)   bade   slow   data
  than   when   but   quickly   dived

7. Look up the following words to see whether they are written with a hyphen, as two words, or as one word.

drawback   drawingroom   coffeecake   Jacobsladder
  gunrunning   doublejointed   touchback   dragonshead

8. Who or what it?

Hapsburg   pimpernel   upbraid (*verb*)   pillory (*noun*)
  Biarritz   ringworm   lug (*noun*)   Lancastrian

GL
GLOSSARY

This Glossary presents a list, alphabetically arranged, of trouble-some words and constructions, along with certain terms that you may find useful in your writing. As we considered each problem of usage, we asked ourselves: "What would the careful writer think about this? What are his choices, and how would he respond to the issue?" We have consulted many authorities (too many to list here), and confess that where they disagreed, we consulted our own experience.

Good writing is what a good writer writes. So if you find that something here contradicts your own experience and the evidence of your reading, feel free to question our advice. The rules of English usage are not carved in stone.

a, an. Use *a* before words that begin with a consonant sound: *a* pole, *a* unit (the sound is *yew*-nit), *a* history. Use *an* before words starting with a vowel sound or a silent *h*: *an* alley, *an* hour, *an* ellipse.

above, below. If you are "pointing" to something graphic on the page, like a chart or an illustration, *above* and *below* are useful: "The table *below* shows you how much money is spent on billiards in Marin

County." If you are referring to ideas, it is wise to use a different expression: "The facts I have just mentioned," rather than "The above facts."

absolute construction.   A phrase that is linked to a sentence by logic but not by any specific grammatical "tie." It may look like a modifier but isn't one:

The play did very well, *considering the circumstances.*
My money having vanished, I decided to leave the hotel.
The last quarter of the game, *everything taken into account,* was better than we hoped.

accept, except.   The verb *accept* means "to receive with approval" or "to answer in the affirmative"; the verb *except* means "to omit or exclude." The preposition *except* means, roughly, "but" or "other than": "All the women *except* Mary came from Denver."

accidentally.   Commonly misspelled as *accidently.* In the correct spelling of this adverb, -ly is added to the adjective *accidental*

adapt, adopt.   *Adapt* means "to adjust to something." *Adopt* has several meanings; the closest to that of *adapt* is "to take or follow a course of action."

adjective.   One of two basic modifiers, the other being the adverb. Adjectives modify nouns or noun elements:

small person (*Small* modifies the noun *person.*)
the woman (*The* modifies the noun *woman.*)
coach *of the year* (*Of the year* modifies the noun *coach.*)
the milk pitcher *that broke* (The adjective clause, *that broke,* modifies the noun *pitcher.*)
Flying at top speed, the squadron overtook the enemy planes. (The participial phrase, *flying at top speed,* modifies the noun *squadron.*)

administrate.   See *commentate.*

adverb.   One of the two basic modifiers, the other being the adjective. Adverbs modify verbs, adjectives, or other adverbs. Most adverbs end in -*ly,* but a few, like *now, very,* and *there,* do not. And not all words ending in -*ly* (the adjectives *slovenly* and *heavenly,* for example) are adverbs. Here are a few typical adverbial constructions:

They spoke *bitterly.* (*Bitterly* modifies the verb *spoke.*)
It was a *bitterly* cold night. (*Bitterly* modifies the adjective *cold.*)
They spoke *very* bitterly. (*Very* modifies the adverb *bitterly.*)

They spoke *in the heat of anger.* (The prepositional phrase is acting adverbially.)

When he beat the rug, the dust made him sneeze. (The subordinate clause is acting adverbially.)

Also see *flat adverb.*

affect, effect.   As a verb, *affect* means "to bring about a change" or "to influence." As a verb, *effect* means "to do or to accomplish something." Example:

"He was *affected* by her attempt to *effect* a change in policy."

As a noun, *affect* is a psychological term referring to emotion or feeling. *Effect* as a noun means "result."

agenda.   A Latin word; the singular in Latin is *agendum.* In modern standard English, you can use *agenda* for the singular and *agendas* for the plural. An *agenda* is a list of things that are to be accomplished or covered at a meeting.

aggravate.   For many years, *aggravate* has carried two meanings—"to make worse" and "to irritate or annoy." Both meanings are acceptable in standard English, although many good writers consider the second too casual in careful writing. Certainly, *irritate* or *annoy* will express the second meaning well enough.

agreement.   The "matching up" of elements in gender, number, case, or person.

1. Subjects and verbs must agree:
   She is a trumpet player.
   They are the boys from Syracuse.

2. Certain adjectives (those that can change form) agree with their nouns:
   Those mice are cowards.
   This mouse is a hero.

3. A pronoun agrees with its antecedent:
   The *quarterback* broke *his* arm.
   Everyone did *his* job. (Some writers prefer *his or her job,* a construction which is not standard now, although it may be in the future.)
   Mrs. Tompkins had *her* way.
   Women should vote for *their* candidates.

alibi.   In Latin, the word meant "elsewhere." For hundreds of years, *alibi* was a technical term in law; you had an alibi for a crime if, when it was committed, you were not on the spot—but elsewhere. The meaning of the term has broadened in two ways, to mean (generally) an *excuse,* and to imply that the excuse may not be a very good one, perhaps even rather shady.

all ready, already.   The first expression, used adjectivally, means "prepared": "We are *all ready* to go." *Already* is an adverb, as in "She has *already* gone ahead."

all together, altogether.   Separate the implications of these words— and their spellings. *All together* means "in a group"; *altogether* means "completely, utterly, entirely."

allusion.   This word is best discussed with a closely related word, *reference.* A reference is a direct remark about something: "She *referred* to his failure to pay for lunch as a sign that he was cheap." An *allusion* is indirect or oblique: "She said that he was a regular *Shylock.*" Allusions are understood only if their origin is known—in this instance, if you know that Shylock is a Shakespearean character who is close with his money.

alot.   An incorrect form for *a lot.*

alright.   A nonstandard spelling; use *all right.*

alumnus, alumna.   These words refer to graduates of educational institutions. The first is a male graduate, the second a female. The plural of *alumnus* is *alumni*; of *alumna, alumnae.* You will probably be better off simply using the term *graduate* in most instances.

among, between.   *Between* implies two things or activities; *among* implies more than two:

He distributed the books *among* the students.
The instructor said that she would decide *between* the arguments of Joan and Carlisle.

Note: *Between* takes the object form in pronouns:

Between you and *me.*
Between *her* and *them.*

and/or.   An expression that almost nobody will say a kind word for, but that some writers will use from time to time. It has an odor of legalese or of business jargon, and the careful writer tends to avoid it.:

Not this: you may be fined *and/or* jailed.
But this: you may be fined or jailed, or both.

angle.   When used to mean "viewpoint," "position," or "approach," the word has a faintly negative connotation, as if you were saying that the person involved is a little tricky or not quite honest. The word is also a bit too *casual* for some contexts.

anxious   (to mean *eager*). *Anxious* implies that you are worried about the future; *eager* that you expect something rather impatiently. For the sake of accuracy, it is wise to keep the two words separate.

anymore.   Should be *any more*: "I don't drink coffee any more."

appositive.   A noun that identifies and explains the noun it is set beside:

> Mr. Smith, our *instructor,* was quite old.
> Our son *John* is a rascal.
> I talked to Sheila, the *director.*

apt, likely, liable.   Good writers often use *apt* or *likely* when a meaning of probability is intended: "If you run in front of a car, you are *apt* (*likely*) to get hit." Used as an adjective, *apt* means "able" or "capable": "She was an *apt* student of burglary."

> *Liable* ordinarily is restricted to matters of responsibility or legal obligation: "*liable* to imprisonment"; "*liable* for military service." Note that *liable* implies a consequence that is not usually considered pleasant.

article.   *A, an,* and *the* are frequently called *articles.* In this book, however, we treat them as adjectives because they modify nouns: *a* tree, *an* omen, *the* part.

as.   Properly used, *as* is a sign of subordination that implies a *time* relation: "I saw you *as* you were coming down the street." Used to indicate a causal relation, *as* is weak and ambiguous: "*As* you are going to stay in the dorm over vacation, would you keep my stereo in your room?" *Since* or *because* is better in statements that imply or show cause.

as to, in respect to.   These expressions are often used as links in a sentence. "*In respect to* Smith's handling of the situation. . . ." "I can't decide *as to* the final disposition of the case." If you need a linking expression in such sentences, the word *about* is simpler and shorter. Sometimes no link is needed at all: "I can't decide the final disposition of the case."

at (as in "Where is she *at*?").   The use of *at* is non-standard in such usages:

> Tell me where they are *at*.
> I know where I am *at*.
> There is where it is all *at*.

author (*verb*).   The careful writer does not use *author* as a verb: "Smith *authored* the new rules for the parking garage." Just say that Smith *wrote* them.

auxiliary verb.   A "helping word"—like *have, had, do, might*—used with the main verb in a verb phrase. The auxiliary allows you to express tense, person, number, mood, and voice:

had written	*will be* writing	*might have been* written
do write	*was* written	*has* written

Modal auxiliaries are important because they supply you with a stock of options to express shades of meaning:

must do	*should* do	*would* do	*might* do	*could* do

Notice the difference between *had* and *must,* for example. *Had* may indicate tense (time) only, while *must* indicates not only time (the future) but also obligation.

Shall and *will* should probably be considered as "dead" modals. A clear distinction between the two no longer exists (if it ever did), and most writers appear to use them merely as signs of tense.

awful, awfully.   As either intensifiers or expressions of disgust, *awful* and *awfully* are badly overworked and too *casual.* Avoid them.

backlash.   A vivid and rather useful metaphorical word, *backlash* ("a violent or sudden reaction") has been worked rather hard in recent years. Try substituting *reaction,* or consider rewriting to avoid the word: "The people are growing hostile to the governor's plans for an increase in taxes."

bad, badly.   With a linking verb, use *bad* (an adjective) in these situations:

> It smells *bad.*
> I feel *bad.*
> It is *bad.*
> It seems *bad.*

Use badly (an adverb) in situations where the verb is a nonlinking one:

They do it *badly.*
Standish needs the money *badly.*
She sang the aria *badly.*
I feel *badly*—my fingers don't work as they should (Better, perhaps, would
   be: My fingers are numb.)

being as (to mean *because*).   There are several related forms that are
   fairly synonymous:

Being as we were absent for the quiz . . .
I explained that *as how* we got the quiz date wrong. . . .
Seeing as we received a zero that day . . .
Avoid such expressions. Ordinarily, you can substitute the word *because*
   for each of them.

between, among.   See *among, between.*

bi-, semi-.   As in *biannual, semimonthly,* etc. Authorities agree that the
   uses of these prefixes have become confused. *Bimonthly,* for instance,
   can mean "every two months," "twice a month," or "every two
   weeks." *Semi-* poses less of a problem—it roughly means "half" ("half-
   monthly" or "twice a month"). To avoid the confusion surrounding
   both prefixes, just say, for example, "every two months" or "twice
   a year."

bug.   As a verb meaning "annoy" or "bother," *bug* is an effervescent
   little word, but too slangy for most situations.

bummer.   Slang for *letdown, disappointment,* or *unpleasant occurrence.* Do
   not use it.

but that, but what.   Both expressions seem unnecessary. Note these
   typical rewrites:

Not this: I do not doubt *but that* she is right.
But this: I do not doubt that she is right.

Not this: I do not know *but what* the Russians have a point in their
              response.
But this: I think the Russians may have a point in their response.

c., ca.   Abbreviations for the Latin *circa,* these mean "about." Used
   with approximate dates or figures: "c. 1670."

can, may.   *Can* refers to ability; *may* to permission or possibility. "I *can*
   do it" means "I am *able* to do it." "I *may* do it" can mean "I have *permission* to do it," or "It is *possible* that I will do it." *Can* and *may* are modal
   auxiliaries. See *auxiliary verb.*

cannot barely, cannot hardly, cannot help but. These are double negatives, and are considered nonstandard. Here are suggested substitutions:

> *Not this:*   I *cannot hardly* believe that.
> *But this:*   I can hardly believe that.
> *Or:*   I cannot believe that.

> *Not this:*   I *cannot help but* wonder about the issue.
> *But this:*   I cannot help wondering about the issue.

caret. A proofreader's symbol (   ), it is used to indicate an insertion in the written copy:

that
I wish ∧ you were here.

case. The customary objection to the word *case* is that it is redundant in many expressions.

> *Not this:*   In some *cases,* the streets were iced over.
> *But this:*   Some streets were iced over.

> *Not this:*   Except in the *case* of Dr. Denny, the surgeons were exonerated.
> *But this:*   All the surgeons but Dr. Denny were exonerated.

Note that no satisfactory alternative has ever been found for "In case of fire, break glass."

casual, casualism. We borrow the term from Theodore M. Bernstein, who remarks in his book *The Careful Writer* that some modern acceptable writing is relaxed and familiar—in a word, *casual.* To call an expression a *casualism* is not necessarily to condemn it because there are gradations of the casual. To use Bernstein's examples, contractions such as *don't* and *can't* and colloquial terms like *face the music* and *skulduggery* may be acceptable casualisms, while *falsies* may not be. Whether a casualism is acceptable depends upon your subject and writer's stance.

censor, censure. Do not confuse these words. To *censor* means to suppress or prohibit a thing or action. To *censure* means to criticize negatively or to disapprove. Generally, ideas are censored while people are censured.

center around. Both a logical and geometrical impossibility. The *center* and the *around* of something are in different places. Write *center* *on,* which suggests a tight grouping; or *cluster about,* which suggests a looser grouping.

cite, site.   When you *cite* (verb) people or ideas, you present them as examples, evidence, or authorities. The noun is *citation. Site* is a noun, referring to a place.

clause.   See pp. 500–502.

cliché.   A cliché is an expression that has grown hackneyed or tired from excessive use. A surprising number of clichés are metaphorical: *slick as ice, knee high to a grasshopper.* Generally, avoid them — unless you can twist them to your advantage:

Slick as the ice in her martini-on-the-rocks.
Knee-high to a rabbit and twice as bouncy.

collective noun.   A word whose form is singular but whose meaning can be singular or plural: *team, group, crowd, family, couple.* (See p. 518 for advice on using singular or plural verbs with this form.)

colloquial, colloquialism.   Technically *colloquial* refers merely to "the language of speech," and a *colloquialism* is an expression typical of speech. Since speech is often more informal than writing, teachers and editors have developed the habit of referring to excessively informal usages in writing as being colloquial (that is, inappropriate). This unfortunate development implies that the language of speech is necessarily inferior to the written language. In many instances, such judgment is obviously untrue: "I didn't do it" (colloquial) is obviously better than a stiffly written version like "This event was not performed by me." From Shakespeare to Hemingway and E. B. White, one finds that the colloquial is, when rightly used, lively and precise. It is objectionable only when it is inappropriate or excessively casual. See *casualism.*

comma splice.   See pp. 540–541.

commentate (*verb*).   Not standard; use the verb *comment.* Similarly, use the verb *administer* rather than *administrate.* "I would rather *comment* on this department than *administer* it."

compare to, compare with.   *Compare to* is most often used when you want to show how two things are similar (particularly in a figurative sense), as in Shakespeare's "Shall I *compare* thee *to* a summer's day?"
    Compare with is the best way to introduce a literal comparison involving both similarities and differences: "I intend to *compare* the freshman course in speech *with* the composition course in English."

comparison of adjectives and adverbs. Adjectives and adverbs change form to indicate three "degrees":

Positive	Comparative	Superlative
low	lower	lowest
good	better	best
honest	more honest	most honest
easily	more easily	most easily

complement. A grammatical term meaning "something that completes." Complements are used to complete ideas (or parts of ideas presented earlier in a sentence).

1. Direct objects as complements:

   You did see *her.*
   You did give her a *present.*

2. Subject complements:

   She is *happy.*
   She is a happy *woman.*

3. Object complements:

   They made him *king.*
   They appointed her *director.*
   I dyed the shirt *green.*

compliment, complement. As a verb, *complement* means "to complete or finish something." As a noun, it means "something that completes or round out another thing."

They are a perfect pair; their personalities *complement* each other.
The *complement* of 60 degrees is 30 degrees.

Compliment, as a verb, means "to say something good," usually about a person. As a noun, it refers to the act of congratulating.

I *compliment* you on your good performance.
I gave him a *compliment.*

compound words. Words made up of two or more words that work together as a unit: *sister-in-law, crapshooter* (or *crap shooter*), *overdrive.* There are no firm rules for determining whether such words should be written separately, together, or with hyphens. When you are unsure of a particular word, check your dictionary.

comprise.   Historically, *comprise* comes from an old French word that meant "comprehend" or "include." The word, in careful usage, still maintains this meaning. The whole *comprises* ("includes") its parts. You may write: "The College of Liberal Arts *comprises* four departments," not "The College of Liberal Arts *is comprised of* four departments." An alternative is to use *compose*: "Four departments *compose* (or *make up*) the College of Liberal Arts"; or "The College of Liberal Arts *is composed of* four departments."

conjugation.   A listing of the forms of a verb, showing tense, person, number, voice, and mood:

Verb: To see   *Principal Parts: see, saw, seen*

ACTIVE VOICE   *PASSIVE VOICE*

INDICATIVE MOOD

Present Tense

I, you, we, or they *see*   I *am seen,* he, she, or it *is seen*
he, she, or it *sees*   You, we, or they *are seen*

Note: In the rest of the table, pronouns are limited to one for each verb form.

Past Tense

I *saw*   I *was seen*
                                                      you *were seen*

Future Tense

I *will* (or *shall*) see   I *will* (or *shall*) *be seen*

Present Perfect Tense

I *have seen*   I *have been seen*
he *has seen*   he *has been seen*

Past Perfect Tense

I *had seen*   I *had been seen*

Future Perfect Tense

I *will* (or *shall*) *have seen*   I *will* (or *shall*) *have been seen*

SUBJUNCTIVE MOOD

Present Tense

that I *see*   that I *be seen*

Past Tense

that I *saw*   that I were *seen*

Present Perfect Tense

that I *have seen*   that I *have been seen*

Past Perfect Tense
(Same as Indicative Mood)

IMPERATIVE MOOD

Present Tense

see   *be seen*

conjunction.   The *conjunction* is a "joiner," a word that is used to connect words, phrases, clauses, or complete sentences. *Coordinating conjunctions* join words and word elements of equal grammatical rank: *and, but, or, nor, so.*

Subordinating conjunctions act as "signs" of subordination. They typically appear just before the subject of the subordinate clause:

When you are near, . . .
Even though the spider plant needs water, . . .

Subordinating conjunctions sometimes are formed by two words: *as if, even though,* etc. To see how the subordinating conjunction works in a sentence, see pp. 499–501.

conjunctive adverb.   A rather clumsy term that grammarians have seized upon to describe what is essentially a sentence modifier:

Accordingly, Mrs. McMinn will not come to work today.
However, work on the project will continue as usual.
The mud is a foot deep across the canal; *therefore,* we will leave all the heavy equipment in the shed today. (Note the punctuation of the conjunctive adverb when it occurs between two main clauses.)

A partial list of conjunctive adverbs: *also, besides, consequently, furthermore, however, instead, likewise, moreover, still, then, therefore, thus.*

connotation, denotation.   *Denotation* refers to the literal, explicit meaning of a word, *connotation* to the associations and suggestions of a word. The former madam of a bawdy house was able to employ both rhetorical devices in her book title: *A House Is Not a Home.* For more discussion of denotation and connotation, see pp. 247–248.

consensus. A *consensus* is an agreement reached by most (but not necessarily all) of the people involved. "The consensus of the student editors was to run the editorial unchanged." *Consensus of opinion* is redundant, since the notion expressed by *of opinion* is built into the idea of *consensus.*

contact (*verb*). People have been debating the uses of this word for many years: "*Contact* Mrs. O'Leary when you get to Chicago." For those who dislike such uses, here is the typical reaction: "Really, I don't know the lady well enough to *contact* her — I will *call* her, *write* her, or *go to see* her." Since *contact* carries the idea of touching ("the coming together or touching of two objects or surfaces," runs a typical dictionary definition), the careful writer may well avoid it when touching is not meant. Many educated people consider the use of *contact* instead of *call* or *write* to be improper. (See *shibboleths of usage.*)

continual, continous. *Continual* means that an event recurs at different times; *continuous* that the event occurs without interruption. Thus, if Jerry's bar was *continually* open from 1936 to the present, it was occasionally closed. If Jerry's stayed open *continuously,* he never closed the place.

contractions. *Contractions* (*isn't, won't, weren't,* etc.) are acceptable in standard English. They tend to be somewhat colloquial and casual, and are perhaps not suitable for very formal occasions. Yet it is impossible either to embrace or denounce contractions in any blanket fashion. Their use depends on your stance and subject — not to mention the tone and rhythm of words in the surrounding passage. It is usually true that too many contractions will make your prose seem excessively casual and familiar, and that avoiding them entirely may make you seem stuffy and Victorian. Hit a happy medium, and listen to the *sounds* of your writing.

cope. (1) *Cope* is a casualism, and you should bear that fact in mind. (2) It also requires *with* — one *copes with something.*

correlatives. These are conjunctions that are used in pairs: *either . . . or; neither . . . nor; not only . . . but also; whether . . . or; both . . . and.*
Generally, use the expression *whether . . . or not* only when you wish to give equal stress to both ideas: "We will vote on this issue *whether* you like it *or not.*" Otherwise, omit the *or not,* which is unnecessary here: "*Whether* Smith will be chosen is up to the committee."

could of, should of, would of. Nonstandard verb forms that incorrectly use the preposition *of* rather than the auxiliary verb *have.*

council, counsel.   A *council* is a governing body. *Counsel* as a noun means "advice."

crisis.   A badly overworked word. A *crisis* is a crucial point or condition, a major turning point in human affairs. A strong word for strong situations, save it for a time when the wolves are at the door. Otherwise, when you yell "Crisis!" people may merely yawn and turn away.

criterion.   An overworked, voguish, and rather pedantic word. Try *standard, rule, test, judgment*. If you must use *criterion*, employ the proper form — singular: *criterion*; plural: *criteria*.

dangling modifier.   See pp. 530–531.

data.   As used in most situations, *data* is a pompous word for *information, evidence, facts, figures,* or *statistics*. It is, in addition, one of those latin words that usage has treated unkindly. Originally, *datum* was the singular; *data,* the plural. (Now *datum* is seldom used, except in certain technical specialties.) In modern English *data* can be both singular and plural, but usually does not sound right as either.

decimate.   An overworked expression that does not mean "to wipe out" or "annihilate." It originally meant "to take a tenth part" of something; now it means "to kill or destroy a large part." Think twice before using the word.

deprecate, depreciate.   *Depreciate* is the opposite of *appreciate,* so when you depreciate a thing you lessen it or belittle it. *Deprecate* (literally, "to pray against") means "to disapprove of or protest a thing." The distinction between the two words is narrowing, but it should still be observed.

desire (*verb*).   Unless you are talking about love or passion, better use *wish, want,* or some other expression. To say "He desired a large plate of ice cream" creates a strange mental picture indeed.

dialect.   "Any one of the mutually comprehensible geographic or social varieties of which a natural language consists." The definition is borrowed from the linguist Joseph Friend. A neutral term, *dialect* refers to a special grouping of linguistic features — words, forms, idioms, grammatical structures, pronunciations, etc. It is not bad to speak a dialect; everyone does.

different from, different than.   *Different from* is preferred in modern English: "My belief is *different from* hers." But when the expression is followed by a clause or "condensed clause," *different than* works well enough: "Don't do this job *differently than* you used to." This is neater than "Don't do this job *differently from* the way you used to."

disinterested, uninterested.   *Disinterested* means "impartial"; *uninterested* means "lacking interest." To be disinterested is to be consciously neutral about an issue; to be uninterested is to be bored or lack interest in it. *Disinterested* sounds stronger and fresher. Perhaps that is why many of us have a sneaking affection for the word, and use it when we shouldn't.

double negative.   Two negatives in a sentence where only one is necessary: "She *never* had *nothing*." Or: "They couldn*'t* put the sofa *nowhere*." A common double negative is made with *hardly:* "There's *hardly nothing* in the refrigerator." All of these constructions are non-standard. Stick to one negative:

She *never* had anything.
They couldn*'t* put the sofa anywhere.
There's *nothing* in the refrigerator.

double possessive.   A strange construction really, because you make the possessive twice, once with an *of* and again with an *'s*, with or without the apostrophe: "a dog *of* Martha*'s*," "a ship *of theirs*," "a photograph *of* Ms. Smith*'s*" Note that the double possessive can have an effect on meaning: "A photograph of Ms. *Smith's*" is different from "A photograph of Ms. *Smith*." With pronouns, however, the double possessive is always natural: "that old gang *of mine*," never "that old gang *of me*."

due to.   Authorities have long objected to this expression when used in this fashion: "*Due to* hard work, she succeeded." The reason usually given is that *due* is adjectival; so one should write: "Her success was *due* to hard work." If you do not find this explanation convincing, consider other options, such as, "She succeeded because she worked hard," or "Owing to hard work, she succeeded."

due to the fact that.   A cumbersome and redundant expression— replace with *because*.

e.g.   Abbreviation for *exempli gratia* (Latin), it means "for example." Use with a comma or colon after. If at all possible, however, use the English phrase.

   Do not confuse *e.g.* with *i.e.,* the abbreviation of the Latin phrase meaning "that is."

elliptical construction.   Such constructions have missing (but understood) parts: "We are getting tired of them, and they [*are getting tired*] of us." "[*You*] Stop doing that." "His purpose was evil and his mind [*was*] disordered." Elliptical constructions are normal in English usage.

end result.   If you have a series of results, and you wish to mention the last of them, *end result* (or *final result, last result*) is not a bad choice. But in most instances, all you need is *result,* and tacking *end* to the word does not help.

enormity.   Refers to something that is greatly wicked or outrageous, not to something huge or enormous in size.

enthuse.   This verb is nonstandard and, therefore, not recommended. Instead of "She was enthused about going to college," write:

> She was very *happy* about . . .
> She was *enthusiastic* about . . .
> She was *pleased* with . . .

etc.   Abbreviation for *et cetra* (which implies "and other things of the same kind"). *And etc.* is redundant.

exists.   Often a sign of deadwood: "a feeling like that which *exists* in the heart." This probably means: "a feeling in the heart."

expedite.   Jargon. Sometimes used with modifiers, as in "to *expedite* more quickly." Since the words means "to do something faster," the modifiers are unnecessary, as are most uses of the word.

expletive.   A grammarian's term for the "filler phrases" that begin sentences like these:

> *There is* a new house going up on Bleeker Street.
> *It's* too bad we must live in this neighborhood.

facet.   Literally, a polished "cut" face on a gemstone, such as a diamond. Used figuratively, it is badly overworked for *phase* or *aspect.* Do not use unless desperate.

factor.   Jargon for *cause, event, fact, idea, occurrence,* the word contributes to wordiness and vagueness: "His good looks were a great *factor* in his success."

farther, further.   *Farther* usually is reserved for physical distance ("She threw the ball *farther* than anyone else"), *further* for all other uses ("That explanation couldn't be *further* from the truth").

fewer, less. Use *fewer* for items that you can count: "If you have *fewer* spoons after a friend leaves your house, he should no longer be your friend." Use *less* for degree or amount: "I have *less* money (*fewer* dollars)."

finalize. Jargon. Write *finish* or *complete*.

firstly. Write *first* (and *second, third, fourth,* etc.). *Firstly* used to be thought adverbially urbane. But *first* is a legitimate flat adverb, and the *-ly can be awkward: fourthly, fifthly, eleventhly, twelfthly*.

flat adverb. An adverb without the *-ly*: "Drive *slow*." Often used in somewhat poetic contexts: "They played the song *low* and *sweet*."

flaunt, flout. *Flaunt* means "to show off something or act ostentatiously" ("Not only was the embezzler unashamed of his crimes, he actually *flaunted* them."). *Flout* means "to show disregard or contempt for" ("If she continues to *flout* the rules, she should go elsewhere"). When using either, make sure you know the difference in meanings.

former, latter. Avoid, where possible. When you use them, you make your reader hunt back through the sentence or paragraph looking for the first thing, and then the second one; after which the reader has to find the place where you interrupted with *former* or *latter*. Using either is seldom worth the trouble.

fulsome. Can mean "offensive," "insincere," "odious," or "repulsive." It does not mean "abundant." The expression *fulsome praise,* besides being a cliché, is often misused.

fun. Never use it as an adjective: "*fun* time," *fun* person," "*fun* course."

fused sentence. See p. 542.

gender. In grammar, *gender* refers to the classifying of nouns and pronouns as masculine, feminine, or neuter.

generic pronoun. See *pronoun*.

gerund. A verbal noun that ends in *-ing:* "*Losing* worried him." "He liked *winning*."

get. Avoid it in its slangy meanings: "I'll *get* you for that." "What do you mean? I don't *get* you." "Their way of doing things really *gets* me."

gobbledygook. Congressman Maury Maverick's term for jargon and nonsense, particularly of the bureaucratic kind. It employs expressions like *function, maximum, inoperative, in terms of, expertise,* and so on.

good, well.   *Good* is ordinarily an adjective: "a *good* child," "She is *good*." Do not use it in this fashion: "She shoveled coal *good*." Rather, use the adverb *well*: "She shoveled it *well*." *Good* and *well* have a complex relationship; check your dictionary if you are unsure of a particular usage.

his/her, his or her.   See p. 595.

hopefully.   Try to avoid overworking this "floating adverb" tied to the front of a sentence: "*Hopefully,* the new rule will help us do a better job." Two suggestions:

a. Tie the word to what it modifies:

She said *hopefully* that the new rule will help. . . . (This means she *said* it hopefully, that is, in a hopeful tone.)

b. Identify the person(s) being hopeful:

She hoped that the new rule . . .
They hoped that the new rule . . .
McTavish hoped that the new rule . . .

identify with.   A vague cliché. Say what you mean; be specific.

Not this: She *identified with* the feminist movement.
But this: She believed that ERA should be adopted.

if and when.   Redundant. In most statements, use either *if* or *when.*

image.   It can mean "a likeness," "a reflection," "a personification" ("she is the *image* of grace"), or "a mental picture." It is also a literary device (see p. 445). Although recently it has come to mean "reputation" or "public impression," the careful writer will avoid these vague usages:

They were worried about the company's *image.*
The child had a poor *self-image.*

impact.   Use it sparingly, and only when a great force or collision is implied. To call every result or effect an *impact* is, as Theodore Bernstein remarks, to employ "a flamethrower to light a cigarette." Do not use *impact* as a verb:

They studied ways the new freeway would *impact* upon the neighborhood.

implement (*verb*).   Jargon.

Not this: The library will *implement* greater use of desks in the reading room.
But this: The library will use more desks in the reading room.

imply, infer.   The speaker or writer *implies* ("Wilkens *implied* that he was going to quit."); the hearer or reader *infers* ("I *inferred* from his remark that he was going to quit."). When you put forth an idea, you may also put forth *implications*; when you guess or interpret the ideas of others, you draw *inferences*.

in regards to.   See *in terms of.*

in terms of.   "Tripled" idioms like *in terms of, in regard to, in relation to,* etc. are usually unnecessary and wordy (they all have three parts— "tripled").

> *Bad:*   "I'll see you *in terms of* next week."
> *Better:* "I'll see you next week."
>
> *Bad:*   "*In regard to* his writing, John improved."
> *Better:* "John improved his writing."

See *as to, in respect to.*

infinitive.   A verbal using this form: "*to* win," "*to* do," "*to* be," "*to* illuminate."

inside of, outside of (as compound prepositions).   The *of* is redundant in these expressions: "Put it inside *of* the car." "Take it outside *of* the house."

inter-, intra.   *Inter-* (as in "*inter*-company trade") means "between units or groups." *Intra-* (as in "*intra*-company memos") means "within or inside of."

irony.   See *sarcasm.*

irregardless.   Never use; always write *regardless.*

it's, its.   See pp. 553–554.

jargon.   Although for some time it has meant "the special language of a group or trade," *jargon* has long implied something closer to gibberish. Its primary definition in *The American Heritage Dictionary* is "nonsensical, incoherent, or meaningless utterance." Such expressions as *conceptualize, maximization, parameters, and implementation* are examples of recent jargon.

Kind of, sort of.

> (1) Keep the number of these pronouns straight:
>
> *Bad:*   These *kind* of persons *are* a delight.
> *Corrected:* *That kind* of person *is* a delight.
>   *Those kinds* of persons *are* a delight.
>   Such *persons are* a delight.

(2) Do not use *a* or *an* after *kind of* and *sort of*:

    Bad: That sort of *a* play won't work.
  Corrected: That sort of play won't work.

(3) These usages are too *casual*:

    I'm *kind of* tired today.
    My car just *sort of* fell apart.

lend, loan.   When writing about money or other material things, use the verbs *lend* in the present tense and *loaned* in the past. As a noun, *loan* is standard.

liable. (to mean likely).   Current usage suggests that *liable* should be restricted to unfortunate or unpleasant events: "The design of that airplane is so bad that it is *liable* to crash." In a legal usage, *liable* means subject to legal action: "You may well be *liable* if a neighbor's child is hurt in your swimming pool."

like, as.   *Like* used as a preposition: "*Like* the Bears, the Cardinals are slowly improving." Observe that *like* takes the object form of the pronoun: "like *me*," "like *them*," "like *her*."

    When *as* is used as a conjunction, the preposition *like* should not be substituted for it:

    Not this: The tree is blooming, *like* it should in the spring.
    But this: The tree is blooming, *as* it should in the spring.

This sentence shows a typical distinction made between *like* and *as*:

He speaks *as* his father does, but he looks *like* his mother. (That is, he looks *like her*.)

linking verb.   This type of verb ties, relates, or "links" the subject to a *complement* (a "completer") in the sentence. The test for a linking verb is to answer this question: "Can I substitute a form of *seem* for it?"

We *are* [*seem*] happy.
That *was* [*seemed*] a perfect day.
It *tasted* [*seemed*] good.

literally.   *Literally* means "verbatim, word for word; prosaic." It can also mean "nonfigurative." If you say, "The facts she read in the newspaper *literally* floored her," you mean that she fell down after she read them.

    The word is not an intensifier and does not mean "very" or "very much." If you write "Sam's blood *literally* turned to ice water," in the next paragraph you had better mention that Sam died shortly after.

mad.   Don't use for *angry, irritated,* or *annoyed. Mad* means "insane," or apparently so.

massive.   Journalese for *big.* Use (only when necessary) for physical objects. Also consider using these words: *solid, bulky, heavy, huge, large.*

maximum, minimum.   Both words are jargon, and ordinarily unnecessary. Instead of writing "*Maximum* effort will be put forth by the students," write "The students will work as hard as they can."

medium, media.   Vogue words. Note that *media* is the plural of *medium.* Do not use these nouns as adjectives: "*media* study," "*media* analysis." It will clear the mind if you try to substitute the real things for *media: newspapers, magazines, television,* and *radio.* Given the logic of classification, you will seldom refer to all of these at once—to claim that "the media" are responsible for something or other is probably a false generalization.

misplaced modifier.   See p. 529.

modifier.   The only modifiers available in English are adjectives and adverbs. A modifier describes, qualifies, or limits another word or word group.

mood.   Refers to the attitudes one has about the meaning expressed by a verb:

Indicative mood (the verb expresses *fact* or *reality*):
I *see* that you *are* here.

Imperative mood (the verb expresses a *command* or *request*):
Let me in!
Do your work immediately.

Subjunctive mood (the verb expresses a *wish* or *possibility*):
I wish that you *were* here.
If she *were* here, we would do the work.
Let the work *begin.*

Ms., ms.   As a title of courtesy before a women's name. *Ms.* has created considerable controversy. Some women dislike it intensely. One well-known American novelist, for instance, remarks that she will not accept mail addressing her as *Ms.*

Ordinarily, however, it seems safe to use *Ms.* when you don't know whether the woman addressed is single or married. We ask our own female students what they want to be called in class, and they vote about four to one in favor of *Mrs.* or *Miss.* It doesn't matter to us, of course—if it matters to the woman involved, we will accept her wishes.

Without the capital *m, ms.* is the standard abbreviation for *manuscript.*

must (noun and adjective).

> *Noun:* "Knowledge of mathematics is a *must* for this job."
> *Adjective:* "Mathematics is a *must* requirement for this job."

Both usages are fairly *casual,* and authorities disagree on whether they should be considered standard usage. Because *must* as noun and adjective is overworked, we suggest avoiding it and rewriting:

> You need to know mathematics for this job.
> *Or:* A knowledge of mathematics is necessary for this job.

myself (to mean *I* or *me*). Avoid this usage.

> *Not this:* Mary and *myself* agree.
> *But this:* Mary and *I* agree.
>
> *Not this:* Give it to Mike and *myself.*
> *But this:* Give it to Mike and *me.*

nice. An overworked, vague casualism. Use a more vivid and specific word.

none. Because this pronoun means "no one," it is technically singular and takes a singular verb. But usage allows the plural "none are," if the pronoun stands for more than one thing.

nonstandard English. See *standard English.*

noun. A part of speech that names something: *woman, building, sweetness, Angela, Houston, covey.*

nowhere near. Slang for *not nearly, far from.*

off of. In "He got *off of* the couch," the preposition *of* is unnecessary: "He got *off* the couch." Sometimes the construction should be changed:

> *Not this:* He fell *off of* the top of the car.
> *But this:* He fell *from* the top of the car.

OK. *OK* (or *okay*) has been in the language for about 140 years, but it remains too slangy for all uses except the most casual.

on account of. Use *because*: "He stole the bread *because* he was hungry."

one . . . his.   *"One* must do what *he* has to do" is normal and idiomatic. It is a bit stiff and old-fashioned to write *"One* must do what *one* has to do," but such constructions may be acceptable in certain contexts. For the problem of gender implied by *he,* see p. 595.

only.   When you can, put *only* next to the word or element that it modifies:

> She likes *only* men wearing beards. (She does not like clean-shaven ones.)
> *Only* she likes men wearing beards. (She is the sole member of the group who likes them.)

The rule is not very firm, however; and you don't have to worry much about *only* unless a reader might mistake your meaning:

> She likes men wearing *only* beards. (And nothing else?)

opt.   A vogue word for *choose* or *select.* Avoid it.

oral, verbal.   Make a distinction between the two words. *Oral* refers only to speech; *verbal* refers to speech, writing, or both. In legal matters, a *verbal* agreement is unwritten.

out of.   Retain the *of* in certain idioms meaning "away from":

> She walked *out of* my life.
> They stumbled *out of* the burning building.

Otherwise, avoid using *of*:

> He ran *out* the door in a hurry.

overall.   A vogue word for the idea expressed by *main(ly), general(ly),* or *usual(ly).*

> *Not this:*   Their *overall* attitude was poor.
> *But this:*   *Usually,* they had a poor attitude.
> *Or:*   Their *general* attitude was poor.

parallelism.   A grammatical balancing of similar elements:

> *She and I* are both here.
> *To be right* and *to be righteous* are not the same thing.
> *Believe what we say* and *watch what we do.*

See also pp. 275–277 and 352–353.

participle.   A verbal that serves as an adjective or as a part of a verb phrase; it ends usually in *-ing, -ed, -t, -en*:

Adjective	*Verb Phrase*
The *abandoned* house	They *had abandoned* it.
The *burned* (or *burnt*) toast	It *was burned* (or *burnt*).
The *running* elephant	It *is running*.
The *sunken* living room	The boat *had sunk*.

passive voice.   In the passive voice the subject of the sentence receives the action:

Mrs. Blount was astonished by his appearance.
Something must be done.

The passive construction consists of a form of *be* and a past participle: *were made, will be accomplished, are riveted.* See pp. 298–300 for more discussion of how the passive voice works.

pejorative.   When referring to words, *pejorative* implies a negative connotation. One might write: "I do not use *communist* in a pejorative sense, but rather as a name for a philosophy of government."

person.   A grammatical term that refers to the form of verb and pronoun indicating whether someone is speaking, spoken to, or spoken about:

First person:	*I see* Fritz.
Second person:	Do *you see* Fritz?
Third person:	*She sees* Fritz.

personnel.   Avoid this jargon, if possible. Say *people,* or when necessary, state specifically who is involved:

Not this:	Why aren't the cleaning *personnel* working on the second floor this week?
But this:	Why aren't the *janitors* working on the second floor this week?

phenomenon.   Can be applied to any fact or occurrence that is observable. But in most instances, you can replace it with more exact or specific wording.

Not this:	It was a strange natural *phenomenon.*
But this:	It was the largest flood in twenty years.

And note that the plural of *phenomenon* is *phenomena.*

phrase.   See pp. 504–505.

predominant, predominate.   *Predominant* is an adjective; *predominate* is a verb.

preposition.   A part of speech that links nouns to other parts of the sentence:

He was mentioned *in* the terms *of* the will.
No one would dare go *over* the hill.
I found some old letters *among* the pages *of* the book.

Although some purists object to ending a sentence with a preposition, the construction can be idiomatic and useful:

What did you hang the picture *on*?
That is the kind of behavior I will not put *up with*.

principal, principle.   A *principal* (noun) is the main thing among lesser things. A *principal* of a school runs the school; a financial *principal* that draws interest is the main sum of money involved. The adjective *principal* likewise makes a suggestion of pre-eminence: "The *principal* idea" refers to the main idea among lesser ones.
The noun *principle* means a rule of conduct or a general truth.

prior to.   Jargon; do not use. Say *before*.

pronoun.   A part of speech that "replaces" or stands for a noun (*this, she, us,* etc.). **Generic pronouns** refer to a group or class. Many nouns and pronouns can be used as generics (*doctors, pilots, coaches*). The singular generic pronoun is frowned upon when it is masculine only: "Any doctor who isn't afraid of malpractice suits must be very sure of *his* abilities." To avoid the problem: (1) Use the plural—*Those* doctors . . . *their* abilities. (2) Use *his or her*—Any doctor . . . *his or her abilities. (3) If your writer's stance allows it use you . . . your.* Use *his or her* and *he or she* sparingly. *He/she* and *his/her* are not standard usage.

proved, proven.   Authoritative opinion is divided on the use of these words. The following advice, however, seems more or less safe: For the verb forms, use *proved*: "I have *proved* my point." For the adjective, use *proven*: "She is a *proven* candidate for the presidency."

quote (*noun*).   Use the full form: *quotation*.

raise, rise (*verbs*).   *Raise* means "to elevate, lift up, or increase." *Rise* means "to get up." *Raise* used to be condemned in the expression "raising children" or "raising a family," but this is considered acceptable usage nowadays.

real (*adverb*).   Should not be used as an adverb to mean "very." This is poor usage: "They did a *real* good job raising the ship from the ocean floor."

reason is because.   One of the most condemned expressions in written English, yet (oddly enough) it is at certain times useful. There are two objections to it: (1) It is wordy: "The *reason* they are deserting the Army *is because* they never get leave." This can be shortened simply to "They are deserting the Army *because* they never get leave." (2) It is ungrammatical. "Because they never get leave" is technically an adverb clause, yet it is being used (in *reason . . . is because*) as a noun clause. The grammatical clause here would be: "that they never get leave."

reference.   See *allusion*.

relative pronoun.   A substitute for a noun that acts as a sign or signal for a subordinate clause:

I have a husband *who* never picks up a hammer.
A house *that* never needs painting would be wonderful to own.

respectfully, respectively.   *Respectfully* means "acting deferentially, with respect." *Respectively* means "singly, in the order mentioned."

"I must *respectfully* tell you," she said, "that I consider your three actions yesterday *respectively* irritating, flatly unnecessary, and illegal."

résumé.   a *résumé* is a short account of one's experience and qualifications. It is usually written as part of a job application. Note the accent marks. Without the accent marks, *resume* is a verb that means "to begin again."

run-on sentence.   See p. 543.

sarcasm, irony.   *Sarcasm* is a bitter and cutting expression of contempt. If, when your roommate knocks over your study lamp, you say, "*That* was a bright thing to do," your remark is sarcasm. The meaning is clear, and your roommate is perfectly aware that you are on the attack. By contrst, *irony* is more indirect and subtle, and the reader or listener may not get its underlying meaning at the time or later. When Ambrose Bierce defined *bride* as "a woman with a fine prospect of happiness behind her," he was being ironical.

sensual, sensuous. *Sensual* refers to the gratification of the physical appetites, particularly the sexual. Typical synonyms are *carnal, voluptuous,* and *licentious. Sensuous* means "appealing to the senses." Clearly, something can be sensuous without being sensual.

sentence. A unit of expression that ordinarily presents at least one complete thought. In writing, it starts with a capital letter and ends with a period. For further discussion of the sentence, see Chapters 13, 14, and 15, and the various entries under "Sentence Structure," pp. 522–544.

shall, will. There used to be a distinction made between these two verb auxiliaries or helpers, but authorities do not accept it now. To many writers, *shall* appears more dignified (or expresses a greater degree of determination), but such opinions are more a matter of tone and style than of grammar.

shibboleths of usage. In the Bible, we learn that the Gileadites used the word *shibboleth* to distinguish the fleeing Ephraimites, who could not pronounce *sh. Shibboleth* has become a word symbolizing the idea of a password, or the "test" of a militant group or party.

Each generation has its own shibboleths of usage. For various reasons, they are used to divide writers of "good" English from writers of "bad." Some shibboleths last a long time. *Ain't* is an old one; *contact* is more recent, and *hopefully* (as in "Hopefully, it won't rain") more recent still. *Hopefully* so irritated novelist Jean Stafford that she placed this sign on the back door of her house: "The word 'hopefully' must not be misused on these premises. Violaters will be humiliated."

situation. Avoid if it creates padding, as in the jargon of sports announcers: "Now we have a passing *situation.*"

slang. The mainly oral vocabulary—often employing quite popular words—found in a culture or subculture. Examples: *uptight, slaphappy, screw up, turkey* (referring to a person), *fatso, What's the diff (difference)?, smooch.* As the last two examples show, slang tends to go out of date quickly. Avoid it in your writing, except when using dialogue.

split infinitive. You "split" the infinitive by putting a word (or words) between the sign of the infinitive (*to*) and the main verb: "to *quickly* run," "to *sharply* define," "to *clearly and without ambiguity* state." The split infinitive is often awkward. Do not use the construction unless your "splitting" improves the meaning and rhythm of the sentence. See p. 528.

standard English.   The language that educated people generally accept as proper and suitable. Nonstandard English is often a deviation "downward" from standard—it is perhaps too casual, slangy, vulgar, or otherwise inappropriate. By contrast, some nonstandard English is too formal or pedantic. See our discussion in Chapter 12. Also see *casualism; colloquial, colloquialism; dialect; jargon; shibboleths of usage; slang; vogue words.*

structure.   A vogue word, often employed as a loose synonym for *organize* or *organization. The Harper Dictionary of Contemporary Usage* says: "*Structure* is very popular with people who use words like *crunch, thrust,* and *seminal.* Such people are best avoided." Perhaps the word is most usefully employed to describe physical objects like buildings.

> *Not this:*   His ideas were *unstructured.*
> *But this:*   His ideas were *disorganized.*

sure (to mean "certainly").   Example: "I'm *sure* happy you came." The word is trite and too *casual.* Rewrite:

> I am very happy you came.
> I am extremely happy you came.
> I am overjoyed you came.

that, which, who.   Much of the time these words take care of themselves, and no particular notice of them need be taken. Generally, you can rely on the old rule: *Which* refers to things, *who* to persons, and *that* to persons or things.

try and.   Not standard; use *try to.*

> *Not this:*   Please *try and* see me tomorrow.
> *But this:*   Please *try to* see me tomorrow.

type (of).   Use *type* as a noun, not as adjective:

> *Not this:*   This *type* person is a blessing to humanity.
> *But this:*   This *type of* person is a blessing to humanity.
> *Not this:*   We need a *new-type* antenna.
> *But this:*   We need a new *type of* antenna.

unique.   Means "one of a kind," and so something cannot be "more unique" or "most unique." *Unique* does not mean *unusual, remarkable,* or *excellent.*

up (*verb*).   *Up* should not be used as a verb.

Not this: Please *up* my salary.
But this: Please increase my salary.

Not this: My final grade was *upped.*
But this: My final grade was raised to a B.

utilize, utilization.   Jargon for *use.* Never use either word.

verb.   A *verb* is a word which *states*:

They *returned.*
These *are* the questions.
I *will be* home when you *arrive.*
The old stump *had been decaying* for years.

Transitive verbs pass the action over from the subject to an object; *intransitive verbs* do not pass any action to an object.

Transitive: The farmer *plowed* his field.
Intransitive: He *plowed* happily.

As the examples imply, most verbs can be either transitive or intransitive, depending on whether the object is present in the sentence. Some verbs are by nature transitive (*ignore*) or intransitive (*snore*). *Ignore* always takes an object—one always ignores *something*—a person, a slight, a distraction. By contrast, one never "snores" anything, at least not in normal idiom. See also *auxiliary verb* and *linking verb.*

verbal.   (1) See *oral.* (2) A *verbal* is a word that is derived from a verb but that cannot act as the main verb in a sentence. A verbal can take complements, objects, modifiers, and in some instances subjects. There are three kinds of verbals: *participles, infinitives,* and *gerunds.*

vogue words.   These are words and phrases that seem to appear everywhere at once in magazines, newspapers, public speeches, and on television and radio. Like new clothing styles, they are a matter of fashion; and so they are picked up (and dropped) by the public with alarming rapidity. Examples: *détente, structure* (verb), *crunch, meaningful, thrust, Back to Basics*—several of these are going out of style even as we write. *Relevant,* perhaps the most popular vogue word of a few years back, is now completely unfashionable.

whether.   See *correlatives.*

who, whom.   Good writers nowadays don't appear to have much trouble with *whom,* partly because they don't use it a great deal, except with prepositions. Authorities appear to be confused themselves and are certainly confusing to others. In his last book, however, Theodore Bernstein suggested "whom's doom," saying that *whom* is "useless and senseless; the word is in addition — a complicated nuisance." Bernstein asked 25 teachers, consultants on dictionaries, professional writers, and linguists if they agreed. Fifteen did agree, six did not, and four were "in between" (*Dos, Dont's and Maybes of English Usage,* 1977).

Our own desire for order and common sense inclines us to agree with Bernstein. So our rule is:

Always use *who* — except with prepositions, as in: *by* whom, *for* whom, *with* whom, *to* whom.

will.   See *shall, will.*

ACKNOWLEDGMENTS

Nelson Algren. From "Down with Cops" by Nelson Algren, *The Saturday Evening Post*, October 1965. Copyright © 1965 by Nelson Algren. Reprinted by permission of Candida Donadio & Associates, Inc.

Excerpt from "Ants," *Réalités*, September 1952. Reprinted by permission of Agence Photographique TOP.

William E. Blundell. Reprinted by permission from *Natural Enemies*, "To Loggers, the Woods Are Dark and Deep—But Far From Lovely" by William E. Blundell, *The Wall Street Journal*, December 8, 1981. Copyright © 1981 by Dow Jones & Company, Inc., All rights reserved.

Daniel J. Boorstin. Excerpt from "Too Much, Too Soon" by Daniel J. Boorstin, *TV GUIDE,*® December 1972. Copyright © 1972 by Daniel J. Boorstin. Reprinted by permission.

Warren Boronson. From "The Workaholic in You," *MONEY*, June 1976. Copyright © 1976 Time Inc. All rights reserved. Reprinted by permission.

Jo Brown. From "Indian Traders of North America" by Jo Brown. *Arizona Highways,* May 1973. Copyright © 1973. Reprinted by permission.

Shannon Brownles. From "What's in a Face" by Shannon Brownles, *Discover* Feb. 1985.

Henry Steele Commager. Excerpt from "Taxes" *Forbes,* April 13, 1981.

Harry Crews. Harry Crews, *A Childhood: The Biography of a Place.* New York: Harper & Row, Publishers, Inc., 1978, p. 51.

George Daniels. From pp. 62–3 in *The Awful Handyman's Book* by George Daniels. Copyright © 1966 by George Daniels. Reprinted by permission of Harper & Row, Publishers, Inc.

Emily Dickinson. "Because I Could Not Stop for Death" by Emily Dickinson. Reprinted by permission of the publishers and the Trustees of Amherst College from *The Poems of Emily Dickinson*, edited by Thomas H. Johnson, Cambridge, Mass.: The Belknap Press of Harvard University Press. Copyright © 1951, 1955, 1979, 1983 by the President and Fellows of Harvard College.

J. Frank Dobie. J. Frank Dobie, *A Vaquero of the Brush Country.* Dallas: The Southwest Press, 1929, pp. 264–65.

Gerald Durrell. From *The Overloaded Ark.* Copyright © 1953 by Gerald M. Durrell. Copyright © renewed 1981 by Gerald M. Durrell. Reprinted by permission of Viking Penguin Inc. and Faber and Faber Ltd.

Bergen Evans and Cornelia Evans. Entry for *lead a dog's life.* From *A Dictionary of Contemporary American Usage* by Bergen Evans and Cornelia Evans. Copyright © 1957 by Bergen Evans and Cornelia Evans. Reprinted by permission of Random House, Inc.

Charles Foley. Excerpt from "The Leap from Golden Gate Bridge: Who Jumps? And Why?" from the *Washington Post* June 1, 1975. Copyright © 1975 by The Washington Post Company. Reprinted by permission.

Ken Follet. From "A Moscow Mystery" by Ken Follet. *Saturday Review,* April, 1981. Copyright © 1981 by Saturday Review magazine. Reprinted by permission.

Robert Fuerst. From "Inference Peddling" by Robert Fuerst. *Psychology Today,* March 1979. Copyright © 1979 by the American Psychological Association. Reprinted by permission.

INDEX

planning and writing,
116–17
as strategy of develop-
ment, 77, 81
as writing strategy, 109
promise pattern, 211, 217,
221
pronouns, 498, 595
agreement of, 520
defined, 595
forms of, 509–10
generic, 595
vague, 508–9
proofreading, methods of,
207
of research paper, 399
proved, proven, 595
punctuation, 545–60
apostrophe, 553–54
colon, 551–52
comma, 547
dash, 552–53
exclamation mark, 547
hyphen, 554
italics, 555–56
mechanics of, 545–58
parentheses, 552
period, 547
question mark, 547
quotation marks,
554–55
rhetoric of, 558–60
semicolon, 550–51
of sentence units, 267,
272, 546

qualifiers, 122
qualifying devices in
sentences, 285
question mark, use of,
547
quotation marks, use of,
547, 554–55
quotations, use of, in research paper, 377–79
quote (noun), 595

raise, rise (as verbs), 595
reader, analysis of, 22,
25–26

identifying, 31–33
*Readers' Guide to Periodical
Literature,* 367–68
real, as adverb, 596
reason is because, 596
redundancy, 259
reference, 596
reference works, 385–92
bibliography form for,
371–74, 402
general, 385–87
note form for, 373–74
special, 365, 387–92
use of, in research,
364–70
refutation argument, 348,
354–56
relative pronoun, 596
research paper
bibliography for,
371–72, 401–3
check list for rough
draft, 398–99
documentation for,
396–97
endnotes, 406–8
footnotes, 408
interviews for, 372
documentation of,
403
librarian as source of
information for,
370
note taking for, 371–72,
372–79
paraphrasing in, 376
parenthetical documen-
tation for, 404–5
plagiarism in, 376–77
procedure for, 361
reference works for,
364, 385–92
sample, 410–21
steps in writing,
393–411
subject for, 362–64
thesis of, 394–96
using card catalog for,
365–66
using encyclopedias for,
364–65

using on-line computer
card catalog
for, 366–67
using on-line data base
computer for, 370
using periodical indexes
for, 367–68
works cited, 401–3
writer's stance in, 363
respectfully, respectively, 596
résumé, 477–78
defined, 596
revising
example of, 197–99
overview, 206
sentences, 306–11
rhetorical question, 341
use of, in classification
papers, 134
rhetorical strategies, for
business writing,
466–68. *see also*
strategies of develop-
ment
rhetoric of punctuation,
558–60
rise, raise, 595
role, in developmental
strategy, 78
role, of writer, 22, 24–25
30–31
rough draft, check list for,
398–99
"rule of nearness," 527–28
"ruling principle" in classification, 131–36
run-on sentences, 543
defined, 596

sarcasm, irony, 596
satire, 445
search strategy, for re-
search paper, 364
*Sears List of Subject Head-
ings,* 366
semi-, 577
semicolon, use of, 550–51
sensory images, 85–87
in description, 93
sensual, sensuous, 597

Key to the Handbook